Adventure Guide™ to

Maine

Earl Brechlin

HUNTER

HUNTER PUBLISHING, INC,
130 Campus Drive, Edison, NJ 08818
732-225-1900; 800-255-0343; Fax 732-417-1744
hunterp@bellsouth.net

1220 Nicholson Road, Newmarket, Ontario
Canada L3Y 7V1
800-399-6858; Fax 800-363-2665

The Boundary, Wheatley Road, Garsington
Oxford, OX44 9EJ England
01865-361122; Fax 01865-361133

ISBN 1-55650-860-3

© 1999 Earl Brechlin

This guide focuses on recreational activities. As all such activities contain elements of risk, the publisher, author, affiliated individuals and companies disclaim any responsibility for any injury, harm, or illness that may occur to anyone through, or by use of, the information in this book. Every effort was made to insure the accuracy of information in this book, but the publisher and author do not assume, and hereby disclaim, any liability for any loss or damage caused by errors, omissions, misleading information or potential travel problems caused by this guide, even if such errors or omissions result from negligence, accident or any other cause.

Cover photo: Acadia National Park shoreline, Bob Thayer
All other photos by author, unless specified.
Maps by Kim André, © 1999 Hunter Publishing, Inc.

2   3   4

www.hunterpublishing.com

 Hunter's full range of guides to all corners of the globe is featured on our exciting website. You'll find guidebooks to suit every type of traveler, no matter what their budget, lifestyle, or idea of fun. Log on and join the excitement!

Adventure Guides – There are now over 40 titles in this series, covering destinations from Costa Rica and the Yucatán to Florida's West Coast, New Hampshire and the Alaska Highway. Complete with information on what to do, as well as where to stay and eat, *Adventure Guides* are tailor-made for the active traveler, with a focus on hiking, biking, canoeing, horseback riding, trekking, skiing, watersports, and all other kinds of fun.

Alive Guides – This ever-popular line of books takes a unique look at the best each destination offers: fine dining, nightlife, first-class hotels and resorts. In-margin icons direct the reader at a glance. Top-sellers include: *The Cayman Islands, St. Martin & St. Barts,* and *Aruba, Bonaire & Curaçao.*

Our ***Romantic Weekends*** guidebooks provide a series of escapes for couples of all ages and lifestyles. Unlike most "romantic" travel books, ours cover more than charming hotels and delightful restaurants, featuring a host of activities that you and your partner will remember forever.

One-of-a-Kind travel books available from Hunter include *Best Dives of the Western Hemisphere; The African-American Travel Guide; Golf Resorts; Chile & Easter Island Travel Companion* and many more.

Full descriptions are given for each book, along with reviewers' comments and a cover image. Books may be purchased on-line using our secure transaction facility.

About the Author

A registered Maine Guide who designed and built his own energy-efficient home, Earl D. Brechlin lives in Bar Harbor on Mount Desert Island. He is an avid hiker, backpacker and whitewater paddler and author of several guidebooks to Acadia National Park.

During winter he enjoys snowshoeing and cross-country skiing in Acadia and snowmobiling near his vacation home in Greenville on Moosehead Lake.

Brechlin has been the editor of the *Bar Harbor Times*, a weekly newspaper, for 15 years. He is a past president of the Maine Press Association, a former Journalist of the Year in Maine, and is on the executive board of the New England Press Association.

■ ■ ■ ■ ■

Contents

■ Maps

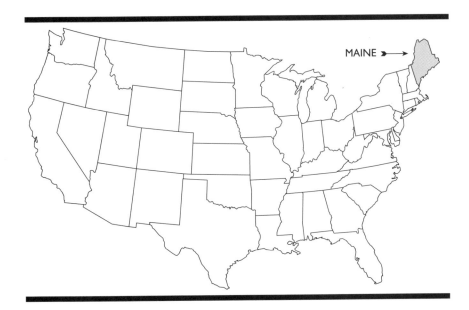

MAINE ➤➝

Dedication

To those who have come before.
To those who will follow.
Live the adventure.

Introduction

Discovering Maine

Adventure is worthwhile in itself. – Amelia Earhart

The farthest east of any state, and the largest and wildest of any in New England, Maine is often perceived as the literal end of the line. In many ways it is.

But that is not the entire story.

Granted, there is only one major interstate highway in and out. Regular passenger rail service is only now coming to fruition. Only two airports – Bangor and Portland – have regular service by commercial jets, although scheduled flights by commuter air serve most larger towns.

West Quoddy Head with its distinctive red-and-white-striped lighthouse near Lubec is the easternmost point in the United States. The Appalachian Trail, a 2,158-mile footpath that begins on Springer Mountain in Georgia, ends atop mile-high Katahdin in Baxter State Park. More than a thousand hikers begin down south each year. Fewer than 200 will finish the entire journey. Yet even as one path ends, another begins. A new, International Appalachian Trail, which heads north to Mount Jacques Cartier in Quebec, begins at the base of Katahdin.

Maine is the only state in the lower 48 that borders only one other state. Except for a long frontier with New Hampshire the only way in or out is through another country – Canada – or by sea.

Just over one million year-round residents are spread out over more than 20 million acres of land. With most major population centers located in the southern part of the state, the farther north you go the faster the population density drops. It's not long before moose and loons begin to outnumber humans.

Popular trends, fads and crazes seem to hit Maine last – if at all.

Distance both physically and culturally has created a land rich in closely held tradition. Yet a steady stream of visitors, connections to the world at large, and an almost institutional rejection of insular attitudes has resulted in a society remarkably open to embracing new ideas, methods and fashions – providing they bring with them sufficient utilitarian purpose or practical application to stand the test of time.

For it is time that is the sole witness and arbiter of change in this ancient landscape. Here the vagaries of climate and the arc of seasons can be discerned not just on the land but also in the faces and hands of those whose lives and livelihoods are tied to it each day.

In Maine the story is not one of the land, or the sea, or the people but rather of the land, *and* the sea, *and* its people. The story of one cannot be told without the telling of the tales of the others.

While Maine has long been settled, it is not by any means an "old" state.

Its origins date back to the1600s, although it did not officially join the Union until 1820 when it formally severed ties with Massachusetts. While forts are many, notable armed skirmishes here were few. Still, the first naval battle of the revolutionary war was fought off the Down East coast near Machias.

Maine's makeup today is a study in contrasts. Cosmopolitan cities, such as Portland, Lewiston and Bangor, jostle for attention with the trendy tourist towns of Kennebunkport, Camden and Bar Harbor. Like a mother wood duck, venerable L.L. Bean in Freeport sits surrounded by a brood of factory outlets and mini-malls competing not for cracked corn but rather the plastic nourishment lining the wallets of visitors.

Meanwhile fourth-generation, family-owned general stores from Rangeley to Greenville stock everything from live bait to the Boston papers (each in season, of course).

Most of all, Maine is a seemingly timeless rural place. The names of families in the oldest cemeteries can still be found in the phone books today. Tiny villages on back roads continue on as always with little more than late model pickup trucks in the driveways and the occasional satellite dish in the dooryard to betray the fact they are not the exact same community you could have experienced six generations ago.

Still, even those who live in what urbanites might consider "wilderness" cherish the wildness of the country deeper in. Many families own backwoods and lakeside camps or cabins to which they can retreat.

In the Great North Woods, the ghost of naturalist Henry David Thoreau still speaks in whispers above the white froth of wild rivers sporting rapids with names like "Hulling Machine" and "The Cribworks." Today he would smile, undoubtedly, at the thought that a state which boasts millions of acres of undeveloped private timberlands open to public recreation would still insist on preserving 205,000 acres in Baxter State Park; most of which by law must remain free of the artificial cacophony of internal combustion engines, radios or cellular phones.

From north to south, east to west, tall white pines compete with granite spires to frame the cosmic flame and crackle of the northern lights.

Mountains, rivers, forests, and shores harbor quiet glens, undiscovered waterfalls and a lifetime of explorations.

Mist rises at dawn from jewel-like ponds with names known but to a few. It may have been days or even weeks since a dry fly, paddle or anything more than the cry of a loon has broken the mirror-flat surface. Barren mountain tops, where snow lingers long into June, wrap themselves each day in the embrace of wind and cloud. Moose wander through backwaters in search of succulent water plants. As night descends, the call of the Eastern coyote echoes from nearby ridges.

All around the state the stony yet fertile soil provides for those who till fields of potatoes, blueberries and hay. For others who accept its Faustian bargain, the cold, fog-shrouded Atlantic Ocean holds constant danger as well as the prospect of nets brimming with fish and traps teeming with lobster.

Information Sources

For general information on activities in Maine contact one of the following sources (area code 207):

The Maine Publicity Bureau, PO Box 2300, 325B Water Street, Hallowell 04347; ☎ 800-533-9595 or 623-0363; E-mail mpbinfo@mainetourism.com.

Maine Office of Tourism, State House Station, Augusta 04330; ☎ 287-5710.

Maine Innkeepers Association, 305 Commercial Street, Portland 04101; ☎ 773-7670.

Maine Publicity Bureau Welcome Centers:
18 Mayville Road, Route 2, Bethel; ☎ 824-4582.
US Route 302, Fryeburg; ☎ 935-3639.

State of Maine Visitor Information Centers:
I-95 and US 1, Kittery; ☎ 439-1319.
US 1, Exit 17 off I-95, Yarmouth; ☎ 846-0833.
I-95, Mile 169, Hampden (North); ☎ 862-6628.
I-95, Mile 172, Hampden (South); ☎ 862-6638.
7 Union Street, Calais; ☎ 454-2211.
Ludlow Road, Houlton; ☎ 532-6346.

Along the Down East coast the endless surge of the briny Atlantic scours rocky shores or rhythmically thumps Southern Maine's miles of fine sandy beaches. The state's 30 lighthouses stand guard along more than 3,000 miles of coastline. Here, on almost any day, the capricious fog plays hide and seek with all your senses.

This book is not designed to be the be-all and end-all guide, a metaphorical holding of your hand if you wish, to reach a specific Maine destination. Rather, think of it as a resource to jump-start the journey. While the major byways and even many of the roads seldom traveled are mentioned, there are still plenty of people, places, and diversions awaiting discovery. After all, you can't call a trip an adventure if everything goes according to plan. Pick a date, pick a road, pick a trail and let the fun begin.

Is Maine then, in fact, the end of the line? Many – artist, industrialist, farmer, fisherman – have found inspiration in the state's great natural beauty, a grounding in its history and a spiritual kinship with its proud, independent people. But it has often proved also to be a new beginning. Maine then, is perhaps paradoxically both the end of the line and a place of beginnings. What better place then to find adventure?

A Land of Fire & Ice

Maine is a landscape literally born both of fire and ice. Titanic forces from deep within the earth have forced mountains of magma through the earth's crust to create the massive rock "plutons" of granite that form most of the state's ancient mountain ranges.

Elsewhere, ridges of dark slate and rugged hills of schist and basalt formed tough barriers for the earliest settlers to cross.

While legend and myth may try to link some mountains in Maine directly to volcanoes, there is no one peak that can clearly be said to be the remnants of a central cone. Still, many of the state's more distinctive hills, such as Mount Kineo and Big Spencer near Moosehead Lake, are volcanic in origin, composed largely of dense volcanic rock that is even tougher than granite. This landscape has been carved and worked by eons of ice and the slow, steady, wearing action of swift streams and rivers.

■ Minerals

Throughout the state those with a careful eye can discern "veins" of basalt which was forced up in a molten state into cracks in the overburden. Maine is not considered a mineral-rich state. Except for limestone quarry operations for cement processing there are no commercial mining ventures in operation. In the late 1800s and before, small operations mined iron, such as those at Katahdin Iron Works along the Pleasant River near Brownville, and sporadic wildcat gold and silver mines were put down. Copper and lead for a while were mined near Blue Hill. In recent years a nickel mine was proposed for the Union area, although it never opened. Prospecting for copper, tin and other minerals has been done in Aroostook County.

Tourmaline

Perhaps the most famous mineral from Maine is tourmaline, which, along with garnets and other gem-quality crystals, can be found in areas in the mountains of Western Maine. Tourmaline, which is crafted into exquisite jewelry, comes in several colors, including black, green and pink. Dozens of minerals can be found in the hills of Oxford County near Newry and Paris.

■ Granite & Stone

Maine more than made up for its lack of minerals by producing prodigious amounts of building stone. Great slabs of slate were mined for roofs, chalk boards, countertops, sinks and walls in Monson. A limited operation continues today.

Granite was king along the Maine Coast during the 1800s, supporting quarries that bustled with immigrants on Vinal Haven, North Haven, on Crotch Island off Stonington, and in Hall Quarry on Mount Desert Island. Granite quarries were busy too in the Sullivan and Franklin areas.

 DID YOU KNOW? *Some of the largest buildings in the biggest cities on the East Coast were made of Maine stone. And many an American street was paved with granite cobblestones, rounded rocks collected from the beaches on the coast of Maine. Cobblestones were also used as ballast in ships carrying everything from lumber to livestock.*

Most stone was shipped out by schooner (the stone was skidded or winched directly from the rock face to the nearby edge of the sea).

Fossils

Fossils, mostly of plants and small marine animals, while not common, can be found primarily in the slate and shale prevalent in the northern part of the state.

■ Glaciers

The 2,000-foot headwall of Katahdin looms over the crystal-clear waters of remote Chimney Pond in Baxter State Park.

Scientists believe the land in Maine has uplifted several times in the past few hundred million years, although no one imagines the area as Vulcan's nursery with volcanoes spewing lava as far as the eye can see.

In marked contrast to Maine's relatively sedate experience with geologic fire, the most easily observed affects on the land have come from ice. Several times, the most recent only about 10,000 years ago, a mere split second in geologic time, great walls of ice more than a mile high have pushed their way from north to south across the state. The sheer weight of the ice alone is believed to have compressed the land nearly a mile below its present contours.

The comings and goings of glaciers have left many distinct signs. Mountains with long, gradual north slopes, and abrupt, broken-away south faces show evidence of glaciation. The ice rode slowly up the back of the mountains and then fractured pieces from the front.

The distinctive multiple peaks of Mount Desert Island, where nearly all ridges run north to south, resulted from glaciation. The island was literally a long east-west ridge at one time. The glacier groaned out of the north, came up against a bulwark of pink granite and pushed through in several areas carving deep valleys now filled with deep lakes.

INTERESTING FACT: *Glacial movement created Somes Sound, the only true fjord on the east coast of the United States and a fissure which nearly cuts Mount Desert Island in two.*

On many high hills the rock has been worn smooth creating flat areas of "glacial polish." In other places deep grooves, like saw marks on the flat surface of fine furniture, help trace the glacier's path.

Erratics

Rocks picked up and transported hundreds of miles by the glaciers were left behind as the ice receded. Bearing no semblance to the nearby bedrock, they were dubbed glacial "erratics" and posed great puzzlement to 18th-century scholars in an age before the effects of great sheets of ice were even suspected much less accepted and understood. One of the most famous is **Bubble Rock** in Acadia National Park. This truck-size boulder, perched it almost seems precariously on the edge of a cliff, is believed to have come from the top of a mountain more than 100 miles away.

Eskers & Kettle Ponds

But the glaciers did not work their magic only on solid rock. Along the way they pushed up massive deposits of loose gravel and rocks. In some places outwash streams under the receding icepack built up their own deposits of sand and smooth, rounded rocks. These long sinuous hills, which scientists refer to as eskers, became known around Maine as "whalesbacks." With the wealth of building material readily available these routes quickly became roads and railroad right-of-ways as settlement progressed. One of the most famous whalesbacks can be found on Route 9 between Brewer and Calais. Glacial sediments also helped dam valleys, creating lakes and bogs and carve deep valleys. Glaciers also left distinctive "kettle" ponds; places where chunks of ice melted last as sediment built up around them.

 DID YOU KNOW? *Most rivers in Maine, except those in the far north or those dammed by humans, flow from the north to the south. In all, there are more than 31,000 miles of rivers and streams throughout the state.*

■ Heaths

Another remarkable feature of the Maine landscape are the massive peat bogs, dubbed heaths. They are the result of the natural death of lakes, where plants slowly creep in from the edges until the entire depression once filled only with water becomes clogged with slowly decaying vegetation. The water flowing from these areas is stained the color of tea from tannins in the peat. The state's largest peat bog, **The Great Heath**, is near Columbia Falls in Washington County. It is several miles across. While canoeist can pass through it along the Pleasant River, most exploration is limited to the winter months when cold and ice keep visitors from quickly sinking into a spongy vegetation. For a while an energy company mined peat on nearby Denbo Heath along the Narraguagus River. The peat was dried and burned to generate electricity.

The Sea

The other great "hand" that has worked the face of Maine's landscape is the sea. The state has more than 3,500 miles of coastline and 6,200 offshore islands.

INTERESTING FACT: *Researchers have discovered that Maine's rugged coastline is longer than originally thought – about 600 miles longer, in fact. The latest information provided by Geographic Information System (GIS) computers puts the length, when all island shores are included, at 5,500 miles.*

All along the state's coastline the relentless waters of the Atlantic scour away the rocks, creating the prominent headlands and pocket rocky beaches. Except in the southern part of the state in York County, where long, wide beaches stretch for miles, sandy intertidal zones are few and far between. Even Sand Beach in Acadia National Park is somewhat misnamed. A good percentage of the material that comprises the beach is really shattered sea shells.

Maine's thousands of offshore islands and ledges, many which are home to nesting seabird and seal colonies, are literally a range of drowned mountains with only the tops exposed.

On rocky beaches the ceaseless action of waves works the stones, shaping and rounding them into distinctive cobble shapes.

WISE WORDS: *Refrain from collecting these rocks. While many visitors fancy taking home "just one" as a souvenir, officials have begun discouraging the practice as some easily accessible locations are being picked clean.*

Despite all the sea's power however, the stubborn granite, born of fire and ice, only reluctantly yields. In several places along the coast the erosion first of nearby softer rock has created natural bridges or unique chasms. a good example of this is **Thunder Hole** in Acadia National Park where, when a wave hits just right, air is trapped up under the rock ledge, and compressed until the water begins to wane and the air sends out a massive column of spray with a loud "boom."

*Salt spray flies from the angry maw of Thunder Hole
along Ocean Drive in Acadia National Park.*

In other spots, long narrow ledges across channels refuse to budge. This has created "reversing" falls where, depending on the height of the tide, which can range as much as 20 feet in Washington County, the water foams, froths and falls in opposite directions twice each day. The most famous can be found at Pembroke on Cobscook Bay in Washington County, in Damariscotta and in Blue Hill.

◾ Coastal Sentinels

What is it about lighthouses that so fascinates people? Is it the romantic notion of the self-reliant keeper and his family marking long days and nights on isolated islands? Is it the altruistic notion of doing a job where countless lives can literally depend on you?

Perhaps it is the tenacity shown by keepers like those on Mount Desert Rock. Here, 25 miles off Mount Desert Island, winter storms each year scour the granite ledge clean of every spoonful of soil. Still, keepers each spring replace the dirt, a bushel basket at a time, most brought out by friendly fishermen, so that a tiny garden can bloom again each summer.

In recent years there appears to be a resurgence in interest in these earliest of aids to navigation. Ironically, it comes at a time when all lights in operation along the coast have been automated and many lighthouses and stations have been handed over to the care of private organizations.

Most plan to operate them for many purposes ranging from inns to whale watching stations.

Maine sports nearly 70 lighthouses and major beacons beginning in the southwest at the New Hampshire border at Isles of Shoals and ending on the border with New Brunswick at West Quoddy Head.

 INTERESTING FACT: *Portland Head Light, which is accessible by car, is the third oldest in the United States. It was erected in 1791.*

Prior to the mid 1800s, lighthouses were constructed of local stone or wood. Around 1850 Congress directed the US Army Corps of Engineers to standardize designs. This resulted in six basic shapes using stone, brick or iron plates that can be seen today.

Placement and tower height was determined by a variety of factors, including exposure to the sea during times of violent storms and visibility. A light 50 feet above the sea can be seen from a distance of approximately eight miles. To double that distance to 16 miles, the height of the tower must increase by a factor of four.

To avoid confusion among mariners, the colors and flash pattern of lighthouses are varied. Charts reveal the frequency of the flash and note when beacons may be blocked by shore-side obstacles.

The Fresnel Lens

In the early years lighthouses often burned sperm whale oil and later kerosene to generate light. Eventually all were electrified. Winslow Lewis' invention in 1810 of the Fresnel lens, which magnifies and concentrates the light from the multiple lamps, made lighthouses much more efficient. The beacons could be seen from farther away and the amount of oil needed was reduced significantly. Polished glass monstrosities standing up to 10 feet tall and weighing thousands of pounds, each Fresnel lens is unique. One of the finest collections of Fresnel lenses can be found on display at the Shore Village Lighthouse Museum in Rockland. ☎ 594-0311.

Directly offshore, from Rockland, some 25 miles out to be exact, is Matinicus Light. First put into service in 1827, it was nearly destroyed by a fierce winter storm in 1839. While all lighthouses have a rich and often well-documented history, Matinicus Rock's is perhaps the most famous, thanks to the heroic efforts of lighthouse keeper Samuel Burgess' 17-year-old daughter Abbie.

Lighthouses of Maine ☀️⛵

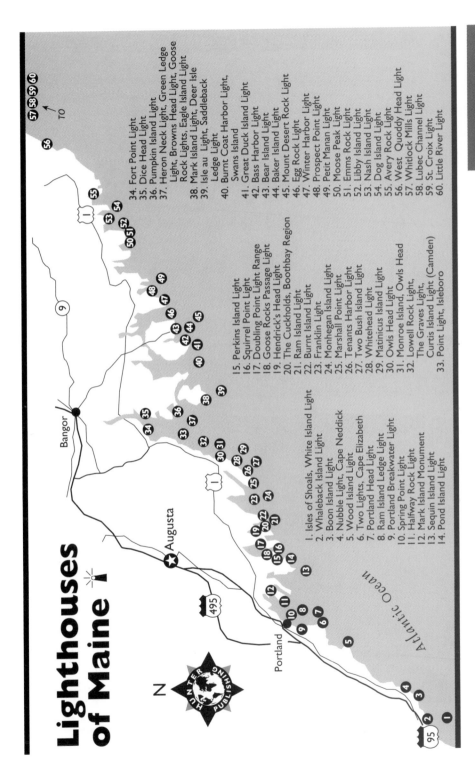

1. Isles of Shoals, White Island Light
2. Whaleback Island Light
3. Boon Island Light
4. Nubble Light, Cape Neddick
5. Wood Island Light
6. Two Lights, Cape Elizabeth
7. Portland Head Light
8. Ram Island Ledge Light
9. Portland Breakwater Light
10. Spring Point Light
11. Halfway Rock Light
12. Mark Island Monument
13. Sequin Island Light
14. Pond Island Light
15. Perkins Island Light
16. Squirrel Point Light
17. Doubling Point Light Range
18. Goose Rocks Passage Light
19. Hendrick's Head Light
20. The Cuckholds, Boothbay Region
21. Ram Island Light
22. Burnt Island Light
23. Franklin Light
24. Monhegan Island Light
25. Marshall Point Light
26. Tenants Harbor Light
27. Two Bush Island Light
28. Whitehead Light
29. Matinicus Island Light
30. Owls Head Light
31. Monroe Island, Owls Head
32. Lowell Rock Light, The Graves Light, Curtis Island Light (Camden)
33. Point Light, Isleboro
34. Fort Point Light
35. Dice Head Light
36. Pumpkin Island Light
37. Heron Neck Light, Green Ledge Light, Browns Head Light, Goose Rock Lights, Eagle Island Light
38. Mark Island Light, Deer Isle
39. Isle au Light, Saddleback Ledge Light
40. Burnt Coat Harbor Light, Swans Island
41. Great Duck Island Light
42. Bass Harbor Light
43. Bear Island Light
44. Baker Island Light
45. Mount Desert Rock Light
46. Egg Rock Light
47. Winter Harbor Light
48. Prospect Point Light
49. Petit Manan Light
50. Moose Peak Light
51. Emms Rock Light
52. Libby Island Light
53. Nash Island Light
54. Dog Island Light
55. Avery Rock Light
56. West Quoddy Head Light
57. Whitlock Mills Light
58. Lubec Channel Light
59. St. Croix Light
60. Little River Light

Abbie Burgess & the Matinicus Light

On some occasions wild winter waves as high as 40 feet would sweep across Matinicus Rock, often taking parts of structures with them. In January of 1856 there was such a storm. Sam Burgess, who had gone in for supplies (keepers in those days rowed and sailed to the mainland), was trapped ashore by the weather. Abbie bravely keep the lights burning for a week and kept her family safe as well.

When Sam Burgess was replaced by President Abraham Lincoln, he and his family remained on Rock for a time to train the new keeper. Abbie ended up falling in love and marrying the new keeper's son Isaac Grant. The couple lived on the barren rock and had four children over 14 years.

Portland Head Light guards the entrance to one of the busiest harbors on the East Coast.

Whether it is picturesque Nubble Light in York, perched on a rocky nob, Pemaquid Light near Damariscotta, with its dramatic position astride long fingers of granite bedrock stretching out to a frothy sea, Southern Island Light, home for a time to renowned artist Andrew Wyeth and subject of his spectacular painting "Groundwire," or any of the "lesser" beacons of the Maine coast, lighthouses are places where human endeavor, great natural forces, and the tidal wash of history inevitably meet.

For Lighthouse Buffs

The **Shore Village Museum** is Maine's Lighthouse Museum. It is located at 104 Limerock Street in Rockland. It claims to have the largest collection of lighthouse artifacts on display in US. It also has other marine exhibits such as ship models and a scrimshaw display. Open daily June through October. Admission is free; donations are accepted. ☎ 594-0311.

For people who just can't get enough lighthouses, Maine boasts the **Lighthouse Depot**, which claims to have the largest collection of lighthouse gifts, books, images and collectibles in the world. Just one quick look at the store and mail-order headquarters on US 1 in Wells will be enough to convince you their claim is true.

Founded by lighthouse lovers Tim Harrison and Kathy Finnegan, the Lighthouse Depot features two floors of items covering lighthouses everywhere from Maine and Florida to Canada, the Great Lakes and indeed from all around the world. Items include original art, prints, books, calendars, postcards, replicas, clothing and working lighthouse models up to six feet tall! The shop is open daily year-round, although hours vary with the season. For store hours, ☎ 646-0608.

In addition to the retail store, Lighthouse Depot also publishes a 48-page, full-color mail order catalog and has its own Website, www.lhdepot.com.

> 📖 The Lighthouse Depot publishes *Lighthouse Digest*, a monthly color magazine full of stories and pictures about lighthouses all over the world.

Lighthouse Depot is located one US 1, off Exit 2 from the Maine Turnpike. To order a catalog, ☎ 800-758-1444.

Maine has nearly 70 lighthouses and light stations, many accessible from the mainland. A brief description of each can be found in the appropriate chapter of this book.

■ Lobster Lore

Lobster is synonymous with Maine. And why not? Maine lobster is the tastiest in the world. Whether boiled or baked, broiled or sautéed, millions of pounds of lobster are consumed with great relish annually.

While most visitors to the state will eat at least one lobster during their stay, few know much about these delectable crustaceans beyond the fact that they come from the ocean and fishermen in small boats use funny-shaped traps to catch them.

Maine has more than 6,000 lobstermen. Many fish more than 1,000 traps each. Each year, more than 20 million pounds of lobster are landed. Fishermen work long hours, often leaving the harbor before dawn so they can reach offshore traps in order to begin hauling at daybreak. The independent nature of lobstermen is the stuff of legend Down East. You cannot help but admire the spunk of an independent businessman who goes down to the ocean each day never knowing what awaits. Lobstermen, and an increasing number of women, are at risk of fickle weather, being tangled in their own lines, or simply being tossed from their boats. Fishing off the coast of Maine is one of the most hazardous occupations in New England. And, yet, with no boss, surrounded by a bountiful sea, with wildlife and spectacular scenery all around, there is a romantic aspect to it as well.

Long a symbol of Down East Maine's fierce independence,
a lobsterman goes about tending his traps along the rocky shore.
Photo courtesy of *The Bar Harbor Times*

Lobster History

Despite lobsters' popularity today, it wasn't always so. More than 100 years ago lobsters were considered unfit for eating. A commercial fishing industry for lobster did not even begin until 1860.

Even during the late 1800s most folks turned up their noses at the thought of eating the creature. In fact, after fierce storms, dubbed "Nor'easters" due to direction of the strongest winds, lobsters would often be tossed up on shore in great numbers. Most people would collect them to be put in compost piles for the garden. The lobster was so lowly that owners of stately shorefront mansions, which they called "cottages," often considered lobsters fit only for consumption by their domestic staff!

In those early years fishermen, in dories they rowed from shore, or in small sailing vessels like Friendship Sloops, tended their traps by hand.

Over the years, the high-prowed, motorized vessel familiar today developed. In recent years, coated wire traps have replaced wooden ones. Wood and glass buoys have been replaced by Styrofoam.

Lobster Trivia

■ Maine has more than 6,000 licensed lobstermen.

■ A female lobster lays anywhere from several thousand to 100,000 eggs at a time, but only one-tenth of one percent of those eggs will develop and live past six weeks in the larva stage.

■ It takes a lobster four to seven years to reach one pound in weight.

■ The largest known lobster caught in Maine measured 36 inches from the rostrum (back) to the end of the tail. One of the largest known ever caught is a 42 lb, 7 oz monster on display (dead and mounted) at the Museum of Science in Boston.

■ A lobster can be right or left-handed. Some have the large crusher on the left, others on the right.

■ A lobster can drop a claw as a defense mechanism and grow another over a period of years.

■ An adult male lobster will grow a new shell and shed its old one about once a year, females once every two years, increasing an average of half an inch and a third of a pound with each molt. During its early growth stages, a lobster is believed to shed some 25 times over five to seven years.

■ After a molt, a lobster's shell takes about eight weeks to harden.

■ Maine coastal waters have provided over 105 million lobsters over the past five years.

Data provided by the staff of the Mount Desert Island Oceanarium in Southwest Harbor and Bar Harbor Oceanarium on Route 3.

Lobster Buoys & Traps

Colorful lobster buoys float in great number along rocky shores and ledges. Each fisherman registers his uniquely colored and patterned buoys with the state. No two license holders have the same buoys. When a fisherman is hauling his traps he must have one of his buoys prominently displayed on the top of his wheelhouse to prove he's pulling the right ones.

Traps are "set" by throwing them over the side with a piece of "pot warp" or rope attached to a buoy. Some fishermen use a small, plain, doughnut-shaped float called a "toggle" down line from the buoy. Traps are set in lines along familiar landmarks or underwater ridges. They are moved seasonally as the lobsters come inshore in summer and head offshore to deeper water in winter. Sometimes, when a particular area is producing plenty of "keeper" or legal-sized lobsters, a fisherman will put more than one trap on a single buoy. That is so other fishermen don't notice a sudden increase in the number of a competitor's traps and realize where the hot spot is.

Ghost Traps

When a buoy is cut from a trap, either accidentally by a passing power boat, by bad weather, or during feuds over fishing territories called "lobster wars," a trap will continue to catch lobsters. Such a trap is called a "ghost trap."

Traps, which are weighted down with bricks or concrete blocks, are baited with a dead fish mixture hung in a mesh "bait bag" in the interior compartment or "parlor" of the trap. Lobsters crawl up the sloped mesh entrance of the trap, called "heads," and drop into the first compartment, called the "kitchen." The only easy way out for the crawling lobsters is into the parlor from which, for larger lobsters, there is little chance of escape. Open vents in the sides of the parlor allow smaller ones to get away.

Lobstermen can fish all year, but most stop in high winter when conditions are rough and demand way down. Also, when a lobster is taken out of the water when the air temperature is below zero, it will often respond by "shooting" a claw, dropping it off. This is part of their natural defense and escape mechanism. The loss of a claw makes the lobster less marketable.

In the waters around Matinicus Island, lobstermen have a closed season and all set their traps on the same day.

Lobstermen haul their traps by snagging the buoy line with a gaff, winding it once around a hydraulic winch, and pulling it up. Once aboard the boat the trap's top is opened, and bycatch, such as crabs, sea urchins, starfish and even an occasional fish, is tossed back into the sea. The fishermen then uses a brass gauge to measure the foreshell of the lobster. If it is too big or too small (called a "short") it is returned to the water. Possession of a short lobster is a crime.

Fishermen must also cut a notch in the tail of egg-bearing female lobsters. V-notched lobsters can not be taken, which serves to insure a continued strong breeding population.

Most lobstermen work alone or hire the services of a sternman, who usually fills the bait bags and tends the traps. During summer, lobsters molt and shed their shells. While a new one forms the vulnerable lobsters hide in crevices and under rocks on the sea floor.

New shells quickly form. During July, many of the lobsters caught have soft shells and are referred to as "shedders." While the price for shedders is lower than for hard shell, many prefer their taste, claiming it to be sweeter.

Lobsters with only one claw, which are destined to be cooked for lobster meat, are called "culls." Those which are perfect and just the right size for cooking are called "selects." Lobstermen hold the "keepers" in floating wooden boxes called lobster "cars." Buyers often deal with dozens of fishermen and pool their purchases for storage purposes in a large saltwater holding facility called a "pound."

Lobster Terms	
Cull	inferior quality lobster
Ghost trap	buoy-less trap
Head	nylon mesh net at opening of trap
Keeper	legal-size lobster
Kitchen	first opening or "room" in a trap
Parlor	interior room of a trap
Selects	the best size lobsters
Shedder	soft-sided lobster forming new shell
Short	illegal lobster that is too small
Toggle	doughnut-like buoy between main buoy and trap

Lobster at the Table

The most common cooking method is boiling, preferably in sea water. The meat is then removed and dipped in melted butter. Most eateries also offer broiled, baked stuff, or sautéed lobster, as well as lobster Newburg, lobster rolls, lobster stew and lobster chowder or bisque. Chowder features pieces of meat, whereas lobster bisque usually does not.

 DID YOU KNOW? *The average lobster served in a Maine restaurant weighs a pound to a pound and a quarter. Picked by experienced hands, a lobster that size will yield five ounces of meat.*

Half the fun of a trip to the Maine Coast can be seeing how many ways you can enjoy this feast from the sea. Sautéed lobster is usually the best value. While a boiled lobster may have five ounces of meat if you get every shred, most cooks will put six to eight ounces of lobster meat in a serving when it is ordered sautéed.

WISE WORDS: *Large lobsters taste great, but when they get to weigh over three pounds, the tail meat can sometimes be tough. For maximum dining pleasure, order two smaller ones instead!*

There is no discreet way to eat a boiled lobster. The best place to dig in is at an informal establishment or at an outdoor or pier-side lobster shack where everything comes on a tray with a paper plate and plenty of napkins.

The Green Stuff

You might ask, what's that "green stuff" in a boiled lobster? That is tomale, the cooked internal parts of the lobster. Many people simply wipe it out of the shell, although some find it a delicacy and spread it on crackers or bread.

Transporting Lobsters

While lobsters are best when eaten fresh, they travel well. Most fish markets and wharfs can pack lobsters in coolers on ice or cold packs with either newspapers or seaweed for the ride home. They will keep for more than a day.

At Christmas time, major lobster suppliers often fill cargo planes at Bangor International Airport with tens of thousands of lobsters headed for markets in England and France.

Climate

Visitors to Maine frequently inquire about the climate. Many people conjure in their minds images of people wearing fur coats all year.

Maine, in fact, sports many different climate zones. Within these zones weather can vary greatly even over distances of a few miles, making the Mark Twain quote of, "If you don't like the weather in New England wait a minute – it'll change," extremely apropos.

■ Seasons

Along the ocean, the deep waters of the Gulf of Maine act as a moderating influence, especially Down East. June can be downright chilly. Summer temperatures are generally milder near the shore than a few miles inland. Usually by noon each day, a sea breeze kicks up as warm air over land rises and is replaced by cooler ocean air. This generates an onshore breeze. At night the process is often reversed, generating an offshore breeze with a calm period right around sunset. Many canoeists and sea kayakers take advantage of this phenomenon and wait out paddling on choppy lake waters until periods of calm during the early morning and evening.

Even along the south coast, where temperatures routinely climb above 90°F in summer, the breeze along the wide sandy beaches helps keep things bearable.

No matter how hot it may seem on shore, however, be sure to bring warm clothing along on any tour or whale-watching boat ride. Just offshore things can be downright cold, as chilly as 48°, even in August.

In winter along the coast the slow-to-cool ocean generates the opposite effect. Winter days close to the sea are often noticeably warmer than elsewhere, although a week or two of sub-zero temperatures in late January or early February is not unusual.

Still, those offshore islands sporting year-round populations find they have very small snow-plowing budgets; most of their winter precipitation is rain.

Inland, things can heat up in summer, sending most folks to the lakes and ponds for cool dips and welcome breezes. Summer temps hit the 80s and 90s regularly, but most often things moderate a bit at night. This pattern helped popularize what has become an overused phrase by television meteorologists who like to say it's going to be "good for sleeping."

By that measure it must be great for insomniacs come dead winter inland, particularly in the western mountains and in northern Aroostook County. Temperatures, not wind chill mind you, can hit 25 to 30 degrees below zero. (Those electrical plugs hanging from the front of vehicles in Presque Isle aren't used to recharge the batteries. Many people have small electric heating elements in their car's engine which they plug in at night to insure an easy start come morning.)

Remarkably, winter is when "The County," as it is known, really comes alive. Many residents commute to work, shopping or school on snowmobiles. Hundreds of miles of trails are enjoyed by thousands of recreational riders. Many hotels are booked months in advance for February and March.

Because temperature falls on average one degree for each 300 feet in elevation gain, the summits of the many mountains in Maine are usually cooler, particularly if the wind is blowing.

*Hikers have been known to get **hypothermia**, the sometimes fatal lowering of their body's core temperature, even in summer when they have been caught unprotected by a passing shower and then chilled by brisk winds on exposed trails.*

In June and September, temperatures drop as the sun sets. If you are planning an evening outing, make sure you bring a jacket or sweater. The first frost can come anytime after the full moon in September. Although rare, snow has fallen in Maine in early September and early June, particularly at higher altitudes. Ice-out, or the day on which a boat can travel freely from one end of Moosehead Lake to the other without being blocked by floes, occurs in early May. Rivers throw off winter's chains earlier, making wet or dry suits mandatory equipment for early season paddlers and rafters.

The fall foliage begins peaking in mountains of Western Maine and the northern part of the state around the last week of September and moves south hitting the Down East Coast and mid-Maine around Columbus Day. It peaks a little later in the very southern areas.

Extreme weather phenomena such as tornados are extremely rare in Maine. Occasionally hurricanes batter the coast but they can often seem anti-climactic in an area when fall and spring storms frequently mean wind gusts in excess of 55 miles per hour.

Weather Statistics

- Maine averages 120 inches (10 feet) of snowfall in winter.
- Total annual precipitation equals 40 to 50 inches of rain.

Tides

With the Atlantic waters ebbing and flowing twice every 24 hours, tides are a force to be reckoned with in Maine. The gravitational pull of the moon and the sun produce dramatic changes in scenery along the coast. What was sparkling blue water one minute can be gray, aromatic mud flats just a few hours later. The process creates great places to explore as the falling water strands numerous sea creatures in tidal pools perfect for wading, soaking and exploring.

▪ Beating the Tide

When planning excursions along the coast be sure to check a reliable tide chart. Most visitor guides and newspapers have them. The time shifts by roughly 45 minutes each day. Many places, such as sea caves, small islands, etc., can be accessed only at certain times. An error in calculating the tide can mean a wet trip back or even death. Sometimes a hike along cliffs and ledges can be cut short by rising water.

Several people have died in sea caves in Acadia when the tide caught them. A visit to Bar Island off Bar Harbor is a great trip, but each summer dozens of visitors fail to heed signs warning of the tides and become trapped on the island until the next ebb tide – a wait of at least six hours. Some who drive across try to race back and frequently get stuck in mud. All they can do is swim for it as their vehicle, and pride, slowly submerges.

Many factors affect the tide, including wind direction, barometric pressure, and seasonal fluctuations that can bring surprisingly higher water levels.

The change in water level can vary widely. While there may be a difference of eight to 10 feet in Southern Maine tides in the Acadia Region average 12 feet of change. As you work your way Down East the shift is even more dramatic. Cobscook Bay, near Lubec and Eastport, have typical Bay of Fundy tidal shifts of as much as 30 feet.

Some places even experience a tidal "bore," which is a wave created when water rushing out of a cove or estuary meets fast tidal water coming back in. Other hazards, particularly in the Quoddy area, are whirlpools and reversing falls, where water pours over restrictive underwater ledges going in both directions.

 WISE WORDS: *Where the water comes in fast, it is often better to wait until the tide falls rather than try to wade across fast-rising water. Not only is the ocean colder than you think, but it is easy to find yourself off good ground and get caught in the mud. Currents can also make swimming difficult.*

Rockweed

Keep an eye out for rockweed. This most common seaweed grows below the high tide line is extremely slippery when the tide is out, even if it appears dry on the surface. Air bladders in the plant allow it to float free when the water is up. But, beneath the dry upper layer there is plenty of slippery stuff. People breaking arms, legs and cracking heads after slipping on rockweed is one of the most common reasons for emergency room visits along the coast.

Fauna

Seeing animals and birds in the wild is one of the most exciting parts of any Maine adventure. The woods and waters of the state are home to a wide variety of species ranging from the regal and majestic moose to the sleek and extraordinarily fast Peregrine falcons.

As the tourism industry shifts more toward what officials call "ecotourism," bird- and animal-watching tours are gaining in popularity.

While moose safaris (hunt here with cameras only please) are now big business around the Greenville and Moosehead Lake region, by far the greatest amount of interest is found along the coast. Numerous ports now feature companies offering whale-watching tours. In Bar Harbor alone three companies vie for the business with a total of nearly 3,000 seats a day available.

Whale-watching in Maine was once an all-day affair, but now sleek catamarans and multi-prop mono-hulls speed passengers out to the whale grounds offshore and back in just a few hours. All tours offer spectacular visibility as you scan the horizon for finbacks or watch as massive humpbacks soar straight up, nearly out of the water, in a move called breaching.

Smaller tour operators specialize in everything from harbor seal- and eagle-watching to lobster-fishing demonstrations, and there are even glass-bottomed boats where a diver wearing a television camera shows passengers life along the sea bottom. Live sea creatures such as spiny urchins and the mysterious sea cucumber are brought aboard for passengers to examine and then carefully put back unharmed where they were found.

■ Feathered Friends

Puffins

While their image is everywhere, the sometimes comical-looking puffin is actually difficult to see and found only on remote offshore ledges. Some tour operators do offer special trips to see these frisky feathered friends.

Save the Puffin

Puffins represent one of Maine's finest wildlife restoration efforts. The bird had been hunted to extinction during the 1800s to feed the flames of fashion for featured hats. But researchers recently captured young chicks in Eastern Canada and transplanted them to select offshore islands along Maine's coast in a successful attempt to revive the population.

Loons

Most undeveloped lakes in Maine sport breeding populations of loons. These ancient birds with their distinct black and white plumage and red eyes, long ago lost their ability to take off or land on dry ground. Their haunting cries echo down misty lakes at night as they call out to their mates. One of the greatest thrills of wildlife watching in early summer is to see a mother loon with young. The startled chicks will head straight for mom and literally run right up on her back!

Marvel when you see them dive at their ability to "fly" long distances underwater in search of small fish.

Ospreys

Ospreys, also called fish hawks, are fascinating to watch. They will circle and hover over a lake or the sea, spot a fish, and dive at tremendous speed right into the water with a huge splash. They must be careful to correctly judge the size of their prey because their talons cannot release until they set a fish down on something solid. If their claws slice into too big a fish and they cannot lift it from the water, they can drown.

Birds of Prey

Many magnificent birds of prey call Maine home, including the spectacular bald eagle to the osprey, red-tailed hawk, sharp-shinned hawk and Cooper's hawk. In Acadia National Park, the reintroduction of the endangered peregrine falcon has been so successful officials are considering dropping their status to threatened.

■ Woodland Creatures

While trips to see marine mammals and seabirds are more dependent on *where* you go, the chances of seeing some of Maine's many land mammals vary greatly depending on *when* you go.

Most woodland creatures – beaver, deer, fox, porcupine, raccoons – are more active at dawn and dusk, and that is when you have the best chance of spotting them.

Moose on paper company dirt road near Kokadjo in Northern Maine.
Photo by Joe Lamonica

Moose

Moose may be more active at dawn and dusk, but can often be spotted at almost any time of the day. They prefer boggy areas or lakes where they love to wade and feast on aquatic plants. The water running off a bull moose's antlers in late season, after the creature has put its entire head underwater to reach succulent vegetation, can sound from a distance like rapids on a river.

Bears & Wolves

Seeing a bear is a rare event, and the jury is still out whether or not some larger mammals call Maine home at all. Officials now do not believe that there is a breeding population of wolves in Maine (they were hunted to eradication more than 100 years ago). Still, two hunters in recent years have killed what they thought were coyotes, but turned out to be stray wolves. The official state word is that wolves are welcome if they wander back here by themselves, but no outright effort to reintroduce them will be made, despite efforts by at least one group to promote reintroduction.

Mountain Lions

Officials are also on the fence as to whether there are mountain lions in Maine, but reports and sightings are being made with increasing frequency. Some towns in the Western Mountains now post warnings that

Introduction

big cats may be in the area, but no one has brought in photographic or physical proof of that.

Caribou

Another animal hunted to eradication a century ago in Maine was the caribou. Efforts to reestablish these tundra dwellers to a plateau in Baxter State Park in the 1970s failed.

■ Calls of the Wild

There are plenty of vocal creatures in the wilds of Maine that you may never get a good look at but who will reveal themselves to attentive listeners with their hoots and calls.

Coyotes

Coyotes communicate over great distances with their yelps and howls. While these shy predators will take great pains to avoid humans, the intensity of their calls often betrays a close approach.

While camped one winter on some high ground in the middle of a vast frozen peat bog, our party was serenaded by coyotes all night long. Their calls came from widely separated ridges surrounding the lowland. Each call was repeated in succession across the valley. Despite calls that indicated one group was only 50 yards or so behind out tents, we never caught sight of the beast.

Birdsongs

Whip-poor-wills call from the edges of fields and woods at dusk. They sound just like their name, although most call so fast it is like hearing it on a high-speed tape.

From the deep woods the lilting call of the **wood thrush** fills the evening air. In high places, even above treeline, the lonely call of the **white-throated sparrow** can fill an ancient silence. In the forest and at feeders the scolding "dee, dee, dee" of the **chickadee** can be heard year-round.

The staccato call of the **kingfisher** is a familiar friend to paddlers as the bird scolds them for disturbing its river-side perch.

The **great horned owl** provides a shocking welcome to the woods the first night it begins to screech from the top of a tall pine above your tent.

WILDLIFE & BIRD CHECKLISTS

Land Birds

❏ Bald eagle	❏ Great horned owl	❏ Purple martin
❏ Bluebird	❏ Grosbeak	❏ Raven
❏ Canada jay	❏ Hermit thrush	❏ Red-tailed hawk
❏ Cedar waxwing	❏ Indigo bunting	❏ Red-winged blackbird
❏ Chickadee	❏ Junco	❏ Robin
❏ Common redpoll	❏ Mourning dove	❏ Ruffed grouse
❏ Crow	❏ Nuthatch	❏ Hawk
❏ Downy woodpecker	❏ Peregrine falcon	❏ Snowy woodpecker
❏ Flicker	❏ Pileated woodpecker	❏ White-throated sparrow
❏ Fox sparrow	❏ Pine siskin	❏ Wood thrush
❏ Goldfinch	❏ Purple finch	❏ Yellow-rumped warbler

Sea Birds

❏ Arctic tern	❏ Gannet	❏ Leach's petrel
❏ Black duck	❏ Greater shearwater	❏ Old squaw
❏ Black-backed gull	❏ Guillemont	❏ Puffin
❏ Common tern	❏ Herring gull	❏ Roseate tern
❏ Cormorant	❏ Laughing gull	❏ Sandpiper
❏ Eider		❏ Sea coot

Freshwater Birds

❏ American golden-eye	❏ Great blue heron	❏ Mallard
❏ Blue-wing teal	❏ Kingfisher	❏ Osprey
❏ Common loon	❏ Least bittern	❏ Wood duck

Mammals

❏ Beaver	❏ Gray squirrel	❏ Rabbit
❏ Black bear	❏ Hare	❏ Raccoon
❏ Bobcat	❏ Moose	❏ Red squirrel
❏ Brown bat	❏ Mountain lion?	❏ Skunk
❏ Chipmunk	❏ Otter	❏ White-tailed deer
❏ Coyote	❏ Pine martin	❏ Wolf?
❏ Fox	❏ Porcupine	❏ Woodchuck

Marine Mammals

❏ Bottlenose dolphin	❏ Hooded seal	❏ Pilot whale
❏ Finback whale	❏ Humpback whale	❏ Right whale
❏ Gray seal	❏ Killer whale	❏ Sei whale
❏ Harbor porpoise	❏ Minke whale	❏ Sperm whale
❏ Harbor seal	❏ North bottlenose whale	❏ Striped dolphin
❏ Harp seal		❏ White-side dolphin

▪ Tracks & Other Evidence

Careful observers will keep a sharp eye out for signs that an animal has recently been in an area. Deer, moose and black bear prints in the mud near a stream crossing are a giveaway. Here are some tracks you might see.

| **Bleak Bear** | **Deer** | **Moose** | **Raccoon** |

The crow-sized **pileated woodpecker** can be heard for more than a mile as it drills its beak into wood in search of boring insects. The pile of wood chips at the base of the tree, coupled with the distinctive rectangular holes, is a sure sign that this majestic "cock of the woods" has been busy.

▪ Whales

Adopt-A-Whale Program

Allied Whale, the marine mammal research lab at College of the Atlantic in Bar Harbor, has selected several of their 70-ton friends to be part of an Adopt-a-Whale project.

When they receive your $30 donation, or $50 for a mother and her calf, the research group will send an 8x10 color photograph of an individually identified whale and a certificate of your adoption. You can also get T-shirts and clothing with your whale's picture for an additional charge. Donors also receive the whale's biography, sighting history and the *Adopt a Finback Whale* book, 16 pages of photographs and information about whales and whale research. Included with every adoption is a subscription to Allied Whale's newsletter, which keeps donors updated on sightings of

A humpback breaches off the coast of Bar Harbor.
Photo by Michael McGuire

their whale and contains other interesting articles about Allied Whale activities.

Finbacks are among the biggest animals ever to live on earth. The largest may reach lengths over 80 feet. In this century more than a million may have been hunted and killed in the world's oceans. For the time being, they are protected from hunting throughout most of the world, but researchers say this poorly understood endangered species faces new threats to its long-term survival.

The whales in the adoption project are part of the *North Atlantic Finback Whale Catalogue*, a large database of information about individual finback whales which are identified by natural markings and scars. It is a cooperative effort by dozens of marine-mammal researchers in the United States and Canada. The photographic-identification technique developed by these scientists is currently one of the best tools available for studying these animals, because each whale can potentially be tracked over its whole lifetime.

To adopt a finback whale, ☎ 288-5644 and charge your contribution on VISA or MasterCard. Or mail your $30 or $50 donation to Finbacks, College of the Atlantic, Bar Harbor, ME 04609. Include your name and address and, if it's a gift, the name and address of the person receiving the gift.

Maine Endangered Species

Birds: Golden eagle, Peregrine falcon, piping plover, roseate tern, Least tern, sedge wren, American pipit, grasshopper sparrow.
Reptiles & Amphibians: Blanding's turtle, box turtle, black racer.

Maine Threatened Species

Birds: Bald eagle, razorbill, Atlantic puffin, harlequin duck, Arctic tern, upland sandpiper.
Mammals: Northern bob lemming.
Reptiles & Amphibians: Spotted turtle, loggerhead turtle.

Source: Maine Department of Inland Fisheries and Wildlife

Flora

 Many may joke that there is no such thing as spring in our fair state, since often we just go straight from winter to mud season.

Lupine shown here along the shore in Bar Harbor,
is one of dozens of species of wildflowers that bloom each spring.

■ Wildflowers

But spring does happen here, bringing with it a fresh green breath of life to the land. With the reappearance of leaves and blades of grass come the wildflowers. There are literally hundreds of species in microhabitats all across the state.

Roadsides explode with daisies, black-eyed Susans and bright purple, pink and white lupine.

In the woods, pink, yellow, and white lady-slippers favor damp places with lots of shade, often with the graceful blossoms of trillium for neighbors. Orange day lilies wave from ditches and from abandoned cellar holes.

Along the shore, the Rugosa rose's prickly stalks await those who venture too close to admire and inhale the sweet offerings of its pink and white flowers.

■ Alpine Flowers

There are several small areas on some of Maine's windswept, barren peaks where true alpine flowers can be found in abundance. They include

Bigelow in Western Maine, and on Katahdin and other nearby peaks in Baxter State Park.

In Acadia National Park, many of the open peaks there sport sub-alpine flowers shows in spring as well.

Alpine flowers are among the hardiest survivors on the planet. They cling to life under harsh conditions. The frail and fragile nature of their flowers and stalks seems at odds with the niche they occupy.

Learning to identify and admire alpine flowers is an acquired taste, particularly because of the effort required get to the areas where the flourish. Most "blooms" occur in early spring, often when there are still large patches of snow at altitude. This is also the time of year when blackflies are most voracious.

Still, the clusters of tiny white diapensia blooms, particularly on Katahdin, are spectacular. Nearby, bright pink lapland rosebay and Alpine azalea also thrive.

Mountain sandwort, wine-leaf cinquefoil await intrepid hikers in early July on many of Acadia's summits. Later, as blueberries ripen, the single-stalked orange wood lilies provide interesting contrast.

 WISE WORDS: *Alpine vegetation, including lichens, mosses and sedges, is fragile. Heavy bootsteps damage plants and also foster erosion. Staying on the marked trail minimizes damage and limits adverse impacts to a small area.*

■ Wild Berries

Maine's most famous wild berry is the **blueberry**, which grows on vast open barrens and rocky fields from central Maine to Down East. The area west and east of Ellsworth is particularly productive. Each year, Maine ships tens of millions of pounds of this succulent, sweet, blue fruit around the world.

 INTERESTING FACT: *Scientists have recently discovered blueberries have high levels of powerful cancer-fighting anti-oxidants.*

Most berries are harvested in August. Some farms where you can pick your own are listed in individual area chapters throughout this book. While removal of vegetation is illegal in Acadia, picking blueberries for your own consumption is allowed. Many hikers have suddenly wondered where an afternoon went after they have become distracted collecting this delicious berry.

Raspberries and **blackberries** also grow wild in Maine and are most fond of the tangled web of vegetation following a timber harvest. The commercial production of **cranberries** has also recently increased.

■ Forest for the Trees

Maine sports several distinct types of forest. In southern and western areas most forests are filled with Eastern hardwood trees such as maple, beech and birch. As you head north, or gain elevation in mountainous areas, this changes.

In the north, east and at higher elevations the forest is primarily Northern softwoods with a predominance of **spruce** and **fir**. **Pines** are found primarily on sandy, well-drained sites. Most of the tallest were felled in Colonial times after being marked with an axe to indicate they were "the King's trees," reserved for use by the Royal Navy for masts and spars.

In wetland areas **cedar** and **larch**, the latter the only evergreen tree to shed all its needles each year, can be found.

TREES OF MAINE CHECKLIST		
❒ Ash	❒ Hemlock	❒ Sugar maple
❒ Aspen	❒ Hickory	❒ Walnut
❒ Balsam fir	❒ Hornbeam	❒ White birch
❒ Basswood	❒ Horse chestnut	❒ White cedar
❒ Beech	❒ Jack pine	❒ White oak
❒ Black oak	❒ Larch	❒ White pine
❒ Chestnut	❒ Red maple	❒ White spruce
❒ Elm	❒ Red oak	❒ Willow
❒ Gray birch	❒ Red pine	❒ Yellow birch
	❒ Red spruce	

The Forest Ecosystem

The composition of forest stands and the distribution of species can be affected by many factors besides climate and moisture. After a major upheaval, such as forest fire or clear cut, hardwood species like maple and birch quickly colonize an area. Softwoods such as pine and spruce prefer shady areas. New hardwood growth creates ideal habitat for moose and deer, as well as upland game birds such as spruce grouse.

As the hardwoods mature they create a canopy which encourages the growth of softwoods. These will eventually take over in a process known as forest succession. If allowed to grow unmolested, eventually a tall, mature stand of large conifers will result. This is called a **climax forest**.

The forest ecosystem is never static, however. Eventually disease, insects, high winds or fire will fell the giants, allowing sunlight the penetrate to the forest floor and begin the process anew. The dead or dying giants make good homes and food sources for birds and small mammals.

INTERESTING FACT: *Some species, particularly the low, gnarled Jack pine, actually use the heat generated by a forest fire to help free seeds from its tough, wood cone.*

Woods - Uses & Growth

While the term softwoods is used as a synonym for conifers (needle-bearing), remember that not all conifer wood is soft. Hemlock, for instance, is tougher than poplar, also known as aspen, even though the latter is classified as a hardwood. Hardwoods, a term generally used for deciduous or leaf-bearing trees that shed their leaves in fall, even though some species bear soft wood. And, all conifers are not necessarily "evergreen." Conifers lose about 30% of their needles every year. The needles of larch, which is also known as tamarack and hackmatack, turn orange-yellow each fall and drop just like their leaf-bearing neighbors. In Maine, softwoods are the primary raw material used for making paper and construction lumber. Hardwoods such as maple and oak are used for pallets, furniture and wood products such as toothpicks. Popsicle sticks and trophy parts are made from odorless white birch, a tight-grained wood, made so by its distinctive bark which grows at a right angle to the stem.

Balsam fir is the tree with the traditional "Christmas tree" smell, although its flat needles make it a rare choice for a full, decorative tree. The dried needles are used in fragrant balsam pillows and in incense.

DID YOU KNOW? *Maine cuts and ships more than 350,000 Christmas trees each year. In addition, softwoods, including fir and spruce, are "tipped" to gather enough brush to create 2.5 million wreaths.*

Treeline, the elevation above which trees no longer grow, is much lower in Maine and New England due to the strong weather patterns that converge here. This is especially true in Western Maine and on Katahdin. At higher elevations, balsam fir and spruce, buffeted and shaped by fierce winds, struggle to maintain a tenuous hold in the shallow soil. Nature has created her own bonsai trees here. Despite their small, shrub-like appearance, these dwarf trees, called krummholz, are often very old.

Studies have shown that the bitter cold temperatures at higher elevations in the winter is not the key factor in determining where the treeline will be. A failure to warm up sufficiently in summer, when trees theoretically should have the best season to grow, has a larger effect.

LARGEST TREES IN MAINE			
SPECIES	CIRCUMFERENCE	HEIGHT	TOWN
Ash	19'-1"	81'	South Waterford
Aspen	17'-11"	70'	Bridgton
Balsam fir	6'-1"	104'	Albion
Basswood	13'-11"	97'	Phippsburg
Beech	16'-2"	72'	Rockport
Black oak	6'-11"	73'	New Gloucester
Chestnut	7'-3"	44'	Orono
Elm	19'-0"	115'	Yarmouth
Gray birch	2'-8"	53'	Unity
Hemlock	14'-4"	100'	TWP 37MD*
Hickory	9'-4"	66'	Kittery
Hornbeam	2'-4"	21'	Gray
Horse chestnut	7'-3"	44'	Orono
Jack pine	9'-0"	25'	T1 R9 Wels*
Larch	6'-4"	107'	Solon
Red maple	12'-10"	55'	Westbrook
Red oak	21'-4"	80'	Vienna
Red pine	7'-4"	96'	Weld
Red spruce	9'-5"	102'	Clifton
Sugar maple	17'-9"	80'	Palermo
Walnut	13'-0"	80'	Camden
White cedar	4'-2"	47'	Appleton
White oak	19'-11"	64'	Pittston
White pine	19'-1"	132'	Morrill
White spruce	8'-7"	83'	Troy
Willow	15'-6"	56'	Troy
Yellow birch	21'-0"	76'	Deer Isle

*Source: Maine Dept. of Conservation. * See page 50 for explanation of road designations.*

Introduction

Firewood

When camping, remember that softwood, which is full of resins and pitch, will help get a fire going quickly but will leave few coals and lasting heat. Pine, spruce, and fir branches pop and snap excessively, sending showers of hot embers into the air and onto the ground around the fire ring.

Dry hardwood burns best and longest and leaves a good bed of coals for cooking or getting a fire going again in the morning. It also produces the fewest flying embers. Of all the hardwoods, ash, which is used for axe and tool handles, is the hardest and is believed to burn hottest and longest.

■ Fall Foliage

From mid-September through mid-October Maine is ablaze with autumnal colors. This colorful current begins in the north and almost imperceptibly wends its way slowly south, peaking last along the South Coast.

Foliage Hotline: The Maine foliage hotline, in service each fall, offers the latest color-peaking information for leaf-peepers. ☎ 800-932-3419.

Due to sheer size alone, Maine provides foliage lovers with no end of spectacular landscapes. Every view – the wave-tossed coast, the towering peaks of the Western Mountains, tumbling streams and wind-swept lakes – comes alive with the vivid reds, oranges and yellows of fall.

Foliage season in Maine, indeed in all New England, is one of the busiest tourist times. What many leaf peepers do not understand is that the leaves really don't change color so much as simply reveal their true stripes. The pigments that produce the reds and yellows are present in the leaves all summer long. In fall, a reduction in daylight prompts leaves to form scar tissue where they attach to a branch. Cut off from a source of water, the chlorophyll in the leaves, which gives them their green color, fades away, revealing in a sense the leaf's inner beauty.

Many factors, such as an early frost or a dry August, can affect just how vivid the colors will be. Also, if a storm with heavy winds and rain moves through at just the wrong time, most of the leaves can be blown down in a single night.

In Aroostook County colorful hardwoods ring potato fields that have only been recently harvested.

Towering over the Great North Woods, Katahdin, itself mostly devoid of trees, becomes a gray mass in contrast to the surrounding ocean of color.

Down East, in Acadia and along the border with New Brunswick, colorful trees are mirrored in rush rivers and surging sea.

In the Western Mountains, the foliage creates a colorful carpet that hugs the rounded terrain. While in the Mid-Coast area, lines of vivid hardwoods create a maze of patterns among fields that cover rolling hills.

PEAK FOLIAGE
September 24 through September 30
The northern sections of Aroostook County and the Katahdin-Moosehead-Penquis regions.
October 1 through October 7
Maine Lakes and Mountains, Kennebec Valley, and southern portions of the Katahdin-Moosehead-Penquis regions.
October 8 though October 14
The Southern Maine Coast, Mid-Coast, and Down East/Acadia regions.

Source: Maine Department of Tourism

Things that Go Bump in the Night

Every state or region has some flora and fauna most visitors would just as soon not run into. Maine is no exception, although the list here of undesirable creepy crawlies is thankfully short and the likelihood of major problems very slight.

■ Insects

Mosquitos, of course, are found everywhere in Maine and are usually in generous abundance about two weeks after a good rain. They fade by August and disappear pretty much for good after the first frost.

Poor fliers, mosquitos favor damp, dark, windless areas. There have been no documented cases of mosquitos transmitting any dangerous diseases to humans in Maine.

Blackflies are at their worst in mid-May and early June when they have been known to drive bull moose out of the deep woods. While not out at night when the mosquitos are about, they can be especially bad in windless areas during the day. Unlike mosquitos, which puncture the skin and drink blood, blackflies rip a tiny tear and literally lap up their meal. Bites itch like crazy and can swell greatly, especially the day after.

Deer flies appear in July and like to circle their victims incessantly before gently landing to chomp down.

 INTERESTING THEORY: *One old woodsman theorized that deer flies were the reason the Indians wore feathers in their head bands. Flies seem to circle the highest point, and the feathers were higher than the head.*

A larger version of the deer fly, dubbed the **moose fly**, is similar to the common horse fly seen around farms.

Maine also has "**no-see-ums,**" tiny winged insects known as "midges," which can bite.

It is believed there are no poisonous spiders or "killer bees" in Maine, but **honey bees**, **wasps** and **yellow jackets** are common.

Ticks can be found all around the state, including some that have tested positive for Lyme disease, a virus that can produce arthritis and immune system problems in humans. Their strategy is to climb on nearby vegetation and hop on any passing animal, be it human, dog or deer. Check for ticks after an outing, before they have a chance to burrow in.

Beating Those Bites

The best defense against biting insects and ticks is a commercial repellent containing **DEET**, such as Ben's. The 100% concentration will literally melt plastic (say goodbye to that new camera or binoculars). The backyard formula with less than 30% DEET seems to work fine. DEET is not recommended for use on children.

Wearing **light-colored clothing** seems to help as well. Some entomologists theorize that biting insects are drawn to large dark shapes because that is what they are most likely to feed off in the wild. Avoid using perfume or shampoo with a strong floral scent. Mosquitos and black flies home in on body heat and carbon dioxide in breath. That is why they seem to pester hot, sweaty people the most. **Head nets** can be a blessing.

Time outings to coincide with windy weather. Baxter State Park Ranger Greg Hamor, who staffs a cabin at Chimney Pond, says his bug strategy involves finding the person wildly waving their arms to drive the bugs away. "I stand right next to him and the bugs seem to leave me alone," he says.

By late July bug populations begin to wane, making them only a minor annoyance.

■ Reptiles

Maine boasts that it is completely free of poisonous **snakes**. Except for the odd sighting of a rattlesnake in the western part of the state near the New Hampshire border, this appears to be true. There are snakes here, but most would rather get out of your way than tangle any day.

Snapping turtles, which can grow quite large, particularly in warm water lakes and ponds, have extraordinarily strong jaws and a very quick lunge. They should be given wide berth.

■ Mammals

As in any natural setting, all animals should be given plenty of room. Maine is home to **black bears**. The black bear is the University of Maine's mascot. Normal camp precautions to prevent bears linking humans with food is recommended. Leave no food lying around, take none in tents and tree the food and garbage when necessary.

Bears here, which can get as large as 600 pounds, are never to be considered tame. Extra precaution should be taken when a mother with cubs is spotted. Black bears can climb trees. Thankfully, attacks are very rare.

Coyotes can often be heard howling in the wildlands of the state. They are shy, wary predators and are seldom seen by humans.

Wolves are believed to occasionally stray into Maine from Quebec, although biologists do not believe there is a breeding population in the state.

Moose are majestic animals easily viewed around marshy areas and ponds. Do not get too close, however, as they have been known to tire of human presence.

DID YOU KNOW? *The largest cause of human fatalities connected with wildlife in Maine comes from vehicle collisions with moose. More than 700 crashes are reported in an average year. Six or seven people are killed.*

These largest members of the deer family are big, dark, difficult to see at night and will often run away from a car or truck and then cut right in front of the vehicle at the last second. Because of their height and weight they land atop the roof of the car, injuring the occupants. Slow down and pass Moose with care. Also, when you see one moose or deer, be sure to look on the opposite side of the road as well; there may well be more.

 Any animal, no matter how cute or cuddly, should not be handled and should be left alone. Fox, raccoons, skunks and other animals are potential rabies carriers.

■ At Sea

While Maine waters are home to small **sharks**, commonly called dogfish, they are not a threat to humans. Larger sharks are sometimes caught offshore, but no beach has been closed in recent times due to concerns over shark attacks.

Keep an eye out for the numerous small red and clear **jellyfish** that often school in saltwater. While not as life-threatening as the Portuguese man-of-war found in warmer climes, they can still sting, even if touched after they have washed up on the beach.

■ Plants

Maine has **poison ivy**, which can be found almost anywhere. It is a three-leaved vine and is most commonly found in roadside ditches and on trees. Poisonous **mushrooms** grow in Maine. Telling them apart from edible species is difficult. Authorities urge only experts to pick any for human consumption.

■ Two-Legged Varmints

The crime rate in Maine is thankfully low. Random violence is rare, with most criminal activity involving petty theft and vandalism. Like most places, more caution is urged in larger population centers. Many people in Maine still do not lock the doors of their homes at night and often leave their keys in the car all the time. The fact that Maine also has one of the highest rates of personal firearm ownership has sociologists wondering if that may be a factor considered by would-be ne'er-do-wells.

The low crime rate, however, does not mean that tourists should let down their guard. Visitors should take these basic precautions.

Introduction

- Keep vehicles locked and place valuables such as purchases, purses, cameras, etc., out of plain view in parked vehicles.
- Don't leave cash lying around in motel rooms.
- If you are alone and involved in a minor accident on a remote stretch of the Interstate, remain in your car until the police arrive.

Vandalism or thefts from vehicles left at river put-ins or trailheads is the exception rather than the rule, although there seem to be a few "smash and grab" thefts from some of the more remote parking areas in Acadia National Park each summer. Most involved items left in plain view.

 WISE WORDS: *Report suspicious activity or any thefts or loss of articles to authorities. Don't take the matter into your own hands. There is a lot more fun than danger out there. Don't be afraid – just be careful.*

Just in Case

Most larger towns have their own police departments and there are sheriff's departments in all counties. Developed areas have 911, but the service is not state-wide. Also, there are a lot of places where cellular telephones will not get a signal. Northern Maine is particularly bad. Get up as high as possible to try and connect. Truckers and other recreational wilderness users often monitor CB channel 9, although the range of CB units is limited. If you are truly stuck, call one of these agencies:

Emergency Telephone Numbers
Maine State Police . . . . Cell phone *77
South & West. . . . . ☎ 800-482-0730
Mid-Coast & Northwest . . . . ☎ 800-452-4664
Down East & North Central. . . . . ☎ 800-432-7381
Far North . . . . ☎ 800-924-2261
Maine Warden Service, ... ☎ 800-322-2033
Search and Rescue
US Coast Guard, ... ☎ 207-244-5121
Search and Rescue
Poison Center. . . . . ☎ 800-442-6305
Crisis Intervention . . . . ☎ 800-245-8889
Maine Turnpike (road conditions) . . . . ☎ 800-675-7453
Whale/Seal Stranding Network. . . . . ☎ 207-288-5644

History

Being the easternmost of the United States, Maine is the place where the rays of the rising sun hit America first. For years, exactly where the dawn can be seen from first has been in dispute. Some claim it is mile-high Katahdin in Baxter State Park. Others claim it is Cadillac Mountain in Acadia National Park along the coast.

In fact, it all depends on the time of year. No one place can rightfully lay ultimate claim to the honor. On some days the sun can be seen first from Mars Hill in Aroostook County; on others an observer in the lighthouse at West Quoddy Head, the nation's easternmost point, would be first.

■ Native Americans

The fact that the sun rises first somewhere over this part of North America was undoubtedly understood by the area's earliest inhabitants – Native Americans known by other tribes as **Wabanaki**, "those living at sunrise." The modern English spelling of the overall name for the tribes who called Maine home is **Abnaki**, or Abenaki. The more literal translation of the name is now "people of the dawn."

The ancestors of these native peoples, whose tribes sported names still used in geography today – the Penobscots, Passamaquoddies, the Sacos, Kennebecs, and Micmacs – were the mysterious **Red Paint People**. Scant evidence of their lives has been found.

What is generally known is that later Indian settlements were found both along the coast, where shell heaps, called middens, were fairly common, and in the interior, where the area's maze-like network of lakes, ponds and streams allowed routine travel by birch-back canoe.

■ Europeans

The earliest contact between European explorers and native peoples sent the French and English back to the continent with tales of great riches and of **Norumbega**; a legendary city of gold. The true wealth, of course, lay in millions of acres of virgin timber, rivers and bays overflowing with fish, and rich fertile land.

There is no end of speculation that Norse explorers were the first white people to visit Maine. A Viking coin uncovered at an excavation of a Native American site near Blue Hill earlier in this century gave backers of that theory hope. Most experts, however, believe the coin arrived at the site through the Indians' elaborate trading network with tribes to the north. Still, a Harvard researcher believes an inscription on a rock on Crow Island, off Deer Isle, is a message written in Bronze-age Nordic Tifinag script, advising fellow Vikings that the nearby waters make for a good anchorage.

The first recorded look by Europeans at what would become the State of Maine, came in 1524 when famed explorer Giovanni da Verrazano labeled a point of land, near present day Penobscot Bay, as Oranbega.

Samuel de Champlain sailed along the Down East Coast in 1604, passing by Mount Desert Island in September. Seeing the rocky mountain tops from the sea he named the place "Isle de Monts Desert," literally island of barren mountains. A French attempt to establish a colony on St. Croix island near present day Calais failed in that year.

The first attempt to establish a colony, made by the English, came four years later in 1608. But, after only one winter the Popham colony, not far from present day Bath at the mouth of the Kennebec River, failed. Starvation, pestilence and cold were not the culprits. The untimely deaths of key leaders and the bungled efforts of financial backers caused its failure, according to historian Charles E. Clark. It was not until a year later, in 1609, that the first permanent settlement in North America, Jamestown, was established.

In 1613 a French party attempted to settled on Mount Desert Island not far from what is now Southwest Harbor. The settlement of St. Savuer was short-lived however. The settlers and priests were quickly driven off by English raiding parties.

Throughout the early 1600s English fishermen used islands far off the Maine coast as remote bases. After spending months at Monhegan and Damariscove Islands and the Isles of Shoals they would return home, holds brimming with salted and dried fish. Europeans also had presence at Pemaquid and other points, where they traded with Indians.

Attempts to colonize Casco Bay, near present-day Portland, failed in 1623 and 1624. Before the decade was out, however, trading and fishing settlements were successful along the entire coast from the Piscataqua River (modern border with New Hampshire) to Pemaquid.

■ Modern History

Kittery became Maine's first incorporated town in 1647. During the next 100 years coastal communities grew and settlers pushed inland following major rivers.

During the Revolutionary War, Maine played a small and often overlooked role, although the first naval battle of the conflict was fought off the Down East Coast. In June of 1775 townspeople in Machias stormed and took over the British schooner *Margaretta*, using a trusty sloop and little more than an odd collection of hunting flintlocks and pitchforks. In October of that year, the British Navy, on orders to harass non-loyalists, bombarded the town of Falmouth, now Portland.

Benedict Arnold's March on Quebec

Perhaps the most notable local operation of the war, immortalized in Maine author Kenneth Robert's novel *Arundel*, was Benedict Arnold's march on Quebec. Beginning with 1,100 men in the early fall of 1775, Arnold and his expedition headed up the Kennebec River in leaky bateau and with provisions and equipment he would soon learn were extraordinarily sub-standard. The plan was to haul the boats and supplies a short ways overland from the northern reaches of the Kennebec and then use north-flowing rivers in Canada to approach the city of Quebec. Winter snows came early. The expedition, with men weakened by disease and malnourishment, became lost and disorientated after hauling the boats literally up the side of a mountain. After eight excruciating weeks Arnold was left with only a handful of men. His attack was repulsed. Despite the capture of hundreds of his men he lay siege to Quebec for several months before ultimately giving up and going home. The raging rapids, falls, and the massive mountains the expedition had to cross can be easily viewed today from Route 201 now named the **Arnold Trail**, with interpretive signs and roadside rest areas.

Also during the revolution, in 1779, American Naval forces suffered a disastrous defeat off Castine in Penobscot Bay.

During the War of 1812, much of Maine east of the Penobscot, including Bangor, was occupied by British forces.

Residents of Maine, then a territory of Massachusetts, were not happy with what little protection and attention they received during the war. The issue sowed the seeds of separatism that resulted in Maine becoming its own state. On July 26, 1891 Mainers voted 17,091 to 7,132 to separate from Massachusetts. The new state, with a population of just under 300,000, officially joined the Union as a free state on March 3, 1820 as part of the Missouri Compromise.

Maine Counties

Maine has 16 counties. They are: Androscoggin, Aroostook, Cumberland, Franklin, Hancock, Kennebec, Knox, Lincoln, Oxford, Penobscot, Piscataguis, Sagadahoc, Somerset, Waldo, Washington, York.

Maine was barely 20 years old as a state when it appeared it might be the setting for another war with the British Empire. A festering boundary dispute with New Brunswick over timber and land in 1839 resulted in both sides sending troops to "the county." Dubbed the Aroostook War, the conflict never came to any major outright battles and was eventually settled by treaty.

■ Industrial Growth

With the state at peace, Mainers set about satisfying their industrious natures. By the middle of the 1800s Maine was building more **ships** than any other state. Between 1851 and 1854, Maine launched 77 graceful clippers from yards in Kittery, Bath, Damariscotta, Rockland and elsewhere.

Hundreds of **sawmills** sprung up as Maine's white pine was exported to cities around the world.

Paper mills were established in Millinocket and other places where towns soon followed.

In the north woods, loggers cut **wood** all winter and piled it on the shores of rivers and lakes. Come ice out in the spring the raw logs were sent tumbling towards the mills of Bangor and Orono.

In the far north, engineers dammed and diverted lakes and streams to force some waterways to flow "backward," allowing timber and pulp logs to be sent south to mills in Maine rather than north, through Canada, which charged a hefty duty.

The United Society of Believers in Christ's Second Coming, commonly known as the "Shaking Quakers," or Shakers, established three communities in Maine beginning in the late 1700s. A small handful of believers continue the old ways to this day and do a brisk business selling seeds and handicrafts to thousands of tourists at Sabbathday Lake.

In Aroostook a favorable report on the land's ability to grow things, particularly potatoes, shipped raw and as starch, launched a major industry.

Maine's connections with the Civil War are many. Harriet Beecher Stowe wrote part of *Uncle Tom's Cabin* at her home in Brunswick at the edge of the Bowdoin campus. Maine Senator Hannibal Hamlin was Abraham Lincoln's first running mate and vice president. Colonel, later to become General Joshua Chamberlain of Brewer commanded the 20th Maine on Little Round Top at the Battle of Gettysburg and held the line on the high point of the Confederacy on the second day of battle. Months later he was appointed by General Ulysses S. Grant to accept the surrender of the rebel army.

French Canadians from Quebec flowed into Maine in the late 1800s, giving mill towns like Lewiston a multi-cultural flair that continues today.

■ Tourism

Around the late 1800s the first seeds of Maine's tourism industry were sowed. Paintings by members of the Hudson River School, like Frederick Church, inspired wealthy city dwellers to foray Down East. Picturesque harbors like Bar Harbor, Camden, Boothbay Harbor and Kennebunkport soon became seasonal watering holes for the wealthy and powerful.

Wide beaches in Southern Maine drew thousands seeking relief from the heat of cities. **Old Orchard** quickly became a favorite playground for visitors from Quebec.

The Plus Side of Tourism

During the early 1900s numerous benefactors began to work to save many of Maine's natural wonders. George B. Dorr and Charles Eliot put together the Hancock County Trustees of Public Reservations and began acquiring land that would become Acadia National Park.

By mid-century, Governor Percival Baxter privately amassed nearly 200,000 acres in the middle of the state, including its highest point, Katahdin. He created a privately endowed preserve that carries his name. The spirit of conservation continues unabated. Paper companies allow public recreational use of their land either for free or a modest fee. Other land protection efforts have created many preserves, including the **Appalachian Trail Corridor**, the **Bigelow Mountain Preserve** and numerous locales protected by the Nature Conservancy, Maine Coast Heritage Trust and other groups.

Tourism has now become one of Maine's top industries, ranking right up there with pulp and paper, agriculture and fisheries.

■ Political People

"As Maine goes so goes the nation," is a popular political maxim first coined in the late 1800s. It stems from the state's motto – *Dirigo*, "I lead," and from the fact that for many years the general election was scheduled in Maine before voting in other states.

Maine has contributed many great leaders to the nation. Hamden Maine native **Dorothea Dix** championed the cause of hospitals for the mentally ill. **Henry Wadsworth Longfellow** called Portland home, while the poet **Edna St. Vincent Millay** lived in Camden. Harborside was the place picked by authors **Helen and Scott Nearing** for living the good life. The late Senator **Margaret Chase Smith**, whose declaration of conscience helped stop Senator Joseph McCarthy's communist witch hunt, brought Maine's homespun wisdom to national attention. It was former Senate Majority Leader and Maine Senator **George Mitchell** who brought the best hope for peace to Northern Ireland. Secretary of Defense and former Maine Senator and Representative **William Cohen** continues to serve. Former President **George Bush** cherishes time spent at his summer retreat at Walkers Point in Kennebunkport.

And finally, while Maine has been at a least seasonal home for too many notable authors and artists to mention, one of the best selling of all time, horror-meister **Stephen King**, lives in a suitably Gothic mansion in Bangor.

■ Ghosts & Legends

Every state has its ghosts and legends. Maine is no exception. From tales of undiscovered pirate treasure on offshore islands to witches and curses the harbors and hollows of Maine sport no shortage of the unexplained and supernatural. Shipwrecks too have left their mark, with drowned souls reportedly still searching the earth for peace.

Many country inns are also said to be haunted, but how much of that relates to matters spiritual and how much to matters of marketing remains undecided.

Haunted History

In the early 1700s **Judith Howard**, a woman familiar in the ways of herbal healing, was reported to be a witch. Children living nearby in Casco Bay, off modern-day Portland, were warned to keep their distance. When she died in 1769, islanders did not follow her wishes when they buried her. Strange occurrences and unexplained phenomena followed for two years until she was dug up and moved two miles to the place where she had asked to be buried.

In Bucksport, **Col. Jonathan Buck** was local magistrate when the body of an unidentified woman was found cut to pieces. One leg was missing. Being it was the mid-1800s and the justice system not yet refined, Col. Buck quickly produced a culprit, a hermit living on the edge of town. As the hermit was being put to death he reportedly called out to his accuser that "the leg will follow you to your grave."

When Col. Buck died a fine granite obelisk was erected over his grave. Soon after, however, a stain, which some say resembles a woman's leg, appeared on the base stone. Several attempts to wash, blast, or scrape it away over the years have been unsuccessful. Each time the stain returns; some say darker than before.

You can see the stone for yourself today in Bucksport. Just after you cross over from Verona Island on Route 1A, take a right. The cemetery is just a few hundred yards up on the left.

Buried Treasure

Many pirates have sailed Maine waters. Legend has it that remote islands off the coast still harbor chests of gold, jewels and other booty. A great stock of buried treasure was reportedly found on **Jewell Island** in Casco Bay during the late 1800s. An island resident moved the rectangular box full of gold for save keeping. He died soon after and no one has found the relocated stash.

In 1840, a farmer near **Castine** found a scattering of 400 coins along the banks of the Bagaduce River.

Islands off **Stonington** are reported to still harbor treasure.

Gold was once reported to hidden on some islands in **Frenchman Bay** off Bar Harbor as well. In the 1950s a Boy Scout beachcombing on one of the islands found a shiny gold doubloon. No other trace of treasure was found.

Pirate loot is also reportedly buried on islands off **Machias**. Because most islands are now privately owned, treasure hunting without permission is not recommended.

Also in Washington County, searchers have for years attempted to locate a **ghost** that may have left its tattered skeleton behind. In 1927, just 12 days before Charles Lindberg made his heroic solo flight across the Atlantic from the United States to Europe, two Frenchmen, Francis Coli and Charles Nungesser, left from the opposite direction in a biplane called *The White Bird*. They disappeared, as one observer said, "like a midnight ghost."

Years later interviews with residents of the Machias area revealed tales of the noise of an airplane overhead (a rare event in those days) about the time the French heros would be expected over North America. Other stories of the engine sputtering and hunters telling of a huge engine rusting in the woods fueled several expeditions to the wild forested lands in search of a wreck site. Proof has yet to be found.

Indian Legends

Native American legends also feature prominently in Maine lore. Perhaps foremost is the mythical figure **Pamola**, a creature with the head of a moose, wings of a bat, body of a man and legs of an eagle, that reportedly ruled on top of Katahdin in Baxter State Park. Pamola lived in a cave on the peak that bears his name. He controlled the weather and was quick to show his wrath if angered.

Legend has it that it was Pamola who each night pushed the moon up into the sky over Chimney Pond and rolled it along the Knifes Edge before letting it sink below the summit prior to daybreak.

> Stories about Pamola are profiled in the book *Chimney Pond Tales, Yarns told to Leroy Dudley* (North Country Press).

In the Far North, at **Allagash Falls** where the famed Allagash River drops 35 feet over jagged ledges, legend holds that a spectre appears some nights in the mist. Supposedly, an Indian maiden died in the churning water and returns each year on the anniversary of her death. She appears at the top of the falls, hovers for a moment, and then disappears into the froth.

What's In a Name?

■ The Name of Maine

While some historians who employed questionable logic have tried to tie the name of Maine, the state, with a province of the same name in France, historian Charles Clark in *Maine, A History*, believes the term is North American in origin.

The area known as Maine today was first described in 1622 as "Province of Maine." The name can be researched from a variety of early land grants and documents.

"These island-studded waters were customarily called 'the main,' spelled alternately *maine, maigne, mayn, mayne*, and even *meign*," Clark writes.

During the debate over statehood some suggested the name Ligonia or Columbia but Maine ultimately prevailed.

■ Where is Down East?
(You Can Get There From Here)

Most everyone knows "Down East" is in Maine, but confusion sometimes prevails over exactly where "Down East" Maine is really located.

Most observers agree Down East refers to the communities east of the Penobscot River and Penobscot Bay along the northeastern coast of Maine. But few people, however, understand why to go "Down" East you must go "up" the coast.

Although there are numerous explanations of the origin, the most satisfactory is that "Down East" is a seafaring term that had foundations in the fact that the prevailing wind along the coast is from the southwest. Schooners and clipper ships arriving from the southwest sailed before the wind. It was easy sailing, an act described as "running downhill."

Vessels running before the wind were said to be "running their easting down." Thus, a sailing vessel bound to Maine would "run" before the wind and go "downhill to the eastward," or, if you will, go "Down East."

■ Who Were the Acadians?

With their plight immortalized in Henry Wadsworth Longfellow's epic poem *Evangeline*, the Acadian people played an important role in Maine's history. Maine's Acadians are the descendants of people who settled in Nova Scotia in the mid-1600s when that area was controlled by France. The British took over in the early 1700s and allowed French-speaking settlers to remain. The relationship soured in mid-century during the French and Indian War. Worried about the Acadian's loyalties, the British forcibly dispersed the population. Some went to Louisiana and became the people we know today at the Cajuns. Others went to New Brunswick. They soon were uprooted from there and settled in the St. John Valley in Aroostook County around 1780.

Today, a visitor to that part of Maine is as likely to hear people speaking in French as in English.

"Acadia"

The name Acadia, as applied to the national park on Mount Desert Island, stems, according to historian Samuel Eliot Morison, from the French term "La Cadie." That is the French translation of the Indian name which is defined as "the place." La Cadie referred to the original French claim to most of Northeastern North America from Philadelphia to Montreal.

■ Place Names

Maine sports a marvelous diversity of place names. Many have Indian or geographical origins. In fact, in a state with thousands of lakes, streams and mountains it is no surprise that more than one body of water or hill has the same name.

The most popular by far is **Mud Pond**. There are 65 scattered about the state (a state which is best known for its sparkling clear water!).

There are 46 Long Ponds, 37 Bog Brooks and 19 Bald Mountains. Someone apparently found the time to name 21 Lost Ponds and there are 14 Bar Islands. There are two Pleasant Rivers and two Machias Rivers, one each in Northern Maine and one each in Eastern Maine.

In Maine, the terms lake and pond are used interchangeably. Often, and to many visitors' confusion, ponds are much larger than nearby water bodies referred to as lakes.

Great Ponds

Great Ponds are any water body more than 10 acres in size. These are owned by the state, even when surrounded by private land. Landowners cannot block foot access to great ponds. Quite a controversy erupted several years ago when wealthy landowners around a particularly productive trout lake placed log booms on the water to keep unauthorized float planes from landing and disgorging fishermen. The state ordered the booms removed.

Many Indian place names are difficult to pronounce. Try saying Mooselookmeguntic Lake (Moose-look-meah-gun-tic) real fast. Many people stumble over Nesowadnehunk Lake (Ne-Sow-deh-hunk). When in doubt, ask. Most folks will be happy to help. If not, they may admit they don't have any idea either.

Gores

Perhaps the most interesting "slice" of land in Maine is famed **Misery Gore**. Gores are unusual triangular or rectangular areas of land that suddenly appeared when various survey results didn't jive (a sort of surveyor's equivalent of not being able to balance a checkbook). Most were absorbed into nearby townships over the years, but a few remain. Misery Gore is a long narrow strip with an end on the west shore of Moosehead Lake. Another fabled wedge is **Coburn Gore**, an irregular piece of land formed by the circuitous boundary with Canada in Western Maine.

Mount Desert or Mount Dessert?

An ongoing debate rages concerning the proper pronunciation for Mount Desert Island. Is it Mount Desert or Mount Dessert? The question of this island's pronunciation and its answer have been tossed around, probably since 1604, when French explorer Samuel de Champlain named it.

"The island," Champlain wrote, "is very high, and cleft into seven or eight mountains, all in a line. The summits of most of them are bare of trees, nothing but rock. I named it l'Isle des Monts Deserts" (island of bare mountains). Since then, people have been unable to agree whether we should be saying Mount Desert, as in the arid wasteland, or Mount Dessert, as in the tasty epilog to a good meal. Old maps are inconclusive.

One school says even though Dessert is probably an Anglicized version of the original French, it is closer to the original than Desert. Another school says Champlain indicated the mountaintops were bare like deserts and we must call a desert a desert. Still other folks say Mount Desert Island and in the same breath call it the Island of Mount Dessert.

Bangor is another name the pronunciation of which seems to confound folks. Some say "Bang-gah," others "Bang-ger," but the correct way is "Bang-gor," so that the last syllable rhymes with door.

■ Place Numbers

You know you may not be at the end of the world but you might have a chance of seeing it from a place where folks run out of names and resort to numbers. These wilderness areas are broken down into townships, "T," and ranges, represented by an "R." Hence the designation T2-R11. Some explorers will find brightly painted posts with the letters and numbers at key road, river, crossing and at township line junctions. They are very useful for navigation purposes in areas with few landmarks.

The letters WELS are added to some townships and stand for West of the East Line Survey or West of the Easterly Line of the State. Other groups of letters are used to help reduce confusion over townships of similar number.

Introduction

Stuff O' Maine

Here is Maine's list of official mascots and symbols.

Capital . . . . Augusta

Population. . . . . Approximately 1.2 million

Motto. . . . . *Dirigo* (I lead)

Bird . . . . Chickadee
(*Parus atricapillus*, adopted in 1927)

Floral Emblem. . . . . White pine cone and tassel
(*Pinus strobus, linnaeus*, adopted in 1895)

Animal . . . . Moose

Tree . . . . White Pine (adopted in 1945)

Berry . . . . Wild blueberry

Gemstone/mineral . . . . Tourmaline

Fossil . . . . Fern (*quadrifaria*)

Cat . . . . Maine coon cat

Insect . . . . Honeybee

Fish. . . . . Landlocked salmon

Song . . . . *State of Maine Song* by Roger Vinton Snow

Vessel . . . . Schooner *Bowdoin*

State Nickname . . . . The Pine Tree State

Flag . . . . Maine's coat of arms sits on a blue field
(the same shade of blue is found on the US flag).
Adopted by the Legislature of 1909.

Getting There from Here

Most people have probably heard the old Maine expression "you can't get there from here." That may seem like nonsense nowadays, but during the era of settlement it rang all too true. With few roads, fewer bridges, and tough terrain, many people on the move would often find themselves in sight of their destinations but with no way to get there.

Basically, there are few options for travel in Maine other than by car. Buses do serve major metropolitan areas and in season run along Coastal Route 1 and down to Bar Harbor.

Rail service from Boston to Portland is slated to begin in the fall of 2000. Commercial air service is outlined a little later.

■ Car Travel

The best approach when traveling by car is to get as close to your destination as possible via feeder routes and then home in. Because Maine has so few main roads, choosing which one to take is seldom a difficult decision.

While many visitors arrive with a romantic notion of taking a day to drive up the coast on old US 1, traffic, stop lights, and slow-moving recreational vehicles soon turn that dream into a nightmare. You cannot get up US 1 from Kittery to Bar Harbor in a single day. Instead, you may want to consider just including a piece of it in your itinerary.

Main Roads

The most basic feeder route is **Interstate 95** from Kittery to Houlton. The lower section is the **Maine Turnpike**, a toll road, which branches in Portland. To shift to I95, and its connections with locations such as Freeport (L.L. Bean) and Coastal Route 1, take Exit 9 just north of Portland.

Interstate 295 is the highway through Portland that eventually becomes I-95 north of the city. You can get on 295 in South Portland at Exit 6A, but it carries much local traffic and really doesn't save any time.

The Maine Turnpike continues north from Portland and slightly west through Lewiston. In this section it carries the route designation 495. Interstate 95 and the Turnpike rejoin just south of Augusta

This old postcard shows the major road routes still in use in Maine today.

where tolls end. The divided highway then continues on through Waterville, Bangor, Old Town, Lincoln and Medway on its way north. The divided highway ends in Houlton.

Key feeder roads maintained by the state include **Route 302**, which runs northwest from Portland toward the White Mountains, and **Route 26**, which, when accessed in Gray, makes for a scenic direct route to the Sunday River, Bethel area.

Route 3 runs east from Augusta to Belfast, Bucksport, Ellsworth and on to Bar Harbor and Acadia National Park. **Route 4** from the Lewiston region heads north toward the Western Mountains.

Route 201, which heads north from Waterville toward the remote Jackman region, is a busy road for people coming and going to Quebec.

Other good north-south roads include **Route 15** from Bangor to Greenville and **US 1**, the main road from Houlton north to Presque Isle, Caribou and Fort Kent.

Billboards

One thing you won't find in Maine are billboards. Off-premise signs are limited to a single, wide, short standardized design. Most places that cater to tourists will have such signs near key intersections as you near your destination. In many communities, signs at individual businesses are also regulated. No large signs are allowed in the state highway right-of-way.

From Bangor, the best way to get to **Acadia National Park** is to take Exit 45 off I-95 and head south on 395. The divided highway ends in Brewer but it is only another 40 miles or so south through Ellsworth on Route 1A to the coast. **Ellsworth** is the crossroads Down East, with Routes 1 and 3 intersecting (Route 3 heads to Mount Desert Island while US 1 continues along the coast further east to the towns of Machias, Lubec and Eastport).

Debate is currently raging in Maine about establishing an official east-west highway. Currently, there is no such route, so a patchwork of two-lane roads will have to do.

Route 2 heads West from Bangor to Bethel and can be accessed from Route 201 or from Pittsfield.

From Brewer, **Route 9**, also known as the Airline, winds through long, lonely miles on its way to the Canadian border at Calais. This road has been slowly improved with wide, smooth sections interspersed with older sections where sharp turns and the lack of paved shoulders make driving an adventure.

Farther north, **Route 6** is a good easterly byway from Lincoln to Vanceboro on the border.

Most state routes in Maine are well marked and engineered. Route signs and distances are provided at most major intersections.

It's The Law

While Maine has pretty much the standard list of motor vehicle laws, some are different than other states. These include:

■ Seat belt use is mandatory for everyone in a vehicle. If minor children up to age 19 are unsecured, the adult driver can be charged. Car seats must be used for infants and small children up to age four.

■ Headlights must be on when a vehicle's windshield wipers are in use.

■ Motorists must stop and grant right of way to pedestrians in a marked crosswalk (wide white or yellow bands painted on the street).

■ The blood alcohol level at which a driver is legally intoxicated in Maine is .08. For those under age 21, the limit is .02. The penalty for being over this limit is a minimum of two days in jail, a $750 fine and loss of license for 180 days. Sheriff's departments and state police regularly conduct safety roadblocks to look for drunk drivers.

■ The fine for passing a stopped school bus, from any direction, when its red lights are flashing, is $250.

Dirt Roads

Much of interior Maine is accessible only by private gravel roads maintained by paper companies. Some of them, such as the Golden Road which runs west and north from Millinocket, and the Stud Mill Road in Eastern Maine, are broad, straight and smooth. While visitors are allowed on these roads, logging trucks have the right of way.

 Logging trucks are big, fast, and can come up on you quickly. Also, dirt roads can be surprisingly slippery after a rain. Moose and downed trees may lurk around the next corner.

Maine

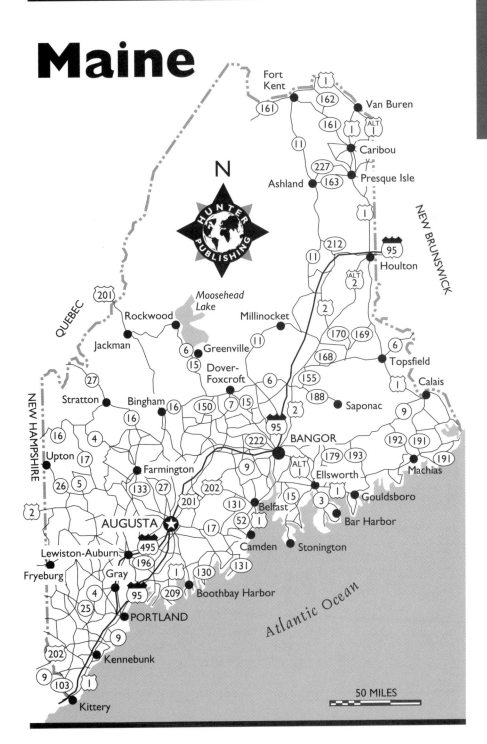

N

Fort Kent
Van Buren
Caribou
Ashland
Presque Isle
NEW BRUNSWICK
Houlton
Moosehead Lake
QUEBEC
Rockwood
Millinocket
Jackman
Greenville
Topsfield
Dover-Foxcroft
Calais
Stratton
Bingham
Saponac
NEW HAMPSHIRE
Upton
BANGOR
Machias
Farmington
Ellsworth
Gouldsboro
Belfast
Bar Harbor
AUGUSTA
Camden
Stonington
Lewiston-Auburn
Fryeburg
Gray
Boothbay Harbor
PORTLAND
Atlantic Ocean
Kennebunk
Kittery

50 MILES

A few tips for safe driving on dirt roads:

- In some places, the gravel roads are in better shape than some paved stretches. But, to be safe, don't travel here unless your tires, suspension, exhaust system, etc., can take a pounding. Ridges form up in the dirt over time and can shake a car apart. Some drivers advocate going slow on rough stretches. Others urge a faster speed arguing, you'll bounce enough to miss half the bumps! It is harder for the dust clouds and flying rocks to catch up to you as well.

- Muddy stretches are common and some "puddles" may be as much as a foot deep. When in doubt, stop (off the travel way) and check ahead on foot.

- Some log and plank bridges on lesser-used logging roads are not for the faint of heart. Bridges are moved, washed out, or sometimes just rot away, so plan routes carefully.

Navigational Aids

Most paper company roads are not well marked and it is surprisingly easy to get turned around. Get a good reference, take your time, and be sure top off the gas tank in town before you hit the dirt.

The best all-round collection of detailed maps for navigating on paved and dirt roads is *The Maine Atlas and Gazetteer.* Published by DeLorme of Freeport, they are available in almost every gas station, convenience store and bookstore. As actor Karl Malden used to say in the American Express commercials, "Don't leave home without it."

In-State Traveling Distances to Portland (miles)			
Augusta	60	Freeport	15
Bangor	130	Greenville	155
Bar Harbor	165	Houlton	250
Bethel	70	Kittery	50
Boothbay Harbor	55	Machias	210
Camden	85	Madawaska	350
Caribou	300	Old Orchard	18
Eastport	250	Presque Isle	290
Fort Kent	315	Rangeley	120

Out-of-State Traveling Distances to Portland (miles)

Atlanta, GA	1,230	Miami, FL	1,675
Baltimore, MD	500	Minneapolis/St. Paul, MN	1,475
Boston, MA	110	Montreal, PQ Canada	270
Chicago, IL	1,050	New Orleans, LA	1,730
Cincinnati, OH	960	New York, NY	330
Cleveland, OH	720	Philadelphia, PA	420
Denver, CO	2,100	Pittsburgh, PA	700
Detroit, MI	790	Portland, OR	3,180
Halifax, NS Canada	550	St. Louis, MO	1,260
Hartford, CT	200	Salt Lake City, UT	2,500
Houston, TX	2,075	San Francisco, CA	3,270
Kansas City, MO	1,510	Seattle, WA	3,115
Los Angeles, CA	3,200	Toronto, ONT Canada	575
Memphis, TN	1,475	Washington, DC	570

Note: To go from Kittery in the south to Madawaska in the far north requires a drive of nearly 400 miles.

■ Travel by Bus

Bus service is very limited in route and schedule. Most service is concentrated along the I-95 corridor from Boston, through Portland, Lewiston, Augusta and on to Bangor. Most firms do run buses up US 1 from Portland to Bangor. Year-round, buses run from Bangor to Caribou with stops in between. Seasonally, buses run from Bangor to Bar Harbor with one run each way daily.

Taking the bus these days is a much more pleasant experience than it was 20 years ago. Some bus companies now offer "in-flight" movies on video monitors overhead as well as snacks and a beverage. Each seat also sports multiple channels of music. Passengers can listen with private headsets.

Most express bus service can take people from one downtown to another faster than you can make it in a private car.

Major cities such as Portland, Lewiston and Bangor have city bus lines.

On Mount Desert Island, a new shuttle bus service connecting hotels, campgrounds and Acadia National Park trailheads and areas of interest began operation in the spring of 1999. It features frequent service and stops in major island towns as well.

Bus Companies

For detailed schedule information contact the following companies:

Concord Trailways . . . . ☎ 800-639-3317
Terminals in Bangor, Portland

Vermont Transit (Greyhound) . . . . ☎ 800-537-3330

Cyr Bus Lines . . . . ☎ 207-942-3354
Bangor, connect to northern towns

The Calais Line . . . . ☎ 800-596-2823
Connecting Ellsworth, Calais and other towns Down East.

Downeast Transportation . . . . ☎ 207-667-5796
Acadia National Park shuttles, regular several times weekly routes between Hancock County towns.

■ Travel by Air

The Maine Department of Tourism furnishes the following information to visitors. In addition to flights directly into Maine, some visitors also fly into Logan Airport in Boston and rent a car to drive up to Maine. Others fly into Manchester, New Hampshire and then drive over. Beware, though, the drive can take several hours. Many small towns, such as Jackman, Bethel, Greenville and Millinocket, have paved airfields best suited for smaller private aircraft.

Airlines

Business Express . . . . ☎ 800-345-3400

Colgan Air . . . . ☎ 800-272-5488

Continental Express . . . . ☎ 800-525-0280

Delta Air Lines . . . . ☎ 800-221-1212

United Airlines . . . . ☎ 800-241-6522

USAir . . . . ☎ 800-428-4322

Airports

Augusta: Augusta Municipal Airport, ☎ 287-3185. Served by Colgan Air.

Bangor: Bangor International Airport, ☎ 947-0384. Served by Business Express, Continental Express, Delta Air Lines, USAir. Good for visits to Acadia, Greenville, Down East.

Bar Harbor: Bar Harbor Airport (located in Trenton, ☎ 667-7329. Served by Colgan Air. Good for visits to Acadia.

Portland: Portland International Jetport, ☎ 772-0690. Served by Business Express, Continental Express, Delta Air Lines, United Airlines, USAir.

Presque Isle: Northern Maine Regional Airport, ☎ 764-3108. Served by Business Express, United Airlines.

Rockland/Owls Head: Knox County Regional Airport, ☎ 594-4131. Served by Colgan Air. Best for visits to Camden, Mid-Coast.

Airport Car Rental

Most major airports have fully-staffed rental car desks. Also, most major cities have outlets. It is advisable to reserve a car in advance. Especially on busy holiday weekends, and during the peak summer season (July-August), cars may be in short supply or the selection limited.

Airport Car Rental Agencies

Avis, ☎ 1-800-331-1212. Serving Bangor International Airport, Bar Harbor Airport, Portland International Jetport, Northern Maine Regional Airport, Knox County Regional Airport.

Budget, ☎ 800-527-0700. Serving Augusta Airport, Bangor International Airport, Bar Harbor Airport, Portland International Jetport, Northern Maine Regional Airport, Knox County Regional Airport.

Hertz, ☎ 800-654-3131. Serving Bangor International Airport, Bar Harbor Airport, Portland International Airport.

National, ☎ 800-227-7368. Serving Bangor International Airport, Portland International Jetport.

■ Travel by Ferry

Ferry rides in Maine are more than just a form of transportation to off-shore islands. They are an adventure unto themselves. Rides range from the Maine Ferry Service's regular vehicle runs to year-round communities such as Swans Island and Vinalhaven, to trips on privately operated mail boats, which often are little more than overgrown lobster fishing vessels.

Either way, the scenery can't be beat, the salt air is great and there is no limit on the amount wildlife you may spot. Many folks take ferry rides just to enjoy the salty air and crashing waves.

Maine State Ferry Service

Ferry Routes

Fares vary slightly depending upon the route you take, but expect to pay $25-30 (round trip) for your car and $9 per adult (round trip).

To Vinalhaven and North Haven: Vinalhaven crossing of 15 miles. Trip time one hour and 15 minutes. North Haven crossing of 12.5 miles. Trip time of one hour. Terminal on Main Street in Rockland. Multiple trips daily. ☎ 596-2203.

To Matinicus: 23-mile crossing. Trip time of two hours and 15 minutes. Several times monthly in season; once monthly in winter. ☎ 596-2203.

To Islesboro: Three-mile crossing. Trip time of 20 minutes. Terminal on US 1 Lincolnville Beach. Multiple trips daily. ☎ 789-5611.

To Swans Island: Six-mile crossing. Trip time of 40 minutes. Terminal in Bass Harbor. Multiple trips daily. ☎ 244-3254.

To Frenchboro: Eight-mile crossing. Trip time of 50 minutes. Terminal in Bass Harbor. Twice weekly. ☎ 244-3254.

Schedule information. . . . . ☎ 207-624-7777
Daily operations update . . . . ☎ 800-491-4883
Rates, exact schedules and fares are available at all terminals.

Rules & Regulations

VEHICLE RESERVATIONS: Vehicle reservations are not accepted more than 30 days in advance, and you can also try just showing up. Payment must accompany requests for reservation, including the non-refundable reservation fee. Requests should be addressed to the terminal from which transportation is to begin. Drivers with reservations must have their vehicles in line 15 minutes before scheduled departure, or forfeit their reservation and reservation fee.

The $24 reservation fee for vehicles being transported to Matinicus will be applied to the purchase of the ticket, or refunded if canceled at least 72 hours in advance of travel date, or if the trip is canceled by the Maine State Ferry Service.

Drivers of vehicles in line must be in their vehicles when the vessel is at the dock to prevent other vehicles from being blocked in.

BICYCLES: Bicycle drivers have the same rights and responsibilities as other vehicle operators on roadways in Maine. On some of the more popular biking destinations, like Isleboro and Vinalhaven, residents often become frustrated by bicyclists who hesitate to get out of the way on narrow, winding roads. The Maine Ferry Service makes no warranty or guarantee as to the suitability of the roadway condition or fitness for bicycling.

HOLIDAYS: Service is limited on Thanksgiving, Christmas, and New Year's Days. Contact the appropriate Ferry Service terminal for specific schedules for these days.

DISABLED PERSONS: Handicapped passengers who need help boarding or disembarking should notify terminal personnel so they can have someone assist them.

PETS: Dogs, cats, small birds and other pets must be held secure by leash, crate, cage, etc.

PASSENGER SAFETY: Parents or guardians are responsible for the safety and conduct of minor passengers. All passengers should keep well clear of moving vehicles.

Passengers should be prepared for a possible jolt when the vessel is being docked. Ferries are equipped with life jackets for all passengers, as well as rafts.

Missing the Boat

Trips may be canceled due to unsafe weather, sea conditions, or mechanical failure. Passengers should be aware that the ferry vessels remain at the island overnight with the exception of the *Gov. Curtis*, operating to Vinalhaven. Those missing the last trip will be stranded on the island overnight.

Private Ferries

A number of private ferries also offer service.

Private Ferry Routes

To Great Chebeague, Peaks Island & Long Island: Casco Bay Lines, from Maine State Pier, Portland. To Peaks, 20 minutes; to Long Island, 30 minutes; to Chebeague, one hour and 15 minutes. Multiple trips daily. ☎ 774-7871.

To Great Chebeague: Chebeague Island Transportation, from Cousins Island in Yarmouth. Multiple trips daily. ☎ 846-3700.

To Monhegan: *Balmy Days II*, from Commercial Street, Boothbay Harbor. One trip daily in season. ☎ 633-2284. *Laura B.*, Monhegan-Thomaston Boat Line, from Port Clyde. 15-mile trip, one hour and 15 minutes. Multiple runs daily in season. ☎ 372-8848. *Hardy III*, North Edgecomb. Multiple runs in season from New Harbor. ☎ 677-2026.

To Isle au Haut: *Mink*, from Atlantic Ave. in Stonington. Ten-mile trip, 45 minutes. Four trips daily in season. ☎ 367-5193.

To Great Cranberry Island, Islesford: *Sea Queen*, *Double B*, operated by Beal and Bunker from town pier, Northeast Harbor. Five miles to Great Cranberry, 25 minutes. Multiple trips daily (more in-season). ☎ 244-3575. Cranberry Cove Boating Company, from Southwest Harbor. Multiple trips daily all season aboard the *Island Queen*. Captain Chuck Liebow often sports a live parrot on his shoulder. "Polly want a tourist?" ☎ 244-5882.

To Deer Island(New Brunswick), Campobello: East Coast Ferries from Water Street, Eastport. Six miles, 25 minutes to Deer Island in New Brunswick, Canada. 1.5 miles, 10 minutes to Campobello (50 miles by road). Multiple trips daily in season. ☎ (506) 747-2159.

Large Ferries to Novia Scotia

Deep ocean-going ferries to Yarmouth, Canada, take roughly 900-1,000 passengers and hundreds of vehicles each.

Leaving from Commercial Street in Portland, the **Scotia Prince** is operated by Prince of Fundy Cruises Ltd. You have 11 hours to shop, sleep, dine or gamble. One trip daily in season. ☎ 775-5616.

The Cat, a fast catamaran operated by Bay Ferries Ltd., leaves from Eden Street, Bar Harbor. The 100-mile trip takes 2.5 hours. Two round-trips daily in-season. Duty-free shop, cafeteria, casino. *The Cat* also offers day-trip (no car) rates. They have 10 package tours for day-trippers in Nova Scotia, ranging from historical tours to panning for gold. ☎ 288-3395.

■ US Customs

The border crossings listed below are open 24 hours a day, seven days a week. All vehicles, including snowmobiles, must stop. For opening times at other crossing points where schedule varies, or for appointments (which must be made for all flights or boat trips making first stop in US), telephone the Bangor Office at ☎ (207) 942-7239 or 780-3328.

WISE WORDS: *When crossing into New Brunswick, Canada, you pass into a different time zone. Remember to adjust your watches and alarm clocks accordingly (back by one hour).*

At Customs you will probably be asked if you are a US citizen, as well as where you are going, how long you will be there, and if you have any live plant materials in your vehicle (a definite no-no). You will need at least two forms of identification to get back in to the country (a passport is not necessary unless you are a non-US citizen) and you will be asked if you have made various purchases.

CAUTION *Under no circumstances try to bring a firearm into Canada without the proper paperwork in-hand. Firearms are serious business, and you should treat them as such.*

24-Hour Customs Checkpoints

Aroostook County: Fort Kent, Madawaska, Van Buren, Limestone, Fort Fairfield, Bridgewater.

Somerset County: Sandy Bay (Jackman).

Franklin County: Coburn Gore.

Washington County: Vanceboro, Calais, Lubec.

Hancock County: Bar Harbor (hours depend on Nova Scotia ferry schedule).

Cumberland County: Portland (hours depends on Novia Scotia ferry schedule).

■ While You're on the Road

You won't find you favorite local radio station while on the road, so here is a list of select radio stations, categorized by music style/content.

Select Radio Stations

Rock: WTOS Skowhegan 105.1; WBLM Portland 102.9; WCYY Portland 94.3; WMDI Bar Harbor 107.7.

County: WQCB Brewer 106.5; WPOR Portland 101.9; WEBB Augusta 98.5; WMCM Rockland 103.3.

Sports/News/Talk: WZON Bangor 620AM; WGAN Portland 560AM; WVOM Bangor 103.9; WZAN Portland 970AM.

Adult Contemporary: WDEA Ellsworth 1370AM; WEZQ Ellsworth 92.9; WALZ Machias 85.3; WQSS Camden 102.5; WWBX Bangor 97.1; WMGX Portland 93.1.

Christian: WHCF Bangor 88.5; WLOB Portland 1310AM; WMDR Augusta 1340 AM.

Top 40: WKSQ Ellsworth 94.5; WMME Augusta 92.3; WJBQ Portland 97.9.

Public Radio/Classical: WMEH Bangor 90.9; WMEA Portland 90.1; WAVX Thomaston 106.9.

Community: WERU Blue Hill 89.9.

Oldies: WWMJ Ellsworth 95.7; WABI Bangor 910AM.

Ayuh, Been Theyah

■ Maine Humor

In addition to its spectacular scenery and pristine wilderness Maine has also earned a reputation as a homeland for quirky characters born with quick wits and extraordinarily dry senses of humor. Combined with the famous Down East accent, (basically substitute "ah" for "er" or "or") it forms the foundation for a truly original experience.

Marshall Dodge

The late Marshall Dodge, who was part of a team that produced the famous *Bert and I* recordings, took Maine humor mainstream. Dodge liked to say that the difference between Western humor and Eastern humor is that out West, the storyteller laughs at the audience for believing a tall tale. Back here in the East, the audience laughs at the storyteller's wit and homespun wisdom, with the punch line often aimed at deflating the pompous and skewering the stuck-up. *Bert & I* recordings are sold at giftshops and bookstores throughout the state.

A good example of this difference is when a wind-bag rancher brags that "my ranch in Texas is so big it takes three days to drive around it in my car."

A Maine farmer would counter, according to Dodge, "Ayuh, back on my fahm in Maine we gottah cah just like that."

Visitors to Maine often expect to find such colorful characters at every turn. In fact, Governor Angus King once said if he could just strategically position a suitably crusty yet benign "Mainah" on the porch of every general store or end of every lobster wharf, giving people asking for directions the standard reply of "You can't get theyah from heyah," tourism revenue would triple.

Still, there's a good chance if you ask some fisherman-type "Have you lived here your whole life?" he'll respond matter-of-factly "not yet."

■ How to Avoid Being Labelled a "Flatlander"

One of the standard jokes, repeated often by Maine humorist and author of *How to Talk Yankee*, Tim Sample, tells of a native taking offense at a person from away calling his or her children born in Maine natives. "Just because my cat had kittens in the oven I wouldn't call 'em biscuits," Sample says.

For the most part, natives and residents (which includes "people from away" who were born "out-ah-state" and folks born elsewhere in Maine but not in the town in which they are presently living), get along with visitors just fine. Occasionally a vehicle may sport a "Welcome to Maine, now go home!" bumper sticker, but they amount to little more than a 1990s Down East version of the '60s classic "Don't laugh – your daughter could be in this van."

Visitors, often referred to as "flatlanders," must bear the brunt of several stereotypes. You, however, as an educated and informed tourist, can avoid doing most of the things that drive the locals nuts.

Pet Peeves

Driving seems to bring out the worst in visitors. First and foremost is the assumption that everyone on busy highways is also on vacation. There are no backroads for the locals to use – in most areas of the state there is only one way to get to anywhere and back, and you may be today's rolling roadblock. Look in the rearview mirror from time to time and pull over if it's beginning to look like you are at the head of the 4th of July parade, especially if it isn't July 4th. Other pet peeves include:

- Stopping in the middle of an intersection to consult a map.
- Driving well below the speed limit and pointing a lot.
- Wearing black socks and tie dress shoes with Bermuda shorts.
- Entire families with matching t-shirts and retired couples with cute his 'n hers outfits.
- Illegal parking and turning around in private driveways.
- Assuming all woodland or undeveloped areas are public property – they're not.
- Not stopping for pedestrians in crosswalks (it is the law).
- Not using the crosswalks.
- Any general anti-social behavior, such as speeding, littering, blasting stereos, flinging lit cigarette butts out of car windows (especially dangerous when the forest fire danger is extreme).

Asking for Directions

Most Mainers are more than happy to help visitors find their way. Only a very few will send you on a 20-mile circuitous route to first see if you are smart enough to follow their directions.

Be prepared for some unusual landmarks. You may be told to go down this or that road "apiece" and "turn at the Shell Station, then go three miles north 'til you pass Doc Wheaton's place, then take the third right after the second left." The only problem may be that it hasn't been a Shell Station for 20 years (it's now an Irving truck stop) and Doc Wheaton's been dead for a decade and some family named Murdy lives there now.

Relax, remain flexible and be prepared to stop and ask someone else a few miles farther on.

Also remember that few Mainers refer to distances in terms of miles. Because road and weather conditions can vary widely most people will express distance as time. How far is Bar Harbor from Bangor? On a map it looks like 44 miles but in truth, it's "about an hour, hour-and-a-half."

A few years ago while taking a canoeing expedition to far Eastern Maine I hired some local folks to shuttle our vehicles around to the take-out point. I ask the old woman in our truck, a cook at the sporting camp where we stopped one night, how far it was from there to Vanceboro. Staring straight ahead and without missing a beat she replied "about three beers." I suggested she might like to drive my friend's new Explorer after they dropped us off.

Be prepared for some creative answers to your route-finding queries.

Asking Questions

Go ahead and ask as many questions as you like. How straight an answer you get can be gauged by the twinkle in the eye and smirk on the face of the person giving you an answer. By now most people in the popular tourist areas have heard them all and then some.

Among the actual Bar Harbor waterfront classics:

- You must have a pretty tough harbormaster! I noticed how he makes everyone park their boats at the moorings facing the same way. (The wind does it.)
- Have you had a dry summer? Last time I was here the water was clean up to there (said while man was pointing to the ocean at low tide).
- How do you make boiled lobster? (Pot, water, heat, lobster.)
- How do we get to Bar Harbor from here? (Don't move.)

WISE WORDS: *Basically, like anywhere else, respect private property, drive safely, treat people as you'd like to be treated and don't pester them if they don't seem like they want to chit-chat.*

■ Other Things Visitors Should Know...

Maine has a general **sales tax** of 5.5%. The tax on lodgings is 7%.

Smoking is against the law in any enclosed public space, including stores, hotel lobbies, etc. No smoking is permitted in hospitals. Maine's legislature just passed a bill banning smoking in restaurants, although it will still be permitted in some cocktail lounges.

It is illegal for anyone under the age of 18 to possess **tobacco** products in Maine. Store clerks must – by law – ask to see identification of anyone purchasing tobacco products who appears to be under the age of 27.

While it is seldom enforced, Maine law restricts people coming into the state from bringing with them more than one gallon of whiskey, one gallon of wine or liquor, or one case of beer. State police have been known to skulk around New Hampshire's State Liquor Store (where booze is cheaper) and jot down the license plate numbers of northbound vehicles if they leave the store with mass quantities of liquor. They radio ahead and the cars are pulled over in Maine.

The legal **drinking age** is 21.

Parks & Preserves

Maine sports dozens of parks and literally hundreds of nature and wildlife preserves scattered along the coast and inland. Some have only a few short trails while others would take weeks or even years to completely explore. Most are administered by a handful of agencies and organizations.

■ State-Managed Lands

Many nature preserves and wildlife areas do not charge fees, although donations are appreciated. Where fees are charged, they run from $1 per adult (over age 12) per day to $5.

Camping fees for a tent site averages $15, with some additional reservation fees. Individual preserves and private parks are described in the various chapters throughout this book. Maine parks have a carry-in, carry-out policy. Trash cans are not provided.

For one-stop shopping to find out more about the more popular preserves and public lands as well as private lands open to the public, contact the agencies below.

- All area codes are 207.

Acadia National Park
PO Box 177, Bar Harbor 04609
☎ *288-3338*

Allagash Wilderness Waterway
☎ *941-4014*
Water level (seasonal) or emergencies
☎ *435-7963*

Baxter State Park
64 Balsam Drive, Millinocket 04462
☎ *723-5140*

Damariscotta River Association
PO Box 333, Damariscotta 04543
☎ *563-1393*

Great Northern Paper Woodlands
1024 Central Street, Millinocket 04462
☎ *723-2119*

West Branch Water Flow (recording)
☎ *723-2328*

Maine Audubon Society
PO Box 6009, Falmouth 04105
☎ *781-2330*

Maine Appalachian Trail Club
PO Box 283, Augusta 04332
☎ *799-5312*

Maine Bureau of Parks and Lands
22 State House Station, Augusta 04333
☎ *287-3821*

Camping Reservations
☎ *287-3824 or 800-332-1501*

Maine Department of Inland Fisheries and Wildlife
41 State House Station, Augusta 04333
☎ *287-8000*

Maine Forest Service (fire permits)
☎ 287-2791

Nature Conservancy of Maine
14 Maine Street, Brunswick 04011
☎ 729-5181

North Maine Woods
PO Box 421, Ashland 04732
☎ 435-6213

White Mountain National Forest
Box 2270, Bethel 04217
☎ 824-213

■ Public Reserve Lands

Gulf Hagas, "Grand Canyon of the East," sports waterfalls, rapids & rugged hiking trails.

The State of Maine also holds more than 500,000 acres in Public Reserve Lands, which are open to the public. These generally lack facilities beyond hiking trails or the occasional gravel road to a hand-carry boat launch site. Some are almost inaccessible. A good way to picture these places are as undeveloped state parks.

Public Reserve Lands are open to hunting and are also harvested for timber for pulp, paper, and saw logs.

All together, there are 29 areas ranging in size from about 500 acres to more than 40,000. Fees are not charged.

For more information, write or call the Bureau of Parks and Lands, 22 State House Station, Augusta 04333. ☎ 287-3821.

Adventuring In Maine

■ Hiking

Maine has the best forest, mountain and above tree-line hiking in the East. Dozens of state parks preserve the best peaks, while the White

Mountains National Forest has extensive holdings in the state with many well-marked trails.

Maine is the northern terminus for the **Appalachian Trail** (AT), which ends atop mile-high Katahdin in Baxter State Park. Here, rare alpine flowers, usually found only in the sub-Arctic in Canada, can be seen each spring. Baxter itself has more than 100 miles of deep, backcountry hiking. Its hills and lakes are home to numerous rustic log lean-tos, which can be reserved in advance but can be reached only by a long, all-day slog.

The AT in Maine is famous for its traverse of the Bigelow Range, its winding remote section known as the "100-mile Wilderness," and for Mahoosuc Notch, reputed to be the AT's toughest mile.

A hiker in Acadia National Park crosses a rugged footbridge at the north end of Jordan Pond.

Along the coast, **Acadia National Park** offers more than 120 miles of outstanding mountain and seashore hiking, much of it on open mountain tops where views extend 360° for more than 100 miles.

The International AT

A new extension of the AT, dubbed the **International AT**, is presently being constructed. Plans call for it to be finished on Earth Day, April 22, 2000. It will run from the base of Katahdin 434 miles to Mount Jacques Cartier in Quebec.

Be sure to read the following sections that will help make your hiking in Maine more safe and enjoyable.

While many trails in Maine are literally "walks in the park," others are extremely difficult. Steep rises and drops where hikers are expected to use their hands to grab roots, rocks or anything they can hang onto are common. In most mountainous areas, the terrain is so rugged that it is nearly impossible to stray off the trail. Bushwacking, and therefore shortcuts, are ill-advised if not impossible.

Heading Out

Proper preparation for a day in the wild means being prepared for every eventuality. With so much to choose from, it is easy to select a route for your individual fitness level and the abilities of those in your party. Take it slow, there is plenty of time. If you set out to "Just do it," you are missing the point and won't get to savor much of what Northern New England has to offer. Accurately assess your physical condition and ability to complete the hike you have chosen.

Weather conditions can change several times in a day. Conditions can vary greatly depending on one's proximity to the ocean and change in altitude.

Daylight fades quickly in autumn, so make sure you have plenty of time to complete your walk before dark. It doesn't hurt to put a small flashlight in your day pack along with other essentials.

Studies have shown that the average temperature drops a degree or two for each 300-400-foot elevation gain. Add in a steady wind and most summits are markedly cooler than the surrounding lowlands.

Clothing

Even on the hottest days be sure to pack a windproof and waterproof jacket. A hiker soaked in a passing shower and then buffeted by high winds can succumb to hypothermia, the sometimes deadly lowering of the body's core temperature, even when the mercury is above 60°. A large percentage of body heat is lost through the head. Packing a **hat** is also a good idea. A disposable **"space blanket"** is also a popular pack item.

Proper footwear is vital. Many trails traverse slippery ledges that become treacherous after a rain. In some areas the dark algae that flourish in the runoff after rains is particularly slippery. A good, solid, hard-soled boot that also provides ankle support is vital. Sneakers or sports sandals offer little protection to the bottoms of feet while leaping from boulder to boulder on some trails.

 WISE WORDS: *To prevent blisters, wear a polypropolyne under-sock under a heavy boot sock. The inner sock helps wick moisture away from your feet; the outer layer reduces abrasion. Keep a small piece of moleskin foam in your first aid kit; it is invaluable for covering hot spots before they develop into blisters.*

Water

Maine is laced with scores of brooks and numerous large lakes. And, although one of the real treats of hiking through the backcountry is a refreshing drink from a mountain stream, bring some water with you on a hike. Even the most reliable mountain springs can go dry in high summer.

 DID YOU KNOW? *Alcoholic beverages and most sodas may seem to quench your thirst, but they actually end up increasing your body's need for water.*

Few pollutants threaten the pristine quality of most of the state's water, although some evidence of *Giardia*, a naturally-occurring parasite that can cause serious intestinal problems known as "beaver fever," has been detected. The chance of you contracting this problem even when drinking unfiltered water is small, but officials in all outdoor areas advise filtering or treating water before consumption. If the choice is between dying of thirst and a sip from an unfiltered yet clear running source, by all means drink up. But, to be safe, pack a lightweight filter for extended trips.

Iced Water For The Trail

The night before a hike, fill a water bottle one-third full and place it on its side in the freezer. Top it off before you leave in the morning and your beverage should remain icy all day. Vary the amount of ice with experience. (Do not try with glass containers or those that will not accept the expansion of the ice.)

Finding the Trail

Most trails in Maine, particularly in parks such as Baxter and Acadia, are clearly marked on the ground and show up well on the many maps that are available. Very often terrain is so severe that it seems nearly impossible to walk anywhere but on the trail. Still, care must be taken not to get off the beaten track. Staying on the trail reduces environmental damage and keeps you from getting lost.

A good, water-repellent map, a small compass and the knowledge of how to use them are invaluable. Study the trail before you head out and refer to the map often. Note landmarks along the way and look back once in a while so some scenes will seem familiar on your return trip.

Trailheads in **Acadia** are marked with lettered signs carved into wooden posts. Blue paint blazes on bare ledge, stone cairns, and metal markers fastened to trees help lead the way when the worn footpath or evidence of brush cutting is less apparent.

Trail intersections are marked with carved wooden signs on posts giving directions and distances. Occasionally, some signs may be missing, so follow the map carefully as you walk.

In Maine, the Appalachian Trail is marked with white blazes and signs at major intersections. Sharp or obscure turns are marked with double blazes.

In **Baxter State Park**, trails use blue blazes except where the path is also part of the AT. Cairns mark the way above treeline on Katahdin where fast moving clouds can lower visibility to less than 30-feet in just seconds.

In any alpine zone hikers should endeavor to remain on the trail to avoid crushing fragile vegetation and displacement of soil which hastens erosion.

MAINE'S HIGHEST MOUNTAINS			
RANK	NAME	ELEVATION (FT)	LOCATION
1	Katahdin	5,267	Great North Woods
2	Sugarloaf	4,237	Western Mountains
3	Old Speck	4,180	Western Mountains
4	Crocker	4,168	Western Mountains
5	Bigelow	4,150	Western Mountains
6	North Brother	4,143	Great North Woods
7	Saddleback	4,116	Western Mountains
8	Abraham	4,049	Western Mountains
9	The Horn	4,023	Western Mountains
10	Spaulding	3,988	Western Mountains

Hazards

- If you **lose the trail**, return to the last obvious marker and have a member of your party fan out to find the next one before proceeding. Sometimes, so many people take wrong turns at the same spot that it creates a false trail which quickly fades or stops abruptly. Piles of logs or rocks are often used by trail crews to block passage on false or closed trails. Hikers sometimes spot the remains of abandoned paths called "ghost trails."

- **Bushwacking** off the trail can be very hazardous. Even a map with 50-foot contour lines does not show a lot of deadly 40-foot drops! From the top, the slope from the Knifes Edge on Katahdin looks steep but not impossible to negotiate. But the incline increases quickly until it ends at a 1,000-foot cliff passable only to those with technical rock-climbing gear and skills.

- **Stick together** or at least make arrangements to regroup members of your party at major intersections or summits. Take a head count before proceeding. Scores of people become separated from their group or are reported overdue in Maine each year. Most are quickly located by Park Rangers, game wardens or members of a volunteer search and rescue group.

- If hiking alone, be sure to **leave a note** detailing your route, and the time of your expected return. That way, should you have a problem on the trail, someone will be able to summon assistance.

- Do not rely on a **cellular phone** to get you out of a jam. While they can be invaluable to speed a rescue, too many hikers now use them in place of proper preparation and common sense. Batteries die quickly, signals are not precise and incorrect information or a sketchy location transmitted by cell phone can delay vital rescue resources. If you do carry one, use it only for emergencies and bring the right numbers to call in event of an accident. Cell phones are banned in Baxter State Park (they are considered a noise-making electronic device).

- When you hike always be prepared for worst-case **weather** and to spend an unexpected night in the wild. If, after all the basic gear is stashed in your pack, you feel the need for a phone, then put it in.

- If **darkness** falls and you have not found your way, stay put and help will come. Most of the serious injuries from falls involving lost hikers in Maine have occurred after dark. The best motto – a favorite of the warden service – is "find a space and show your face."

- Forgetting to use **sun block** while hiking or basking in the sun along the shore has ruined more vacations that any other affliction. Use of a lotion with at least an SPF of 15 or higher is critical during prime sunburn time between the hours of 10 am and 2 pm.

In 1947 devastating forest fires swept across many areas of Maine, including much of Acadia. When fire dangers rise, traditionally in late

Introduction

summer and early fall, state officials will sometimes ban smoking on the trails.

 Use all smoking materials carefully at all times, but especially when fire danger is high. Field strip all cigarettes and pack out the butts.

▪ Mountain Biking

Mountain bikers are just beginning to discover the fun that awaits in riding the maze of paper company haul roads that crisscross the northern and eastern portions of the state.

Back roads beckon in nearly every county. Old railroad rights of way, often used by snowmobiles in the winter, offer perfect forest riding. Many old logging roads in the Western Mountains also offer exciting ride possibilities.

Major ski areas are now stepping forward and have modified their lifts to take bicycles for thrilling downhill runs during the summer.

Acadia National Park – with its 50 miles of groomed, gravel carriage roads that are off-limits to motor vehicles, its 22-mile scenic Park Loop Road, and four-mile road to the summit of 1,532-foot Cadillac Mountain – is a biker's paradise.

Most bike shops around the state will rent bikes. Rates range from $9 to $25 per day, depending on model.

One good source for backcountry biking information is the Maine Department of Conservation. During the last 20 years hundreds of miles of old railroad lines have been abandoned and converted into multiple-use trails. Snowmobiles use them in winter and bicyclists and ATVs are allowed on them the rest of the year. While no official bike maps exists, you can request a map of ATV trails, which will do just fine. Snowmobile trail maps are not as reliable as they often include river and lake crossings on ice or across rough and swampy areas when there is four feet of snow to smooth out rocky terrain.

You can get the ATV map by contacting the Conservation Department at 22 State House Station, Augusta 04333. ☎ 287-4968.

Biking Safety

Dressing for the weather, preparing to deal with bugs and sun, bringing adequate water, and proficiency with map and compass are all required before taking to the backcountry. With few repair shops, especially in the

North, those who fail to bring basic tools or a tire patch kit may not want to ride further in than they are willing to walk out.

Also, Maine is famous for having just three seasons; summer, winter, and mud. Because the ground thaws from the top down in the spring, water cannot soak deep into the ground. This results in thick mud up to two feet deep in some places. Many areas close trails and roads until the thaw is complete and roads and bikeways can dry out. This prevents ruts, which contribute to erosion and increased maintenance costs.

Several firms in Maine offer biking tours, including a company that offers a trip to watch the sunrise on top of Mount Cadillac and then a glide down on special bikes with high-tech brakes.

Most major tourist towns, such as Bar Harbor, Camden, Bath, Bethel, Kennebunkport, Ogunquit, Orono, Searsport and Southwest Harbor have rental and repair shops.

As the popularity of mountain biking has increased, so has the number of clashes between bikers and other user groups. Most state and national parks ban bicycles from hiking trails.

Suggested rides can be found in the individual chapters throughout this book.

Information Sources

The state-wide **Bicycle Coalition of Maine** is active in promoting the sport. They can be reached at PO Box 5275, Augusta 04332. ☎ 865-3636.

The **Maine Bicycle Trail Association**, based in Portland, offers several inexpensive trail-riding maps of the Portland and Mid-Coast areas. They can be contacted at 43 Carleton Street, Portland 04102. ☎ 879-7440.

■ Canoeing

Canoeing is an ancient art in Maine. Its roots reach back thousands of years to the Native Americans who were the first humans to call the region home.

With thick forests and high mountains everywhere, rivers and streams provided the best routes between seasonal encampments and rich hunting and gathering grounds. With relatively short carries between lakes or over coastal peninsulas, the Indians, who fashioned rugged canoes from single sheets of bark from "canoe birch," (aka white birch), could quickly and safely access most of the state.

The potential for trips is endless. It ranges from short day trips on meandering streams Down East (such as the Narraguagus and Pleasant) to two-week expeditions on the fabled Allagash in Northern Maine.

For paddlers who don't shrink from having to endure repeated lengthy portages, there is the East Branch of the Penobscot, with its aptly-named Hulling Machine where no pulp or saw log that entered upstream came out below with a shred of bark left on.

Maine's hundreds of small lakes and ponds and thousands of miles of slow-moving streams offer endless variety for quiet water paddling.

For those seeking a more transcendental experience there are leisurely float trips on the sandy Saco in Western Maine or week-long adventures on the St. Croix on the boundary with New Brunswick. There are few canoeable places in North America where river left is one country and river right another. And, because each country is in a different time zone, it is possible to get up in Canada, paddle for nearly an hour, and stop for breakfast in the US before you actually got up!

Use of Maine's rivers shifts with the seasons. Smaller coastal rivers with limited watersheds often get too low for decent paddling by late June. Bigger rivers, many of which are dam controlled, often sport rapids too dangerous for paddlers in open boats. Still, drifting down a wild stream never knowing if a moose may be lingering just around the corner is one of life's great pleasures in the Maine outdoors. On most lakes loons call each night and serenade tired campers to sleep.

Recommended canoe trips are covered in the individual area chapters.

700-Mile Paddle Route

In recent years, a man from Waldoboro, Maine, has been championing the idea of a 700-mile Northern Forest Canoe Trail from Fort Kent in northern Maine to Old Forge in New York. Mike Krepner has founded **Native Trails Inc.** to push the idea. He and fellow paddlers have spent years exploring and in some cases re-opening old Native American portage routes between major watersheds in Maine. He can be reached at PO Box 240, Waldoboro 04572. ☎ 832-5255.

River Classification

The International River Classification system rates rapids on a scale that includes Class I, Class II, Class III, Class IV and Class V. There is no Class VI, but if there were it would probably be something totally unrunnable, such as Niagara Falls. Water conditions, distance and time from rescue, and air temperature combine to determine what class a rapid should be. While high water may flood out Class I rapids, it can make a Class IV into a V very easily.

Classification Chart

Class I – Very easy. Waves small, regular; passages clear; sandbanks, artificial difficulties such as bridge piers; riffles.

Class II – Easy. Rapids of medium difficulty, with passages clear and wide; low ledges.

Class III – Medium. Waves numerous, high, irregular; rocks, eddies; rapids with passages that are clear though narrow, requiring expertise in maneuvering; inspection usually needed.

Class IV – Difficult. Long rapids; waves powerful, irregular; dangerous rocks; boiling eddies; passages difficult to reconnoiter; inspection mandatory first time; powerful and precise maneuvering required.

Class V – Very Difficult. Long and very violent rapids, following each other almost without interruption; riverbed extremely obstructed; big drops, violent current; very steep gradient; reconnoitering essential but difficult.

The standard joke among paddlers is to pass a drainage ditch with some water in it and say "it looks runnable." Use detailed guidebooks and acquaint yourself with International River Classification System before setting off on a river trip.

Canoe Clinics

Each June, **L.L. Bean** sponsors a canoe symposium on Moose Pond in Bridgton. Dozens of different models are available to test. Clinics include topics such as choosing a canoe, paddle technique, and how to pole. To find out the exact dates and more information, ☎ 800-341-4341.

Maine Sports in Rockport and **Cadillac Mountain Sports** in Bangor (see page 118) also sponsor annual paddling clinics and demonstrations.

Canoeing Safety

- Conditions can change rapidly. Spring and fall temperatures require use of **wet or dry suits**. The rule of thumb is that when the air and water temperature added together doesn't equal 100, on go the suits.

- The most important piece of equipment, after a good attitude, is a **life jacket**. Forget the old orange ones that are uncomfortable and bulky. Get, rent, beg, borrow, or steal a good vest-type life jacket and then wear it. Once you are overboard it is too late to put it on.

- If you should **hit a rock** or come up against a tree leaning out over the river, resist the urge to lean away. When you hit, the current will be pushing the bottom of the canoe downstream. If you lean upstream, you are just helping it tip you over faster. This goes against instinct and is hard to do but necessary.

- If you do **flip**, take steps to keep from getting pinned between the canoe and any rocks downstream. Stay upstream of the canoe. Even moderate current pressing on a canoe can exert thousands of pounds of pressure. Don't worry about the gear, it can be replaced. Make sure you and your canoe partner are safe first.

- If caught in **rapids**, work your way to shore by aiming your feet downstream to fend off any rocks or other obstacles. Always carry an extra paddle as it is surprisingly easy to lose one or have it pulled from your hands in a rapid.

- When **camping**, pull all canoes well up on shore and tie them off. Freak wind gusts can send your only transportation sailing out over the lake with surprising ease. Also, water levels or waves can pick up at night and are responsible for the loss of many a canoe. Exercise judgement when considering setting up camp on a sandbar or shallow beach. When camping near falls or other obstacles that may require portaging, make sure your canoes, tents, tarps, and clotheslines do not block the path for others.

■ While Maine is seldom prone to **flash floods**, water levels can change quickly, particularly below dams or after thunderstorms upstream. Most dams, which use water for power generation, may release high flows unexpectedly. Usually, a horn will sound to warn fishermen and boaters immediately downstream, but even a half-mile away the signal may not be heard.

These rusting steam locomotives, once used to haul logs between lakes in the Allagash Waterway region, are visited today by the occasional paddler.
Photo by Kirsten Stockman

MAINE'S LARGEST LAKES *(includes connecting water bodies)*			
RANK	NAME	SURFACE AREA (MILES)	LOCATION
1	Moosehead	117	Great North Woods
2	Sebago	45	South Coast
3	Chesuncook	36	Great North Woods
4	Mooselookmeguntic	26	Western Mountains
5	Twin Lakes	25	Great North Woods
6	East Grand Lake	24	Down East Coast
7	Grand Lake	23	Down East Coast
8	Spednik Lake	23	Great North Woods
9	Chamberlain Lake	17.5	Far North
10	Churchill Lake	17	Far North

■ Kayaking

Kayaking is without a doubt the fastest growing outdoor sport in Maine. In many areas it has surpassed mountain biking in the number of new aficionados it has attracted.

With its 3,500 miles of rocky shoreline, thousands of small offshore islands, most uninhabited, Maine is a kayaker's paradise. Wildlife abounds, seldom startled by the presence of a slim boat not powered by a noisy, polluting motor.

In fact, Maine was the first place to create an "island trail," a coastal water route open to conservation-minded boaters.

Kayakers can use any public boat launch ramp in Maine to get to sea. There are literally hundreds from which to choose. Most communities have several. The best place to check is with the local harbor master. He or she can also help with a related problem – where to safely leave the car for a few days.

Among the most popular coastal destinations for kayakers are Casco Bay off Portland, Penobscot Bay off Rockland, Deer Isle, and the waters surrounding Mount Desert Island, including Frenchman and Blue Hill Bays.

Most islands in Maine are privately owned. Others are owned by conservation groups or subject to easements that allow day visits, but no overnight camping.

See individual area chapters for recommended kayak routes and lists of tour operators.

Kayak Clinics

More and more companies are now offering guided kayaking tours with Registered Maine Guides. The tours include instruction in how to handle a kayak as well as important safety lectures. Half- and full-day trips are possible. Guides schedule trips to take into account wind and tides and also know where to find the best beaches, wildlife locales, and scenic areas. Outfitters are listed in each chapter.

Each July, **L.L. Bean** sponsors a sea kayaking symposium at the Maine Maritime Academy in Castine. To find out the exact dates and more information, ☎ 800-341-4341.

Kayaking Safety

Kayaking is not a sport you can simply take up without proper instruction or at the very least going a few times with experienced hands. The cold Atlantic waters are too unforgiving to take such a chance. Be sure you are prepared, both mentally and physically, for the trip you have planned. Inform someone of your plans so they can contact authorities if you are overdue.

Build plenty of time into your schedule to **weather-related delays** and pay especially close attention to winds, current and tides. Whenever possible, time trips to paddle with the tide or wind so you do not have to fight both on a return trip.

When it comes to paddling safety the simplest advice is still the best – wear that **life jacket**! How many times have we heard that admonishment? Yet how often it is ignored.

Exploring Maine's freshwater and coastal waters in a person-powered watercraft is one of the best ways to enjoy the state's unparalleled natural beauty. Yet each year scores of people die needlessly because they did not take the time to put on their personal floatation device before stepping aboard a boat. Trying to put it on in an emergency is often futile.

In tests with expert swimmers, all had difficulty trying to put on a life jacket once they were in the water. With Maine's historically chilly waters that quickly take the breath and sap the strength of even the strongest individual, there is no time to spare.

Maine law requires that there be an approved floatation in the boat for each adult occupant. Life jackets must be worn at all times by anyone under the age of 12. But go the extra step and be sure to have everyone wear them. Find a model appropriate for the type of activity you enjoy and make sure it fits comfortably. If you don't like the old standby orange around-your-neck models then get a vest type. Life jackets for very young children should include a crotch strap to make sure they cannot slip out.

Except on some of the smaller lakes, be sure to bring a **compass**; especially when paddling on the ocean (even if you are going only a short distance). Fog can move in almost instantaneously. While you don't need to be able to plot a complicated course, keep an eye on your heading and be ready to find and follow a back bearing if necessary.

Sea kayakers should consider adding an inexpensive **radar reflector** to their vessels. Reflective tape on life jackets and boats is also a good idea. One local harbormaster attaches his radar reflector to a fiberglass rod used to fasten indicator flags to bicycles. Up to date **nautical charts** are also indispensable.

Coastal waters and the waters of larger lakes teem with recreational and **commercial boat traffic**. And some of the larger whale watch vessels are capable of very high speeds. Even though smaller vessels theoretically have the right-of-way, make sure yours can be seen.

Always inspect your canoe or kayak for damage or excess wear before putting in. A roll of that old standby – duct tape – can be invaluable for making minor field repairs in the field.

When trying out a new boat for the first time, pick a body of water that is calm and relatively warm. Give yourself time to adjust to the correct balance and adjust to how the boat handles before tackling anything big.

Watch the tide! Each year scores of kayakers along the coast are stranded when the incoming tide carries off their boats. Tides in the Mid-Coast area average 12 feet. Near Eastport they can rise and fall as much as 40 feet. Take the time to carry your boat above the high-water mark and tie it to a heavy object.

Carry a **rescue rope** throw bag and practice how to use it.

Be honest to yourself about your **skill level**. Most paddling problems happen when people, metaphorically, get in over their heads. Trying something new or challenging is half the fun in paddling, but let weather, your physical condition, and equipment dictate when and where.

Respect other paddlers' **privacy**. Solitude and escape from crowds is why many people take up paddle sports. There is plenty of shoreline out there.

Maine Island Trail

Originally conceived as a sort of Appalachian Trail in the sea, the Maine Island Trail is a network of more than 80 public and privately owned islands along a 300-mile stretch of Maine coast open to recreational use. Some islands are as large as several hundred acres, while others are basically bare ledges which can be awash during storms. All state islands are open to use by the public while privately owned trail islands are open to members of the Maine Island Trail Association in exchange for members sticking to a low-impact use ethic. Users can arrive by kayak, sailboat, or motorized craft.

Members support the work of the association through dues and also through volunteer efforts to keep popular campsites clean and damage free.

Contact the **Maine Island Trail Association** to learn more. PO Box C, Rockland 04841. ☎ 596-6456.

Weather conditions can vary greatly depending on one's location. Daylight fades quickly in autumn, so make sure you have plenty of time to complete your paddle before dark. It doesn't hurt to put a small flashlight in your duffle along with other essentials.

Especially during summer, afternoon thunderstorms can whip the water into a maelstrom that is impossible to navigate, even for seasoned paddlers. Most thunderstorms brew up out of the west or north and head east or southeast. Watch for black clouds gathering on horizon and pay particular attention to those that rise suddenly behind nearby mountains.

Lightning is often more of a danger to small boats than wind. Get off the water, and stay away from taller trees. Avoid seeking shelter in caves, bunkers or near tree roots that can conduct lightning strikes underground from trees. Several years ago some boaters sought refuge from a thunderstorm in a World War II-era blockhouse on an island off Portland. Lightning hit nearby, traveled through the ground, and one person was killed.

Before setting out on any paddle trip check the weather forecast and watch for any deviation from the prediction. When in doubt, hole up, ride it out... and live to tell about it.

Clothing

See the *Hiking* section, above, for details on jackets and headwear that should be worn.

A disposable "**space blanket**" is also a popular, yet light-weight, pack item. Good **paddling gloves** are also important.

Most experienced paddlers bring a small waterproof river bag with a few essentials even on a modest day trip. Wind, rain, rough water or equipment problems and other hazards can easily conspire to force you to spend a night in the open.

For those paddling freshwater in early or late season, or on the ocean even in high summer, consider wearing a **wet suit** or a dry suit. An unexpected dunking when the water temperatures are down is the first step in what can easily become a life-threatening situation.

Resource Protection

One of the great joys of paddling is being able to see wildlife close up. However, even good-intentioned visitors can disturb nesting aquatic birds or birds of prey. Keep a respectful distance from eagle, osprey, or loon nests and ledges and rocks used as nesting and resting sites by birds, seals, and other sea life. Don't feed the birds; they will fast see humans as a source of food, which can dull their most important survival instinct – fear of people.

Camping

On freshwater lakes, ponds and rivers, camping is allowed only at designated sites. Usually a fire permit is required. You can pick one up at any forest warden's headquarters on the way to your put-in. In periods of high fire danger all campfires are banned.

*If you plan to gather shell fish for a meal, be sure you check before leaving for warnings concerning **red tide**, a toxic algae bloom which can poison humans. After heavy rains, state officials often close mud flats to clamming to allow any pollution that may have washed down from the land to dissipate.*

Some islands along the coast are open to camping and have designated sites. Others are privately owned and permission must be secured before going ashore.

WISE WORDS: *Never pull a lobster trap, even out of curiosity. Most caught doing so by fishermen wish they had been nabbed by a warden instead. Fishermen are often willing to sell some of their fresh catch to sea kayakers, so just ask.*

Introduction

General Tips

- Stay away from alcohol or other drugs. Not only do they impair judgement and balance, but alcohol dilates blood vessels in the skin, creating the sensation of warmth but actually speeds the cooling the body's core. This can lead to hypothermia.
- Always remember to use sunblock.

RANK	NAME	LENGTH (MILES)	LOCATION
MAINE'S LONGEST RIVERS			
1	St. John	331	Far North
2	Penobscot	325	Great North Woods
3	Androscoggin	240	Great North Woods
4	Kennebec	170	Great North Woods
5	Saco	121	Western Mountains
6	Aroostook	100	Far North
7	Mattawamkeag	83	Great North Woods
8	Dead	74	Western Mountains
9	Sebasticook	72	Great North Woods
10	Allagash	69	Far North

■ Whitewater Rafting

All whitewater rafting in Maine is done on three rivers in the north-central part of the state. They include the **West Branch of the Penobscot**, which offers fleeting glimpses of Katahdin, and the **Kennebec and Dead Rivers**, which meet at **The Forks**, a village along Route 201 that is the center of rafting in Maine. It takes about five hours to reach The Forks from Boston. Nearly all trips take less than a day, with an average cost of around $80 to $90 per adult. Water levels are guaranteed – all rivers used by rafting companies are controlled by major dams.

DID YOU KNOW? *The highest rapid rating is Class V, found in places on the Dead River and at the Cribworks on the Penobscot. Magic Falls is a Class IV "hole" on the Kennebec.*

*Each year thousands of visitors enjoy a safe and exciting rafting trip
on the Dead, Kennebec and Penobscot Rivers.*
Photo courtesy of Northern Outdoors

With guides licensed by the state, all trips on Maine rivers, while exciting, are comparatively safe. All paddlers are given a safety lecture and
shown how to paddle as a team before putting in. Instructions include
what to do if you are tossed out of the boat.

These trips are on big water and should not be considered lightly.

Most outfitters provide life jackets, paddles, rafts, and transportation to
the put-in point. Wet suits may be rented, although in high summer they
are not needed. Most operators also offer a hearty lunch cooked either
riverside or back at their base camp.

Check to see if your outfitter offers still photos or video of your wild ride.
Some even put on a slide presentation or video show and take orders before your departure.

When to Go & What to Bring

The rafting companies will hate to read this, but I say forget about going
in the spring. Early on it is just too cold and, even with wet or dry suits, it
is far from an idyllic experience. By early June these rivers are swarming
with ravenous black flies that will chew rings around any flesh left bare
by your wet suit.

Go in late July or early August, when the days are warm and sunny and when half the fun is jumping off the raft in the quiet water sections to float along with the river. Reserve early as this is the most popular time and outfitters have set allocations on how many people they can take each day. (It's usually easier to get reservations during the week.)

Autumn too can be spectacular. Most people don't think of leaf peeping from a raft, but it really doesn't get any better. The water is warm and sunlight just right.

Make sure you have packed the following:

❏ Wet suit (optional)
❏ River sandals, shell shoes
❏ Towel
❏ A change of clothing
❏ Hat
❏ Sunscreen
❏ Bug repellent
❏ Strap for glasses
❏ Waterproof camera

Rafting Outfitters

BETHEL
Raft Maine, PO Box 3, Bethel 04217. Reservations and information, ☎ 800-723-8633.

BINGHAM
Maine Whitewater, PO Box 663, Bingham 04920. Base facility at Gaddibout Gaddis Airport, Route 201. ☎ 800-345-MAIN.

BRUNSWICK
Unicorn Rafting Expeditions, PO Box T, Brunswick 04011. Base facility on Parlin Pond has cabins, swimming, windsurfing, lake canoeing. ☎ 800-UNICORN.

EAST VASSALBORO
AAA Whitewater, PO Box 47, East Vassalboro 04935. Whitewater rafting on the Penobscot, Kennebec and Dead Rivers in Maine. ☎ 800-348-8871.

THE FORKS
Magic Falls Rafting, PO Box 9, The Forks 04985. Duckie (inflatable kayak) trips on the lower Kennebec and Dead. ☎ 800-207-RAFT.

Crab Apple Whitewater and Lodge, HC 63, Box 25, The Forks 04985. Operates inn, lodge, luxury suites and cottage. Prime location for Nordic skiing, snowmobiling, whitewater rafting and hiking. Specializes in romantic getaways, family vacations and corporate outings. ☎ 663-2218.

Northern Outdoors, Route 201, PO Box 100, The Forks 04985. Whitewater rafting on Maine's Kennebec, Penobscot and Dead Rivers. Rock climbing, kayak touring, team-building ropes courses. Also, corporate/meeting retreats. Wilderness resort features deluxe lakeside log cabins, riverside campsites, heated pool, hot tubs, paddle tennis court, meeting/function rooms, restaurant and Kennebec River microbrewery. ☎ 800-765-7238.

Moxie Outdoor Adventures, HC 63, Box 60, Forks 04985. Whitewater rafting adventures from mild to wild on the Kennebec, Dead and Penoscot Rivers. ☎ 800-866-6943.

MILLINOCKET
New England Outdoor Center, 240 Katahdin Avenue, Millinocket 04462. Canoe and kayak school, wilderness rescue courses, self-guided trips. ☎ 800-766-7238.

JACKMAN
Windfall Rafting, Route 201, Box 505 Jackman 04945. Professionally guided rafting trips down the Kennebec and Dead Rivers. Accommodations and packages to suit every need. A family-oriented outfitter with safety and enjoyment of the rivers being the prime concern. ☎ 800-683-2009.

ROCKWOOD
Wilderness Expeditions, PO Box 41, Rockwood 04478. Based at The Birches Resort on Moosehead Lake; year-round wilderness recreation. ☎ 800-825-WILD.

WEST FORKS
Professional River Runners, PO Box 92, West Forks 04985. Overnight camping trips along major rivers. ☎ 800-325-3911.

■ Hunting

Maine offers a variety of game animals and birds for hunters of every persuasion. The big action comes in the fall when nearly 200,000 residents and out-of-staters purchase hunting licenses to pursue the elusive **white-tailed deer**.

Except for hunters who apply for and get an "any deer" permit, Maine has a bucks-only rule when hunting season opens at the beginning of November. The first day of the season is for Mainers only. No hunting is allowed on Sunday. The season ends at dusk on the Saturday after Thanksgiving. Archers may hunt earlier; muzzleloaders later.

Moose are hunted as well, with 2,000 permits being issued by lottery each year. The season runs for one week in October.

Black bear hunting seasons vary with technique, use of dogs, etc. Wildlife officials estimate there are approximately 22,000 bruins in the state.

The open seasons and bag limits for **small game** such as rabbit, hare, raccoon, squirrel, etc., vary by date and area.

Upland **birds** such as woodcock, pheasant, quail and ruffed grouse, can be hunted beginning October 1.

The season on **duck** and **geese** varies and is set by an oversight board each year in late August.

Licenses & Rules

Hunting licenses can be purchased at town offices across the state. Types of licenses include small or large game. They can be obtained in combination with fishing licenses at an impressive discount. Fees for non-residents vary from $55 to $85.

Separate licenses are required for bow hunting or use of muzzleloading firearms.

Also, special stamps or permits are required for bear, moose, waterfowl and turkey.

Rule books are provided when a hunting license is purchased. Among the more important regulations are those dealing with safety.

- All firearm hunters must wear two items of blaze orange clothing, one of which must be a hat.
- No firearm can be discharged in proximity of a home, building or school.
- No hunting is allowed from a motor vehicle or from a paved road. Those found with loaded firearms in a vehicle, or concealed loaded firearms in a vehicle, face heavy fines and time in jail.
- Hunters who fail to completely identify their targets and cause injury or property damage can face criminal charges.

People who suspect someone is poaching can call game wardens toll-free at **Operation Game Thief**, ☎ 800-253-7887.

Hunting & Fishing Guides

ASHLAND
Libby Camps, PO Box V 28 Main Street, Ashland 04732. A full-service Orvis-endorsed guiding/lodging operation. Many log cabins throughout the North Maine Woods. A century-old family operated business. Winter lodging now available. Experienced guides, seaplane on location, home cooking, first-class wilderness accomodations. ☎ 435-8274.

BELGRADE
Maine Wilderness Tours. RR 1 Box 462, Belgrade 04917. An adventure travel planning service specializing in booking guided or unguided trips ranging from hunting and fishing to hiking and wildlife photography. ☎ 495-7729.
Whisperwood lodge and Cottages, Taylor Woods Road, Belgrade 04917. Fishing lodge. Enjoy fine dining, lakeside cabin, swimming, boats. ☎ 800-355-7170.

BLAINE
#9 Lake Outfitters, PO Box 267 Blaine 04734. ☎ 429-9632.

BINGHAM
Sunrise Ridge Guide Service and Cabins PO Box 435, Bingham 04920. Offers the excitement of the hunt coupled with pure outdoor fun set in the beautiful mountains of Western Maine. ☎ 672-5551.

BURLINGTON
Nicatous Lodge and Camps, PO Box 100S, Burlington 04417. Lake and stream fishing, game and bird hunting, hiking, canoeing and bird watching. ☎ 732-4771 (let it ring!).

CARROLL
Lukacik's Inn Beyond, RR 1 Box 991 Carroll 04487. Prime smallmouth bass fishing. Black bear hunts with hounds or bait, white-tailed deer, bobcat, coyote, bird hunting. Professional guides. Full-service accommodations. ☎ 738 5315.

DOVER-FOXCROFT
The Foggy Mountain Guide Service, RR 2 Box 1140 Dover-Foxcroft 04426. ☎ 564-3404.

EAGLE LAKE
Fish River Lodge, PO Box 202, Old Main Street, Eagle Lake, 04739. Recreation and vacation cottages located in beautiful Northern Maine. Eight cottages with all utilities. Fish, vacation, hunt or photograph moose and bald eagles. Easy access off Route 11, private and quiet. ☎ 444-5207.

GRAND LAKE STREAM
Weatherby's... The Fisherman's Resort, PO Box 69, Grand Lake Stream 04637. One of the country's oldest and most famous fishing lodges, with origins stemming from before the turn of the century. It has become a way of life for anglers in search of a remote spot. Many grandchildren of the original guests return for their fishing vacations. ☎ 796-5558.

GREENVILLE
Little Lyford Pond Camps, PO Box 1269, Greenville 04441. Century-old sporting camp in back-woods location offering outstanding fly fishing for native brook trout. In winter a vast network of backcountry trails entices the serious cross country skier and naturalist. ☎ 534-2284.

HARRISON
Deertrails Guide Service, 6 Deertrails Road, Harrison 04040. Deertrails offers trophy hunts in the Western Foothills of Maine. Low hunter-to-guide ratio. For bear, deer or bobcat; with firearms, bow, or camera. Contact John Strickland, Registered Maine Guide. ☎ 888-558-HUNT (4868).

THE FORKS
Northern Outdoors, Route 201 PO Box 100 The Forks, 04985. This company prides itself on providing guests with the best hunting experience the Northeast has to offer. Specializing in Trophy Whitetail hunts. Comfortable wilderness lodge or remote tent camps. ☎ 765-7238.

ISLAND FALLS
Bear Creek Guide Service and Lodge, Box 288, Island Falls 04747. Registered Maine Guide John Schmidt offers trophy game hunts for bear, deer, moose, coyote and grouse as well as fishing trips. ☎ 463-2662.

JACKMAN
Cedar Ridge Outfitters, PO Box 744 HF, Jackman 04945. Master Guide Hal Blood and wife, Registered Maine Guide Debbie Blood, offer fishing and hunting trips of any persuasion. Cabins and lodge with housekeeping camps or American plan. Trophy deer hunting in the Boundary Mountains area a specialty. ☎ 668-4169.
Long Pond Camps and Guide Service PO Box 815, Route 15, Jackman 04945. Complete guide service as well as camp and cabin rentals in the Jackman area. ☎ 668-4872.
Red Buck Sporting Camps, Box 114 HF, Jackman 04945. Offers guided bear hunts, fly fishing trips to remote ponds as well as family vacations and mountain bike rentals. ☎ 800-308-2017.

LOVELL
Rocky Ridge Guide Service, 1 Ridge Road, PO Box 76 Lovell 04051. Fish in Southern, Central and Western Maine for large- and smallmouth bass, salmon and lake trout. Hunt in the beautiful foothills of the White Mountains for woodcock, Grouse and white-tailed deer. ☎ 925-6262.

MADISON
Miller's Guide Service, RR 1, Box 754 HF, Madison 04950. Upland game and trophy big game hunts. Hunt from main lodge or remote camps. Robert and Raymond Miller, Master Guides. ☎ 474-3730.

MILLINOCKET
Nahmakanta Lake Camps, PO Box 544 Millinocket 04462. ☎ 746-7356.

NEW SHARON
Gary C.'s Guiding, PO Box 22 New Sharon 04955. A full-service hunting and fishing guide booking clients into a number of traditional sporting camps in northwestern Maine. Fish for brook trout, salmon, lake trout, blueback trout or hunt trophy white-tailed deer in remote North Maine Woods. ☎ 778-0529.

PORTLAND
Calendar Islands Guide Service, PO Box 10513 Portland 04104. Fly fishing for trophy striped bass along Maine's scenic tidal rivers. Claims to be the state's only guaranteed guide service. If you don't land a fish, the trip is free. ☎ 829-4578.

ROCKWOOD
Gentle Ben's Hunting and Fishing Lodge, Box 212 MG, Rockwood 04478. Trophy hunts and fishing trips in the Moosehead Lake and Allagash regions. Main facility and remote wilderness camps. ☎ 534-2201.
Sundown Cabins, PO Box 129 Jackman Road, Rockwood 04478. Waterfront cottages on the shore of crystal clear Moosehead Lake. Open year-round for fishing, hunting, snowmobiling, skiing, relaxing, moose and deer watching, all outdoor activities. ☎ 534-7357.

UNION
Captain Don Kleiner, Master Maine Guide, Maine Outdoors, PO Box 401, Union 04862. Professional guide services providing quality outdoor experiences for all ages and confidence levels. Canoe trips, spin or fly fishing; for trout, bass, stripers, bluefish. Nature programs, cross-country ski or snowshoe trips. Hunting; upland birds, puddle and sea ducks. Trips range from a half-day to multi-day by reservation only. ☎ 785-4496.

Introduction

WEST BUXTON
Raio's Guide Service, 268 Mary Jane Road, West Buxton 04093. Bass fishing adventures with fully equipped jetboats, bassboats, and all tackle required for an excellent day of fishing. ☎ 727-3215.

WILTON
North Woods Adventures, PO Box 812 55 Woodland Avenue, Wilton 04294. ☎ 645-3575.

Source: Maine Department of Tourism

For more information and a free list of top guides, contact the **Maine Professional Guides Association** at PO Box 847, Augusta 04332. ☎ 785-2061.

■ Fishing

Fresh or salt? That is the question that confronts anglers in Maine. The state maintains more than 130 launching ramps on lakes, rivers and along the coast to facilitate recreational boating and fishing.

Saltwater

No license is needed to fish in the ocean. Most saltwater fishing is done from boats. Fishing from shore, which includes dropping lines from bridges, wharfs or rocks, is seldom productive. Sure, a harbor pollock, passing mackerel, or even an occasional flounder may be hooked, but pollock are not considered good to eat. Still, most anglers consider just catching something, *anything*, worth the time spent savoring the fresh salt air or watching the sun dance on the water.

In Southern Maine traditional **surf casting** can be done from the broad sandy beaches, provided it doesn't impinge on swimmer safety. Striped bass and blue fish are the favorite targets here.

Is This Beach Private?

Many beaches may be marked private, but laws harking back to Colonial days prohibit barring the public from the intertidal area (zone from mean low to mean high tide) for the purposes of "fishing, fowling or navigation." Basically, this means that shorefront property owners don't have to give you access to the shore, but once you are there, provided you stay below the high tide line (usually a line of seaweed) they cannot force you to leave. Constant respect for privacy and private property, however, make for the best landowner relations.

Fishing near shore is a favorite pastime, with mighty **striped bass** being the quarry of choice. They can be found well into rivers and estuaries and, like their predatory neighbors, the blue fish, often terrorize schools of bait fish, occasionally even driving them right up on shore.

Nothing beats a good "mess" of **mackerel**, usually caught by trolling with multi-hooked jigs. When a school is crossed it is not unusual to have three or even four strikes at once. When the mackerel are running, the fishing is fast. Children especially like the fast-paced action. Because mackerel are an oily species, they are usually served fried.

Flounder, which frequent muddy bottom in coves and harbors, are usually hooked on hand lines dropped from boats at anchor or on a mooring. Watch for a subtle tug on the line – this savvy prey will easily steal the bait off the hook of the unwary angler.

Offshore fishing is best pursued by hooking up with the captain of one of the many **deep-sea fishing charter boats** that work the coast. Full- and half-day trips are available. In most cases the trip includes tackle, bait, and transportation. Food and beverages are usually available for an additional charge.

Once offshore, lines are dropped overboard in the search for **cod, haddock, halibut** and **hake**, which are usually fished on bottom or just off bottom. It is also not unusual to catch one of the Gulf of Maine's ugliest fish, the **sculpin**, which, because of its mangled appearance and extraordinarily large maw, was long ago nicknamed "the mother-in-law fish."

Small sharks, referred to as "dogfish," are frequently hooked and put up a good fight.

For those thirsting for even greater adventure, some charters go further offshore in pursuit of giant **tuna**.

Don't Help Yourself

You must have a license to dig clams, even for personal consumption. They are available at most town offices for a nominal fee. No one can take lobsters out of the sea, either by hand or while diving, without a license. You have to be a permanent resident and serve an apprenticeship to get one. The penalty for taking lobsters from a trap or storage car (officially called trap molesting) is severe, although being caught by authorities is usually preferable to being caught by the lobsterman whose livelihood you intended to steal.

Freshwater

Casting a fly with pinpoint accuracy into a deep pool along a rushing stream or watching the trout rise during a Mayfly hatch on a remote northern lake are among the most beautiful experiences in Maine.

Nationally, freshwater fishing is the most popular sporting activity.

Maine, which boasts both cold water lakes (home to trout and land-locked salmon), and warmer ponds (home to such game fish as large- and smallmouthed bass and perch), has something to offer every angler.

Anyone over the age of 16 must have a state-issued license to freshwater fish. Licenses, which can be issued for the entire season, 15 days, one week, three days or one day, can be obtained at most town offices and at many outfitting stores and sporting camps. Prices for non-residents range from $9 to $38.

THERE ARE SOME FISH AROUND HERE.

Greetings from SOUTH CHINA, Maine.

An old postcard gets the message out that the fishing is good in the South China / Belgrade Lakes area.
From the collection of Barbara Saunders

When you pick up a license be sure to get the rule book. Maine fish and wildlife officials will be the first to admit that the state has some of the most complex and often confusing regulations in the country. In some areas, almost every pond has different restrictions on which techniques may be used, what types of baits may be employed, as well as shifting bag and size limits. Many lakes have restrictions on the use of motors or set restrictions on motor horsepower ratings.

📖 For a free rule booklet, write to the **Department of Inland Fisheries and Wildlife**, State House Station #41, Augusta, Maine 04333.

Maine is open to fishing nearly all year long. The open water season begins April 1 and ends, for the most part, on September 30. Some season extensions exist for specified waters for bass and other warm water game fish through October. Some trout and salmon fishing is allowed in early fall in specific waters.

Deep Sea

When deciding which boat and skipper to hire for a deep-sea fishing excursion. don't be bashful about asking for details. Find out what kind of success the vessel routinely enjoys and what folks have been catching lately. Boats should be US Coast Guard certified and the skipper licensed by the coast guard. Legitimate outfitters won't be offended if you ask. Basic questions might include:

■ How long is the trip?

■ How many others will be on the boat?

■ What's the crew-to-passenger ratio? Many a trip has been ruined when passengers spend too much time untangling their lines.

■ Are refreshments offered? Some boats have rules prohibiting passengers from bringing their own.

Also, check the weather yourself. If a change is imminent, consider a shorter trip.

 WISE WORDS: *The effects of sea sickness are often worsened on a bobbing stationary boat. If you're prone to seasickness, consider joining a regular tour boat that maintains a steady speed.*

Ice Fishing

Ice fishing is allowed for some species on most lakes as soon as the ice is safe to walk on (at least two inches of clear, solid ice). Ice fishing for all species is open on January 1 and runs until the end of March. In winter, many lakes sport transient communities of ice tents and houses, some with bunks, wood stoves and even television sets! Because of easy access to all reaches of a lake, fishing pressure in many places is much higher in winter than in summer.

Before venturing on unfamiliar ice, check with local residents to find out where traditional thin spots might lurk. After a light snow, the new layer of white can hide dangerously thin ice. After a rain, the warm water rushing into holes left by ice fishermen can create a "Swiss cheese" effect, making any ice travel hazardous.

 Pressure ridges are often treacherous, as are areas around inlets and outlet streams. And, springs may well up anywhere on a lake bottom, creating an area of thin ice above.

Game Wardens

For the most part, Game Wardens, who are responsible for enforcing all fish and wildlife laws, are understanding and will usually take inexperience into account when considering whether or not a violation deserves a warning or a summons. The law requires a fishing license to be produced upon the order of a game warden.

Be courteous. Among the violations for which wardens traditionally have the least tolerance are fishing without a license, exceeding bag limits or fishing in closed areas.

One tip to keep in mind is that the length of a fish is determined by the amount of the fish measurable when you are contacted by the warden. Don't cut the head or tail off a barely-legal length fish until you are just ready to cook it. If stopped and the body in your possession is undersized, you could be charged.

Wardens, particularly in Northern Maine, routinely run roadblocks to search vehicles carrying illegally-caught fish cargo, catch limit violations, and undersize fish.

Fishing of the Future

Two recent practices may have a profound impact on the future of Maine's freshwater fisheries. One is the practice of **catch and release**.

Officials encourage anglers to gently release fish they do not intend to eat so that they can continue to grow and be sport for people in the future. Often, the trip up from deeper water on the end of a hook is traumatic for the fish. Hold it gently just under the surface of the water until it can rest and swim free from your hand.

The other practice, **introduction of non-native species**, is worrisome. In some ponds species preferred by some anglers have been deliberately introduced in the mistaken belief they will provide additional fishing.

What these species do is compete with native fish for habitat and feed until the natives die off. That is why many key ponds are off-limits to the use of live bait, which could swim free and establish alien breeding populations.

Consumption Advisory

All anglers in Maine should also be aware that concerns about mercury in fish have prompted the state to issue advisory consumption limits for fish from certain rivers, particularly large rivers in the southern part of the state downstream from paper mills and large industries. These warnings, which outline how many fish per year can be safely eaten are detailed in the guidelines booklet.

Fishing Safely

A small fishing boat is found circling in a lake or at sea with no one aboard. Sometime later warden service divers make a disheartening discovery – the body of the fisherman who failed to wear his life jacket. The tragedy repeats itself far too many times each year in Maine. Always wear a **life jacket**.

Another boating safety tip is to keep a good eye on the **weather**. It can change rapidly. If a boat does overturn or swamp, officials recommend staying with it as long as it is afloat. If it sinks, use the wind and current to your advantage as you head for shore.

All motorized craft are required to have **lights** when running at night and to carry flares or similar emergency signaling equipment.

Maine has a tough law when it comes to operating a watercraft under the influence of **alcohol**. It can lead to heavy fines, loss of automobile driver's license, and time in jail. As state officials like to remind boaters "Water and alcohol don't mix."

Personal Watercraft Banned

In 1998 Maine banned the use of personal watercraft, popularly known by the brand name "Jetski," from hundreds of lakes and ponds, primarily in the more undeveloped northern and eastern parts of the state. Several municipalities are considering their own ban in several places. Check locally before using personal watercraft. Also, laws prohibit riding these craft at greater than minimal headway speed within 200 feet of shore. No one under the age of 16 may drive a personal watercraft unattended by an adult.

FISH SPECIES CHECKLISTS		
Cold Water Species		
❏ Brook trout ❏ Brown trout	❏ Land-locked salmon	❏ Atlantic salmon ❏ Togue (lake trout)
Warm Water Species		
❏ Smallmouth bass ❏ Largemouth bass	❏ Pickerel ❏ White perch	❏ Yellow perch ❏ Sunfish

■ Camping

Sitting around a crackling campfire while loons, owls, or even coyotes call in the distance is one of the great outdoor pleasures in Maine. Possible camping experiences vary widely in the state from infrastructure-intensive RV parks to remote backcountry sites sporting little more than a circle of stones for a fire pit. Some, if you are lucky, have privies. While many of the backcountry sites are located along logging roads, others are accessible only by boat.

List of commercial campgrounds can be found in the individual area sections. Tent site fees start at around $14 per night, with additional costs for electric hookups, etc. A comprehensive list can also be obtained from the **Maine Campground Owners Association** at 655 Main Street, Lewiston 04240, ☎ 782-5874.

While it would be nice, there is no one source for information on campsites run by state government. State park campgrounds are noted throught the text. Camping opportunities in Baxter State Park and Acadia are covered in detail in those park sections. For information on backcountry sites maintained by the **Bureau of Public Lands**, ☎ 287-3821.

For information on the nearly 90 sites overseen by the **Maine Forest Service** you can call regional headquarters in Old Town (☎ 827-6191), Greenville (☎ 695-3721), or Island Falls (☎ 463-2214).

For state park campground information and policies regarding sites along the Allagash Wilderness Waterway, contact the Bureau of Parks and Lands at the telephone number above.

Campfires

After overall resource degradation the primary regulatory concern as far as camping goes in Maine is fire. Except for fires in approved campgrounds or at Maine Forest Service approved campsites, no fires may be kindled in the state without a permit from the forest warden. Permits are available across the state at forest service field offices. If the warden is not there; no worry. Most facilities have a small box outside the office with directions and forms for filling out a permit.

> 📖 The excellent map book, *The Maine Atlas and Gazetteer*, published by DeLorme, shows fire warden headquarters as a small red house on the maps.

If you are caught having a fire without a permit you can be fined. Fire wardens patrol in trucks, on foot, by canoe, and often by airplane looking for violators. The permit boxes also have another useful purpose – you can see if there are other parties ahead of you that plan to stay at the same spot. If privacy is your major concern, you can alter your plans.

Pay attention to fire danger signs scattered across the state. When the danger hits extreme, usually early spring before the land "greens up," in mid-August or late fall, all fires and even smoking may be banned in the wild areas. In some years officials have also taken the step of banning the use of picnic grills.

Fire Safety

Low impact camping ethics dictate use of a stove for most cooking chores. However, having an occasional campfire is part of the wilderness experience. When building a campfire be sure the spot you select is cleared down to mineral soil – not the decaying vegetation known as "duff."

Even with a ring of rocks, fires on duff can smoulder underground and erupt later. Softwood, such as branches from pine, spruce or fir, burns quickly and throws numerous sparks. Hardwood, from maple or ash, burns hottest, throws few sparks, and leaves the best bed of coals for cooking.

It is considered common practice to let a fire burn down overnight. Watch it until there are no major flames and see that all burned ends are within the rocks or steel ring. When leaving a site, douse all fires with water, stir, and douse again when breaking camp. Never leave a fire unattended.

Gathering Wood

At popular sites you may have to walk aways back to find good, dry wood. Big soggy logs lying on the ground won't burn, so pass them by. Look for good dry tinder in the small, dead branches under softwood trees. Cedar bark and birch bark make excellent fire starters. Some backpackers I know pick it up as they hike and arrive at camp with a pocket full of good fire starter. Be careful not to strip a tree too closely, which leave it vulnerable to insects and disease. Many places only allow the taking of wood that is "dead and down." But, at others, look for small (two inches or so in diameter), dead, standing hardwood trees. The broken, leafless branches at the top will be the give-away. Watch as you saw that upper branches don't break off and hit your head! Cut off at the base and haul the entire piece back to camp for cutting into smaller pieces (a practice called "bucking up").

When planning how much wood you think you'll need for a nice, cozy fire, collect as much as you think would be good – then double it. You'll end up having just enough!

WISE WORDS: *Never, never, cut a live standing tree. It hurts the forest, and green wood doesn't burn worth a darn anyway. As a courtesy, try to leave some firewood and kindling behind so if the next person coming along is tired, wet or hypothermic, they can quickly get a fire going.*

Food & Animals

Being sloppy with food at campsites can result in the appearance of several uninvited quests – insects and animals.

While ants and yellow jackets are manageables, dealing with a ravenous raccoon or bear rummaging through your gear is not a pleasant experience. Unfortunately, many campground animals are very clever and will find a way to get at your larder unless you leave it locked in a vehicle or building.

First and foremost, maintain a clean campsite. Wash all dishes thoroughly. In the backcountry it is advisable to "bear-bag" your food and cooking utensils. This involves suspending them in a bag tied to the center of a rope run between two trees at least 15-20 feet from the ground. In Baxter State Park, all food must be bear-bagged by rule. Since everyone does it, animals seldom bother to search, although the mice at many backcountry lean-tos can be real pests.

Never leave food, dishes or pots in your tent or sleeping bag. Many campers have returned from a day hike to find their brand new tent shredded and the sleeping bag torn to bits.

Leaving food around, or worse, actually feeding wild creatures, can create another problem – imprinting. When animals lose their natural fear of humans it exposes them to harm from others who may not appreciate their friendly ways. It also adversely affects their ability to find food naturally and survive in the wild. It may be tough to ignore that charming chipmunk, but don't feed it.

On the Appalachian Trail on Bigelow Mountain, the Canadian jays are so bold that not only to they eat out of hikers' hands but they also swoop at their faces when a spoonful of food is heading for a mouth. They apparently do this so campers will drop something they can then eat.

In certain circumstances, feeding or baiting wild animals in Maine can be a crime. It is also illegal to shine a spotlight on an animal at night, even if you do not intend to harm it.

While camping try to leave a site as clean, or cleaner, than when you found it. The most basic rule is "If you pack it in, pack it out." Don't throw cans or foil-faced items into the fire; they won't burn. Don't put nails in trees, leave rope or twine between trees, carve up picnic tables or trample vegetation.

When tenting, fluff up matted vegetation and scuff up the ground compacted by your passing.

Outhouses of the Wild

Most approved backcountry sites are equipped with privies. Don't throw food, trash, and unbiodegradeable items down an outhouse. While most campground managers try to keep toilet paper in good supply, it is not unusual for some of the hike-in locations to run out. Bring some along. If you are hiking out and have extra, leave it behind for those coming along next.

A Solar-Powered Privy

At Horn's Pond on Bigelow Mountain, the privy is solar powered! Users cross a draw bridge to the throne tower and throw a handful of wood chips and peat moss down the hole after they go. Bins in the bottom, which are rotated regularly and heated by the sun, turn everything into a rich compost which is then used to fertilize the surrounding forest.

In areas without outhouses officials advise digging or scuffing a six-inch-deep cathole for the disposal of human waste. Make sure it is located at least 100 feet back from any water source. Don't dig it too deep or it will be located in mineral soils, which lack the bacteria and detritus feeders needed to break down waste. After you are done, cover the hole.

While some experts urge people to pack out used toilet paper, I think that's crazy. Toilet paper is biodegradable wood fiber. It will decay if properly buried with other waste.

■ Swimming

With more than 3,500 miles of coastline, thousands of lakes and ponds, and miles and miles of rivers and streams, Maine has no shortage of places to swim. Terrain and topography, however, conspire to limit the number of really good spots. Prime swimming locations are listed in the individual area chapters.

A brave swimmer endures the icy cold runoff water in Screw Auger Falls near Gulf Hagas.

Swimming Safety

Most lake or ocean beaches maintained by the state have lifeguards during the summer season. The same goes for Echo Lake and Sand Beach on the ocean at Acadia National Park.

The rest of the time, however, swimmers are usually on their own. Below are a few advisories that can make your swim safer.

- Don't dive into water you have not checked first for depth and obstructions.
- Avoid areas above and below dams. In addition to trick currents, water levels can change rapidly and without warning.
- Do not swim in remote, abandoned quarries. In addition to access difficulty the water is often extraordinarily deep, cold, and filled with debris such as old derricks and steel cables.

■ If caught in a rip tide (sudden surge of water away from land) while swimming at an ocean beach, don't fight it. You will only tire and get nowhere. Swim parallel to the shore. You will eventually swim out of the rip and into water where you can easily make your way to dry land.

■ Skiing

For many residents of Maine and visitors alike, winter is the season when things really come alive. Years ago, winter was a time to "hive up," and avoid going outdoors. Hearty trappers ventured out to tend their lines and the woods buzzed with activity as loggers felled trees in anticipation of Spring's thaw and the rush of wood downstream to mills. Sporting camp owners and entrepreneurs hit the lakes to cut massive blocks of ice to stash in ice houses insulated with sawdust. Winter's bounty kept the bourbon cool all summer and was often shipped by schooner to big cities all along the Eastern Seaboard.

By November, most of those "snowbirds" who will flee to Florida have left. But, as the first flakes of snow begin to mount and deep, clear ice stills the waters of northern lakes, a new season of visitation sets in.

Fishermen take to the lakes in their cozy, wood-heated shacks. With thousands of miles of trails, Maine's more than 75,000 snowmobiles hit the road.

Still, even where there is an emphasis on motorized travel, the wilds of Maine offer millions of acres of pristine snow for snow shoeing or winter camping. Ice skating and ice boating are also popular pastimes.

Maine is home to some of the finest alpine skiing in North America. Mountains and resorts range from the comparatively tame Shawnee Peak in Bridgeton to lofty Sugarloaf, which offers the only above-treeline skiing in the North. More than a dozen major ski areas boast some of of the longest trails and shortest lift lines in the country. Smaller "family" mountains may not offer the longest vertical drops, but hold their own prospect of fun for those on tighter schedules or budgets.

Skiing under the lights is offered at many mountains. Snowboarding areas are growing in number. Most areas offer good weekend discount deals on rooms and meals as well as family packages.

An adult lift ticket for a weekend day at one of the larger resorts like Sugarloaf or Sunday River is poised to break the $50 mark. The cost is much lower at smaller mountains.

With some mountains getting more than 200 inches of natural snow a season the base is always great. Still, snowmaking operations at major

A pair of cross-country skiers takes in the view from the summit of Cadillac Mountain in Acadia National Park.

mountains are extremely sophisticated and add a degree of insurance. As soon as nighttime temperatures begin to dip regularly below 20°, the big snow guns come out. Resorts race each fall to see who opens the first trail. Likewise, spring skiing is spectacular. It takes a long time for the solid base on the bigger mountains to melt and nightly grooming keeps trails fun. Racing downhill in shirt sleeves in May is considered by many to be the epitome of the sport.

Many towns and ski areas also offer excellent Nordic opportunities. In Acadia National Park, there are nearly 50 miles of groomed trails, most without snowmobile access.

Fees for cross-country ski touring centers start in the $10-$12 per day range, less for children.

Baxter State Park allows winter use with provisos that those who seek the deep solitude of its backcountry be experienced and that their condition, attitude, and gear pass muster by tough wardens. While more remote and not as popular as Tuckerman's Ravine on Mount Washington in New Hampshire, extreme skiers flock each spring to Chimney Pond in Baxter's backcountry. Some skiable snowfields last into early June, and in 1997 the snow stayed deep. Campgrounds opened late in the month and some small patches of snow persisted in deep shade until the 4th of July.

Winter visitors to Maine need to be prepared to weather extremely harsh conditions in the out of doors. Driving can be hazardous, especially when a driving Nor'easter whips snow into white-out conditions.

Road crews do their best, but sometimes the smart thing is to retreat and wait until morning to tackle drifting snow.

Snow conditions vary widely from area to area and change rapidly. Two feet of fluffy powder can be six inches of slush in less than a day. The general rule is that the farther north one travels, the more reliable the snow. Acadia's great in the snow, but several times each winter rain moves in and makes things too messy for good skiing or snowmobiling. Especially along the coast, call a chamber of commerce first to check on conditions.

Snow remains on the ground reliably all winter in Mid-Maine, the Western Mountains, and in the zones we've decided to call the Great North Woods and the Far North. Even when the ground is bare in Bangor, there can be two feet on the ground in Greenville. Winter comes earliest and stays longest in Aroostook County's Far North.

Even though many may consider winter the "off" season, reservations are recommended, particularly in popular ski areas and snowmobile destinations.

Winter Recreation Outfitters

For more information on winter recreation contact the following organizations (all are in area code 207).

Ski Maine Association
PO Box 991, Portland 04104; ☎ 761-3774

Maine Nordic Ski Council
PO Box 645, Bethel 04217
☎ 800-SKI-XC (754-9263); office 824-3694
Ski reports and information

Maine Snowmobile Association
PO Box 77, Augusta 04332; ☎ 622-6982
E-mail mesnow@mint.net

Snowmobile Trail Conditions
☎ 626-5717 (24 hours)

Alpine Ski Conditions
☎ 800-533-9595

Nordic Ski Conditions
☎ 800-754-9263

■ Snowmobiling

Whether it is an extended multi-day trip in Northern Maine on some of the state's 12,000 miles of trails or a day of riding in Acadia National Park, snowmobiling is big business.

Officials estimate the sport pumps tens of millions of dollars into the state's economy each year. Those who do not own sleds can rent them.

Maine has more than 75,000 registered snowmobiles. On any given weekend in winter when the weather is good, many riders are out enjoying the winter wild lands of Maine. At Mount Kineo on Moosehead Lake wardens have counted in excess of 3,000 snowmobiles a day passing just one checkpoint. In fact, for most winter weekends hotels and sporting camps from Rangeley to Fort Kent are often booked weeks in advance.

Because of riding's soaring popularity, state officials and groups such as the Maine Snowmobile Association have joined forces to increase safety and improve riding habits. While the machines themselves are quieter and less smoky than in the past, they are also more powerful, sporting bigger engines. Safety training is helping to lower accident rates and fatalities.

Common sense, courtesy and safety are the basis of snowmobiling regulations in the State of Maine. If you know the laws, respect other people's rights and sled safely, you'll have fun, rather than problems, note officials of the Maine Snowmobile Association (MSA).

Snowmobiling is one of Maine's most popular winter pastimes.
Photo courtesy of Northern Outdoors

Snowmobiling Safety

Snowmobile safety is largely common sense. Don't ride too fast; don't drink alcohol and ride; do not cross ice you are not sure is thick enough; and dress for the weather. Still, scores of people each year forget these most basic tenets, often with tragic results.

- Always wear a helmet and dress in layers of warm clothes. Tooling along at 40 miles per hour on a cold day can often send the wind chill factor off the scale.
- Ride in a group or let someone know your plans.
- Carry some basic survival gear, such as a space blanket, matches, first aid kit and flashlight, in case you break down or get the machine stuck in deep snow or slush.
- Check the mechanical condition of your snowmobile regularly and fuel up regularly. Never assume you will be able to find fuel at the extended range of your sled's tank. Wrong turns or side trips can sip away at fuel reserves. Especially in Northern areas, where fuel stations are few and far between, stations can run out of gas by mid-afternoon on busy weekends as thousands of snowmobilers enjoy the day.

Registration & Rules

All snowmobiles must be registered to ride the trails in Maine. Resident registration is $25 (one year), commencing July 1. Non-residents have some options – a three-consecutive-day registration is $35; 10 consecutive days is $50; and a full season will run $60.

You can register at numerous agent locations throughout the state. Check with the local chambers of commerce or call the MSA office. You can also register through the Maine Department of Inland Fisheries and Wildlife.

Snowmobile Trail Fund

A portion of all registration money is credited to the Snowmobile Trail Fund of the Department of Conservation, Bureau of Parks and Lands, where it is distributed through grants to snowmobile clubs, towns, etc., to develop, construct and maintain snowmobile trails.

 DID YOU KNOW? *If you are a resident of New Hampshire and have registered your sled in that state, you do not need to register it in Maine. The reverse goes for Maine sledders who ride in New Hampshire.*

Riding is prohibited in a cemetery or within 200 feet of a dwelling, hospital, nursing home, convalescent home or church. Snowmobiles can't be operated on a road except to cross as directly as possible, which is defined as no more than 300 yards and always staying on the extreme right.

Get a trail map and a law handbook. Park the trailer. Ride the trails only where landowner permission has been obtained for everyone, snowmobile laws have been complied with, trails have been cut, snow has been groomed, and signs are in place.

Maine has a tough under-the-influence law, with stiff penalties for operating snowmobiles under the influence of alcohol or drugs. Operators who are convicted of operating under the influence face a minimum of a mandatory 48 hours in jail and a $300 fine; second offenses carry a minimum of a mandatory seven days in jail and a $500 fine; and third offenses earn the offender a minimum of a mandatory 30 days in jail and a $750 fine.

It is also against the law to operate a snowmobile in such a manner that you endanger a person or property. Harassing wildlife is also illegal.

Excessive speed can bring charges. While there are currently no speed limits on Maine trails, sledders are judged by the standard of "reasonable and prudent speed for the existing conditions."

Headlights are mandatory at night.

Children under 10 must be accompanied by an adult unless on their parents' land with parental permission. No child under the age of 14 may cross a road maintained for travel while operating a snowmobile. If a person under 18 years old has a snowmobile accident, the owner of the sled, the person who furnishes the sled and the parent or guardian responsible for the minor are jointly liable for damages caused in the operation of that sled.

 TAKE NOTE: *Sledders who have an accident must report it to the nearest law enforcement officer if there are injuries requiring medical attention or which result in a fatality and/or property damage of more than $300.*

Where to Ride

Most riders stick to mapped and marked routes on the Interconnected Trail System (ITS) or on regularly maintained club trails. Regulations governing crossing or use of roads can be confusing. Check the rule book.

📖 A snowmobile law handbook is available from the Maine Department of Inland Fisheries and Wildlife and the Maine Department of Conservation.

Customs

You must stop at Customs to cross the Canadian border. The penalty for not stopping is $5,000 and the loss of the sled. In Quebec and New Brunswick you need a trail pass to ride. There is an exception for a direct route from the border checkpoint near Jackman to a nearby clubhouse inside Canada. Contact the Federation of Clubs for Snowmobiles in Quebec and/or the New Brunswick Federation of Snowmobile Clubs for information. Trails which cross the border, including 89/75 in Jackman and 85/19 in Fort Kent, are open 24 hours a day, seven days a week, as are major New Brunswick crossings.

Snowmobile Rentals

Renting a snowmobile can be a great way to introduce yourself to a growing sport without investing thousands of dollars. New snowmobiles cost from $3,000 all the way up to $10,000 – a lot of money to lay out if you later discover you're really not that interested.

The cost of renting snowmobiles varies but usually runs between $100 and $150 per day, depending on model. Half-day rates are sometimes available. Those that carry two people, referred to as "two-up" machines, usually cost more. Some companies require that rental sleds be returned to their facility overnight, even on multiple-day rentals.

Don't get hung up on make or model for your first time out, but ask about age of the units and make sure they have basic features, such as hand and thumb warmers. Electric start is nice too, especially if you don't have a lot of experience pull-starting a balky two-cycle motor. Remember, rental sleds that are more than three or four years old may be in great shape or may be beat to hell. Ask if the rental agent guarantees mechanical soundness.

Especially for new riders, avoid the super fast muscle sleds in favor of more comfortable, easy-riding, touring models. The power may seem attractive, but is the last thing someone with little experience really needs while out riding on crowded trails.

Most rental places include helmets in the price and will also provide snowmobile suits and other warm clothes either as part of the rental or for a nominal fee. Check with your rental agent to find out what type of insurance coverage and other services they provide.

WISE WORDS: *Two of the best places to rent sleds are the **Kokadjo Trading Post** north of Greenville and almost anyplace in the **Patten area***. *These are located in some pretty remote country, but the trails are good, access to scenic vistas unsurpassed, and the trails will not be as crowded as you might find around other snowmobiling Meccas such as Greenville and Millinocket.*

Especially on fair weather weekends rental sleds go fast. Call ahead and make sure you have a reservation before heading north.

Snowmobile Outfitters

BETHEL
Sun Valley Sports Snowmobile Rentals, 129 Sunday River Road. ☎ 824-7533.

CARIBOU
Crystal Snowmobile Tours, Fort Fairfield Road. ☎ 498-3220.
Earl's Snowsled Sales and Service (Polaris). ☎ 492-5281.
Jordan Ski Doo Rentals, US 1, Box 255. ☎ 455-4410.
Four Seasons Yamaha, 20 Van Buren Road. ☎ 496-6912.

FORT KENT
Top of Maine Rentals, Eagle Lake Road. ☎ 834-3098.

GREENVILLE
Evergreen Lodge, Bed & Breakfast, Route 15. ☎ 695-3241.
Greenwood Motel, Route 15. ☎ 800-477-4368.

JACKMAN
Dana's Rentals. ☎ 668-7828.
Sky Lodge, Route 201. ☎ 668-2171.

KOKADJO
Kokadjo Trading Post, Lily Bay Road. ☎ 695-3993.

LINCOLN
Richard's Sport Shop, Outer West Broadway. ☎ 794-3363.

LOVELL
Lovell Hardware, Route 5. ☎ 925-2101.

MADISON
T-K Sun'n Snow, Route 201. ☎ 474-0199.

MILLINOCKET
Destination Sports. ☎ 723-8336.

Introduction

New England Outdoor Ctr, Rice Farm Rd. ☎ 800-766-7238.
Sport Shop Express, 10 Balsam Drive. ☎ 723-5333.

PATTEN
Bowlin Camps, Bowlin Pond Road. ☎ 528-2022 (radio phone).
Mount Chase Lodge, Route 159. ☎ 528-2183.
Matagamon Store & Camps, Matagamon Lake. ☎ 528-2448.
Shin Pond Village, Route 159. ☎ 528-2900.
UFF DA Rentals, Shin Pond. ☎ 528-2452.

PRESQUE ISLE
The Sled Shop, 108 Main Street. ☎ 764-2900.

RANGELEY
City Hill Rentals (Arctic Cat). ☎ 864-3758.
Dockside Sports Center, Rangeley (Ski-Doo, Arctic Cat).
☎ 864-5477.
River's Edge Sport Shop, Route 4, Oquossoc (Polaris). ☎ 864-5582.
Rev-It-Up Sport Shop, Route 4 (Yamaha). ☎ 864-2452.

ST. AGATHA
Northern Sno Sled and Watercraft Rentals, Route 162.
☎ 543-7355.

STRATTON (SUGARLOAF USA)
Flagstaff Rentals, 141 Main Street. ☎ 246-4276.

THE FORKS
Northern Outdoors, Route 201. ☎ 663-4466.

■ The Price of Adventuring

WHALE-WATCHING: A typical two- to four-hour whale-watching trip costs $25-$35 per person. Many operators offer money-back guarantees if no whales are seen.

WHITEWATER RAFTING: Nearly all trips take less than a day with an average cost of $80-90 per adult. Most include a riverside lunch. Lifejackets are provided but wetsuit rentals cost extra.

BIKE RENTALS: Rates range from $9 to $25 per day, depending on model.

DEEP-SEA FISHING: When the weather is rough a half-day of deep-sea fishing is plenty. That will set you back $25-35. A full day runs from $40 to $55. Most trips include rod, reels and bait. Beer, other beverages and snacks will cost extra. Deckhands will usually fillet your catch should you choose to keep it (be sure to tip for this service).

SIGHTSEEING, BY AIR, LAND & SEA: Depending on duration sightseeing and sunset cruises range anywhere from $15 to $25 for adults; less for children. Sightseeing bus or trolley tours cost in the vicinity of $15 per adult, $5-7 per child. Float plane, glider, hot air balloon and single-engine plane sightseeing trips cost from $20 to $45 per person, depending on the amount of time spent in the air. Per-person fees may be lowered if a group participates.

WINDJAMMER TOURS: A windjammer trip can run anywhere from $350 to $750 per person, per week, less for shorter trips with fewer amenities. Fees include cabin and meals.

GUIDED CANOE/KAYAK TRIPS: Overnight trips average $100-150 per person, per day. Half-day guided trips run in the vicinity of $50.

CANOE/KAYAK RENTALS: Basic rentals for either cost between $25 and $45 per day. Most rentals include life jackets, paddles and cartopping gear.

HUNTING & FISHING GUIDES: Registered Maine Guides charge between $100 and $200 per day for their services, depending on how far you plan to travel and how many people are in your party. Half-days can also be arranged.

GOLFING: Greens fees vary greatly according to the popularity of the course and the time of year. For instance, fees at Kebo Valley Golf Club in Bar Harbor, the country's ninth oldest course, are $30 for 18 holes in May, but jump to $60 July through mid-September. Meanwhile, you can play all day at the nine-hole Castine Golf Club course for just $20. In Rockland, greens fees for the municipal course are $30 for 18 holes; at the nearby Samoset course, which fronts open ocean, peak-season fees top out around $100 for 18 holes (resort guests do qualify for a discount). On average, expect to be charged $15-20 for 18 holes.

■ Maine's Top Ten Adventures

If, to use native parlance, you'd like to tell your friends that when it comes to experiencing the outdoors in Maine you've "been theyah, done that," here is a list of what we consider to be be the top 10 destinations/activities.

Acadia National Park

New England's only national park protects 40,000 acres of spectacular rocky shoreline and numerous mountain peaks. More than 120 miles of hiking trails, 50 miles of car-free, groomed, biking paths, cobble beaches and fresh and saltwater swimming. Many summits are bare and sport spring wildflowers.

Baxter State Park/Katahdin

From the top of Katahdin, Maine's highest windswept peak at just shy of a mile, to rocky ponds brimming with moose, this 205,000-acre preserve offers the outdoors the way it should be – by reservation with the gates shut when the parking lots fill. You have to go hundreds of miles north into Canada to find comparable wilderness.

The Allagash

A designated National Wild and Scenic River, the Allagash provides a rare opportunity on the East coast for extended canoe trips of a week or more. From grand Chamberlain Lake with its wind-whipped waters, to the challenging Class II whitewater of Chase Rapids, to campsites where loons serenade you to sleep, this is a first-class canoeing experience.

Whale Watching

Boats running from ports all along the coast from Portland, to Boothbay and especially from Bar Harbor take thousands of people daily to visit marine mammals. Nothing compares to the thrill of seeing finbacks surfacing right next to the boat, the spray from their blowholes wetting the decks. Watching humpbacks broach – they literally shoot right up out of the water and seem to stand on their tails – has been compared to a religious experience. Trips are quick, safe, and most offer money-back guarantees if no whales are sighted.

Kokadjo/Greenville

Greenville is the gateway to spectacular Moosehead Lake, but if you haven't been to tiny Kokadjo (population 3), a half-hour up the road, well, you haven't been to the Great North Woods. Just south of Kokadjo is where the utility poles end and real wilderness begins. The entire region is prime moose-watching territory. Greenville is famous for fishing, swimming, boating, snowmobiling in winter, and for being a jumping off place for hikers using the nearby Appalachian Trail, heading up Squaw Mountain or the flint monolith, Mount Kineo, part-way up the lake.

Pemaquid Point

The stunning lighthouse and ledges of Pemaquid Point comprise the quintessential Maine seashore scene. This is vintage coastal Maine dripping with history – Fort William Henry is just a few miles away. Public access to the shore is good and the back roads and byways of this portion of the coast are lined with pretty farms, antique houses, unique shops and restaurants and lobster piers that offer up Maine's most delectable crustacean in dozens of ways.

Rafting/Kennebec

Once you've bagged a few peaks and beachcombed along the coast, it's time to test yourself against one of Maine's mightiest rivers. Dozens of rafting companies offer safe trips down a steep-sided gorge and through "Magic" falls, a potentially-perilous Class V rapid unrunnable by open boats. After learning the fine points of paddling as a team, and running the maelstrom, relax, and enjoy the remainder of the trip floating alongside the boat in fast, yet smooth water. All trips include a delicious lunch.

Moose River Bow Trip

The circuitous Moose River Bow Trip has to be the quintessential canoe trip in Maine. With just a single mile-long portage, you can paddle for four days yet end up back right where you began. This is wild country, home to the river's namesake. The boredom of long, flat-water stretches is broken by challenging yet fun rapids. Some of the best river-side camping in Maine is found along the Moose.

L.L. Bean

It might as well be the law that all visitors to Maine stop at L.L. Bean on their way into or out of the state. This is the most complete outfitter around. You can literally step through the door of the main store in Freeport any time of the night or day with little more than the shirt on your back and a credit card and be fully outfitted for any adventure within minutes. At L.L. Bean, all merchandise is top quality and field-tested. Knowledgeable and friendly sales people will always point you in the right direction.

Mahoosuc Notch

How would you fare tackling the Appalachian Trail's toughest mile? You won't know until you've hiked Mahoosuc Notch in the rugged mountains of Western Maine. It's an adventure just getting to the top or bottom of the notch to begin with. This is a long slot canyon, 20-yards wide at the base with steep slopes rising 600 feet up each side. The bottom is a jumble of car-sized boulders where snow and ice linger into late June. The trail slabs over and under these moss- and tree-covered rocks. In the caves, where packs must be taken off to allow hikers to crawl through, listen for an unseen stream rushing deep underground.

Two experienced hikers I know took more than four hours to traverse its one-mile length. Seasoned AT through-hikers have been known to do it at night, with full packs and no flashlight in the rain (definitely don't try this at home, besides, what fun would that be?).

Outfitters & Guides

Literally hundreds of businesses in Maine sell clothing and equipment for the active outdoor life. But only a handful are true full-service, one-stop outfitters either offering an incredible variety of outdoor merchandise or the best selection of specialty gear. If you've only got time to stop at one or a handful of outdoor stores, or even if all you want to do is browse and dream about your next gear acquisition or upgrade, here's where to go.

■ The Best Outfitters

Cadillac Mountain Sports, *Cottage Street, Bar Harbor,* ☎ *288-4532; High Street, Ellsworth,* ☎ *667-7818; Downtown Bangor,* ☎ *941-5670.*

From kayaking and canoeing gear to one of the largest selections of hiking boots and sleeping bags anywhere, Cadillac Mountain Sports caters to those who discover a non-consumptive outdoor pursuit and practice it for life.

A wide selection of clothing and outer wear, backpacks and swimming gear. Well-trained sales staff, perhaps the best in Maine, use and test what they sell.

DeLorme, *US 1, Yarmouth (just off Interstate 95, south of L.L. Bean.)* ☎ *846-7000.*

No one in the know even considers venturing into the wilds of Maine without a *Maine Atlas and Gazetteer,* a comprehensive map book published by this Maine firm. When someone asks where somebody has been in Maine it is not unusual for the reply to be "Map 54," in reference to the book. One of the largest mapping software and publishing firms in the world, their map store offers the widest selection of maps/guides found anywhere. They stock a complete set of USGS topos for the entire state. The lobby of this building contains "Eartha," the largest free-standing, rotating globe in the world.

Kittery Trading Post, *US 1, Kittery,* ☎ *439-2700.*

Since 1938, the Kittery Trading Post has been serving a loyal clientele heading for adventure in Maine. Most of the clothing tends to hunting and work-oriented pursuits, and the equipment tends toward hunting and fishing. The Trading Post offers the largest selection of new and used firearms, scopes and accessories on the East Coast, as well as ammunition and reloading supplies. Fishing equipment runs the gamut from saltwater tackle to fish finders, trolling motors, rods, reels and flies.

L.L. Bean, *Main Street, Freeport, just off Interstate 95. There are also factory outlet stores in Portland and Ellsworth and in nearby North Conway New Hampshire. ☎ 800-431-4341.*

By far the most complete outfitter in Maine, if not the entire Northeast. You can literally come into Maine with little more than a rental car and a credit card and find everything you need here – clothing, footwear, equipment, advice. There actually is an indoor fish pond in the building. Kayaking and canoeing gear, biking stuff, tents, coolers, outer wear, climbing gear and a wide selection of books and field guides make this the top spot. Open 24 hours, 365 days a year. Factory store with first-quality end lots, returns, and close-outs across the street.

Maine Sport Outfitters, *US 1, Rockport, ☎ 236-7120.*

This is the Mecca of paddle sports equipment in Maine (you can tell when you pull onto the property as it is literally surrounded by hundreds of canoes and kayaks of various brand names). They even have their own pond so you can test before you buy.

Inside, the multi-level retail store is packed with every piece of equipment and clothing you can think of for paddling, hiking, camping, mountain biking and more. They also have a highly-trained bicycle servicing department and rentals. Although production was moved from nearby Camden to the West Coast years ago, you can still buy top-of-the-line Moss Tents at Maine Sports. This outfitter also offers guided trips and has a paddling equipment rental operation. Open year-round.

Old Town Canoe, *Middle Street, Old Town, ☎ 827-5513.*

Sooner or later they all come to the Old Town Canoe Factory Outlet. Great deals on factory seconds, including the popular Discovery models, which are virtually indestructible. Hundreds of dollars in savings possible on canoes and kayaks rejected by inspectors, often for minor cosmetic scratches or color blemishes. The knowledgeable sales staff can help you pick out just the right boat. Prices are often below what people advertise for used canoes in newspapers and shoppers. I dare anyone to find the original defect after just one run down a rock-strewn river!

The factory store features broad selection of accessories and repair kits ranging from replacement thwarts and cane seats to dozens of different-sized paddles, to life jackets, spray skirts, hardware, books, maps, and company memorabilia.

■ Maine Guides

Maine is one of the few places left that requires people offering their services as guides to be licensed. Registered Maine Guides must submit to rigorous background checks, must be proficient in first aid, and must get passing grades on detailed written and oral examinations on everything from weather, to animals and plants, water safety, firearm and fishing laws. Oral exams are given by a panel of experienced guides and game wardens. You can't pass that test by simply reading a book. If you don't know survival and safety in the wild, and are not familiar with Maine's backcountry, don't even try.

In fact, the testing is so tough about half of the entrants fail on their first attempt. Still, there are many who yearn to proudly wear the distinctive red, green and white patch that is issued only to genuine Registered Maine Guides.

 DID YOU KNOW? *While traditionally a majority of guides have been men, women are increasingly represented in the wild. In fact, the very first Registered Maine Guide more than 100 years ago was **Cornelia, "Fly rod" Crosby**, who was famous for her skill at fishing and guiding "sports" through the backcountry.*

Guide categories include hunting, fishing, recreational (canoeing, kayaking, snowmobiling, backpacking, etc.), whitewater rafting and master (a combination of all). A separate test and process is used to grant guides licenses to operate motorboats.

Maine has nearly 3,000 men and women registered as guides. They offer trips ranging from traditional hunting and fishing expeditions to extended canoe trips, winter camping and sled dog excursions. In most cases retaining the services of a guide saves time and hassle. They know the best areas for your favorite recreation and will usually handle all the arrangements and provide communal gear.

For more information, contact the **Maine Professional Guides Association** at PO Box 847, Augusta, Maine 04332. ☎ 785-2061.

The Basics

■ Sleeping In

There are literally thousands of places to stay in Maine, from some of the finest five-star inns and hotels to cozy bed and breakfast establishments and roadside motels straight out of the 1950s.

Seasons

What does "in-season" and "off-season" mean when it comes to rates for lodgings and restaurants? In most cases, rates are high when the season is in and lower when it's off. Generally, the season in Maine runs from Memorial Day until Labor Day, although the fall remains strong and bargains may be few and far between on busy foliage weekends. In recent years the times formerly referred to as the "off-season" (anything not in season) have changed. Late spring and most of fall are now referred to as the "shoulder-seasons."

Most chambers of commerce produce new information-packed booklets each year and will also have websites with the latest details on lodging and meal rates and dates.

Hotels, Motels & House Rentals

Quiz the owners or staff before deciding where to stay. Key words that may mean one thing in your state may mean something totally different in Maine. Rustic to you may mean no HBO, while in some rural areas it means a longer-than-normal walk to the outhouse. Do not assume all motels offer cable television and in-room phones. Also, do not assume all rural cabins have electricity.

Cabins and rental houses can run from as little as $400 in the Greenville area to as much as $2,000 a week on the coast. Most areas have a wide price and amenity selection. The standard weekly rental runs from Saturday to Saturday, with check-out time around 10 am and check-in around 3 pm. Some places will not accept reservations for a single week until after a certain date in late spring to allow those wishing longer stays an advantage.

Many popular places will book up months in advance.

Above all, remember that reservations are a necessity in high summer. It is not unusual for visitors to have to drive 100 miles back from Bar Harbor in late July and in August to find an available room. In Northern Maine it is risky to go to Greenville, Millinocket or Rangeley in high winter (snowmobiling and ski season) without reservations. And, like anywhere else, you will probably get what you pay for. Prices in excess of $95 dollars a night for a hotel room with no view along the coast are average. When the sign says "$26 per night for two," don't expect room service and a mint on your pillow. You might want to give the room a close inspection before flashing your plastic.

The national "no smoking" trend has been quickly adopted in Maine and most places either ban smoking entirely or have non-smoking rooms.

WISE WORDS: *If you are a non-smoker and decide to settle for a smoking room, especially in an older motel, check it out first. In one establishment in Greenville the smoking room had seen heavy use by multi-pack-a-day smokers, leaving it distinctively odorous.*

Among the questions to ask in addition to amenities are polices on deposits (most are non-refundable if a cancellation is not made by a certain date), views, pets, and smoking. Also, standards for what is considered "private" change. Along the beaches of Old Orchard, most motels and cottages are barely two feet apart. And that wonderful room with an ocean view may indeed have one, as do your 120 new closest friends on the balconies surrounding you on all sides. In fact, many seasoned travelers find that paying extra for an ocean view, unless it is a special occasion, is a waste of money. With all there is to do in Maine, what makes you think you'll be spending that much time just sitting around indoors looking out the window?

Check on proximity to the water, downtown, and other attractions. As comedian Stephen Wright once noted "Everywhere in the world is within walking distance if you have the time." Ask for specifics.

One odious practice that is beginning to permeate the state is charging people's credit cards when the reservation is made, even if it is weeks away from the actual visit. This seems to be standard practice at the larger ski resorts.

Every place takes cash and most will accept traveler's checks and major credit and debit cards. Most larger towns have at least one or two ATMs, but don't figure on finding one at every corner. On one canoe trip to Northern Maine some years back, we were on a very long dirt road north of Patten with only miles and miles of trees in any direction and with utility poles a distant memory when someone in the car said "Let me know if anyone sees a cash machine." We had passed the last chance to find one about an hour earlier. To again paraphrase the late Karl Malden: "Cash; don't leave a paved road without it."

Another practice to watch for is sweeping through some of the more popular inns in Southern Maine. They often require a minimum three-night stay. At $250 a night for a room with a fireplace, that quickly eats into the vacation budget.

When booking a cottage or camp, inquire if linens, towels and dishes are furnished. In addition to 50% down payment, most rental cabins or houses require the balance shortly before arrival as well as a separate check for a security deposit, which is returned upon departure inspection.

Sporting Camps

One of the state's most enjoyable traditions is a stay at a Maine Sporting Camp. Back at the turn of the century, before logging roads opened up much of the interior, such establishments were the main gateways to the wild.

Usually located on lakes or rivers, sporting camps offered hunters and fishermen rugged comforts such as cozy log cabins, clean sheets and warm blankets, home-cooked meals, equipment and boat rentals, as well as the services of a stable of reliable Registered Maine Guides. Entire families or parties returned year, after year, after year.

The names of these camps are legendary: Packard's on Sebec Lake, Nugent's North in the Allagash, or Bowlin Camps on the East Branch of the Penobscot River south of Matagamon Lake.

During the 1960s and 1970s many smaller sporting camps fell into disrepair or went out of business. Since that time, however, there has been a renaissance of sorts as a new generation has taken over these camps, or started new ones. In Princeton, on Long Lake, one enterprising couple rescued a run-down property that had been subdivided by developers for condominiums and recreated Long Lake Camps. Here you can sit on the porch of a weathered log cabin while the waters of the lake literally lap at the posts.

In Western Maine, guide Greg Drummond and his wife established Clay Brook Mountain Lodge, an old farm house that has become a favorite with ski-touring fans and a mandatory lunch stop for hungry snowmobilers.

In Jackman, Hal and Debbie Blood, both registered guides, have established Cedar Ridge Outfitters, offering traditional hunting and fishing trips, family vacations, as well as clean, cozy modern cabins and efficiencies.

These new owners have injected new energy and capital, and shifted use patterns to include non-consumptive outdoor recreation such as photography, hiking, mountain biking, cross-country skiing and nature walks.

Most camps feature a main lodge or dining hall, and small cabins, some with cooking facilities. Guests can simply pay for lodging or purchase an American Plan that includes meals.

For a detailed list of sporting camps contact the **Maine Sporting Camp Association** at PO Box 89, Jay, Maine 04239. ☎ 800-305-3057.

■ Dining Out

After lobster buoys and motels, perhaps the most common sights in Maine are restaurants. The selection ranges from fast food like McDonalds and Burger King to elegant five-star bistros where both the food and the prices are out of this world. Luckily, most places post their menus outside, giving strollers a chance to peruse.

In high season most busy places will serve dinner until at least 10 pm. In spring and fall the sign will probably say "Serving 5 pm until Closing," which means "we close whenever we dang well feel like it." If you want a nice, long, dinner with wine, dessert and all the trimmings, you may want to start no later than 7 pm in the off season.

While cuisine of almost any country can be found in most Maine towns, I happen to favor the flavor of distinctive local dishes. And you have to try lobster at least once if you visit Maine. While every place serves lobster, forgo the white tablecloths and stuffy waiters and head for a lobster pier or, as they are called, lobster pound. Put that stupid white plastic bib on, twist the cap off a frosty brew, crack into that steamy devil, and let the juice, shells and drawn butter fly where it may. (See the section on lobster, pages 13-18, for more detail on how important the lobster industry is to Maine.)

Other delicacies on the must-try list are blueberry pancakes and muffins, "bean-hole" baked beans (preferably slow cooked in a stone-lined pit in the ground), lobster bisque, steamed mussels, and fried clams and fresh crabmeat roll. Be sure to take a Maine baked potato on the side.

Often, items such as baked beans and pancakes are the focus of public suppers, breakfasts and festivals. Not only will the food be good, it will be cheap and your attendance will help support worthy local causes as well.

Prices for dining out vary widely across the state. While a two-item small pizza delivered to your hotel will set you back only about $5 in Greenville, that same pie comes with an $11 price tag in Bar Harbor.

Most restaurants feature nightly specials as well as early-bird deals and low, low prices for twin-lobster dinners used as loss leaders.

The drinking age in Maine is 21.

What About Tipping?

Ask about tipping in Down East Maine and some folks will think you are talking about the process of cutting spruce and fir brush for Christmas wreaths each November. For most folks in the tourist industry though, tips from patrons comprise an important part of their wages.

Restaurant servers are paid sub-minimum wage with the expectation they will make up the balance with gratuities. Servers in many establishments also share tips with table-clearers, bartenders and hosts.

It has also become the custom to tip chambermaids at hotels and inns. Guides on packaged tours are often rewarded with a gratuity.

The standard restaurant tip is 15%. In the case of exceptional service a higher amount is encouraged. At motels and inns, the traditional amount is $2 per day. Many establishments provide envelopes for tipping the maid. On bus and similar guided tours the usual gratuity for the guide is $1 per person.

While tips are not always expected, those on individual guided tours are encouraged to tip whatever amount they feel appropriate.

Visitors on package tours should consult their trip leaders before tipping (often, gratuities are included in the price).

Special Needs

More and more communities and businesses in Maine are moving ahead with a barrier-free approach to assist visitors with physical disabilities. Check with specific chambers of commerce for details. Most brochures note handicapped accessibility, and each year more and more outdoor activities are opening up for people with disabilities.

■ Handicapped-Accessible Adventures

The whale watch vessels *Friendship V* and *Atlantis* in Bar Harbor are handicapped-accessible.

In Acadia National Park, a recent grant from the Shelby Cullum Davis Foundation helped Friends of Acadia bring two high-quality, handicapped-accessible **horse-drawn carriages** to the riding stables there. Special wheelchair ramps and viewing areas have also been created at the popular attraction, **Thunder Hole** along the Ocean Drive.

National Park Tours, which offer narrated bus rides through Acadia National Park, has a wheelchair-accessible bus.

In Portland, the group **Portland Trails**, which oversees a 30-mile network of paths and bike trails in and around the city, has made several areas suitable for wheelchair access. They can be reached at PO Box 17501, Portland 04101. ☎ 775-2411.

Also in Portland, the **Maine Narrow Gauge Railroad Company and Museum** operates a museum dedicated to the history of the state's two-foot gauge trains. Operating equipment provides train rides daily in season. Museum entrance and trains are handicapped-accessible.

In Jackman, the non-profit group **Disabled Outdoor Experiences** have planned a **nature center** and wheelchair-accessible trails through the woods and along a river. They can be reached at PO Box 607, Jackman 04946. ☎ 465-3064.

At Greenville the restored lake steamer ***Katahdin,*** which offers tours of various durations on Moosehead Lake, is wheelchair-accessible.

In Presque Isle, the town's recreation department operates an **indoor pool** on Mechanic Street that includes a handicapped lift as well as handicapped-accessible showers and restroom facilities. ☎ 764-2564.

Several parks and recreational areas sport nature trails and paths for those with handicaps. Look in the various chapters throughout this book for details. They include:

- Wells National Estuary Reserve, Wells.
- Rachel Carson Wildlife Refuge, Wells.
- Wolfe's Neck State Park, Freeport.
- Department of Inland Fisheries & Wildlife Game Farm, Gray.
- The Moosehorn National Wildlife Refuge in Washington County has a handicapped-accessible nature trail, restrooms and an observation and fishing pier.

Country Fairs

With its strong rural communities, Maine is home to scores of country fairs. While they are scheduled throughout the warmer months, most are held in August and September.

Fairs range from traditional agricultural events, where local cooks enter their best pies and farmers their strongest oxen, to the Common Ground Fair, which is run by the Maine Organic Farmer's Association and is as much a celebration of New Age counterculture as it is a place to exhibit vegetables and gardening techniques. More than 50,000 people turned out for that popular fair in 1998.

Maine is also home to many popular festivals throughout the summer. Some of the major ones include the Lobster Festival and the Blues Festival on the Waterfront in Rockland, the annual Blueberry Festival in Machias, the Salmon Festival in Eastport and the annual Clam Festival in Yarmouth.

Most fairs belong to the Maine Association of Agricultural Fairs. They maintain the exact calendar of dates, which change each year. The fairs listed below are in order from earliest in the month until latest. The association can be reached at **Maine Association of Agricultural Fairs**, PO Box 200, Litchfield 04350-0200. ☎ 268-2032.

■ When & Where

June

Pittston Fair, Pittston
Smaller than average, family oriented country fair. Games for children and pulling events. ☎ 582-0037.

Twelve Oaks Fair, Chester
Very small traditional fair with pulling events, small midway and lots of local flavor. ☎ 794-8408.

July

Houlton Fair, Houlton
Good-sized event that includes standard agricultural exhibits, arts and crafts displays, midway and Independence Day fireworks. ☎ 532-4315.

Ossipee Valley Fair, South Hiram
Good, old-fashioned country fair with horse shows, exhibition halls and nightly entertainment. ☎ 793-8434.

World's Fair, Waterford
This is a pretty big name for a relatively small event. Notice they don't call themselves "The" World's Fair. Exhibits, displays and exhibitions. ☎ 583-4054.

Bangor State Fair, Bangor
Old-fashioned fair with traditional exhibits, displays and competitions. Very large midway with lots of rides and nightly big-name entertainment (with a slant toward Country and Western). Local demolition derby is also popular. ☎ 942-9000.

August

Monmouth Fair, Monmouth
On of the major events on the fair circuit with large midway, livestock, special events and evening entertainment. ☎ 933-2157.

Northern Maine Fair, Presque Isle
Premier fair for Maine's largest county. Events and lots of livestock, 4-H presentations and four-wheel-drive pulling events. ☎ 764-1830.

Topsham Fair, Topsham
Agricultural exhibits, circus acts and harness racing. ☎ 725-2735.

Union Fair, Union
Famous for its Friday night Blueberry Festival that has attracted the likes of lifestyle maven Martha Stewart. Agricultural exhibits, livestock, events and entertainment. ☎ 785-3281.

Piscataquis Valley Fair, Dover Foxcroft
All the usual fair attractions plus a working milking parlor. Milk is then used by kids to make ice cream right at the fair. Agricultural exhibits and livestock. ☎ 564-8862.

Acton Fair, Acton
About as country as a country fair can get in Maine. Livestock, exhibitions, flower show, pulling events and 4-H competition. ☎ 636-2026.

Windsor Fair, Windsor
Long running fair with extensive agricultural exhibits, competitions, arts and crafts displays, parade and carnival midway. ☎ 549-7121.

September

Blue Hill Fair, Blue Hill
One of Down East Maine's most popular fairs. Midway, exhibits, racing, nightly entertainment, fireworks. Pulling and sheep dog trials. ☎ 374-3701.

Springfield Fair, Springfield
Horse show, auto show, exhibits, livestock, midway and lots of Country and Western entertainment mark this popular agricultural fair. ☎ 738-2165.

Clinton Lions Fair, Clinton
Low-key family fair with agricultural exhibits, crafts displays, pulling events and 4-H competition. ☎ 426-8013.

Litchfield Fair, Litchfield
One of the largest midways around mark this country fair with exhibits, displays and "Old MacDonald" farm for the kids. ☎ 683-2487.

Lion's Fair, North New Portland
Large exhibition hall, horse and pony pulling, Saturday night dance and livestock events with a midway. ☎ 628-2052.

Farmington Fair, Farmington
A major fair at the gateway to the Western Mountains, this event features a top-notch exhibition hall, covered pulling ring, harness racing and plenty of livestock. ☎ 778-2684.

Common Ground Fair, Unity
This event is billed as celebration of rural life. Wide selection of Maine-

made foods and other products. Organic farming and low-impact, simple lifestyle products and techniques predominate. ☎ 623-5115.

Cumberland Fair, Cumberland Center
This fair boasts that is has the largest Holstein Futurity in the United States. 4-H competition, displays and exhibits, livestock. ☎ 829-6647.

October

Fryeburg Fair, Fryeburg
Maine's largest agricultural fair is held at prime foliage time in one of the Western Mountains' prettiest towns. Permanent exhibition halls, museum, logging equipment displays, midway, livestock, pulling events. ☎ 935-3268.

Antiques

When big city antique dealers in Boston and New York want to find merchandise for their clientele, where do they look? Why, Maine of course.

For collectors who have discovered this secret, the main drags and byways of Maine hold good hunting. From flea markets and yard sales to formal shops, Maine literally brims with quality antiques and collectibles.

From Maine's "Antique Mile," US 1 through Searsport on the coast (the area bristles with shops and flea markets) to the back roads of Aroostook County, there is a lifetime of exploring. Does that dusty box of books in what appeared to be a junk store really harbor an autographed first edition of Truman Capote's *In Cold Blood*? Does that dealer realize that reasonably priced old print of a winter scene in the country is a Currier and Ives original? Come early; stay late; bring money and be prepared to haggle with some of the cagiest characters around.

> 📖 The official chronicle of antiques, in fact the Bible of antiquing in the state, is the monthly *Maine Antiques Digest*, published in Waldoboro. It is a 400-page newspaper chock full of the latest news and advertisements on auctions, estate sales and shows.

Shops and dealers mentioned in this guide are official members of the Maine Antique Dealers Association (MADA).

A copy of MADA's guide to their membership is available by sending a stamped, self-addressed envelope to Nancy Prince, Secretary, MADA, PO Box 604, North Turner, Maine 04266. ☎ 224-7823.

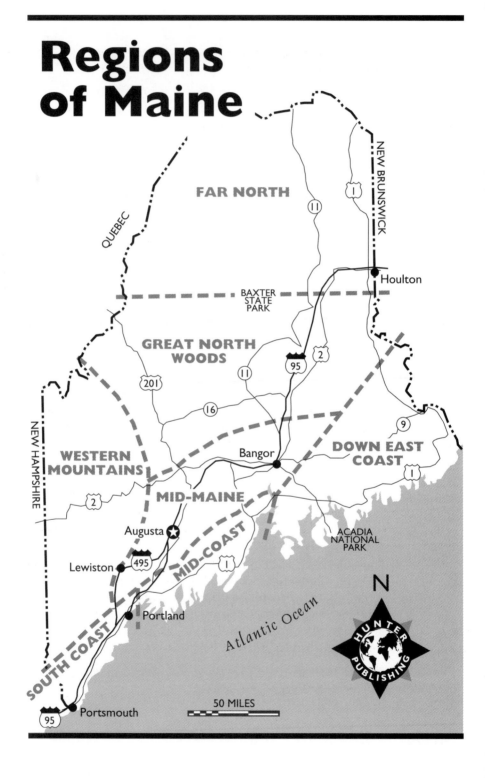

Regions of Maine

The South Coast

SOUTH COAST

Unlike much of the rest of Maine, which is famous for its rock-bound coast, the South Coast of the state is best characterized by its long, flat, sandy beaches.

Great swimming and sunning begins in Kittery, just across the border from New Hampshire, and continues north up the coast through York, Ogunquit, Well, Kennebunk, Biddeford and, of course, the grand dame of South Coast beaches, Old Orchard. Here the amusement pier and honky-tonk main drag attract visitors by the thousands, including scores of Canadians who shed the cooler climes of Quebec and flee down Routes 201 and 302 in search of fresh sea air, the scent of sun tan oil, and the feel of fine white sand under foot.

But the South Coast is more than just beaches. There are scores of picturesque harbors, quaint shops, cozy inns and bed and breakfast establishments, as well as outlet shopping in Kittery, which is also home to the renowned Kittery Trading Post, an outfitter selling everything from cross-country ski wax and tents to firearms and hunting apparel.

Portland, Maine's largest city, reigns over the region. Too poor during the 1960s to afford the type of urban renewal that leveled historic structures in many New England towns of similar size, Portland was perfectly positioned when the restoration boom of the 1980s took root. Its famous Old Port section, characterized by gas-lit cobblestone streets, now bustles with trendy shops and charming restaurants and bars.

Portland, along with the docks in South Portland to the west, is one of the busiest seaports on the Eastern Seaboard. Here the waters of Casco Bay are traversed daily by tiny lobster boats and sprawling ocean-going bulk carriers. The city is also home to a major art museum and the **Seadogs**, the state's only minor-league baseball team. The state's largest retail shopping complex, the **Maine Mall**, is located in South Portland.

To the northwest is one of Maine's premier freshwater playgrounds, **Sebago Lake**. The towns that surround it boast long, proud histories predating the Revolutionary War and are themselves the gateway to New Hampshire's lofty White Mountains.

Boats bob at their moorings at Ogunquit.
Photo by Nancy Horton, Courtesy Ogunquit Chamber of Commerce

At the northeastern end of this region lies **Freeport**, home to the legendary **L.L. Bean** and dozens of other outlet and factory stores. **DeLorme**, the homegrown mapping company that has now become an information and software giant, is headquartered here with Eartha, the world's largest three-dimensional globe, which spins silently in the three-story glass atrium lobby of their company superstore.

Still, despite its urban and suburban nature, the South Coast still has plenty to offer those who seek to cast off the cloak of civilization. From nature centers, bird sanctuaries and state parks in Scarborough to the Rachel Carson National Wildlife Refuge in Kennebunk to Bradbury Mountain State Park in Pownal, escape from the hustle and bustle is only minutes away.

Parks, Preserves & Beaches

■ State Parks

 Crescent Beach State Park, Cape Elizabeth. Small family seaside park not far from Portland. A fine sand beach nearly a mile long with one rocky section. Ocean swimming and fishing.

Major Parks & Preserves Along the South Coast

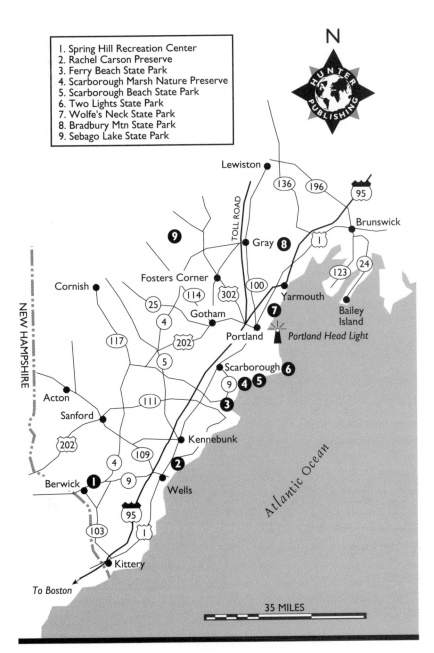

1. Spring Hill Recreation Center
2. Rachel Carson Preserve
3. Ferry Beach State Park
4. Scarborough Marsh Nature Preserve
5. Scarborough Beach State Park
6. Two Lights State Park
7. Wolfe's Neck State Park
8. Bradbury Mtn State Park
9. Sebago Lake State Park

South Coast

Parking, picnic tables, snack bar and an entrance fee. ☎ 799-5871.

Two Lights State Park, Cape Elizabeth. This park features picnic areas and a walking path, from which you can admire the two lighthouses and the Atlantic beyond. Site of a shore battery and two anti-aircraft gun emplacements in WWII. Fishing from rocky shore. Plenty of parking. Entrance fee. Two Lights Road off Route 77. ☎ 799-5871.

Wolfe's Neck Woods State Park, Freeport. Small busy park on peninsula just minutes from the outlet mall hustle and bustle. Scenic location on river and bay. Forested area features self-guided nature walk along the Harraseeket River and Casco Bay. Fee parking, picnic area, fishing allowed. Just offshore is an active osprey nest. ☎ 865-4465.

Maine Wildlife Park, Gray. Maine Deptartment of Inland Fisheries and Wildlife Game Farm and Visitors Center on Route 26. A great place to view and learn more about wildlife. The 200-acre park has 25 species of wildlife, including moose, black bears, lynx, mountain lions, wild turkeys, bald eagles, owls, a show fish pool and more. Open daily May through November. Picnic and grill areas, bookstore and gift shop. Adults $3.50, children $2. ☎ 657-4977.

Deering Oakes, Portland. Portland's largest city park features many stately old trees, footpaths, and ponds. Skating in winter. Flower garden and duck pond. At Park and Forest Streets. ☎ 874-8793.

Bradbury Mountain State Park, Pownal. Located on Route 9, the centerpiece of this park is a granite cliff at the 484-foot bald summit that overlooks Casco Bay. There are hiking trails, cross-country ski trails, a picnic area, a softball field and a public campground. ☎ 688-4712.

Ferry Beach State Park, Saco. A small park with a fine sand ocean swimming beach, toilet, bathhouse, picnic areas and hiking trails. There is an entrance fee. Open from mid-May until mid-October. On Route 9 near Camp Ellis. ☎ 283-0067.

Mackworth Island, Falmouth. Located off US 1 this island features a circular walking trail that skirts the shore with good views of Portland. (No telephone.)

Scarborough Beach Park, Scarborough. A very popular fine sand beach with good surf, dunes, and a salt marsh. There is a bathhouse, picnic tables, grills. Fishing is allowed. Entrance fee. On Route 207 on way to Prout's Neck. ☎ 883-2416.

Sohier Park, York. Tiny park on Cape Neddick sports interesting geology and good views of Nubble Light. Birdwatching along the shore. ☎ 363-7608.

■ Maine has one area code – 207.

■ Beaches at a Glance

Fortunes Rock Beach, Biddeford. Fine sand beach nearly two miles long. Scant parking.

Hills Beach, Biddeford. On sandy peninsula. Fine sand beach 1,500 feet long. Facilities nearby. Scant parking.

Gooch's Beach, Kennebunk. Mile-long crescent beach of fine sand. Nearby rocky point, limited parking.

Kennebunk Beach, Kennebunk. Fine sand beach about a half-mile long. Park along road.

Parsons Beach, Kennebunk. Mile-long string of beaches and salt marshes. Good birding area. No facilities, scant parking.

Goose Rocks Beach, Kennebunkport. Fine sand beach nearly two miles long. Birdwatching in nearby salt marsh. Scant parking.

Cresent Beach, Kittery. 1,200-foot sand beach on tiny headland with scant parking.

Seapoint Beach, Kittery. Half-mile crescent of fine sand on quiet side of penninsula. Favorite birding area. No facilities, scant parking.

Ogunquit Beach, Ogunquit. Mile-long fine sand beach at famous artist colony. Facilities nearby, fee parking.

Old Orchard Beach, Old Orchard. Two miles of white sand with famous 475-foot honky-tonk amusement pier. Facilities nearby. Parking (fee).

Wide sandy beaches, like this one at Old Orchard, characterize the shore in Southern Maine.

Higgins Beach, Scarborough. Popular resort beach with facilities, 1,000-feet long. Adequate parking.

Pine Point Beach, Scarborough. Mile-long fine sand beach and sand spit. Facilities nearby, fee parking.

Western Beach, Scarborough. Small sheltered white sand beach with dunes. No facilities. Parking nearby but difficult.

Drake's Island Beach, Wells. 2,700-foot sand beach with dunes, nature area. Scant parking.

Moody Beach, Wells. Good swimming beach at traditional summer community. 8,200 feet long, facilities nearby, fee for parking.

Wells Beach, Wells. Maine's longest beach at nearly 2½ miles. Fine sand, salt marsh nearby. Facilities on beach, fee for parking.

Long Beach, York. Busy fine sand beach 1½ miles long. Scant parking.

Short Sand Beach, York. Quarter-mile fine sand beach near summer homes. Facilities nearby, scant parking.

■ Wildlife Refuges

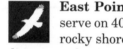 **East Point Sanctuary**, Biddeford. Ocean walk and bird preserve on 40 acres owned by the Audubon Society. Trail traverses rocky shore, pebble beach, and field. Small parking area. Short distance to beginning of trail. ☎ 781-2330.

Fore River Sanctuary, Portland. 70-acre Audubon Society preserve featuring several miles of hiking and walking trails, a 30-foot waterfall on the Fore River, and a stroll along the abandoned Cumberland and Oxford Canal. Adequate parking off the end of Rowe Avenue off Route 25. Trails marked with colored blazes. Maps available at parking area. Day use only. ☎ 781-2330.

Kennebunk Plains, Kennebunk. Nearly two square miles of prime habitat for endangered grasshopper sparrow and other endangered animals and plants. Controlled jointly by the Nature Conservancy and the Maine Department of Inland Fisheries and Wildlife. Conservancy office at 14 Maine Street, Brunswick 04011. ☎ 729-5181.

Vaughn's Island Preserve, Kennebunkport. A 40-acre island separated from mainland by creek (tidal). Hardwood forest covers cellar holes and other evidence of former settlement. Hiking trails. Access by foot or boat, but pay attention to tides. (No telephone.)

Back Cove, Portland. Hugh tidal basin that separates city from suburbs. Very attractive to birds. Paralleled by I-295 on South and Baxter

Blvd. on the North. Running, biking track circles entire basin. Picnicing allowed. (No telephone.)

Goosefare Brook, Saco. A 300-acre parcel purchased by the Nature Conservancy for eventual inclusion in the Rachel Carson National Wildlife Refuge (see above). Conservancy office at 14 Maine Street, Brunswick 04011. ☎ 729-5181.

Saco Heath, Saco. An 800-acre bog environment protected by Nature Conservancy. Nature and hiking trails, including boardwalk through the heath. Benches for walkers and bird watchers. Adequate parking off Buxton Road. Conservancy office at 14 Maine Street, Brunswick 04011. ☎ 729-5181.

Prout's Neck Bird Sanctuary, Scarborough. Access to this private sanctuary in the middle of summer is difficult. There is no parking. Self-guided nature trail and boardwalk through woods. At end of Route 207. (No telephone.)

Vaughn Woods Memorial, South Berwick. A self-guided nature trail threads through this 250-acre preserve along the Salmon Falls River. Trail was once an Indian trade route. Picnicking, parking area. ☎ 384-5160.

Wells Estuary Reserve, Wells. 1,600 acres of fields, forest, wetlands, and beach comprise the Wells Estuary Reserve. Three rivers meet the sea here, including the Merriland, Webhannet, and the Uttle. Created around historic Laudholm Farm, which features exhibits and visitor centers. Seven miles of hiking trails. Hours vary. Access is free. Fee for parking in July and August. RR 2, Box 806, Wells 04090. ☎ 646-4521.

Rachel Carson National Wildlife Refuge, Wells. Established in 1966, this collection of estuary preserves will eventually total more than 7,000 acres. It is dedicted to author Rachel Carson, whose seminal work *Silent Spring* helped awaken the world to the environmental dangers of pesticides.

More than 250 species of birds can be seen in or near the refuge over the course of a year, including upland, migratory and shore birds. A one-mile nature trail built specially for handicapped access begins at the headquarters site on Route 9 on Wells/Kennebunk border. This main area of the preserve boasts 3,600 acres. Literature and maps also available at headquarters. Refuge open daily all year. Office open weekdays. RR 2 Box 751, Wells 04090. ☎ 646-9226.

Wood Island, Biddeford. A 42-acre offshore island with lighthouse, this is an Audubon Society preserve. Access restricted during nesting season. Terrain includes shrubs and some woods. Boardwalk bisects island. Water access only. Permission must be obtained to visit. ☎ 781-2330.

■ Natural Areas/Preserves

 Basket Island, Cumberland. Nine-acre island maintained by the Cumberland Mainland and Islands Trust. Partially forested. Occasional osprey sightings. Picnicking and day use allowed. Boat access. (No telephone.)

Gilsland Farm, Falmouth. This former farm is the headquarters for the Maine Audubon Society. It is open dawn to dusk year-round. There are 2½ miles of trails through the farm's 70 acres – which border the Presumpscot River – and a gift shop. Easy bike ride from Portland. ☎ 781-2330.

Mast Landing Sanctuary, Freeport. This 150-acre preserve is the Audubon Society's summer day camp. Self-guided nature walk through the woods and along streams. Good place to see beavers. Free parking, picnicking. ☎ 781-2330.

Scarborough Marsh, Scarborough. Maine's largest salt marsh (3,000-acres) features guided canoe trips (rentals available) as well as birding walks. There is a mini-museum and visitors center with exhibits and slide show. Operated by the Maine Audubon Society. ☎ 781-2330.

 WISE WORDS: *Saltwater mosquitos can be brutal on calm days with no wind. Remember to bring along plenty of bug repellent to deter them.*

Douglas Mountain Preserve, Sebago. This 169-acre preserve protects a hill with remarkable views of the surrounding lands. On a clear day view reaches from the Atlantic Ocean to the White Mountains. Interpretive display on top of old stone tower on 1416-foot summit. Parking area on Douglas Mountain Road (limited), trails, picnic area. ☎ 729-5181.

Waterboro Barrens, Waterboro. Unique scrub oak and pitch pine forest located on sandy glacial outwash deposit. 2,300 acres with wide, easy to follow, gentle terrain trails. Parking lot. Self-guided nature walk. Owned by the Nature Conservancy. Office at 14 Maine Street, Brunswick 04011. ☎ 729-5181.

Sightseeing

■ Historic Sites/Museums

Biddeford

 Biddeford Historical Society, McArthur Library, 270 Main Street. Local memorabilia, including town records of Biddeford (1653-1855) plus common council, alderman and assessors' reports. ☎ 283-4706.

First Parish Meeting House (1759), 3 Meeting House Road. Owned by the Biddeford Historical Society. Boxed pews, cricket kneelers, late 19th-century organ and lighting. ☎ 283-4706.

Buxton

Tory Hill Meeting House (1822), Route 202 and 112. ☎ 929-8573.

Cape Elizabeth

Fort Williams Park-Museum at Portland Head Light, 1000 Shore Road. Grounds of former military installation now open as picnic, play area. Ocean access (swimming pool). Picturesque lighthouse perched on rocky outcropping. ☎ 799-2661.

Casco

Friends Schoolhouse (1841), Raymond/Casco Historical Society, Route 121. One-room school house retained as last used. Many school-related items of local historical interest. ☎ 655-4231.

Nathaniel Hawthorne's Boyhood Home (1812), Hawthorne Road. ☎ 655-3349.

South Coast

Chebeague Island

Chebeague Island Historical Society. ☎ 846-5140.

Cumberland Center

Cumberland Historical Society. ☎ 829-5423.

Freeport

Desert of Maine, Desert Road, Freeport 04032. Severe soil erosion from a mismanaged farm years ago exposed underlying sand left by a glacier. Dunes shift between forested sections. Camel statues, gift shop, admission fee. ☎ 865-6962.

Gorham

Baxter House Museum, (1797), South Street. Birthplace of James Phinney Baxter, former Mayor of Portland, father of Percival Baxter, founder of Baxter State Park. Articles and records of local interest. ☎ 839-5031.

Gray

Gray Historical Society. ☎ 657-4492.

Windham Historical Society, 26 Dutton Hill Road. ☎ 892-9667.

Kennebunk

Brick Store Museum, 117 Main Street. Historical, fine and decorative art exhibits in block of restored 19th-century buildings. ☎ 985-4802.

Taylor-Barry House (1803), 24 Summer Street. Elegant federal home of sea captain and adjoining early 20th-century artist's studio. ☎ 985-4802.

Kennebunkport

Kennebunkport Historical Society, Nott House (White Columns), Maine Street. Victorian house with period furnishings occupied by Nott family. Greek Revival architecture from the mid-19th century. ☎ 967-2513.

Seashore Trolley Museum, 195 Log Cabin Road. Turnpike exits 3 and 4. World-wide collection of trolleys, narrated tours, rides, museum store. More than 200 cars in the collection. Museum established in 1939 to save an old Biddeford and Saco Railroad open trolley. Bills itself as the oldest and largest electric railway museum in the world. ☎ 967-2712.

South Coast

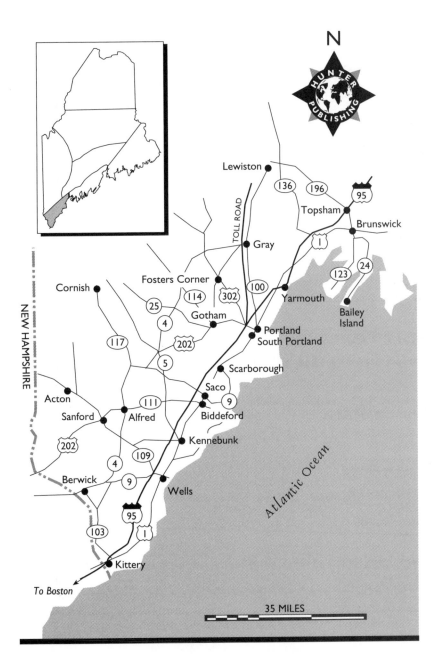

N

NEW HAMPSHIRE

Lewiston

136 196

95

Topsham

Brunswick

TOLL ROAD

Gray

1

Fosters Corner

123 24

Cornish

100

25 114 302

Yarmouth

Gotham

4

Bailey Island

Portland
South Portland

117 202

5

Scarborough

Saco

Acton

111

9

Sanford

Alfred

Biddeford

202

Kennebunk

Atlantic Ocean

4 109

Berwick

9

Wells

95

103 1

Kittery

To Boston

35 MILES

South Coast

Town House School, North Street. Contains various exhibits and files of local history and genealogy. Clark shipyard office, maritime exhibit, jail. ☎ 967-2751.

St. Anthony Monastery, Beach Avenue. ☎ 967-2011.

Kittery

Kittery Historical and Naval Museum, Rogers Road Ext. Portrays the history of the seacoast area and Kittery, Maine's oldest incorporated town. Location of oldest US Naval Shipyard in the country. ☎ 439-3080.

Railway City U.S.A., Model Railroad Museum, Route 236. ☎ 439-1204.

Kittery Point

Fort McClary Blockhouse, Off Route 103. Fort McClary was used for nearly 275 years to protect the approaches to the Piscataqua River. Buildings and fortifications remaining on the site represent several periods of construction. ☎ 384-5160.

Newfield

Willowbrook Museum. Large 19th-century museum, off Elm Street. Restored village of 37 buildings and hundreds of displays. 1894 Armitage-Herschell carousel. Open May through September. ☎ 793-2784.

North Berwick

Hussey Seating Company Museum (1831), Dyer Street Exit. ☎ 676-2271.

Ocean Park

Ocean Park Historical Society. ☎ 934-2526.

Ogunquit

Ogunquit Museum of American Art (1952), Shore Road. Houses an extensive permanent collection of important 20th-century American art. ☎ 646-4909.

Old Orchard Beach

Old Orchard Beach Historical Society Museum, Harmon Memorial, 4 Portland Avenue. ☎ 934-4485.

Porter

Parsonfield-Porter Historical Society, History House (1875); **Porter Old Meeting House** (1823), Main Street. Route160. Local memorabilia, old flags, books, clothing, maps. Portland-built piano from Longfellow's birthplace. Large collection of foreign dolls. ☎ 625-4667.

Portland

Children's Museum of Maine,142 Free Street. Interactive and hands-on displays engage children's hands as well as their minds. Exhibits explore arts, nature, humanities. Permanent exhibits include a space shuttle, news center, fire engine, lobster boat and computer center. ☎ 828-1234.

First Parish Church (1825), 425 Congress Street. Oldest stone building in the state. ☎ 773-5747.

Maine Coastal Museums, Fore Street. ☎ 828-0814.

Maine Historical Society, 485-489 Congress Street. Includes Maine Historical Society Library. Extensive research collections on genealogy and Maine history. ☎ 879-0427.

Maine History Gallery. Artifacts from Maine history and collections of the Maine Historical Society. ☎ 879-0427.

Wadsworth Longfellow House. Childhood home of the poet, Henry Wadsworth Longfellow, the house is the oldest brick residence in Portland. ☎ 879-0427.

Neal Dow Memorial (1829), 714 Congress Street. Late Federal-style mansion of Civil War General Neal Dow. National Historic Landmark. ☎ 773-7773.

Portland Fire Museum (1829), 157 Spring Street. Collection of artifacts and photos relating to Portland's fire fighting history, located in granite Greek Revival building. ☎ 929-5352.

Portland Museum of Art, 7 Congress Square. Maine's oldest art museum. Regular traveling exhibitions of work by world-famous artists. Designed by I.M. Pei and Partners, the museum opened in 1983. It houses an extensive collection of fine and decorative arts. Among the notable artists whose works are on display are Winslow Homer, Rockwell Kent, Marsden Hartley, John Singer Sargent and Andrew Wyeth. Parking nearby. ☎ 775-6148.

Portland Observatory (1807), 138 Congress Street. Last remaining 19th-century signal tower on the Atlantic Coast. Built of wood. ☎ 774-5547.

Portland Public Library, George I. Lewis and Family Gallery, 5 Monument Square. ☎ 871-1758.

Tate House (1755), 1270 Westbrook Street. Architecturally significant Georgian house accurately restored and furnished to reflect lifestyle of a successful Colonial merchant. George Tate was agent for a British firm which provided masts for the Royal Navy. ☎ 774-9781.

U. S. Customhouse (1872), 312 Fore Street. Of French Second Empire style, building is the finest of its type and period in Maine. A symbol of Portland's importance as a 19th-century shipping center. ☎ 780-3326.

University of Southern Maine Art Gallery and Center Gallery, 37 College Avenue. ☎ 780-5409.

Victoria Mansion, Morse-Libby House (1858), 109 Danforth Street. One of the finest surviving examples of a 19th-century house and furnishings in the United States. ☎ 772-4841.

Wiscasset, Waterville, and Farmington Railway Museums. ☎ 774-4971.

Women's Christian Temperance Union, 714 Congress Street. ☎ 773-7773.

Raymond

Raymond-Casco Historical Society, Main Street. ☎ 627-4350.

Saco

Bower Mansion Inn, 408 Main Street. ☎ 284-1734.

MacDonald's Mineral Museum, 34 Moody Street. ☎ 284-4633.

York Institute Museum, 371 Main Street. Exhibitions explore regional and natural history, art, culture, and industry. Adjacent Dyer Library has extensive Maine history collection, local genealogy, city of Saco records. ☎ 282-3031.

Scarborough

Jacqueline Designs - The 1840 House, 237 Pine Point Road. ☎ 883-5403.

Scarborough Historical Society, 649 US 1. ☎ 883-3539.

Sebago

Jones Museum of Glass and Ceramics, Douglas Mt. Road off Route 107. Major collection dating from the first century B.C. to the present. ☎ 787-3370.

Shapleigh

Acton-Shapleigh Historical Society, Route 109. Converted old school house. Museum room built on to meeting room. Local artifacts. ☎ 636-2606.

South Berwick

Counting House/Old Berwick Historical Society, Route 4. ☎ 384-8041.

Hamilton House (1785), Vaughan's Lane, off Route 236. Georgian mansion, overlooking Salmon Falls River, built by shipbuilder-merchant Col. Jonathan Hamilton. Owned by the Society to Preserve New England Antiquities. ☎ 617-227-3956.

Old Berwick Historical Society, Counting House (1830). Route 4. Greek Revival commercial structure contains collection of shipbuilders' tools, gundalow models, navigational instruments, and items of local nature. ☎ 384-8041.

Sarah Orne Jewett House (1774), 5 Portland Street. Jewett, famed author of *Country of the Pointed Firs* and other works, spent most of her life in this stately Georgian mansion. Owned by the Society to Preserve New England Antiquities. ☎ 617-227-3956.

South Portland

Maine Aviation Historic Society, 19 Fickett Street. (No telephone.)

South Portland-Cape Elizabeth Historical Society. ☎ 799-1977.

Spring Point Museum, Campus of Southern Maine Technical College, Fort Road. Museum of local history. ☎ 799-6337.

Standish

Daniel Marrett House (1789) Route 25. Preserved by the Marrett family in the 1880s when they celebrated its centennial with restoration efforts and an elaborate family reunion. Owned by the Society to Preserve New England Antiquities. ☎ 642-3032.

Standish Historical Society, Oak Hill Road. Old Red Church Museum. ☎ 642-4443.

Wells

Meetinghouse Museum, US 1. Artifacts and memorabilia relative to Old Wells. Genealogical and historical research library. Historic meeting house at site of first church built 1662 and burned by Indians in 1692. On the National Register of Historic Places. ☎ 646-4775.

Wells Auto Museum, US 1. Over 80 vehicles dating from 1900-1963. Nickelodeons and antique arcade. ☎ 646-9064.

Wells Historical Society, Post Road. ☎ 646-4775.

West Buxton

Buxton-Hollis Historical Society. ☎ 727-3368.

Yarmouth

Yarmouth Historical Society, Museum of Yarmouth History and Merrill Memorial Library, Main Street. ☎ 846-6259.

Old Ledge School (1738), West Main Street. A pre-revolutionary war one-room school house which was reconstructed by the Yarmouth Historical Society in 1973. ☎ 846-6259.

York

Sayward-Wheeler House (1718), 79 Barrel Lane Ext., York Harbor. Remodeled and enlarged in the 1760s by Jonathan Sayward, a local merchant and civic leader. Owned by the Society to Preserve New England Antiquities. ☎ 603-436-3205.

Old York Historical Society, Lindsay Road, ☎ 363-4974. The Old York Historical Society offers guided tours of the following historic buildings.

- **Elizabeth Perkins House** (1730), South Side Road, Colonial Revival House retains Perkins family furnishings, plus antiques collected from world travels.
- **Emerson-Wilcox House** (1742), Lindsay Road and York Street (Route 1A). Served as a general store, tailor shop, tavern, post office, and dwelling in 18th and 19th centuries.
- **George A. Marshall Store Building**, Lindsay Road. 19th-century general store situated on the Hancock Wharf serves as a gallery for revolving exhibits relating to the history of York.
- **Jefferds Tavern**, Lindsay Road, just off Route 1A. Saltbox tavern (mid-18th century) originally located in Wells.
- **John Hancock Warehouse**, Lindsay Road. 18th-century warehouse with exhibits on life and industry on the York River.

- **Old Gaol Museum**, Lindsay Road and York Street (Route 1A). Built in 1719 as the King's prison for the Province of Maine.
- **Old Schoolhouse** (1745), Lindsay Road, just off Route 1A. One-room school with exhibits of early school life.

List Source-Maine Department of Tourism.

■ Lighthouses

White Island Light, Isles of Shoals. First light erected in 1820 on White Island, a barren rock outcrop. Boat access only.

Whaleback Island Light. Granite tower built in 1872 is second on offshore ledge site. Boat access only.

Nubble Light, Cape Neddick. Cast-iron tower 40-feet high on rock nubble just offshore in York. Car/walking access.

Boon Island Light. This granite tower built in 1811 and rebuilt in 1855 is 130-feet high. On offshore island. Boat access only.

Wood Island Light. 50-foot granite tower at entrance of Saco River. Established in 1808, rebuilt in 1858. Boat access only.

Two Lights, Cape Elizabeth. Twin cast-iron towers 70-feet high. East light active, west light inactive and privately owned. Small state park at site.

Portland Head Light. 80-foot fieldstone and brick tower built in 1791 in Cape Elizabeth. Good road and foot access. Scenic rocky coast.

Ram Island Ledge Light. Granite 75-foot tower built in 1905. Boat access only. View from Portland Head.

Portland Breakwater Light. Cast-iron 20-foot tower on octagonal base. Founded in 1855 and rebuilt in 1875. Boat access only.

Spring Point Light. Built in 1897, this 55-foot brick and cast-iron tower is located on a breakwater off Portland with land access from South Portland.

Halfway Rock Light. Granite tower, 65-feet high on ledge. Established in 1871. Boat access only. View from Portland Head or Land's End on Bailey Island.

Mark Island Monument. Marker light on 60-foot granite pedestal. Boat access only.

■ Covered Bridge

Covered bridges are a quintessential symbol of New England. Typical of Yankee frugality, the spans were covered over to afford the structure protection from wind and rain, make it easier to keep the decking free of snow and ice, and to help keep horses calm while crossing high over rushing streams.

At their high point there were hundreds of covered bridges throughout the region. Most succumbed to old age, fire, or flood.

 DID YOU KNOW? *In an era when chaperones kept a constant eye on courting couples, young lovers particularly liked the privacy afforded by covered bridges, as a trip across one was the perfect opportunity to steal a kiss!*

Babb's Bridge, 1843, Presumpscot River. Maine's oldest covered bridge. It is located off the River Road, 2½ miles north of South Windham, then a half-mile west between the towns of Gorham and Windham. Burned in 1973, it has since been rebuilt.

Shopping

The south coast area has without a doubt the highest concentration of shopping opportunities in Maine. They range from the sprawling Maine Mall just off the Maine Turnpike and I-295 in Portland to trendy shops and boutiques in the quaint villages of Kennebunkport and Ogunquit. What most visitors seek, however, are outlet and factory stores.

The Difference Between An Outlet & A Factory Store

Outlets are usually taken to mean a store selling regular merchandise at a discount. Factory stores often feature incredible deals on close-outs, discontinued items and or seconds and returns.

■ Outlets & Factory Stores

Two towns vye for the title of outlet capital, with **Freeport**, home to venerable outfitter L.L. Bean, slightly edging **Kittery** for total sales (even though Kittery has a larger number of shops and its own outdoor standby, the Kittery Trading Post).

In Freeport, most shops are in a small radius and walking distance of L.L. Bean or in small plazas nearby. In Kittery shops are clustered in more than a dozen individual malls.

Both towns have outlet or factory stores by Anne Klein, Bass, Big Dog, Boston Traders, Brooks Brothers, Bugle Boy, Calvin Klein, Carter's Childrenswear, Corning Revere, The Cosmetic Company, Dansk, Dexter Shoe, Donna Karan, Eagle's Eye, Famous Brand Housewares, Foreside Co.,

Billed as the largest globe of its kind, Eartha graces the lobby of the the DeLorme retail store in Freeport.
Photo courtesy of Delorme Mapping

GAP, Golf Day, J. Crew, Jockey, Jones New York, Jones New York Sport, L'eggs/Hanes/Bali/Platex, Levi's, Liz Claiborne, London Fog, Maidenform, Mikasa, Nautica, Nine West, Olga/Warner's, OshKosh B'Gosh, Pepperidge Farms, Perfumania, Polo, Reebok, Samsonite, Soccer Mania, Sunglass World, The Sweatshirt Shop, Timberland, Totes and Yankee Candle.

Shoppers in Kittery have 80 other stores to pick from, including Crate & Barrel, Esprit, Eddie Bauer, Lenox and Old Navy.

Shoppers in Freeport have 60 other shops to pick from, including J.L. Coombs Shoes, Patagonia, Nordictrak, Delorme Map Store and Shermans Books Store.

■ Antiques

Alfred

DeWolfe and Wood, Route 202. Books, postcards, ephemera, and antiques with large selection of Shaker material. In summer, open daily 9-4. ☎ 490-5572.

Arundel

The Front Porch (owner: Julianne Blocksom), 21 Old Post Road and US 1. Located in 1850 Farmhouse. ☎ 985-1233.

Berwick

Patricia Fulton Antiques, 310 Blackberry Road. Large shop featuring furniture from 1700-1950. American and French antiques, decorative objects, paintings, photography, ceramics. Summer, Mon.-Sat., 10-5. Winter, by appointment. ☎ 384-2474.

Cornish

Cornish Trading Company (owner: Francine O'Donnell), Main Street. Multiple dealer shop with furniture and accessories. Emphasis on Americana, garden and architectural. April-Oct. ☎ 625-8387.

Cumberland

Meadowood Farm Antiques (owner: Barbara and Henry Milburn), 18th-century furniture and accessories. Large items in barn. View by appointment. ☎ 829-5318. Showing at MacDougall-Gionet, US 1, Wells.

Falmouth

Port N' Starboard Gallery (owner: Michael Leslie), 53 Falmouth Road. Marine antiques, paintings and folk art. By appointment. ☎ 781-4214. Showing at MacDougall-Gionet, US 1, Wells.

Gorham

Country Squire Antiques (owners: Jane and Ed Carr), 105 Mighty Street. Early American refinished country furniture, pine, maple, cherry. Early hooked rugs a specialty. Appointment preferred. ☎ 839-4855.

Kennebunk

Cattails Antiques, The Ellenberger Gallery, 154 Port Road. Country furniture, accessories, folk art, nautical, wicker, Shaker, hooked rugs, linens. Open all year. Summer hours, daily, 10-4. ☎ 967-3824.

Heritage House Antiques (owner: Fae Weiss), 10 Christensen Lane. Specializing in clocks, porcelain, art glass, cut glass, silver, pottery and silverplate. Open all year. ☎ 967-2580.

Kennebunkport

Old Fort Antiques (owner: Shelia Aldrick), Old Fort Avenue. Country furniture, primitive art, tin advertising items. Call for hours. ☎ 967-5353.

Windfall Antiques (owner: Anne and Ken Kornetsky), Ocean Avenue. American and English silver, Orientalia, 19th-century art, bronze and selected antiques. Call for hours. ☎ 967-2089.

Portland

F.O. Bailey Antiquarians, 141 Middle Street. Auctions, appraisals, showroom of find furniture, paintings, rugs, etc. Open all year. ☎ 773-8288.

Heller and Washam Antiques, 1235 Congress Street. 18th- and 19th-century furniture, accessories, paintings, folk art, textiles and garden furnishings. By appointment. ☎ 773-8288.

Nelson Rarities Inc., Estate Jewelers, One City Center. Extensive collection of estate jewelry. Specializing in art deco, art nouveau and period jewelry, stones, watches, silver. Open daily year-round. ☎ 775-3150.

Renaissance Antiques and Fine Art (owner: Richard Smith), 382 Commercial Street. 18th- and 19th-century Americana. Paintings, architectural, garden and nautical items. Open daily year-round. ☎ 879-0789.

Venture Antiques (owner: Isabel Thacher), 101 Exchange Street. General line of antiques, decorative accessories. Lamps a specialty. Open all year. ☎ 773-6064.

Wilma's Antiques and Accessories (owner: Wilma Taliento). Country pine and formal furniture, porcelains, pattern glass, hooked and braided rugs. By appointment (no shop). ☎ 772-9852.

Geraldine G. Wolf, 26 Milk Street. Antique jewelry, silver, and selected antiques. Tues.-Sat., 10:30-5, or by appointment. ☎ 772-8994.

South Coast

Scarborough

Centervale Farm Antiques (owners: Steve and Pat Center), 200 US 1. Large New England barn with antique furniture, china, accessories, art and collectibles. Open daily summer. Closed Mondays in winter. ☎ 883-3443.

South Portland

Mulberry Cottage (owner: Mary Alice Reilley), 45 Western Avenue. English, Irish and continental furniture and accessories. ☎ 775-5011.

Wells

Peggy S. Carboni Antiques, 1755 Post Road. Wide variety of furniture and decorative items for home and garden. Open year-round. ☎ 646-4551.

Douglas N. Harding Rare Books, US 1 North. ☎ 646-8785.

R. Jorgensen Antiques, 502 Post Road (US 1). Eleven rooms of fine period 17th- and 18th- and early 19th-century furniture and accessories. ☎ 646-9444.

Yarmouth

Marie Plummer and John Philbrick, 68 East Main Street. 17th- and 18th-century furniture and accessories displayed in room settings. Open all year by chance or appointment. ☎ 846-1158.

A.E. Runge Jr. Oriental Rugs, 108 Main Street. Buying and selling Maine's largest selection of decorative and collectible semi-antique and antique oriental rugs. ☎ 846-9000.

W.M. Schwind Jr., Antiques, 51 East Main Street. 1810 house featuring country and formal furniture, paintings, prints, ceramics, glass, rugs and accessories. Open all year. ☎ 846-9458.

York

Rocky Mountain Quilts (owner: Betsey Telford), 130 York Street. More than 400 antique quilts from 1780-1940. ☎ 363-6800.

Withington-Wells Antiques (owners: Bob and Nancy Withington), 191 Cider Hill Road. 19th- and 20th-century garden furniture, accessories and decorative arts. By appointment. ☎ 363-7439.

York Antiques Gallery (owners: Gail and Don Piatt), 746 US 1 North. Multiple dealer shop offering diversified selection. Emphasis on American country furniture and accessories. Open year-round. ☎ 363-5002.

Nancy T. Prince. Showing at gallery above or by appointment at home in North Turner. Specializing in Native American art, American folk art. ☎ 224-7823.

Adventures On Foot

■ Hiking & Walking

Bradbury Mountain, Pownal: Numerous trails ascend this 485-foot summit from parking areas in the state park at the base. The shortest, steepest route is only .2 miles long. Some trails are open to mountain biking and cross-country skiing. Good views. Old stone cattle pound and other sites along the trails. Easy to moderate. Located on Route 9. Camping, water is available at the park. ☎ 668-4712.

Douglas Mountain, Sebago: For a short hike this trip offers great panoramic views of the surrounding landscape, including Sebago Lake to the east and the White Mountains to the west. The trailhead, which is located in a Nature Conservancy preserve, is on an unmarked dirt road off the Douglas Hill Road (check a map). While the summit is at 1,416 feet, it is only a half-mile and 300 feet or so of elevation gain to the top from the parking area. A boulder on top bears a Latin inscription meaning "Not for one, but for all." Moderate effort required.

Hedgehog Mountain, Freeport: As the town's only major hill, Hedgehog Mountain may pale in comparison to larger mastiffs to the west, but it is a little bit of wilderness in a largely suburban community best known for its outlet shopping. The trail network is accessed from a parking area near the recycling center off the Pownal Road. A sign board at the trailhead contains a map of the trails to the top of the 308-foot hill. Good views in all directions. Walks of half an hour to nearly two hours possible. Easy to moderate.

Marginal Way, Ogunquit: One of the most popular village/shore walks in Maine, this mile-long stroll is especially scenic when the swells coming in off the Atlantic are made angry by offshore storms.

> **INTERESTING FACT:** *Ogunquit is a Native American word meaning "pretty place by the sea." Take this walk and you'll see why it is so named.*

Begin at small parking area across from Barnacle Billy's Restaurant on Cove Road and head north along cliffs. Good access to the shore at several spots. To return, retrace your steps or walk back through town on Shore Road. Easy (paved). Don't stray on the land side as it is private property.

Rachel Carson Preserve, Wells: This easy one-mile nature walk stays level and is accessible to wheelchairs. It winds through woods and over salt and fresh-water marsh areas and along the Merriland River and later Branch Brook (some boardwalk sections). Fixed observation stations and wooden bridges. At one point the open ocean is visible in the distance. Boulder with plaque notes dedication of preserve to Rachel Carson, US Fish and Wildlife Service Biologist and author of the seminal environmental work *Silent Spring*. Easy. Begin and end at parking area off Route 9. ☎ 646-9226.

■ Golfing

Greens fees vary greatly according to the popularity of the course and the time of year.

Dutch Elm Golf Course, 5 Brimstone Road, Arundel, ☎ 282-9850. 6,250 yards, par 72. 18 holes. April-November.

Great Chebeague Golf Club, Wharf Road, Chebeague Island, ☎ 846-9478. 2,234 yards, par 33. 9 holes. Memorial Day-Columbus Day.

Val Halla Golf & Recreation Center, off Route 9, Cumberland, ☎ 829-2225. 6,324 yards, par 71. 18 holes. April-November.

Freeport Country Club, 2 Old Country Road, Freeport, ☎ 865-4922. 2,960 yards, par 36. 9 holes. April-November 1.

Frye Island Golf Course, Frye Island on Sebago Lake, ☎ 655-4551. 3,255 yards, par 36. 9 holes. May 1-October 31.

Gorham Country Club, 134 McLellan Road, Gorham, ☎ 839-3490. 6,509 yards, par 71. 18 holes. April-November.

Salmon Falls Resort, Salmon Falls Road, Hollis, ☎ 929-5233. 2,643 yards, par 35. 9 holes. April-November.

Webhannet Golf Club, Old River Road, Kennebunk Beach, ☎ 967-2061. 6,248 yards, par 71. 18 holes. May-November.

Cape Arundel Golf Club, 19 River Road, Kennebunkport, ☎ 967-3494. 6,000 yards, par 69. 18 holes. Mid-April-November 10.

Dunegrass Golf Community, Wild Dunes Way, Old Orchard Beach, ☎ 521-1029. Public. 9 and 18 holes.

Riverside Municipal Course, 1158 Riverside Street, Portland, ☎ 797-3524. 6,520 yards, par 72. 18 holes. April 15-November 15.

Biddeford-Saco Country Club, Old Orchard Road Saco, ☎ 282-9892. 6,196 yards, par 71. 18 holes. April 15-November 15.

Sanford Golf Club, Route 4, South Sanford, ☎ 324-5462. 6,666 yards, par 72. 9 holes. April-October.

Pleasant Hill Country Club, 38 Chamberlain Road, Scarborough, ☎ 883-4425. 2,400 yards, par 34. 9 holes. April-November.

Willowdale Golf Club, US 1, Scarborough, ☎ 883-9351. 5,980 yards, par 70. 18 holes. April 15-October 30.

Sable Oaks Golf Club, 505 Country Club Drive, South Portland, ☎ 775-6257. 6,359 yards, par 70. 18 holes. April-November.

South Portland Municipal Golf Course, Route 9, South Portland, ☎ 775-0005. 2,285 yards, par 33. 9 holes. April-November.

River Meadow Golf Course, 216 Lincoln Street, Westbrook, ☎ 854-1625. 2,900 yards, par 35. 9 holes. April 1-November 15.

Twin Falls Golf Club, 364 Spring Street, Westbrook, ☎ 854-5397. 2,440 yards, par 33. 9 holes. April-November.

Westerly Winds, 853 Cumberland Street, Westbrook, ☎ 854-9463. 1,163 yards, par 27. 9 holes. April-October.

Wilson Lake Country Club, Weld Road, Wilton, ☎ 645-2016. 9 holes in a wooded setting.

Highland Farm Golf Club, 301 Cedar Hill Road, York, ☎ 363-4677. 9 holes, par 36.

Adventures On Wheels

■ Mountain Biking

 The **Bicycle Transportation Alliance of Portland** offers three bike route maps, including a seven-mile route through Historic Portland, two trips on Islands of Casco Bay, and a 21-mile Lighthouse Tour. The maps are available for $1 each from the Alliance at PO Box 4506, Portland 04112. ☎ 773-3053.

A fine, off-road ride follows the old bridle trail along the Mousam River in **Kennebunk**. Park at the edge of the entrance road to the Sea Road School. Head in either direction. This former rail line ends in the north at the old railroad depot. It heads southeast along the Mousam River and then cuts back north to end at the Webhannet Golf Course. The entire path is just over three miles long. Much of it is wheelchair accessible.

Bradbury Mountain State Park, ☎ 688-4712, on Route 9 in Pownal has about seven miles of trails on its 450 acres. Most riders agree the trails are intermediate.

There is the **Knight Woods Loop** east of the paved road, a boundary ride and one to the 485-foot summit of Bradbury Mountain, which offers excellent views. Trails open to bikes are also used by hikers, who have the right of way. Trails closed during mud season. Call to check, ☎ 688-4712.

Mount Agamenticus in York (parking area off the Mount Agamenticus Road) A variety of trails ascend this 691-foot peak just west of I-95. Many more traverse the nearby woods and fields and run alongside ponds. Difficulty of trails varies from beginner to expert.

Medicine Man Gravesite

A mound of rocks with a cross at the top of mount Agamenticus reportedly marks the grave of a Pawtucket Indian medicine man who converted to Christianity. He was named St. Aspinquid.

Trail are multiple use. Hikers and equestrians are likely to be encountered. ☎ 363-1040.

Bike Rentals

Cape-Able Bike and Rentals
83 Arundel Road, Kennebunkport 04046, ☎ 967-4382.
Rentals bikes, helmets, sales and service. Bills itself as Maine's biggest bike shop. Free maps. Open daily year-round.

Cycle Mania
59 Federal Street, Portland 04101, ☎ 774-2933.
Complete bicycle shop offering rentals of bikes and helmets, sales, service and repairs.

Wheels and Waves
579 Post Road, Wells 04090, ☎ 646-5774.
Surf, fishing and bicycle shop with rentals of bicycles, helmets, sales and service. Open year-round.

■ Foliage/Motor Tours

 You can drive for days along the South Coast and never tire of the beautiful landscape, quaint fishing villages and craggy coastline. The following routes are provided courtesy of Maine Department of Conservation.

Beaches & Boutiques

95 miles, 2¼ hours, one way

Highlights: *This tour winds you along Maine's colorful southern coast, where stunning fall foliage meets cozy harborside towns, wide sandy beaches, superb outlet shopping and vibrant arts and culture communities.*

Route: Start in **Kittery**, where you can go outlet shopping and find something to suit any taste. Head north along US 1 through The Yorks, Ogonquit, Wells and **Kennebunk**, where you'll find shops, period homes, art galleries and sweeping ocean beaches. Plan a side trip to **Cape Elizabeth**, site of Maine's famous lighthouse,

> **Foliage Hotline:** The Maine foliage hotline, in service each fall, offers the latest color-peaking information for leaf-peepers. ☎ 800-932-3419.

Portland Head Light. Visit **Portland**, and choose between historic Old Port shopping, fine dining, museum and gallery art viewing, or strolling the Eastern Promenade for stunning views of island-studded Casco Bay. Take US 1 north to Route 88 in **Falmouth**, passing the marinas and waterside restaurants of Falmouth Foreside and Yarmouth. Continue on US 1 to **Freeport**, home of L.L. Bean and a myriad designer outlets. Continue on through Brunswick to **Bath**, whose shipbuilding heritage is evident today in **Bath Iron Works**, the **Maine Maritime Museum** and historic **Front Street.** Continue toward **Phippsburg**, and the wide sandy beaches and historic fort at **Popham**.

Apples & Antiques

85 miles, 2 hours, round trip

Highlights: *This region is known for its wealth of antiques shops, beautiful period architecture, superb pick-your-own apple orchards and numerous roadside stands, which feature everything from fresh apple cider and maple syrup to family farm-grown vegetables and pumpkins.*

Route: From Sanford, go east on US 202 through historic **Alfred Village,** with its period architecture and rustic antiques shops. At Hollis Center, go north on 35 to **Standish**, keeping an eye out for the **1806 Old Red Church**. Head west on 25 through Kezar Falls, along a scenic route that includes numerous apple orchards and the **Porter Covered Bridge**. In Porter follow 160 south to **Limerick** for more antiquing, then head south on 11, past Newfield's gracefully restored 19th-century Victorian village of Willowbrook. Stay on 11 to Emery Mills, then continue on 11/109 back into Sanford.

The Pros & Cons of "Old" Route 1

Mention the idea of driving through Maine on "Old" Route 1 and images of the romance of the open road and a simpler time before Interstate highways come to mind. In reality, that can often be far from the truth as everyday traffic and starry-eyed tourists clog that route.

If you are in the mood to explore on older roads, allow yourself plenty of time for traffic, particularly around the pervasive strip malls that seem to spring up near main byways.

US 1, Kittery to Portland

75 miles, 3 hours, one way

Highlights: *A modified route up the coast is your best bet for experiencing that old-style coastal drive. Combining travel on "Old" Route 1 with occasional detours on Route 9 and other state roads that will actually get you closer to the shore and to the best scenery.*

Route: If you want to avoid the outlet malls, discount liquor store and the Kittery Trading Post traffic, hop on US 1 in **York** by taking Exit 1 off the Maine Turnpike. Turn right and go a mile or so, then turn left onto Route 1A, which takes you through the village itself, by the harbor and along the sandy shores. Eventually the road loops back north to rejoin US 1 as it heads to Ogunquit.

North of Wells, turn left onto Route 9 near the headquarters for the Rachel Carson National Wildlife Preserve. Side roads lead to some of the prettiest beaches in the state as you near **Kennebunkport**. After crossing the Kennebunk River, in the middle of the village turn left again onto side streets and pass **Walker Point**, summer home of former President George Bush. Ocean Avenue and the Wildes District Road will bring you back out to Route 9 near Cape Porpoise.

Stay on Route 9 as it continues to hug the shore and loops through the bustling town of **Biddeford**. The route then takes you along more beaches, through the honky-tonk downtown of **Old Orchard** to **Pine Point**, where it turns north back toward US 1, passing through the **Scarborough Marsh** with its Audubon Nature Center.

Take a right on US 1 and go about 3½ miles. Turn right onto Route 207. Straight takes you to the **Prouts Neck Sanctuary**. A left turn onto Route 77 after a few miles loops you around **Cape Elizabeth** with its Crescent Beach State Park and numerous lighthouses. Eventually you end up in busy downtown **South Portland**. Take 77 across the new bridge into **Downtown Portland** and stop by the **Old Port shopping district** with its cobblestone streets, unique shops and restaurants and antique buildings.

Signs in Portland will direct you back toward I-295 and other highways headed north.

Orrs Island/Bailey's Island

15 miles, 30 minutes, one way

Highlights: *Traveling out to the tip of Bailey's Island in Harpswell from Brunswick is one of the unique driving experiences in Maine. Boat launch ramps and places to picnic abound on this 15-mile, one-way trip. Unless you have a boat waiting, there's only one way back – the way you came.*

Route: Get on Route 24 where it crosses US 1 in **Brunswick** and head east. The road soon cuts south around the end of the Brunswick Naval Air Station and heads out onto a narrow finger of land left over from the time when glaciers gouged out Maine's many bays. Between Orrs and Bailey Islands the road crosses the unique **Cobwork Bridge**, which is registered as a National Civil Engineering Landmark. The criss-crossed granite "logs" of the bridge, which sit on a ledge, allow the tidal waters to course through with little impedance.

On the way back, take a right onto the Cundy's Harbor Road and visit, where else, **Cundy's Harbor**. This is the quintessential Maine fishing village is there ever was one.

■ Riding the Rails

 Maine Narrow Gauge Railroad Company and Museum, 58 Fore Street, Portland 04101. ☎ 828-0814. Maine two-foot gauge operational museum and railroad. Celebrates the history and tradition of Maine's tiny two-foot trains. Train rides daily in season on three-mile stretch along Casco Bay. Museum and train ride are handicapped accessible. Adults $5, children $3. Open May-October, with some runs offered on weekends and school vacations throughout the rest of the year.

Adventures On Water

■ Whale Watching

 A typical whale-watching trip runs two to four hours and costs between $25 and $35 per person. Keep in mind that many operators offer money-back guarantees if no whales are seen.

Kennebunk

First Chance Whale Watching, 4A Western Avenue, Kennebunk 04043. Two, four-hour trips daily with guaranteed sightings (free future trip if no whales are seen). Naturalists on board. Bring your own lunch or buy snacks and beverages from the galley. ☎ 967-5507.

Indian Whale Watch, PO Box 2672, Ocean Avenue, Kennebunkport 04046. Daily trips in season with sunset cruises on 75-foot *Indian*. Leaves from Arundel Wharf Restaurant. Guaranteed sightings. Running in July, August and September. Adults $25, children less. ☎ 967-5912.

Nautilus Whale Watch Company, PO Box 2775, Kennebunkport 04046. Two trips daily with naturalist on the *Nautilus*. Sailing from Kennebunkport Marina. Scenic cruises of coastal area four times daily on *Deep Water II*. Seasonal. ☎ 967-0707.

Ogunquit

Deborah Ann Cruises, PO Box 1671, Ogunquit 03907. Climb aboard the 40-foot *Deborah Ann* for a 4½-hour trip to Jeffery's Ledge to see whales. Two trips daily from Perkins Cove. Adults $30, children less. ☎ 646-3632.

■ Boat Trips, Charters

Freeport

 Atlantic Seal Cruises, 25 Main Street, Freeport 04032. Seal watching, Eagle Island, lobstering, osprey, foliage and sunset cruises. Boat leaves from Freeport town wharf. Seasonal. ☎ 865-6112.

Freeport Sailing Adventures, PO Box 303, Freeport 04032. Crewed sailing charters on Casco Bay by the half-day or full day. Longer charters along the coast possible. Passengers can crew or just relax. ☎ 865-6399.

Friendship Sloop Charter Company, PO Box South Freeport 04032. Half- and full-day trips aboard a classic Friendship Sloop – the boats once used by lobstermen and fishermen before motor-powered vessels arrived on the scene. Passengers can help sail the boat or just relax. Three trips daily in season. ☎ 865-3736.

Ogunquit

Finestkind Scenic Cruises, PO Box 1828 Ogunquit 03907. Leaving from Barnacle Billy's dock in Perkins Cove, boats offer scenic cruises daily from May through mid-October. See Nubble Light, go on lobstering trips, cocktail cruises, sailing trips, and even a breakfast cruise. Charters available, reservations urged.☎ 646-5227.

Kennebunk

Bellatrix Sailing Trips, PO Box 2762, Kennebunkport 04046. A 37-foot ocean racing sailing yacht offering sailing instruction or trips charged by the hour. ☎ 967-8685.

Second Chance Lobster Cruises, 4A Western Avenue, Kennebunk 04043. Five cruises of area daily with evening sunset cruise. See seals, former President George Bush's summer home at Walker's Point, as well as lobstermen going about their daily routine. ☎ 967-5507.

LazyJack Sailing Trips, Schooners Inn, Ocean Avenue. PO Box 572, Kennebunkport 04046. Operated by Capt. Rich Woodman. Regular sailing excursions in season. ☎ 967-8809.

Kennebunkport Marina, 67 Ocean Avenue, Kennebunkport 04046. Canoe and fishing equipment sales and rentals, bait. ☎ 967-3411.

Portland

Bay View Cruises, 184 Commercial Street, Portland 04101. More than 100 passengers can enjoy a tour in Casco Bay aboard the 66-foot *Bay View Lady*. Snack and beverage service available. ☎ 761-0496.

Casco Bay Lines. Year-round narrated cruises and charter service run by a company that also operates ferries to offshore islands. Special lobsterbake trips. Offerings vary by season. ☎ 774-7871.

Eagle Tours, Inc., 1 Long Wharf, Portland 04101. Daily cruises to Eagle Island or by Portland Head Lighthouse. Seal watching trips also offered . Charters for groups. Seasonal. ☎ 774-6498.

Olde Port Mariner Fleet, Long Wharf, Commercial Street, Portland 04101. Regular sightseeing, seal watching and deep-sea fishing trips in season. Evening entertainment and Casablanca Dinner cruises. Seasonal. ☎ 775-0727.

Palawan Sailing Cruises, PO Box 9715, Portland 04101. Up to 24 passengers can sail the waters and see the sights of Casco Bay during several trips daily aboard this 58-foot ocean racing yacht. Seasonal. ☎ 773-2163.

York Harbor

Lobstering Trips, 10 Organug Road, York 03909. Operated by Capt. Tom Farnon. Twice-daily trips from town dock to see lobstering in progress. Six-person maximum. ☎ 363-3234.

■ Deep-Sea Fishing

 PRICING: When the weather is rough a half-day of deep-sea fishing is plenty. That will set you back $25-35. A full day runs from $40 to $55. Most trips include rod, reels and bait. Beer, other beverages and snacks will cost extra. Deckhands will usually fillet your catch should you choose to keep it (be sure to tip for this service).

Bailey Island

Casco Bay Boat Charters, Box 233, Bailey Island 04003. Capt. Don Trott. Vessel *Sandy J.* leaves from Mackerel Cove, April thru October. ☎ 833-5024.

Kennebunkport

Chicks Marina, 75 Ocean Avenue, Kennebunkport 04046. ☎ 967-2782.

Cape Arundel Cruises, PO Box 2775, Kennebunkport 04046. Capt. Ben Emery. Vessel *Deep Water* leaves from Arundel Boatyards, Memorial Day through Columbus Day. ☎ 967-4938.

Lady J Charters, PO Box 2544, Kennebunkport 04046. Small private charter boat plying the waters of the Kennebunk and Mousam Rivers. Half- and full-day trips. Fully licensed. Catch and release encouraged. All bait and tackle provided. Leaves from the Arundel Wharf Restuarant. ☎ 967-8097.

Nereus, 4 Western Avenue, Kennebunk 04043. Capt. Dee Giguere. Leaving from dock at 4 Western Avenue, with daily trips offered from May through October. ☎ 967-5507.

Venture Inn Charters, Inc., 4A Western Avenue, Kennebunk 04043. Leaves daily from Western Avenue dock on half- and full-day fishing trips. Special fireworks and foliage cruises. Galley has hot and cold foods as well as beverages. ☎ 967-0005.

Kittery

Eliot Charter and Marine Services, 8 Forest Avenue, Eliot 03903. Capt. Orris Scribner. Vessel *Content* leaves from Seaview Lobster with daily trips, June-September. ☎ 439-5233.

Seafari Charters, 7 Islands Avenue, Kittery 03904. Capts. Barry and Bryan Bush. Daily trips from Island's Avenue dock. Runs April through the end of November. ☎ 439-5068.

Ogunquit

Bunny Clark, Box 837, Ogunquit 03907. Capt. Tim Tower. Leaves from Perkins Cove daily, mid-May-early November. ☎ 646-2214.

Bluefishing Plus, PO Box 1211, Ogunquit 03907. Capt. Bernie Stein. Vessel *Ms. Lainey* leaves from Perkins Cove daily between mid-May and October. ☎ 646-5046.

Ugly Anne, PO Box 863, Ogunquit 03907. Capt. Ken Young Sr. Leaves Perkins Cove daily, April-October. Run on a 44-foot wooden boat. Full day costs $45 per person (half-day trips also). Rod, reel, bait furnished. ☎ 646-7202.

Portland

Devil's Den Charters, PO Box 272, Scarborough 04070. Capt. Harry Adams. Vessel *Devil's Den* leaves DiMillo's Marina on Portland waterfront. Open daily, April-October. ☎ 761-4466.

Olde Port Mariner Fleet, Inc., 634 Cape Road, Standish 04084. Capts. Dan and Kathryn Libby. Vessel *Indian II* leaves from Long Wharf on Commercial Street in Portland. Daily, April-October. ☎ 642-3270.

South Harpswell

Happy Hooker II, RR 1, Box 842, South Harpswell 04079. Capt. Jerry Sullivan. Trips leave town dock at end of Route 123 daily, May-September. ☎ 833-5447.

York Harbor

Mainely Fishing Charter Service, 41 Emus Way, York 03909. Leaves daily in season from town dock 2. ☎ 363-6526.

Seabury Charters Inc., PO Box 218, York 03909. Capt. Herbert Poole. Vessel *Blackback* leaves York town dock 2 daily, May-October. ☎ 363-5324.

Shearwater Fishing, PO Box 472, York Harbor 03911. Capt. Bill Coite. Vessel *Shearwater* leaves daily from town dock 2, May-October. ☎ 363-5324.

■ Places to Paddle

Saco River, Biddeford Pool

 The lower, tidal reaches of the Saco River, below the dams in downtown Biddeford/Saco, as well as the nearby Biddeford Pool, await exploration by paddlers. The one-mile-wide pool is mostly a mud flat at low water.

 Watch the current at the breakwaters at the mouth of the river. It can be quite strong in these areas and is therefore dangerous.

Several beaches, the East Point Wildlife Sanctuary and nearby islands await discovery. Call ☎ 781-2330 for permission to visit. There are numerous small boat-launching areas at Biddeford Pool and along the river in both Biddeford and Saco.

 WATCHABLE WILDLIFE: *The pool is very attractive to wading birds and other species. Wood Island, with its lighthouse, is an Audubon Sanctuary and is closed for parts of the year during nesting season.*

Mousam River

Two sections of the Mousam River, one tidal, the other fresh, both separated by dams, await paddlers. The lower, tidal section is best accessed from the boat launch ramp along Route 9. Ride the incoming tide upstream as the river meanders toward downtown Kennebunk. There is also a salt marsh area just downstream of the ramp to explore. Tidal currents can be strong.

The second section, above several dams, is best accessed from the bridge on the Thompson Road. You can paddle three miles upstream on barely moving water until you hit a rapid just below the Old Falls Pond dam. There is also a boat ramp on the nearby Kennebunk River which allows ocean and upstream access.

Scarborough Marsh

Considered prime bird watching territory, the 3,000-acre Scarborough Marsh offers a seemingly endless number of channels and sloughs to explore by paddle. Special attention should be paid to the strong tidal currents and winds, since they will often dictate your route. Many who have misjudged these natural forces have had a good day ruined by trying to get back against the wind and tide.

 Don't go too far up small channels on an outgoing tide or you'll become mosquito chow for a few hours after your boat is stranded on the seemingly bottomless mud.

A good place to start explorations of the marsh is at the Audubon Nature Center and canoe rental shop on Route 9. There are displays and exhibits and the staff will advise you on the best routes and how to avoid hazards.

Vaughn's Island, Kennebunkport

A 40-acre island separated from mainland by tidewater. Hardwood forest covers cellar holes and other evidence of former settlement. Hiking trails. Access by foot or boat (pay attention to tides). Hand-powered boat put-in located on side road off Ocean Avenue. Kayakers can also explore the shores of a ring of several nearby islands, including Trott, Cape, Goat, Folly and Green Island. All are approachable from the comparatively protected waters of Cape Porpoise Harbor. Be sure to respect private property.

Webhannet River Marsh, Wells

Another extensive salt marsh ecosystem is the Webhannet River Marsh, which is protected from the pounding surf by the barrier beach of Wells Beach. There is a public launch ramp at the end of Lower Landing Road. There are literally dozens of miles of channels to explore as well as abundant bird life.

 Pay attention to the tides to avoid being stranded in the deep, rather aromatic mud. Only the northern sections and the center of the southern channel have water at low tide.

South Coast

Canoeing & Kayaking Outfitters

Overnight trips average $100-150 per person, per day. Half-day guided trips run in the vicinity of $50. Basic rentals cost between $25 and $45 per day. Most rentals include life jackets, paddles and car-topping gear.

Gone with the Wind
524 Pool, Biddeford 04005.
Ecological kayak tours of the South Coast on 14-foot open-top kayaks, which are considered unsinkable and stable. For all skill levels from beginner on up. Three-hour afternoon tour ranges from $50 to $40 per person. Sunset tour is slightly less expensive. Half- and full-day kayak rentals available. Tours and rentals include life jackets and wet-suit shorts. Lessons scheduled. Seasonal and subject to weather. ☎ 283-8446.

Kittery Rent-All and Sales
432 US 1 North, Kittery 03904.
Canoe rentals, year-round. ☎ 439-4528.

Sebago Lake Lodge and Cottages
PO Box 110, White's Bridge Road, North Windham 04062.
Canoe rentals. May 1-October 31. ☎ 892-2698.

Maine Island Kayak Co.
70 Luther Street, Peaks Island 04108.
Sea kayak trips ranging from half a day to a full week. ☎ 766-2373.

Maine Waters
76 Emery Street, Portland 04101.
Canoe trips, kayak trips. ☎ 871-0119.

Sebago Lake Camps
Box 905, Route 11 and 114, North Sebago 04029.
Canoe rentals, year-round. ☎ 787-3211.

World Within Sea Kayaking
746 Ocean Avenue, Wells 04090.
Complete kayak outfitter with full- and half-day rentals, lessons and equipment sales. ☎ 646-0455.

■ Scuba Diving

Adventures Inc., PO Box 943, Kennebunkport 04046. Scuba lessons, sales and service. Underwater guided tours to exotic locations. Kayak trips also. ☎ 967-5243.

The Diver's Locker, 460 Old North Berwick Road, Lyman 04002. Diving supplies, equipment. Certified instruction and air station. Guided tours of area underwater attractions such as shipwrecks, Nubble Light, etc. ☎ 985-3161.

York Beach Scuba, 19 Railroad Avenue, York Beach 03901. Dive charters, lessons, equipment rental, sales, air station. ☎ 363-3330.

■ Parasailing

 Watersports of Wells, Atlantic Avenue, Wells 04090. Powerboat tows raise adventurous souls high into sky. Call for trip times and rates. Seasonal. ☎ 646-2222.

■ Fishing

 Northeast Angler, 181 Port Road, Kennebunk 04043. Guided fly-fishing trips on the Kennebunk and Mousam Rivers for some of the finest striped bass fishing in Maine. Wading trips in backwater estuaries also available. Fishing gear, snacks and beverage provided. Four-hour trip for two people – $275. ☎ 976-5889.

Adventures In the Air

■ Hot Air Balloon Rides

Gliding silently and gently across Maine's spectacular countryside in a hot air balloon is a very special adventure. Your ears will ring during the silence after the propane burner is extinguished. Even the faintest sounds from the world below become easily audible and crystal clear. Most trips average an hour of time aloft with excursions set for the times of day when the air is calm, such as morning and early evening. Both tethered and free-flight trips are offered; all with experienced operators. Most firms require reservations and deposits. Check with your outfitter for the maximum number of people per gondola and for recommended clothing.

Cape Elizabeth

Hot Fun. One-hour flights include picnic and champagne celebration. Cost is $175 per person. ☎ 799-0193.

Kennebunk

Balloons Over New England. Trips of one hour leave at 6 am and 6 pm. The cost of $175 per person includes champagne, and selection of fresh fruit and pastries. ☎ 800-788-5562.

Portland

Balloon Rides, 17 Freeman Street, Portland 04103. One-hour trips scheduled for 6 am and 4 pm. Cost of $150 per person. ☎ 800-952-2076.

Pownal

Freeport Balloon Company. This company offers one-hour trips scheduled to begin at 6 am and 5 pm. Of course, the obligatory champagne and snacks is included. The cost of $150 per person although discounts are offered for children ages 12 and under. ☎ 865-1712.

Adventures On Snow

■ Cross-Country Skiing

Dayton

 Harris Farm XC Ski Center, 25 miles, 252 Buzzell Road, Dayton 04005. Groomed ski trails. Skating, snowshoeing, lessons, rentals, snack bar, warming hut and maple sugaring in March. ☎ 499-2678.

Limerick

Mountains and Meadows, 10 miles, PO Box Limerick 04048. Backcountry trails, lessons, rentals, snack bar. ☎ 793-4846.

Scarborough

Beech Ridge Farm XC Ski Center, 10 miles, 193 Beech Ridge Road, Scarborough 04074. Snowshoeing, lessons, rentals, night skiing, snack bar. ☎ 839-4098.

South Berwick

Vaughn Woods State Park, six miles of trails. ☎ 624-6080.

West Buxton

Ski-a-Bit, 16 miles, RFD 1 Box 115, West Buxton 04093. Lessons, rentals, snack bar. ☎ 929-4824.

Westbrook

Smiling Hill Farm, 22 miles, PO Box Westbrook 07092. Skating, snowshoeing, rentals, lessons, snack bar. ☎ 775-4818.

■ Snowmobiling

Lasting snow is often a fleeting quantity in Southern Maine. However, just a few miles inland where the foothills rise, riding is pretty reliable. Interstate Trail System (ITS) 89 begins in the village of **Emery Mills** and cuts up the west side of Sebago Lake. It leads directly to the **Fryeburg** area and on into the **White Mountains National Forest**. ☎ 824-2134.

Eco-Tours & Cultural Excursions

■ Ghost Tours

Ghostly Tours, 250 York Street, York 03909. Evening candlelit tours of quaint village with hooded figure as guide. Guide relates authentic ghost stories, witch tales and folklore of 18th and 19th centuries. Weekdays June through August. Saturday during the fall. $5 per person. ☎ 363-0000.

■ Apple Picking

Fall is the season for picking your own fresh apples. Load up a basket and take some home for friends. Here are the pick-your-own farms in the South Coast area.

Pick Your Own Apples

Acton

- **Blueberry Hill Farm**, Milton Mills Road, ☎ 457-1151.
- **Kelly Orchards**, Route 109, ☎ 636-1111.
- **Romac Orchard**, H Road, ☎ 636-3247.

Alfred

- **Gile Orchards**, Route 202, ☎ 324-2944.

Buxton

- **Snell Family Farm**, Route 112, ☎ 929-6166.

Hollis Center

- **Derring Ridge Orchard**, Route 202, ☎ 727-3405.

Raymond

- **Meadow Brook Farm**, Route 85, ☎ 627-7009.

Wells

- **Spiller Farm**, 1123 Branch Road, ☎ 985-2575.

Where to Stay & Eat

Rate Scale

All rates are for entrée or complete dinner, per person.

Inexpensive. . . . . under $10

Moderate . . . . $10-$20

Expensive . . . . More than $20

■ Favorite Restaurants

Camp Ellis

Captain Maxie's, 11 Bay Avenue, Camp Ellis, Saco 04072. Great restaurant in the diner tradition with big menu full of sandwiches, burgers, lobster and shrimp rolls, salads, crabmeat and an ice cream smorgasbord (28 flavors and 15 toppings). Breakfast menu includes lobster omelets and lobster and seafood crêpes. Waterfront seating as well as outdoor deck. Open seven days in season. Inexpensive to moderate. ☎ 284-5275.

Freeport

The Corsican Restaurant, 9 Mechanic Street (near L.L. Bean), Freeport 04032. Eclectric lunch and dinner menu featuring tasty clam chowder, lobster sandwiches, pizza, pasta, homemade soup and breads, expresso, desserts, beer and wine. Open year-round. Inexpensive to moderate. ☎ 865-9421.

Gray

Cole Farms, Route 100, Gray 04039. For nearly 50 years Cole Farms has been a favorite with local residents and visitors alike. Casual, diner-like atmosphere with breakfast being served from 5 am. Usual menu items such as burgers, sandwiches, fried seafood. Specials, too. Cole Farms makes all their own soups, chowders, pastries and ice cream. Prime rib on weekend nights. Open year-round. Inexpensive. ☎ 657-4714.

Kennebunkport

Bartley's DockSide, by the bridge, Kennebunkport 04046. Serving fresh seafood either outside on the deck or inside by candlelight with water views. Wide-ranging menu from steaks and lobster to seafood and Italian dishes. Jumbo lobsters available if ordered in advance. Large cocktails. Open daily in season. Air-conditioned. Moderate to expensive. ☎ 967-5050.

The Kennebunkport Inn, One Dock Square, Kennebunkport 04046. Relaxed, elegant dining room with fireplace indoors or casual terrace dining outdoors. Traditional New England fare includes pan-roasted Maine salmon with potato-horseradish crust, bouillabaisse, baked stuffed lobster, smoked game hen or roast rack of lamb. Delicious homemade desserts. Piano music nightly in the pub. Moderate to expensive. ☎ 967-2621.

Windows on the Water, Chase Hill Road, Kennebunkport 04046. Bills itself as Southern Maine's "casual gourmet restaurant." One reviewer said "a must for people looking for something a little upscale and out of the ordinary." Try the lobster bisque, prosciutto-wrapped shrimp, free-form vegetable pedestal along with fresh-baked breads, a classic Caesar salad and a fine dessert. Water views. Open for lunch and dinner daily. Moderate to expensive. ☎ 967-3313.

South Coast

Ogunquit

Mike's Clam Shack, US 1, Moody. When it's a "mess" of something you crave, why fool around with cloth napkins and stuffy waiters? Open for lunch and dinner year-round, Mike's Clam Shack features fresh broiled, baked or fried seafood, BBQ ribs, steamed clams and original desserts. Air-conditioned. Indoor and outdoor dining. Beer and wine. Take-out available. Wheelchair accessible. Inexpensive to moderate. ☎ 646-5999.

Vinny's East Coast Grille, US 1, Ogunquit 03907. With more than 100 menu items under $10, a kid-friendly dining room as well as outdoor terrace, sports bar and lounge, Vinny's has something for everyone. Menu ranges from bacon-wrapped shrimp and scallops to quesadillas, burgers, pizza, sirloin, ribs, fettuccine, seafood and chicken alfredo, to traditional seafood and lobster dishes. Casual atmosphere. Breakfast buffet daily. Open seasonally. Inexpensive to moderate. ☎ 646-5115.

Portland

DiMillo's Floating Restaurant, 25 Long Wharf, Portland 04101. A truly unique dining experience. There is a harbor view from nearly every seat in this converted ferry boat that's tied securely to the dock. The only thing that will sway is your appetite from ravenous when you arrive to fully satisfied when you leave. Traditional American menu strong on seafood, lobsters, beef and chicken. Also, wide selection of Italian dishes. Full cocktail service. Open year-round for lunch and dinner. Handicapped access. Moderate. ☎ 772-2216.

F. Parker Reidy's, 83 Exchange Street, Portland 04101. Every menu item from seafood to pasta, chicken, sandwiches and salads is delicious in this tastefully-decorated Old Port establishment. Prime rib on weekends. Full cocktail service. Open daily for lunch and dinner, year-round. Children's menu. Moderate. ☎ 773-4731.

Snow Squall Restaurant and Lounge, 18 Ocean Street, Portland 04101. American grill menu features steaks, chicken, chowders, vegetarian dishes, lobster rolls and fresh haddock. Try the lobster fettuccine or grilled salmon fillet. Full cocktail service. Open daily year-round. Children's menu. Moderate. ☎ 799-2232.

Wells

Lord's Lobster Harborside Restaurant, Harbor Road, Wells 04090. Dockside restaurant featuring – you guessed it – lobster. So fresh they are picked live from saltwater tanks on premises. Lord's is famous for their chowder. Wide-ranging menu includes steaks, sandwiches, lobster, shrimp and clam rolls, seafood pasta. Open for lunch and dinner every day but Tuesday. Nice views from dining room. Seasonal. Inexpensive to moderate. ☎ 646-2651.

The Maine Diner, US 1, Wells 04090. For five years running The Maine Diner has won first place in the local chowder taste off. Famous for lobster pie and for breakfast, which includes blueberry pancakes, eggs benedict and corned beef hash. Good spot for lobster and clam rolls. Open daily from 7 am until 9:30 pm. Take-out available. Beer and wine. Children's menu, handicapped accessible. Open year-round. Inexpensive to moderate. ☎ 646-4441.

York

Foster's Down East Clambake, US 1, York Harbor 03911. A veritable seafood feast, including lobster, clam chowder, steamed clams, mussels, sweet corn on the cob, potato, onions, rolls, drawn butter and blueberry crumb cake. Full restaurant open in season for lunch and dinner. Moderate. ☎ 363-2213.

Lighthouse Restaurant, 181 Nubble Road, York Beach 03910. Great view of Nubble Light out the dining room window. Menu features seafood, lobster, steak, chicken and vegetarian dishes. Full cocktail and beer and wine service. Casual attire, air-conditioned. Open seven days a week in season for lunch and dinner. Moderate to expensive. ☎ 363-4054.

■ Brew Pubs/Microbreweries

Portland

 Portland is taken out of the usual alphabetical order here because it is a brew fan's dream town. The first three breweries are located close to each other, making for a beer-lover's once-in-a-lifetime treat.

Allagash Brewing Company, 100 Industrial Way. Belgian-style beer – Allagash White Beer and Allagash Double Ale. Tours by appointment. Gift shop. ☎ 878-5385.

Casco Bay Brewing Company, 57 Industrial Way. Katahdin Golden, a clean, crisp-flavored lager, with light color and body. Katahdin Red Ale, a hearty Irish-style brew. Katahdin Stout, creamy texture and smooth taste. Also Katahdin Pale Ale and seasonal spiced brews. Tours Wednesday evenings or by appointment. ☎ 797-2020. Gift shop open weekdays.

D.L. Geary, 38 Evergreen Drive. Geary's Pale Ale, a classic British ale. Geary's London Porter, Geary's American Ale, Geary's Hampshire Special Ale, rated one of the top 24 beers in North America. Tours (call ahead on weekdays). Gift shop open weekdays. ☎ 878-2337.

Gritty McDuff's Brewpub, 396 Fore Street, Portland, and Lower Main Street, Freeport. McDuff's Best Bitter, Portland Head Light Pale Ale, Black Fly Stout, Lion's Pride Brown Ale and Sebago Light Ale. Many seasonal brews. Boasts of being Maine's first brewpub. Often voted best of Portland in annual surveys. The establishment offers traditional pub food. The gift shop, which its owners like to refer to as a "brewtique," is open Thursday-Monday (half-days on Sunday). ☎ 772-2739 (Portland), ☎ 865-4321 (Freeport).

Al Diamon Headquarters

Gritty McDuff's is the official headquarters of news columnist and television commentator Al Diamon. Look for this bearded curmudgeon at the end of the bar. It is okay to feed him, just keep your hands away from his mouth.

Shipyard Brewing Company, 86 Newbury Street. Shipyard Export Ale, Old Thumper Extra Special Ale, Blue Fin Stout, Goat Island Ale, Shipyard Brown Ale, Chamberlain Pale Ale, Mystic Seaport Ale. Many seasonal brews. Afternoon tours daily. Gift shop open daily in summer. Other times call ahead. ☎ 761-0807.

Stone Coast Brewing Company, 14 York Street. An offshoot of the Sunday River Brewing Company's founders, this establishment offers brew, music, and billiard tables. Brews include Cannery Kolsch, 420 IPA, Stone Coast Sessions, J.B. Brown Ale and Stone Coast Stout. Food includes Cajun entrées, seafood, sandwiches and appetizers.

Kennebunk

Federal Jack's Restaurant and Brewpub, Western Avenue. All Shipyard brews on tap. Prelude Ale offered for Prelude Weekend in December. Menu includes seafood and traditional pub fare. Call for tour times. Gift shop in same complex. ☎ 967-4322.

■ B&Bs, Hotels & Motels

Price Scale

All rates are based on double occupancy.

Inexpensive . . . . Under $65

Moderate . . . . $66-$100

Expensive . . . . Above $100

Freeport

 Harraseeket Inn, 162 Main Street, Freeport 04032. Without question "the" place to stay in Freeport. Tastefully decorated comfortable rooms, many with fireplaces and canopy beds. Rooms, restaurant and lounge housed in two period buildings just a few minutes' walk from L.L. Bean and other outlet shopping. 54 rooms, six suites, all with private bath (either steam, standard or jacuzzi tubs). Telephone, cable TV, air-conditioning, complimentary afternoon tea. Open all year. Weekend, off-season and Modified American Plan available. Moderate to expensive. ☎ 865-9377.

Kennebunkport

The Colony Hotel, Ocean Avenue, Kennebunkport 04046. Smoke-free rooms, most with great views of the ocean and nearby river. Cable TV, phones, air-conditioning. Private sandy beach, fitness center, heated saltwater pool, flower gardens. New England fare offered in award-winning restaurant. Sunday jazz brunch. Lounge with dancing nightly. Open seasonally. Moderate to expensive. ☎ 967-3331.

The Maine Stay Inn and Cottages, 34 Maine Street, Kennebunkport 04046. Exquisite 1860s Victorian Inn and newer cottages on spacious grounds in heart of village's historic district. All rooms have private bath, cable TV, air-conditioning; some have fireplaces. Suites and one-bedroom cottages with kitchens available. Rooms include full breakfast and afternoon tea. AAA three diamonds. One mile to beach, golf, tennis. Open year-round. Moderate to expensive. ☎ 967-2117.

The Rhumb Line, PO Box 3067, Kennebunkport 04046 (on Ocean Avenue). Modern luxurious rooms with cable TV, phones, air-conditioning. Indoor and outdoor heated pools, sauna, hot tub, fitness facilities. Quiet wooded setting; short walk to ocean. Lobster bakes and poolside dining seasonally. Rates include continental breakfast. Open year-round with off-season package rates. Moderate to expensive. ☎ 967-5457.

Ogunquit

Meadowmere Resort, PO Box 2347, Ogunquit 03907. Located on US 1, within walking distance of the village, the beach, and Perkins Cove, the Meadowmere boasts 85 air-conditioned rooms, two swimming pools (one inside, one outside), sauna, outdoor whirlpool, exercise and game rooms. Pub serving light fare and beverages. On-premise laundry. Moderate to expensive. ☎ 646-9661.

Old Orchard

There are literally hundreds of lodging places in Old Orchard, from tumble-down cottages to modern, concrete high-rises.

Beachwood Motel, 29 West Grand Avenue, Old Orchard 04064. The Beachwood has the flavor of what this sandy resort town was like before it became overbuilt. Small, two-story, motel-style establishment right on the beach. Heated freshwater pool. 44 units with air-conditioning, phones, cable TV. Some units have kitchenettes. Seasonal. Moderate. ☎ 934-2291.

Echo Motel and Cottages, 8 Traynor Street, Old Orchard 04064. The beach is only a short walk over a dune from this comfortable oceanside establishment. Modern rooms, some with kitchenettes and all with air-conditioning, cable TV, phones, and refrigerators. Units available with up to three beds. Studio apartments and cottages also offered. Open seasonally. Moderate. ☎ 934-5174.

Portland

Holiday Inn by the Bay, 88 Spring Street, Portland 04101. More than 200 rooms and suites, all with phone, cable TV, air-conditioning. Fitness center, restaurant and lounge, gift shop, indoor pool, sauna and free covered parking. Close to Old Port District with its trendy shops, restaurants, night life. Bayside rooms have great view of Portland's bustling working harbor. Open year-round. Moderate to expensive. Airport shuttle service. ☎ 775-2311.

The Marriott, 200 Sable Oakes Road, Portland 04101. 227 guest rooms and five suites all with phone, cable TV, air-conditioning. Indoor pool, sauna, whirlpool, health club and golf. Room and valet service. Airport transportation. Restaurant on premises open for breakfast, lunch and dinner. Cocktail lounge. Moderate to expensive. ☎ 871-8000.

The Regency, 20 Milk Street, Portland 04101. Located in the heart of the historic Old Port District, the Regency sports 95 charming rooms and suites nestled in a remodeled turn-of-the century stone armory. Phones, cable TV, health club, restaurant and lounge. Moderate to expensive. Open year-round. ☎ 774-4200.

Wells

The Midway Motel, PO Box 1360, Wells 04090 (Route 1). Like most hotels in Wells, the Midway is located back from the barrier beach. Still, it's close enough to put you in the action yet away from the higher prices. Suites and efficiencies are available, all with cable TV, air-conditioning and phone. Outdoor heated pool. Cottages offered. Open seasonally. Moderate. ☎ 646-6066.

Misty Harbor Resort Hotel, Mile Road, Wells 04090. Modern one- and two-bedroom suites with cable TV, phone and air-conditioning. Heated pool, sauna, hot tub and exercise facilities. Pub with dancing and entertainment. Open year-round. Not far from beaches, village. Laundry area. Outdoor picnic area with grills. Moderate to expensive. ☎ 646-8373.

York

Long Beach Inn, PO Box 615, York Beach 03910 (Route 1A). Two-story modern hotel set on three seaside acres. Efficiency units all have full baths, cable TV, and phones. Heated pool. Ocean and lighthouse view out front. Moderate. ☎ 363-5481.

Stage Neck Inn, PO Box 70, York Harbor 03911 (Stage Neck Road). Small, European-style resort featuring fine dining (open to the public), golf, tennis, indoor and outdoor pools and deluxe guest rooms. Situated on a narrow spit of land. Cable TV, phones, air-conditioning. AAA Four-Diamond rating. Open year-round. Moderate to expensive. ☎ 363-3850.

■ Camping

Facilities indicated as "nearby" are located within one mile of the campground.

Acton

Apple Valley Campground, PO Box 92, Acton 04001. Apple Valley Campground is a family-oriented campground nestled in the hills of Acton on Route 109. Enjoy friendly camping for a day, week, month or season. 145 sites, 30 amp, sewer, dump station, store, laundry, recreation hall, swimming, fishing, pool, LP gas. Pets allowed. Open May 15-October 15. ☎ 636-2285.

Alfred

Bunganut Lake Camping Area, PO Box 141, Alfred 04002. Located on Anderson Road. 110 sites, tenting area, 30 amp, dump station, store, laundry, rec hall, swimming, boating, fishing, on-site rentals, LP gas. Pets allowed. Open May 1-October 1. ☎ 247-3875.

Scott's Cove Camping Area, PO Box 761, Alfred 04002. Relax and enjoy quiet family camping on a beautiful spring-fed lake with great fishing, swimming and boating. 50 sites, tenting area, 30 amp, sewer, dump station, store, rec hall, swimming. Laundry nearby. Open May 1-Columbus Day. ☎ 324-6594.

Walnut Grove Campground, 599 Gore Road, Alfred 04002. A friendly family campground. Large open and wooded sites. Small groups welcome. Can accommodate any size trailer. 93 sites, tenting area, 30 amp, dump station, store, laundry, rec hall, pool, group area. Pets allowed. Open May 1-October 13. ☎ 324-1207.

Arundel

Fran-Mort Campground, 111 Sinnott Road, Arundel 04046. 130 sites, tenting area, 30 amp, sewer, dump station, laundry, rec hall, LP gas. Pets aallowed. Open May 12-October 12. ☎ 967-4927.

Biddeford

Shamrock RV Park, 391 West Street, Biddeford 04005. Quiet, secluded campground situated in a rural area, near some of the finest scenery along Maine's south coast. Close to major attractions. 60 sites, tenting area, 30 amp, sewer, dump station, fishing, pool. Store nearby. Pets allowed. Open May 1-September 30. ☎ 284-4282.

Cape Neddick

Cape Neddick Oceanside Campground, PO Box 1, Cape Neddick 03902. Tent and small pop-up sites shaded by pines on Route 1. Oceanside beaches and great views of the Atlantic. Close to Ogunquit, York, and Kittery shopping malls. Many sports activities nearby. Some seasonal sites. 80 sites, tenting area, 30 amp, dump station, store, swimming, boating, fishing. Open May 15-October 12. ☎ 363-4366.

Dixon's Campground, 1740 Route One, Cape Neddick 03902. A natural wooded and open area offering beauty and quiet solitude for tenters and small RVs. Free transportation to Ogunquit Beach (late June to Labor Day). No pets. 100 sites, tenting area, 20 amp, dump station, store, dryers. LP gas nearby. Open Memorial Day-September 15. ☎ 363-2131.

East Lebanon

Heavenlee Acres Campground, RR 2, Box 503, East Lebanon 04027. 58 sites, tenting area, 20 amp, sewer, pumping, laundry, rec hall, swimming, pool, on-site rentals. Pets allowed. Open May 1-Columbus Day. ☎ 457-1260.

Kings and Queens Court Resort, RR 1, Box 763, East Lebanon 04027. Two heated pools, four hot tubs and a 360-foot watersilde. The campground with everything. 400 sites, tenting area, 30 amp, sewer, dump station, store, laundry, rec hall, swimming, fishing, pool, on-site rentals, group area, LP gas. Pets allowed. Open May 15-September 27. ☎ 339-9465.

East Waterboro

Blackburn's Campground, PO Box 356, East Waterboro 04030. Located on Route 5 in Waterboro on Ossipee Lake, which has been tested and found to be one of the cleanest lakes in Maine. 85 sites, tenting area, 20 amp, sewer, dump station, rec hall, swimming, boating, fishing. Pets allowed. Open May 1-October 1. ☎ 247-5875.

Freeport

Cedar Haven, 39 Baker Street, Freeport 04032. Two miles from I-95 and L.L. Bean. Accommodates all size units. Full hook-ups, 30 amp service; some sites have cable. Large private tent sites and rentals. 58 sites, tenting area, sewer, dump station, store, laundry, rec hall, swimming, on-site rentals, group area, LP gas. Pets allowed. Open May 1-October 25. ☎ 454-3403.

Desert Dunes Of Maine, 95 Desert Road, Freeport 04032. Clean, quiet camping with wooded and open sites, showers, badminton, volleyball, and horseshoes. Just 2½ miles to L.L. Bean. Free pass to famous Desert of Maine. 50 sites, tenting area, 30 amp, sewer, dump station, store, laundry, pool, LP gas. Pets allowed. Open May 9-October 15. ☎ 865-6962.

Florida Lake Campground, 82 Wardtown Road, Freeport 04032. RV and tent sites with a swimming pool, lake for fishing, pedal boats, recreation field and snack bar. Located about 3½ miles from L.L. Bean. 40 sites, tenting area, 20 amp, dump station, rec hall, swimming, boating, group area. Store nearby. Pets allowed. Open May 15-October 15. ☎ 865-4874.

Flying Point Campground, Lower Flying Point Road, Freeport 04032. A unique, tranquil setting on the shores of Casco Bay, three miles east of L.L. Bean. 38 sites, tenting area, 30 amp, dump station, laundry, swimming, boating, fishing, on-site rentals. Pets allowed. Open May 1-October 15. ☎ 865-4569.

Kennebunk

Yankeeland Campground, PO Box 829, Kennebunk 04043. Seasonal and transient sites available. 200 sites, tenting area, 50 amp, sewer, dump station, store, laundry, rec hall, swimming, boating, fishing, pool, LP gas. Pets allowed. Open May 1-Columbus Day. ☎ 985-7576.

Kennebunkport

Kennebunkport Camping, 117 Old Cape Road, Kennebunkport 04046. "The way camping should be." Large wooded sites, free hot showers, play area and friendly, helpful service. Close to many popular attrac-

South Coast

tions. 82 sites, tenting area, 30 amp, sewer, dump station, store, group area. Laundry, swimming, boating, and fishing nearby. Pets allowed. Open May 15-October 15. ☎ 967-2732.

Salty Acres Campground, 277 Mills Road, Kennebunkport 04046. Salty Acres is located near beautiful Sandy Goose Rocks Beach. Scenic, peaceful, wooded campsites. A great affordable family vacation spot. 260 sites, tenting area, 30 amp, sewer, dump station, store, laundry, boating, fishing, pool, on-site rentals, group area. LP gas and swimming nearby. Pets allowed. Open May 15-Columbus Day. ☎ 967-8623.

Lebanon

Potter's Place Adult Park, RR 2, Box 490, Lebanon 04027. A unique park developed for the adult camping community, featuring wooded nature trails, a seven-acre pond, floral gardens and an arboretum. Spacious, uncrowded sites. 100 sites, tenting area, 20 amp, dump station, rec hall, swimming, boating, fishing, on-site rentals. Pets allowed. Open May 1-October 15. ☎ 457-1341.

Moody

Outdoor World, US 1, Box 477, Moody 04054. 136 sites, tenting area, 50 amp, sewer, dump station, store, laundry, rec hall, pool, on-site rentals. Pets allowed. Open Memorial Day-Columbus Day. ☎ 646-4586.

Old Orchard Beach

Acorn Village, 42 Walnut Street, Old Orchard Beach 04064. A small unique family vacation spot with camping and cabins that is close to the beach and center of town, yet quiet and private. 75 sites, tenting area, 15 amp, sewer, dump station, laundry, swimming, pool. Store, boating, and fishing nearby. Open Memorial Day until Labor Day. ☎ 934-4154.

Hid'n Pines Campground, PO Box 647, Old Orchard Beach 04064 (Route 98). 260 sites, tenting area, 20 amp, sewer, dump station, laundry, rec hall, pool. Store, LP gas, swimming, and fishing nearby. Pets allowed. Open May 15-September 15. ☎ 934-2352.

Ne're Beach Family Campground, PO Box 537, 38 Saco Avenue, Old Orchard Beach 04064. Clean, quiet campground just a short walk to seven miles of sand, surf, and amusements. Convenient for day trips to area attractions and outlet malls. 60 sites, tenting area, 30 amp, sewer, dump station, store, laundry, pool. Swimming, boating, fishing, and LP gas nearby. Pets allowed. Open Memorial Day-Labor Day. ☎ 934-7614.

Old Orchard Beach Campground, 27 Ocean Park Road, Old Orchard Beach 04064. Sites with or without hook-ups. Campstore, gameroom, recreation fields, swimming pools, shuttle bus, laundry, phone, hot showers – all within a mile of Maine's finest sandy beaches, seven miles of them. 300 sites, tenting area, 30 amp, sewer, dump station, laundry, rec hall, pool, group area, LP gas. Swimming, boating, store, and fishing nearby. Pets allowed. Open May 1-October 15. ☎ 934-4477.

Paradise Park Resort, Box 4, Old Orchard Beach 04064. Located on 40 wooded acres only 800 feet from downtown Old Orchard Beach, with its pier, shopping, amusements, and seven miles of beach. 200 sites, tenting area, 30 amp, sewer, dump station, store, laundry, rec hall, swimming, boating, fishing, pool, on-site rentals, group area. LP gas nearby. Pets allowed. Open May 15-October 15. ☎ 934-4633.

Powder Horn Family Camping, PO Box 366, Old Orchard Beach 04064 (Route 98). Enjoy family camping at its best. Three pools, two jacuzzis, 18-hole mini golf, playgrounds, laundromat, store and paved roads. 450 sites, tenting area, 30 amp, sewer, dump station, rec hall. Pets allowed. Open Memorial Day-Labor Day. ☎ 934-7058.

Virginia Tent Trailer Park, Box 242, Old Orchard Beach 04064. Quiet family camping with clean restrooms and grounds. Free hot showers, Down East lobster bakes, swimming pool, spa and playgrounds. A half-mile to sandy, ocean beach and activity center. 130 sites, tenting area, 30 amp, sewer, dump station, store, on-site rentals, group area, laundry, rec hall, swimming. Boating, fishing and LP gas nearby. Pets allowed. Open Memorial Day-September 27. ☎ 934-4791.

Wagon Wheel Campground and Cabins, #3 Old Orchard Road, Old Orchard Beach 04064. Sites with or without hook-ups, recreation hall, campstore, swimming pools, playground, laundry, phone, hot showers, set in a charming pine grove environment within a mile of the ocean. 200 sites, tenting area, 30 amp, sewer, dump station, swimming, on-site rentals, group area, LP gas. Boating and fishing nearby. Pets allowed. Open May 1-October 15. ☎ 934-2160.

Wild Acres Family Camping, 179 Saco Avenue, Old Orchard Beach 04064. Wild Acres is the closest resort family campground to Old Orchard's beautiful beach. A first-class family vacation sure to please all ages. 360 sites, tenting area, 50 amp, sewer, dump station, store, laundry, rec hall, swimming, fishing, pool, LP gas. Pets allowed. Open Memorial Day-September 15. ☎ 934-2535.

Parsonfield

Windsong Campground, PO Box 547, Parsonfield 04047. Located in a quiet mountainside pine grove near rivers and ponds. Centrally located for easy access to the ocean (30 miles) and Sebago Lake (20 miles). 35 sites, tenting area, 30 amp, dump station, store, laundry, rec hall, pool, on-site rentals, group area. Swimming, boating, and fishing nearby. Pets allowed. Open year-round. ☎ 625-4389.

South Coast

Portland

Recompence Shore Campsites, 844 Stevens Avenue, Portland 04103. Breathtaking oceanfront campground. Comfortable camping facilities, tidal swimming, fishing, recreation, nearby Wolfe's Neck Woods State Park, and Freeport outlet shopping. 105 sites, tenting area, 15 amp, dump station, store, laundry, swimming, boating, fishing, group area, LP gas. Pets allowed. Open May 15-October 15. ☎ 865-9307.

Pownal

Blueberry Pond Campground, 218 Poland Range Road, Pownal 04069-6205. Large sites for tenting or RVs in a peaceful, nature-filled environment off the main road just 4½ miles from Freeport, L.L. Bean and outlets. 35 sites, tenting area, 30 amp, sewer, dump station, pool. Store and laundry nearby. Pets allowed. Open May 15-October 15. ☎ 688-4421.

Saco

Saco Portland South KOA, 814A Portland Road, Saco 04072. A quiet vacation destination offering blueberry pancakes and desert nightly. Whale watching, lobster cruise, amusement park, rock-bound coast and L.L. Bean are nearby. A+ KOA rated. Handicap accessible. 120 sites, tenting area, 30 amp, sewer, dump station, store, laundry, pool, on-site rentals, group area, LP gas. Rec hall, swimming, boating, and fishing nearby. Pets allowed. Open May 14-October 13. ☎ 282-0502.

Silver Springs Campground, 705 Portland Road, US 1, Saco 04072. Silver Springs is located only 1½ miles from the ocean. Full hook-ups with up to 50 amp service. Swimming pools, game room and much more. 50 sites, tenting area, 50 amp, sewer, dump station, store, laundry, pool. Swimming, boating, fishing, and LP gas nearby. Pets allowed. Open May 1-October 15. ☎ 283-3880.

Sanford

Apache Campground, Bernier Road, Box 1400, Sanford 04073. Family campground with a lake, pool, large sites, good fishing, ball field, pavilion, playground, shuffleboard, and planned activities. 150 sites, tenting area, 30 amp, sewer, dump station, store, laundry, recreation hall, swimming, boating, fishing, pool, group area. Pets allowed. Open May 15-October 15. ☎ 324-5652.

Sand Pond Campground, PO Box 741, Sanford 04073. Situated just 12 miles west of Wells, on a clean spring-fed pond off Sand Pond Road in Sanford. Sand Pond Campground appeals to ocean lovers as well as wilderness lovers. 38 sites, tenting area, 50 amp, sewer, dump station, rec hall, swimming, boating, fishing, group area. Store, laundry, and LP gas nearby. Pets allowed. Open May 15-Columbus Day. ☎ 324-1752.

Yogi Bear's Jellystone Park, 1175 Main Street, Sanford 04073. Game room, playground, horseshoes, volleyball, bocci court, ball field, group area, hay rides. Tourist attractions nearby. Wells Beach – 10 minutes. 131 sites, tenting area, 50 amp, sewer, dump station, store, laundry, rec hall, pool. Pets allowed. Open May 15-September 15. ☎ 324-7782.

Scarborough

Bayley's Camping Resort, Box M8, 27 Ross Road, Scarborough 04074. Offers three heated pools, four jacuzzis, planned activities, professional entertainment and a beach bus. 400 sites, tenting area, 50 amp, sewer, dump station, store, laundry, rec hall, swimming, fishing, pool, on-site rentals, group area, LP gas. Boating nearby. Pets allowed. Open May 1-Columbus Day. ☎ 883-6043.

Wassamki Springs Campground, 56 Saco Street, Scarborough 04074. Closest campground to Portland. Family camping at its best. Clean and quiet campground with something to do for everyone – or just come and relax. 160 sites, tenting area, 50 amp, sewer, dump station, store, laundry, rec hall, swimming, boating, fishing, group area, LP gas. Pets allowed. Open May 1-October 15. ☎ 839-4276.

Wild Duck Campground, 39 Dunstan Landing Road, Scarborough 04074. In the middle of Scarborough Marsh Nature Area. Clean wooded sites, three miles to ocean beach. 60 sites, tenting area, 30 amp, sewer, dump station, canoe rentals, cable TV, laundry, boating, fishing. Store nearby. Pets allowed. Open May 15-Columbus Day. ☎ 883-4432.

South Lebanon

B & B Family Camping, Route 202, RR 2, Box 1115, South Lebanon 04027. A small but great campground offering fun for all with a game room, horseshoes, ping-pong and bikes for kids. Located near two malls. Good season rates. 56 sites, tenting area, 50 amp, sewer, dump station, pool, store, rec hall, swimming. Laundry, boating, fishing, and LP gas nearby. Pets allowed. Open Memorial Day-Columbus Day. ☎ 339-0150.

Wells

Beach Acres Campground, 563 Post Road, Wells 04090. 380 sites, tenting area, 50 amp, sewer, dump station, store, laundry, swimming, pool, group area. LP gas, boating, and fishing nearby. Open Memorial Day-Labor Day. ☎ 646-5612.

Gregoire's Campground, 697 Sanford Road, Wells 04090. First campground off Maine Turnpike, Exit 2 in Wells. Can accommodate trailers of

40 feet and longer, plus motor homes. Trolley runs daily during peak season. Pets on leash welcome. 130 sites, tenting area, 30 amp, sewer, dump station, store, rec hall. Laundry nearby. Open May 15-October 15. ☎ 646-3711.

Ocean Overlook, PO Box 309, US 1, Wells 04090. Large sites, family oriented, one mile to beach, quiet peaceful area, restaurant on premises. No pets. 50 sites, tenting area, 30 amp, sewer, dump station, pool. Store, laundry, swimming, boating, and fishing nearby. Open May 15-Columbus Day. ☎ 646-3075.

Pinederosa Campground, 128 North Village Road, Wells 04090. Located just north of Oqunquit Village, Pinederosa offers family camping at its best. Campsites are scattered throughout the Pinederosa's 35 acres of woods and field. 152 sites, tenting area, 30 amp, sewer, dump station, store, laundry, swimming, pool. Open May 15-September 15. ☎ 646-2492.

Riverside Park Campground, 2295 US 1, Wells 04090. Centrally located between Kennebunkport and Ogunquit, near ocean beaches with cable, phone hook-ups, modern showers, reasonable rates and seasonal sites. 130 sites, tenting area, 50 amp, sewer, dump station, store, swimming, fishing, pool, group area. Pets allowed. Open May 15-October 15. ☎ 646-3145.

Sea Breeze Campground, 2073 Post Road, Wells 04090. 58 sites, tenting area, 50 amp, sewer, store, laundry, swimming, pool, on-site rentals, LP gas. Boating and fishing nearby. Pets allowed. Open May 15-October 15. ☎ 646-4301.

Sea-Vu Campground, PO Box 67, Wells 04090. Ideally located to experience Maine. The village atmosphere of Ogunquit and Kennebunkport, summer theaters, rocky coast, sandy beaches, and the delectable Maine lobster. 220 sites, tenting area, 50 amp, sewer, dump station, store, laundry, rec hall, swimming, pool, LP gas. Boating and fishing nearby. Pets allowed. Open May 15-Columbus Day. ☎ 646-7732.

Stadig Mobile Park Campground, 146 Bypass Road, Wells 04090. Stadig Campground has a quiet wilderness atmosphere located within two miles of beautiful beaches. Tent, RV, and seasonal sites available. 150 sites, tenting area, 30 amp, sewer, dump station, store, laundry, rec hall, group area. Swimming, boating, and fishing nearby. Open Memorial Day-October 1. ☎ 646-2298.

Wells Beach Resort, 1000 Post Road, Wells 04090. Premium camping facility located on US Route1 between Kennebunkport and Ogunquit, one mile from Wells Beach. 212 sites, tenting area, 50 amp, sewer, dump station, store, laundry, rec hall, swimming, pool. LP gas, boating, and fishing nearby. Pets allowed. Open May15-October 15. ☎ 646-7570.

Windham

Highland Lake Park Campground, 19 Roosevelt Trail, Route 302, Windham 04062. Small quiet lakeside family campground with great fishing, boating and swimming. From I-495 take Exit 8 to Route 302 (Roosevelt Trail). 40 sites, tenting area, 30 amp, sewer, dump station, swimming, boating, fishing, on-site rentals and group area. LP gas, rec hall and pool are nearby. Pets allowed. Open year-round. ☎ 892-8911.

York Beach

Flagg's Trailer Park Inc., PO Box 232, York Beach 03910 (Route 1A). Small quiet park, 500 ft. to beach. Seasonal and daily rates, self-contained RVs. Close to all conveniences, restaurants, and shopping malls. 83 sites, 30 amp, sewer. Store, laundry, swimming, boating, and fishing nearby. Open May 15-October 1. ☎ 363-5050.

Wayside Trailer Park, PO Box 83, York Beach 03910. Across from ocean on Route 1A. Near shopping, dining, churches and recreation. 38 sites, 15 amp, sewer. Store, laundry, swimming, boating, fishing, and LP gas nearby. Pets allowed. Open May 13-September 30. ☎ 363-3846.

York Beach Camper Park, PO Box 127, 11 Cappy's Lane, York Beach 03910. 46 sites, tenting area, 50 amp, sewer, dump station, laundry. Swimming, boating and fishing nearby. Pets allowed. Open Memorial Day-Columbus Day. ☎ 363-1343.

York Harbor

Camp Eaton, PO Box 626, York Harbor 03911. Located next to 1½-mile Long Sand Beach on Route 1A. Wooded tent sites, grassy RV sites, and extensive recreation for all ages. 307 sites, tenting area, 50 amp, sewer, dump station, store, fishing, rec hall, swimming. Laundry, boating, fishing, and LP gas nearby. Pets allowed. Open May 1-October 1. ☎ 363-3424.

Libby's Oceanside Camp, PO Box 40, York Harbor 03911. Open grassy campground adjacent to 1½-mile sandy beach on Route 1A. Two lighthouses in view. Assistance with parking and connecting sewage. 95 sites, tenting area, 50 amp, sewer, fishing, swimming. Laundry and boating nearby. Pets allowed. Open May 15-October 15. ☎ 363-4171.

Maine's Mid-Coast

MID-COAST

Maine's Mid-Coast, an area stretching roughly from Brunswick in the south to Belfast in the east, is a region just now coming into its own. For most of the latter half of the 20th century only a few towns along the coast here, such as Boothbay Harbor and Camden, were known as tourist magnets. But all that has changed.

While the traditional stops are busy as ever and still retain their charm, older, working-class harbors such as Belfast and Rockland have enjoyed a renaissance of sorts. Belfast has shed its past as a chicken-processing port and sports a lively downtown, picturesque harbor, and popular train rides on the Belfast and Moosehead Lake Railroad.

Rockland, once best known for the odors emanating from its many fish processing plants, now hosts more windjammers than any other port on the coast. It is home to the Farnsworth Museum and the Wyeth Center, which harbor fine collections of Wyeths.

Camden's harbor is as crowded with visiting yachts as ever. And, the entire region has benefited from the largess of credit card giant MBNA. This success has translated into thousands of jobs in processing centers in Camden and Belfast.

To be sure, quaint fishing villages such as Friendship, home of the beloved design class of the sloop of the same name, remain timeless in their beauty and nod to tradition. Damariscotta, despite the growth of the standard commercial strip outside of town, still boasts one of the friendliest old-style downtowns in Maine.

Standing on the tower of the lighthouse at Owls Head, a gentle sea breeze out of the southeast, you may be lucky enough to spy the gray silhouette of Matinicus Island off on the horizon. Here it takes little imagination to picture what life was like here more than 100 years ago when most cargo and passengers went by schooner or steamship.

Long narrow fingers of land, which escaped the mighty glacier's gouging power, reach out into the sea at Phippsburg, Harpswell and Bailey's Island. Intimate beaches and small state parks and natural areas await discovery.

Pemaquid Point, with its stately lighthouse perched literally only feet away from were the rock disappears beneath the sea, is a mandatory stop.

Visits to Monhegan, Matinicus, North or Vinal Haven or Isleboro, all reachable by mailboat or scheduled ferry, provide not just a brief journey at sea but also a trip back to a simpler time when life was indeed slower and the most important news didn't come from Washington or New York.

Inland from the shore all along the Mid-Coast tiny towns await discovery. Many of the north-south state routes connecting US 1 along the coast with Routes 17 and 3 in the interior wind through pastoral valleys past sagging barns filled with antique treasures and farm stands overflowing with fresh produce.

Camden Hills State Park, which boasts it is "where the mountains meet the sea," features some fine day hikes and great views from the auto road that winds to the stone tower atop Mount Battie.

While the Mid-Coast may lack a major park or preserve such as Baxter or Acadia, there are an equal number of places worth discovering and exploring.

■ Maine has one area code – 207

Parks, Preserves & Beaches

■ State Parks

 Barrett's Cove Beach, Camden. Located on Route 52 beneath the towering granite of Maiden Cliff that is part of Camden Hills State Park, this facility includes a freshwater swimming beach on Megunticook Lake. There are restrooms, picnic tables, a play area and a public boat launch ramp. Good parking.

Birch Point State Park, Owls Head. Small, 56-acre state park located on the shore of Owls Head. It has a 220-yard pocket beach near high headland with freshwater marsh. No facilities, limited parking. Swimming, fishing and picnicking. Open during summer season. Good kayak launching spot.

Camden Hills State Park. This 900-acre park off US 1 bills itself as being "where the mountains meet the sea." The beauty of this area inspired the poet Edna St. Vincent Millay. While trails and access do not actually go from summits to the sea, it's pretty close. There is an extensive 30-mile trail system with access from several state routes. Maps can be obtained at the park office off US 1. There is a paved toll road to the top of 900-foot

Mount Battie, which features a stone tower on top and fine panoramic views of the surrounding ocean and hills. Good views of Megunticook Lake from Maiden Cliff, an 800-foot precipice. Park facilities include camping (112 sites), picnic tables, toilets, hot showers, a dumping station and plenty of parking. In winter, cross-country ski trails make this a popular spot. Snowmobiling is allowed. ☎ 236-3109.

Damariscotta Lake State Park, Jefferson. This small lakeside "parklet" on Route 32 sees heavy use in summer. It has a fine sand beach for swimming, access for fishing, picnic tables and grills and toilets provided. Good access for winter users. Parking is limited so get there early. ☎ 549-7600.

Eagle Island State Park, Harpswell. This island state park is located several miles off the coast of Harpswell. It can be reached only by boat (see below). In summer, the island is open seven days a week. There is an admission fee. Call ☎ 624-6080 for more park information. There is a public ramp and floats and moorings available for private boats.

Admiral Robert Peary

Eagle Island was once home to famous polar explorer Admiral Robert Peary, whose claim of having been the first to discover the North Pole has come under fire in recent years. The cliff-top house built by the explorer has recently been refurbished. About 6,000 visitors annually come to see where Admiral Peary spent most of his summers.

Several tour companies offer round-trips. These include:

- **Atlantic Seal Cruises**, South Freeport, ☎ 865-6112
- **Casco Bay Boat Charters**, Bailey Island, ☎ 833-2978
- **Dolphin Marina**, South Harpswell, ☎ 833-2978
- **The Coast Watch Guiding and Light Navigation Co.**, Portland, ☎ 774-6498

Fort Knox State Park, Prospect. Route 172. Massive granite fort and gun emplacements constructed to guard approaches to Bangor on Penobscot River. Complex includes maze of deep underground tunnels and caves. Bring a flashlight. Toilets and picnic area. Entrance fee. Plenty of parking. Fort is popular spot with Civil War re-enactors.

Fort Point State Park, Stockton Springs. On Fort Point Road at the end of scenic peninsula at northern end of Penobscot Bay. Fishing allowed off pier which also provides boat access. Picnicking and a nice drive in. Site features location of Fort Pownall, which was built in 1759. Some earthworks remain.

Fort Popham State Park, Popham. Site of Fort Popham, a semicircular stone fort begun at onset of Civil War but never finished. Scenic drive. Fishing allowed. Picnic area. At end of Route 209. Beginning of Arnold Trail, where Benedict Arnold began ill-fated expedition to Quebec in fall of 1775.

Johnson Memorial Park, Rockland. Town-run freshwater swimming beach on Chickawaukie Lake on Route 17 west of town. Swimming beach, picnic area with grills, restrooms and public boat access. Free parking.

Lake St. George State Park, Liberty. Lakeside beach located on edge of busy Route 3. Backcountry area to the north is a favorite with hikers, cross-country skiers and snowmobilers. Fishing and freshwater swimming. Bathhouse, toilets, pump station and launching ramp. Camping area. ☎ 589-4255.

Moose Point State Park, Searsport. Small seaside picnic area off US 1. There are open fields, a softwood grove and plenty of parking. ☎ 548-2882.

Mullen Head Park, North Haven. Located on Mullen Head Road. Town-operated park on offshore island that sports a year-round community. Hiking trails leave from dirt road. Views of ocean, Deer Isle to north.

Pemaquid Beach State Park, Bristol. Snowball Hill Road. Favorite family swimming beach with warmer water, usually free of any major wave action. In village of New Harbor. Facilities include bathhouse, toilet, picnic tables, a snack bar and paid parking. Fort William Henry, historical sites nearby.

Popham Beach State Park, Phippsburg. Route 209. One of the state's finest preserves, featuring fine, white sand beaches, tide pools, rocky ledges and a nature walk. Off Route 209. All activities, including swimming, surfing, surf casting, etc., are pursued here. Picnic area. Plenty of parking for a fee. Park includes Fort Baldwin, complex of batteries and observation towers built in early 1900s and during WW II on Sabino Hill. Good views from old tower. Old pilings from former steamboat piers.

Reid State Park, Georgetown. Large park with just about everything: sandy beach, hiking, salt marsh, rocky ledges and warm tidal pool. Bathhouses, toilets, snack bar, picnic tables, grills, and parking for a fee. On Sequinland Road off Route 127. ☎ 371-2303.

Rockland Breakwater, Rockland. Located off the Samoset Road, this small park, named in memorial for Marie H. Reed, includes a tiny sand beach and the 4,300-foot-long harbor breakwater itself which forms a long rocky, yet relatively flat walk in good weather to the historic lighthouse on the south end. Great views of the harbor and nautical traffic.

Royal River Park, Yarmouth. Two sets of falls delineate this riverside park that offers woods, a bike path, a fish ladder and picnic area. In the heart of downtown Yarmouth.

Major Parks & Preserves Along the Mid-Coast

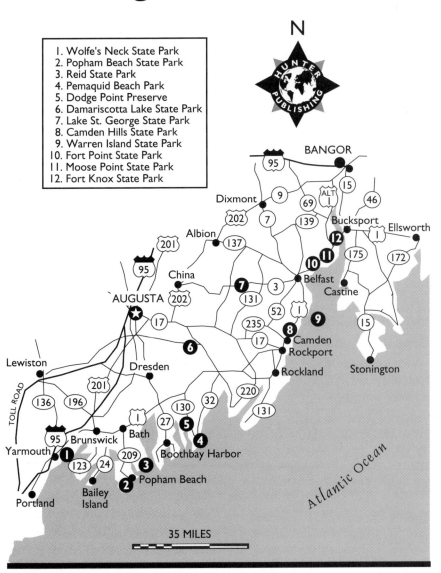

1. Wolfe's Neck State Park
2. Popham Beach State Park
3. Reid State Park
4. Pemaquid Beach Park
5. Dodge Point Preserve
6. Damariscotta Lake State Park
7. Lake St. George State Park
8. Camden Hills State Park
9. Warren Island State Park
10. Fort Point State Park
11. Moose Point State Park
12. Fort Knox State Park

N

BANGOR

Dixmont
Albion
China
AUGUSTA
Belfast
Castine
Ellsworth
Bucksport
Buckport
Lewiston
Dresden
Camden
Rockport
Rockland
Stonington
Yarmouth
Brunswick
Bath
Boothbay Harbor
Popham Beach
Bailey Island
Portland

TOLL ROAD

35 MILES

Atlantic Ocean

Swan Lake State Park, Swanville. Small recently opened park on lake includes swimming beach, toilets. Scant parking. Off Frankfort Road off Route 141. ☎ 525-4404.

Warren Island State Park, Isleboro. A saltwater island park with boat access only. In Penobscot Bay. Heavily forested with spruce. Hiking, picnicking, fishing are allowed. Overnight camping is permitted. Dock and moorings available for day users. Best access is from Lincolnville, or take the ferry to Isleboro and kayak from there. ☎ 236-3109.

■ Beaches at a Glance

As a rule, the farther north and east a visitor goes in Maine, the fewer the fine sand beaches.

Pemaquid Beach, Bristol. Small, crescent-shaped, sand beach 1,500 feet long. Dunes. Snowball Hill Road.

Thomas Point, Brunswick. Back bay swimming area has privately run beach about 1,000 feet long on Meadow Road. Picnic and play areas. Facilities, fee for parking.

Half-Mile Beach, Georgetown. Open sand barrier spit with salt marsh on Seguinland Road. Fine sand beach nearly 2,000 feet long.

Mile Beach, Georgetown. Dunes and marsh back up this coarse sand beach just shy of a mile long. Rocky areas. Located on Seguinland Road.

Lincolnville Beach, Lincolnville. Half-mile long sand and gravel beach near Ducktrap on Route 1. Scant parking. No facilities.

Crescent Beach, Owls Head. Favorite beach near Rockland on Crescent Point Road. 3,000 feet long. Facilities nearby. Parking not great.

Head Beach, Phippsburg. Crescent-shaped, fine sand beach 1,000 feet long. Parking with fee at nearby campground. On Small Point Road.

Birch Point, Owls Head. Small pocket beach between rocky headlands. Scant parking. Accessed via a dirt track off Ballyhac Road.

Sandy Point, Stockton Springs. Gravel and sand beach and nature area off US 1. About a mile long. No facilities, limited parking.

■ Wildlife Refuges

Todd Wildlife Sanctuary, Bremen. Sanctuary is operated on Hogg and Bremen Long Islands in Muscongus Bay by the Audubon Society as part of their continuing education programs. Boat access only. ☎ 781-2330.

Josephine Newman Sanctuary, Georgetown. Trails and nature walks through woods and along the shore. Good views of Sheepscot Bay to the east. Off Route 127.

Pond Island National Wildlife Refuge, Popham Beach. Located about 16 miles northeast of Portland, this treeless, 10-acre island sports an automated lighthouse and fog signal. Water access only. Limited sheltered landing areas. Numerous nesting seabird colonies. ☎ 546-2124.

Armbrust Hill Wildlife Reservation, Vinalhaven. Small refuge near town behind the medical center. Site of abandoned quarries. Small pond, hiking trails, picnic area. Small parking area.

Osborn Finch Preserve, Waldoboro. A small, 11-acre preserve on the bank of the Medomak River. Parking on Dutch Neck Road off Route 32. Hiking trails lead to shore.

Seal Island National Wildlife Refuge, Penobscot Bay. Once used for Navy gunnery practice, this 65-acre treeless island 21 miles south of Rockland offers prime seabird nesting habitat. The island once harbored a large puffin colony, but it was killed off by hunters by the late 1800s. Administered by the US Fish and Wildlife Service. Tern, puffin and other seabird restoration project underway in cooperation with Maine Audubon and other agencies. Water access only. Shore access may be limited. ☎ 546-2124.

■ Natural Areas & Preserves

Damariscove Island, Boothbay. This 209-acre island is maintained by the Nature Conservancy. Located far offshore, it was once used as a base for fishermen in the late 1600s. Long narrow cleft in rock serves as rudimentary harbor. Caretakers present in season. Visitors must avoid seabird nesting areas. Contact the Conservancy office at 14 Maine Street, Brunswick 04011, for transportation details. ☎ 729-5181.

Ovens Mouth Preserve, Boothbay. 146-acre parcel overseen by the Boothbay Region Land Trust, which serve to protect scenic shoreline, quiet coves and a salt marsh. It has 1.6 miles of trails on the east peninsula and 3.1 miles on the west peninsula. Trails do not connect. On Dover Cross Road. Adequate parking. The trust also has several other smaller preserves (under 25 acres) in the Boothbay Region. ☎ 633-4812.

> A map to all area preserves is available by mail from the Boothbay Regional Land Trust office at PO Box 183, Boothbay Harbor 04538.

Mid-Coast

Linekin Preserve, East Boothbay. 100-acre area that stretches from Route 96 to the Damariscotta River. It has 2.35 miles of hiking trails and 650 feet of shore frontage. Some parking. ☎ 633-4812.

Hockomock Nature Trail, Bremen. Self-guided nature tour along shore, through woods and fields. Operated by the Audubon Society. Free parking are nearby Audubon camp. Located at end of Keene Neck Road off Route 32. ☎ 781-2330.

La Verna, Bristol. Rocky shoreline and long gravel beach are the prime features of this 119-acre Nature Conservancy preserve. Dense forest along with freshwater marsh bordering Muscongus Bay not far from Pemaquid Lighthouse. Water access only. Contact the Conservancy office at 14 Maine Street, Brunswick 04011, for transportation details. ☎ 729-5181.

Witch Island Preserve, Bristol. Small, 18-acre wooded island with two beaches, a trail and ruins of a house. Easy quarter-mile paddle from South Bristol town landing. Owned by Audubon Society. ☎ 781-2330.

Fernald's Neck Preserve, Camden. 315-acre forested peninsula in Megunticook Lake just west of Camden. Nature Conservancy maintains large network of color-coded trails. Maps available at trailhead. View of Camden Hills. Conservancy office at 14 Maine Street, Brunswick 04011. ☎ 729-5181.

Merryspring Horticultural Nature Park, Camden. Located off Conway Road, this nature 66-acre preserve is a favorite for hiking and cross-country skiing. More than a dozen trails. Gazebo for picnics and lectures. Open year-round during daylight hours. ☎ 236-2239.

Salt Bay Farm, Damariscotta. Home of the Damariscotta River Association, which manages numerous preserves and island in the area. Office in house. Maps and brochures available. 90 acres of fields, woods and salt marsh with walking trails. On the Belvedere Road. ☎ 563-1393.

Nelson Nature Preserve, Friendship. Operated by Mid-Coast chapter of the Audubon Society, this marsh and wooded preserve sports just under four miles of hiking trails. Off Route 97. Scant parking.

St. Clair Preserve, Northport. 250-acre Nature Conservancy preserve protecting most of the shoreline of pretty Knight's Pond. Ducktrap Mountain on south shore. Not far from US 1. Conservancy office at 14 Maine Street, Brunswick 04011. ☎ 729-5181.

Dodge Point, Newcastle. More than 500 acres of land with 8,000 feet of shoreline along the wide Damariscotta River make up this recent addition to Maine's Public Reserve Lands. No facilities. No overnight use. Many relatively easy trails criss-cross the property and offer access to the shore. Great place to spend half a day or so. Parking area off the River Road, just a few miles south of US 1.

Rachel Carson Salt Pond, New Harbor. Salt marsh, pond and tidal pool where famed environmental author Rachel Carson once came to study marine life. 78 acres are now protected by the Nature Conservancy. Along Route 32. Trail through fields and forest on mainland side of road lead to a pond where ice was once cut. Conservancy office at 14 Maine Street, Brunswick 04011. ☎ 729-5181.

Morse Mountain Preserve, Phippsburg. 600-acre preserve off Route 216. Park near main road and walk private road through salt marsh, woods to sandy beach and natural rock seawall.

Bradley Pond Preserve, Topsham. More than 160 acres of private land are open to the public, thanks to the generosity of the owners. More than two miles of nature trails wind through marshes, woods, fields and by a pond. Please stay on trails. Adequate parking off the Bradley Pond Road. Protected by the Brunswick-Topsham Land Trust. ☎ 729-7694.

Areys Neck Woods, Vinalhaven. Nice moderate hike through spruce woods along the shore, marsh. Scant parking at end of dirt road.

Big Garden Island Preserve, Vinalhaven. This 25-acre island was given to the Nature Conservancy in the late 1960s by Charles and Anne Morrow Lindbergh. Densely forested and accessible only by small craft. Conservancy office at 14 Maine Street, Brunswick 04011. ☎ 729-5181.

Lane's Island Preserve, Vinalhaven. 43-acre Nature Conservancy preserve on small island joined to Vinalhaven by a stone causeway. Rudimentary trails. Good ocean views. Conservancy office at 14 Maine Street, Brunswick 04011. ☎ 729-5181.

Meadow Mountain Preserve, Warren. 300-acre mountainside with swamp and frontage on Quiggle Brook. Scant parking. Dirt access road difficult to find. Take Upper Beachwood Street north off Route 90. Drive 1¼ miles and turn left on a dirt road. You'll reach the preserve after .75 miles.

Montsweag, Woolwich. Operated by the non-profit Chewonki Foundation, this preserve protects woods and ledgy shoreline along a tidal creek which runs into Montsweag Bay. Loop trail takes in highlights. Access by land or by canoe/kayak. RR 2, Box 1200, Wiscasset 04578. ☎ 882-7323.

Robert Tristam Coffin Wildflower Sanctuary, Woolwich. Operated by the New England Wildflower Society. 180-acre preserve off Route 128 with more than 200 species of trees, shrubs, flowers, and grasses. Trails follow shores of Merrymeeting Bay.

Mid-Coast

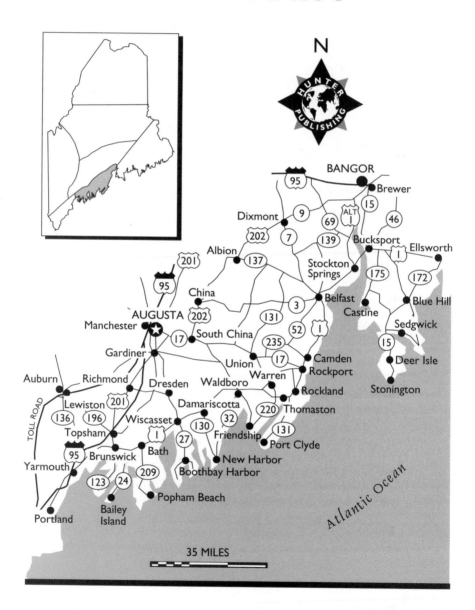

N

BANGOR
Brewer
95
15
Dixmont
9
69
ALT
1
46
202
7
139
Bucksport
Albion
137
Stockton
Springs
Ellsworth
1
201
175
172
95
China
Belfast
Blue Hill
AUGUSTA
202
3
Castine
Manchester
131
Sedgwick
17
South China
52
1
15
Gardiner
235
Camden
Deer Isle
Union
17
Rockport
Auburn
Richmond
Dresden
Waldboro
Warren
Rockland
Stonington
Lewiston
201
Damariscotta
220
Thomaston
136
196
Wiscasset
32
131
Topsham
130
27
Friendship
Port Clyde
95
Bath
1
Yarmouth
New Harbor
Brunswick
123
24
209
Boothbay Harbor
Popham Beach
Portland
Bailey
Island

Atlantic Ocean

TOLL ROAD

35 MILES

Sightseeing

■ Historic Sites/Museums

Alna

 Alna Center School House Museum (1795), Route 218. Second-oldest one-room school house in Maine. On the National Register of Historic Places. ☎ 586-6928.

Alna Historical Society, Old Alna Meeting House (1789), Route 218. 18th-century meeting house. Original box pews and hand-hewn pillars supporting balcony. On the National Register of Historic Places. ☎ 586-6928.

Old Head Tide Church (1838), off Route 194. ☎ 586-5643.

Bath

Maine Maritime Museum, 243 Washington Street. Institution dedicated to preserving and interpreting materials and implements relating to Maine's maritime heritage. Located on the Kennebec River. Nautical art galleries, exhibitions and exhibits, shipyard site, special events and children's program. Occasional river and coastal excursions. Open daily except Thanksgiving, Christmas, New Year's. ☎ 443-1316.

Belfast

Belfast Museum, 10 Market Street. Local area artifacts and displays. Includes paintings by Percy Sanborn. ☎ 338-2078.

Boothbay

Boothbay Railway Village, Route 27. Turn-of-the-century village containing historical exhibits, including the Thorndike (1870) and Freeport

(1911) railroad stations. Explore and see period buildings and rides on old steam trains. ☎ 633-4727 for hours.

Marine Resources Aquarium, located in W. Boothbay Harbor, is operated by the Maine Department of Marine Resources. A collection of regional fish and invertebrates can be seen within the rocky shore setting. Interactive displays include petting tanks for sharks and skates and seven touch tanks for many invertebrates. The Marine Resources Aquarium provides visitors with an exciting opportunity to learn about the ocean and the richness of life that it supports. Educational programs, presentations and tours of our research laboratory are offered daily. A picnic lunch can be enjoyed at the waterfront site that overlooks picturesque Boothbay Harbor. ☎ 633-9542 for hours.

Kenneth E. Stoddard Shell Museum, Hardwick Road and Route 27. ☎ 633-4828 for opening times.

Boothbay Region Historical Society, 70 Oak Street. Italianate house (1874), local historical artifacts, photographs, papers. ☎ 633-3462.

Bristol

Fort William Henry is a round stone tower situated on a point at the wide mouth of the Pemaquid River. Detailed archaeological excavations over the years have unearthed more than a dozen foundations of 17th- and 18th-century structures and the officers' quarters for Fort William Henry and Fort Frederick. A museum displays hundreds of artifacts found on the site, dating from prehistoric times through the Colonial period. Musket balls, coins, pottery, and early hardware are among items of interest. Good views of the surrounding countryside and ocean bays from the top of the fort. Guided tours during summer. Call for opening hours. ☎ 677-2423.

Brunswick

Bowdoin College Museum of Art, Upper Park Row, Walker Art Building, Bowdoin Campus. Housed in a Charles Follin McKim-designed building, constructed in the 1980s, the collection numbers over 12,000 objects and represents the art of ancient Assyria, Greece, Rome, Asia, Africa, Europe and America. ☎ 725-3275.

Curtis Memorial Library, 23 Pleasant Street. ☎ 725-5242.

First Parish Church (1846), Maine and Bath Road. Inspiration place for Harriet Beecher Stowe's *Death of Uncle Tom*. Pres. William Howard Taft, Henry Wadsworth Longfellow, John Masefield (Poet Laureate of England), Mrs. Franklin D. Roosevelt and Martin Luther King have spoken from the pulpit here. ☎ 729-7331.

Peary-MacMillan Arctic Museum, Hubbard Hall, Bowdoin Campus. Artifacts and equipment relating to Arctic explorations of Robert E. Peary and Donald B. MacMillan. ☎ 725-3416.

Pejepscot Historical Society Museum (1858), 159 Park Row. Local history of Brunswick, Topsham and Harpswell. ☎ 729-6606.

Joshua L. Chamberlain Museum, 226 Maine Street. Home of Joshua Chamberlain, former Governor of Maine, President of Bowdoin College, Civil War General and hero of Little Round Top. Artifacts of the Civil War. ☎ 729-6606.

Skolfield-Whittier House Museum (1858), owned by the Pejepscot Historical Society, 161 Park Row. Former home of a sea captain, the house contains items from his voyages to Europe and Asia. ☎ 729-6606.

Camden

Camden-Rockport Historical Society Conway Homestead (1770) – **Mary Meeker Cramer Museum**, US 1, Rockport. The Conway Homestead is an 18th-century furnished, restored farmhouse. The complex also includes a barn, blacksmith shop, Victorian privy and maple sugar shop. Guided tours are given in the house. Adjacent is the **Cramer Museum**, which has changing exhibits and local memorabilia. ☎ 236-2257.

Cushing

Cushing Historical Society Museum, Hathorn Point Road. ☎ 354-8262.

Olson House, Hathorn Point Road. Saltwater farmhouse (circa 1800) of Hathorn and Olson families, subjects of artist Andrew Wyeth. Most famous for being used as backdrop in painting *Christina's World*. Operated by the Farnsworth Museum in Rockland. Open daily Memorial Day through Columbus Day. Fee charged. ☎ 596-6457.

Damariscotta

Chapman Hall House (1754), Main Street. (No telephone.)

Dresden

Dresden Historical Society, Dresden Brick School House Museum (1816), Route 128. ☎ 737-2839.

Pownalborough Court House, Route 128. Oldest pre-Revolutionary Court House in Maine. Exhibits include judges' chambers, spinning room, tavern, Revolutionary cemetery.

Mid-Coast

Durham

Durham Historical Society, 15 Cyr Road. (No telephone.)

Edgecomb

Fort Edgecomb (1808-09), Fort Road, Davis Island. Quiet, scenic, historic site with shoreside family picnic area. ☎ 882-7777.

Friends of Fort Edgecomb, ☎ 882-7157.

Freeport

Freeport Historical Society, Harrington House Museum Store, 45 Main Street. Greek Revival transitional house. On the National Register of Historic Places. ☎ 865-0477.

Pettengill Farm (1810), Pettengill Road. Saltwater farm located on 140 acres. Location for educational programs about 19th-century rural life and natural history. ☎ 865-3170.

Friendship

Friendship Museum (1851), Route 220 and Martin's Point Road. Former schoolhouse. Local memorabilia, mostly marine related. Historical information on the history of the Friendship sloop. ☎ 832-4818.

Harpswell

Adm. Robert E. Peary Home, Eagle Island. Eagle Island State Historic Site, Casco Bay. Summer home of Admiral Robert E. Peary, discoverer of the North Pole. Boat access only, landing pier, nature trails. See *Parks* section, above, for more details. ☎ 693-6231.

Harpswell Historical Society, Old Meeting House (1757), Route 123. ☎ 721-8950.

Islesboro

Islesboro Historical Society, Main Road. Old Town Hall/School. Exhibits, programs and genealogical material. ☎ 734-6733.

Sailor's Memorial Museum and Lighthouse (1850), Grindle Point. Open Tues.-Sun., July through Labor Day. ☎ 734-2253.

Lincolnville

Lincolnville Historical Society Museum, US 1. ☎ 789-5445.

Monhegan Island

Monhegan Museum, 1 Lighthouse Hill. Housed in former lighthouse keeper's home. Collection includes exhibits on flora, fauna, marine life, and human history of island. Limited ferry access. ☎ 594-5646.

Newcastle

St. Patrick Roman Catholic Church (1808), Academy Hill Road. Oldest surviving Catholic church in New England. Revere bell. ☎ 563-3240.

Nobleboro

Nobleboro Historical Society, 198 Center Street. Old Route 1. 1818 school house restored for museum. Detailed records of early Nobleboro families. ☎ 563-5874.

Owls Head

Owls Head Transportation Museum, Route 73, Knox County Airport. Landmark, operating collection of World War I-era aircraft, automobiles, motorcycles, bicycles and carriages. Special events featuring a World War Airshow and rallies of classic autos, foreign autos, trucks, tractors, commercial vehicles and military vehicles most summer and fall weekends. Several aerobatic shows each summer. Regular antique vehicle auctions. ☎ 594-4418.

Pemaquid

Fishermen's Museum, Route 130, Pemaquid Point Lighthouse. Located in former lighthouse keeper's home. Artifacts connected with Maine's fishing industry. ☎ 677-2726.

Pemaquid Historical Society, 23 Old Harrington Road. (No telephone.)

Colonial Pemaquid State Historic Site (1600s), Fort William Henry (1692), off Route 130. Historic artifacts and maps exhibited inside the restored, round, cobblestone fort. Panoramic view at top.

Harrington Meeting House and Museum (1772), Old Harrington Road, Bristol.

Phippsburg

Fort Popham (1861), terminus of Route 209. Semi-circular stone fort begun just before Civil War, but never completed. ☎ 389-1335.

Mid-Coast

Phippsburg Historical Museum, Parker Head Road. 1859 one-room schoolhouse portraying life in Phippsburg from days of Indians through World War II. ☎ 442-7606.

Port Clyde

Marshall Point Lighthouse Museum, Port Clyde Harbor entrance. Located in a lighthouse, this museum displays memorabilia from area lighthouses. Open in summer season. ☎ 372-6450.

Pownal

Pownal Scenic and Historical Society, Minot Road. Drop by to make an appointment (no telephone).

Rockland

Farnsworth Art Museum, 352 Main Street. Permanent and changing exhibits of American art (18th-20th centuries) focusing on the role of Maine. ☎ 596-6457.

William A. Farnsworth Homestead (1850s), 21 Elm Street. Greek Revival home with original Victorian furnishings. National Register of Historic Places. ☎ 596-6457.

Shore Village Museum, Maine's Lighthouse Museum, 104 Limerock Street. Largest collection of lighthouse artifacts on display in US Marine exhibits. ☎ 594-0311.

The Wyeth Center, Union Street. In Summer 1998, the Board of Directors of the Farnsworth Museum opened this new gallery and study center devoted to the Maine-related works of Andrew Wyeth and other members of the Wyeth family. ☎ 596-6457.

Searsport

Penobscot Marine Museum, Church Street at US 1. Housed in eight historic buildings, the museum's collection of marine paintings, photographs, art and artifacts is one of the finest in the country. The **Stephen Phillips Memorial Library**, the museum's research center, open year-round, serves scholars and amateur historians of all ages. Rich stores of papers, photographs, ships' logs, nautical charts and genealogical information are among its diverse collections. The reading room features selected artwork from the museum's collections. Museum shop. ☎ 548-2529.

Searsport Historical Society, Main Street, US 1. ☎ 548-0245.

South Bristol

Old Walpole Meeting House (1772), South Bristol Road, Route 129. ☎ 563-5318.

Thompson Ice House (1826), Route 129, 12 miles South of Damariscotta. On the National Register of Historic Places. ☎ 644-8551.

Southport

Southport Historical Society/Hendricks Hill Museum, Route 27. ☎ 633-3942.

Tenants Harbor

S. O. J. School House, Port Clyde Road. ☎ 372-8012.

Thomaston

Knox Building (1789-1793), Lower Knox Street. Original farmhouse of the Gen. Henry Knox estate, later used as a railroad station. Currently restored as a meeting place and museum for collections of local memorabilia. ☎ 354-2295.

Montpelier, High Street, off US 1. Replica of original 1793 home built by General Henry Knox, US Secretary of War in George Washington's cabinet. ☎ 354-8062.

Union

Matthews Museum of Maine Heritage and "Hodge" One Room School, Fairgrounds. ☎ 785-3281.

Unity

Maine Tribal Museum, Unity College. ☎ 948-3131.

Vinalhaven

Vinalhaven Historical Society Museum, High Street. Exhibits highlighting island life and industries. Ferry access. ☎ 863-4410.

Waldoboro

Old German Church, Bremen Road, Route 32. Old German church and burying ground.

Waldoboro Historical Society Museum, Route 220 South. Open daily, June-Labor Day. (No telephone.)

West Southport

Southport Historical Association. ☎ 244-5856.

Wiscasset

Castle Tucker Museum (1807), Lee Street at High Street. Built by Judge Silas Lee in 1807; remodeled in 1858, when a distinctive portico was added. ☎ 882-7364.

Lincoln County Historical Association, Lincoln County Museum (1839) and Old Jail (1811), Federal Street. Early 19th-century prison houses artifacts of Lincoln County. ☎ 882-6817.

Musical Wonder House, Music Museum (1852), 18 High Street. World's finest museum of restored antique music boxes. ☎ 882-7163.

Nickels-Sortwell House (1807), corners of US 1 and Route 218. ☎ 882-6218.

Woolwich

Woolwich Historical Society and Museum, Nequasset Road. The 11 rooms of this circa 1810 farmstead feature antique quilts and old-fashioned clothing. ☎ 443-4833.

List Source-Maine Department of Tourism.

■ Lighthouses

Sequin Island Light. 55-foot stone tower established in 1795 and rebuilt in 1887. At mouth of Kennebec River. Boat access only. View from Popham Beach in Phippsburg.

Pond Island Light. 20-foot stone tower in center of island. Light established in 1821. Boat access only. Phippsburg.

Perkins Island Light. Octagonal wooden tower built in 1898. Boat access only. View from Parker Head Road in Phippsburg.

Squirrel Point Light. Octagonal wooden tower built in 1898 in Georgetown. No access. View from Parker Head Road in Phippsburg.

Doubling Point Light Range. 15-foot wooded octagonal tower built in 1898 on banks of Kennebec River in Arrowsic. No access.

Hendricks Head Light. Square stone 40-foot tower built in 1875. In Southport. Privately owned.

The Cuckholds, Boothbay Region. 50-foot wooden octagonal tower on stone base, which is part of the keeper's house. Boat access only. View from town dock, Newagen.

Ram Island Light. Small 30-foot stone and masonry tower once reached by long catwalk from shore of this offshore island. Boat access only. View from Route 96, Boothbay.

Burnt Island Light. Squat 26-foot tower on high point on offshore island in 1821. Boat access only. View from Spruce Point, Boothbay Harbor.

Pemaquid Light. Perhaps the most spectacular lighthouse in Maine. 32-foot stone tower erected in 1857 on striking granite finger. Easy road and foot access. On Route 130 in Bristol.

DON'T MISS

Franklin Light. Lonely 40-foot stone tower on island in Muscongus Bay. Erected in 1857. Boat access only.

Marshall Point Light. Built in 1858, this 25-foot granite tower is reached by a catwalk from the mainland. Good road access from Route 131 in St. George.

Tenants Harbor Light. Privately owned 26-foot stone tower on island. Light built in 1857.

Two Bush Island Light. Square masonry tower built on offshore island in 1897. Just off Tenants Harbor. Original keeper's house fell into the water and was used for target practice by the Green Berets. Boat access only.

Monhegan Island Light. 50-foot granite tower on island with year-round community 10 miles offshore. Built in 1850. Access by ferry or mailboat from Boothbay Harbor, Port Clyde or New Harbor. Light is on island's high point, about a 15-minute walk from the wharf. Keeper's house used as museum.

Whitehead Light. Granite 35-foot tower on island off St. George. Built in 1852. Boat access only.

Owls Head Light. 20-foot brick tower erected in 1825. On mainland on south side of Rockland Harbor. View from Lighthouse Road.

Monroe Island, Owls Head. Steel skeleton tower.

Matinicus Rock Light. Twin 50-foot towers on barren ledge five miles off Matinicus Island. Only one light in use. Built in 1857. Kept burning by teenage heroine Abbie Burgess when her father was trapped ashore by weather (see page 12). Boat access only. Ferry and mailboat service available to Matinicus from Rockland.

Lowell Rock Light, Rockport. 25-foot tower on island at entrance to harbor. Boat access only.

Mid-Coast

The Graves Light. 25-foot pedestal on barren, wave-tossed ledge. No access.

Curtis Island Light. Picturesque 26-foot stone tower on island at entrance to fabulous Camden Harbor. Boat access only. View from Bayview Street, Camden.

Grindel Point Light, Isleboro. 32-foot sloping tower built in 1874 on this offshore island with year-round community. Privately owned. Take ferry from Lincolnville Beach. View from Gilkey Harbor.

Fort Point Light. 28-foot stone tower on mainland in Searsport. Built in 1857. View from Fort Point Road, Stockton Springs.

Browns Head Light. 25-foot round brick tower built in 1857. On Fox Island Thorofare, Vinalhaven, offshore island with year-round community and ferry service from Rockland. Used by town as living quarters for town manager.

Goose Rock Lights. Distinctive spark-plug-shaped steel tower on masonry base in Northaven. Located on wave-tossed ledge. Access, view by boat.

Saddleback Ledge Light. 30-foot granite tower built in 1839. Boat access only. Vinalhaven.

Shopping

■ Antiques

Bailey Island

James and Nancy Glazer Antiques, Route 24. 18th- and 19th-century furniture and folk art. Good collections of smalls. Open by appointment in season. ☎ 833-6973.

Bath

Brick Store Antiques (Polly Thibodeau, proprietor), 143 Front Street. A wide range of country and Victorian decorative pieces large and small. Open daily, year-round. ☎ 443-2790.

Belfast

Kendrick's Collectibles (Al and Carol Kendrick), US 1. Specializing in formal and country furniture in cherry, walnut, pine, mahogany and oak.

Primitives, books, lamps. Open all year. Daily in summer, off-season by chance. ☎ 338-1356.

Boothbay

Sweet Woodruff Farm (Evelyn and Mel Shahan), Route 27. A 1767 barn filled with painted country and garden antiques. Open May-December. ☎ 633-6977.

Boothbay Harbor

Bay Street Antiques (Tom Cavanaugh), 2 Bay Street. Extraordinary art glass and pottery, fine art, lamps, furniture, rugs. American Indian, African and pre-Columbian artifacts. Open daily in-season. ☎ 633-3186.

Gleason Fine Art Inc. (Dennis and Martha Gleason), 7 Oak Street. Regional, contemporary and vintage paintins and sculpture. Open Tuesday-Saturday or by appointment. ☎ 633-6849.

Camden

Downshire House Ltd. (Alan Spanswick), 49 Bayview Street. Antique longcase clocks, wall regulators, telescopes and barometers as well as furniture. Monday-Saturday or by appointment. ☎ 236-9016.

Rufus Foshee Antiques, US 1. Specializing in English and American pottery and porcelain 1650-1880. Open daily. ☎ 236-2838.

Richards Antiques (Chad Richards), 93 Elm Street. Furniture and accessories for the discriminating collector. Lamps a specialty. Open in season. Appointment suggested. ☎ 236-2152.

Schueler Antiques, 10 High Street. American period and country furuniture, paintings, accessories, folk art, decoys. Open seasonally. ☎ 236-2770.

Suffolk Gallery (Marjorie Jones), 47 Bayview Street. Fine English silver, blue and white transfer ware, porcelains, Staffordshire figures, furniture, paintings and decorative accessories. Open daily or by appointment. ☎ 236-8868.

Cushing

The Barometer Shop, Pleasant Point Road. Barometers purchased, sold and repaired. Fine English and Chinese porcelains and paintings. By appointment. ☎ 354-8055.

Mid-Coast

Damariscotta

Arsenic and Old Lace Antiques (Shirley Frater), Main Street. Large selection of restored vintage linens, tablecloths, napkins, dresser scarves, pillowcases and hand towels. Clothing, china, silver and silverplate. Open year-round, Monday-Saturday. ☎ 563-1414.

The Ditty Box

Muriel Lewis, US 1. Country and period furniture, Staffordshire portrait figures, Currier and Ives lithographs, samplers. Open in season. ☎ 882-6618.

Patricia Anne Reed Fine Antiques, 148 Bristol Road. 18th- and 19th-century furniture and accessories, paintings, folk art, Americana, toys, rugs, architectural. Open daily in season. ☎ 563-5633.

Jefferson

Bunker Hill Antiques (Joanne and Erland Johnston), 18 Vose Road. Early painted country furniture and accessories, folk art, paintings, hooked rugs, French Jaspe pottery. Call ahead. ☎ 563-3167.

Lincolnville Beach

Mainely Antiques (Bev and John Black), US 1. Large selection of refinished country pine furniture, advertising items, ironware, tinware, baskets and primitives. Open year-round by chance or appointment. ☎ 236-6809.

Newcastle

Kaja Veilleux Antiques, Inc., Newcastle Square, Business Route 1. Large store filled with antique paintings, furniture, jewelry, clocks, etc. Hours vary with season. ☎ 563-1002.

Rockland

Bruce Gamage Jr., Antiques, 467 Main Street. large selection of American period furniture, paintings and rugs from local estates. Open all year by chance or appointment. ☎ 594-4963.

Rockport

Early Times Antiques (George Martens), Route 90. Select group of dealers with diverse offerings, including postcards, furniture, accessories and books. Open all year, Monday-Saturday. ☎ 236-3001.

Folklore Antiques (Raymond Cushing), Birch Street. Period and country furniture and accessories in original surfaces. Early ceramics, textiles, spatter, sponge and yellow-ware. Home shop, call ahead. ☎ 236-2735.

Antique Treasures (Sue Hopkins and Martha Martens), Route 90 in West Rockport. Group shop featuring wide variety of furniture and smalls, silver, china and books. Open daily year-round. ☎ 596-7650.

Searsport

Antiques at the Hillmans (Les and Alma Hillman), US 1. Fine china, furniture, lamps, and dolls. Specializing in old ivory china. Open daily in-season or by appointment. ☎ 548-6658.

Hart-Smith Antiques (Scott Smith), US 1. Country and formal American furniture, unusual accessories, paintings, folk art, frames, architecturals. Open in-season by appointment. ☎ 548-2412.

Primrose Farm Antiques (Liz Dominic), US 1. Shop and barn full of country antiques, fine glass, china, mochaware, Shaker smalls, folk art. Open in-season or by appointment. Hours vary. ☎ 548-6019.

Thomaston

Anchor Farm Antiques (Muriel Knutson), US 1. Silver, estate jewelry, china and tools. Open daily in season. Other times by appointment. ☎ 354-8859.

Ross Levett Antiques, 131 Main Street. Objects from ancient to modern times from America, Europe, Asia; Islamic items. Open Wednesday-Saturday or by appointment. ☎ 354-6227.

David Morey-American Antiques, 103 Main Street. Period and country American furniture of the 17th and 18th centuries. Fine accessories, glass, pottery, textiles and useful arts. Hours vary. ☎ 354-6033.

Wiscasset

Dianne Halpern Antiques, corner of Main and Pleasant Streets. Painted furniture, related accessories, toys, advertising items. Daily April-December or by appointment. ☎ 882-7725.

John Henry Antiques, 12 Summer Street. New England Country Furniture and accessories. Open year-round. ☎ 882-6420.

Priscilla Hutchinson Antiques, 62 Pleasant Street. Coach house filled with 18th- and 19th-century furniture, paintings, hooked rugs, weathervanes and folk art. Open most days in-season or by appointment. ☎ 882-4200.

Lilac Cottage (William Waters), US 1. American and English furniture, porcelains, metals and decorative items. Open Monday-Saturday, June-October. ☎ 882-7059.

Merndale Antiques (Marian and Bill Merner), US 1. 18th- and 19th-century American furniture, painted and refinished rope beds, quilts, folk art, Pris Mfg. Co. sleds and wagons and decorative items. Open daily, May-October. ☎ 882-9292.

Part of the Past (Peter Pardoe), Water Street. Early country furniture, folk art, toys, stools, Shaker smalls, metalware, prints, nautical, scientific and sporting items. Open daily. ☎ 882-7908.

Bill Quinn Antiques, corner of Main and Water Streets. Country painted furniture and accessories, folk art, garden, architectural items. Open year-round. ☎ 882-9097.

The Marston House (Sharon Mrozinski), corner of Main and Middle Streets. Painted country furniture, smalls, textiles, folk art, garden tools. Open daily. (Also a bed and breakfast.) ☎ 882-6010.

Margaret Ofslager, corner of Main and Summer Streets. Painted furniture and appropriate 19th century accessories. Call for hours. ☎ 882-6082.

Debra Schaffer, 50 Water Street. Selected samplers, silhouettes, watercolors, 18th- and 19th-century painted furniture. Open daily in season or by appointment. ☎ 882-8145.

Doris Stauble Antiques, corner of Main and Summer Streets. Country painted furniture, paintings, folk art, decoys and nautical items. Open all year. Appointment advisable. ☎ 882-5286.

Patricia Stauble Antiques and Associates, corner of Pleasant and Main Streets. American country painted furniture, 18th- and 19th-century art, early china, pottery, folk art, hooked rugs, quilts and children's items. Monday-Saturday in season or by appointment or chance. ☎ 882-6341.

James Welch Antiques, Main Street. Country furniture in original paint, folk art, country accessories. Open daily in-season. ☎ 529-5770.

Parker's of Wiscasset. Group shop on US 1. Open daily April-December. ☎ 882-5520. Parker's features the following dealers:

> **Different Drummer Antiques** (Judy Waner, ☎ 563-1836) – Country and formal furniture and accessories, toys to textiles, specializing in early lighting; **Jane Brown Antiques Unique**, ☎ 633-6956 – Early quilts, hooked rugs, sewing items, baby clothes, Victorian white clothes, other textiles, painted smalls and folk art; **Head Tide Antiques** (Helen Keating, ☎ 586-6214) – Country smalls, pewter, frass, copper, blue willow, iron-

stone, baskets, stoneware; **Meadowside Farm Antiquest** (Dick and Jane Pickering, ☎ 832-0538) – Country furniture, woodenware, baskets, china, flass, primitives and other decorative treasures; **New England Antiques** (Marion Redlon, ☎ 442-8000) – American country furniture in original paint and decoration, wicker, accessories, hooked rugs, quilts and fine linens; **Bette Zwicker,** ☎ 563-3897 – Country furniture, appropriate smalls, hooked rugs, spongeware, garden and early toys. French quimper and Christmas items a specialty.

Adventures On Foot

■ Hiking & Walking

 Bald Rock Mountain, Lincolnville. One of the less-traveled peaks of the Mid-Coast area, 1,100-foot Bald Rock Mountain offers great views of Penobscot Bay to the east and the rolling peaks of Camden Hills to the south. Park at the gate on the Ski Lodge Road off the Youngstown Road. Follow the dirt road 1.25 miles to the trailhead. The trail to the top of this mountain, which once had a ski area, is about a half-mile long and features switchbacks and several stone steps. It is a moderate, steady climb through attractive woods. There is a lean-to and a few small tent areas at the summit where overnight camping is permitted. Check first at Camden State Park headquarters, ☎ 236-3109. There is also a longer route to the top from US 1. No water along this trail.

Cathedral Woods, Monhegan Island. Although it is just under two miles long, Monhegan Island, which sits 10 miles out to sea, has nearly 20 miles of hiking trails that wind through deep spruce forest and along spectacular sea-facing cliffs. An almost endless number of loops and circuits can be mapped out. Difficulty ranges from easy to strenuous.

> **WISE WORDS:** *All trails are numbered and well marked, but watch out for false trails made by the island's many deer.*

The Cathedral Woods Trail begins near the east end of the Main Road and runs for a quarter-mile through virgin woods to emerge on the shore near Squeaker Cove. The woods are deep, dark, moist and have a primeval feel to them. Access is by ferry only. There are three seasonal inns on the island (**Island Inn,** ☎ 596-0371; **Monhegan House**, ☎ 594-7953;

The Trailing View, ☎ 596-0440) and one that's open all year (**Shining Sails**, ☎ 596-0041). No camping is permitted.

Mount Megunticook, Camden. The trail that traverses the wooded ridge of Mount Megunticook in Camden Hills State Park offers the best views of the entire surrounding area. The trail begins in the park's campground off US 1 in Camden. The path steeply ascends the east end of the mountain, rising 900 feet and crossing the tableland area at about 1,385 feet. After one mile it comes to the Ocean Lookout, which looks down on Penobscot Bay and nearby Mount Battie with its stone tower. You can make a loop by taking the Tablelands Trail down towards Mount Battie and turning left onto the Mount Battie Trail to return to the campground. Or, you can continue west, descending gradually to the Maiden Cliffs Loop Trail, which overlooks Megunticook Lake. It is nearly five miles from the campground to the Cliffs, so you may want to park a car on the Maiden Cliffs Trail parking area or plan on having a long day. There is no reliable water. Moderate to strenuous.

DON'T MISS   **Mount Battie, Camden**. Most people drive the auto road to the top of Mount Battie, with its stone tower overlooking Camden Harbor and Penobscot Bay. But some purists insist on hiking. Like Cadillac Mountain to the east in Acadia National Park, the reward of sweating it out to the top seems somehow diminished when you find idling recreational vehicles and crowds from tour buses at a summit.

The Mount Battie Trail leaves from the campground access road in Camden Hills State Park and roughly parallels the auto road to the col between Mount Battie and Mount Megunticook. At the intersection with the Tablelands Trail turn left, cross the auto road, and quickly reach the summit with its great views of the nearby mountains and countryside. Retrace your steps to return. The total distance is about 1.25 miles, one way. Elevation gain of 550 feet. Moderate to strenuous.

Rockland Breakwater. A walk on the massive stones that form this breakwater looks deceptively easy from the starting point off the Shore Access Road.

It is a long mile to the lighthouse on the end and the weather can change quickly. Still, if you don't mind slippery rocks and the occasional crevasse, you'll be rewarded with good views of the harbor as well as lobster boats, ferries and sailboats going about their business in Penobscot Bay. This is an excellent outing. Seals, porpoises and seabirds can also be observed. The breakwater, which is a popular fishing spot, was built in the late 1800s. Easy to moderate.

Watch out for freezing salt spray in winter, and if dark thunderclouds begin building in the west get back to shore immediately.

Sears Island, Searsport. Time was when the State of Maine wanted to turn this wild island in the upper reaches of Penobscot Bay into a world-class, deep-sea cargo port. Environmental concerns halted that effort. Now, the causeway from the mainland is used only by hikers and nature lovers. Park just over the causeway for the road reaching into the center of the island is gated. A rough five-mile loop skirts the shore of the entire island, making a large circuit. Views on the west side include a cargo port at Mack Point. From the southern tip you can see Isleboro; from the east side the village of Castine across the bay and nearby Cape Jellison are visible.

■ Golfing

Greens fees vary greatly according to the popularity of the course and the time of year.

Bath Country Club, Wiskeag Road, Bath. 6,216 yards, par 70, 18 holes. Season: April 15-November. ☎ 442-8411.

Sebasco Lodge, Shore Acres Golf Club, Route 217, Bath. 2,109/1,715 yards, par 33/31, 9 holes. Season: May 12-October 22. ☎ 389-1161.

Boothbay Region Country Club, Country Club Road, Boothbay. 3,125 yards, par 35, 9 holes. Season: May-October. ☎ 633-6085.

Country View Golf Club, Route 7, Brooks. 2,856 yards, par 36, 9 holes. Season: April-November. ☎ 722-3161.

Brunswick Golf Club, River Road, Brunswick. 6,300 yards, par 72, 18 holes. Season: April 1-November 15. ☎ 725-8224.

Northport Golf Club, 581 Bluff Road, Northport. 3,400 yards, par 36, 9 holes. Season: April-October. ☎ 338-2270.

Rockland Golf Club, Old Country Road, Rockland. 6,300 yards, par 70, 18 holes. Season: April 1-October 31. ☎ 594-9322.

Goose River Golf Club, Simonton Road, Rockport. 2,910/2,871 yards, par 36/35, 9 holes. Season: May-November. ☎ 236-8488.

Samoset Resort, 220 Warrenton Street, Rockport. 6,567 yards, par 70, 18 holes. Season: Mid-April through mid-November. ☎ 594-2511.

Wawenock Country Club, Route 129, Walpole. 5,680 yards, par 35, 9 holes. Season: May 1-November 15. ☎ 563-3938.

Adventures On Wheels

■ Mountain Biking

Camden Hills State Park, Camden. Located off US 1, this park protects the hills in a town which bills itself as being "Where the Mountains Meet the Sea." A 10-mile out-and-back run is possible on a snowmobile trail and summer bypass section that runs from the campground just off US 1 to the Youngston Road just off Route 173. It passes through attractive woods. You can combine your ride with hikes up the park's peaks, but bikes are not allowed on hiking trails. Bike route closed in mud season. ☎ 236-3109.

Camden Snow Bowl, off the Barnstown Road, Camden 04843. Several rides of varying difficulty are possible at this popular family ski area. Lots of single-track routes through woods and swamps in addition to ski trails. Intermediate skill level. No lift service but views from top of 1,300-foot Ragged Mountain are worth the pump. ☎ 236-3438.

Bike Rentals

Tidal Transit, PO Box 743
Boothbay Harbor 04538, ☎ 633-7140
Mountain bike rentals.

Fred's Bike Rentals, 53 Chestnut Street
Camden 04843, ☎ 236-6664
Full-service bicycle sales, repair and rental shop offering delivery to area hotels and inns. Tandem bikes a specialty.

Maine Sport Outfitters, US 1
Rockport 04856, ☎ 236-7120
Open year-round. Sales and rentals of biking equipment and accessories.

Birgfeld's Bike Shop, US 1
Searsport 04974, ☎ 548-2916
Mountain bike, trailer and car rack rentals. Open year-round.

■ Foliage/Motor Tours

Maine's coast offers days of driving tours to suit every traveler. Take your pick from waterfront vistas, seaside towns and winding country roads with spectacular scenery.

Foliage Trip – Windjammers & Water Views

126 miles, 3 hours, round trip,

Highlights: *Mid-Coast Maine is known for its unsurpassed shore dinners, historic lighthouses, quaint fishing villages, classic harbors and unique galleries and shops. In the fall, imagine all of this framed in a palette of autumn reds, oranges and golds, and finished off with a stroke of oceanic blue.*

Route: From **Wiscasset**, take US 1 north to Newcastle and into the shop-lined streets of **Damariscotta**. Take 130 south to the fishing village of **New Harbor** and the lighthouse and crashing surf at **Pemaquid Point**. In Pemaquid, visit the **Fishermen's Museum, Fort William Henry** and the **Colonial Pemaquid Restoration**. Take 32 north to Waldoboro, then 220 south to **Friendship**; go northeast on 97 and Upper Cross Road through Cushing to **Thomaston**. Drive down the **St. George Peninsula** to **Port Clyde**; pick up US 1 to **Rockland**, where the **Farnsworth** and **Wyeth museums** display the works of Andrew Wyeth and Winslow Homer. Continue east to **Camden**, a classic seacoast village complete with windjammers, old captains' houses, unique shops and fine restaurants. Go east to Lincolnville for dramatic foliage views of **Mt. Battie**. Take 173 west to Lincolnville Center, then south on 235 to Hope; northwest on 105 to 131; then south on 105/131 through Appleton to 17 at Union. Continue on 17, then on 206 south, to **Jefferson**, then southwest on 213 to 215. Take 215 northwest, then 194 northwest to **Head Tide** and its picturesque white-steepled church. Cross the river and go south on 218 through the rolling hills of Sheepscot back into Wiscasset.

> 🌿**Foliage Hotline:** The Maine foliage hotline, in service each fall, offers the latest color-peaking information for leaf-peepers. ☎ 800-932-3419.

Route courtesy Maine Department of Conservation.

Mount Battie Auto Road

The toll road to the top of Mount Battie in **Camden Hills State Park** is one of the few places in Maine where you can drive a short distance and be on top of a superb lookout with great views of land and sea. The road heads west from the park entrance on US 1 just north of the downtown. It is only 1½ miles to the parking area at the summit. A stone tower here is an interesting landmark. Below lies the peaceful village and harbor. Megunticook Lake is to the southwest. All the islands of Penobscot Bay lay to the east with the rounded hills of Mount Desert Island and Acadia National Park easily visible on clear days. On some foggy days you can

Mid-Coast

get above the mist and observe the spectacle of hilltops floating on a white sea like isolated islands. Not open in winter.

Country roads and quiet villages, such as Appleton, shown here,
characterize the inland regions of the Mid-Coast.
Photo by David Grima

Routes 131/235

Approx. 20 miles, 45 minutes

Route 3 at Belmont Corner to US 1 in Waldoboro

Higlights: *Seldom travelled by people zipping by on the main drags, the north-south trip afforded by State Routes 131/235 is one of the picturesque in the state. This is the quintessential driver's road – winding, hilly, views of lakes and far hills, with the occasional farm tractor moving at three miles per hour in your lane thrown in to make it interesting. It is almost like these roads were designed with two-seater sport scars in mind. Both these roads have been repaved in recent years, so you don't have near as many potholes and frost heaves as nearby routes.*

Route: At Belmont Corner turn south off Route 3 onto Route 131 and plunge quickly through wooded countryside of old farms. The road snakes through Searsmont, past a lumber mill and over a small bridge over the upper reaches of the St. George River. 131 follows the side of a major ridge with good views of the river valley and occasional lakes to the east. Slow down for the tiny village of Appleton. Leave 131 where it joins

Route 17. Proceed east (left) on 17 a short ways and go right on Route 235. Pass the village green in Union and check out the state boat launch area and picnic ground at Seven Tree Pond. Watch for the hard right turn as the road leaves the pond and heads in a more westerly direction. It continues through wooded and open rural country before meeting coastal US 1 in Waldoboro. Take a right and just a mile or so down Route 1 stop at the infamous Moody's Diner, home of good food and a fine roadhouse tradition.

Route 220 (3 to 1)

Approximately 20 miles, 45 minutes

Route: Another good back road with a north/south slant is Route 220, where it runs between Route 3 and Route 1. It traverses similar country to 131/235, although the views and scenery are different. Take a little side trip in the quiet village of **Liberty** to visit the **Old Tool Barn**, crammed with tens of thousands of antique hand tools and metal implements.

There is another interesting antique store and junk barn in the tiny village of **Washington** just down the road. Detour a little west from the village on Route 105 to picnic on the shore of **Washington Pond**, or continue south through local landmarks such as **Stickney Corner, Bogues Corner, Davis Corner** and **Feyler's Corner** before hitting Route 1 in **Waldoboro**. Most likely none of those folks still live on those corners, but it's fun to make note of them as you pass by.

River Road Newcastle to Boothbay

15 miles, 30 minutes

Highlights: *While there is only one way to get to most places in Maine, there is a back way to get to the bustling tourist town of* **Boothbay Harbor**. *Route 27, just east of Wiscasset is the obvious choice, but for folks coming from the east the sneak route begins in* **Newcastle**, *just over the river from its overshadowing sister Damariscotta.*

Route: Simply known as the **River Road**, this route follows the **Damariscotta River** south, although to call it a river at this stage is somewhat of a misnomer. It is really a long, narrow, tidal salt water bay. The road is characterized by its narrow width and its lack of shoulders. It is mostly forested with the occasional historic farm or old sea captain's house. Not far from Newcastle you'll pass the **Dodge Point Preserve**, with its many hiking and ski trails and thousands of feet of natural shoreline. The parking areas are well marked. Ten miles from your start you'll hit Route 27 anyway. A left will take you into the picturesque harbor. Stay on Route 27 for a round trip to **Southport Island** and the many water views it offers. A left on Route 96 just before entering the village will take

Mid-Coast

you out to **Linekin Neck**. The public boat launching ramp at the tip of the peninsula is a great oceanside place to "sneak" a picnic.

Route 130 Damariscotta to Pemaquid

18 miles, 45 minutes

Highlights: *This trip is short on distance but long on scenery.*

From Main Street in **Damariscotta** (Route 1B) go south on Route 130. The turn is right next to Seacoast Texaco, one of the best garages in the Mid-Coast.

Route 130 roughly parallels the east side of the **Damariscotta River** for a few miles before cutting east toward **Bristol**. Pass through this quiet village and head another seven or eight miles to **New Harbor**. Here you will find **Pemaquid Beach State Park**, which offers good saltwater swimming with minimal wave action. **Fort William Henry** is also nearby. A short detour to the east on Route 32 takes you to the **Rachel Carson Salt Pond Preserve**.

From New Harbor, **Pemaquid Point**, inarguably the most spectacularly situated lighthouse in Maine, is another three miles ahead. There's also a fishermen's museum here.

131 Thomaston to Port Clyde

15 miles, 30 minutes

Highlights: *Often overlooked by those in a hurry, State Route 131 from Thomaston to Port Clyde (once named Herring Gut) is a fun road trip.*

You begin off US 1 where the historic **Henry Knox Mansion** sits (now upstaged by the giant cement plant behind it). Route 131 is a winding narrow road that seems more the type that inspired the old Maine expression "you can't get there from here." Don't worry, you'll do just fine. About six miles from the start the road begins a series of twists and turns as it starts to wind from one side of the narrow peninsula to the other. **Tenants Harbor** is a busy fishing village with numerous lobster boats. Next comes **Martinsville** and finally **Port Clyde**. This is where passenger ferries can be taken to **Monhegan**. Long-term parking rates are not bad – about $4 per day. Be sure to pop into the **Port Clyde General Store**. It's been around for more than 100 years and you'll find just about anything you can imagine inside.

■ Riding the Rails

Maine Coast Railroad, Water Street, Wiscasset 04578. Railtrips of up to two hours along the coast are offered by this firm. It uses the freight line between Portland and Rockland to take passengers along the tidal flats, over steel truss bridges, along rivers and through the scenic forested flatlands in vintage passenger cars. Trips run from the waterfront in Wiscasset to Newcastle next to Damariscotta. Picnic tables at stations. Beverage service, light lunch and snacks are available on the trains. Family rates. Trains run daily in season and on weekends in early June and late September. Foliage trips are especially popular. ☎ 882-8000.

Belfast and Moosehead Lake Railroad, Belfast. The Belfast and Moosehead Railroad was originally conceived as a way to link the booming Northwoods gateway community of Greenville, at the southern end of massive Moosehead Lake, with the coast at Belfast. Financial problems beset the line and it was never completed farther than Burnham Junction, where it interchanged with the Maine Central just north of Waterville. The stubborn line never really died, although it fell on hard times by the latter half of the 20th century.

Luckily for rail fans the Belfast and Moosehead Lake Railroad does a bustling excursion business throughout the tourist season and well into the fall.

A steam engine on the Belfast and Moosehead Lake Railroad.
Photo by Jennifer Thorburn

The B&MLRR offers many combinations of trips, including excursions on fine passenger coaches and open cars pulled by a working Swedish steam locomotive and others in cars pulled by a trusty diesel.

The tracks wind through attractive countryside, by lakes and along the Pasagasawamkeag (say that five times real fast; the locals call it the "Passy" for short) River, see Belfast Harbor and endure a mock train robbery conducted by a bunch of good-natured desperados.

The train is an especially good way to take in the foliage and the crowds are smaller in the autumn; especially mid-week.

The B&MLRR also offers package deals that include an ocean trip on the *Chippewa*, a stately steamship replica, as well as dinner and overnight lodging deals.

Together with the Belfast Comfort Inn, the B&MLRR offers overnight packages, including Rail/Sail tickets, lunch aboard the train, and an overnight stay with a deluxe continental breakfast. Package prices ($169 in season) are based on two adults. Custom packages are also available with options like lobster dinners and additional nights at the hotel. The Belfast Comfort Inn is a new hotel complete with an indoor swimming pool, hot tub, and a beautiful view of Penobscot Bay. Prices vary according to the season.

Trains carry First Class Cars, Coach Cars, Swedish Dining Cars, and Open Air Cars. Gift shops located at both stations feature railroading memorabilia and other local treasures. The Maskers Theater is located at the Belfast Station for an extra evening activity. Inquire about schedules.

Trips leave several times daily from downtown Belfast and from the line's headquarters at Unity Station inland. ☎ 948-5500.

Adventures On Water

■ Windjammer Cruises

 Aside from staying in a logging camp or an old sea captain's house which has been converted into an inn, the only real way to physically return to Maine's past for more than an hour or so is to book yourself onto a Maine Windjammer for a cruise along the coast.

History, lore, old-time sailing skills, and outdoor adventure await those who step aboard one of these majestic vessels. Not only will they transport you to another time, they will surely sail you away from all your work-a-day woes and worries. Some vessels are veterans of the coast trade, and are over 100 years old. Others are skillfully handcrafted reproductions. Most people can't tell the difference. All of the windjammers meet strict safety standards and are Coast Guard approved.

Most windjammers offer cruises ranging from three days to a week; some have overnight trips and day sails. The ships take varying courses, depending on the weather, events planned in Downeast harbors and, of course, the whim of the skipper. Most cruises leave from Camden,

Rockland and Rockport. The sailing season extends from Memorial Day to Columbus Day, and numerous special events are scheduled throughout the summer.

Six-day cruises promise total immersion in the restful routine of shipboard life, varied ports of call, and a night of all the lobster you can eat. Three-day getaways mix seafaring adventure with the majestic beauty and serenity of the Maine coast. The usual schedule calls for several hours of sailing each day, followed by a stop at a remote island or quaint harbor where the vessels will anchor for the night. Passengers can go ashore and explore, sail a small boat, swim, or just relax on board. Cruise prices range from $350-$765, including three hearty meals each day, all accommodations, activities and parking.

You can do as much or as little as you wish on a windjammer vacation. Most folks like to take a turn at the helm, assist with hauling the sheets and lines (by the end of the trip you'll know one from the other) and help keep things spit-and-polished. Berths are plain, but comfortable, and the fresh, home-cooked food is out of this world.

Opportunities for wildlife watching are numerous; you might see seals, puffins, eagles, ospreys, and even an occasional whale. You'll also have great views of many historic lighthouses. Be sure to bring along your binoculars.

Finding Your Sea Legs

Seasickness is seldom a problem on the windjammer cruises, due to the easy motion of the vessels and the protected waters they cruise. Still, if you're prone to seasickness you might want to obtain prescription medication from your doctor in case you feel queasy; although usually just staying on deck, keeping busy, and keeping your eyes on the horizon will help you feel better.

The **Maine Windjammer Association**, with 13 member vessels, represents the largest fleet of merchant ships operating under sail in America. More than half of them are National Historic Landmarks and were built around the turn of the century, when these tall sailing ships were the primary method of transporting lumber and other cargo along the Northeast coast. These individually owned vessels have experienced captains and all ships are impeccably maintained. The oldest vessel in the fleet is the *Lewis R. French*, launched in 1871 at Christmas Cove, Maine. The 64-foot schooner carries 22 passengers. The *Victory Chimes*, at 132 feet, is the last three-masted schooner on the East Coast, and the largest passenger sailing vessel under the US flag. Built in 1900 in Bethel, Delaware, the ship carried lumber along the Chesapeake Bay. She now accommodates 40 passengers. The 92-foot schooner *American Eagle* carries 28 passengers. She was built in Gloucester, Massachusetts in 1930, and was a working member of the famed Gloucester fishing fleet for 53 years. All three of these vessels are designated National Historic Landmarks. Contact the association for a complete packet of brochures on all of their member vessels.

Maine Windjammer Association, PO Box 1144, Blue Hill, ME 04614. ☎ 800-807-WIND. Website www.sailmainecoast.com. Member vessels: *American Eagle, Angelique, Grace Bailey, Heritage, Isaac H. Evans, J. & E. Riggin, Lewis R. French, Mary Day, Mercantile, Nathaniel Bowditch, Stephen Taber Timberwind, Victory Chimes.*

A partial list of windjammers plying the Mid-Coast waters appears below, organized by port, and includes some vessels that are not members of the Maine Windjammer Association.

Windjammers, by Port

Camden

Angelique, Box 736, Camden 04843, ☎ 800-282-9989; E-mail sailypc@midcoast.com. Built 1980, 95 feet, 31 passengers. Captains Mike and Lynne McHenry.

Grace Bailey, Box 617, Camden 04843, ☎ 800-736-7981; E-mail mwc@midcoast.com. Built 1882, 81 feet, 29 passengers. Captains Ray and Ann Williamson.

Lewis R. French, Box 992, Camden 04843, ☎ 800-469-4635. Built 1871, 64 feet, 22 passengers. Captains Dan and Kathy Pease.

Mary Day, Box 798, Camden 04843, ☎ 800-992-2218. Built 1962, 90 feet, 29 passengers. Captains Barry King and Jen Martin. E-mail maryday@midcoast.com.

Mercantile, Box 617, Camden 04843, ☎ 800-736-7981; E-mail mwc@midcoast.com. Built 1916, 78 feet, 26 passengers. Captains Ray and Ann Williamson.

Roseway, Box 696, Camden 04843, ☎ 800-255-4449. Built 1925, 112 feet, 36 passengers. Captains George and Lesley Sloane.

Rockland

American Eagle, ☎ 800-648-4544; E-mail schooner@midcoast.com. Built 1930, 28 passangers. Captain John Foss.

J & E Riggin, Box 641, Rockland 04841, ☎ 800-869-0604; E-mail riggin@midcoast.com. Built 1927, 90 feet, 26 passengers. Captains Jan Finger and Ann Mahle.

Nathaniel Bowditch, Box 459, Warren 04864, ☎ 800-288-4098. Built 1922, 82 feet, 24 passengers. Captains Gib and Terry Philbrick.

Heritage, PO Box 482, Rockland 04841, ☎ 594-8007; E-mail schooner@midcoast.com. Built 1983, 94-foot schooner, 30 passengers. Captains Doug and linda Lee.

Isaac H. Evans, PO Box 482, Rockland 04841, ☎ 877-238-1325; E-mail evans@midcoast.com. Built 1886, 65-foot schooner, 20 passengers. Captain Brenda Walker.

The Stephen Taber, Windjammer Wharf, PO Box 1050, Rockland 04841, ☎ 800-999-7352 or 236-3250. Built 1871, 22 passengers. Captains Ken and Ellen Baines.

Victory Chimes, Box 1401, Rockland 04841, ☎ 800-745-5651; E-mail vchimes@sunline.net. Built 1900, 132 feet, 44 passengers. Captains Kip Files and Paul DeGaeta.

Flying Fish, RR 1, Box 670, Jefferson 04348, ☎ 549-3908. Built 1936, 45-foot schooner, six passengers.

Kathryn B., PO Box 133, Hope 04847, ☎ 800-500-6077, 763-4109. Built 1995, 80-foot, three-masted schooner, 12 passengers.

Schooner Yacht Wendameen, North End Shipyards, Rockland 04841, ☎ 594-1751. Built 1912, 67-foot schooner, 14 passengers, overnight trips.

Rockport

Timberwind, Box 643, Rockport 04856, ☎ 800-759-9250; www.schoonertimberwind.com. Built 1931, 70 feet, 20 passengers. Captain Rick Miles.

■ Whale Watching

A typical two- to four-hour whale-watching trip costs $25-$35 per person. Many operators offer money-back guarantees if no whales are seen.

Boothbay Whale Watch, PO Box 547, Boothbay Harbor 04538. Multiple trips daily aboard the vessel *Harbor Princess*. Leaves from Pier 6. Naturalist on board. Food and beverage service. If no whales are seen, your next trip is free. ☎ 633-3500.

■ Boat Trips, Charters

See pages 114 and 115 for costs.

Union

 Maine Outdoors Guide Service, PO Box 401, Union, Maine 04862. Active in the Maine Professional Guides Association, Master Maine Guide and licensed captain Don Kleiner has shared his knowledge of the woods and waters of the Mid-Coast area with hundreds of satisfied visitors.

His specialties are freshwater and saltwater fishing within a close radius of his base of operations just off Route 17. Half- and full-day trips are available. Stripers, bass, trout and perch are the usual fish of choice. Capt. Kleiner also specializes in introducing children to fishing and will supply all rods, reels, and bait. Price vary with length of trip and number in party. ☎ 785-4496.

Boothbay Harbor

Balmy Days Cruises, 62 Commercial Street, Boothbay Harbor 04538. Regular trips aboard the *Balmy Days II* and *Novelty* to sightsee in the harbor or travel to Monhegan Island way offshore. Another alternative: go at night to see moon, stars and flashing lighthouses. Supper and picnic cruises. *Bay Lady* Friendship sloop trips. ☎ 633-2284.

Boothbay Steamship Company, Fisherman's Wharf, Boothbay Harbor 04358. Sixty-foot steamship replica carrying 128 passengers. Tours of 1½ to three hours. Meals and snacks available. ☎ 633-2500.

Cabbage Island Clambakes, Pier 6, Boothbay Harbor 04538. Regular cruises several times daily in season aboard the 65-foot power vessel *Argo*. Up to 126 passengers. Adult tour price $8. Clambake cruise $37.50. ☎ 633-7200.

Cap'n Fish's Cruises, PO Box 660, Boothbay Harbor 04538. A variety of vessels offer puffin and whale watching cruises, seal and lighthouse trips as well as lobster trap hauling and sunset trips. Multiple trips daily leaving from Cap'n Fish's Motel dock. ☎ 633-3244.

Eastward, Pier 6, Boothbay Harbor 04538. Half- and full-day sailing trips with Captain Alec S. Duncan. This 32-foot Friendship sloop can take up to six passengers. Half-day rate is $25 per person. ☎ 633-3406.

Miss Boothbay, 5 Williams Street, Boothbay Harbor 04538. Hands-on lobster fishing trips aboard a working 33-foot Maine-built lobster boat with Captain Dan Stevens. Leaves from Pier 6. About 1½ hours. $10 for adults, less for children. 30 passengers maximum. Also available for charters. ☎ 633-6445.

Schooner *Appledore*. Four trips daily aboard authentic two-masted sailing vessel. Leaves from Fisherman's Wharf. Just sit back and relax, enjoy a cocktail or take a turn at the wheel of this 86-foot windjammer. ☎ 633-6598.

Midcoast Power Boat Rentals, Pier 8, Boothbay Harbor 04538. Outboard power boat rentals of vessels in the 19-22-foot range. Available by hour, half- or full day, or week. ☎ 633-4188.

Camden

Appledore, Lily Pond Drive, Camden 04843. A 65-foot schooner offers two-hour sailing trips in season. Children allowed, snacks and cocktails available. ☎ 236-8353.

Olad and *Northwind*, Box 432, Camden 04843. Classic sailing schooners offering two-hour tours in season. Children allowed, snacks available. ☎ 236-2323.

Penobscot Bay Cruises, 35 Pearl Street, Camden 04843. The 38-foot power vessel *Betselma* takes 30 passengers on one- and two-hour cruises along the coast. ☎ 236-2101.

Lively Lady Too, PO Box 127, Rangeley 04920. A 40-foot excursion vessel with room for 40 passengers. Two-hour cruises out of Camden. ☎ 236-6672.

Surprise, PO Box H, Camden 04843. This 57-foot schooner takes 18 passengers on two-hour sailing tours in season. Snacks available. ☎ 236-4687.

New Harbor

Hardy Boat Cruises, Monhegan Island Express, PO Box 326, New Harbor 04554. Offering a variety of ferry options to Monhegan as well as ocean safaris, puffin watches, seal watches, lighthouse cruises and private charters. ☎ 677-2026.

Nobleboro

Muscongus Bay Cruises. Private charter fleet offering trips ranging from deep-sea fishing to sailing to sightseeing. Vessels which can take from four to 34 people. Bareboat or captained. ☎ 529-4474.

Mid-Coast

Port Clyde

Monhegan Boat Line, PO Box 238, Port Clyde 04855. Ferry company (to Monhegan daily aboard *Laura B.*) also offers summer day trips aboard the motor vessel *Elizabeth Ann*. Charters for groups, families, special events. Fall foliage trips and dinner cruises. Leaves from wharf off Route 131. ☎ 372-8848.

Rockland

Bay Island Yacht Charters, 120 Tillson Avenue, Rockland 04841. Sailing school, day sailer rentals and bareboat charters. ☎ 596-7550.

Flying Fish, RR 1, Box 670, Jefferson 04348. Lobster dinner cruises, schooner sailing and sightseeing trips of four hours in season from Rockland. Meals available. ☎ 549-3908.

Midcoast Boat Rentals, Rockland Landings Marina, Rockland 04841. Powerboat rentals by hour, half- and full day, and longer. ☎ 594-7714.

Monhegan, Harbor Park, Rockland 04841; Capt. Ray Remick. Daily harbor tours with beverage service. Vessel is large enough to charter for weddings and functions. ☎ 596-5660.

Pauline, PO Box 1050, Rockland 04841. A 83-foot motor yacht offering multi-day cruises for up to 12 people. Leaves from Windjammer Wharf. ☎ 236-3520.

Sunshine, 274 Limerock Street, Rockland 04841. This 32-foot classic motor yacht can take six people on one-hour tours from the Public Landing. ☎ 596-0108.

Rockport

The Wooden Boat Company, PO Box 623, Rockport 04856. Six people can sail aboard the 40-foot classic yacht *Shantih II* for up to six hours. Children allowed, meals, snacks available. ☎ 236-8605.

Timberwind, PO Box 247, Rockport 04856. This 74-foot windjammer takes up to 25 passengers on four-hour tours in season. ☎ 236-0801.

Tenants Harbor

Goddess of the Sea Cruises, 107 Western Avenue, Waterville 04901. Sailing trips from small working harbor to see whales, dolphins and seals, Enjoy meals with fresh lobster, mussels or spend overnights aboard a sloop, schooner or on a small offshore island with private cabin. ☎ 888-724-5010.

Thomaston

Phantom, 4 Knox Street Landing, Thomaston 04861. A 22-foot classic runabout that can carry up to six people. One-hour tours, or available by charter. ☎ 354-0444.

Pride of Rockland, 4 Knox Street Landing, Thomaston 04861. This 30-foot Friendship sloop can take six on several-hour sailing cruises. ☎ 354-0444.

■ Deep-Sea Fishing

 PRICING: When the weather is rough a half-day of deep-sea fishing is plenty. That will set you back $25-35. A full day runs from $40 to $55. Most trips include rod, reels and bait. Beer, other beverages and snacks will cost extra. Deckhands will usually fillet your catch should you choose to keep it (be sure to tip for this service).

Bath

Kayla D., Clifford Road, Phippsburg 04530. Capt. David Dooley. Leaves waterfront park in Bath daily, June-September. Tackle provided. ☎ 443-3316.

Obsession, 4 Patricia Drive, Thopsham 04586. Capt. David Pecci. Leaves waterfront park in Bath daily, May-October. Tackle provided. ☎ 729-3997.

Boothbay Harbor

Bingo, PO Box 463, Boothbay Harbor 04538. Capt. Jeff Ritter. Leaves Tugboat Inn dock daily, April-October. Tackle provided. ☎ 633-3775.

Breakaway, Royall Road, Box 860B, East Boothbay 04544. Capt. Pete Ripley. Leaves daily from Fishermen's Wharf. June-September. Tackle provided. ☎ 633-6990.

Cap'n Fish's Cruises, PO Box 660, Boothbay Harbor 04538. Multiple Captains. Vessels *Buccaneer* and *Yellow Bird* leave daily from Pier 7, May-September. Tackle provided. ☎ 633-3244.

Charger Sport Fishing, Capt. George Warren. Leaves daily in season from the Tugboat Inn dock. Tackle provided. ☎ 882-9309.

Lucky Star II Charters, PO Box 161, Boothbay Harbor 04538. Capt. Matt Wilder. Leaves daily from Pier 8, June-September. Tackle provided. ☎ 633-4624.

Shark Five, 4 Puritan Road, Beverly, MA 01915, Capt. Barry Gibson. Leaves daily from Brown's Motel dock, June-October. Tackle provided. ☎ 633-3416.

North Edgecomb

Catch 22 Sport Fishing, RR 1, Box 3265, Union 04862. Capts. Bob Groess and Russell Troy. Leaves Eddy Marina on Sheepscot River daily (May-October). Tackle provided. ☎ 785-2408.

Small Point

Yankee Cruises, 42 Front Street, Bath 04530. Capt. Sewall Holbrook. Nature and bird-watching and sunset trips leave from Hermit Island Campground daily, mid-May through mid-September. Tackle provided. ☎ 389-1788.

Wilderness & Laughter

Wilderness Ways, 15 Knowlton Street, Camden 04843. Master guide and respected outdoor columnist Ken Bailey conducts custom half- or full-day trips for fishing or sightseeing on local lakes and ponds. Complete fishing and paddling gear provided. No charge for tall tales and humorous stories. ☎ 236-4243.

■ Places to Paddle

Damariscotta River

 The Damariscotta River, really more of a long, narrow, saltwater bay, offers semi-sheltered paddling all the way from downtown Damariscotta to East Boothbay and South Bristol. Lovely forests and graceful saltwater farms line the shores. On the western shore, about three miles south of the boat launch ramp in Damariscotta, is the **Dodge Point Preserve,** with its attractive sand and pebble beaches and its hiking trails. Just 10½ miles out is a campsite on **Fort Island**, which also boasts the remains of a small fortification. The best sheltered take-out on the south end of this trip is in South Bristol at the east end of "The Gut."

Watch the tidal currents throughout this area as they are strong enough to pull navigation buoys underwater at times.

Duckpuddle Pond, Waldoboro

Most of the ponds and streams in the Mid-Coast area were long ago developed, but Duckpuddle Pond and its outlet stream to Pemaquid Pond seem as remote as any in northern Maine. Access the pond where the outlet stream flows under the Duckpuddle Road. The 300-acre pond, with its lily pad-choked inlet and quiet shores, is to the north. The two-mile outlet steam – which flows south – is also worthy of exploration.

Megunticook Lake, Camden

Located literally in Camden's backyard, Megunticook Lake offers fun paddling from a variety of put-in locations. There are launch ramps on the north side on Route 52, on the south on Route 105 and at the north there is a hand-carry site on **Norton Pond**, which connects to the main lake. Although there are numerous camps and year-round homes on Megunticook, it still has a wilderness flair.

There are many small islands to explore as well as a large nature preserve in the center of the lake at **Fernald's Neck**. From almost any spot on the lake you'll have great views of Camden Hills and the spectacular Maiden Cliffs.

Orrs Island

The Orrs and Bailey islands and Harpswell areas are a sea kayaker's delight. There are numerous coves and ledges to explore along the narrow peninsulas which stick far out into the Atlantic. More than a dozen public boat launch ramps are available, providing sheltered paddling when the wind is coming from nearly any direction. **Basin Cove Falls** in Harpswell is a popular tidal reversing rapid popular with kayakers. Between Orrs and Bailey islands a unique causeway made up of interlaced granite blocks allows the strong tidal currents to ebb and flow. Kayakers also like to visit the numerous offshore islands, including **Eagle Island**, a preserve which protects the cliff-top home of polar explorer Adm. Robert Peary (see page 189).

St. George River

Once proposed for the site of a canal and freight railroad, the St. George River is now allowed to run free through bucolic rolling hills impeded only by the occasional abandoned dam. Trips of up to 30 miles are possible, depending on water levels. There is also a popular canoe race on the St. George each spring. The 21-mile section from **Woodman's Mills**, which begins on Route 173, contains a mixture of Class I and II rapids, flat water and an occasional portage around old dams or tricky channels through broken dams. A good place to take out is at the picnic area on Route 235 in Union at Seven Tree Pond.

Canoeing & Kayaking Outfitters

Overnight trips average $100-150 per person, per day. Half-day guided trips run in the vicinity of $50. Basic rentals cost between $25 and $45 per day. Most rentals include life jackets, paddles and car-topping gear.

Seaspray Kayaking, Bath, ☎ 888-349-7772. Trips on the New Meadows River. Guided trips, instruction, sunset and moonlight paddles, canoes and kayak sales.

Tidal Transit, PO Box 743, Boothbay Harbor 04538, ☎ 633-7140. Kayak rentals, kayak trips. Also mountain bike rentals.

Dragonworks, Inc., RR 1, Box 1186, Bowdoinham 04008, ☎ 666-8481. Kayak trips.

Ducktrap Sea Kayaking, US 1, Lincolnville Beach 04849 (Camden area). ☎ 236-8608. Kayak trips on Penobscot Bay for two hours or half-day. Sales and rentals.

Indian Island Kayak Co., 16 Mountain Street, Camden 04843, ☎ 236-4088. Kayak trips.

Lake Pemaquid Camping, PO Box 967, Egypt Road, Damariscotta 04543, ☎ 563-5202. Canoe rentals, kayak rentals. May 15-Columbus Day.

Duck Puddle Campground, PO Box 176, Duck Puddle Road, Nobleboro 04555, ☎ 563-5608. Canoe rentals. May 1-October 15.

H2Outfitters, PO Box 72, Orrs Island 04066, ☎ 833-5257. Exciting kayak instruction and adventures for beginners and advanced paddlers.

Outward Bound Hurricane Island, PO Box 429, Rockland 04841, ☎ 594-5548. Canoe trips, kayak trips.

Maine Sport Outfitters, US 1, PO Box 956, Rockport 04856, ☎ 236-8797. Canoe trips, kayak trips, canoe rentals. Memorial Day-Columbus Day.

Ocean Kayak, PO Box 375, US 1, Rockport 04856, ☎ 594-2428. Sit-on-top ocean kayaks for sale or for rent. Shuttle service to nearby Megunticook Lake or car-top gear available.

Canoe Me, 27 Knox Street, Thomaston 04861, ☎ 354-8975. Canoe trips on Allagash, St. John, Penobscot and Moose Rivers. May-October.

Maine Outdoors, RR 1, Box 3770, Union 04862, ☎ 785-4496. Custom canoe trips.

Sandy Shores Campground, RR 1, Box 754, South Pond, Warren 04864, ☎ 273-2073. Canoe rentals. Memorial Day-Labor Day.

Mt. Pleasant Canoe and Kayak, 650 Mount Pleasant Road, West Rockport 04865, ☎ 785-4309. Half- and full-day kayak trips, or canoe trips. Longer trips possible. Sunset trips on Megunticook Lake.

Chewonki Foundation, RR 2, Box 1200, Wiscasset 04578, ☎ 882-7323. Canoe trips, kayak trips, on the Allagash, St. John, St. Croix, and West Branch of the Penobscot. Sea kayak trips.

■ Parasailing

X-treme Water Sports, PO Box 990, Rockport 04856. Parasailing on Chickawauklie Lake off Route 17. Seasonal. ☎ 236-7272.

Adventures In the Air

■ Air Charter/Transport

Belfast

Ace Aviation, Belfast. Located at the Belfast Municipal Airport, Ace Aviation offers scenic flights and 24-hour charters in single and dual-engine light aircraft. Flights over islands of Penobscot Bay a specialty. ☎ 338-2970.

Appleton

Coastal Helicopter, Appleton. FAA certified chopper on floats operating out of the Belfast Airport. Sightseeing, surveying and aerial photos are specialties. Service to any location in Maine. ☎ 236-4774.

Rockland

Penobscot Air Service, Rockland. Operates fleet of small planes from the Knox County Regional Airport in Owl's Head. Operates charter flights for up to six people at a time to the offshore islands of Penobscot Bay. Available year-round, weather permitting. ☎ 596-6211.

Adventures On Snow

■ Downhill Skiing

Camden

 Camden Snow Bowl, PO Box 1207, Camden 04843. 950-foot vertical drop, 11 trails, 3 lifts, night skiing, 40% snowmaking, ski shop, rentals, lessons, cafeteria, lounge, toboggan shoot with annual championship, Nordic skiing nearby. The Snow Bowl is the closest ski mountain for tens of thousands of residents in the Mid-Coast area. Even with snowmaking, the influence of the comparatively warm Atlantic waters can make the slopes a slushy mess. Adult lift tickets: $28 weekend, $18 mid-week. To be sure, call for conditions. ☎ 236-3438.

■ Cross-Country Skiing

Camden

 Camden Snow Bowl Ski Area, Camden 04856. In Camden Hills State Park. Twenty miles of trails open to skiing, snowshoeing and snowmobiling. ☎ 236-0849, 236-3438.

Liberty

Lake St. George State Park, 30 miles of trails open to skiing and snowmobiling. ☎ 589-4255.

Lincolnville

Tanglewood 4H Camp, 10 miles of ski trails. ☎ 789-5868.

Newcastle

Dodge Point Preserve, River Road. Five miles of trails open to skiing and snowshoeing. ☎ 287-3061.

■ Snowmobiling

Spotty snow leaves Mid-Coast snowmobilers ready to rock and roll as soon as the white stuff hits. It may last only a day or two. There are no ITS trails in the region. However, there is a maze of local and club trails stretching from Camden to Augusta. Consult snowmobiling clubs in the *Appendix*.

Adventures On Horseback

Ledgewood Stables, Bradford Road, Wiscasset 04578. Trail rides through wooded areas. Suitable for all skill levels, both adults and children. Open daily in season. ☎ 882-6346.

Eco-Tours & Cultural Excursions

■ Farms

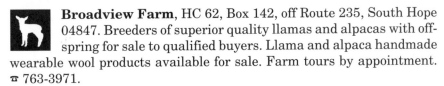

Broadview Farm, HC 62, Box 142, off Route 235, South Hope 04847. Breeders of superior quality llamas and alpacas with off-spring for sale to qualified buyers. Llama and alpaca handmade wearable wool products available for sale. Farm tours by appointment. ☎ 763-3971.

Kelmscott Farm, RR 2, Box 365, Lincolnville 04849. Working farm dedicated to breeding and preserving rare livestock, particularly sheep, but also pigs, cows, goats, horses and poultry. Open daily Memorial Day through Labor Day. Heirloom gardens, wagon rides, special events, farm shop and museum. Admission fee. ☎ 763-4088.

■ Apple Picking

Fall is the season for picking fresh apples right off the tree. Here are the pick-your-own farms in the Mid-Coast area. Fill up your basket!

Pick Your Own Apples

Damariscotta

■ **Biscay Orchards**, Biscay Road, ☎ 563-3026.

Dixmont

■ **Maine-ly Apples**, Route 7, ☎ 234-2043.

Hope

■ **Hardy Farms Apple Orchard**, Church St., ☎ 763-3262.

■ **The Apple Barn**, Route 105, ☎ 763-4080.

Jefferson

■ **Country Fair Farm**, Route 32, ☎ 549-5662.

Lincolnville

■ **Sewall Orchard**, Masalin Road, ☎ 763-3956.

Morrill

■ **Bear Well Orchard**, Higgins Road, ☎ 342-5471.

■ **Schartner's Farms**, Route 220, ☎ 568-3668.

■ Blueberry Picking

 Late July and early August is blueberry harvest season in Maine. From the flat windswept barrens of Washington County, to the rolling hillside fields in Hancock, Waldo and Knox Counties, rakers begin their seasonal labors.

 INTERESTING FACTS: *Recent studies have shown that blueberries have the highest concentration of cancer-fighting antioxidants of any fruit native to North America. Maine, which harvests millions of pounds of blueberries each year, produces 98% of the country's crop and about half of the amount produced in the world. Canadian maritime provinces produce the rest.*

While pints and quarts of fresh-raked berries are available at most stores and farmstands, there is nothing like picking them yourself. Commercial picking fields charge visitors a small fee, usually by the pint.

WISE WORDS: *If picking blueberries in the wild while hiking or camping, be sure to bring a sturdy container to take your wild bounty home. You'll be surprised at the size of your harvest.*

Pick Your Own Blueberries

Lincolnville

■ **Sewall Orchard**, Masalin Road. Open daily, Tuesday-Sunday. ☎ 763-3965.

Stockton Springs

■ **Staples Homestead**, County Road. Open daily in season. ☎ 567-3393.

Where to Stay & Eat

Rate Scale

All rates are for entrée or complete dinner, per person.

Inexpensive	under $10
Moderate	$10-$20
Expensive	More than $20

■ Favorite Restaurants

Belfast

Darby's Restaurant and Pub, 155 High Street, Belfast 04915. Casual affordable menu with fresh seafood, chicken, beef and vegetarian dishes. Fresh bread. Menu selection goes far afield to include Moroccan lamb and Pad Thai. Daily specials and great dessert selection. Cocktails and micro-brews. Open year-round, seven days a week, lunch and dinner. Inexpensive to moderate. ☎ 338-2339.

Young's Lobster Pound, Mitchell Avenue, Box 4, Belfast 04915. The best place to eat lobsters is right at the shore at Young's. Shore dinners, live and boiled lobsters and crabs, lobster and crab rolls and lobster and crab stew. Live lobsters can be packed for travel. Nothing fancy in this 250-seat establishment – and that's the way it should be when eating lobster. Open daily in season for lunch and dinner. Cocktails served. Moderate. ☎ 338-1160.

Camden

O'Neils, 21 Bayview Street, Camden 04843. From this establishment's wood-fired oven, rotisserie and grill comes a wide variety of menu items to tempt any palate. Selection includes lobsters, seafood, pasta, pizza, Caesar salad and great expresso. Cocktails. Open all year. Outside seating available. Moderate to expensive. ☎ 236-3272.

Peter Ott's, 12 Bayview Street, Camden 04843. Home of the best teriyaki steak this side of the Mississippi River. Casual atmosphere with elegant food. Black Angus beef, fresh local fish, pastas, lobsters, award-winning desserts and extensive wine list. Open all year, full cocktail service, wheelchair access. Moderate to expensive. ☎ 236-4032.

Boothbay

Chowder House Restaurant, 49 Townsend Avenue, Boothbay Harbor 04538. Located in an old granary at end of the scenic footbridge that crosses the inner harbor, this establishment offers hearty New England and Maine fare prepared in an open kitchen. Dine indoors or out. Cocktails and appetizers served outside at the Boat Bar, literally a small sailboat hauled up onto the dock and remodeled for service. Menu includes lobster, seafood, pasta, chicken, surf and turf, crab melts, sandwiches, salads. Cocktails served. Open daily in season for lunch and dinner. Moderate. ☎ 633-5761.

Lobsterman's Co-op, Atlantic Avenue, Boothbay Harbor 04538. Why not eliminate the middle man? The best way to eat lobsters, clams and crabs is to wade right in and make a big mess, and what better place than a working fishermen's pier. Also serving hot dogs, hamburgers, sandwiches and other fare. Tables outside on dock and inside when weather threatens. Open daily in season for lunch and dinner. Closes at 8:30 pm. Seafood also packed to travel. Inexpensive to moderate. ☎ 633-4900.

Rocktide Inn, 35 Atlantic Avenue, Boothbay Harbor 04538. Pick and choose from any of five different dining rooms in this waterfront hotel/restaurant. The Seadeck, Chart Room and Buoy Room are casual dining without reservations. The Dockside and Harborside require gentlemen to wear jackets and reservations are suggested. Large-scale train runs along the ceiling in one. Inn sports more than 100 ship models, including a seven-foot model of *Titanic*. Sit on the deck and watch the comings and goings in the harbor. Standard lobster, seafood and steaks and other fare such as prime rib and duckling; salad bar. Cocktail lounge. Moderate to expensive. ☎ 633-4455.

Rockland

Café Miranda, 15 Oak Street, Rockland 04841. A truly unique eatery for the coast of Maine. The menu changes daily at this intimate bistro where the kitchen sports a real brick oven, and the entrées range from fresh pasta to seafood to grilled and international dishes. Closed for two weeks at the end of April and another two weeks at the end of October. Cocktail service, microbrews. Outdoor dining in season. Inexpensive to moderate. ☎ 594-2034.

The Brown Bag, 606 Main Street, Rockland 04841. This bakery and sandwich shop is open daily year-round for breakfast and lunch. Delicious homemade foods, breads, cookies. Vegetarian as well as healthy selections for all. Fresh roasted turkey a specialty. Storefront dining room with some views of working harbor. Inexpensive. ☎ 596-6372.

Rockport

The Sail Loft, 1 Main Street, Rockport 04856. Extremely cozy dining room overlooking picturesque Rockport Harbor. Nearby dock, boatyard frame the view. Menu ranges from seasonal gourmet selections to standard coastal fare with lobsters, chowders, soups and prime rib leading the way. Open year-round (schedule varies). Moderate to expensive. ☎ 236-2330.

Waldoboro

Moody's Diner, US 1, Waldoboro 04572. You suspect something is up when you drive by this US 1 institution and notice the parking lot is full of pickups and police cars. Moody's serves good, old-fashioned diner food ranging from burgers and pot roast to breakfast and liver and onions with French fries. Open 24 hours a day, every day except Christmas Day. We'd say inexpensive, but the folks at Moody's would probably have us say "damn cheap." No need to call first; just come on down.

Wiscasset

Muddy Rudder Restaurant, US 1, Edgecomb 04556. Open daily 11 am until 11 pm, year-round, this full-service establishment offers one of the widest menu selections on the coast. Traditional Maine fare, lobsters, chowder, seafood, steaks. Children's menu. Cocktails. Turn right on the east shore of Sheepscot River after you cross the bridge. Good sunset views. Moderate. ☎ 882-7748.

Mid-Coast

Sarah's Café, US 1, Wiscasset Village 04556. Open daily for hearty breakfasts, lunches and dinner. Eclectic menu features diverse items, including lobster 12 different ways, Mexican, vegetarian, pizza and sandwiches as well as soup and bread buffet. Surprises for kids. Microbrews and wine served. Open year-round. Inexpensive to moderate. ☎ 882-7504.

▪ Brew Pubs/Breweries

Camden

Sea Dog Brewing Company, 43 Mechanic Street. Black Irish Winter Stout, Penobscot Maine Pilsner, Windjammer Blonde Ale, Owl's Head Light, Old East India Pale Ale, and nearly a dozen others. Lunch at the Sea Dog's dining room, located in a renovated mill that is bisected by the rushing Megunticook River, is an experience. The menu includes plenty of fresh Maine seafood as well as traditional pub fare. Alcohol-free beverages are available. This place is a favorite with locals and with workers from credit card giant MBNA, which occupies most of the mill complex. Call for tour times. ☎ 236-6863.

▪ B&Bs, Hotels & Motels

Price Scale
All rates are based on double occupancy.
Inexpensive . . . . Under $65
Moderate . . . . $66-$100
Expensive. . . . . Above $100

Belfast

Comfort Inn, US 1, Box 5290, Belfast 04915. Belfast's newest motel offers all the latest amenities and a great water view. All 52 rooms boast cable TV, phones with free local calls and fresh salt air. Facilities include indoor pool, hot tub, sauna, game room, and guest laundry. Microwaves and refrigerators in some rooms. Complimentary continental breakfast. Open year-round. Moderate. ☎ 338-2090.

Wonderview Cottages, RR 5, Box 5339, Belfast 04915. Cluster of 20 cottages spread among 10 acres on the shore of Penobscot Bay. Cottages have two or three bedrooms, complete kitchens, fireplaces and TV. Private beach. Open seasonally. Moderate to expensive. ☎ 338-1455.

Boothbay

Cap'n Fish's Motel, 63 Atlantic Avenue, Boothbay Harbor 04538. Smaller and less ostentatious than other harborfront motels. Not all rooms have water view. Nice sunset views. 53 rooms in the inexpensive to moderate price range. Air-conditioning, cable TV, many local cruises leave from pier. Handicapped access. ☎ 633-6605.

Tugboat Inn, 80 Commercial Street, Boothbay Harbor 04538. Right on the waterfront with its own marina, the Tugboat Inn is a quintessential lodging establishment for Boothbay Harbor. Short walk to village center. Spacious air-conditioned rooms, balconies, phones, cable TV. Boat trips leave from inn pier. 64 rooms open seasonally. Full-service restaurant and lounge. Moderate to expensive. ☎ 633-4434.

Camden

Norumbega, 61 High Street, Camden 04843. High Street in Camden offers six unique country inns to choose from, but Norumbega, also known as the "castle by the sea," is the flagship. This turreted stone mansion is set on wide lawns reaching to the bay. It boasts 12 rooms, all with private baths, and is open year-round. A full breakfast is served. Phones. Some rooms have fireplaces, some have TV. Rates are very expensive. If you have to ask, you probably shouldn't consider staying here. ☎ 236-4646.

The Black Horse Inn, US 1, Lincolnville (just north of Camden). This cross between traditional country inn and hotel features 21 elegantly furnished rooms, full-service restaurant and cocktail lounge. Romms have phones, TV, air-conditioning. The four suites have two-person jacuzzis, wet bars, refrigerators and come with a complimentary bottle of champagne. Open year-round. Wheelchair access. Moderate to expensive. ☎ 236-6800.

Monhegan

The Monhegan House, PO Box 345, Monhegan 04852. 100-year-old, three-story, wood-frame island inn with relaxed atmosphere. Great place from which to explore this remote yet beautiful offshore island. Sit on the front porch and watch very little of the world go by. 33 rooms, seven with private baths. Breakfast, lunch and dinner served. Café and bakery. Open in season. Access by ferry only. Moderate to expensive. ☎ 594-7983.

Mid-Coast

Phippsburg

Sebasco Harbor Estates, Route 217, Sebasco Estates 04565. A combination of old seaside resort and modern amenities. Nearly 100 guest accomodations spread out among dozens of buildings, cottages and duplexes. Four-story squat "Lighthouse" is among the most unique. Pool, tennis, golf, bowling and swimming make for fun on this 650-acre property. Restaurant on property. Open seasonally. Modified American Plan available. Lobster and sightseeing cruises aboard 38-foot *Ruth* leave from Estates' dock. Moderate to expensive. ☎ 389-1161.

Rockport

Strawberry Hill Motor Inn, US 1, Rockport 04856. 20 rooms overlooking Glen Cove off Penobscot Bay, although this establishment is not on the water. Private balconies, cable TV, outdoor heated pool, air-conditioned, continental breakfast, phones, no pets. Open year-round. Moderate to expensive. ☎ 594-5462.

The Samoset Resort, 220 Warrenton Street, Rockport 04856. 150 luxury rooms on sprawling grounds that include championship golf course and mile-long breakwater to Rockland Harbor Lighthouse. Indoor pool, sauna, hot-tub and health club. Restaurants, lounges, outdoor patio dining. Indoor tennis. Open year-round. Occupancy rate is so high be sure to reserve early. Moderate to expensive. ☎ 594-2511.

Rockland

Captain Lindsey House Inn, 5 Lindsey Street, Rockland 04841. Nine nicely appointed rooms with private baths in the harbor district. Open year-round and serving breakfast and dinner. Phones, TV, some water views, fireside cordials. Adjaceant to Waterworks Restaurant and Pub. Moderate to expensive. ☎ 596-7950.

Searsport

Captain A.V. Nickels Inn, 127 East Atlantic Coast Highway (US 1), Searsport 04974. Eat your heart out Bob Newhart. This is an inn to remember in the classic sense. Listed on the National Register of Historic Places, it boasts rooms furnished with antiques, great breakfasts, formal gardens and a ballroom that has been the setting for many weddings. Open year-round. Moderate to expensive. ☎ 800-343-5001.

Vinalhaven

The Tidewater Motel, PO Box 546, Vinalhaven Island 04863. This fairly modern motel perched right on the water's edge bills itself as the island's largest motel. No dispute, however, since it is the island's only motel. 11 rooms are open year-round. Televisions, phone. Moderate. ☎ 863-4618.

Wiscasset

Edgecomb Inn, US 1, Wiscasset 04556. A combination of 40 traditional motel rooms, efficiencies and cottages on the east shore of Sheepscot River overlooking village of Wiscasset. Phones, cable TV, restaurant on premises, continental breakfast, tennis, guest laundry. Nice sunset views. Open year-round. Walking trail to nearby Fort Edgecomb. Moderate. ☎ 882-6343.

■ Camping

Facilities indicated as "nearby" are located within one mile of the campground.

Appleton

Sennebec Lake Campground, PO Box 602, Appleton 04862. 65 sites, tenting area, 30 amp, sewer, dump station, store, laundry, rec hall, swimming, boating, fishing, group area. Pets allowed. Open May 15-October 15. ☎ 785-4250.

Belfast

Moorings Ocean Campground, RR 5, Box 5334, Belfast 04915. An oceanfront campground with a million-dollar view of the water. 39 sites, tenting area, 30 amp, dump station, store, laundry, rec hall, swimming, boating, fishing, group area. Pets allowed. Open May 1-October 20. ☎ 338-6860.

Boothbay

Camper's Cove Campground, PO Box 136, Boothbay 04537. Prettiest little campground on the coast of Maine. Clean and quiet. Camp at the water's edge. Everything from tents to big rigs welcome. Nature at its best. 56 sites, tenting area, 30 amp, sewer, dump station, swimming, boating, fishing, group area. Pets allowed. Open May 15-October 15. ☎ 633-5013.

Little Ponderosa, RR 1, Box 915, Boothbay 04537. A private unspoiled campground with a national park flavor. 96 sites, tenting area, 30 amp, sewer, dump station, store, laundry, rec hall, swimming, boating, fishing, group area, LP gas. Pets allowed. Open May 15-October 15. ☎ 633-2700.

Shore Hills Campground, RR 1, Box 448, Boothbay 04537. "No rig too big." 150 open, wooded or waterfront sites, 30-50 amp, cable TV. Also welcome small RV's, pop-ups and tents. 150 sites, tenting area, 50 amp, sewer, dump station, store, laundry, rec hall, swimming, boating, fishing, group area, LP gas. Pets allowed. Open May 1-Columbus Day. ☎ 633-4782.

Brunswick

Thomas Point Beach, 29 Meadow Road, Brunswick 04011. Beautiful 84-acre park located on Thomas Bay. Secluded pine grove campsites. Hot showers, snack bar, gift shop, arcade, playground and lifeguards. Special summer events throughout the season. 75 sites, tenting area, 15 amp, dump station, store, laundry, rec hall, swimming, fishing, group area. Boating and LP gas nearby. Open Memorial Day-August 24. ☎ 725-6009.

White's Beach and Campground, PO Box 696, Durham Road, Brunswick 04011. 45 sites, tenting area, dump station, swimming, group area. Pets allowed. Open May 15-October 15. ☎ 729-0415.

Damariscotta

Lake Pemaquid, PO Box 967, Damariscotta 04543. Waterfront sites, cabins and cottages on beautiful Pemaquid Lake. Jacuzzis, sauna, playgrounds, and tennis courts. 277 sites, tenting area, 30 amp, sewer, dump station, store, laundry, rec hall, swimming, boating, fishing, pool, on-site rentals, group area, LP gas. Pets allowed. Open May 15-Columbus Day. ☎ 563-5202.

Georgetown

Camp Seguin Ocean Camping, HC 33, Box 287, Georgetown 04548. Crashing surf, soaring osprey, rocky coastline – adjacent Reid State Park's sandy beach. Fishing, playground, hiking trails nearby. Private wooded sites, tent platforms, enforced quiet time. 30 sites, tenting area, 20 amp, dump station, store, rec hall, fishing. Swimming nearby. Pets allowed. Open Memorial Day-September 15. ☎ 371-2777.

Jefferson

Town Line Campsites, 483 East Pond Road, Jefferson 04348. A family tradition since 1960. Located on 14-mile-long Damariscotta Lake in Nobleboro. Old-fashioned camping in a heavenly place to relax. 55 sites, tenting area, 15 amp, dump station, store, laundry, rec hall, swimming, boating, fishing, on-site rentals, group area. Pets allowed. Open Memorial Day-Labor Day. ☎ 832-7055.

Lincolnville Beach

Old Massachusetts Homestead, PO Box 5, US 1, Lincolnville Beach 04849. Historic site abuts nature conservancy park with nature trail, access to lake. Ocean beaches, restaurants one mile away. A mature forest scented with fresh salt air. 68 sites, tenting area, 30 amp, sewer, dump station, store, laundry, rec hall, swimming, pool, on-site rentals, group area. Boating and fishing nearby. Pets allowed. Open May 1-November 1. ☎ 789-5135.

New Harbor

Sherwood Forest Campsite, PO Box 189 Pemaquid Trail, New Harbor 04554. 800 feet to Pemaquid Beach. Quiet, safe and patrolled. Sunday service at 9 am. 62 sites, tenting area, 30 amp, dump station, store, laundry, pool, rec hall, swimming. Boating, fishing and LP gas nearby. Pets allowed. Open May 15-October 1. ☎ 677-3642.

Newcastle

Sherman Lakeview Campground, One Campground Road, Newcastle 04553. Grassy, shaded sites offering a view of the lake. Excellent TV reception, nice meadows, privacy, walking paths, quilt shop on premises. 30 sites, tenting area, 30 amp, sewer, dump station, pool, on-site rentals, laundry. Store, swimming, boating, and fishing nearby. Pets allowed. Open Memorial Day-Columbus Day. ☎ 563-3239.

Nobleboro

Duck Puddle Campground, PO Box 176, Nobleboro 04555. Lakefront camping on seven-mile-long Pemaquid Lake. "Small enough to be friendly – large enough to accommodate you." 95 sites, tenting area, 30 amp, sewer, dump station, store, rec hall, swimming, boating, fishing, on-site rentals, group area, LP gas. Laundry nearby. Pets allowed. Open May 1-Columbus Day. ☎ 563-5608.

Northport

Northport Travel Park Campground, 14 Chelsea Lane, Northport 04849. Halfway up the Maine coast. Convenient for sightseeing coastal Maine. Easy access directly off US 1, six miles south of Belfast – 10 miles north of Camden. 77 sites, tenting area, 30 amp, sewer, dump station, store, laundry, rec hall, fishing, pool, LP gas. Pets allowed. Open May 15-October 15. ☎ 338-2077.

Mid-Coast

Orrs Island

Orrs Island Campground, RR 1, Box 650, Orrs Island 04066. Family camping on a 42-acre point of land reaching into Casco Bay and surrounded by a half-mile private beach and ocean breezes. 70 sites, tenting area, 30 amp, sewer, dump station, store, laundry, swimming, boating, fishing. Pets allowed. Open Memorial Day-September 15. ☎ 833-5595.

Phippsburg

Meadowbrook Camping, HC 31, Box 2280, Phippsburg 04562. The managers sometimes cook lobsters and clams for you. Close to ocean beaches. Heated pool, mini golf, large sites, nature trail. 100 sites, tenting area, 50 amp, dump station, store, laundry, rec hall, pool, LP gas. Pets allowed. Open May 1-October 15. ☎ 370-2267.

Popham Beach

Ocean View Park, Inc., PO Box 129 Popham Road, Popham Beach 04562. Campground, cottages, rental trailer on site on two miles of sandy beach. Beautiful views of ocean, islands, and lighthouses. Striped bass, bluefish, and mackerel fishing. 48 sites, tenting area, 15 amp, sewer, dump station, store, swimming, fishing, on-site rentals. Pets allowed. Open May 15-September 21. ☎ 389-2564.

Rockport

Megunticook By The Sea, PO Box 375, Rockport 04856. Enjoy outstanding facilities in a quiet, wooded setting on the ocean, just three miles south of Camden Harbor. 80 sites, tenting area, 30 amp, dump station, store, laundry, rec hall, swimming, boating, fishing, pool, on-site rentals, group area, LP gas nearby. Pets allowed. Open May 1-Columbus Day. ☎ 594-2428.

Searsmont

Aldus Shores Lakeside Campground, PO Box 38, Searsmont 04973. Family-oriented, fun-filled campground. Seasonals welcome. 150 sites, tenting area, 15 amp, dump station, store, laundry, rec hall, swimming, boating, fishing, on-site rentals, group area, LP gas nearby. Pets allowed. Open May15-September 15. ☎ 342-5618.

Searsport

Searsport Shores Camping, 216 West Main Street, Searsport 04974. Magnificent views of Penobscot Bay in a quiet atmosphere. Private ocean beach with easy access for swimming, beachcombing, lobster bakes, and fishing. Perfectly located for day trips. 100 sites, tenting area, 30 amp, dump station, store, laundry, rec hall, swimming, boating, fishing, on-site rentals, group area, LP gas, pets allowed. Open May 15-October 15. ☎ 548-6059.

Smallpoint

Hermit Island Campground, Hermit Island Road, Small Point 04562. Ocean camping on Maine's beautiful rockbound coast, for tents, tent trailers, and small pickup campers. Eight white sand beaches. 275 sites, tenting area, store, dryers, rec hall, swimming, boating, fishing. Pets allowed. Open May 15-Columbus Day. ☎ 443-2101.

South Thomaston

Lobster Buoy Campsites, 280 Waterman Beach Road, So. Thomaston 04858. Old-fashioned camping, no planned entertainment or game rooms. Oceanfront – easy access for kayaks and small boats. June and September are beautiful, quiet months. 40 sites, tenting area, 30 amp, dump station, store, swimming, boating, fishing, on-site rentals, group area. Pets allowed. Open May 15-October 15. ☎ 594-7546.

Southport

Gray Homestead Oceanfront Camping, HC 66, Box 334, Southport 04576. Beautiful, peaceful, small beach, tent and RV sites with clean bathhouse. Kayaker's paradise. Fishing off the point. Live or cooked lobsters for sale. Reasonable rates. Oceanview cottage and apartments. 40 sites, tenting area, 30 amp, sewer, dump station, laundry, swimming, boating, fishing, on-site rentals, group area. Store nearby. Pets allowed. Open May 1-Columbus Day. ☎ 633-4612.

Thomaston

Saltwater Farm Campground, PO Box 165, Thomaston 04861. A small, quiet, family-owned campground on the shores of the St. George. Serene beauty on the water, large grassy sites. Large rigs welcome. 35 sites, tenting area, 30 amp, sewer, dump station, store, laundry, rec hall, swimming, fishing, pool, on-site rentals, group area. Boating nearby. Pets allowed. Open May 15-October 15. ☎ 354-6735.

Union

Mic Mac Cove Family Campground, PO Box 545, Union 04862. 82 sites, tenting area, 30 amp, dump station, store, rec hall, swimming, boating, fishing, group area, LP gas. Pets allowed. Open April 24-October 4. ☎ 785-4100.

Warren

Loon's Cry Campground, 2559M Atlantic Highway, Warren 04864. L.L. Bean and Freeport with all the outlets close (one-hour drive) and Acadia National Park and Bar Harbor just two hours away. Kayak sales and rentals. 50 sites, tenting area, 30 amp, dump station, store, laundry, swimming, boating, fishing, group area, LP gas. Pets allowed. Open Memorial Day-Columbus Day. ☎ 273-2324.

Sandy Shores RV Park, 459 Sandy Shores Road, Warren 04864. An exceptional RV community designed for long-term camping and site ownership. Campers welcome on a limited number of the 25 sites. 50 amp electric service, sewer, laundry, rec hall, swimming, boating, fishing, pool. Pets allowed. Open May 1-October 31. ☎ 273-2073.

West Rockport

Robert's Roost, PO Box 170, Route 90, West Rockport 04865. Nestled in whispering pines, this campground offers a tranquil setting and a good base from which to explore the Camden-Rockport area. 50 sites, tenting area, 50 amp, sewer, dump station, laundry, rec hall, group area, LP gas. Pets allowed. Open May 1-November 15. ☎ 236-2498.

Wiscasset

Chewonki Campgrounds, PO Box 261, Wiscasset 04578. 47 clean, spacious sites on 50 acres overlooking a saltwater inlet. Full hook-ups, tennis, saltwater pools, fishing, nature trail. 47 sites, tenting area, 30 amp, sewer, dump station, store, rec hall, swimming, boating, fishing, pool, group area. Laundry nearby. Pets allowed. Open May 15-October 15. ☎ 882-7426.

Down East Family Camping, Gibbs Road, Wiscasset 04578. Family camping as it used to be. Sites spaced for privacy. Always a quiet night's sleep. Majestic pines surrounding lake with beach. Free hot showers. 43 sites, tenting area, 15 amp, rec hall, swimming, boating, fishing, group area. Pets allowed. Open June 12-September 12. ☎ 882-5431.

Down East Coast

DOWN EAST COAST

While many areas claim to represent "Down East" Maine, those in the know understand the real Down East does not begin until you cross over to the eastern side of the Penobscot River. The lofty suspension bridge that takes Routes 1 and 3 across the river at Bucksport is the true portal, although Ellsworth (a half-hour farther east) claims to be "The crossroads of Down East Maine." This is a place with wild, undeveloped forests, long, wide, and often shallow lakes strewn with massive boulders, rocky detritus from the glaciers that ruled the great ice age.

As Maine grew in the 1800s access to this region was primarily by schooner and later by steamship and then train. It is no wonder then that communities here developed around safe harbors or on rivers where rapids, falls or rocks stemmed inland progress.

Towns grew where paper mills sprang up. The Champion Paper Mill in Bucksport anchors the western side of this region, while on the eastern end another – the Georgia Pacific Paper Mill in Woodland – is the major employer.

The land in this part of Maine is very different. Much of it is sandy and characterized by blueberry barrens and gravel pits. The rest is mostly the opposite extreme – low and swampy. Still, two ancient granite ridge lines, their rise to the sky cut short by glaciers, are much in evidence on Mount Desert Island and in the Franklin area.

For most visitors interested in the outdoors, Acadia National Park on Mount Desert Island is the top destination. It has more than 50 miles of groomed gravel carriage roads, where motorized traffic is banned. Nearly 120 miles of hiking trails traverse seven major barren mountaintops. There is much to see and do here, and plenty of places to explore. The island's many lakes invite paddlers and swimmers of all skill levels. Pocket cobblestone beaches in hidden coves await discovery by those who wish to avoid the crowds at Sand Beach.

With thousands of motel rooms, a similar quantity of campsites, and plenty of private cottages and cabins to rent, Mount Desert Island easily accommodates the throngs of visitors, although traffic can get heavy in late July and in August. Towns surrounding Acadia brim with galleries and shops offering interesting wares from around the world. Bar Harbor alone boasts more than 100 restaurants.

While many come back year after year to stroll Bar Harbor's shore path, gazing out at some of the more than 40 ocean liners that visit each year, others prefer to visit more traditional fishing villages such as Bass Harbor.

Elsewhere along the coast in Hancock and Washington Counties you'll find picturesque fishing villages. To the west sits Castine, home to the Maine Maritime Academy and several historic sites. Just south is Deer Isle and Stonington, both home to busy commercial harbors bustling with lobster and fishing boats. Here, more and more galleries are tucked into the weathered buildings every year.

Ellsworth is a major commercial center, home to a typical shopping strip with major grocery stores, clothing and department stores, a Wal-Mart, fast food and traditional restaurants and some outlet stores such as L.L. Bean. Still, just a few miles from the inviting Main Street area of downtown, the waters of Green, Graham and Branch Lakes are popular recreational destinations.

One of the undiscovered gems of this region is Schoodic Point, near Winter Harbor. Schoodic is part of Acadia National Park, and offers spectacular scenery and rough surf crashing into rocks on stormy days.

Washington County to the east may be the first place in nation to be lit by dawn's early light, but in many ways it ranks last in economic prosperity. The friendly, hardworking people here still wrest their living from the fields, forests and sea. Few tourists venture this far east, making it an ideal place to explore. There are plenty of preserves, small parks and wildlife refuges, and no shortage of spectacular scenery.

Lofty radio antenna towers in Cutler form the nucleus of the US Navy's communications system staying in contact with nuclear submarines.

Machias, which is an Indian name meaning "bad little falls" is a former sawmill center wedged now between the sea and the flat open barrens of the blueberry barrens to the north.

Lubec and Eastport, which sit astride the border with Canada, have bustling marine industries and many aquaculture operations growing salmon for markets to the south. From Lubec, a bridge crosses into Canada to Campobello Island and an international park that preserves Franklin Roosevelt's summer home there.

Up US 1 in the town of Perry, a stone marker at the roadside demarks the 45th parallel. There is a picnic area nearby. People in Maine may wonder how to get somewhere or other, but here you'll know precisely where you are – exactly halfway between the North Pole and the equator.

In this region there are few roads running west to east. Low population is one reason for that.

> **INTERESTING FACT:** *Washington County may cover 1.5 million acres, but is home to only 30,000 people or so – less than the population of Bangor.*

US 1 runs west to east along the coast. Route 9, also known as "The Airline," which ends at the Canadian border in Calais, runs due west to Brewer. The road sports a famous feature known as "The Whalesback," a glacial esker (long, winding, narrow sandhill), which proved to be the ideal roadbed for early builders looking for ways across swampy, wet ground.

In this area, the trout and salmon of renowned West Grand Lake await the patient angler. The village of Grand Lake Stream, tidy in its preserved Victorian splendor, is in marked contrast to the poverty and economic disadvantage just a few miles down the road.

The only other cross-region route lies farther north, a wide, dirt paper company road known simply as "The Stud Mill Road." Open to the public, this private highway offers access to the deep interior and to put-in points for spring canoe trips on the region's many modest-sized rivers. With no road signs and many feeder roads it is easy to get lost in the maze of haul roads in this area. But for many who venture here armed with little more than a full tank of gas, a good DeLorme road atlas, and a thirst for adventure, getting lost, and finding your own way out, is half the fun.

■ Note: Maine has one area code – 207.

Parks, Preserves & Beaches

■ Acadia National Park

Acadia National Park is without a doubt the crown jewel of accessible wildness in Maine. The park encompasses 54 square miles and covers more than 40,000 acres. There are few places in New England, much less Maine, offering as many recreational opportunities as Acadia. From more than 100 miles of spectacular hiking trails, to groomed-gravel carriage roads ideal for leisurely bicycle rides, to quiet shores and lakes for paddling and picnicking, Acadia has it all. There is a stable that provides carriage rides, several fresh-water swimming areas, a saltwater swimming beach and numerous small boat launching ramps.

With three million visitors annually it is one of the most-visited parks in the country. Still, even in the peak season of late July and the month of August, there is stillness and solitude available to those willing to get up a little earlier, explore some of the less-visited parts of the park, or wait until evening when few cars and even fewer hikers and bikers venture out.

Most of Acadia is located on Mount Desert Island, a knob of pink granite sitting just offshore and connected to the mainland by a short bridge.

 INTERESTING FACT: *MDI, as the island is called, encompasses some 110 square miles, making it the nation's third-largest island outside Hawaii and Alaska. Of the lower states, only Long Island in New York and Martha's Vineyard in Massachusetts are larger.*

Acadia is intertwined with the year-round communities of Bar Harbor, Mount Desert, Southwest Harbor and Tremont. Isle Au Haut to the west, reachable only by ferry or mail boat, and Schoodic Peninsula to the east, a lovely rocky headland more than an hour's drive from the main portion of the park, also attract many visitors.

Unique in the country, Acadia was a gift to the nation from early summer residents. Appreciating the rare combination of rugged coastline, towering hills and crystal lakes, they set the land forever aside for the enjoyment and pleasure of all. In 1919, Acadia became the first park east of the Mississippi River. Its visitors following a tradiion of "rusticating," whereby early cottage dwellers spent their days in leisurely walks through the hills and mountains engaged in serious conversation. The island's network of trails was started privately by Village Improvement Associations in the various towns.

John D Rockefeller, Jr.

Most prominent and generous of the donors who helped create Acadia was the late John D. Rockefeller Jr., who donated more than a third of the park's acreage. He also built some 55 miles of beautifully engineered carriage roads, on which people bicycle, walk, ride horses, and cross-country ski. Each graceful granite arch bridge on the carriage roads is unique and worth a visit in itself.

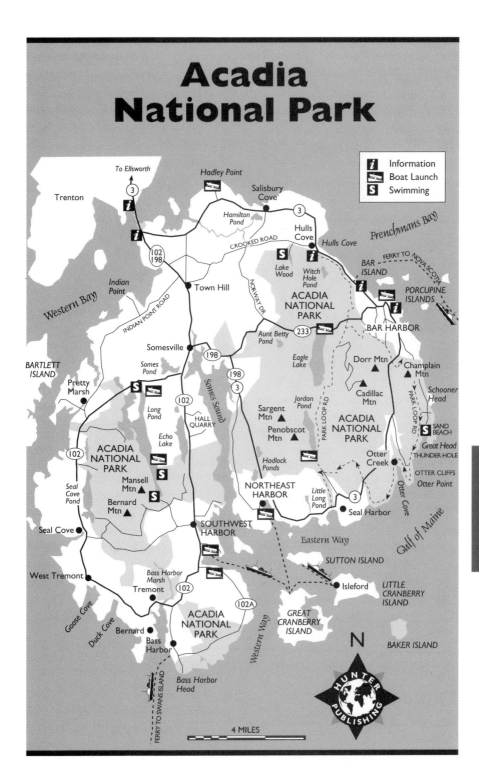

Acadia National Park

Information
Boat Launch
Swimming

To Ellsworth
Hadley Point
Salisbury Cove
Trenton
3
Hamilton Pond
Hulls Cove
Hulls Cove
Frenchmans Bay
102
198
CROOKED ROAD
Lake Wood
Witch Hole Pond
FERRY TO NOVA SCOTIA
BAR ISLAND
PORCUPINE ISLANDS
Indian Point
Town Hill
ACADIA NATIONAL PARK
BAR HARBOR
Western Bay
INDIAN POINT ROAD
NORWAY DR
233
Somesville
Aunt Betty Pond
Eagle Lake
Dorr Mtn
Champlain Mtn
BARTLETT ISLAND
Pretty Marsh
Somes Pond
198
Cadillac Mtn
Schooner Head
Long Pond
102
198
3
Jordan Pond
ACADIA NATIONAL PARK
PARK LOOP RD
PARK LOOP RD
SAND BEACH
Echo Lake
HALL QUARRY
Somes Sound
Sargent Mtn
Penobscot Mtn
Great Head
THUNDER HOLE
ACADIA NATIONAL PARK
Mansell Mtn
Hadlock Ponds
Otter Creek
OTTER CLIFFS
Otter Point
Seal Cove Pond
Bernard Mtn
NORTHEAST HARBOR
Little Long Pond
3
Seal Harbor
Otter Cove
Gulf of Maine
Seal Cove
SOUTHWEST HARBOR
Eastern Way
West Tremont
Bass Harbor Marsh
Tremont
102
SUTTON ISLAND
Goose Cove
Duck Cove
Bernard
Bass Harbor
102A
Isleford
LITTLE CRANBERRY ISLAND
ACADIA NATIONAL PARK
GREAT CRANBERRY ISLAND
BAKER ISLAND
N
Western Way
Bass Harbor Head
FERRY TO SWANS ISLAND
HUNTER PUBLISHING
4 MILES

Down East

Sand Beach in Acadia is a popular swimming location. Much of the "sand" is comprised of bits of broken shells.

Some folks like to say that Acadia now includes more scenic variety per square mile than any other unit of the national park system. It includes a dozen major mountain summits, the longest stretch of publicly owned rocky coast in Maine, many lake shores, and extensive forest and wetland areas.

The park maintains two campgrounds, one at Seawall in Manset and the other at Blackwoods in Otter Creek. Both are just a short stroll from the rocky shore. There are numerous private campgrounds on the island. ☎ 800-365-2267.

Isle Au Haut

The only real backcountry camping allowed at Acadia is on remote Isle Au Haut. Reservations for five six-person lean-to sites on beautiful Duck Harbor must be made by mail after April 1 (see address below). Each lean-to is $25, which allows a maximum stay in the shoulder seasons of five nights. In season (June 15-September 15) the maximum stay is three nights. No camping is allowed after October 15 or before May 15.

From mid-June until Labor Day the mail boat from Stonington docks at Duck Harbor dock, meaning an easy carry for the gear. At other times it is a five-mile backpack trip from the village to the campground. ☎ 367-5193 for ferry information.

Only 48 day visitors are allowed in addition to campers each day. The island, which has a small village and a ranger station on the north end, has 12 miles of dirt roads open to bicycles and 20 miles of hiking trails that traverse low hills, swamps, and along the rocky headlands.

Hiking

Along with the carriage roads, which have been undergoing major renovation, there are more than 120 miles of hiking trails, including those up majestic Mount Cadillac.

INTERESTING FACT: *Mount Cadillac was named for the French adventurer, Antoine de la Mothe Cadillac, who once held title to the island and went on to found Detroit and govern Louisiana.*

Most summits on Cadillac are ledges with scrub growth and blueberry bushes, making for great views. Trails rise quickly in Acadia and there are spectacular vistas at nearly every turn. This is in marked contrast to most mountain hiking trails which, for much of their lengths, are little more than tunnels through the trees.

The difficulty of trails ranges from easy, flat, self-guided nature hikes along the shore at Ship's Harbor, to the challenging Precipice, which is more of a non-technical climbing route featuring iron rungs and handrailings cemented into tall cliffs to aid in the ascent.

Acadia Mountain, Acadia National Park: Offers hundreds of miles of trails and many splendid views and summits. It is hard to choose between them, but if you must, **Acadia Mountain** would be my recommendation.

Beginning on Route 102, at the trailhead across the road from the parking area, the route heads north, crosses the Man 'O War Fire Road and then begins to ascend toward the 681-foot summit. There is only one place where hands are needed as you climb through fragrant pine woods on this half-mile trail. There are numerous open ledges at the top with great views of the surrounding mountains as well as Somes Sound, the only Fjord on the east coast of the United States. Retrace you steps to return or continue down to Man 'O War Brook on a very steep and rocky trail. Follow the fire road a mile back to Route 102.

Cadillac Mountain, Acadia National Park: No visit to Acadia is complete without a hike up Cadillac Mountain, the highest point within 50 miles of the sea from Maine to Rio de Janeiro. There are four trails up this 1,5320-foot edifice. The **South Ridge Trail** is the least steep. Begin at the well-marked trailhead on Route 3 near the Blackwoods Campground in Otter Creek. The trail rises slowly through deep woods until emerging in a loop at Eagle's Crag. The best views come with taking the right fork.

Soon the trail hits barren ledge areas with low jack pine woods. Views are great in all direction. The trail dips for a while to the shallow, weed-choked pond called the Featherbed, which is a major trail intersection offering log benches if you need a rest. Continue up steeply and then rise steady on the open, treeless spine of the mountain until reentering forest just near the top. Views are great in all directions, but you'll have to share. There is an auto road to the top as well as a gift shop and restroom. Distance one-way is 3.5 miles. Elevation gain is 1,300 feet. Strenuous.

Gorham Mountain, Acadia National Park: Although this hill tops out at less than 500 feet, its proximity to the ocean and other loftier peaks makes it a favorite. The one-mile trail to the summit begins in the corner of the Gorham Mountain Parking Lot on the Ocean Drive section of the Park Loop Road. It rises very gradually on bare ledge through jack pine woods. Soon, a plaque honoring Waldron Bates, one of the earliest trail architects on the island, is seen. You can continue straight here and gradually ascend or go right on the spur Cadillac Cliffs Trail, which skirts interesting caves and cliffs that were once under the sea. It reconnects with the main trail which then rises steeply to the summit plateau. The views extend out to sea, north to Cadillac and east to Sand Beach and Frenchman Bay. Moderate.

Huguenot Head, Acadia National Park: This is considered one of the park's lesser lights and many people hike Huguenot Head only on the way to the top of nearby Champlain Mountain. Still, at 731 feet, this mountain is no slouch. Begin at the trail sign on the east side of Route 3 across from the Tarn. There is a parking area several hundred feet north. The trail winds gradually on stone steps and easy grades until it breaks out of the trees and becomes a pathway lined bottom and sides with massive slabs of granite. There are switchbacks up the west side with continual good views of nearby Dorr Mountain and the Tarn below. Called the Beachcroft Trail by the association that built it, this route is reminiscent of a "Hobbit road" from the novel *Lord of the Rings*. When the trail hooks east and breaks out level near the top there are wonderful ocean views to the south. Falcons and eagles frequently soar overhead at these ledges and wildflowers bloom in spring. A short unmarked path leads to the nondescript summit.

Precipice, Acadia National Park: Actually more of a non-technical climbing route than a hiking trail, the Precipice on Champlain Mountain's sheer east face is a very difficult route.

 Drop-offs of several hundred feet are common. For the upper third of the 800-foot ascent iron bars hammered into the cliff face form hand and foot holds. Anyone with fear or heights or not in good shape should avoid this trail.

The way begins at the trailhead parking area on the Park Loop Road. After several hundred yards hikers reach "The Eliminator," an iron pull-up bar to assist your ascent up an eight-foot ledge. If you can't make it, turn back. The trail then has switchbacks up the cliff crossing a boulder field with several small caves. Narrow ledges are common, some with no hand holds. The rocks can also be very slippery when wet. Once at the top of the cliff the trail rises more gradually to the open and rocky summit with good views in all directions. Several alternative trails without the ladders are available for descent.

TAKE NOTE: *In most years the Precipice is closed until late August to allow for endangered peregrine falcons nesting there to fledge their young undisturbed.*

The elevation gain is nearly 1,000 feet. The flat-land distance is only about a mile. Very strenuous.

Ship's Harbor Nature Trail, Acadia National Park: Ship Harbor is an easy and fun walk for people of all abilities. It is comparatively level and has numerous numbered nature exhibits that are explained with the help of a booklet available from the park. A figure-eight loop of under two miles is possible. The trail begins at the well-marked parking area on Route 102A not far from Bass Harbor Head Light and heads east to the rocky ocean shore. For a time it runs along the edge of Ship Harbor.

INTERESTING FACT: *Ship Harbor was the scene of a tragic shipwreck in 1739 when a vessel full of settlers mistook the dead-end harbor for a river mouth and went aground. This is how the harbor got its name.*

Mountain Biking

Although bicycling is prohibited on Acadia's 150 miles of hiking trails and off-road trails, there are an endless number of bicycle trips possible both on the park's 22-mile Park Loop Road, as well as the 50 miles of groomed gravel carriage roads and on dirt fire roads on Mount Desert Island's western side. One company based out of Bar Harbor also offers Cadillac Mountain Downhill rides. First, participants watch the sunrise, then they hop on custom bikes with super disc brakes for the ride down the three-mile road that twists its way down the mountain. Riders then change to road-friendlier bikes to continue a guided trip.

Carriage Roads: The carriage roads were built largely through the largess of John D. Rockefeller Jr., who was upset when the Maine legislature voted to allow motor vehicles into Bar Harbor in 1913 and onto the rest of Mount Desert Island in 1915.

Stop by the park visitor center in Hulls Cove in Bar Harbor or by one of the island's many bicycle shops for maps and tips on good rides.

The roads wind among the woods, mountains and lakes of the island with scenic vistas at nearly every turn. A myriad of different loops of almost any length are possible. Motor vehicles are banned on the carriage roads, but hikers, equestrians, carriage drivers and the occasional dog walker with a long lead are likely to be encountered. See courtesy rules below.

The grades are very easy as the roads were designed for horse and carriages. Numerous trails, waterfalls and unique granite arch bridges are encountered.

> 📖 Local guide books, such as Diana Abrell's *Carriage Road Guide* and Audrey Minutolo's *Biking Guide to Mount Desert Island and Acadia* are invaluable (see Appendix). Numbers at carriage road intersections connect to the books and to maps distributed by the park.

Among the more popular loops are:

Witch Hole Pond. This four-mile circuit begins and ends at a graceful stone arch bridge over Duck Brook off the New Mills Meadow Road. Most riders go left as the path gradually rises through forests and fields with distant mountain views. The route passes by Half-Moon and Witch Hole Ponds before curving back around to the bridge. As one of the most popular routes with the locals it is apt to be very busy in the early morning and late afternoon.

Eagle Lake. Perhaps the most popular carriage road ride in the park, if not in Maine, the Eagle Lake loop offers six miles of gradual hills and a trip along a lake. No swimming is allowed; the lake serves as Bar Harbor's reservoir. Begin at the parking lot along the Eagle Lake Road and cut under the stone arch bridge. Your toughest decision of the day is just ahead at intersection 6. If you go left you'll bike along the lake first and then slowly climb the hills. Right turns at each intersection will bring you back to the start. Staying straight will bring you around the west side of the lake in the opposite direction. Staying left will bring you back to the start. Most bikers prefer to do the west side first (straight under the bridge) as the layout of hills and grades seems friendlier.

Day Mountain. Day Mountain is the one place where a carriage road leads right to the top of a mountain. Begin at the Jordan Pond Gate House and head east along the Triad. Soon you'll see Wildwood Stables. Turn south at intersection 17, which brings you across a stone bridge over the Park Loop Road. You can go left or right here.

If you go right stay straight at intersection 38 you'll continue to the south end of Day Mountain at intersection 36. A left here will take you up a graceful and winding road with good views to the 583-foot summit.

TAKE NOTE: *Several park carriage roads in the Seal Harbor area pass onto private land owned by the Rockefeller family yet open to the public. While dogs are permitted off-leash (which is against the law in the park) bicycles are not allowed following several incidents of bikers riding too fast around horses and walkers. Bikers on Rockefeller property without permission can be summonsed to court.*

The Amphitheater. This is a natural headwall in a valley between two of Acadia's major peaks. While it is not visible from the carriage road, it does take its name from it. For a five-mile trip begin at the Brown Mountain Gate House parking area on Route 198/3 and take a right at intersection 18, another right at intersection 19 and curve around the south end of Cedar Swamp Mountain. Go straight at intersection 20 and curve around the Amphitheater. Right turns at intersections 21 and 22 and a left when you get back to 20 will allow you to retrace your steps to the start.

Long Pond Fire Road. An easy five-mile ride with only small hills and an occasional motor vehicle can be had on the Long Pond Fire Road, which traverses park land on the Western side of Mount Desert Island. Park at the Pretty Marsh Parking area off Route 102. The entrance to the dirt fire road is just down the road on the left.

This dirt track, which can get quite dusty in summer, winds through damp forest and over barren ledges as it approaches the west side of Long Pond. Along the lake is a favorite casual swimming spot and canoe and kayak launching area. The road cuts back inland with only short side spurs to Duck Pond and around Pine Hill. Before rejoining Route 102 it crosses a low, wet area between Seal Cove and Hodgdon Ponds. A right on Route 102 will bring you back to the start.

Breakneck Road. This three-mile-long abandoned dirt road cuts through a portion of Acadia National Park, but is owned by the town of Bar Harbor. Therefore, mountain bikes are allowed. Beginning on the Eagle Lake Road, just uphill from the Eagle Lake Road Carriage Path Parking Area, the Breakneck road heads downhill through deep washouts and over rocks and roots. It passes between two ponds where the road often floods in spring. Eventually the Breakneck Road comes out in Hulls Cove. You can take a right to the nearby Park Visitor Centers and follow carriage roads back to the parking area for a loop trip.

Isle au Haut. You have to take a boat out to this wild and unspoiled island off the coast of Stonington. The mailboat/ferry, which takes passengers and freight, will also take bikes for a nominal fee.

Down East

A 12-mile circumnavigation of the island, nearly half of which is controlled by Acadia National Park, is possible by starting in the village. There is a small village with tiny store and ranger station where the ferry docks. In summer the boat continues onto Duck Harbor, carrying campers with reservations for the lean-tos (it does not take bikes). Bikes are banned on the park's hiking trails.

Head east out of the village on sole paved road. The area is privately owned but the road is public. It will eventually curve south out toward Eastern Head. As you approach Duck Harbor on the island's southwest side, a side road leads two additional miles out to Western Head, with its fine ocean views. The around-island road continues from Duck Harbor back to the village, winding slightly more inland through deep, damp forest and up several hills. This a moderate ride suitable for in-shape beginners. Be sure to watch the clock – you don't want to miss the last ferry back to Stonington.

Acadia is also a favorite spot for technical climbers, who test their skills against sheer cliffs on the Precipice and South Bubble. Acadia is one of the few places where the cliffs go right down to the sea. At Otter Cliffs the park has installed permanent climbing anchors to save trees and vegetation that was being worn by ropes used on the more popular routes.

Sightseeing

Central to the park is the 22-mile Park Loop Road (see below), which begins in Hulls Cove in Bar Harbor. The park also maintains and staffs a helpful information center here, with audio-visual presentations and free maps.

> 📖 Pick up a copy of *The Beaver Log*, a park publication containing the schedule for the scores of free or low-cost ranger and naturalist talks held each day. Topics range from tide pool life, to astronomy, to learning about and watching endangered peregrine falcons that nest on Acadia's cliffs.

Acadia National Park Park Loop Road

28 miles, 1½ hours (without stops), round trip

Highlights: *At just 22 miles long, the Acadia National Park Loop Road and spur up Cadillac Mountain is, mile-for-mile, the most scenic drive in Maine.*

Route: It begins at the park visitor center just off State Route 3 in **Hulls Cove**, a few miles north of downtown Bar Harbor. The visitor center is worth a stop, with exhibits, free maps and displays, helpful volunteers and interpretive staff.

For the next several miles the Loop Road is two-way. Scenic vistas out over **Frenchman Bay** at handy pullouts begin almost immediately. Interpretive plaques at the pullouts explain the terrain and give snippets of history. One describes the devastating Great Fire of 1947, which blackened tens of thousands of acres in October of that year. Much of the present vegetation on the eastern side of Mount Desert Island shows the natural succession that follows such a disaster.

 As you near Cadillac Mountain, bear left where the Loop Road becomes one-way. The speed limit is 35 miles per hour. On the one-way sections parking is allowed anywhere in the right lane, so watch the Mario Andretti moves around slower traffic.

The road skirts the base of several mountains with great views out over the bay and of forests, fields and marshes. If you have time, stop by **Suier de Monts**, a natural spring where the park has built a nature center. You'll discover the **Wild Gardens of Acadia**, with their self-guided tour of area flora, and the **Abbe Museum of Stone Age Antiquities**.

All along the Loop Road parking areas, small streams, and hiking trailheads beckon to be explored.

Continue eastward up the north flank of **Champlain Mountain**. The large industrial-like complex to the left is the **Jackson Laboratory**, one of the foremost cancer and genetics institutions in the world. The next pullout is called the **Champlain Overlook** after French explorer Samuel de Champlain, who visited the area and named the island in 1604. The road continues past the 800-foot cliffs on the east side of Champlain. A trail, which is really more of a non-techinical climbing route, goes up the face. Called the **Precipice**, this route is often closed in summer when endangered Peregrine falcons nest upon the high rock ledges (see page 254 for more details).

Soon you'll hit the Acadia fee station, which collects entrance fees of $10 per car for a seven-day pass. If you want to duck out early, go left just before the station and follow the signs back to Bar Harbor. This is also the way to the **Schooner Head Overlook**. The view is great, and from the parking area a winding path heads down to one of the park's secret wonders – **Anenome Cave**.

Down East

Anemone Cave

No longer marked on maps, the Anemone Cave harbors tiny pink sea anenomes in its tide pools. When the cave was marked with signs, so many people visited that the park service worried about the anenomes being harmed. Caution is in order though, and not just due to environmental concerns. The rocks are very slippery and water fills the cave at high tide. The cave is not off-limits, but should definitely be treated with respect.

Just past the entrance station the **Ocean Drive** section of the Park Loop Road begins. Here, the scenery really explodes. Sand Beach with its chilly waters is on the left, offering facilities and a parking area. The road soon hugs the top of ocean-side cliffs, passing by **Thunder Hole**, where the incoming waves when the tide is just right (an hour or two before high tide) compress air under rocky overhangs and send the water back out with a loud boom. **Otter Cliffs**, a granite headland more than 100 feet high, is just ahead. The road continues past the **Fabbri Picnic Area**, where one of the first wireless radio stations was once located, and around **Otter Cove** on a graceful causeway. It continues along the rocky shore for several more miles past more parking areas, some of which lead down to pretty pocket stone beaches.

Heading inland, the Loop Road passes **Wildwood Riding Stables**, which offer guided carriage rides on the park's 50 miles of motorless paths. Here it returns to two-way traffic and then passes the **Jordan Pond House**, a gift shop, restaurant and hiking hub famous for afternoon tea and popovers on the lawn. The road then begins to climb as it clings to the west side of **Pemetic Mountain**. Wonderful views of Penobscot and Sargent Mountains to the west and the Bubbles to the north entice the eyes. Jordan Pond immediately below frames the scene.

Bubble Rock

On top of South Bubble sits Bubble Rock. This truck-sized boulder is a "glacial erratic." Composed of rock different from the granite upon which it sits, it was actually torn from another mountain by the mile-high glacier that once covered most of Maine. The melting ice left the massive rock where it sits today.

As the Loop Road winds through attractive forests with occasional views, it begins to climb up the western side of Cadillac as you head back to the intersection where you first joined the one-way road.

But you're not done yet. Take a right onto the **Cadillac Mountain Summit Road** and being the 2½-mile climb to the top of this 1,532-foot peak. Views are spectacular as you switch from one side of the mountain to the other. There are many places to pull off and take photos or admire the scenery. Watch for the hairpin turn, especially if there is a bus or other large vehicle coming the other way!

Just before reaching the summit parking area you will pass the **Blue Hill Overlook** on the left.

 DID YOU KNOW? *Blue Hill Overlook used to be called the Sunset Overlook. The name attracted so many people (in the hundreds every night) to watch the colorful sunsets that its name was changed. It is still a fun way to end the day, and the crowds will likely be smaller.*

At the top of Cadillac Mountain views extend for miles. On a clear fall day mile-high Katahdin can be seen more than 150 miles to the north. A hotel once was located here and a cog railway once brought people to the top before an auto road was built.

The First Rays of Sunlight

Some folks like to say Cadillac is the first place touched by the rays of the rising sun each day. But geographers say that the first ray shines on different places, depending on time of year. Still, you may be the first person in the United States to see a new day dawn. The idea of seeing the sunrise from Cadillac is not original however. Some summer days more than 100 people are there to await first light. With plenty of room to spread out however, it doesn't have to feel crowded.

After a careful trip down the mountain, taking it easy not to overheat the brakes, turn right back onto the Loop Road. In less than a mile you'll notice a familiar intersection and your tour of the Park Loop Road will be complete.

The only entry fee station is on the Loop near Sand Beach. The fee is $10 per car for seven days. If you want to skip that part of the park, which I don't advise, there are no fees for other areas.

Cross-Country Skiing & Snowmobiling

Acadia National Park features more than 50 miles of groomed carriage roads that wind through mountains and across graceful granite arch bridges. Many excellent views possible. Most carriage roads off-limits to snowmobiles and other motorized travel.

One lane of the Park Loop Road along **Ocean Drive** is not plowed to allow oceanside skiing and snowmobiling when weather permits. Many

Down East

more miles of ungroomed fire roads on western side of Mount Desert Island.

Also, the road to the top of **Cadillac Mountain** is open for skiing and snowmobiling. High drifts and possible bare or icy spots at higher elevations. ☎ 288-3338.

Park Rules

- Dogs must be kept on a leash at all times.
- No parking on vegetation or natural ground.
- No firearms.
- No fires except in designated picnic areas.
- Bicycles are prohibited on hiking trails.
- Hang-gliding is prohibited.
- In-line skating and skate boarding are banned on park roads and parking lots.
- Do not remove rocks or plants from the park.
- Do not harm standing vegetation or pick anything but blueberries in season. You can be fined.

Swimming

The park runs swimming beaches at **Echo Lake**, where there are lifeguards, restrooms and changing rooms, and at **Lakewood**, where there are no facilities. Other popular swimming spots include the west side of **Long Pond** (off the Seal Cove Fire Road) and at "**the ledges**" just downhill from the Acadia Mountain Parking area on Route 102. The only lifeguarded saltwater beach is **Sand Beach**, along the Park Loop Road. It has changing rooms and restrooms. Swimming is allowed in other small ponds and in the ocean wherever visitors feel it looks inviting and it is safe.

Swimming Holes

Many lakes in Acadia are public water supplies, which means they are off-limits to swimmers. In summer, many have regular patrols and violators can be summoned to court. While boating and fishing are allowed, swimming is banned in the following lakes: Eagle Lake, Bubble Pond, Upper and Lower Hadlock Ponds, Jordan Pond, Long Pond (south end extending north to one mile beyond pump station).

One of the favorites for hikers is **Sargent Mountain Pond**. Located at 1,000 feet in a valley between Sargent and Penobscot Mountains, the dark, iron-rich waters of this one-acre pond stay cold well into summer. There is a small place to jump in along a trail and several log sitting benches.

Rules of the Road for Bikers

User conflicts are inevitable in any popular area, and increasing fondness for Acadia National Park's carriage roads has led to the formation of user courtesy rules. Park officials urge walkers to yield to horses, and bicyclists to yield to both walkers and horses. Most of the suggested rules are aimed at reducing bicycle-related complaints. Concerns about reckless cyclists have prompted the closing of 10 miles of carriage paths located on private land adjacent to the park roads. Other steps may be needed, as signs requesting bicycles not use the area have been repeatedly damaged or removed. Heed all signs and respect private property. Among the following are some suggestions for avoiding conflict:

- **Access** – Ride on open trails only. Carriage roads and motor roads are open to bikes. Hiking trails are off-limits.

- **Low impact** – Don't leave skid marks or cause ruts.

- **Control** – Excessive speed threatens everyone. Don't take up the entire road by riding abreast.

- **Yield** – A friendly greeting warns others that you are approaching from behind. Bells are recommended.

- **Speed** – Go slowly when passing, or stop altogether.

- **Never spook animals.**

- **Plan ahead** – Bring water, food and clothing for rapid weather changes.

Down East

Park Fees

The Acadia National Park entrance fee is $10 per vehicle, which buys a permit good for seven days. An individual entering on foot or by bicycle will be charged $5 for a seven-day pass. An annual pass to Acadia is $20.

Nationwide, the cost of a *Golden Eagle Pass*, which allows unlimited access for a year to any national park or monument, is $50.

Some of the more popular interpretive programs charge a nominal fee. Call the park for details at ☎ 288-3338.

Winter in Acadia

Acadia is open year-round. All parts of the park remain open, although gift shops, restaurants, nature centers and restrooms are closed once cold weather hits. A winter visitor center is set up at park headquarters on the Eagle Lake Road in Bar Harbor.

The Park Loop Road remains open until closed by snow. In winter it is kept snow-covered and is used by skiers and snowmobilers.

Except for two short sections, the 50 miles of carriage roads are off-limits to snowmobiles. Local volunteers groom the trails after snowfalls leaving a perfect double cross-country track.

Blackwoods Campground in Otter Creek has a limited number of sites open in winter for hardy campers. There is no fee. You can ski from the campground to the Ocean Drive section of the Park Loop Road when snow conditions permit. Often though, snow quickly turns to rain because of the proximity to the comparatively warm ocean.

Contact Acadia National Park, PO Box 177, Bar Harbor 04609, ☎ 288-3338. Blackwoods Campground, ☎ 800-365-2267; Emergencies, ☎ 288-3369.

Friends of Acadia

Friends of Acadia is an organization created to allow citizens to help care for Acadia National Park. The nonprofit group is dedicated to the everlasting preservation and appreciation of the park and its surroundings. It actively recruits volunteers to work on the park's trails (see the *Coming Events* section of the weekly *Bar Harbor Times* for days and times). The group raises funds to support an Acadia Youth Conservation Corps, and are responsible for a large-scale restoration of the park's carriage roads. They have also started an innovative program of "Resource-Sensitive Tourism" to allow those who benefit from Acadia's resources to help in their protection.

Friends of Acadia was established in 1986. It works in partnership with park management, government, special-interest groups and local communities to:

■ Promote understanding of Acadia National Park;

■ Protect resources that cannot be protected by the Park Service alone;

■ Involve citizens in park management and planning;

- Protect Acadia from overuse;

- Provide fund-raising support for special projects.

For more information about the group, write Friends of Acadia, PO Box 725, Bar Harbor 04609 or ☎ 288-3340.

Many nature tour companies offer trips into Acadia as well as other destinations Down East. These are listed under *Eco-Tours & Cultural Excursions*, pages 300-301.

■ State & Town Parks

 Cobscook Bay State Park, Edmunds. Scenic and less-visited park with campsites right along the bay where tides roil and boil twice each day (current can be very dangerous). Off US 1. Hiking and nature trails through 900 acres. Other activities include fishing, picnicking, berry picking, boat launching ramp, winter use. Showers and dump station. ☎ 726-4412.

Holbrook Island Preserve, Brooksville. This state-owned preserve covering nearly two square miles is one of the best kept secrets in Down East Maine. Hiking trails, including several along the bay, picnicking and good views. Nearby is Goose Falls, a tidal rapid that switches direction with the tide. Parking available. ☎ 326-4012.

Lamoine State Park. Located off Route 184 in Lamoine, this park is a favorite with locals seeking to escape the crush of the crowds in Acadia. The surf may never be up but the views of Acadia's mountains are spectacular. There are changing and bathroom facilities, a campground, dock, and public boat launching area. Plenty of parking. There is an entrance fee. ☎ 667-4778.

McLellan Park, Milbridge. Local recreation area with campsites, toilets, hiking, picnicking and good views of the coast Down East. Adequate parking. Make camping arrangements at the town office. ☎ 546-2422.

Quoddy Head State Park, Lubec. You can't get any farther east than this and still be in the United States. Picturesque red-and-white striped lighthouse on spectacular rocky headland. Hiking trails through 475 acres and along towering cliffs at seaside. Some of the highest tides on the east coast. Mile-long bog boardwalk. Entrance fee. Good parking. ☎ 733-0911.

Shackford Head, Eastport. Great views of Eastport and vicinity from the point on Cobscook Bay near Eastport after a 10-minute walk through the woods. Picnicking, hiking, adequate parking. A 90-acre park. Outhouse at trailhead. ☎ 726-4012.

Reversing Falls Park, Pembroke. This small (140-acre) town-owned park provides a front-row seat for an unusual tidal phenomena. Twice-daily tides surge over the ledge, causing rapids to run in two directions. Parking, picnicking and hiking. Pit toilets. Time your visit within an hour or two of high or low tide for the best show.

Major Parks & Preserves Down East

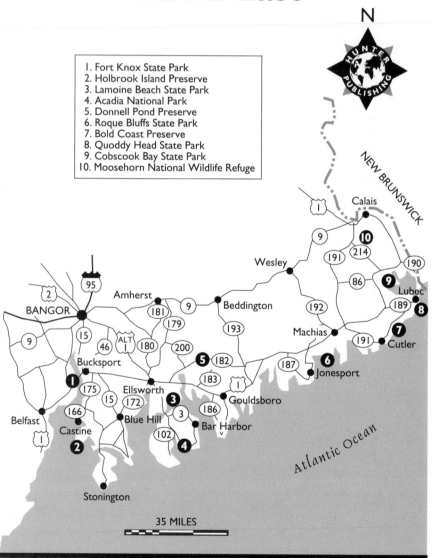

N

1. Fort Knox State Park
2. Holbrook Island Preserve
3. Lamoine Beach State Park
4. Acadia National Park
5. Donnell Pond Preserve
6. Roque Bluffs State Park
7. Bold Coast Preserve
8. Quoddy Head State Park
9. Cobscook Bay State Park
10. Moosehorn National Wildlife Refuge

NEW BRUNSWICK

Calais

Wesley

Amherst

BANGOR

Beddington

Machias

Lubec

Cutler

Buckport

Jonesport

Ellsworth

Gouldsboro

Belfast

Blue Hill

Castine

Bar Harbor

Stonington

Atlantic Ocean

35 MILES

DID YOU KNOW? *The entire bay around Reversing Falls was once planned to be the site of massive WPA tidal power project during Franklin Roosevelt's presidency. However, the project was never completed.*

Roque Bluffs State Park, Roque Bluffs. The last good public place to swim as you head east. Pebble swimming beach has saltwater on one side and a warm, shallow, freshwater pond on other. A total of 300 acres on which to picnic and relax. Fishing allowed but probably not very productive. Bathhouse, toilets, tables, grills, ample parking for fee. ☎ 255-3475.

St. Croix Island, Calais. Small, six-acre island in river was site of one of the first attempted settlements in North America by the French in 1604. Under control of National Park Service through Acadia National Park. Boat access only but strong currents and high tides make small boat passage risky. Plans call for mainland visitor center and boat shuttle across. ☎ 288-3338.

Campobello, New Brunswick. Why mention a Canadian location in a guidebook about Maine? Simple. Campobello is an international park administered by a commission with members from both countries. It preserves the 34-room summer home of Franklin D. Roosevelt which is open for tours and filled with FDR memorabilia. The park itself comprises nearly 3,000 acres and features seaside picnic sites and hiking trails. Open seasonally. No fee. Access by passing through the border checkpoint at the international bridge in Lubec. ☎ (506) 752-2922.

■ Beaches at a Glance

Lamoine Beach. Nearly one mile of sand, gravel and pebble. A family beach at north end of Frenchman Bay in Lamoine State Park. Adequate parking. Fee.

Roque Bluffs Beach. Curved beach 2,700 feet long with steep drop-off. Saltwater is usually frosty but there is a warm, shallow, freshwater pond behind. Outhouse, picnicking, fee parking.

Sand Beach, Acadia National Park. A 1,000-foot-long beach between headlands. Not so much sand as bits of crushed shells. Lifeguards on duty in season. Parking, changing houses, toilets, no dogs. Fee to enter park, beach free.

Seal Harbor Beach. Town-run family beach in village of Seal Harbor on Mount Desert Island. It's 1,000 feet long, set right along the road. In protected cove with very little wave action. Good place to look for sand dollars after a storm. No facilities.

Sandy River Beach, Jonesport. Small gravel and cobblestone beach east of Jonesport. Tidal stream nearby. Public access but surrounded by private property. Scant parking.

■ Wildlife Refuges

Birdsacre Sanctuary, Ellsworth. Quiet, wooded, 200-acre parcel adjacent to busy commercial strip on Route 3 in Ellsworth. Numerous nature trails wind among boulders and three small ponds. Preserve headquarters once home of ornithologist Cordelia Stanwood. Privately run non-profit. Collection of mounted birds in museum. Adequate parking. ☎ 667-8460.

Cross Island National Wildlife Refuge, Cutler. This 1,703-acre island complex is located just offshore and includes the satellites of Mink, Scotch, Old Man and the Double Head Shot Islands. Islands are densely forested and home to deer, eagles, waterfowl and sea birds. Terrain includes rocky cliffs 100 feet high. Several anchorages. Tour boat trips scheduled out of Cutler. ☎ 546-2124.

Moosehorn National Wildlife Refuge, Baring. Way down in Washington County near Calais this massive 24,400-acre preserve is half the size of Acadia National Park. Features woods, fields, bogs and streams. Two sections – Baring Unit is 17,200 acres; Edmunds Unit bordering tidal waters of Cobscook Bay near Dennysville is more than 7,000 acres. Moosehorn is open daily, year-round. Visitor center in Baring on the Charolette Road. ☎ 454-7161.

> **WATCHABLE WILDLIFE:** *Moosehorn is home to more than two dozen species of mammals and 200 varieties of birds, including many endangered species. Woodcock studies are now underway. Deer hunting is allowed.*

Petit Manan National Wildlife Refuge, Milbridge. Large 3,335-acre set aside on Petit Manan peninsula and on Nash, Petit Manan and Bois Bubert Islands. Some public-use restrictions in nesting sea bird areas. Good birding throughout. Mainland portion is wooded with ledges and swampy areas. Islands are windswept and accessible by private boat. Bois Bubert offers some possibility of sheltered anchorage. Petit Manan with its tall stone lighthouse is quite far offshore. ☎ 546-2124.

Schoodic Island, Winter Harbor. Part of Acadia National Park, this 61-acre island just off the tip of Schoodic Peninsula is home to bald eagles and nesting sea birds. Water access only. Very large swells, strong currents.

Fish Hatcheries

Craig Brook National Hatchery, Orland. Located a short way off Route 3 (follow the signs). Raises Atlantic salmon for stocking in several Down East rivers including the Penobscot and Union. Visitor center, nature trail, picnicking and swimming. ☎ 469-2803.

Grand Lake Stream State Fish Hatchery. Located in a picturesque village. This state-run facility raises landlock salmon for lake stocking program. Limited access to public. (No phone.)

■ Natural Areas/Preserves

The following preserves are all under the management of the Nature Conservancy. Their main office is at 14 Maine Street, Brunswick 04011. ☎ 729-5181.

Blagden Preserve, Bar Harbor. Located on Indian Point this 110-acre preserve features wooded trails and a dirt road (foot travel only) to the shore. Property once was a private estate.

WATCHABLE WILDLIFE: *Blagden offers good views of seals hauled out on rocks on nearby islands and ledges. Good birding, too.*

Crockett Cove Woods, Stonington. Coastal rain forest preserve of 100 acres just west of downtown Stonington. Mature spruce, swampy area. Self-guided nature trail and good bird watching.

Great Wass Island, Beals. Give yourself plenty of time to explore this 1,500-acre preserve in Beals, just off Jonesport. Good parking. Maps and information at the trailheads. Numerous hiking routes skirt ocean and pass through lush forests with peatlands and rare plants. Day access only. No camping, fires or pets. No facilities.

Mistake Island, Jonesport. A 21-acre island with lighthouse. Old Coast Guard boardwalk allows touring without damage to rare vegetation. Boat access only.

Wreck Island Preserve, Stonington. An 80-acre island halfway between Stonington and Isle au Haut. Water access only with good anchorages. Mix of abandoned fields, woods, ledges.

Down East

Sightseeing

> **NOTE**
>
> *Many museums and historic sites in Maine are small, and operate for only part of the year, staffed by volunteers. The opening days and times of these institutions vary, depending upon weather, available staff and other factors; some are open by appointment only. We recommend that you call ahead to find out the latest opening times.*

■ Historic Sites/Museums

Alexander

 Alexander-Crawford Historical Society, Pokey Road. ☎ 454-7476.

Bar Harbor

Acadia National Park Nature Center at Sieur de Monts Spring. Natural history exhibits relating to Acadia National Park and Mount Desert Island and hands-on activities for children. ☎ 288-3338.

Bar Harbor Historical Society Museum, 33 Ledgelawn Avenue. Large collection of early photographs and artifacts of local history. Original *Life* magazine photos and personal accounts of the Great Fire of 1947. ☎ 288-0000.

Natural History Museum, College of the Atlantic, 105 Eden Street. Route 3. Housed on campus of award-winning college, this musuem features prize-winning exhibits depicting animal and plant life indigenous to Mount Desert Island and the Gulf of Maine. Special programs for children. ☎ 288-5015.

Abbe Museum, Sieur de Mont Spring, Acadia National Park (Mount Desert Street, downtown Bar Harbor). Native American artifacts from the Frenchman and Blue Hill Bay areas. 10,000-year-old stone tolls, ornaments, bone implements, basketry and clothing. Authentic wigwam reproduction. Gift shop, programs. ☎ 288-3519.

Bar Harbor Oceanarium, Route 3. Houses the Maine Lobster Museum, a lobster hatchery, Thomas Bay marsh walk, large seal exhibit. ☎ 288-5005.

Bar Harbor Whale Museum, 52 West Street. For-profit museum that serves as ticket office for the *Sea Bird Watcher,* which runs whale and bird watching tours offshore. Displays on whales, the history of whaling as well as exhibits with displays of dolphin, seal and Minke whale skeletons. Gift shop. Open seasonally. ☎ 288-2025.

Down East Coast

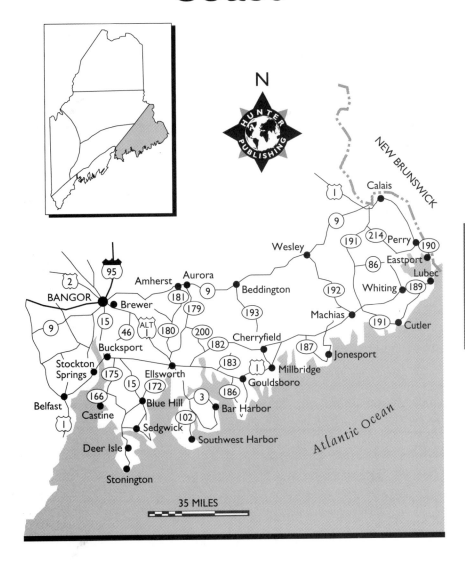

Bass Harbor

Tremont Historical Society, ☎ 244-3410.

Bernard

Nancy Neale Typecraft, Steamboat Wharf Road. Old wood and metal printing type and cases. ☎ 244-5192.

Blue Hill

Holt House (1815), Blue Hill Historical Society, Water Street. Federal period home. Artifacts, and other memorabilia relating to the history of Blue Hill. (No phone.)

Jonathan Fisher Memorial (1814), Main Street. Route 15. House built by Jonathan Fisher, the town's first settled minister. ☎ 374-2161.

Brooksville

Brooksville Historical Society Museum, Route 176, Brooksville Corner. Area memorabilia, genealogical records, period clothing, farm tools, household items. ☎ 326-4900.

Bucksport

Bucksport Historical Society Museum (1874), Main Street. Railroad station containing items of local history. ☎ 469-2591.

Northeast Historic Film, 379 Main Street. Archive of films and footage from newsreels, television stations and libraries from across the Northeast. Located in old theater. ☎ 469-0924.

Calais

St. Croix Historical Society, 245 Maine Street. On the National Register of Historic Places.

St. Croix Island International Historic Site. Island is the site of the first French settlement in the New World. Established by explorer Samuel de Champlain in 1604, the settlement was unsuccessful. Info via Acadia National Park. ☎ 288-3338.

Campobello Island (New Brunswick, Canada)

Roosevelt Campobello International Park Commission. International memorial to Franklin D. Roosevelt. On Campobello Island, New Brunswick, Canada, across bridge from Lubec, Maine. FDR's summer home. Visitor center offers video and interpretive display. Beautiful flower gardens. Scenic vistas, picnic and observation areas, walking trails, and beaches in 2,800-acre natural area. No fees. Day use. ☎ (506) 752-2922.

Castine

Castine Historical Society, Abbott School, Town Common. ☎ 326-8786.

Fort George. Earthworks constructed in 1779 by British to protect their interests in the Province of Maine and Canada. Located in the village proper.

Fort Madison Site (1811). A small grassy area located in the village proper.

State of Maine, Maine Maritime Training Academy ship, Sea Street. ☎ 326-4311. Half-hour tours are offered in season. ☎ 326-4311.

Wilson Museum, John Perkins House (1763-1783), Perkins Street. Only pre-Revolution building in area, restored and furnished in period style with family and local pieces. On the grounds of the Wilson Museum, pre-historic artifacts from North and South America, Europe and Africa. Ship models and local historic items, rocks and minerals. ☎ 326-8545.

Cherryfield

Cherryfield-Narraguagus Historical Society, Main Street. Photographs of early Cherryfield. Tools and household items of 1850-1920 era. Genealogical information. ☎ 546-7979.

Columbia Falls

Ruggle's House (1818), off US 1. Federal-style home features intricately hand-carved interiors and magnificent flying staircase. Restored and furnished with period pieces. ☎ 546-7429.

Deer Isle

Salome Sellers House (1830), Route 15A, Sunset. Restored and furnished period home. Adjacent to museum of Deer Isle-Stonington Historical Society. ☎ 348-2886.

Eastport

Barrack's Museum of the Border Historical Society, Washington Street. Part of the barracks and officers' quarters of the original Fort Sullivan (1809). ☎ 853-2328.

Down East

Raye's Mustard Mill, 83 Washington Street. ☎ 853-4451. Oldest stone-ground mustard mill still in use in the US.

Ellsworth

Colonel Black Mansion, Woodlawn (1827), West Main Street. Route 172. Modified Georgian-type period home, richly furnished, on 300-acre grounds. Authentic period furniture, china, glass. Collection includes rare volume of Massachusetts Colonial Laws. Restored garden, carriage house. Open daily Monday-Saturday. Season: June-October 15. ☎ 667-8671.

Ellsworth Historical Society (1886), State Street. This brick and granite structure served as the county jail, sheriff's home and office. The angular gables and asymmetrical elevations bespeak a style once common throughout New England. ☎ 667-4468.

Stanwood Homestead Museum & Wildlife Sanctuary – Birdsacre (1850), Route 3, Outer High Street. Country home of pioneer ornithologist Cordelia J. Stanwood, photographer and author. 200-acre woodland sanctuary. Bird rehabilitation building. ☎ 667-8460.

Franklin

Franklin Historical Society, Sullivan Road, Route 200. Old Baptist church. Local photographs, documents, tools relating to the granite, lumbering, and ship building industries. Old post office and school. On the National Register of Historic Places. ☎ 565-3635.

Gouldsboro

Old Town House (1884), Gouldsboro Historical Society, US 1. Historical collection of photographs, artifacts, newspapers, maps and books. ☎ 963-5530.

Hancock

Hancock Historical Society, Hancock Corner. ☎ 422-3080.

Isleford (Little Cranberry)

Isleford Historical Society. ☎ 244-7853.

Islesford Historical Museum, Little Cranberry Island. Exhibits on early history of region known as Acadia. Artifacts, pictures, household tools of Mount DeseRoute Records of Cranberry Isles families. ☎ 288-3338 (Acadia National Park).

Machias

Burnham Tavern Museum (1770), Main and Free Streets, Route 192. Oldest building in eastern Maine, only one with Revolutionary War history. Reputed to be place where plot to engage in first naval battle of Revolution was hatched. ☎ 255-4432.

Fort O'Brien Site (Fort Machias 1775), Route 92. The British drove the earliest defenders of Fort O'Brien from the site in 1775. Refortified in 1777 and destroyed during a British naval offensive in 1814. ☎ 941-4014.

Machiasport

Gates House (1807), Machiasport Historical Society, Route 92. Federal-style house furnished in period fashion. Maritime room. ☎ 255-8557.

Milbridge

Milbridge Historical Society, S. Main Street. ☎ 546-7479.

Mount Desert (Somesville)

Mount Desert Island Historical Society Museum, Main Street. Route 102. Collection of documents and artifacts from the island's early settlements. ☎ 244-9012.

Northeast Harbor

Great Harbor Collection at the Old Firehouse (1916), Main Street. Historical museum and cultural center. Exhibits of fire-fighting equipment, clothing, sleighs, machinery and tools from another time. Nautical exhibits. ☎ 276-5262.

Petite Plaisance, South Shore Road. Home of the late Madamme Youcennar, first woman writer to be admitted to prestigious French Academy. ☎ 276-3940.

Orland

Orland Historical Society, Main Street, Route 175. Tools, housewares, pictures and documents of local area. Mineral collection. Military uniforms from several wars. Native American artifacts. ☎ 469-2476.

Sedgwick

Sedgwick-Brooklin Historical Society Museum, Route 15. Caterpillar Hill. Located in the Rev. Daniel Merrill House (1795), town's first minister and a founder of Colby College. On the National Register of Historical Places. ☎ 359-2251.

Down East

Southwest Harbor

The Wendell Gilley Museum of Bird Carvings, 4 Herrick Road. Life-size wood carving of a bald eagle is often mistaken for a mounted bird. It, and the other 200+ pieces in the collection, were created by renown carver Wendell Gilley. Demonstrations, classes, shop. ☎ 244-7555.

Sullivan

Sullivan-Sorrento Historical Society, US 1, West Sullivan. ☎ 422-6253.

Swans Island

Sea Side Hall Museum, Atlantic. Atlantic, Swan's Island, near ferry terminal. Local records, artifacts. ☎ 526-4350.

Tremont

Seal Cove Auto Museum, Route 102, Seal Cove. More than 100 vintage vehicles, including Rolls-Royce, a steam fire engine and Stutz Bearcat. ☎ 244-9242.

Winter Harbor

Old School House (1855). ☎ 963-5832.

List Source-Maine Department of Tourism.

■ Lighthouses

Dice Head Light. A 45-foot stone tower erected in 1829. View from end of Lighthouse Road in Castine. Privately owned.

Pumpkin Island Light. Stone tower 25 feet high, built in 1854. On offshore island. Boat access only. View from Eggemoggin Road in Little Deer Isle.

Heron Neck Light. A 25-foot round tower erected in 1854. Boat access only.

Isle au Haut Light. 50-foot stone and brick tower with footbridge to shore of this offshore island, much of which is part of Acadia National Park. Keeper's house used as an inn. Ferry access from Stonington. ☎ 367-2261.

Eagle Island Light. 30-foot stone tower built on this offshore island in 1858. Island once thickly settled. Boat access only.

Mark Island Light, Deer Isle. Square 28-foot stone tower build on off-shore island in 1857.

Green Island. 25-foot stone tower built in 1856 on offshore island in Blue Hill Bay. Boat access only. Privately owned.

Burnt Coat Harbor Light, Swans Island. 35-foot brick tower erected in 1872. Car, bicycle access after ferry ride from Bass Harbor on Mount Desert Island.

Great Duck Island Light. 40-foot round stone tower on windswept off-shore island. Tower erected in 1890. Boat access only.

Baker Island Light. 45-foot round stone tower built in 1855 in center of island. Boat access only. Much of island is Acadia National Park. Regular naturalist tours daily in summer by boat Mount Desert Island.

Mount Desert Rock Light. Known locally simply as "The Rock." 60-foot granite tower erected in 1830 on this barren ledge 18 miles out from Mount Desert Island. Boat access only. Owned by College of the Atlantic as a marine mammal observation station.

Bear Island Light. 25-foot round stone tower erected on offshore island in 1889. Privately owned. View from mailboat, ferry ride to Cranberry Isles from Northeast Harbor on Mount Desert Island.

Egg Rock Light. Square wooden building built in 1875 on barren ledge in middle of Frenchman Bay. Red light 40 feet above ground. View from Champlain Overlook and Schooner Head Overlook in Acadia National Park on Mount Desert Island.

Winter Harbor Light. 20-foot round stone tower built in 1856 on Mark Island at entrance to Winter Harbor. Privately owned. Boat access only.

Prospect Harbor Point Light. 30-foot round stone tower built in 1891 on east side of harbor. Privately owned. View from across harbor on Route 186.

Narraguagus Light. 55-foot stone tower built on Pond Island in 1853. Privately owned. Boat access only.

Libby Island Light. 40-foot tapped stone tower built on offshore island at entrance to Machias Bay in 1817. Boat access only.

Petit Manan Light. Graceful 119-foot granite tower erected on treeless offshore island in 1855. Island used for seabird research. Boat access only.

Emms Rock Light. 28-foot high stone tower erected at the entrance to Moosabec Reach in mid-1800s. Boat access only.

Dog Island Light. Steel skeleton tower 32 feet high. Built on east side of Eastport riverbank in 1919. Marks site of second-largest tidal whirlpool in the world.

Down East

Whitlock Mill Light. 32-foot tapered stone tower erected in 1892 on American side of St. Croix River in Calais.

Nash Island Light. 30-foot square masonry tower built on offshore island in 1838. Boat access only.

Moose Peak Light. 60-foot tapered tower built in 1827 on offshore island off Beals Island. Boat access only.

The lighthouse at Quoddy Head sports a distinctive red and white striped pattern.

Little River Light. 40-foot cast-iron tower built on small island at the entrance of Cutler Harbor in 1817. Boat access only. View from trails on Western Head.

West Quoddy Head Light. Distinctive 50-foot red and white brick tower on high headland on the United States' easternmost point. Built in 1808. Good road and foot access.

Lubec Channel Light. 50-foot iron and brick tower built on a ledge on the west side of the St. Croix River channel in Lubec in 1890. View from Lubec.

St. Croix Light. 40-foot stone tower on island bisected by the international boundary with Canada. Built in 1857. Boat access only.

Shopping

▪ Antiques

Blue Hill

Blue Hill Antiques, 8 Water Street. Large shop featuring furniture from 1700-1950 with American and French antiques, decorative objects and paintings. Monday-Saturday, 10-5. Winter by appointment. ☎ 374-8825.

Liros Gallery (Serge L. Liros), Main Street. Fine paintings, Russian icons, old prints, maps. ☎ 374-5370.

Deer Isle

Blecher's Antiques, Reach Road, Deer Isle. Country furniture, folk art, toys, advertising signs, rugs, nautical and sporting items. Open June-October. Off season by chance or appointment. ☎ 348-9938.

Ellsworth

Cindy's Antiques (Lawrence Clough), Bucksport Road (Route 3). General line. Open by appointment or chance. ☎ 667-4476.

Sargentville

Old Cove Antiques (Peg and Olney Grindall), Route 15. Formal and country furniture, accessories, paintings, nautical, hooked rug, folk art, decoys. Memorial Day-Labor Day, 10-5 daily. Off season by appointment. ☎ 359-2031.

Southwest Harbor

Marianne Clark-Fine Antiques, Main Street, Route 102. Select 18th- and 19th-century furniture, country and formal, paintings, folk art. ☎ 244-9247.

Trenton

Tiffany's Antique Center (Gregory Betz), Route 230. Three floors of quality furnishing, miscellaneous. ☎ 667-7743.

West Sedgewick

Thomas Hinchcliffe Antiques (Tom and Daphne Hinchcliffe), Route 176. Country furniture in original paint, prints, rugs, quilts, boat models, accessories. Open most days May-September. Off season by chance or appointment. ☎ 326-9411.

Down East

Adventures On Foot

■ Hiking & Walking

For details on hikes in Acadia National Park, see the special Acadia section at the beginning of this chapter.

Bar Harbor Shore Path, Bar Harbor: For more than a century the Shore Path in Bar Harbor has attracted strollers to spend a leisurely afternoon or evening by the sea. Stretching nearly a mile from the municipal pier to Hancock Street, the easy walkway is maintained by the Village Improvement Association and remains open through the generosity of business and private land owners.

Sights along the way include Balance Rock, an egg-shaped boulder perched on ocean side ledges, and Grant's Park, with its sweeping lawn reaching to the edge of the sea. Offshore lobster boats and sail boat ply the waters of Frenchman Bay. There is no better place to view the ocean-going cruise ships calling at Bar Harbor. Walkers can do the path as an out-and-back route or take Wyman Lane at the south end back west toward Main Street and walk back to the start through the village.

Black Mountain, T-10 SD: Located in the Donnell Pond Public Reserve lot, Black Mountain offers everything its sister hills in nearby Acadia do – except the high number of hikers.

Begin by driving to the clearly marked trail by taking the first dirt road on the left after crossing the old railroad tracks on Route 183 in Sullivan. A signboard contains a good map of the area. The trail begins a steep ascent through thick aromatic woods with only intermittent views. As it levels off on the top, stay right. The left trail leads back down to Donnell Pond. By heading right you stay fairly level before heading down to a small hidden waterbody, Wizard Pond. The trail goes back up the other side to the true summit at 1,094. Total elevation gain is about 800 feet; distance is roughly two miles.

The view from the top of Black runs 360° with spectacular glimpses of Mount Desert Island and Acadia National Park to the south. Strenuous.

Blue Hill, Blue Hill: Looming over the village that is its namesake, Blue Hill sports a moderate hike to its 935-foot summit. The trail begins in a parking area marked "Fire Tower Trail," just off the Mountain Road. The path heads northwest through open blueberry fields and stands of hardwood. It then hooks around to the east and passes through stands of softwoods before reaching the summit with its fire tower and radio antennas after about a mile, total. There are good views all around, including the village to the south, Mount Desert Island to the southeast, and Castine and towns along Penobscot Bay to the west. Moderate.

Bold Coast, Cutler: Here is another recent addition to lands open to the public in Maine that has yet to be discovered and overrun. Its location, way Down East in the Washington County coastal town of Cutler, also insures that this preserve with spectacular rocky ocean frontage and cliffs will probably never see large numbers of visitors.

Pickup a map from the box at the parking area along Route 191 north of the village. This is a 1.5-mile hike through gently rolling forested terrain to the shore. The trail ends atop a 100-foot cliff with surf crashing below and Grand Manan Island on the horizon.

Trails continue along the five miles of shorefront, offering several dips to the water's edge on major coves. At the three-mile mark a cutoff trail returns to the road. You can continue on to Fairy Head at 3.8 miles, where there are three rough backcountry campsites (first-come, first-served) and a pit toilet. No fires are allowed. There is a dark water bog nearby where you can filter water. Alternately, use rain pools in the ledges.

Deer Isle: The Deer Isle Walking Trails Group offers a handy map showing all the walking, hiking, and bicycling paths on Deer Isle. Preserves and wildlife refuges are also shown. It costs $1 and is widely available locally or by telephoning ☎ 367-2448.

Schoodic Mountain, T-9 SD: Schoodic Mountain is the major peak to the northeast seen from most summits in Acadia National Park. The 1,070-foot summit is open and barren and contains the remains of an abandoned radio antenna, generator house, and other debris. Still, the views of the surrounding countryside make this a popular day hike destination.

The trailhead is off Route 200 between two bridges. It begins on asphalt road and then quickly turns to dirt as it heads east, eventually crossing an abandoned rail line. Here it turns hard right for a short ways before breaking left and ascending in earnest. The actual trail is very steep, exposed for much of the way, and very buggy in spring. Total distance is 2.5 miles, one way. The elevation gain is 1,000 feet. Moderate to strenuous.

∎ Rock Climbing

Bar Harbor/Acadia

 Atlantic Climbing School, 24 Cottage Street (inside Cadillac Mountain Sports), Bar Harbor 04609. Personalized rock climbing instruction with courses for all abilities. Experienced climbers Chris Kane and Jeff Butterfield stress safety and wilderness ethics.

Accredited by the American Mountain Guides Association and licensed to operate in Acadia National Park. ☎ 288-2521.

Acadia Mountain Guides, 198 Main Street, Bar Harbor 04609. Half- , full- or multiple-day instruction. Accredited by American Mountain Guides Association. Owners Jon Tierney and Liz Dunn-Tierney. Trips custom-tailored to group size and experience. Licensed to operate in Acadia National Park. ☎ 288-8186.

■ Golfing

Greens fees vary greatly according to the popularity of the course and the time of year.

Kebo Valley Golf Club, Route 233, Eagle Lake Road, Bar Harbor. 6,102 yards, par 70/men, 72/ladies. 18 holes. May-October. ☎ 288-3000.

Bucksport Golf Club, Bucksport. Route 46. 3,413 yards, par 36. April-November. ☎ 469-7612. 9 holes.

St. Croix Country Club, River Road, Calais. 2,735 yards, par 34. 9 holes. May 1-Oct. 30. ☎ 454-8875.

Castine Golf Club, Battle Avenue, Castine. ☎ 326-8844. 2,977 yards, par 35. 9 holes. May 15-October 15.

Island Country Club, Route 15A, Deer Isle. 3,865 yards, par 31. 9 holes. Memorial Day weekend-September 30. ☎ 348-2379.

White Birches Motel, Thorsen Road, off US 1, Ellsworth. 2,622 yards, par 34. 9 holes. April-October. ☎ 667-3621.

Lucerne Hills Golf Club, Route 1A, Lucerne-in-Maine. 3,205 yards, par 36. 9 holes. April 15-October 30. ☎ 843-6282.

Northeast Harbor Golf Club, Sargeant Drive, Northeast Harbor. 5430 yards, par 69. 15 holes. April-October. ☎ 276-5335.

Great Cove Golf Course, Jonesboro, Roque Bluffs. 1,694 yards, par 30. 9 holes. May-October. ☎ 434-2981.

Causeway Club Golf Course, Fernald Point Road, Southwest Harbor. 4,718 yards, par 65. 9 holes. May 1-October 31. ☎ 244-7220.

Bar Harbor Golf Course, Route 3, Trenton. 6,631 yards, par 71. 18 holes. April-October. ☎ 667-7505.

Grindstone Neck Golf Course, Grindstone Avenue, Winter Harbor. ☎ 963-7760. 3,000 yards, par 36. 9 holes. June 1-September 15.

Adventures On Wheels

■ Mountain Biking

For details on the many mountain bike trails in Acadia, see the special Acadia section at the beginning of this chapter.

Moosehorn National Wildlife Refuge, Baring

Two different units of this massive (24,400-acre) preserve are laced with more than 50 miles of dirt roads perfect for mountain biking. Terrain includes woods, fields, bogs and streams. There are two sections – the Baring Unit covers 17,200 acres; the Edmunds Unit, bordering tidal waters of Cobscook Bay near Dennysville, is more than 7,000 acres. Terrain throughout is rolling hills. Roads are open to hikers and, in winter, snowmobilers. Wildlife is abundant throughout the year. Deer hunting, however, is allowed in November.

There's a Visitor Center in Baring on the Charlotte Road. It has maps, water and restrooms. ☎ 454-7161.

Acadia-Area Bike Rentals

Acadia Bike and Canoe Shop
Cottage Street, Bar Harbor 04609, ☎ 88-9605.
Full-service shop featuring sales, service, clothing, tandems, trailers, and accessories. Also offers guided kayak trips, canoe, kayak rentals.

Bar Harbor Bicycle Shop
Cottage Street, Bar Harbor 04609, ☎ 288-3886.
Full-service shop featuring sales, service, clothing and accessories.

Maine Mountain Bike
Route 3, Ellsworth 04605, ☎ 667-3223.

Southwest Cycle
Main Street, Southwest Harbor 04679, ☎ 244-5856.
Full-service shop featuring sales, service, clothing and accessories. Jogging strollers, car racks. Open daily in season.

■ Foliage/Motor Tours

 One of the best scenic drives in the state is the **Park Loop Road** in Acadia National Park. For complete details, see the Acadia section at the beginning of this chapter.

Acadia Harbors & Heights

210 miles, 5¼ hours, round trip

Highlights: *Winding around the breathtaking Acadia National Park, this tour offers mountains, lakes and ocean as its autumn backdrop. Discover the charming islands, quiet harbors, and dramatic vistas that have made this one of Maine's most enchanting fall destinations.*

Route: In **Bucksport**, travel east on Route 3, then on 175 to **Deer Isle bridge**, suspended over scenic Eggemoggin Reach. Head south on 15 to **Stonington**, a traditional lobstering community, and return as far as **Sargentville**. Go east on 175 to **Sedgewick**, then north on 172 to the arts community of **Blue Hill**. Continue north on 176 to **Surry** and 172 to **Ellsworth**; head south on 230 to the **Mount Desert Island** bridge. Take 102 south through **Bass Harbor** and **Southwest Harbor** to **Somesville** along Somes Sound, the only fjord on the US Atlantic coast. Drive east and south on 198 and 3 through **Northeast Harbor** and **Seal Harbor** to **Bar Harbor**. Enjoy the mountains-to-the-sea views of Acadia National Park, taking time to bike the carriage paths, hike the scenic trails, and enjoy an island tradition of tea at the Jordan Pond House.

Take 3 north through **Hulls Cove** on to Ellsworth, then northwest on 1A to Brewer. Take 15 south back to Bucksport.

Downeast Villages & Vistas

180 miles, 4½ hours, round trip

Highlights: *This getaway will take you through the true "Downeast." It's quintessential coastal Maine, especially in autumn, when scarlet wild blueberry barrens blanket the landscape and the rugged coastline becomes softened by nature's colorful transition from summer to fall.*

Route: From **Ellsworth**, the site of the Georgian Black Mansion, take Route 179 northwest to **Aurora**. Take 9 east through the lakes, rivers and forest region of Washington County, passing through **Beddington**, **Wesley** and **Alexander**. Take US 1, watching for the **Moosehorn National Wildlife Refuge**, where a short

> **Foliage Hotline:** The Maine foliage hotline, in service each fall, offers the latest color-peaking information for leaf-peepers. ☎ 800-932-3419.

walk could reward you with eagle or moose sightings. Drive to 191 south on a local road, then go east on 191 to 214. Take 214 south to **West Pembroke**, site of the Reversing Falls, then go south on US 1 through **Machias**, the site of Burnham Tavern, where the first naval battle of the Revolutionary War was planned. While in Machias, plan a side trip to **Jasper Beach** and **Roque Bluffs** for beach combing. Continue on U.S. 1 to **Cherryfield**, then west on 182 through Franklin to US 1; drive south on 1 back to Ellsworth.

Routes courtesy Maine Department of Conservation

Route 15, Orland to Stonington

35 miles, 1 hour, one way

Highlights: *Poet Robert Frost would love to have driven on Route 15 from Orland to Stonington. From a visitor's perspective it is truly the road less travelled.*

Route: Jump on Route 15 where it meets Route 1/3 about five miles east of **Bucksport**. Also called the **Blue Hill Road**, this minor highway sticks to the high ground as it heads south toward the coast, passing the small village of North Penobscot. Route 15 takes hard right in North Blue Hill and drops quickly past the town's namesake mountain (with its open fields and hiking trails) toward the quaint yet trendy harbor village of **Blue Hill.**

From Blue Hill Route 15 makes another hard right and courses inland and for a while (here the road also has Route 176 markers). Apparently Maine has more routes than roads and one road often carries more than one numerical designation for part of its run.

Bear left at the next "t" intersection and begin a straight southerly shot toward **Deer Isle**. Watch for the picnic area on the right a couple of miles south of where Route 175 joins from the west.

Soon open fields provide spectacular glimpses of the **Eggemoggin Reach Suspension Bridge,** with its high arch and graceful towers.

Down East

Suspended Safely?

Like the suspension bridge over the Penobscot River between Prospect and Verona Island at Bucksport, the Deer Isle bridge is similar in design to the famous one Tacoma Narrows, which was twisted apart when high winds set up harmonic vibrations. Both Maine bridges have been altered to diminish this potential problem, but the Deer Isle bridge is known to sway in high winds, prompting many squeamish local residents to avoid it on windy days.

In season, there is a small information center on Little Deer Isle just after you cross the bridge.

On its way to Stonington Route 15 crosses a narrow, man-made causeway and then passes through the attractive town of Deer Isle. At **Stonington** there are numerous small preserves to visit. It is also the jumping-off place for the ferry to remote Isle au Haut, which is part of Acadia National Park. Just off the town wharf in Stonington dozens of attractive small islands are peppered in the sparkling sea. This is a quintessential fishing village without a doubt, but it also boasts one of the highest concentrations of art galleries per capita in the state. This area once sported a thriving granite trade, and stone is still quarried from time to time on Crotch Island, just offshore.

 INTERESTING FACT: *Stonington granite was used in building the Brooklyn Bridge and Rockefeller Center in New York City, and the Kennedy Memorial in Boston.*

Route 9, Brewer to Calais

100 miles, 2½ hours, one way

Highlights: *Reputed to be the rough route of an old stagecoach line, Route 9 is such a legendary Maine road that it has its own nickname – The Airline. While some argue that was the name of the old stage line, others claim it stems from the amount of time a vehicle spends in the air while vaulting over the road's many bumps and turns.*

In recent years road crews have been hard at work to ease the curves and smooth the bumps resulting in some of the best motoring in the state. With several years of work ahead to complete the entire 100-mile-long road, there are still plenty of rough places left to remind modern travellers of yesteryear.

Route: While Route 9 runs through much of the state, the Airline itself really begins in **Brewer** and heads due east toward Calais on the border with New Brunswick. Head north on Main Street in Brewer as the road follows the east side of the Penobscot River. Route 9 takes a hard right in **Eddington** and heads through picturesque woods and by open fields before passing through the village of **East Eddington**. Just head is the proud village of **Clifton**. Here, Route 9 heads through some respectable hills. Through Amherst and just past Aurora, Route 9 climbs atop and follows an unusual geological formation dubbed "The Whalesback." It is actually an esker, a sinuous mound of sand and gravel deposited by glacial outwash streams 10,000 years ago. A pullout overlooks the marshy twists and turns of the Middle Branch of the Union River. Watch out for moose!

Route 9 from the Whalesback on can be a very lonely road. For much of its length it is even abandoned by telephone and electric poles and wires. It crosses the upper reaches of most of the canoeable rivers in Down East Maine, including the Narraguagus, Pleasant, Machias and East Machias. Lead Mountain to the north is the dominant hill.

 INTERESTING FACT: *Prior to the outbreak of the Civil War, Confederate President Jefferson Davis came to Lead Mountain to spend the summer tenting near the top in the belief the airs and waters would help his ill health.*

About the only bright lights on this stretch come from the **Airline Snack Bar**, which is a small sit-down restaurant and convenience store. They also rent a few rooms and cabins.

 AUTHOR'S TIP: *Keep an eye out for Viola Sargent. The 92-year-old Maine Guide likes to drop by for a sandwich and cup of coffee between trips guiding her "sports" on moose and deer hunts.*

The next place to rest up or get some gas is in Wesley. There is also a small state picnic area on the north side of the road about halfway between Brewer and Calais.

The real jewel as far as stops go, however, is where Route 9 crosses over the **Machias River**. On the east bank there is a small campground with a handful of drive-in sites and one or two obscure carry-in sites closer to the highway. These may take a little bushwacking to find, but there are obvious paths from the road between the river and the campground entrance. One particularly nice site sports a lean-to only 50 feet from the river. There are pit toilets, fire rings and picnic tables and best of all-no fees. The water in spring flows fast here as it courses through the Airline Rapids (Class III in high flows).

There is also a nice launch ramp for hand-carry boats just below the rapids at the south end of the campground. Look carefully for the entrance road, especially in the off-season when the road side sign is removed for safe keeping.

Along Route 9 several state routes peel off to right and head south straight to US 1. All offer good scenery, especially Route 193, which heads to **Cherryfield**. Along the way it passes through **Deblois** with its hundreds of acres of wide open blueberry fields. When the plants turn bright crimson in the fall its almost like standing on Mars.

Down East

Back on Route 9 town signs disappear and township markers, which designate land with numbers and letters, become common.

The return of power and phone lines in **Crawford** and **Alexander** hint that you are nearing the end of the Airline in Calais. You can make a long day trip out of it by turning left (north) and heading up US 1 to **Topsfield** and then right again on Route 6, which traverses attractive countryside as it heads back to **Lincoln** and access to Interstate 95, which can return you south to the Bangor/Brewer area.

Or, you can turn right in Calais and follow US 1 back along the coast through quaint fishing villages and more blueberry barrens. As you head west, leave US 1 in Cherryfield and head to Ellsworth via Route 182, which takes you through the mountains and past the lakes of the **Tunk Lake Unit** of Maine Public Reserve Lands with its seldom-visited campsites and hiking trails. Route 182 rejoins US 1 just east of Ellsworth. From Ellsworth Route 1A will take you straight north back to the Bangor/Brewer area.

Adventures On Water

■ Whale Watching

 A typical two- to four-hour whale-watching trip costs $25-$35 per person. Many operators offer money-back guarantees if no whales are seen.

Bar Harbor

Bar Harbor Whale Watch Company, *Friendship* **V.** A fast catamaran with handicap accessibility that offers three trips daily to an offshore whaling area near Mount Desert Rock lighthouse. Food, film, etc., available on board. Money back guarantee if no whales seen. Dock: Regency Hotel, Eden Street Bar Harbor; Ticket office located on Cottage Street. ☎ 288-2386.

Whale Watcher Inc., *Atlantis.* A new, fast monohull that can accommodate 300 passengers in comfort. Visits offshore whale-watching grounds. Food, film, etc., available on board. The vessel is handicapped accessible. Money back guarantee if no whales seen. Docks: Harbor Place, West Street, Bar Harbor; Bay Ferries, Ferry Terminal, Eden Street. ☎ 288-3322.

Sea Bird Watcher Co., *Acadian Whale Watcher.* Multiple trips daily to see whales, marine mammals, puffins, seals and rare sea birds. Beverage and snack service. Dock: 55 West Street Bar Harbor. ☎ 288-5033.

∎ Boat Trips, Charters

Bar Harbor

 Harbor Boat Rentals, Harbor Place, West Street. Rent a Boston Whaler by the hour, half-day, or full day. Includes charts, life jackets and emergency radios. Fuel not included. $45 per hour and up. ☎ 288-3757.

Mt. Desert Island Sail Charters, 2 Kavanaugh Place, Bar Harbor 04609. Sail the coast of Maine in a 36' ketch *The Rose.* ☎ 288-3056.

Acadia Nature Cruise aboard *The Acadian.* Tour shores of Bar Harbor with stately mansions and see islands, lighthouse in Frenchman Bay. Dock: Harbor Place, West Street, Bar Harbor. ☎ 288-3322.

Bar Harbor Sightseeing and Sealwatch aboard *The Seal.* Trips to offshore ledges to see seals, seabirds and other wildlife. Dock: Bar Harbor Inn pier. ☎ 288-4585.

Bay Lady Schooner Cruise aboard *Bay Lady.* Sail the scenic waters of Frenchman Bay. Several trips daily with sunset cruise. Beverage service. Dock: Harbor Place, West Street, Bar Harbor, ☎ 288-3322.

Downeast Windjammer Cruises. Vessels: *Margaret Todd, Young America, Sylvina W. Beal.* Restored schooners and windjammers offer several trips daily and sunset cruises on Frenchman Bay. Winds and tides dictate the route. Dock: Bar Harbor Inn pier. ☎ 288-4585.

Seaventure Custom Boat Tours. Custom private boat tours for sightseeing, photography or wildlife observation. ☎ 288-3355.

Cutler

Bold Coast Charter Company, PO Box 364, Cutler 04626. Capt. Andrew Patterson. Offers regular nature cruises aboard the *Barbara Frost* to Cross Island Wildlife Preserve and puffin cruises to Machias Seal Island, nine miles offshore. Shortest sea trip possible to the popular puffin watching site. Weather permitting. Also, narrated trips along the remote Down East Bold Coast. ☎ 259-4484.

Down East

Jonesport

Norton of Jonesport, RR 1, Box 990, Jonesport 04649. Capts. Barna and John Norton. Daily trips, weather permitting, to Machias Seal Island and its famous puffin colony. Naturalist on board. ☎ 497-5933.

Machias

Machias Bay Boat Tours, Kayaking, PO Box 42, Machias 04654. Capts. Rick and Martha Jordan. Half- and full-day trips aboard the 34-foot motor vessel *Martha Ann*. See seals, lobster fishing, lighthouses ancient petroglyphs and spectacular scenery. Kayak and freshwater fishing trips also offered. ☎ 259-3338.

Mount Desert

Blackjack Sail Boat Charters aboard *Blackjack*. Small, intimate sailboat leaves from small harbor full of million-dollar yachts and sails the scenic waters of the Great Harbor of Mount Desert. Dock: Northeast Harbor. ☎ 276-5043.

Southwest Harbor

Acadia Cruises, aboard *Ranger*. Dock: Great Harbor Marina, Southwest Harbor. Tour nearby shores, islands and lighthouse from vessel based in authentic working harbor. ☎ 244-7399.

Mansell Boat Co. Inc., Box 1102 Main Street, Southwest Harbor 04679. Small boat rental, sailing lessons in waters around Mount Desert Island and Acadia National Park. ☎ 244-5625.

Manset Yacht Service, Shore Road, Manset 04679. Rentals of sail and power boats by half-day, day, week, month. ☎ 244-4040.

MDI Water Taxi. Private motor launch service for tours of local waters or transport to nearby islands. Seal watching. Small boat rentals available. ☎ 244-7312.

Schooner *Rachel B. Jackson*, PO Box 1252, Southwest Harbor 04679. Working replica of an 1890s topsail schooner sailing the waters off Mount Desert Island and Acadia National Park. Breakfast tours and sunset sails. Overnite guests have choice of berthing at marina in harbor or at anchor in Somes Sound. ☎ 244-7813.

Stonington

Isle au Haut/Stonington Dock Company, Sea Brezze Avenue, Stonington 04681. Regular scheduled passenger ferry, freight and mail trips to Isle au Haut. Daily seasonal runs to Duck Harbor campground, operated by Acadia National Park. Daily excursions in season among the islands of Penobscot Bay on the *Miss Lizzie*. Tour includes narrated talk on history and wildlife. Charter excursions and other trips to points of interest can be arranged on the vessel *Mink*. ☎ 367-5193 days, 367-2355 evenings.

Jericho Bay Charters, PO Box Stonington 04681. Private cruises for up to six people can be arranged on the lobster yacht *Lady Michele*. Trips include Jericho Bay, Western Way and even over to the eastard toward Swans Island and Bass Harbor (which includes portions of Acadia National Park). Enjoy the flying bridge on a four-hour tour. ☎ 348-6114.

Palmer Day IV, PO Box Stonington 04681. Capt. Reg. Greenlaw. Daily trips covering a 16-mile route among islands and offshore ledges. See wildlife, including sea birds, ospreys and eagles from this 49-passenger motor vessel. Leaves from dock in Stonington. ☎ 367-2207.

Tremont

Bass Harbor Island Cruises. Regular trips from working harbor on Mount Desert Island's quiet side. Aborad the 41-passenger vessel *R.I. Gott* and 21-passenger *Christina*. 3½-hour lunch cruise to the tiny island community of Frenchboro. Two-hour afternoon nature cruise. Rates, $14-$17 for adults, children less. Dock: Bass Harbor. ☎ 244-5785.

■ Deep-Sea Fishing

PRICING: When the weather is rough a half-day of deep-sea fishing is plenty. That will set you back $25-35. A full day runs from $40 to $55. Most trips include rod, reels and bait. Beer, other beverages and snacks will cost extra. Deckhands will usually fillet your catch should you choose to keep it (be sure to tip for this service).

Eastport

Harris Point Shore Cabins, Eastport 04631. Capt. George Harris. Vessel *Quoddy Dam* leaves daily from the Harris Point Wharf from June-September. ☎ 853-4303.

Jonesport

Aclid Aventures, RR 1, Box 990, Jonesport 04649. Capts. Barna and John Norton. Daily trips aboard vessels *Chief, Chief III* or *Harpoon* leaving from the Jonesport Marina. June-September. ☎ 497-5933.

Down East

The lighthouse at Bass Harbor Head has been a beacon to mariners for generations.

Northeast Harbor

R.M. Savage and Sons, PO Box 582, Northeast Harbor 04662. Capt. Rick Savage. Custom charter trips aboard *Poor Richard* leave from the town pier on Sea Street, Northeast Harbor. June-October. ☎ 276-3785.

Southwest Harbor

Masako Queen, Beal's Wharf, Clark Point Road, Southwest Harbor 04679. All-day trips eight to 12 miles offshore in pursuit of mackerel, blue fish (when they are running) sharks, and cod. ☎ 667-8493.

Next Time. A 29-foot sportfisher. ☎ 244-7044.

■ Places to Paddle

Blue Hill Falls

This reversing tidal rapid is a favorite whitewater play spot for covered boaters. It is located under the Route 175 bridge just southeast of the village. About 300 feet long, this falls runs best beginning about three hours after low tide. It builds over the next several hours to a Class IV run. Limited parking available near the bridge.

Donnell Pond

This gem of a lake was recently protected and much of the shoreline became public reserve land. Paddlers can begin in the cove at the west end of the lake where a rough, hand-carry ramp is located. Be sure to put a donation into the lock box for maintenance.

The cove is lined with many camps but just beyond lies open country. Mile Island is a great place to picnic and explore. It has a small gravel landing and swimming beach on the southeast side. Most of the eastern and southern shores are public with broad sandy and gravel beaches. Swimming and camping is allowed. The best beaches at the southern end tend to get quite worn by summer's end. There are great mountain views, opportunities to paddle to trailheads for nearby Black Mountain, and Loons to serenade you to sleep at night.

Long Pond, Mount Desert Island

Most people who paddle Long Pond, Mount Desert Island's largest lake, put in at the small town beach at the north end. Forget that. For an un-crowded paddle take the Long Pond Fire Road off Route 102 and park several miles in where the edge of the road skirts the lake. This is the lake's western cove. It is generally sheltered from the high winds that can plague the main body of the lake. Paddle straight across the cove to the east to Southern Neck. There are great wide ledges here for picnicking and swimming in the lake's clear, cool waters. No camping or fires.

Machias River, Route 9 to Northfield

Especially in spring and early summer when its headwater lakes are still discharging a good flow, the Machias River is a major stream.

A good trip begins at the state-run camping area just east of the Route 9 bridge. There are many flat water sections, but major Class II and above rapids are encountered at Little Falls, the Wigwams and Upper Holmes Falls (which must be portaged). Hidden in trees on an island just below Holmes Falls is a grave marker erected to memorialize Obadiah Hill a pi-oneer who drowned in the river in 1786. There is mostly flat water below Lower Holmes Falls which leads you to the best takeout at Smith's Land-ing. A scenic 23-mile trip. Paddlers can elect to continue but must portage a major waterfall.

Narraguagus River, Deblois to Cherryfield

The "Guagus," as it is affectionately known locally, is a fun river that tests your paddling skills with its twists, turns, blowdowns, and occa-sional rapids. You can begin at the Route 193 bridge by carrying your boats down the portage path on the right for .25 miles. There is a short run, another short carry, and then only a few rips among nine miles of fast-moving flat water.

Major hazards are strainers, trees which have fallen into the stream. They collect debris, and their share of passing canoeists and gear. Lit-tle Falls is a broad, sweeping Class II rapid that should be scouted. There is also an im-pressive ledge drop about a mile downstream.

After several minor rapids the river spends its last few miles winding through an extensive marsh. Watch for false channels. Go left when you can see a house straight ahead and the takeout point near Stillwater Dam is just around the corner. This 17-mile route makes for a long day trip. There are no authorized campsites along the river.

Northeast Creek, Bar Harbor

Northeast Creek is the only real stream of any size on which to paddle on Mount Desert Island. Park at the paved pullout along Route 3 in Salisbury Cove where the stream runs under a small bridge and into the sea. This very slow-moving water meanders past a farm into the island's interior. After a few bends the stream widens out into a massive marsh. Stick to the main channel and you will eventually come to a high ground island which can be explored. Further still, in fall, wild cranberries wait to be picked. A total of two miles of stream are navigable by hand-carry boats.

Somes Pond, Mount Desert Island

A small body of water by Maine standards but what this lacks in size if more than makes up for in features. Put in at one of the small roadside pullouts on either the south or north end. There is a wildlife sanctuary on the south shore, a small private island in the center, and on the west end some good swimming ledges. A small stream meanders nearly a half-mile from the west side. The east side is very shallow and weed-choked. Watch out for seaplanes.

St. Croix River, Vanceboro to Kelleyland

The Saint Croix, from Vanceboro to the hydro dam on Grand Falls Flowage at Kelleyland, is one of the finest river trips in the Northeast. Because it is dam-controlled there is enough water to paddle (500 CFS minimum) all summer long. The ride at that level may be somewhat bony, but it gets better when the water is up.

The best place to begin is Russell's Landing (☎ 788-3980) near a railroad bridge which German spies once tried to blow up in WWII. For a small fee Russell will let you park for several days and launch your boats. You can camp there and there is a restroom. He can also arrange car shuttles.

This 33-mile trip (shorter if you take out at Loon Bay) features some long flat stretches but also mile upon mile of fun Class I and Class II rapids. There are only two spots – Little Falls and Canoose Rips – that are tougher and must be scouted or portaged. There are numerous campsites along the way on both the Canadian and American side.

WISE WORDS: *Avoid the Canadian sites, at least the ones with road access, during fall hunting season as wildlife sightings will likely include a non-stop parade of beered-up good ole' boys with guns. They are largely harmless but annoying.*

One of the endearing factors on this trip is that river left is one country, river right another. The time zones change too, depending on which side of the boundary you are on.

The St. Croix Waterway is managed by an international commission. They produce an excellent, detailed, full-color map with rules and regulations on the back. You can reach them at St. Croix International Waterway Commission, 435 Milltown Blvd., St. Stephen, New Brunswick, E3L 1J9.

The Hop, Frenchman Bay

This attractive offshore island, which is part of Acadia National Park, is a popular kayak destination in Frenchman Bay. Most paddlers put in at the Bar Harbor Town Pier or nearby town beach and head east across the bay island-hopping among the Porcupine Islands, so named because of their distinctive rounded shapes.

The Hop, located at the eastern end of Long Porcupine Island, is separated from its larger sister by a gravel and stone bar. The Hop features a nice beach on the northwest side, a grassy meadow on top, and tall cliffs on the south. No fires or camping allowed. Paddling across Frenchman Bay, with its high level of nautical traffic including a high-speed catamaran ferry to Nova Scotia, requires an intermediate level of paddling skill. Several companies offer guided trips that include a stop at the Hop.

Union River, Ellsworth

Most people who get stuck in traffic on Ellsworth's commercial strip have no idea there is a lovely sea kayak trip only half a mile away.

Paddlers can park and put in at the town dock on Water Street and head south down the tidal Union River, which after several miles opens up into a broad bay. There are plenty of small coves to explore and wildlife to watch.

Canoeing & Kayaking Outfitters

Overnight trips average $100-150 per person, per day. Half-day guided trips run in the vicinity of $50. Basic rentals cost between $25 and $45 per day. Most rentals include life jackets, paddles and car-topping gear.

Acadia National Park Canoe Rental, Inc.
Box 120, Route 102, Long Pond Road, Mount Desert 04660.
Canoe rentals by half- or full day. Fully equipped fishing canoes available. Guided sunset trips. Car-top the canoes or wheel across road to nearby beach. Mid-May through October. ☎ 244-5854.

Acadia Bike and Canoe
Box 422, 48 Cottage Street, Bar Harbor 04609
Canoe rentals, kayak trips & rentals. May 1-October 1. ☎ 288-5483.

Acadia Outfitters
PO Box 405, Bar Harbor 04609.
Half- and full-day kayak trips in waters off Mount Desert Island and Acadia National Park. ☎ 288-8118.

Coastal Kayaking Tours and Acadia Bike
48 Cottage Street, PO Box 405, Bar Harbor 04609.
Coastal Kayaking Tours was the first outfitter to bring sea kayaking to the Maine coast on a commercial basis. The company has 16 years experience. Acadia Bike has the largest fleet of rental bicycles in New England. ☎ 288-9606.

National Park Sea Kayak Tours
137 Cottage Street, Bar Harbor 04609.
Kayak trips, limited to parties of six tandem kayaks. Beginners welcome. Locally owned and operated. Relaxed pace, routes selected to take maximum advantage of winds, waves, weather. Small group size increased chances of seeing wildlife. Registered Maine Guides with top-quality safety equipment. May-September. ☎ 288-0342.

The Phoenix Centre
Route 175, Blue Hill Falls 04615.
Canoe rentals & trips, kayak rentals & trips. ☎ 374-2113.

Sunrise County Canoe Expeditions, Inc.
Route 191, PO Box, Cooper 04638.
Canoe rentals, canoe trips, on Cathance Lake. Trips on all rivers in eastern Maine, including St. Croix, Machias. Some northern Maine waterways. March-October. ☎ 454-7708.

Tidal Trails Sea Kayak Tours (Eastport)

PO Box 321, Pembroke 04666.
Guided two- to three-hour sea kayak tours. No experience needed. See great scenery, wildlife, eagles. Eco-tours and freshwater canoeing also available. Also a float rafting trip through a tidal reversing falls. ☎ 726-4799, 853-7373.

D-Arrow Wilderness Canoe Trips

PO Box 9, Grand Lake Stream 04637.
Canoe trips, on West Grand Lake, St. Croix River. June-August. ☎ 796-2969.

Eastern Outdoor Adventures

RR 1, Box 160, Machias 04654.
Freshwater, fly, and saltwater fishing and sea kayaking tours throughout Eastern Maine. Book for a few hours, days, or a week. See wildlife along Cobscook, Machias and Chandler Bays. ☎ 255-4210.

Loon Bay Kayak Tours and Livery

PO Box 391, Orland 04472.
A full-service livery and touring center, sea kayaking the shores of Acadia. Rental pickup in Trenton on Route 3. ☎ 266-8888.

Mansell Boat Rental

Box 1102, Shore Road, Manset, Southwest Harbor 04679.
Canoe rentals, canoe trips. May 1-November 1. ☎ 244-5625.

Maine Wilderness Camps

RR 1, Box 1085, Springfield 04487.
Canoe rentals, canoe trips, kayak rentals, kayak trips. May 15-November 15. Location: Washington County, Pleasant Lake-T7 R2. ☎ 738-6052.

■ Scuba Diving

Bass Harbor

 Dive Maine, HCR 33, Box 40, Bass Harbor 04653. Chris and Elaine Eaton of Harbor Divers in Bass Harbor offer morning and afternoon two-tank dive trips in the waters off Acadia National Park. A one-tank night dive is also an option. Snorkling packages for adults and children are also available but, frankly, without a wetsuit it is a very chilly proposition. Rental equipment, air refills available. Harbor Divers, which is located on Route 102 in Bass Harbor, also has a free map of local dive sites. ☎ 244-5751.

Calais/Machias

Kissing Fish Dive Shack, 19 East Main Street, Machias 04654; 165 Main Street, Calais 04619. Guided underwater tours of shipwrecks and ocean wonders from Eastport to Schoodic. Equpiment rental and air. Diving training, underwater video service. Sea kayak rentals, canoe rentals and tours also offered. ☎ 255-3567.

■ Guided Trips

Mooselook Guide Service, Route 186, Gouldsboro 04607. Regular kayak tours for paddlers of all abilities on local waters. Emphasis on wildlife watching. Special sunset tour. Kayak island camping trips can be scheduled. Overnight canoe trips on Washington County's Pleasant River or other rivers Down East.

Canoe, kayak and pedal boat rentals as well as mountain bike rentals. Low rates. Short distance from Schoodic section of Acadia National Park.

Rustic rental camp with only water access on Graham Lake. One-room dwelling with cooking facilities (no running water) on secluded beach. Outhouse. $215 a week. ☎ 963-7720.

North Woods Tours, PO Box 55, Danforth, Maine 04424. From its base in the secluded Chiputneticook Lakes area of Eastern Maine, this company offers remote and relaxed family and group paddling outings as well as lodging opporunties. Regular half-day and multi-day river and lake trips include all non-personal gear. Regular wildlife seminars and trips on St. Croix River. ☎ 448-2300.

Adventures In the Air

■ Scenic Flights & Glider Rides

Bar Harbor/Acadia

Acadia Air, Route 3, Bar Harbor Airport, Trenton 04605. This popular company offers seven route options and varying flight lengths. Low-level overflights of Acadia National Park offered seasonally on a first-come, first-served basis. Lighthouse and foliage tours offered. $15-$37 per person, two-person minimum. ☎ 667-5534.

Island Soaring, Route 3, Bar Harbor Airport, Trenton 04605. Ticket office on Cottage Street, Bar Harbor. Glider overflights for two over the mountains, lakes and shores of Mount Desert Island and Acadia National Park. Many trips daily with special sunset trips. Prices start at $50 per person. ☎ 667-7627.

Adventures On Snow

■ Cross-Country Skiing

For details of cross-country skiing options in **Acadia National Park**, see the Acadia section at the beginning of this chapter.

Baring

Moosehorn National Wildlife Refuge. Nearly 50 miles of unplowed roads open to skiing, snowshoeing and snowmobiling. ☎ 454-3521.

Brooksville

Holbrook Island Sanctuary State Park. Four miles of trails open to skiing and snowshoeing. ☎ 326-4012.

Dennysville

Cobscook Bay State Park. Four miles of trails. Snowmobiling, snowshoeing. ☎ 726-4412.

Skiing & Snowmobiling Outfitters
Cadillac Mountain Sports Cottage Street, Bar Harbor 04609. Cross-country ski and snowshoe rentals, equipment for sale, clothing and gear. Expert advice from salespeople. ☎ 288-4532. Also at High Street, Ellsworth 04605, ☎ 667-7818.

■ Snowmobiling

Because of its proximity to the ocean, and the propensity of snowstorms to often turn to rain before they end, riding Down East is spotty. When the snow is right there is a good half- to full day of snowmobiling possible in Acadia National Park. One lane of the **Ocean Drive** is left unplowed and machines are allowed anywhere on the 22-mile **Park Loop Road**. The trip to the summit of **Cadillac**

Mountain is challenging and rewards intrepid riders with great views and Arctic-like summit conditions.

One **ITS trail**, #81, begins in the Washington County town of Harrington and heads north. There are also uncountable club and local trails. **ITS 84** stretches across Washington County from Calais in the east all the way to Milford across the Penobscot River from Old Town.

Eco-Tours & Cultural Excursions

■ Bird Watching/Nature Tours

Bar Harbor/Acadia

Down East Nature Tours, PO Box 521, Bar Harbor 04609. Naturalist Mike Good offers several varied trips around Bar Harbor and the environs of Acadia National Park. Rates begin at $15 for a four-hour beginners bird-watching session. He also offers Cadillac Mountain sunrise and sunset tours, a wetland ecology trip and custom tours for avid birders looking to expand their life lists. Group rates available, reservations required. ☎ 288-8128.

Wild Gardens of Acadia, Suier de Monts Springs in Acadia National Park. This tiny three-quarter-acre plot of land is a thriving garden containing more than 500 plant species native to Mount Desert Island.

Two features make the garden unique – the range of plant species, including those customarily found in the more northern and southern regions, and the division of the garden into habitats.

As glaciers retreated more than 4,000 years ago, many plants were left behind – mountain cranberry, bunchberry, bearberry, rhodora, chokeberry, mountain sandwort, Labrador tea, early saxifrage, crowberry and three-toothed cinquefoil. Today, hikers find these plants on mountain summits. In the Wild Gardens they are found in the artificially constructed mountain and heath habitats and clearly labelled to aid in indentification.

There is plenty of parking and no fee. Donations are accepted in a box at the entrance of the garden. Nature center and trailside Native American Museum within walking distance. ☎ 288-3519.

Acadia Zoo, Route 3, Trenton 04605. Reindeer, bison, and moose roam the 30 acres of fields of this non-profit educational facility. Inside numerous other animals are on display in simulated rainforest habitat. Open daily in season. Admission charged. ☎ 667-3244.

Mount Desert Oceanarium, Clark Point Road, Southwest Harbor 04679. Considered as one of America's best family destinations, the Oceanarium features nearly two dozen saltwater tanks and even more exhibits about the sea and sea life. Touch tank for children. Open daily except Sunday May through October. Admission fee. Also operates location on Route 3 in Bar Harbor with the Maine Lobster Museum and salt marsh tours. Lobster hatchery on premises. ☎ 244-7330.

Downeast Interpretive Center, 45 Water Street, Lubec 04652. Center contains exhibits, films and interactive displays about Lubec and Down East Maine. Subjects include tides and fog, tide pools, birds and whales and Lubec's past. Free area information and guided nature walks scheduled daily. Open Tuesday-Sunday in July and August. Gift Shop.

■ Lumberjack Show

The Great Maine Lumberjack Show, Route 3, Trenton 04605. It may sound kind of hokey, but the main thing this show provides is fun for the entire family. From the covered bleachers (bring bug repellent in spring) you can watch as the show's team of male and female and child lumberjacks log roll, speed climb, power saw, chop and axe throw the night away. Lots of comedy and games for the kids. Owner "Timber" Tina Scheer has been performing and competing for more almost 25 years. One show nightly at 7 pm, June through September. Admission charged. ☎ 667-0067.

■ Apple Picking

 Fall is the season for picking your own fresh apples. Try **Merrill Farms**, Route 1A, Ellsworth, ☎ 667-9750.

■ Blueberry Picking

 Late July and early August is blueberry harvest season in Maine. From the flat windswept barrens of Washington County, to the rolling hillside fields in Hancock, Waldo and Knox Counties, rakers begin their seasonal labors. While pints and quarts of fresh-raked berries are available at most stores and farmstands, there is nothing like picking them yourself. Commercial picking fields charge a small fee, usually by the pint. If picking in the wild while hiking, use sturdy container to bring your wild bounty home. Here's where to go:

Pick-Your-Own Blueberries

Acadia

Acadia National Park, Mount Desert Island. Blueberries grow wild on most open summits and hills. Park rules allow picking for personal consumption. Birds love to eat berries too. But, they are timid about getting too close to vegetation. (My secret picking spots are the summits of Sargent and Penobscot Mountain. Look for good picking where fields meet forests and clumps of trees.)

Ben's Berry Patch, Long Pond Road, Southwest Harbor. Open all day. No fee. No pesticides. Nice views of nearby Western, Beech Mountains. ☎ 244-3944.

Cherryfield

Beddington Ridge Farm, Route 193. Open through August. Call ahead. ☎ 638-2664.

Where to Stay & Eat

■ Favorite Restaurants

Rate Scale

All rates are for entrée or complete dinner, per person.

Inexpensive. . . . . under $10

Moderate . . . . $10-$20

Expensive . . . . More than $20

Bar Harbor

Bubba's, 30 Cottage Street, Bar Harbor 04609. Without question the best burgers in Eastern Maine; charbroiled with great toppings. Soups, sandwiches, full bar, rich wood decor. Open daily in season for lunch, dinner, nightlife. Inexpensive to moderate. ☎ 288-5871.

Jordan's Restaurant, 78 Cottage Street, Bar Harbor 04609. Open daily between 5 am and 2 pm for breakfast (served all day) and lunch. Famous for blueberry muffins and pancakes, unique omelets. Best coffee in town. Open kitchen. Closes for a few weeks in winter. No charge cards or reservations accepted. Waiting line forms early in season but moves fast. Inexpensive to moderate. ☎ 288-3586.

Porcupine Grill, 123 Cottage Street, Bar Harbor 04609. Upscale establishment with great atmosphere. Menu offerings range from seafood, to Angus beef to their famed "haut-vegetarian." Homemade breads, pastas and desserts. Casual dress. Cocktail lounge. Wide wine list and big by-the-glass selection. Reservations suggested. Open seven days in season, schedule changes during winter. Moderate to expensive. ☎ 288-3884.

The Quarterdeck Restaurant, corner of Main and West Street, Bar Harbor 04609. This is the quintessential Maine waterfront restaurant with great views from two floors of indoor candlelit dining and an outdoor deck. Steaks, seafood, lobster, daily specials. Cocktails. Open seasonally for lunch and dinner. Moderate to expensive. ☎ 288-5292.

West Street Café, corner of West Street and Holland Avenue, Bar Harbor 04609. Family restaurant near the harbor with indoor and some outdoor dining. Early bird specials make this establishment very affordable. Standard menu of fresh seafood, lobster, beef and chicken. Large lobsters available. Children's menu. Cocktail lounge open until midnight. Open seven days a week, seasonally. Moderate. ☎ 288-5242.

Eastport

Waco Diner, Bank Square, Eastport 04631. Small and shopworn but good food, cheap. Traditional diner fare – meatloaf, fried foods, pot roast and bottomless cup of coffee. Try the cheesecake. Inexpensive. ☎ 853-4046.

Hancock

Crocker House Country Inn, Hancock Point Road, Hancock. Intimate dining in a quiet country setting. American cuisine includes poached salmon Florentine, rack of lamb, fresh seafood, lobsters. Cocktails. Open seasonally for dinner. Moderate to expensive. ☎ 422-6806.

Lubec

Waterside Restaurant, on the waterfront, Lubec 04652. Steamed lobster and all-you-can-eat steamed clams can be eaten right on the dock where fishermen land their catch. Eagles soar overhead. Sandwich and standard menu available. Open seasonally. Jazz concerts weekly in August. Inexpensive. ☎ 733-2500.

Down East

Machias

Helen's Restaurant, US 1, Machias 04654. Helen's is Down East Maine's most famous restaurant and a favorite with adventurers on their way into or out of the woods. Steak, seafood, pot roast and daily specials. Strawberry pie is to die for. Open daily year-round for breakfast, lunch and dinner. Also has Ellsworth location. Inexpensive to moderate. ☎ 255-8423.

Mount Desert

Burning Tree, Route 3, Otter Creek. Owned by the chefs, this casually-elegant restaurant specializes in gourmet seafood and vegetarian dishes. Wide menu selection changes frequently. Open daily for dinner (except Tuesdays) throughout the season. Cocktails. Moderate. ☎ 288-9331.

Redfield's, Main Street, Northeast Harbor. Lauded in the top cooking magazines, Redfield's boasts a quiet elegant atmosphere. Gallery on premises. Lightly smoked entrées, lobster, roast quail, sesame-dipped tuna. Impressive wine list. Cocktails. Reservations suggested. Expensive. ☎ 276-5283.

Southwest Harbor

Beal's Lobster Pier, Clark Point Road, Southwest Harbor 04679. You can't get lobsters and seafood any fresher than this. Indoor and outdoor no-frills dining on the dock where fishermen land their catch. Pick your own lobster from the tank. Also: sandwiches, crabmeat, shrimp, chowders, fresh fish, homemade desserts. Open daily 9 am until 8 pm. Live lobsters shipped anywhere. Inexpensive to moderate. ☎ 244-7178.

Deacon Seat, Clark Point Road, near the post office, Southwest Harbor 04679. Best breakfast and lunch in town. Fresh baked goods, bottomless cup of coffee, standard lunch fare and unusual sandwiches. ☎ 244-9229.

Deck House Restaurant, Great Harbor Marina, Southwest Harbor 04679. Dinner theater at its finest with a water view to boot. Diner begins at 6:30 pm and when the sun falls the curtain goes up as waiters and waitresses change into costume for a variety musical and dramatic numbers. Open seasonally. Reservations recommended. Moderate. Also serves lunch. ☎ 244-5044.

Stonington

The Bay View Restaurant, Seabreeze Avenue, Stonington 04681. Lunch and dinner served in dining room with great view of the busy working harbor. Lobster, chowder, lobster stew, fried and broiled seafood, steak, chicken. No alcoholic beverages. Open seven days in summer, five days a week in winter. Inexpensive to moderate. ☎ 367-2274.

Winter Harbor

Chase's Restaurant, Main Street, Winter Harbor 04693. A favorite with local residents, Chase's features good Down East food and real home cooking. It is open every day except Christmas for breakfast, lunch and dinner. Lobster, chowders, diner fare. Great deal on fish and chips. Lunches packed to go. Inexpensive to moderate. ☎ 963-7171.

▪ Brew Pubs/Microbreweries

 If Jed Clampet and the rest of the Beverly Hillbillies were microbrew aficionados they would have loaded up the truck and headed east to Bar Harbor. In recent years this picturesque town by the sea, surrounded on the land side by the mountains and trails of Acadia National Park, has seen a boom in microbreweries and pubs. Even more are in the planning stages.

Bar Harbor

Atlantic Brewing Company/Lompoc Café and Brewpub, 30 Rodick Street. A wide variety of beers are available, including Bar Harbor Real Ale, Bar Harbor Blueberry Ale, Ginger Wheat Ale, Coal Porter, Lompoc's Pale Ale and seasonals. The menu focuses on, of course, Maine seafood as well as Mediterranean entrées and vegetarian dishes. After hours the pub, with its outdoor bocce court, is a favorite hangout for a varied cast ranging from local hippie capitalists to students from the nearby College of the Atlantic. Tours daily at 4 pm. Gift shop open daily in season. ☎ 288-9513.

Bar Harbor Brewing Company, Route 3, Otter Creek. This firm's Cadillac Mountain Stout won a Platinum award in 1996 from the Beverage Tasting Institute. They are also well known for Thunder Hole Ale, named for a feature in Acadia National Park, as well as Harbor Lighthouse Ale and in season Bar Harbor Peach Ale and Ginger Mild Ale. Call ahead for tour times. ☎ 288-4592.

Maine Coast Brewing Company and Taproom, 21A Cottage Street. The small place that is big on beer. Brews include Bar Harbor Gold, Great Head Ale, named for a prominent headland in Acadia, Redneck Ale, Eden Porter and Sweet Waters Stout. Many seasonals. Tours daily; call for times. Gift shop in pub. ☎ 288-4914.

Jack Russell's Brewpub and Beer Garden, 102 Eden Street. Seasonal restaurant and outdoor dining on the lawn featuring Maine Coast

Brewing Company beers (above). Eight beers on draft along with home-made root beer. Menu includes English pub food, lobster, seafood and pizzas. ☎ 288-4914.

■ B&Bs, Hotels & Motels

Price Scale
All rates are based on double occupancy.
Inexpensive . . . . Under $65
Moderate . . . . $66-$100
Expensive. . . . . Above $100

Bar Harbor

 Bar Harbor Inn, 7 Newport Drive, Bar Harbor 04609. A true waterfront resort located right on the harbor. Superb dining in Reading Room Restaurant, which is open to the public for all meals with a special Sunday buffet. Gatsby's Terrace offers outside dining with view of harbor and schooners leaving from inn's dock. Rooms and suites feature phone, cable TV, air-conditioning, continental breakfast. Ocean views. Heated outdoor pool, jacuzzi, complimentary use of nearby health club. Cocktail lounge with nightly entertainment. Open year-round. Package rates available. Moderate to expensive. ☎ 288-3351.

Base Camp Cabin, PO Box 750, Bar Harbor 04609. Cozy housekeeping cabin on edge of Acadia National Park. Rustic, but with all the comforts of home. Built and operated by Registered Maine Guide. Sleeps four-five. Free use of Old Town canoe with car-topping and paddling gear. Fireplace, TV, VCR, phone. Open seasonally. Moderate. ☎ 288-4859.

Emery's Cottages, Box 172C, Bar Harbor 04609. Immaculate cottage colony on the shore in Hulls Cove. Private pebble beach, private baths, cable TV, picnic ground, laundry, some units have kitchens. Spectacular sunset views. Open seasonally. Moderate. ☎ 288-3432.

Inn at Canoe Point, Route 3, Bar Harbor 04609. Located only a mile or so from town, the Inn at Canoe Point is a deliciously isolated spot. This former summer estate perched over the ocean has just five elegant guest rooms each with private bath. Spectacular views of Frenchman Bay. Entrance to Acadia National Park almost across the street. Open year-round (except January). Expensive. ☎ 288-9511.

The Regency, Holiday Inn, Sunspree Resort, 123 Eden Street, Bar Harbor 04609. Oceanfront luxury hotel with ocean views. Outdoor pool, hot tub, sauna, fitness room, three restaurants, pool-side lounge, putting green, lighted tennis courts, docking space. Whale watch boat leaves from property. Rooms include coffee-maker, refrigerator, hair dryers, phone, cable TV. Open seasonally. Moderate to expensive. ☎ 288-9723.

Wonderview Inn, 50 Eden Street, Bar Harbor 04609. Hilltop location gives all modern rooms spectacular views of Frenchman Bay. Phones, cable TV, outdoor pool. Some rooms have private balconies. Award-winning restaurant, cocktail lounge on premises with great views from every seat. Open seasonally. Moderate to expensive. ☎ 288-3358.

Grand Lake Stream

Leen's Lodge, PO Box Grand Lake Stream. Located on shores of massive West Grand Lake famous for its salmon and trout, Leen's offers traditional sporting camp accommodations on the American plan. Great views, wild setting. Boat rentals. Guides available. Open seasonally. Moderate. ☎ 796-5575.

Lubec

Eastland Motel, Route 189, Lubec 04652. 22 units make up this AAA-approved establishment just a few miles out of town. Phones, cable TV, all on ground floor. Four lighthouses within 10-mile radius. Inexpensive to moderate. ☎ 733-5501.

Machias

Machias Motor Inn, East Main Street, Machias 04654. 35 units overlooking the Machias River. All rooms have phone, cable TV, and air-conditioning. Indoor pool, handicapped access. Restaurant on premises. Open year-round. Inexpensive to moderate. ☎ 255-4861.

Mount Desert

Asticou Inn, Route 3, Northeast Harbor 04662. This stately landmark overlooking picturesque harbor is a favorite with the rich and famous from Supreme Court Justices to authors and entertainers. The 48 rooms include those in Cranberry Lodge and cottages on grounds. Tennis, afternoon tea, telephones, no TV. Modified American plan or B&B packages available. Adjacent to famous gardens. Tennis, pool. Cocktail lounge. Open seasonally. Dining room open to public. ☎ 276-3344.

Down East

Orland

Alamoosook Lodge, PO Box 16, Orland 04472. Watch loons on the lake from cozy rooms with private baths. Wonderful views, gardens, swimming and canoeing. Rooms include breakfast. Moderate. ☎ 496-6393.

Princeton

Long Lake Camps, PO Box 817, Princeton 04668. Traditional sporting camp where housekeeping cabins have porches literally on the shore of Long Lake. American plan available for those who want to eat in the main lodge. Swimming, canoeing, fishing and boating. Boat rentals. Guides available. Seasonal. Moderate. ☎ 796-2051.

Southwest Harbor

Claremont Hotel, Clark Point Road, Southwest Harbor 04679. Graceful old inn with broad lawn sweeping down to the ocean. Fine dining (jacket required) in inn or at dockside bistro. Cottages available. Famous for annual croquet tournament. Tennis, afternoon tea. Offers 30 comfortable rooms in inn, all with private baths. Phone but no TV. Close to Acadia National Park. Open seasonally. Rooms with view of Somes Sound (ocean) are modified American plan only. Moderate to expensive. ☎ 244-5036.

Stonington

Inn at the Harbor, PO Box 69, Stonington 04681. A total of 13 cozy rooms (10 overlooking the harbor) make up this rambling, recently remodeled establishment on the shore. All rooms, which are named for famous windjammers, have private baths, phones and TV. Deck overlooking harbor. Complimentary wine and sherry each evening. Homemade breakfast (included), expresso bar with lighter fare for lunch, snacks. Open April 1 through January 1. Moderate to expensive. ☎ 367-2420.

■ Camping

 Facilities indicated as "nearby" are located within one mile of the campground.

Alexander

Pleasant Lake Camping Area, 371 Davis Road, Alexander 04694. With the spring fed Pleasant Lake in the front and scenic Break Neck Mountain on your right, this spot offers excellent swimming, fishing, boating, hiking, and more. 120 sites, tenting area, 30 amp, sewer, dump station, store, laundry, rec hall, swimming, boating, fishing, LP gas. Pets allowed. Open Memorial Day-Columbus Day. ☎ 454-7467.

Bar Harbor

Bar Harbor Campground, RFD1, Box 1125, Bar Harbor 04609. A very quiet, clean family campground. Modern bathrooms with hot showers. Closest to town and Acadia National Park. 300 sites on 100 acres. Choose you own site (pick from 300). Tenting area, 50 amp, sewer, dump station, store, laundry, rec hall, swimming, pool, group area, LP gas. Boating and fishing nearby. Pets allowed. Open Memorial Day-Columbus Day. ☎ 288-5185.

Barcadia Campground, RR 1, Box 2165, Bar Harbor 04609. 3,500 feet of spectacular oceanfront camping for tents to largest RVs. Near Acadia National Park and Nova Scotia ferry. New heated bathhouse, store, seventh day of stay is free. 200 sites, tenting area, 50 amp, sewer, dump station, store, laundry, rec hall, swimming, boating, fishing, on-site rentals, group area, LP gas. Pets allowed. Open May 9-October 15. ☎ 288-3520.

Hadley's Point Campground, RFD1, Box 1790, Bar Harbor 04609. Situated four miles from Acadia National Park entrance. A five-minute walk to public beach. Sunday church services on-grounds. Friendly relaxed family atmosphere. 180 sites, tenting area, 30 amp, sewer, dump station, store, laundry, swimming, pool, group area, LP gas. Boating and fishing nearby. Pets allowed. Open May 15-October 15. ☎ 288-4808.

Mt. Desert Narrows Camping, RR 1, Box 2045, Route 3 Bar Harbor 04609. On the ocean, nightly entertainment (in season), heated pool, and shuttle bus to town (Memorial-Columbus Days). 239 sites, tenting area, 50 amp, sewer, dump station, store, laundry, rec hall, swimming, boating, pool, group area, LP gas. Pets allowed. Open May 1-October 25. ☎ 288-4782.

Spruce Valley Campground, RR 1, Box 2420M, Route 102, Bar Harbor 04609. Centrally located five miles from main entrance of Acadia National Park. Secluded, wooded and open sites, heated bathhouse, cable TV, shuttle bus. 100 sites, tenting area, 30 amp, sewer, dump station, store, laundry, rec hall, swimming, pool, on-site rentals, group area, LP gas. Boating and fishing nearby. Pets allowed. Open May 10-October 31. ☎ 288-5139.

Bass Harbor

Bass Harbor Campground, PO Box 122, Bass Harbor 04653. A friendly family oriented campground adjacent to western portion of Acadia National Park and just a 10-minute walk from picturesque Bass Har-

Down East

bor Lighthouse and the Atlantic Ocean. 114 sites, tenting area, 30 amp, dump station, store, laundry, rec hall, swimming, pool, on-site rentals, group area. Boating and fishing nearby. Open June15-September 30. ☎ 244-5857.

Bucksport

Flying Dutchman Campground, PO Box 1639, Bucksport 04416. Camp beside beautiful Penobscot River. Clean and attractive facilities. Wooded, open, or riverside sites and able to accommodate any size RV. 35 sites, tenting area, 20 amp, sewer, dump station, store, laundry, rec hall, swimming, fishing, pool, group area. Boating nearby. Pets allowed. Open May 1-Columbus Day. ☎ 541-2267.

Masthead Campground, RR 1, Box 1590, Bucksport 04416. A family oriented place with spacious, private sites. Usual campground sports including lake swimming. Fifty minutes to Acadia National Park. A total of 38 sites, tenting area, 15 amp, dump station, laundry, rec hall, swimming, boating, fishing. Pets allowed. Open Memorial Day- September 15. ☎ 469-3482.

Danforth

Greenland Cove Campground, Box 279, Danforth 04424. A quiet family campground on beautiful East Grand Lake. Lakeshore sites, swimming – lake or heated pool. Fishing – salmon, togue, and bass. 37 sites, tenting area, 30 amp, dump station, store, laundry, rec hall, swimming, boating, fishing, pool. Pets allowed. Open May 15-September 30. ☎ 448-2863.

Deer Isle

Sunshine Campground, RR 2, Box 521D, Deer Isle 04627. All camping conveniences off the main roads, on an island (accessible by causeway) in a quiet wooded setting you'll love. Water access near for kayaks. 22 sites, tenting area, 20 amp, dump station, store, laundry, rec hall, on-site rentals, LP gas. Pets allowed. Open Memorial Day-October 15. ☎ 348-6681.

East Orland

Balsam Cove Campground, PO Box C, East Orland 04431. Family camping at its best on beautiful Toddy Pond. Swimming, fishing, boat rentals, play area and 60 wooded sites only 26 miles from Bar Harbor. 60 sites, tenting area, 30 amp electric service, sewer, dump station, store, laundry, rec hall, swimming, boating, fishing, on-site rentals. Pets allowed. Open Memorial Day-September 30. ☎ 469-7771.

Whispering Pines Campground, US 1, East Orland 04431. A clean, very quiet, family-oriented campground in a beautiful natural setting, owned and operated by the Gates family since 1977. 50 sites, tenting area, 20 amp, sewer, dump station, rec hall, swimming, boating, fishing. Store nearby. Pets allowed. Open Memorial Day-Columbus Day. ☎ 469-3443.

East Sullivan

Mountainview Campground, US 1, Box 20, East Sullivan 04607. Quiet and friendly. Close to attractions but away from the crowds. Reasonable rates for one night or the summer. View and sunsets across the bay. 50 sites, tenting area, 30 amp, sewer, dump station, swimming, boating, fishing, group area. Store nearby. Pets allowed. Open Memorial Day-October 1. ☎ 422-6215.

Eastport

The Seaview Campground, 16 Norwood Road, Eastport 04631. On the shores of Passamaquoddy Bay and the Canadian border. Full services, modern campground in a "quiet neck of the woods." 80 sites, tenting area, 30 amp, sewer, dump station, store, laundry, rec hall, on-site rentals, group area, LP gas. Swimming, boating, fishing, and pool nearby, Pets allowed. Open May 15-October 15. ☎ 853-4471.

Ellsworth

Branch Lake Camping Area, RR 5, Box 473, Ellsworth 04605. Beautiful clear lake, great fishing and swimming, boat rentals, clean heated restrooms. Not far to Acadia National Park. 50 sites, tenting area, 30 amp, sewer, dump station, store, rec hall, swimming, boating, fishing. Pets allowed. Open May 1-October 15. ☎ 667-5174.

Lubec

Sunset Point RV Trailer Park, PO Box 217, Lubec 04652. All sites on the water (28-foot tides!). 25 sites, tenting area, 30 amp, store, laundry, swimming, fishing, group area, LP gas. Boating nearby. Pets allowed, Open Memorial Day-Columbus Day. ☎ 733-2150.

Machias River

Machias River, Route 9. This is an informal, state-run campground is located on the banks of the Machias River where it runs under Route 9 at the Class III Airline rapids. There are several drive-in tent sites here and one lean-to along the river. Except for outhouses, picnic tables and fire rings there are no facilities and none nearby. Sites taken on a first-come, first-served basis. There is a primitive hand-carry boat ramp you can drive right to here for put-in for Machias River canoe trips.

Mount Desert

Mount Desert Campground, Route 198, Mount Desert 04660. Traditional camping, tent and tent/trailers only. Quiet, wooded sites located on the saltwater shore of beautiful Somes Sound. Hot showers, canoe/kayak rentals, campstore. 150 sites, tenting area, 15 amp, swimming, boating, fishing. Open June 15-September 15. ☎ 244-3710.

Somes Sound View Campground, 86 Hall Quarry Road, Mount Desert 04660. Small, quiet campground on the rocky, saltwater shores in the heart of Acadia National Park. Beautiful views, close to hiking, saltwater and fresh water swimming. Dock and moorings. 66 sites, tenting area, 30 amp, dump station, rec hall, swimming, boating, fishing. Pets allowed. Open Memorial Day-Labor Day. ☎ 244-3890.

Orland

Shady Oaks Campground, 32 Leachers Point, Orland 04472. Your friendly hosts Joyce and Don Nelson offer a clean quiet family campground where friendships are made and carried home. Stay for a week and remember it for lifetime. 50 sites, tenting area, 30 amp, sewer, dump station, store, laundry, rec hall, swimming, pool. Open May 15-October 1. ☎ 469-7739.

Robbinston

Hilltop Campground, RR 1, Box 298, Robbinston 04671. 84 sites, tenting area, 50 amp, sewer, dump station, store, laundry, rec hall, swimming, fishing, pool, on-site rentals, group area, LP gas. Boating nearby. Pets allowed. Open May 15-October 15. ☎ 454-3985.

Perry

Knowlton's Campground, RR 1, Box 171, Perry 04667. Quiet, eight-tenths of a mile off US 1 on shores of Cobscook Bay. Stores and restaurants are three miles away. Clam digging on shore and deep-sea fishing are just 10 miles away. 80 sites, tenting area, 30 amp, sewer, dump station. Pets allowed. Open May 20-October 15. ☎ 726-4756.

Southwest Harbor

Smuggler's Den Campground, PO Box 787, Southwest Harbor 04679. Located on beautiful Mount Desert Island, next to Acadia National Park, minutes from Bar Harbor. Coastal New England at its best. Comfortable, private and affordable. 100 sites, tenting area, 30 amp, sewer, dump station, store, laundry, swimming, pool, on-site rentals, group area. Boating and fishing nearby. Pets allowed. Open Memorial Day-Columbus Day. ☎ 244-3944.

Steuben

Mainayr Campground, 321 Village Road, Steuben 04680. 30 sites, tenting area, 30 amp, sewer, dump station, store, laundry, swimming, boating, fishing, on-site rentals, group area. Pets allowed. Open Memorial Day-Columbus Day. ☎ 546-2690.

Stonington

Greenlaws RV, Tenting Rentals, PO Box 72, Stonington 04681. A wooded campground in a lobstering community far off the beaten path. Good restaurants and boat tours close by. 24 sites, tenting area, 30 amp, sewer, dump station, store nearby, laundry, rec hall, on-site rentals, group area. LP gas, swimming, boating, and fishing nearby. Pets allowed. Open May 1-October 1. ☎ 367-5049.

Surry

The Gatherings Family Campground, RR 1, Box 4069, Surry 04684. A family campground with wooded oceanfront sites. Clean and quiet. Just 45 minutes from Acadia National Park, Bar Harbor and other treasures of Down East Maine. 110 sites, tenting area, 30 amp, sewer, dump station, store, laundry, rec hall, swimming, boating, fishing. Pets allowed. Open May 1-October 15. ☎ 667-8826.

Topsfield

Maine Wilderness Camps, HC 82, Box 1085, Topsfield 04490. Nestled in the wilderness and unspoiled forest on the northern shores of Pleasant Lake, surrounded by mountains, lakes, streams and trees. 20 sites, tenting area, 15 amp, store, swimming, boating, fishing, on-site rentals, group area. Pets allowed. Open May 15-November 15. ☎ 738-5052.

Trenton

Narrows Too Camping Resort, RR 1, Box 193, Route 3 Trenton 04605. On the ocean with breathtaking views and premiere facilities. Heated pool, shuttle bus to Bar Harbor, exercise room, basketball, volleyball, video gas, mini-golf, and store. 120 sites, tenting area, 50 amp, sewer, dump station, store, laundry, rec hall, swimming, pool, group area, LP gas. Pets allowed. Open Memorial Day-Columbus Day. ☎ 667-4300.

Down East

West Tremont

Quietside Campground and Cabins, PO Box 8, West Tremont 04690. Something for the quiet camper. Well spaced log cabins and screened tent sites. Adjacent to western part of Acadia National Park. Very peaceful atmosphere. 37 sites, tenting area, 30 amp, dump station, on-site rentals, laundry. Store, swimming, boating, and fishing nearby. Pets allowed. Open June 15-Columbus Day. ☎ 244-5992.

Woodland

Sunset Acres Campground, RR 1, Box 427, Woodland 04694. Quiet, clean, all new facility located on Route 9 just 10 miles from Canadian border in good salmon and bass fishing area. 15 sites, tenting area, 30 amp, sewer, dump station, store, pool. Swimming, boating, and fishing nearby. Open May 1-November 1. ☎ 454-1440.

Western Mountains

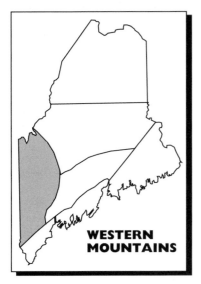

WESTERN MOUNTAINS

With lofty peaks and winding valleys carved by boulder-strewn streams, Maine's Western Mountains evoke a sense of timelessness. The hills here are old, as are the tidy towns and farms that nestle below them. It was not the mountains, but rather the fertile soil on the flood plains of the rivers that first attracted settlers. Even today travelers along the busy state highways look out over fields of corn and hay sandwiched between the riverbanks and the road.

While the forest products industry is strong here with paper mills in Jay and Rumford and wood products mills scattered throughout, the landscape remains largely pastoral with numerous family homesteads and dairy farms.

The Western Mountains are an outdoor recreation paradise. Within this region you'll discover several parks like Mount Blue and Grafton Notch, and portions of the White Mountains National Forest, and the Appalachian Trail's admitted toughest mile through Mahoosuc Notch. Many peaks rise more than 4,000 feet. Paper company roads and off-season ski areas provide for a wide array of mountain biking opportunities.

Depending on water level, streams and rivers are ideal for rafting, canoeing or fly fishing. The renowned Saco River, with its meandering turns and sand bars, is a favorite spot for day-long family float trips.

Golf courses and grand hotels await in towns like Bethel. Jewel-like lakes are a swimmer's delight.

The jewel of all lake regions in Maine has to be Rangeley, whose water areas come with tongue-twisting names like Mooselookmeguntic. The view from Height of Land, along Route 17 on the way into the region, is among the prettiest in the eastern United States.

DON'T MISS

Farmington is a busy commercial hub offering easy access to all major features of the area.

The Western Mountains are big snow country. Located just east of the massive Presidential Range in nearby New Hampshire, the snows come early, stay late, and are apt to lie several feet deep for much of the winter. Often, there is good spring skiing into May.

Houses Adapted for Winter Living

Rather than asphalt shingles or cedar shakes, corrugated tin is the roofing material of choice here. It provides a slippery surface for snow to slide off on its own, so that owners worried about too much snow or ice collapsing the rafters don't need to venture onto a steep roof in February to clear it off.

While summer hikers, bikers and campers keep businesses busy, and the fall foliage is among the most spectacular in New England, ski season is the boom time here. Downhill ski areas such as Sugarloaf in Carrabassett and Sunday River near Bethel boom as soon as nighttime temperatures allow snowmakers to ply their trade. That, combined with bountiful natural snow, makes for a skiing experience many say rivals that offered by resorts in the Rockies. Nordic skiing fans will not be disappointed either, as most major ski areas groom cross-country trails and several establishments cater only to those who seek the solitude and rhythm of kick and glide. Snowmobilers too flock to the trails that traverse the area, running from the New Hampshire border to Canada.

Outfitters abound in this part of Maine. They range from guides who will take you on a "feminist vision-quest" to a company who will take you trekking through the Whites with the gear hauled by llamas.

■ Note: Maine has one area code – 207.

Parks & Preserves

■ National Parks

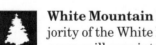

White Mountain National Forest, Bethel. While the vast majority of the White National Forest is in New Hampshire, 50,000 acres spill over into Maine in the Bethel region. This section features spectacular of mountain terrain good for hiking, backpacking, cross-country skiing and canoeing. Major features include more than 150 miles of trails, five campgrounds and scores of roadside rest and picnic spots as well as fishing and swimming. Caribou/Speckled Mountain Wilderness is the centerpiece. Visitors' center located at 18 Mayville Road, Bethel. ☎ 824-2134.

Major Parks & Preserves in the Western Mountains

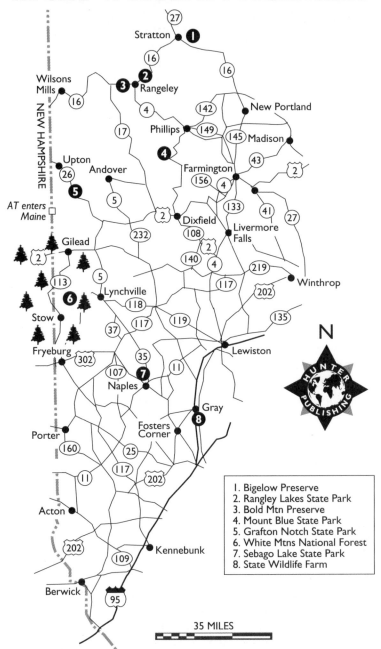

1. Bigelow Preserve
2. Rangley Lakes State Park
3. Bold Mtn Preserve
4. Mount Blue State Park
5. Grafton Notch State Park
6. White Mtns National Forest
7. Sebago Lake State Park
8. State Wildlife Farm

35 MILES

■ State Parks

 Grafton Notch State Park, North Newry. This is one of the wildest and most scenic mountain areas in Maine. On Old Speck (campsites and lean-to at pond near summit), the Appalachian Trail crosses into Maine. Approach to the mountain is via Mahoosuc Notch, reportedly the AT's toughest mile. Numerous roadside parking places to picnic and play among tumbling waterfalls. There are natural bridges and deep gorges in the area. Hiking trails run alongside interesting land features, such as Moose Cave, Table Rock, and falls such as Mother Walker and Screw Auger. Extended backpack trips possible. Elevation gains of 2-3,000 feet in a mile or two are common. On Route 26. ☎ 624-6080.

Mount Blue State Park, Weld. This park near the shore of Lake Webb has 3,187-foot Mount Blue as its centerpiece. Facilities include swimming beach, hiking trails, camping, picnic tables, fire grates, boat launch ramp, ATV trail, rentals and dump station. Fishing allowed. Winter use includes cross-country skiing and snowmobiling. Adequate parking for a fee. Bisected by Route 142. ☎ 585-2261.

Rangeley Lake State Park, Rangeley. Comparatively small state park (700 acres) located in just the perfect place on the south shore of Rangeley Lake. Swimming and fishing are top notch, and there is plenty of hiking nearby. Facilities include a campground, dump station, boat ramp, toilets, showers, boat dock and picnic tables and fire rings. Stores nearby. ☎ 864-3858.

Sebago Lake State Park, Naples. A large, 1,300-acre wooded park on north shore of one of Maine's largest lakes – Sebago. Activities include swimming on sandy beaches, boating, canoeing on the winding Crooked River and fishing. Park personnel schedule talks and other activities. Campground and beach with bathhouse, toilets, picnic tables and grills, dump station, boat rentals and a snack bar. Cross-country skiing in winter. ☎ 693-6231.

■ Wildlife Refuges

 Brownfield Bog Wildlife Management Area, Brownfield. Nearly 3,000 arces of marsh and woodland make up this splendid preserve just off Route 160. Attractive mountain views. Hunting, hiking, canoeing and camping allowed. (No phone.)

Hiram Nature Study Area, Hiram. Self-guided nature trails winds through 60 forested acres along the sandy banks of the Saco River. Occasional nature tours scheduled. There are restrooms and plenty of parking. Hiking, hunting, fishing, picnicking in designated area. No phone.

Hunter Cove Wildlife Sanctuary, Rangeley. Long, narrow cove on north end of Rangeley Lake. Owned by the Audubon Society, this is a great place to birdwatch and look for other wildlife. Parking is adequate. No admission fee. More than two miles of trails. ☎ 781-2330.

■ Natural Areas/Preserves

 Stephen Phillips Memorial Preserve, Rangeley Plantation. The Stephen Phillips Foundation protects several dozen miles of wild lake frontage on the western shore of Mooselookmeguntic Lake as well as the two largest islands, Students and Toothaker. There are numerous paddle-in and a few walk-in campsites (among the prettiest in Maine). There is a nominal fee. Reservations required. ☎ 864-2003.

Bigelow Preserve, Stratton. Skiers on Sugarloaf across the valley look out upon one of the most spectacular mountain ranges in Maine – Bigelow. Traversed by the Appalachian Trail, Bigelow is actually a series of several peaks that includes the Horns (3,800-feet), West Peak (the highest at 4,150 feet) and Avery Peak, with its square wooden fire watchtower (4,088 feet).

 INTERESTING FACT: *Avery Peak is named for Myron Avery, one of the pioneers of the Appalachian Trail.*

In all there are more than 35,000 acres of public land here. They stretch from the highway at Sugarloaf, across the ridge, and down to the shores of massive Flagstaff Lake. This area was saved from development into a ski area by a state-wide referendum vote. There are several lean-tos and campsites along the ridge, the most popular at Horns Pond, where there is a caretaker and fees in season. Very busy on weekends. Site features a unique solar-powered composting toilet! (See page 104.) Good mountain biking on dirt roads. Most hikes feature big elevation gains, rugged terrain, and limited views (except on peaks). Day trips possible for very fit hikers. (No phone.)

Rangeley Lakes Heritage Trust, Oquossoc. This private membership organization has managed to preserve hundreds of acres of land in the Rangeley area as well as many islands in Rangeley and nearby lakes. Call for more detail. ☎ 864-7311.

Snow Falls Rest Area, West Paris. This is a 300-foot gorge with falls on the Little Androscoggin River. Picnic tables at roadside pullout on Route 26.

Step Falls Preserve, Newry. A number of cascading falls and rapids through this 24-acre Nature Conservancy Preserve made it worthy of becoming the group's first acquisition. Stream drops 150 feet in less than an eighth of a mile. Near Grafton Notch State Park. On Route 26. Conservancy office at 14 Maine Street, Brunswick 04011. ☎ 729-5181.

Sucker Brook Preserve, Lovell. Protected by the Greater Lovell Land Trust, these 32 acres feature a brook flowing through marshes between Moose Pond and the lower bay of Kezar Lake. (No phone.)

Sightseeing

▪ Historic Sites/Museums

> **NOTE**
>
> *Many museums and historic sites in Maine are small, and operate for only part of the year, staffed by volunteers. The opening days and times of these institutions vary, depending upon weather, available staff and other factors; some are open by appointment only. We recommend that you call ahead to find out the latest opening times.*

Bridgton

 Bridgton Historical Society Museum, Gibbs Avenue. Former fire station (1902), contains collection of local historic items and artifacts dating from founding of town in 1768 to present day. ☎ 647-3699.

Narramissic/Historic Peabody-Fitch Farm, Ingalls Road, South Bridgton. Federal period home of prominent settling family in unspoiled rural setting. ☎ 647-2765.

Spratt-Mead Museum, Route 37, Bridgton Academy. ☎ 647-3469.

Brownfield

Brownfield Historical Society. ☎ 935-4392.

Bryant Pond

Bryant Pond Telephone Museum, Rumford Avenue. Village was last in United States to have hand-crank phones. ☎ 665-2960.

Woodstock Historical Society Museum (1873-74), Route 26, Main Street. Renovated barn, owned by Capt. Dearborn. Houses a fine collection of old furniture, pictures, and research library. ☎ 665-2450.

Buckfield

Old Church on the Hill (1830-31), High Street. ☎ 336-2191.

Dixfield

Dixfield Historical Society, 4 Mill Street. (No phone.)

Farmington

Nordica Memorial Association, Holley Road. Birthplace of famous operatic soprano Madame Lillian Nordica. ☎ 778-2042.

Red Schoolhouse Museum (1852), Rtes. 2 and 4. Restored 19th-century school building. Desks, books, lunch boxes, and other classroom memorabilia. ☎ 778-7325.

UMF Art Gallery Museum, 102 Main Street. ☎ 778-7001.

Union Meeting House (1826), Route 41. Restored Federal-style church used by four denominations over the years. Now serves as the Farmington Falls Union Baptist Church. ☎ 778-2569.

Fryeburg

Fryeburg Fair Farm Museum (1832), Route 5, Fryeburg Fairgrounds. ☎ 935-3268.

Fryeburg Historical Society Museum (1820), 96 Main Street. Building was the first Registry of Deeds for Oxford County. ☎ 935-4192.

Fryeburg Public Library (1832), 98 Main Street. Located in 1832 stone school house. Paintings by local artists. Lincoln memorabilia. Clarence Mulford collection (creator of Hopalong Cassidy). On the National Register of Historic Places. ☎ 935-2731.

Harrison

Harrison Historical Society, Haskell Hill Road. ☎ 583-6225.

Scribner's Mill Preservation, Scribner's Mill Road. ☎ 583-4298.

Hebron

Hebron Historical Society. ☎ 966-3111.

Western Mountains

Hiram

Hiram Historical Society. ☎ 625-4794.

Jay

Jay Hill Antique Auto Museum, Route 4. ☎ 645-4330.

Kingfield

Kingfield Historical Society, Church Street. Memorabilia of the town including the Narrow Gauge Railroad, the Stanley Family (inventors of the Stanley Steamer car) and Maine's Governor, William King. Country store, school house. On the National Register of Historic Places. ☎ 265-4871.

Stanley Museum, School Street. Museum of local history. ☎ 265-2729.

Lovell

Lovell Historical Society. ☎ 925-3760.

Naples

Naples Historical Society Museum, Route 302, Village Green. Local historical items. ☎ 693-6790.

New Portland

Nowetah's American Indian Museum and Gift Store, Route 27. Open year-round. Educational programs, visits and classes. ☎ 628-4981.

New Sweden

Maine's Swedish Colony, Inc., Capitol Hill Road. A local historical restoration and preservation society presently maintaining three outstanding facilities consisting of a blacksmith and woodworking shop, a two-story log home and Capitol School. ☎ 896-5624.

New Sweden Historical Society Museum, Capital Hill Road. Replica of 1870 Colony's capitol houses three floors of immigrant artifacts that depict the life of the early Swedish settlers. ☎ 896-3018.

North Anson

Embden Historical Society. ☎ 566-0921.

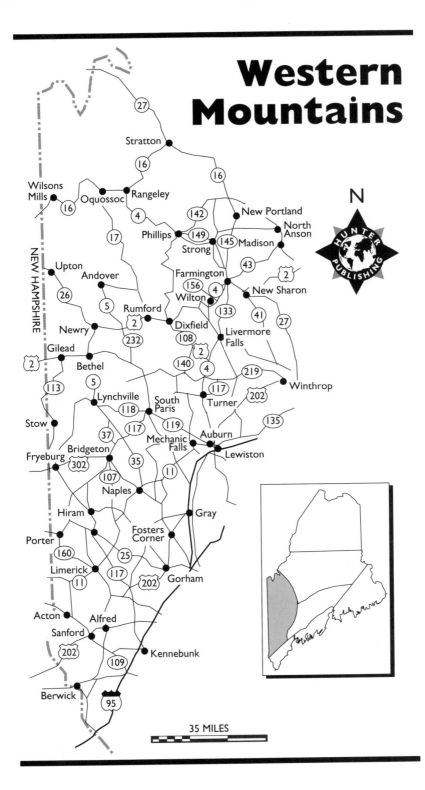

Western Mountains

N

HUNTER PUBLISHING

NEW HAMPSHIRE

27

Stratton

16

16

Wilsons Mills

16

Oquossoc   Rangeley

4

142   New Portland

North Anson

17

Phillips   149   145   Madison

Strong

43

Upton

Andover

Farmington   2

26

156   New Sharon

5   Rumford   Wilton   4

133

Newry   Dixfield   41   27

232

108   Livermore Falls

Gilead   2

2   Bethel   140   4   219

113   5   117   202   Winthrop

Stow   Lynchville   Turner

South   118   135

37   Paris   119   Auburn

Fryeburg   Bridgeton   117   Mechanic Falls

302   35   11   Lewiston

107

Naples

Hiram   Gray

Porter   Fosters Corner

160   25

Limerick   117   Gorham

11   202

Acton   Alfred

Sanford

202   Kennebunk

109

Berwick

95

35 MILES

North Jay

Jay Historical Society, Holmes-Crafts Homestead, Route 4, Jay Hill.
☎ 645-2732.

Norway

Norway Historical Society, 232 Main Street. (No phone.)

Paris

Hamlin Memorial Library and Museum, Old Stone Jail, Paris Hill.
Oxford County Jail until 1896, now houses public library and museum.
Artifacts from Hannibal Hamlin (and family), Lincoln's Vice President.
☎ 743-2980.

Phillips

Phillips Historical Society (1825), Pleasant Street. ☎ 639-3352.

Poland

Maine State Building (1893) & **All Souls Chapel** (1912), Route 26, Poland Spring. Grounds of former Poland Spring Resort. ☎ 582-7080.

Rangeley

Rangeley Lakes Region Historical Society, Main and Richardson
Streets. ☎ 864-3317.

Wilhelm Reich Museum, Dodge Pond Road, off Route 4. Library, scientific equipment, paintings and other memorabilia. The Wilhelm Reich
Museum at Orgonon Estate was Reich's home and workplace. Located in
the Rangeley Lakes Region of Maine and comprising 175 acres of fields
and woodland with a system of trails and two major buildings, the museum represents and interprets the life and work of this renowned yet
controversial physician-scientist and the environment in which he inves-
tigated the energy functions that govern all living things. Reich's views
on orgone energy, UFOs, sexuality, and his energy concentrators won him
some powerful enemies, including the government.

The Orgone Energy Observatory, designed for Reich in 1948, exhibits
biographical materials, inventions, and equipment used in his pioneer-
ing experiments. Reich's library, personal memorabilia, sculpture, and
paintings are also on view, and there is a discovery room for children. The
observatory deck on the roof provides a spectacular vista of the surrounding countryside. Reich's tomb is nearby.

Programs on various aspects of Reich's work and the natural environment take place in the conference center and on the property. ☎ 864-3443.

Source – Reich Museum publications.

Rumford

Rumford Area Historical Museum, Lufkin School, Route 2. Displays of local artifacts, photos, and books. Country store exhibit, old tools. ☎ 364-4007.

South Paris

Paris Cape Historical Society, 19 Park Street. (No phone.)

The McLaughlin Foundation, Main Street. Serene 3½-acre, 60-year-old perennial garden/arboretum and 1840s farmstead located directly on Route 26. The garden is maintained by a nonprofit organization and is open free May-October. Gift shop. Open all year. ☎ 743-8820.

Stockholm

Stockholm Historical Society Museum, Main and Lake Street. Served as town's first store and post office. Houses local history collection. ☎ 896-5731.

Stratton

Dead River Area Historical Society, 172 Main Street. ☎ 246-2271.

Weld

Weld Historical Society, Weld Village. ☎ 585-2586.

Wilton

Wilton Farm and Home Museum, 10 Canal Street. Former "Bass Boarding House" now houses rural and small-town artifacts, 18th-century to present. National Register of Historic Places. ☎ 645-2091.

List Source-Maine Department of Tourism.

■ Covered Bridges

Covered bridges are a quintessential symbol of New England. Typical of Yankee frugality, the spans were covered over to afford the structure protection from wind and rain, make it easier to keep the decking free of

Western Mountains

Hemlock Bridge (1857) crosses the Saco River northwest of Fryeburg.

snow and ice, and to help keep horses calm while crossing high over rushing streams.

At their high point there were hundreds of covered bridges throughout the region. Most succumbed to old age, fire, or flood.

Hemlock Bridge, 1857, Saco River. Located off Route 302, three miles northwest of East Fryeburg in the town of Fryeburg. Spanning an old channel of the Saco River, it is of Paddleford truss construction with supporting laminated wooden arches.

Sunday River Bridge, 1872, Sunday River. The "Artist's Bridge" is the most painted and most photographed bridge in the state. It is located off Routes 2 and 26, about four miles northwest of North Bethel in the town of Newry.

Porter Bridge, 1876, Ossipee River. Built by the towns of Porter and Parsonfield as a joint project, the two-span structure is located off Route 160, a half-mile south of Porter.

Lovejoy Bridge, 1883, Ellis River. This Paddleford truss structure is the shortest of Maine's covered bridges at only 70 feet long. Built by the Town of Andover, it is located off Route 5 at South Andover.

Bennet Bridge, 1901, Magalloway River. This relatively young bridge is just off Route 16, 1½ miles south of the Wilsons Mills post office, then west .3 miles to the Lincoln Plantation.

Shopping

■ Antiques

Farmington

Maple Avenue Antiques (Frank Dingley), 23 Maple Avenue. Fine collection of early country furniture, paintings and great old things from area homes. Open by appointment or chance year-round. ☎ 778-4850.

The Old Barn Annex Antiques (Emery Goff and Bill Carhart), 30 Middle Street. Fine Maine country furniture and accessories. Nineteenth- and 20th-century toys. Showing at Pumpkin Patch in Searsport. ☎ 778-6908.

Rangeley

Blueberry Hill Farm (Stephanie and Don Palmer), Dallas Hill Road. Country furniture, smalls, hooked rugs, decoys and collectible fishing items. Open daily in season or by appointment. ☎ 864-5647.

Moose America-Rustic and Country Antiques (Bob Oestreicher), 97 Main Street. Vintage camp decor and related accessories. Painted country and folk art. Open daily in season. ☎ 864-3699.

Roxbury

Ann McCrillis. Route 17. Large barn with glass, china, pewter, coins, primitives, toys, furniture and paintings. Open daily May-November. ☎ 364-4458.

Rumford

Connie's Antiques (Maurice and Connie Goudreau), 190 Lincoln Avenue. Vintage clothing, linens, postcards, dolls, jewelry, glass, china, primitives, furniture, paintings, books, lamps. Open all year by chance or appointment. ☎ 364-3363.

Sebago

The Gallery Shop, off Route 107. Division of Jones Museum of Glass and Ceramics. Selection of 18th-, 19th- and 20th-century glass and ceramics, American, English, Continental and Far Eastern. Research Library. Call for hours. ☎ 787-3370.

Adventures On Foot

▪ Hiking

Bald Mountain, Rangeley: The name Bald Mountain is particularly popular in Maine, but among the 18 peaks so named this one has no parallel. It stands proudly overlooking Mooselookmeguntic and Rangeley lakes. With an elevation gain of 1,000 feet over a little more than a mile this trip is well worth the effort. Begin on the Bald Mountain Road off Route 4. Footing can be tricky on the wide, well-worn path leading to the 2,443-foot summit. Just over halfway the trail splits (the right side offers a more gradual ascent). The divergent paths rejoin just below the open summit and its fire tower. There are wonderful views of the lakes below, the village of Rangeley nestled in the hills, and of larger mountains in all directions.

Bigelow Mountain, Dead River Township: Bigelow Mountain's twin peaks form Maine's fifth highest Mountain lagging just behind Old Speck at 4,180, Crocker at 4,168, Sugarloaf at 4,237 feet, and Baxter Peak on Katahdin at 5,267. The higher West Peak on Bigelow is 4,150 feet high while the slightly lower East Peak, which sports a wooden fire tower, comes in at 4,088.

This is a big mountain. It makes for a long day hike or, better still, a leisurely, multi-day backpacking trip.

Begin at the Fire Warden's Trail parking area along the dirt Stratton Brook Road. The path rises gradually to an intersection with the Horns Pond Trail. Bear left and begin climbing steeply on an old woods road. Occasional views out over the valley toward Sugarloaf to the southeast can be enjoyed. After a short very steep section the trail joins the Appalachian Trail, which comes in on the left. Go right and follow the white blazes to the Horns Pond Shelter. There is a large lean-to, some tent platforms, tent sites, a spring, pond, and a solar-powered privy here. The elevation gain to this point is 2,000 feet over four miles. The AT then steeply climbs to the top of South Horn and covers several sections where hands must be used. The high point on South Horn is at 3,831 feet. There are great views. It then heads east dropping several hundred feet before rising sharply again to the top of West Peak. There is a small area above treeline here and great 360° views.

Continuing east the trail drops 500 feet into a col, where an old cabin and a lean-to and tent sites are located. A side trail leads from the col to the tower on East Peak, also known as Myron Avery Peak after the man who helped create and maintain the AT in Maine.

To return to the parking area take the Fire Warden's Trail down from the col. Hands must be used near the ridge and one section features a wooden ladder/stair arrangement. Strenuous.

Mahoosuc Notch, Riley Township: Mahoosuc Notch is one of those legendary places many hikers hear and talk about, but few ever visit. While the Appalachian Trail Conference is careful not to dish out too many superlatives when it comes to labeling parts of the AT, it does grudgingly acknowledge in some publications that Mahoosuc Notch is considered to be the trail's toughest mile.

The notch is a long, deep, steep-sided gorge about 20 yards wide in places. The bottom is filled with house- and car-sized boulders covered with moss, trees and detritus. The trail, if you can call it that, slogs over and under these rocks. In places, when down in the caves, you can hear an underground river rushing below. Snow lingers here long into summer.

One legend has it that the skeleton of a bull moose which became trapped among the rocks could be seen for many years by passing hikers.

Several routes access the notch. The easiest involves a 4½-mile approach hike from the Sunday River ski area in Bethel. It passes through an unofficial tenting area at the base of the notch. Climb to the top of the notch to where the AT veers south up Fulling Mill Mountain and then retrace your steps. The total elevation gain in the notch from east to west is about 400-500 feet.

Other day trip approaches include coming in from the west on the Success Pond Road which begins off Route 26 in Maine but quickly enters New Hampshire. From the parking area on that road the Notch Trail leads 2½ miles to the top of the notch. Figure on at least two hours to climb down and two hours to climb back up, plus time for the trail back to the road.

Longer trips are possible by combining a traverse of the notch with a stay at the popular shelter and tent platform site at Speck Pond on Old Speck. The pond is the highest body of water in Maine. Begin further east on the Success Pond Road and take the Speck Pond Trail up for an elevation gain of 2,100 feet over four miles. Follow the AT down into the notch and connect with the Notch Trail to return to the road. It is about 2½ miles back down the road to the first parking area. Water isn't too hard to come by in this area.

 Do not underestimate the endurance needed to tackle Mahoosuc Notch. About the 30th time in the first hour you've taken off your pack to get through a tight spot you may wish you'd taken a different route.

Western Mountains

Mount Blue, Weld: Mount Blue looks the part of the quintessential mountain, rising to a clear peak above the surrounding valleys and nearby ridges.

Follow the signs from the village of Weld to Mount Blue State Park and to the trailhead at the end of a dirt road. The trailheads right off into nearby woods and begins climbing steadily to make the 1,800-foot elevation gain before reaching the summit in just over 1½ miles. About halfway up pass the remains of the old fire warden's cabin. There is a spring nearby. The trail continues steadily upward to the summit, which sports the remains of an old fire tower. The top is forested but there are good views in all directions from various ledges. This is a strenuous hike. Return by the same route.

Mount Will, Bethel and Newry: The Mount Will Trail is a comparatively recent effort on the part of the Bethel Conservation Commission. The 3¼-mile loop includes a rugged ascent to open ledges offering great views of the Androscoggin River Valley.

The trailhead is on Route 2 directly across from the Bethel Transfer Station. Park here and head up an old logging road to the North Ledges Trail, which climbs 630 vertical feet in just under a mile. Several sections are steep and slippery. Blue and green blazes mark the way. Some of the path is on private land and the rest is in the Bethel town forest, which was designed to demonstrate regeneration after timber harvesting. From the North Ledges Overlook the trail continues to ascend to the peak of Mount Will with good views from various ledges. It then drops gradually to an area called the South Cliffs, where you'll have views of the valley and the village of Bethel. It is a long, steady, one-mile descent (of 730 vertical feet) back to the parking area. Strenuous.

Tumbledown Township, North of Weld: There are two choices for ascending and descending this 3,068-foot peak; one that requires only moderate effort and another that requires some non-technical climbing and steady nerves. Both begin from separate trailheads on the Bryon Road, which can be used as a connector to form a long loop hike. Both trails include about 1,400 feet of elevation gain.

The easier of the two, the Brook Trail, is just under 2½ miles long. It starts out on an old logging road and for a time follows Tumbledown Brook as it rises up the hill before becoming very steep. It skirts scenic Tumbledown Pond and cuts west rising more steeply to the summit.

The Chimney/Loop Trail begins with a gradual gradient and seems deceptively easy. After a mile it cuts around a large boulder and rises sharply to some open ledges with good views of the mountain's 700-foot "Tumbledown" cliffs. The defunct Chimney Trailheads left and across broken and loose rocks and ascends up a narrow cleft in the rock. The way is occasionally blocked by fallen chock stones. It is no longer open to hikers, but is listed here as many folks will undoubtedly seek it out.

 Anyone with a fear of heights or who lacks good physical dexterity or the proper gear should avoid this route.

From the top of the chimney it is only a few hundred yards to the summit.

At the intersection with the Old Chimney Trail, the Loop Trail cuts to the right, heads east for a time and then cuts left and rises steeply. As it traverses a rocky slide the trail passes under fallen boulders in a section called "Fat Man's Misery." It then rises steeply to the top and joins the Ridge Trail. It is only a short ways (left) to the summit. From the top there are great views of surrounding peaks.

Both these routes are very strenuous.

■ Rock Climbing

 Bear Mountain Climbing School. Custom rock climbing instruction and four-season hiking in the White Mountains. All-day or multiple-day ski touring. Winter climbing instruction and telmark skiing instruction. ☎ 452-2547.

■ Golfing

Greens fees vary greatly according to the popularity of the course and the time of year.

The Bethel Inn and Country Club, Town Common, Bethel. 6,663 yards, par 72. April-October. 18 holes. ☎ 824-2175 .

Bridgton Highlands Country Club, Lower Ridge Road, Bridgton. 6,039/5,795 yards, par 72 men, par 74 ladies. 18 holes. May 1-October 31. ☎ 647-3491.

Green Acres Inn and Golf Course, Canton. 1,750 yard. 9 holes. ☎ 597-2333.

Sugarloaf Golf Club, Carrabassett Valley. 6,950/6,450/5,376 yards, par 72. 18 holes. May 15-October 15. ☎ 237-2000.

Kennebec Heights Country Club,1 Fairway Lane, Farmingdale. 6,000 yards, par 70. 18 holes. April-October. ☎ 582-2000.

Sandy River Golf Course, George Thomas Road, Farmington. 1,336 yards, par 3. 9 holes. Mid-April through November 1. ☎ 778-2492.

Lake Kezar Country Club, Route 5, Lovell. May-October. 5,961 yards, 9 holes. ☎ 925-2462.

Oakdale Country Club, Route 2, River Road, Mexico. 3,038 yards, par 36. 9 holes. May1-November 1. ☎ 364-3951.

Naples Golf and Country Club, Old Route 114, Naples. 3,277 yards, par 36. 9 holes. April 20 through fall. ☎ 693-6424.

Norway Country Club, Lake Road, Route 118 Norway. May 1-October 15. 2,910 yards, par 35. 9 holes. ☎ 743-9840.

Paris Hill Country Club, Paris Hill. 2,400 yards, par 33. 9 holes. May 1-November 30. ☎ 743-2371.

Province Lake Country Club, Route 153, Parsonfield. 6,343 yards, par 72. 18 holes. April 24-November 1. ☎ 793-9577.

Fairlawn Country Club, Route 11 and 26, Poland. 6,300 yards, par 72. 18 holes. April until first snow. ☎ 998-4277.

Poland Spring Country Club, Route 26, Poland Spring. 6,196 yards, par 71. 18 holes. May 1-October 15. ☎ 998-6002.

Summit Golf Course, Summit Spring Road, Poland Spring. 2,863 yards, par 36. 9 holes. April-November. ☎ 998-4515.

Mingo Springs Golf Course, Proctor Road and Route 4, Rangeley. 5,900 yards, par 70. 18 holes. May 26-October 15. ☎ 864-5021.

Turner Highlands Country Club, Route 117, Turner. 2980 yards, par 36. 9 holes. May-November 1. ☎ 224-7060.

The Original Golf School at Sugarloaf USA

More than 65,000 duffers have gotten off to a better start by learning the basics here. Attendees are grouped by fours according to ability, and work on their stance, grip, alignment and swing. Located in a beautiful mountainous ski resort. The challenging course follows the banks of the Carabassett River. RR 1, Box 5000, Kingfield 04947. ☎ 800-664-6535.

Adventures On Wheels

■ Mountain Biking

Sunday River Mountain Biking Park, Bethel. More than 60 miles of downhill ski trails, paths, and four-wheel-drive routes in this large resort are open to bikers as soon as the snow melts and mud subsides. The vertical drop from the top (there's a chairlift) is more than 2,300 feet. Open weekends at the beginning of June and daily from July 1 through September. Bike and equipment rentals available on mountain. There is a full-service repair shop. During peak times trails are patrolled.

Ten beginners' trails, 15 intermediate trails and 11 expert routes. Maps available at base lodge or from bikes shops around the state. Regular racing circuit in summer. Cost for full suspension biker rental (worth it), helmet, lift and trail fee is $60 per day. Life and all-day trail pass, $15. ☎ 824-3000.

Shawnee Peak Mountain Biking Park, Bridgton. Once the snow leaves this popular ski area the chairlifts are set up to take experienced mountain bikers and their mounts up 1,300 vertical feet to the summit. A wide variety of trails go down. Views from 1,900-foot summit range all the way to White Mountains. Terrain varies from technical descent areas to open fields to wooded lands. Open weekends only June-September. Some racing events in summer. Snack bar, bike and helmet rentals, minor repairs available. ☎ 647-8444.

Sugarloaf USA, Carrabassett Valley. This 7,000-acre resort sports more than 50 miles of trails open to mountain biking. Riding varies from dirt roads to ski trails to single track and there are routes for every skill level. Shuttle service to various riding locations. $5 per day trail fee. Open June through August. Numerous lodging and restaurant options on mountain and nearby. Vertical drops of 1-2,000 feet possible. Several bike shops and service centers on mountain. Bike and equipment rentals available. ☎ 237-2000.

Hebron to Canton Railbed, Hebron. This 18-mile abandoned railroad line offers easy riding on gradual grades through pretty woods and along marshy areas and ponds where frequent wildlife sightings can be made. Passes through village of Buckfield. Used by snowmobiles in winter. ATVs are allowed. Permission must be obtained to ride on one gated section (keeps in livestock) in East Sumner. You can detour around on Route 140 to Hartford. Some wet sections. Ends at Lake Anasagunticook.

Jay to Farmington Railbed. This 15-mile route follows an abandoned railroad bed from the paper mill town of Jay, north through Wilton to West Farmington. It features easy grades and good gravel surface. It is used by snowmobiles in winter. Route passes through woods, fields and wetlands. Some old railway buildings and rusting relics remain. Several attractive picnic spots. Route also passes Troll Valley Cross Country Ski and Mountain Biking center in Farmington. It features 14 miles of single-track riding for a small fee. Troll Valley phone, ☎ 778-3658.

Rangeley Mountain Bike Touring Center, 53 Main Street, Rangeley 04970. This is the headquarters for maps and information on mountain biking in the Rangeley Lakes area. Multi-use trail on abandoned rail bed begins nearby. Maps available. Rentals, sales and service, including mountain bikes, cruisers, kids' bikes, trailers and quadracycles. ☎ 864-5799.

Mount Blue State Park, Weld. There are more than 20 miles of single- and double-track trails through forested mountains with the occasional great view. Designed with riders in mind, some trails have picnic stops and shelters. Grades are moderate and elevation gains modest. ATVs and horses allowed on some trails; Hikers allowed on all trails. Dirt roads offer expanded riding opportunities. Campground in the park. ☎ 585-2347.

■ Foliage/Motor Tours

 A weekend of cruising the countryside in this region will take you from mountains and maple trees to historic towns and some of the very best foliage destinations in the country.

Maples & Mountains

160 miles, 4 hours, round trip

Highlights: *This region features fertile, rolling hills, majestic mountain ranges, sparkling lakes and fish-filled streams. Takes you to Fryeburg, the site of Maine's oldest agricultural fair. This area's historic towns are a living tribute to the simpler lifestyle of a previous era.*

Route: From **Fryeburg**, drive southeast on US 302, stopping to see the **Hemlock Covered Bridge** in East Fryeburg. Continue on 302 to **Naples**, where you can cruise the lake on the *Songo River Queen* (operates weekends in September). Take 35 north to **Harrison**, then 117 north. Take a side trip to **West Paris** for information on tourmaline, the state gem, at Perham's. West of Norway, drive north on Greenwood Road along Lake Pennesseewassee to **Greenwood**, then east on 219 to 26 into the beautiful village of **Bethel**. In Bethel, enjoy a leisurely game of golf. Take US 2/Route 26 north to **Newry**, crossing the covered bridge known as the **Artist's Bridge** (see page 326). Newry is also home to **Sunday River**, a ski resort with chairlift rides offering brilliant mountain views of fall foliage. Go north on 26 to **Grafton Notch State Park**, taking time for short, color-filled hikes to Screw Auger Falls, Moose Cave, Mother Walker Falls, and the Natural Falls.

Take 26 south back through Newry, then on US 2/26 south back to Bethel. Take US 2 west to Gilead, then go south on 113 to **Evans Notch**, with its panoramic views of the White Mountains to Stow. Go east around Kezar Lake, nestled at the foot of the Presidential Range in the White Mountains. Head to north Lovell, then south on 5 through Lovell back to Fryeburg.

Franklin Heritage Loop

133 miles, 3¼ hours, round trip

Highlights: *From its wooded mountaintops and birch-lined riverbanks to its serene lake shores, Maine's western region features a wealth of scenic, historic and cultural attractions. For those seeking a sampling of Maine's Yankee heritage amid breathtaking scenery, this tour features plenty of both!*

Route: From **Farmington**, head north on Route 27 to **Kingfield**, where the **Stanley Museum** honors the Stanley family's Yankee ingenuity in art, music and steam car transportation. Continue on 27 along the winding Carrabassett River to **Sugarloaf USA**, where you can enjoy a leisurely game of golf amid spectacular mountain views. Travel northwest on 27 to Stratton and hike the **Bigelow Mountain Range Trail** to scenic Cranberry Peak. From Stratton, head to Eustis north on route 27 along the **Arnold Trail**, taking note of the historical markers along the way describing the route of Benedict Arnold's army as it traveled through the region in 1775. In **Eustis**, enjoy the sweeping views of Flagstaff Lake and the Chain of Ponds from Eustis Ridge. Return to Stratton via 27 south, keeping an eye out for the **Cathedral Pines** lining the route three miles north of Stratton. Head west on Route 16 to **Rangeley**, where the area's 40 lakes and ponds create a 450-square-mile fishing, golfing, boating and hiking paradise. In Rangeley, visit **Saddleback Ski Resort** for a beautiful view of the region from the lodge. From Rangeley, take Route 4 southeast through **Madrid**, site of the scenic **Small's Falls** picnic area, back to Farmington.

Routes courtesy Maine Department of Conservation

Route 113

28 miles, 45 minutes, one way

Highlights: *A mixture of rolling hills, clear water and nature preserves make this an interesing drive.*

Route: This trip begins north and west of Portland in **Standish**, just west of the village where Route 113 begins with a right turn off Route 25. The road, which traverses the rolling hills west of Sebago Lake, passes by dozens of natural wonders on its way north and slightly west, roughly paralleling the Saco River.

In **Steep Falls** you can visit the town's namesake on the sandy-banked Saco River. The 12-foot drop was the site of several old mills and an abandoned narrow gauge railroad bed runs along the banks.

Farther on, there is a picnic area at **Hiram Falls**, a series of cascades that drop 75 feet just below a Central Maine Power Company dam. As you continue toward Fryeburg, you will also pass the **Hiram Nature Study Area**, the trail to the top of **Mount Cutler** and the **Brownfield Wildlife Management Area**.

To return toward the coast take Route 302, which hugs the opposite side of Sebago Lake and passes near several state parks. Stop in **Naples** and take a ride on the river steamer the *Songo Queen*.

Route 17

43 miles, 1¼ hours, one way

Highlights: *Winding mountain road packed with scenic variety.*

Route: Take Route 17 from the paper mill town of **Rumford**, north, to the lakeside village of **Oquossoc**. This is one of the premier mountain roads in Maine. It starts out gently enough as it climbs along the Swift River, where amateur prospectors can be ably rewarded for time spent panning for gold. Numerous picnic sites and natural wonders are passed, including **Swift River Falls** and **Coos Canyon,** a 1,500-foot-long gorge with smooth sculpted potholes and veins of crystals.

From the canyon north the road gets a little dicier. But the drive is well worth it. Just north of where the Appalachian Trail crosses the pavement is Height of Land, a pullout with spectacular views of the Rangeley Lakes area and the White Mountains to the west.

Route 17 then continues north twisting and turning down the mountains to Oquossoc, passing Rangeley Lakes State Park, the shores of Rangeley Lake and by Bald Mountain, which has a popular hiking trail to the top.

Route 27

105 miles, 2½ hours, one way

Highlights: *Route 27 from Augusta to the Canadian border offers a fine day trip with no end of scenic variety.*

Route: It begins in the heart of Maine's capital, **Augusta**, and heads north through the rolling hills of the Belgrade Lakes Region. There are plenty of scenic turnouts and picnic areas along the way.

In **New Sharon**, Route 27 joins with Route 2, a main east/west artery, and heads into **Farmington**, home to a branch of the University of Maine and gateway to the Western Mountains.

In **New Portland,** Route 27 begins its run along the west bank of the Carrabassett River, passing through Kingfield. North of Kingfield the road hugs the stream with numerous opportunities to pull off and picnic alongside the river. Water can run high with snow melt in the spring, but eases back to a trickle among rounded, smooth boulders in summer.

Just north of the Sugarloaf USA ski area, the road is bisected by the Appalachian Trail. The massive **Bigelow Preserve** with its big mountain hiking lies to the east.

North of **Stratton** the road passes through some pretty wild county with fewer signs of human activity. Occasionally glimpses of the Dead River can be had. When you see Long Pond on your left you are only a few miles from the border checkpoint at **Coburn Gore**. The border checkpoint here is open 24 hours, year-round, although most road-trippers turn here and retrace their route.

 DID YOU KNOW? *Maine has several "gores," which are small, unusually shaped plots of land "left over" after major surveys. (If you want to learn more about gores, see page 49.)*

■ A Foliage Treat

One ski area in Western Maine fires up its chairlifts early for foliage season. **Sunday River** in Bethel runs the lift from 9 am until 3 pm. weekdays and longer on weekends, weather and foliage permitting. The lift is also used by a mountain bike rental company to take customers up the slope. There are great views from the top of the 3,150-foot peak. Check on the policy for rides back

> **Foliage Hotline:** The Maine foliage hotline, in service each fall, offers the latest color-peaking information for leaf-peepers. ☎ 800-932-3419.

down. In some years the lift took people *up*, but not down. It is a long walk to the base, especially if you lack the proper footwear. To be sure, call ahead. The cost is $8 per person and there are restaurants both at the base lodge or nearby. ☎ 824-3000.

■ Riding the Rails

 Sandy River and Rangeley Lakes Railroad, Phillips. Narrow gauge railroad using original equipment and roadbed with a gasoline locomotive dressed up to look like a steam engine. Rides given 1st and 3rd Sundays of each month, June through October. ☎ 639-3352.

Adventures On Water

■ Places to Paddle

Brownfield Bog

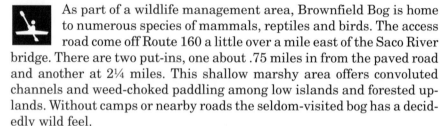

As part of a wildlife management area, Brownfield Bog is home to numerous species of mammals, reptiles and birds. The access road come off Route 160 a little over a mile east of the Saco River bridge. There are two put-ins, one about .75 miles in from the paved road and another at 2¼ miles. This shallow marshy area offers convoluted channels and weed-choked paddling among low islands and forested uplands. Without camps or nearby roads the seldom-visited bog has a decidedly wild feel.

Range Ponds, Poland

Located on the Empire Road off Route 122. Ideal for canoeing and kayaking. There is a 10 horsepower limit on Lower Range Pond, keeping personal watercraft and big boats to a minimum. The water is clear and the shores boast fine sandy beaches, forested glens and weedy coves filled with wildlife. Put in at the park on Lower Range Pond's northeastern end. You'll have to carry your boat across Route 26 if you want to explore Middle Range Pond as well. It connects to Upper Range Pond, although there are more camps and houses in the Middle Range Pond area.

Saco River (Fryeburg to Hiram)

Saco had a reputation for offering a great, easy, float trip. But this image is getting a little tarnished in recent years as Massachusetts fraternity boys have turned weekend trips into drunken brawls. Maine Wardens hold canoe roadblocks during particularly busy times and check floaters for drunkenness, illegal possession of alcohol and other violations. Still, if you go mid-week, and approach a trip on the twisting and turning Saco as an afternoon diversion instead of a wilderness experience, you can have a good time thanks to swift currents, sandy banks and bars, and the fine swimming the river offers. If you don't have your own boat, local liveries can help out. They lease and transport hundreds of canoes daily. Camping is allowed on river; fires by permit. There are also some commercial campgrounds along the way.

The most popular stretch runs from Fryeburg at Swan's Falls just off Route 302 to Hiram, a distance of some 33 miles. The trip takes six to eight hours.

Umbagog Lake

Remote Umbagog Lake sits astride the New Hampshire border. It is a paddle camper's paradise, with much of the surrounding land designated a wildlife refuge and its broad shores dotted with campsites. The best put-in for the southern end of the lake is along Route 26. There is also access on the west side from New Hampshire. The 30 remote and island campsites are too numerous to describe in detail. They are managed by the Umbagog Lake Campground on Route 26. There is a fee and reservations are required. You can contact them at ☎ (603) 482-3415. The lake is comparatively shallow, but big waves can blow up in high winds. There are great views in all directions.

Canoeing/Kayaking Outfitters

Overnight trips average $100-150 per person, per day. Half-day guided trips run in the vicinity of $50. Basic rentals cost between $25 and $45 per day. Most rentals include life jackets, paddles and car-topping gear.

Wild River Adventures
PO Box 754, Bethel 04217.
Canoe rentals, canoe trips, kayak rentals, kayak trips. Trips on the Allagash, Moose River, East/West Penobscot. June-August. ☎ 824-2608.

Camp 'N Canoe-Woodland Acres
Route 160, RR 1, Box 445, Brownfield 04010.
Canoe rentals, canoe trips, May 15-October 15. ☎ 935-2529.

River Run Canoe Rentals and Camping
PO Box 90, Route 160, Brownfield 04010.
Canoe rentals. Mid-May through September 30. ☎ 452-2500.

Mahoosuc Guide Service
Box 245, Bear River Road, Newry 04261.
Canoe trips, year-round. ☎ 824-2073.

Cupsuptic Campground
PO Box 326, Oquossoc 04964.
Canoe rentals, canoe trips. Mid-May through November 30. ☎ 864-5249.

Sundown Boat Rentals
Bald Mountain Road, Oquossoc 04964.
Canoes, fishing and sail boat for rent by hour or day. Pickup and delivery service to all nearby lakes. ☎ 864-3650.

Western Mountains

South Arm Campground (Rangeley)
PO Box 310, Andover 04216.
Canoe rentals, canoe trips. Trips on: Rangeley, Mooselook-
meguntic and Richardson Lakes. Mid-May through Mid-
September. ☎ 364-5155.

Town and Lake Motel
PO Box 47, Main Street, Rangeley 04970.
Canoe rentals. May-October. ☎ 864-3755.

Mount Blue State Park
Webb Beach Campground, Weld 04285.
Canoe rentals, May15-September 30. ☎ 585-2261.

Adventures In the Air

▪ Air Charters

Bethel

 Bethel Air Service, PO Box 786, Bethel 04217. Scenic flights arranged to your schedule at a cost of $20 per person for 20 minutes. Longer flights for higher cost. ☎ 824-4321.

Fryeburg

Dearborn Aviation, PO Box 518, Fryeburg 04037. Flights in a seven-passenger aircraft anywhere in Maine and Northern New England. They carry freight as well. ☎ 935-2288.

Rangeley

Mountain Air Services, PO Box 367, Rangeley 04970. Twenty-minute sightseeing flights arranged at your schedule for $25 per person. Ask about going along on the aerial fire watch patrol. Flight instruction offered. ☎ 864-5307.

Adventures On Snow

■ Downhill Skiing

Bethel

 Sunday River, PO Box 450, Bethel 04217. Offers 2,340-foot vertical drop, 112 trails, 16 lifts, 92% snowmaking (1,300 snow guns on mountain), glade skiing, rentals, ski shops, three base lodges, one summit lodge, restaurants, skier development clinics, snowboard park with 400-foot halfpipe, child care, lounges, slopeside lodging, Nordic skiing nearby, . Sunday River competes head to head with its sister resort Sugarloaf for the title of premier ski destination in Maine. Both are owned by the American Skiing Company, which grew rapidly in the mid-1990s and now owns ski mountains from coast to coast. Discount lodging and lift ticket packages are available. Adult lift ticket $49 (weekend); lower during the week. Reservations, ☎ 824-3000; Snow report, ☎ 824-5200.

Bridgton

Shawnee Peak, PO Box 734, Bridgton 04009. 1,300-foot vertical drop, 31 trails, four lifts, 98% snowmaking, night skiing, rentals, ski shop, lessons, cafeteria, restaurant, lounge, child care. Nordic skiing nearby. Adult lift ticket $39 weekend, $29 mid-week. Information, lodging and snow conditions, ☎ 647-8444.

> ### Shawnee, Once Pleasant Mountain
>
> Some folks may be confused by the mountain's name. Shawnee Peak was called Pleasant Mountain up until 1988, when it was purchased by an out of state group, the Shawnee Group. Still, the relatively wild sounding Indian name has been a better draw. If you ask the locals for directions you may still have to ask for the old name before getting a response.

Carrabassett Valley

Sugarloaf USA, RR 1 Box 5000, Carrabassett Valley, Kingfield 04947. 2,820-foot vertical drop, 107 trails, 14 lifts, 90% snowmaking, above-treeline snowfields (this is the only lift-serviced above-treeline skiing in the Northeast), rentals, lessons, ski shops, health club with indoor pool, complete mountain alpine village with trendy shops and restaurants, on-mountain lodging, Nordic skiing connected to mountain, snowboard park, child care.

 INTERESTING FACT: *The largest snowboarding halfpipe in North America was constructed at Sugarloaf USA in 1995 for the US Snowboard Championships.*

Sugarloaf USA is Maine's largest ski resort and perhaps the most popular non-snowmobile winter destination in the state. You'll spot the resort's distinctive blue and white triangular mountain decal on almost every other vehicle in the state. In the last two years alone more than $4 million has been invested to make this first-class resort even better. Discount lodging and lift packages available. Adult lift ticket, $49 weekend; lower mid-week. Reservations, ☎ 800-THE-LOAF; general, ☎ 237-2000; snowphone, ☎ 237-6808.

Farmington

Titcomb Mountain, PO Box 138, Farmington 04938. 340-foot vertical drop, 14 trails, two lifts, 75% snowmaking, night skiing, Nordic, snowboarding, lessons, rentals, restaurant. Adult lift ticket $14. ☎ 778-9031.

Locke Mills

Ski Mount Abram, PO Box 120, Locke Mills 04255. 1,030 feet vertical, 35 trails, five lifts, 75% snowmaking, lessons, rentals, cafeteria, lounge, Nordic skiing nearby, child care. Adult lift ticket $31 weekends, $20 midweek. ☎ 875-5003.

Rangeley

Saddleback Ski Resort, PO Box 490, Rangeley 04970. 1,830 feet vertical, 41 trails, five lifts, 60% snowmaking, glade skiing, lessons, nastar racing, rentals, ski shop, restaurant, lounge, slopeside lodging, snowboard park, lakeside village, Nordic skiing, child care. The base lodge here is the highest in New England.

Conflict With the Appalachian Trail

Along the Saddleback Ski Resort's ridge line runs the Appalachian Trail. There has been considerable controversy in recent years over the ski area's desire to expand and concerns that expansion at upper elevations may adversely impact the trail's wilderness character.

Saddleback offers big mountain skiing without the crowds you are likely to encounter at Sugarloaf or Sunday River. Adult lift ticket $42 weekends, $29 mid-week. As one wise ski bum suggests: "Ski Sugarloaf and Sunday River on weekdays and Saddleback on the weekends." Not a bad idea. ☎ 864-5671.

Rumford

Black Mountain of Maine, PO Box 239, Rumford 04276. 470 feet vertical, nine trails, two lifts, night skiing, 65% snowmaking, rentals, lessons, cafeteria, Nordic skiing. Adult lift ticket $17. ☎ 364-8977.

■ Cross-Country Skiing

Bethel

 Maine Nordic Ski Council, PO Box 645, Bethel 04217, offers ski reports and information. ☎ 800-SKI-XC; office 824-3694.

The Bethel Inn Touring Center, Box 49, Bethel 04217. Twenty-five miles of backcountry trails, skating, ski school, rentals, snack bar, hot tub/sauna. ☎ 824-2175.

Carter's XC Ski Center, Middle Intervale Road, Bethel 04217. Snowshoeing, ski school, 41 miles of trails, rentals, snack bar, hot tub/sauna. ☎ 539-4848.

Gould Academy, PO Box 860, Bethel 04217. Public skiing by permission of the school. Biathlon Range. Seven miles of trails. ☎ 824-7700.

Sunday River XC Ski Center, Box 1688, Bethel 04217. Part of greater Sunday River downhill ski area including hotels, condos, shops, restaurants, brew pub. Skating, snowshoeing, ski school, rentals, restaurant, hot tub/sauna. Twenty-five miles. ☎ 824-2410.

The Telemark Inn Ski Touring Center, RFD #2, Box 800, Bethel 04217. Private trails for inn guests open to limited number of people from the public each day. Twelve miles of trails. Most trails groomed and 15-feet wide. Warming cottage. ☎ 836-2703.

White Mountains National Forest. A thousand miles on numerous logging roads and trails open to skiing, snowshoeing and snowmobiling. ☎ 824-2134.

Buxton

Ski-A-Bit, PO Box West Buxton 04093. Twenty-five miles of trails. Lessons, rentals, snack bar. ☎ 929-4824.

Carabassett

Sugarloaf Ski Touring Center, Box 5000, Carabassett 04947. Ski and snowshoe rentals, lessons. 56 miles. ☎ 237-6830.

Farmington

Titcomb Mountain Ski Touring Center, Box 138, West Farmington 04992. 16 miles. Equipment rentals available, snack bar. ☎ 778-9031.

Troll Valley XC Ski Center, RR 4 Box 5215, Farmington 04938. 20 miles. Backcountry trails, snowshoeing, lessons, rentals, restaurant, hot tub/sauna. ☎ 778-3656.

Oxford

Carter's XC Ski Center, RR 1, Box 710, Oxford 04270. 14 miles. Snowshoeing, lessons, rentals, snack bar, hot tub/sauna. ☎ 539-4848.

Rangeley

Rangeley Municipal Trails, Rangeley 04970. 13 miles. Backcountry trails. ☎ 864-3326.

Saddleback Touring Center, Box 490, Rangeley 04970. 25 miles. Backcountry trails, skating, lessons, rentals, snack bar, hot tub/sauna. ☎ 864-5671.

■ Snowmobiling

Bethel

White Mountains National Forest. In addition to nearly 100 miles of local trails, the Bethel area provides access to nearly 50 miles of groomed snowmobile trails in the national forest. Snowmobiles must stay on marked trails. Routes include the High Peaks Trail in the former Evergreen Valley ski area in Stoneham near Speckled Mountain. Park at the former ski area. Trails lead into New Hampshire and up to Canada.

Rangeley

Rangeley is one of the premier snowmobiling destinations in Maine with more than 140 miles of groomed trails plus plenty of views and fun destinations. Service and fuel are plentiful. In town, snowmobilers can use trail network to ride from their lodging place to restaurants/shops, and nearby parks.

📖 Map available for $5 from Rangeley Lakes Snowmobile Club. PO Box 950, Rangleley 04970.

Eustis

While often left in the shadow of Sugarloaf to the south, Eustis is a major snowmobiling crossroads in Maine. ITS 89 cuts right through town and leads to Jackman to the north and Rangeley to the south.

Adventures with Pack Animals

■ Llama Trekking

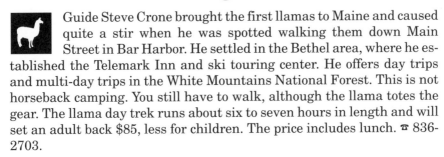

Guide Steve Crone brought the first llamas to Maine and caused quite a stir when he was spotted walking them down Main Street in Bar Harbor. He settled in the Bethel area, where he established the Telemark Inn and ski touring center. He offers day trips and multi-day trips in the White Mountains National Forest. This is not horseback camping. You still have to walk, although the llama totes the gear. The llama day trek runs about six to seven hours in length and will set an adult back $85, less for children. The price includes lunch. ☎ 836-2703.

Eco-Tours & Cultural Excursions

■ Mushing

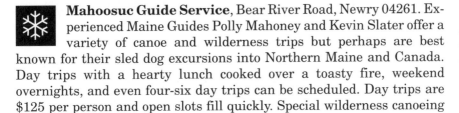

Mahoosuc Guide Service, Bear River Road, Newry 04261. Experienced Maine Guides Polly Mahoney and Kevin Slater offer a variety of canoe and wilderness trips but perhaps are best known for their sled dog excursions into Northern Maine and Canada. Day trips with a hearty lunch cooked over a toasty fire, weekend overnights, and even four-six day trips can be scheduled. Day trips are $125 per person and open slots fill quickly. Special wilderness canoeing and dog sled trips offered throughout the year for women. Longer trips average $100 per day. ☎ 824-2073.

Winter Journeys, RR 1, Box 1105, East Stoneham 04231. Instruction and guided trips by dog sled with winter camping or even staying at a nearby B&B. Day trips cost $150 and average seven hours of instruction and mushing. Half-day trips for $85 available. Trips usually limited to four people. ☎ 928-2026.

■ Panning for Gold

Seeking your fortune in the **Swift River** along Route 17 in Byron is a popular activity. Just swirl gravel from the river around in your pan looking for the flecks of gold, which will settle to the bottom as the lighter materials wash out. Permit required. Pick one up at Mount Blue State Park in Weld or from an area game warden.

■ Rock Hounding

Perham's of West Paris, Route 26, PO Box 280, West Paris 04289. This gem and mineral museum and shop owns four old quarries nearby in the Western Maine area; they are open to rock hunters at no charge. Search for tourmaline, garnet, and amethyst. ☎ 674-2341.

Songo Pond Mine, off Route 5, Bethel, PO Box 864, Bethel 04217. Collectors are allowed to search for aquamarine and other minerals in tailings area. $10 for adults, $5 children under 13. ☎ 824-3898.

■ Apple Picking

Fall is the season for picking your own fresh apples. Here are the pick-your-own farms in the Western Mountains area.

Pick-Your-Own Apples
Limington
■ **Brackett Orchards**, Route 11, ☎ 637-2377.
■ **Dole Orchards**, Dole's Ridge Road, ☎ 793-4409.
South Hiram
■ **Apple Acres Farm**, Durgintown Road, ☎ 625-4777.

Standish

- **Moulton Orchards**, Route 35, ☎ 225-3455.
- **Randall Orchards**, Randall Road, ☎ 642-3500.

Waterford

- **Fillerbrown Orchards**, Plummer Hill Road, ☎ 583-4779.

West Paris

- **Cooper's Farm**, Route 26, ☎ 674-2200.
- **Hungry Hollow Orchards**, Route 26, ☎ 674-2012.

■ Blueberry Picking

Late July and early August is blueberry harvest season in Maine, a time when rakers begin their seasonal labors. And there is nothing like picking them yourself. Commercial picking fields charge a small fee, usually by the pint. If picking in the wild, bring a sturdy container to bring your wild bounty home. Here's one place to try.

Pick-Your-Own Blueberries

Kingfield

- **Richard Oliver's Blueberries**, Route 24. Open daily in season, hours vary. Call ahead, ☎ 696-1044.

Where to Stay & Eat

Rate Scale

All rates are for entrée or complete dinner, per person.

Inexpensive. . . . . under $10

Moderate . . . . $10-$20

Expensive . . . . More than $20

Western Mountains

■ Favorite Restaurants

Bethel

 Matterhorn Wood-fired Pizza, Cross Street, Bethel 04217. Once you've had a pizza baked in a wood-fired oven you'll never go back. A 12-inch, three-cheese pizza will set you back $7.95 and you have your choice of marinara, pesto or garlic parmesan sauce. This establishment offers fresh pasta as well, such as seafood Alfredo Florentine ($16.95). Try the appetizer of fresh focaccia with olive oil for $3.95. Menu available for takeout. Moderate. ☎ 824-6836.

Great Grizzly Bar and Steakhouse, Sunday River Road, Bethel 04217. Watch the flames leap from the blazing firepit as fresh beef hits the hot iron. Casual dress and moderate prices. Full selection of cocktails and microbrews. Open for lunch. Live entertainment on Thursday, Friday and Saturday. Après-ski specials at 3 pm in season. ☎ 824-6271.

Bridgton

Venezia Restorante, Route 302, Bridgton 04009. Fine Italian cuisine open seven days a week in summer and Wednesday through Saturday in winter. Moderately priced. Handicapped access. Reservations accepted. ☎ 647-5333.

Farmington

The Granary, 23 Pleasant Street, Farmington 04938. Relaxed atmosphere characterizes this brewpub and coffee house. Open for lunch and dinner. Handicapped access. Moderately priced. ☎ 779-0710.

Rangeley

The Red Onion, Main, Street, Rangeley 04970. Pizza made from scratch, meal specials and hearty sandwiches make up the heart of the menu. A baked haddock dinner – which includes potato or rice, salad and bread – will set you back $10.95, while the rib eye goes for $9.95. The manicotti at $6.50 is the best buy. Senior (65+) portions available. Orders can be packed to go. ☎ 864-5022.

Road Kill Café, Main Street, Rangeley 04970. Part of a small chain born in Greenville, this establishment hypes up the highway angle by calling menu items by weird names (like "the chicken who didn't make it across the road"). Waitresses are encouraged to sass customers and vice versa. Decor includes old road signs, license plates. Fare tends toward burgers and fried foods with entrées ranging from $7.95 to $13.95. Full bar. Order a "yard" of Bass Ale. It costs $9 and comes in a skinny three-foot tall glass. ☎ 864-3351.

■ Brewpubs/Microbreweries

Bethel

 Sunday River Brewing Company, US Route 2. At entrance to the Sunday River Ski Area, this places rocks in ski season and during summer and fall. The Moose's Tale brewpub serves Pyrite Golden Ale, Mollocket IPA, Redstone Red Ale, Black Bear Porter and many seasonals. Menu features barbecued ribs, pork, chicken and other standard tourist fare. Tours Tuesday afternoons or by appointment. Gift Shop on site. ☎ 824-4 ALE.

Carrabassett Valley

Sugarloaf Brewing Company, Access Road. Theo's Restaurant offers their own special house brews to go along with traditional ski area fare such as burgers and pizza. The establishment features a game room and billiard tables. Call for tour schedule. ☎ 237-2211.

Farmington

Narrow Gauge Brewing Company, 23 Pleasant Street. Beers include Clearwater Cream Ale, Sidetrack Amber, Boxcar Brown and Coal Porter. No tours or gift shop. ☎ 779-0710.

The Forks

Kennebec River Brewery, Route 201 at Northern Outdoors. Penobscot Porter, Magic Ale IPA (named for the famous whitewater rafting falls on the nearby Kennebec River), and Northern Light. Menu includes traditional American food. Call about tours. ☎ 663-4466.

Naples

Bray's Brewpub and Eatery, Route 302. Beers include Brandy Pond Blonde Ale, Old Church Pale Ale, and Pleasant Mountain Porter. plus seasonals. Owner likes to boast the beer comes straight from the brewery into the glass. Menu includes traditional Maine fare, crab cakes, lobster stew, as well as barbecue and gourmet selections. Summer tours daily. Off-season by appointment. ☎ 693-6806.

Western Mountains

■ B&Bs, Hotels & Motels

Price Scale
All rates are based on double occupancy.
Inexpensive . . . . Under $65
Moderate . . . . $66-$100
Expensive . . . . Above $100

Bethel

 The Bethel Inn, PO Box 49, Bethel 04217. A 200-acre resort with stately inn, condominium units, pool and championship golf course. Fine dining as well as a poolside lounge and the Mill Brook Terrace Restaurant. Kids stay free. Close to village and area ski resorts, Nordic centers, hiking, biking. Tennis, health club, lake house and sauna on grounds. Package rates available. Room rates are moderate to expensive. ☎ 824-2175.

Crocker Pond House, 917 Northwest Bethel Road, Bethel 04217. Shingled house set on 50 acres of quiet woods with pond. Each room has private bath, phone and mountain views. Handicapped-accessible room. Rates are $90 per night for two and includes breakfast. Lower rates in off season. Near ski areas, White Mountain National Forest. ☎ 836-2027.

River View Motel, Route 2, Bethel 04217. Clean, modern 32-room motel on banks of river. One-mile walking trail. Close to town and major ski areas. Two-bedroom efficiencies available. This is an affordable option. Rooms feature cable, phone and air-conditioning. Open year-round. Moderately priced. ☎ 824-2808.

Speckled Mountain Ranch, RR 2, Box 717, Bethel 04217. Three-room (2½ baths) bed and breakfast on working farm with riding stable. Great views of nearby hills and close to activities. Carriage rides available. No smoking. Open all year. B&B rates $55 per night, single, $15 per night each additional person. ☎ 836-2908.

Sunday River Summit Motel, PO Box 450, Bethel 04217, on Sunday River Road. A conventional-type motel with lobby, restaurant and lounge on premises and cable television. This slopeside establishment has 230 rooms, some with kitchenettes. Tennis courts, health club, playground heated outdoor pool open year-round. Air-conditioned in summer. Some mountain views. Rates begin (in season) in the expensive range. Packages available. ☎ 824-3500.

Telemark Inn, RFD #2, Box 800, Bethel 04217, on King's Highway. 100-year-old Adirondack-style lodge nestled in the shadow of Caribou Mountain in the White Mountains National Forest. Heated with wood the establishment has been featured in *EcoTraveler* magazine, *Down East*, and *Outside*. Two-day weekend packages, which include meals, run in the range of $220 per adult, based on double occupancy. Sleigh rides, skating and ski touring in winter. Llama trekking, hiking, moose and eagle watching in summer. ☎ 836-2703.

Eustis

Tim Pond Wilderness Camps, Box 22, Eustis 04936. Established in 1860, this camp offers 10 rustic log housekeeping cabins, each with full bath, running water, and wood stoves. Located on the shore of crystal-clear Tim Pond. Camp runs a daily moose watch. American Plan available. Canoes on premises. Inexpensive. ☎ 243-2947.

Farmington

Farmington Motel, PO Box 447, Farmington 04938. Located off Routes 2 and 27, this 40-room hotel is AAA approved and very affordable. It is open year-round, has cable and phones, and is handicapped-accessible. Near snowmobile trails and the Sandy River. Inexpensive. ☎ 778-4680.

Fryeburg

Acres of Austria B&B, RR 1, Box 177, Fryeburg 04037. Located on Fire Lane 48, Route 5. This inn with an Austrian flair overlooks 65 acres, including a half-mile of frontage on the Old Saco River. Owners Candice and Franz Redl speak both English and German to their visitors. There are four rooms, each with a private bath; some are handicapped-accessible. Canoes available. No smoking or pets. Special theme weekends offered throughout the year, such as quilting demonstrations, a murder mystery weekend, and seminars on getting a book or magazine piece published. Rates vary, but they are generally in the moderate range. Discounts for longer stays. Packages available. ☎ 800-988-4391.

Kingfield

The Herbert, PO Box 67, Kingfield 04947. Dubbed "The Ritz of the Woods," the Herbert is a four-story wooden structure in the heart of a quaint village on Main Street. Most rooms boast jacuzzis and are furnished with brass beds, antiques and cozy comforters. Warm apple cider is provided for après ski folks. The hotel also has a sauna and a four-person hot tub.

The award-winning dining room has a fireplace, and there are 100 wines on offer, all at moderate prices. Management boasts that "kids and dogs, even your mother-in-law, will find a warm welcome at The Herbert." Moderate to expensive. ☎ 265-2000.

Rangeley

Saddeback Inn, PO Box 377, Rangeley 04970. Perched out over Rangeley Lake, this establishment is just a short walk from town. Rooms have cable television and phones; some units have kitchenettes. Close to ski area. Moderate. Approximately $60 per night, double. ☎ 864-3434.

Hunter Cove, HC 32, Box 2800, Mingo Loop Road, Rangeley 04970. Eight lakeside cabins finished with rustic wood interiors, just like you'd expect in this part of the state. Some have hot tubs. Open year-round. Moderately priced. ☎ 864-3383.

Grant's Kennebago Camps, PO Box 786, Rangeley 04970. Lakeside sporting camp more than 100 years old. Winner of the *Boston Globe* Travel Award in 1996. Individual cabins and main lodge on the water. Arrive by road or float plane. American plan available. Moderate to expensive. ☎ 864-3608.

South Waterford

Bear Mountain Inn, 35/37 Main, South Waterford 04018. Classic farmhouse (150 years old) with porch overlooking Bear Lake. Sits on large parcel with a natural spring (the inn's water supply) and private beach on the lake. Eight rooms, six baths, buffet breakfast. Rates range from moderate to expensive depending on view, amenities, etc. ☎ 583-4404.

■ Camping

 Facilities indicated as "nearby" are located within one mile of the campground.

Andover

South Arm Campground, PO Box 310, Andover 04216. Great canoeing and fishing for trout or salmon on 17-mile Richardson Lake. Remote camping or RV camping in the main campground on South Arm Road. 102 sites, tenting area, 15 amp, dump station, store, laundry, swimming, boating, fishing, group area, LP gas. Pets allowed. Open May 15-September 15. ☎ 364-5155.

Bethel

Riverside Campground, 121 Mayville Road, Bethel 04217. Located on the Androscoggin River banks in the Western Maine mountains. Canoe, kayak, and bicycle rentals. Call for information on river trips and free river map. 25 sites, tenting area, 50 amp, dump station, store, swimming, boating, fishing, group area. Laundry nearby. Pets allowed. Open May 1-November 1. ☎ 824-4224.

Bridgton

Bridgton Pines Cabins and Campground, RR 2, Box 723, Bridgton 04009. Enjoy life, relax. Camping or cottages with kitchens. Pool with diving board, horseshoes, badminton, volleyball, kids play area. Close to public lakes and restaurants. 30 sites, tenting area, 50 amp, dump station. Pets allowed. Open May 15-October 15. ☎ 647-8227.

Vicki-Lin Camping Area, RR 2, Box 808, Bridgton 04009. Quiet camping area on Long Lake – specializing in seasonal sites with lots of space, boat docks, and swimming. 84 sites, 30 amp, sewer, fishing. Pets allowed. Open May 15-October 15. ☎ 647-8489.

Brownfield

River Run Canoe and Camping, PO Box 90, Brownfield 04010. Primitive campground with secluded riverfront sites on the Saco River, Route 160. Canoe rentals. 20 minutes from North Conway, NH. 22 sites, tenting area, swimming, fishing, group area. Dump station, store, laundry and LP gas nearby. Pets allowed. Open Memorial Day-Labor Day. ☎ 452-2500.

Woodland Acres Camp 'N Canoe, RR 1, Box 445, Brownfield 04010. Relax and enjoy the privacy of a spacious campsite. Delightful choice of canoe trips on the crystal-clear, sandy-bottomed Saco River. 55 sites, tenting area, 30 amp, dump station, store, laundry, rec hall, swimming, boating, fishing, on-site rentals, group area, LP gas. Pets allowed. Open May 15-October 15. ☎ 935-2529.

Byron

Coos Canyon Campground, HC 62, Box 408, Byron 04275. A quiet, natural setting. Tents, pop-ups, and very small campers allowed. Hot showers. Strict no-noise policy – all the time. Pets allowed. 20 sites, tenting area, store, swimming, fishing. Boating nearby. Open April 15-November 15. ☎ 364-3880.

Casco

Point Sebago Golf and Beach Resort, PO Box 712, Casco 04015. Located on Route 302. Beautiful sandy beaches, 18-hole championship golf course and a five-star activities and recreation program, full restaurant and night club. 500 sites, tenting area, 50 amp, sewer, dump station, store, laundry, rec hall, swimming, boating, fishing, on-site rentals, LP gas. Open May 1-October 31. ☎ 266-9840.

Denmark

Granger Pond Camping Area, PO Box 47, Denmark 04022. Located on Bush Row Road. A unique mountaintop campground with beautiful views of the White Mountains. All wooded sites. Close to golf course. Great sunsets. 45 sites, tenting area, 15 amp, sewer, dump station, rec hall, swimming, boating, fishing, on-site rentals. Store nearby. Pets allowed. Open Memorial Day-Labor Day. ☎ 452-2342.

Pleasant Mountain Camping Area, RR 1, Box 941, Denmark 04022. Small family-run campground on shores of Moose Pond. Many seasonal campers with families. Located at the base of Pleasant Mountain. Easy access to White Mountain hiking and nearby lakes. 40 sites, tenting area, 20 amp, sewer, laundry, swimming, boating, fishing, group area. Pets allowed. Open Memorial Day-Columbus Day. ☎ 452-2170.

Dixfield

Mountain View Campground, 208 Weld Street, Dixfield 04224. Any length pull-thru sites, pool, canoes, large rec hall for rental. Full hookups, 32 sites, tenting area, 30 amp, sewer, dump station, store, rec hall, boating, fishing, group area. Pets allowed. Open May 15-October 15. ☎ 562-8285.

East Hebron

Hebron Pines Campground, RR 1, Box 1955, East Hebron 04238. Large campsites, open spaces, great biking. Entertainment includes Annual Bluegrass Festival Memorial weekend. Clean and affordable. 24 sites, tenting area, 30 amp, dump station, store, rec hall, swimming, fishing, pool, group area. Pets allowed. Open Memorial Day-Labor Day. ☎ 966-2179.

Eustis

Cathedral Pines Campgrounds, PO Box 146, Eustis 04936. Located on Route 27. 115 sites, tenting area, 30 amp, dump station, laundry, rec hall, swimming, boating, fishing, group area. Pets allowed. Open May 15-October 1. ☎ 246-3491.

Fryeburg

Canal Bridge Campground, PO Box 181, Fryeburg 04037. Beautifully wooded sites next to a large sandy beach on the Saco River, off Route 5. 40 sites, tenting area, 20 amp, dump station, store, swimming, boating, fishing, on-site rentals, group area. Pets allowed. Open May 15-October 15. ☎ 935-2286.

Gray

Twin Brooks Camping Area, PO Box 194, Gray 04039. Quiet family camping on Little Sebago Lake off Route 85. Sandy beach, boat launch and rentals, swimming, horseshoes, swings, volleyball, basketball. Tent sites to complete hook-ups. 43 sites, tenting area, 20 amp, sewer, dump station, fishing. Pets allowed. Open Memorial Day-September 15. ☎ 428-3832.

Greene

Allen Pond Campground, 102 North Mountain Road, Greene 04236. 65 sites, tenting area, 30 amp, dump station, store, laundry, swimming, boating, fishing, on-site rentals, group area. Pool nearby. Pets allowed. Open Memorial Day-October 1. ☎ 946-7439.

Hanover

Stony Brook Recreation, US Route 2, Hanover 04237. Stony Brook recreation offers year-round camping and recreation opportunities from swimming, hiking, and summer sports to snowmobiling, skiing, and ice skating in winter. 30 sites, tenting area, 30 amp, sewer, group area. Pets allowed. ☎ 824-2836.

Harrison

Vacationland Campsites, RFD #2, Box 95, Harrison 04040. Sits on 1,300 feet of shorefront on beautiful Crystal Lake. Family camping at its best. 110 sites, tenting area, 30 amp, sewer, dump station, store, laundry, rec hall, swimming, boating, fishing, group area, LP gas. Pets allowed. Open year-round. ☎ 583-4953.

Kezar Falls

Locklin Camping Area, Box 197, Kezar Falls 04047. Family camping on a clean spring-fed lake off Tripp Road. Free hot showers, shady sites, excellent fishing, beach for swimming, large field for games, and cottages for rent. 49 sites, tenting area, 50 amp, dump station, rec hall, boating, on-site rentals, group area. Pets allowed. Open Memorial Day-Labor Day. ☎ 625-8622.

Kingfield

Deer Farm Campground, RR 1, Box 2405, Tufts Pond Road, Kingfield 04947. Quiet family campground in the Sugarloaf Mountain area. Trails for casual walks or biking. Weekend activities. Free hot showers. Cabin rentals. Good Sam park. 47 sites, tenting area, 30 amp, dump station, store, laundry, rec hall. Swimming, golf course, boating and fishing nearby. Pets allowed. Open May 9-Columbus Day. ☎ 265-4599.

Leeds

Riverbend Campground, RR 2, Box 5050 State Route 106, Leeds 04263. Family-oriented campground with large open wooded or riverfront sites. Camp store, boat/canoe rentals and planned activities. 80 sites, tenting area, 30 amp, dump station, store, rec hall, swimming, boating, fishing, pool, on-site rentals, group area, LP gas. Pets allowed. Open May 1-September 30. ☎ 524-5711.

Livermore Falls

Rol-Lin Hills Campground, 189 Hathaway Hill Road, Livermore Falls 04253. Lake view. Clean park offering full hook-ups, tent sites, hot showers, pavilion, frisbee golf, mini-golf, horseshoes and hayrides. 30 sites, tenting area, 30 amp, sewer, dump station, store, laundry, pool, group area. LP gas nearby. Pets allowed. Open May 15-Labor Day. ☎ 897-6394.

Locke Mills

Littlefield Beaches, RR 1, Box 4300, Locke Mills 04255. Quiet family campground in a natural environment. Three connecting lakes surround the campground, providing miles to explore sandy beaches with lake trout and bass for anglers. 130 sites, tenting area, 30 amp, sewer, dump station, store, laundry, rec hall, swimming, boating, fishing, on-site rentals, group area, LP gas. Pets allowed. Open Memorial Day-October 1. ☎ 875-3290.

Lovell

Kezar Lake Camping Area, RR 1, Box 246, Lovell 04051. 110 wooded sites on a nine-mile-long sparkling clear lake. Offers a 400-foot sand beach, excellent fishing, store, snack bar and great activity programs. 110 sites, tenting area, 30 amp, dump station, store, laundry, rec hall, swimming, boating, on-site rentals, LP gas. Pets allowed. Open May 15-October 15. ☎ 925-1631.

Naples

Bay Of Naples Family Camping, Route 11/114, Box 240, Naples 04055. Quiet, peaceful family camping in pine forest with large campsites, sandy beach, crystal clear lake, boat slips, playgrounds, adjoining golf course. Cottage rentals, 130 sites, tenting area, 30 amp, sewer, dump station, store, laundry, rec hall, swimming, boating, fishing, LP gas. Open Memorial Day-Columbus Day. ☎ 693-6429.

Colonial Mast on Long Lake, PO Box 95, Kansas Road, Naples 04055. Year-round camping on Long Lake in Naples. Waterfront sites, beach, boat launch, recreation hall, activities and playground. New indoor heated pool. Snowmobilers and skiers welcome. 79 sites, tenting area, 30 amp, sewer, dump station, store, laundry, rec hall, swimming, boating, fishing, on-site rentals. Pets allowed. Open year-round. ☎ 693-6652.

Four Seasons Camping Area, PO Box 927, Naples 04055. A quiet, family-oriented campground on Long Lake, Route 302. Sandy beach, playground, secluded open or waterfront sites, boat docks, seasonal sites. 115 sites, tenting area, 20 amp, dump station, store, rec hall, swimming, boating, fishing, on-site rentals. Pets allowed. Open May 15-Columbus Day. ☎ 693-6797.

K's Family Campground, PO Box 557, Naples 04055. Crystal-clear lake on Route 114. Excellent fishing, two beaches, waterfront sites. 125 sites, tenting area, 15 amp, dump station, store, laundry, rec hall, swimming, boating, fishing. Pets allowed. Open May 15-September 15. ☎ 693-6881.

North Shore Campground, RR 1, Box 153, Naples 04055. 18 sites, tenting area, swimming, boating, fishing, on-site rentals. Pets allowed. Open May 20-October 15. ☎ 693-6326.

North Bridgton

Lakeside Pines Campground, PO Box 182, North Bridgton 04057. A family campground on Long Lake under virgin pines, off Route 117. 1,500 feet of shorefront. Safe beaches and plenty of boating. 185 sites, tenting area, 30 amp, sewer, dump station, store, laundry, rec hall, swimming, fishing, on-site rentals, LP gas. Pets allowed. Open Memorial Day-September 15. ☎ 647-3935.

North Waterford

Papoose Pond Resort and Campground, RR 1, Box 2480, North Waterford 04267. Five-star activities program, spacious sites, housekeeping cottages, half-mile-long sandy beach. Call for free award-winning video brochure. 180 sites, tenting area, 30 amp, sewer, dump station, store, laundry, rec hall, swimming, boating, fishing, on-site rentals. Pets allowed. Open May 15-Columbus Day. ☎ 583-4470.

Oquossoc

Black Brook Cove Campground, PO Box 319, Oquossoc 04964. Nestled in a scenic cove of a pristine 17-mile-long lake off Route 16. Private RV sites, as well as remote wilderness and island campsites. 66 sites, tenting area, 30 amp, dump station, store, laundry, swimming, boating, fishing, group area, LP gas. Pets allowed. Open April 15-November 15. ☎ 486-3828.

Cupsuptic Campground, PO Box 326, Route 16, Oquossoc 04964. Nestled in the pines on the shore of Cupsuptic Lake with sandy beaches surrounded by the mountains. Horseshoes, badminton, volleyball, and canoe and boat rentals. 55 sites, tenting area, 25 amp, dump station, store, rec hall, swimming, boating, fishing, group area. Pets allowed. Open May 1-December 1. ☎ 864-5249.

Stephen Phillips Preserve, PO Box 21, Oquossoc 04964. Located on Briches Beach Road. 60 sites, tenting area, swimming, boating, fishing. Pets allowed. Open May 1-September 30. ☎ 864-2003.

Oxford

Mirror Pond Campground, 210 Tiger Hill Road, Oxford 04270. New electric boxes and water at every site. Pine grove with crystal-clear water for swimming. Three miles to Oxford Plains Speedway. 40 sites, tenting area, 30 amp, dump station, rec hall, boating, fishing, group area. Pets allowed. Open Memorial Day-Labor Day. ☎ 539-4888.

Two Lakes Camping, PO Box 206, Oxford 04270. Located on Hogan Oond Road. The large sandy beach here is just what your toes cry for. Campers are never bored unless they want to be. 114 sites, tenting area, 30 amp, sewer, dump station, store, laundry, rec hall, swimming, boating, fishing, on-site rentals, group area. LP gas nearby. Pets allowed. Open May 1-October 1. ☎ 539-4851.

Peru

Honey Run Beach and Campgrounds, RR 1, Box 1230, Peru 04290. Trailers to rent and a large field with tent and bandstand for reunions. 225-foot sandy beach. 78 sites, tenting area, 30 amp, sewer, dump station, laundry, swimming, fishing, on-site rentals, group area, LP gas. Store nearby. Pets allowed. Open Memorial Day-Labor Day. ☎ 562-4913.

Poland

Range Pond Campground, 94 Plains Road, Poland 04274. They strive to make campers feel welcome, secure and comfortable at all times by providing a peaceful and relaxed atmosphere. 80 sites, tenting area, 30 amp, sewer, dump station, store, laundry, rec hall, swimming, boating nearby, pool, on-site rentals, group area. Fishing and LP gas nearby. Pets allowed. Open Apr 15-October 15. ☎ 998-2624.

Poland Spring

Poland Spring Campground, PO Box 409, Poland Spring 04274. On the lake. A quiet family campground with planned activities, recreation program, large playground, boat rentals and excellent canoeing and fishing. 100 sites, tenting area, 30 amp, sewer, dump station, store, laundry, rec hall, swimming, pool. Pets allowed. Open May 1-October 15. ☎ 998-2151.

Raymond

Kokatosi Campground, 635 Route 85, Raymond 04071. Located on Crescent Lake, planned activities, theme weekends, tent and full hook-up sites, store, rec hall, trailer rentals and boat rentals. 162 sites, tenting area, 15 amp, sewer, dump station, store, laundry, rec hall, swimming, fishing, on-site rentals, group area, LP gas. Pets allowed. Open May 15-Columbus Day. ☎ 627-4642.

Rumford

Madison Riverside Wilderness Camping, Route 2, PO Box 398, Rumford 04276. Pine grove along the river next to the Madison Motel Resort with all motel privileges available. 24 sites, tenting area, dump station, rec hall, swimming, boating, fishing, pool, group area. Pets allowed. Open May 1-November 1. ☎ 364-7973.

Standish

Family-N-Friends Campground, 140 Richville Road, Standish 04084. Located in the Sebago Lakes region. Wooded sites with electric and water. Beautiful pool area and main lodge for activities. 60 sites, tenting area, sewer, pool, dump station, store, rec hall, swimming. Boating, fishing and laundry nearby. Pets allowed. Open May 1-November 1. ☎ 642-2200.

Sebago Lake Family Campground, 1550 Richville Road, Standish 04084. Large wooded sites each with their own barbeque grill, campfire ring and picnic table. Private sandy beach on Sebago Lake with roped-off swimming area. 101 sites, tenting area, 30 amp, sewer, dump station, store, laundry, rec hall, boating, LP gas. Fishing nearby. Pets allowed. Open May 1-Columbus Day. ☎ 787-3671.

Steep Falls

Acres Of Wildlife Campground, PO Box 2, Steep Falls 04085. Family campground, completely private with secluded woods in the Sebago Lake area (on Adams Pond Road). Stocked private lake, free fishing, large sandy beach, activities, restaurant, store and rentals. 200 sites, tenting area, 30 amp, sewer, dump station, store, laundry, rec hall, swimming, boating, on-site rentals, group area, LP gas. Pets allowed. Open May 1-Columbus Day. ☎ 675-3211.

Waterford

Bear Mt. Village Cabins and Sites, RR 2, Box 745, Waterford 04088. 49 sites, tenting area, 30 amp, sewer, dump station, store, laundry, rec hall, swimming, boating, fishing, on-site rentals, group area. Pets allowed. Open May 15-October 15. ☎ 583-2541.

Weld

Dummer's Beach Campground, PO Box 82, Weld 04285. Panoramic mountain views from a private half-mile-long sandy beach off Dixfield Road. Water deepens gradually, making this a good choice for those with children. Plenty of hiking. Located in the center of Tumbledown and Mount Blue ranges. Showers, playground. Near Maine ATV Trails. 200 sites, tenting area, 30 amp, dump station, store, swimming, boating, fishing. LP gas nearby. Pets allowed. Open Memorial Day-Labor Day. ☎ 585-2200.

West Poland

Hemlocks Camping Area, PO Box 116, West Poland 04291. Located on Megquier Hill Road. Can accommodate self-contained large groups. 60 sites, tenting area, 30 amp, sewer, dump station, store, laundry, rec hall, swimming, boating, fishing, LP gas. Pets allowed. Open May 15-October 1. ☎ 998-2384.

Mac's Campground, PO Box 87, West Poland 04291. On Route 11. 30 sites, tenting area, 20 amp, sewer, dump station, rec hall, swimming, boating, fishing. Store and LP gas nearby. Pets allowed. Open May 15-September 15. ☎ 998-4238.

Wilson Mills

Aziscoos Valley Camping Area, HCR 10, Box 302, Wilson Mills 03579. 31 sites, tenting area, 30 amp, dump station, laundry, swimming, boating, fishing, group area. Pets allowed. Open May 15-October 30. ☎ 486-3271.

Mid-Maine

MID-MAINE

The Mid-Maine region literally bisects the center of the state running roughly parallel to Interstate Highway 95 from the Lewiston/Auburn area in the south to the Greater Bangor vicinity in the north.

Most of the major communities, including Augusta, the capital, Waterville, Lewiston, Skowhegan and Bangor sprang up when industrious settlers decided to harness the power of nearby rivers to saw wood, weave fabric, or run machinery to makes shoes, tools and other goods. The rivers provided key transportation to bring raw materials in and ship finished goods out.

Despite the decidedly urban nature of many of these communities their compact suburbs quickly give way to the rural areas that truly characterize this region. It is an area of gently rolling hills, broad farm fields where ancient stone walls divide the boundary between cultivated ground and lush hardwood forests.

Especially in the Augusta/Waterville area, lakes are the primary attraction. In summer, lakeside camps and cottages overflow with people looking to escape the city heat.

Backcountry roads, where farm vehicles often outnumber out-of-state cars, are havens for bicycle riders shell-shocked by heavy traffic on busy US 1.

Deer Alert

While there is less true wilderness here than elsewhere in the state, the number of deer is higher. These animals, which prefer a landscape mottled with fields and forest glens, are a majestic sight stepping warily at the end of a field on a misty morning.

Numerous small streams, such as the Sheepscot River or Cobbosseecontee Stream, offer plenty of paddling opportunities, especially in spring or after a good rain.

Hikers will find no shortage of day hikes. Most are short and relatively easy as they ascend moderate hills like Mount Pisgah with its fire tower in Winthrop or Monument Hill in Leeds. In most cases the views are as spectacular as any from their larger cousins to the west.

Bald Mountain in Dedham, on the eastern end of this region, is also a popular day hike.

The state capitol in Augusta was designed by Thomas Bullfinch.

WATCHABLE WILDLIFE: *The **Sunkhaze Meadows** marsh near Old Town is a wildlife-watcher's dream. You could spend days canoeing its many channels in search of great blue herons, muskrats, beavers and moose.*

▪ Note: Maine has one area code – 207.

Parks & Preserves

▪ State Parks

Peacock Beach State Park, Richmond. Located on Route 201 just 10 miles south of Augusta, this 100-acre park with a fine sand beach features good swimming with lifeguards. Open during summer season. Small fee. Plenty of parking. ☎ 582-2813.

Range Ponds State Park, Poland. Open seasonally. This 750-acre pond is popular with swimmers and paddlers. Good fishing. Facilities include beach, bathhouse, toilets, picnic ground and more than a mile-long nature trail. There is a fee. ☎ 998-4104.

Major Parks & Preserves in Mid-Maine

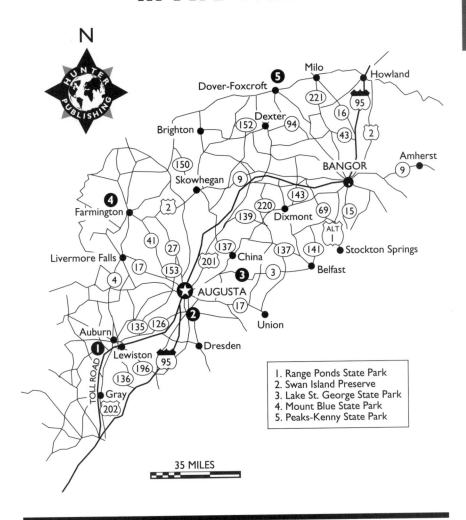

N

1. Range Ponds State Park
2. Swan Island Preserve
3. Lake St. George State Park
4. Mount Blue State Park
5. Peaks-Kenny State Park

35 MILES

■ Wildlife Refuges

Sunkhaze Meadows National Wildlife Refuge, Milford. Established in 1988, this 9,337-acre preserve is located along five miles of Sunkhaze Stream.

DID YOU KNOW? *According to refuge publications, the name Sunkhaze is derived from the Abnaki phrase Wetchi-sam-kassekug. Roughly translated, this means "concealing outlet," referring to the stream's well disguised junction with the Penobscot River.*

Habitats include forests, alder and willow riparian zones, swamps and the second largest peat bog in Maine. Twelve miles of other streams make for great canoeing.

WATCHABLE WILDLIFE: *While canoeing, watch for moose, beavers, and migrating wildfowl. Other wildlife include bears, coyotes, and deers. More than 200 species of birds have been seen at Sunkhaze.*

Hiking is allowed on old logging roads and there is good cross-country skiing in winter. No facilities. Hunting is permitted in season (take care). Put canoes in at Stud Mill Road or Route 2. Office open weekdays at 1033 South Main Street, Old Town 04468. ☎ 827-6138.

Swans Island, Richmond. This 3½-mile-long island in the middle reaches of the Kennebec River is operated by the state as a wildlife refuge and management area. Tidal flats, upland and wetland ecosystems.

WATCHABLE WILDLIFE: *Bald eagles nest on Swans Island, deer live in the woods and migrating wildfowl can be seen.*

Foot access to some areas is banned. Water access only. Day trips are allowed and overnight camping on 10 sites is permitted with reservations. A truck used to transport tours and people to the campground area (☎ 289-1150). Passenger boat access with reservations. ☎ 547-4167.

Hirundo Wildlife Refuge, Alton. Located along the banks of Pushaw Stream, this 1,000-acre preserve has been the site of archeological excavations. Several trails, good wildlife-watching from canoes. Located on Route 43. Open during daylight hours year-round. ☎ 394-4681.

Chesterville Wildlife Management Area, Chesterville. A 470-acre preserve featuring woods, bogs, ponds. Hunting, fishing and canoeing allowed. Access in village. Nearby is Chesterville Esker, a sand and gravel glacial deposit 30 yards tall between two ponds.

Thorncrag Bird Sanctuary, Lewiston. More than 228 acres of wildlands in the middle of a major metropolitan area is a treat. Operated by the Stanton Bird Club, this forested preserve features nearly three miles of color-coded paths that wind through woods, past ponds, and by an old building foundation. Biking, camping, alcohol, and motor vehicles are all banned. Open to skiing and snowshoeing in winter. Fires by permit only. Occasional lectures, field trips. Maps available at the parking area off Montello Street. Open daily. No fee. ☎ 782-5238.

Removal of Edwards Dam

On Friday, July 2nd, 1999, the waters of the mighty Kennebec River for 17 miles above Augusta were allowed to flow freely to tidewater for the first time in 160 years. Workers breached the 917-foot-wide Edwards Dam to allow Atlantic salmon, shad, striped bass and shortnose sturgeon access upstream, including historic spawning regions and feeder streams. Edwards Dam was the first dam in the US ever ordered removed because its economic benefits did not justify its negative environmental impact.

■ Preserves/Natural Areas

Fields Pond Nature Center, Holden. This 200-acre Maine Audubon preserve and wildlife refuge on the site of a former estate features a 20-acre island in the pond. Trails include a walk along the eastern shore of the pond and the Ravine Trail, an easy mile-long excursion through stately white pines along a natural gorge. There are also trails through a marsh and through fields. Plenty of parking at the visitor center and gift shop on Fields Pond Road off the Wiswell Road. Maps available. No pets. Open year-round (hours vary). Special programs. ☎ 781-2330.

Mendall Marsh, Frankfort. Numerous birds and other creatures live in this 250-acre refuge on the South Branch of the Marsh River where it meets the Penobscot. Parking area off Route 1A and boat launch. Hunting and fishing allowed.

Sightseeing

NOTE

Many museums and historic sites in Maine are small, and operate for only part of the year, staffed by volunteers. The opening days and times of these institutions vary, depending upon weather, available staff and other factors; some are open by appointment only. We recommend that you call ahead to find out the latest opening times.

■ Historic Sites/Museums

Athens

 Athens Historical Society Museum, Somerset Academy Community Center, Academy Street Former Somerset Academy. Featuring Somerset Academy memorabilia from 1846 to 1967 with collections of Athens town reports, maps, photos, scrapbooks, and other local antiquities. On the National Register of Historic Places. ☎ 654-2647.

Auburn

The Androscoggin Historical Society, 2 Turner Street, County Building. ☎ 784-0586.

Auburn Fire Department Museum, 550 Minot Avenue. Collection of antique fire equipment from Auburn. ☎ 784-5433.

Knight House Museum (1796), Great Falls Plaza. A 1½-story Cape Cod, oldest frame house in downtown Auburn. Adjacent one-room shoe shop showing tools and methods used prior to 1835. ☎ 783-0584.

Augusta

Blaine House (1833), 192 State Street. Home of James G. Blaine. The house was given to the State of Maine in 1919 to be used as the governor's mansion. Frederick Law Olmsted designed the front entrance, which was completed in 1990. Grounds are being restored in the spirit of the original Olmsted plan. ☎ 287-2301.

Kennebec Historical Society, 14 Smith Street. ☎ 621-3486.

Maine Historical Records Advisory Board, 84 State House Station Cultural Building. The Board maintains a listing of historical societies, museums and archives holding historical records, including location, contact information, visiting hours, types of collections. ☎ 287-5790.

Maine State Archives, 84 State House Station Cultural Building. The Archives maintains the official records of Maine State government, including vital records (births, deaths, marriages) prior to 1922. The 60 million pages in the collection include Civil War photos and correspondence, court records beginning in 1639, state legislative and administrative records from 1820. Access records in databases, on microfilm, or in files. ☎ 287-5790.

Maine Military Historical Society Museum, Camp Keyes, Upper Winthrop Street. Maine's military history from 1763 to the Persian Gulf

War. Firearms, period uniforms, insignia, sabers, awards, etc. Library for military publications on the second floor; by appointment. ☎ 626-4338.

Maine State Museum, State House Complex, State Street. Multi-level displays and exhibitions on Maine history and industry. Home to the *Lion*, the state's oldest steam locomotive. Battle flag of General Joshua Chamberlain who lead the 20th Maine at Little Round Top in Gettysburg is on display. Gift shop. ☎ 287-2301.

Maine State Police Museum, 36 Hospital Street. ☎ 624-7000.

Old Fort Western, 16 Cony Street. A National Historic Landmark. Main house is the oldest surviving wooden fort building in New England (1754). Museum offices in the adjacent City Hall. ☎ 626-2385.

Samantha Smith Statue, in front of the Cultural Building, State House Complex, State Street. Honors young girls from Maine who helped create an atmosphere of peace with the Soviet Union.

State Capitol Building (1829), State Street. Constructed of native granite, the building's portico and front façade with its towering arcade is an example of the work of noted American architect Charles Bullfinch. Building underwent major renovation in Fall of 1998. Maine battle flags, portraits of former Maine Governors. Maine Law Library, Legislative Chambers, and Office of the Governor. ☎ 289-1615.

Bangor

Bangor Historical Society Museum, including Thomas A. Hill House (1834), 159 Union Street. Greek Revival home, designed by Richard Upjohn. ☎ 942-5766.

Cole Land Transportation Museum, 405 Perry Road. Private collection open to the public featuring cars, trucks, boats and an entire BL2 Bangor and Aroostook locomotive. Large collection of early snow removal equipment. Other exhibits include fire truck, blacksmith shop. Thousands of old photos on display. ☎ 990-3600.

Isaac Farrar Mansion (1845), 17 Second Street. Greek Revival, Regency and late Victorian with mahogany paneling and stained glass. ☎ 941-2808.

Bradley

Maine Forest and Logging Museum, Leonard's Mills, Route 178. A recreation of a 1790s logging and milling community. Special events, exhibitions throughout the year. ☎ 581-2871.

Brewer

Brewer Historical Society, Clewley Museum, 199 Wilson Street. Two-story home and barn, antique hearse, diorama of original shipyard, old photos, paintings of former Governor Joshua Chamberlain's family members. ☎ 989-7468.

Canaan

Lindbergh Crate Museum. Very large crate used to transport The *Spirit of St. Louis* back to the US after Lindbergh's historic flight to France. The crate has been turned into a museum. It sits in a field with photos and other memorabilia inside. Go to any store on Route 2 and ask for directions. (No phone.)

Corinna

Stewart Free Library (1897), Pleasant Street. Late Victorian architecture. Legal and personal library of building's donor. Contains photographs of local early settlers. Open by appointment. ☎ 278-4183.

Dexter

Dexter Historical Society, Grist Mill Museum (1853) and **The Millers' House**, Main Street. ☎ 924-5721.

Dixmont

Law Enforcement Museum. The museum follows the progress of the Bangor Police from its first constable in 1792 to the present. Artifacts dating from pre-Civil War include a rare Tramp Chair, turn-of-the-century uniforms, etc. ☎ 234-2394.

Easton

Easton Historical Society, Station Road. ☎ 488-6846.

Francis M. Malcolm Institute, Route 1A. ☎ 488-5451.

Exeter

Memory Lane Museum of Antique Cars, Stetson Road. (No phone.)

Fairfield

History House, Fairfield Historical Society, 42 High Street. Victorian House containing restored painted and stenciled ceilings and borders. ☎ 453-2998.

L. C. Bates Museum, Campus of Good Will, Route 201, Hinckley. Natural history, art, archaeology, Americana, and ethnology. On the National Register of Historic Places. ☎ 453-4894.

Fayette

Fayette Historical Society. ☎ 685-4373.

Mid-Maine

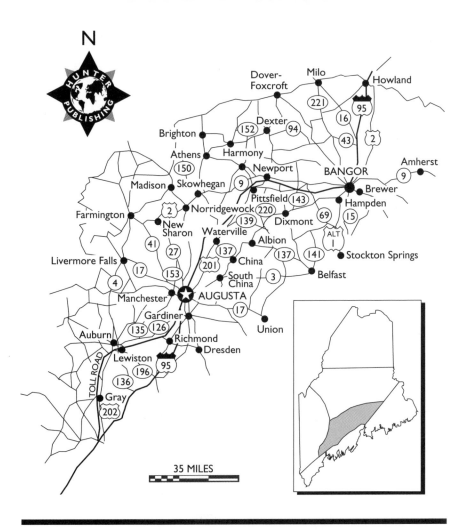

Hallowell

Dr. John Hubbard Office Museum, 116 Second Street. Built around 1835. Furnishings are of the period and were not necessarily owned by the doctor. Books and instruments were used by the doctor in his practice. ☎ 623-4021.

Hampden

Kinsley House Museum, Hampden Historical Society, Museum and Archives, 83 Main Road, Route 1A. 1794 home of Martin Kinsley, Mass. Senator, Judge, and a Member of the Missouri Compromise Commission. Also features the Hannibal Hamlin Law office used from 1831-1860 by Mr. Hamlin. ☎ 862-2027.

Indian Island

Penobscot Nation Native American Museum, Center Street. ☎ 827-4153.

Lewiston

Bates College Museum of Art, Olin Arts Center, 75 Russell Street. Galleries for traveling exhibitions; works from the permanent collection. ☎ 786-6158.

Liberty

Liberty Historical Society, Old Octagonal Post Office (1867), Route 173, Main Street. ☎ 589-4393.

Lisbon Falls

Lisbon Historical Society, 14 High Street. (No phone.)

Livermore Falls

Livermore Falls Historical Society. ☎ 897-4695.

Norlands Living History Center, Norlands Road, north of Route 108. A 445-acre complex that recreates life in the 19th century. Victorian mansion of Maine's famous Washburn family. School groups participate in day-long re-enactments. Adults can sign up for 72-hour "immersion" in history sessions. Drop-in visitors welcome in summer, Wednesday-Sunday. ☎ 897-4366.

Monmouth

Cumston Hall and Public Library (1900), Main Street. Ornate Romanesque-style building houses public library and Theater at Monmouth. The opera house has a hand-carved proscenium arch and ceiling frescoes created by Maine's Harry H. Cochrane. ☎ 933-4788

Monmouth Historical Society, Monmouth Museum, 751 Main Street. Complex of buildings filled with memorabilia dating to the founding of Monmouth. ☎ 933-2287.

New Gloucester

United Society of Shakers, Shaker Museum and Gift Shop, Route 26. Employing the motto "Hands to work, hearts to God," hundreds of celibate believers once worked these fields and farms. Only a handful remain. Sect was famous for their simple approach to life and elegantly simple designs for furniture and other items. A living history museum. Summer and fall workshops and special events. Guided tours. Seed outlet. ☎ 926-4597.

Newburgh

Jabez Knowlton Old Country Store Museum (1839), Route 9 and 202. ☎ 234-2381.

Norridgewock

Norridgewock Historical Society, Mercer Road. ☎ 634-4243.

Old Town

Old Town Museum, 138 South Main Street. Historic waterworks building, permanent logging exhibits. ☎ 827-7256.

Orono

Hudson Museum, Maine Center for the Arts, University of Maine. Exhibits and programs exploring anthropology. ☎ 581-1901.

Page Farm and Home Museum. ☎ 581-4100. Exhibits of farm and domestic life at the turn of the century.

Planetarium, Wingate Hall/UMO. ☎ 581-1341.

University of Maine Museum of Art, Carnegie Hall. Not handicapped-accessible. Museum with campus art galleries and traveling exhibitions for schools. ☎ 581-3256.

Palermo

Dinsmore Grain Co. Mill, Main Street. Branch Mills Village. ☎ 993-2496.

Pittsfield

Pittsfield Historical Society, Depot House Museum, Railroad Plaza. Next to the Maine Central Railroad Line. ☎ 487-2254.

Pittston

Arnold Expedition Historical Society, Major Reuben Colburn House (1765). Off Route 27. Currently being authentically restored. Contains historic batteaux, canoes, and picture panels of Benedict Arnold's ill-fated march to Quebec. ☎ 582-7080.

Readfield

Readfield Historical Society and Museum (1827). Route 17 in Readfield Depot. Extensive genealogical info is available to researchers by appointment. Artifacts from families, businesses, organizations and schools are on display. ☎ 685-3831.

Richmond

T.J. Southard House Museum (1870), 75 Main Street. Local history, tools, toys and housewares in Victorian built by shipping magnate T. J. Southard as a wedding gift. ☎ 737-8202.

Richmond Historical Society, 7 Gardiner Street. ☎ 737-4166.

Skowhegan

History House, 40 Elm Street. ☎ 474-6632.

Margaret Chase Smith Library, Norridgewock Avenue. A non-profit research center and museum of 20th-century political archives and memorabilia as they relate to the ideals and career of Maine's Senator Margaret Chase Smith. ☎ 474-7133.

Skowhegan History House (1839), Norridgewock Avenue. ☎ 474-3140.

Smyrna

Oakfield Railroad Museum. Displays of photos, vintage signs, and other railroad memorabilia. Restored caboose, motor car and a manually propelled pedal car. Wheelchair accessible. ☎ 757-8575.

Strong

Strong Historical Society, Vance and Dorothy Hammond Museum, Main Street. Historical Society collection of artifacts. Adjoining stable. ☎ 684-4137.

Thorndike

Bryant Stove and Music Museum, Route 139 and 220, Rich Road. Collection and sales office for old and restored wood stoves. Parts department. ☎ 568-3665.

Vassalboro

Vassalboro Historical Society Museum (1850), Route 32. ☎ 923-3533.

Waterville

Colby College Museum of Art, 5600 Mayflower Hill Dr. An outstanding permanent collection of 18th-, 19th-, and 20th-century American art and selected European works and collections of oriental, pre-Colombian, and Greek ceramics. ☎ 872-3228.

Redington Museum and Apothecary (1814), 64 Silver Street. Nineteenth-century apothecary, Civil War items, Indian relics, china, and silverware. Library contains local photos, manuscripts and diaries. ☎ 872-9439.

Waterville-Winslow Two-Cent Bridge, Front Street. ☎ 873-7131.

Waterville Historical Society, 64 Silver Street. ☎ 872-9439.

Wayne

Annie Louise Cary Memorial Library, Old Winthrop Road, Route 133. (No phone.)

Whitefield

Whitefield Historical Society. ☎ 549-5064.

Winslow

Winslow Historical Society, 16 Benton Avenue. (No phone.)

Winterport

Winterport Historical Association, 760 N. Main Street. ☎ 223-5556.

List Source-Maine Department of Tourism.

■ Covered Bridges

Covered bridges are a quintessential symbol of New England. The spans were covered over to afford the structure protection from wind and rain, and to keep the decking free of snow and ice. There were hundreds of covered bridges throughout the region, but most succumbed to old age, fire, or flood.

Robyville Bridge, 1876, Kenduskeag Stream. The only completely shingled covered bridge in the state of Maine. Located off Route 15 in Robyville Village in the town of Corinth, about three miles northwest of Kenduskeag Village.

Shopping

■ Antiques

Albion

Cock Hill Farm (Barbara Thornsjo), Bessey Ridge Road. Barn open by appointment. ☎ 437-2345.

Augusta

Pine Tree Stables Antiques and Collectibles (Lois and Harold Bulger), 1095 Riverside Drive. Art glass, cut glass, bride's baskets, primitives, watches, clocks, lamps, lanterns, prints, flow blue, Majolica. Open May-December. Closed Mondays. ☎ 622-4859.

Bangor

Alcott Antiques and Associates (Patricia Alcott), 30 Central Street. Small multi-dealer shop. Focus on primitives, early country items in paint, hooked rugs, baskets and folk items. Tuesday-Saturday, year-round. ☎ 942-7706.

Thomas Jewett Antiques, displaying at Searsport Antique Mall on US 1. Country furniture in original paint, country smalls, Victorian jewelry, American and European art. ☎ 941-8445.

Fairfield

James Julia, Inc., Route 201. Auctioneer conducting specialized catalog auctions; guns, toys, dolls, rare glass and lamps and advertising. ☎ 453-7125.

Gardiner

Kenneth Tuttle, Route 2. Specializing in 18th-century American furniture, formal and high country. ☎ 582-4496.

Hallowell

Newsom and Berdan's (Betty Berdan and Michael Newsom), 151 Water Street. Period and country furniture, pottery, folk art, textiles and accessories. Open by chance or appointment. ☎ 622-0151.

Lisbon

Lisbon Schoolhouse Antiques (Burt and Donna Warren), 273 Lisbon Road. Victorian schoolhouse with wide variety of furniture, decorative items, silver, pottery, rugs. Dealers welcome. Open varied hours April-December. ☎ 353-6075.

Skowhegan

Hilltop Antiques (Greg Salisbury), 55 East Front Street. Wholesale to trade only. Open by chance or appointment. ☎ 474-3972.

Adventures On Foot

■ Hiking

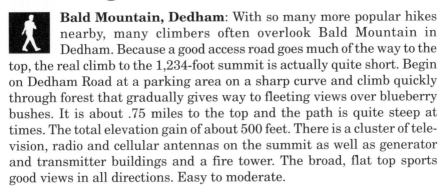 **Bald Mountain, Dedham**: With so many more popular hikes nearby, many climbers often overlook Bald Mountain in Dedham. Because a good access road goes much of the way to the top, the real climb to the 1,234-foot summit is actually quite short. Begin on Dedham Road at a parking area on a sharp curve and climb quickly through forest that gradually gives way to fleeting views over blueberry bushes. It is about .75 miles to the top and the path is quite steep at times. The total elevation gain of about 500 feet. There is a cluster of television, radio and cellular antennas on the summit as well as generator and transmitter buildings and a fire tower. The broad, flat top sports good views in all directions. Easy to moderate.

Mount Pisgah, Winthrop: Mount Pisgah may not be the tallest mountain around, but its proximity to the major metropolitan areas of Lewiston and Augusta make it a favorite escape. From the trailhead off the Pisgah Mountain Road, the route heads quickly up to the summit following a power line for a short distance. The trail to the summit is only a mile long, with an elevation gain of 400 feet. There is a fire tower and some antennas at the top as well as great views of the Western Mountains and the Presidential Range to the far west. Moderate effort required.

Passadumkeag Mountain, Grand Falls Township: Woods roads and foot trails combine to provide fit hikers a long day trip to the top of this 1,463-foot peak. With an elevation gain of 900 feet, this is a very strenuous hike. Begin on the Greenfield Road at a cluster of cabins in a field. Continue another 5½ miles down a rough dirt road to the trailhead near a small cabin and pond. The trail leads steeply 1½ miles to the top. There is an old fire tower and some communications gear at the top. Views extend in all directions.

■ Golfing

Greens fees vary greatly according to the popularity of the course and the time of year.

Natanis, Webber Pond Road, Vassalboro, Augusta. 9,610 yards, par 109. 27 holes. Mid-April through November. ☎ 622-3561.

Western View Golf Club, Bolton Hill Road, Augusta. 5,410 yards, par 70. 9 holes. April-October. ☎ 622-5309.

Prospect Hill Golf Course, 694 S. Main Street, Auburn. 6,000 yards, par 71. 18 holes. April-November. ☎ 782-9220.

Bangor Municipal Golf Course, 278 Webster Avenue, Bangor. 6,350 yards, par 71, 3,215 yards, par 36. 27 holes. April-November. ☎ 941-0232.

Hermon Meadows Golf Club, Billings Road, Hermon. Bangor Area. 6,500 yards, par 72. 18 holes. April-November. ☎ 848-3741.

Pine Hill Golf Club, Outer Mill Street, Brewer. 2,934/2864 yards, par 36/35. 9 holes. April-October. ☎ 989-3824.

Lakeview Golf Club, Prairie Road, Burnham. 3,072 yards, par 36. 9 holes. April 15-October 30. ☎ 948-5414.

Carmel Valley Golf Club, Route 2, Main Road, Carmel. 1,378 yards, par 27. 9 holes. April-November, or first snow. ☎ 848-2217.

Dexter Municipal Golf Course, Sunrise Avenue, Dexter. 2,630 yards, par 35. 9 holes. April 25-November. ☎ 924-6477.

Foxcroft Golf Club, Foxcroft Center Road, off Milo Road, Dover-Foxcroft. 2,922 yards, par 36. 9 holes. April-October. ☎ 564-8887.

Woodland Terrace, Route 1A, East Holden. 1,700 yards, par 30. 9 holes. April 1-October 31. ☎ 989-3750.

Hampden Country Club, Route 9, Hampden. 2,950 yards, par 36. 9 holes. April 20-October 20. ☎ 862-9999.

J. W. Parks Golf Course, 94 Hartland Avenue, Hartland. 5,803 yards, par 70. 9 holes. ☎ 487-5545. May 1-October 15.

Kenduskeag Valley Golf Course, Higginsville Road, Kenduskeag. 2,562 yards, par 34. 9 holes. ☎ 884-7330. May 15-October 15.

Springbrook Golf Course, Route 202, Leeds. Men is 6,408 yards, par 71; women is 5,634 yards, par 74. 18 holes. Mid-April through November. ☎ 946-5900.

Apple Valley Golf Course, 316 Pinewoods Road, Lewiston. 5,037 yards, par 70. 9 holes. April 10-November 15. ☎ 784-9773.

Maple Lane Country Club, River Road, Livermore. 2,420 yards, par 35. 9 holes. April-November. ☎ 897-4453.

Lakewood Golf Course, Madison. 5,729 yards, par 70. 13 holes. April 15-November 4. ☎ 474-5955.

Cobbossee Colony Golf Course, Cobbosseecontee Road, Monmouth. 2,413 yards, par 34. 9 holes. Mid-April until first snow. ☎ 268-4182.

Orchard View Golf Course, Old Corinna Road, Newport. 2,240 yards, par 30. 9 holes. April-November. ☎ 368-5600.

Penobscot Valley Country Club, 366 Main Road, Orono. 6,301 yards, par 72. 18 holes. April-November. ☎ 866-2060.

Palmyra Golf Course, Lang Hill Road, Palmyra. 6,617 yards, par 72. 18 holes. April-November. ☎ 938-4947.

Pine Ridge Golf Course, West River Road, Waterville. 2,570 yards, par 27. 9 holes. April-November 1. ☎ 873-0474.

Waterville Country Club, Country Club Road, Waterville. 6,600 yards, par 70. 18 holes. April-November. ☎ 465-9861.

Adventures On Wheels

■ Mountain Biking

 Lost Valley Ski Area/Bike Park, Auburn. While the lift does not run in summer, bikers have use of miles of ski trails, single-track paths, and four-wheel-drive roads from May until November. Terrain includes rolling hills, streams. Maximum elevation gain of several hundred feet. Riders must check in and out at the ticket counter, where maps are available. Rides for all skill levels. Daily trail pass $5; season, $75. Adult paintball field with equipment provided. Lost Valley is home to the annual L.L. Bean Biking School. ☎ 784-1561.

Corinna to Dover Foxcroft Railbed, Corinna. Twenty miles of packed gravel surface await riders willing to explore the abandoned railbed between these two communities. For a time the path follows the Sebasticook River. There is plenty of parking in Corinna at the intersections of Routes 7 and 43. Several road crossings demand attention to traffic. Very easy ride. ATVs may be encountered in summer, snowmobiles in winter.

University of Maine Woods, Orono. As part of the main campus of the University of Maine System, a large experimental forest provides great recreational opportunities for bikers as well as joggers and walkers. You can access the paved bike path at The Field House and football field area. There is a large visitor's parking lot here , although it is a good idea to get a pass from the university police so they don't tow your vehicle.

The paved portions of the trail form a large "T" with the stem running from the Field House north. The crossbar is a paved bike path running between Stillwater Avenue and Old Town. There are dozens more miles of potential single-track riding. The entire area is relatively level with some low, wet sections. Several four-wheeler roads also make for interesting route possibilities.

Waterville Ridge. There are five miles of trails in this town park located off the West River Road. These wooded single-track trails are characterized by rocks, roots and some muddy stretches. Steep climbs and descents but okay for intermediate skill level.

 📖 For map, contact the chamber of commerce. ☎ 873-3315.

Bike Rentals

Rainbow Bicycles
1225 Center Street, Auburn 04210
Sales, service, accessories. ☎ 784-7576.

Bangor Ski Rack
24 Longview Drive, Bangor 04401
Rentals of mountain bikes and full-suspension bikes. Sales, service and accessories. ☎ 945-6474.

Pat's Bike Shop
373 Wilson Street, Brewer 04412
Wide selection of new and used bikes. Parts, service, accessories. ☎ 989-2900.

Roy's Bicycle Shop
51 Farwell Street, Lewiston 04240
Sales and service, accessories. ☎ 783-9090.

Rose Bicycle
9 Pine Street, Orono 04473
Offers bicycles and service for every budget, as well as parts, accessories and clothing. ☎ 866-3525.

■ Foliage/Motor Tours

 The beauty of Mid-Maine is easily accessible by car. You can explore the state capital and its history, then take off for a scenic road trip.

The Capital & Country Roads

126 miles, 3 hours, round trip

Highlights: *A bit of history and lots of color await you on this inland tour, which winds from Augusta, the state capital, to the antique-filled town of Hallowell, and over quiet country roads through the beautiful surrounding lakes region.*

Route: Start in **Augusta**, site of historic **Fort Western**, the beautiful **Blaine House**, which serves as the Governor's residence, and the **Maine State Museum**. Take Route 27/201 south to **Hallowell**, home to numerous charming antiques shops. Take 201 to **Richmond Corner**, then head west on 197 to **Litchfield Corners**. Head north on secondary road toward Litchfield to the junction of 126; take 126 west to the intersection of 132, just before Sabattus. Take 132 north to **Monmouth,** site of the Queen Anne-style **Cumston Hall**.

🌿 **Foliage Hotline:** The Maine foliage hotline, in service each fall, offers the latest color-peaking information for leaf-peepers. ☎ 800-932-3419.

Continue north on 132 to US 202, then east on 202 into **Winthrop**; take 41 north then 133 north through Wayne to near **Livermore Falls**. Head east on 17 to **Kents Hill**, with its crystal-clear views of surrounding lakes; then take 41 north to **Mt. Vernon**, go east on secondary road and bear left at the fire station in Mt. Vernon, continuing straight to 27. Take a left on 27 to Rome Corner, the site of **Blueberry Hill**, a scenic outlook from which you can see all of the Belgrade Lakes. Travel east on 225 to 8; then south on 8 to 27 again, around Great Pond through quaint **Belgrade Lake Village**. Head back to Augusta on 27 south.

Route courtesy Maine Department of Conservation

Route 2, Bangor to Farmington

80 miles, 1¾ hours, one way

Highlights: *Route 2 from Bangor is really the only way to easily head over to the western part of the state. It is not really a wilderness road, but it does pass through plenty of woods and by rolling farm fields and small towns. A pleasant drive.*

Route: Jump on Route 2 where Interstate 395 ends at its intersection with Interstate 95. After a short area of commercial sprawl the road heads west through **Northern Maine Junction**, the busy marshalling yard for what was formerly the Bangor and Aroostook Railroad. Route 2 then winds through Bangor's bedroom towns like Hermon and, to a lesser extent, Carmel and Etna. Activity picks up again in **Newport**, where Route 2 can also be easily accessed from Interstate 95.

About 10 miles farther, just outside of West Palmyra there is a rest area with picnic tables and pit toilets on the right. Route 2 gently climbs the hills and passes through the villages of mid-Maine as it continues west through **Canaan** and by **Eaton Mountain** ski area. The Kennebec River passes through **Skowhegan** just ahead. There is a shady, attractive riverside picnic area with pit toilets on the right just before you get into town. Following Route 2 through Skowhegan is a little tricky as the small downtown has multi-lane, one-way traffic. It is easy to get into the wrong lane.

WISE WORDS: *Stay in the left lane after the first turn. Stay in the right lane after at the second turn. After you cross the river, be ready to take another right. If you follow the signs, you will do fine.*

Route 2 then roughly parallels the south shore of the Kennebec River for the next 10 miles to **Norridgewock**. Here it leaves the river and turns south-westerly over rolling hills. Watch for Route 27 on the left. It leads to the scenic Belgrade Lakes area.

Continue on Route 2 to **New Sharon**, where it crosses the attractive Sandy River. **Farmington**, home to a branch of the University of Maine, a mountain biking and cross-country ski center, and a great jumping off place for the Western Mountains area, is just ahead. You can continue north on Route 27 or stay on 2 and continue west to Bethel and into New Hampshire.

Route 9/202, Hampden to Augusta

60 miles, 1½ hours, one way

Highlights: *Route 9 and 202 from Hampden to Augusta may bear half the fabled numerical designation of "The Airline," which passes through wild, wild country in Eastern Maine. Here, though, Route 9 and its co-designee denote a very different road.*

Route: Access 202 from Interstate 395, which connects Bangor and Brewer. Head west on the divided highway which quickly narrows to a conventional two-laner. It joins Route 9 with a left turn in **Hampden**. The road is easy to follow as it eases over gentle hills and through woods and by farms. For nearly 30 miles there is barely a major curve as you gently ease to the southwest. In **Dixmont** Route 9/202 crosses Route 7. Two miles south on Route 7 leads to a gated dirt road to the abandoned fire tower on top of **Mount Harris**, which provides spectacular views in all directions.

Twelve miles farther on Route 9/202 you'll reach **Unity** on the shores of Unity Pond. Here is the headquarters of the seasonal **Belfast and Moosehead Lake Railroad**, which offers rail excursion and cruise packages between Unity and Belfast. Unity is also home to the popular **Common Ground Fair** each September, a celebration of organic farming techniques, alternative energy and counter-culture politics and organizations.

The nearby Quaker Hill Road is home to the **Peter Smith Terry Collection of Native American Artifacts**, which includes a research library and exhibits.

In the middle of the village of Unity Route 9/202 takes a southerly heading and assumes a more traditional winding route toward the state capital in Augusta. It passes through **Albion** and **Johnny's Selected Seeds**, a company that specializes in variety of flowers and vegetables that grow best in northern climates.

In the village of **China**, Route 9/202 hooks a hard left before following the east side of China Lake down to Route 3. Route 3 then adds the 9/202 designation as it heads straight into Augusta and across the Kennebec River.

Adventures On Water

■ Places to Paddle

Stevens Pond, Liberty

 You can put in at the town beach near the outlet dam on Route 173 and paddle south across this 300-acre pond. There's a large undeveloped island in its center. Tall pines, massive boulders and deep hardwood forests characterize the shore.

Kenduskeag Stream

From its starting point in the village of Kenduskeag the annual **Kenduskeag Stream Race** each April draws more than 600 canoes and kayaks. (Contact Bangor Parks & Recreation Dept., ☎ 947-1018, for race details). Because it lacks headwater lakes, the best time to paddle the route solo is early spring or after an extended rainy period. The 14-mile trip to the traditional takeout (at an old dam in Bangor near Interstate 95) includes several small rapids and rips. The countryside is wooded with an occasional home. At **Six Mile Falls** the tricky rapids and Class III ledge drop should be scouted. You can spot a vehicle here for an abbreviated trip.

Lower Togus Pond, Augusta

Finding a comparatively wild lake so close to the state capital is not easy. Yet as soon as you launch your boat into Lower Togus Pond from the put-in off Route 105, city cares seem to evaporate. This shallow and sometimes rocky elongated pond is dotted with islands and has little development. Ducks, beavers and other wildlife are in the majority here.

Marsh Stream, Monroe

High water in the spring is the best time to try out this nine-mile trip, which starts at the base of a falls and ends at a dam near tidewater. Begin by Nickerson Mills at the sharp turn on Route 131. The next few miles feature lots of Class I and some occasional Class II action. The fast water lasts until you reach the deadwater backed up behind a dam near the Loggin Road in West Winterport, the takeout point.

Mendall Marsh, Frankfort

Numerous birds and other creatures live in this 250-acre refuge on the South Branch of the Marsh River where it meets the Penobscot. Stream heads south for two miles toward village of Prospect. Parking area on Route 1A and boat launch. Hunting and fishing allowed.

Canoeing/Kayaking Outfitters

Overnight trips average $100-150 per person, per day. Half-day guided trips run in the vicinity of $50. Basic rentals cost between $25 and $45 per day. Most rentals include life jackets, paddles and car-topping gear.

The Villa Vaughn Family Camping
RR 5, Box 205, Bangor 04401
On-site canoe rentals. May 15-October 15. ☎ 945-6796.

Great Pond Marina, Inc.
PO Box 405, Route 27, Belgrade Lakes 04918
Canoe rentals. April-October. ☎ 495-2213.

North Country Rivers
PO Box 47, East Vassalboro 04935
Kayak trips, West Branch Penobscot. May-September. ☎ 800-348-8871.

Lakeside Motel, Cabins and Marina
PO Box 236, Route 202, E. Winthrop 04343
Canoe rentals. ☎ 800-532-6892.

Stetson Shores Campground, Inc.
PO Box 86, Route 143, Stetson 04488
Canoe rentals, kayak rentals. May 1-October 15. ☎ 296-2041.

Adventures In the Air

■ Hot Air Balloon Rides

Gliding silently and gently across Maine's spectacular country-side in a hot air balloon is a special adventure. Your ears will ring of the silence after the propane burner is extinguished. Even the faintest sounds from the world below become easily audible.

Most trips average an hour of time aloft with excursions set for the times of day when the air is calm, such as morning and early evening. Both tethered and free-flight trips are offered; all with experienced operators. Most firms require reservations and deposits. Check with your outfitter for the maximum number of people per gondola and for recommended clothing.

Auburn

Rosebud Balloon Company. One-hour trips include a special celebration with champagne. Cost is $150 per person. ☎ 784-2257.

Augusta

Sails Aloft. One-hour trips include a champagne celebration. Cost is $150 per person on Saturday and Sunday or $125 per person on weekdays. ☎ 623-1136.

Adventures On Snow

■ Downhill Skiing

Auburn

 Lost Valley Ski Area, PO Box 260, Auburn 04212. 240-foot vertical drop, 15 trails, three lifts, night skiing, 100% snowmaking, ski shop, rentals, lessons, cafeteria, lounge, Nordic skiing, snowboard park, child care. Bike park, adult paintball in warm weather. Adult lift ticket $30 weekend, $18 midweek. ☎ 784-1561.

Hermon

New Hermon Mountain, PO Box 1347, Searsport 04974. 350-foot vertical drop, 18 trails, two T-bar lifts, one chair lift, night skiing, 100% snowmaking, ski shop, ski school, rentals, cafeteria. Nordic skiing nearby. Adult lift ticket $18. ☎ 848-5192.

Skowhegan

Eaton Mountain, HCR71, Box 128, Skowhegan 04976. 600-foot vertical drop, 15 trails, one lift, night skiing, 100% snowmaking, glade skiing, rentals, lessons, cafeteria, lounge, snowboard park. Adult lift ticket $18. ☎ 474-2666.

∎ Cross-Country Skiing

Vassalboro

 Natanis Ski Center, PO Box Vassalboro 04989. Eight miles of trails. Rental equipment available, snack bar. ☎ 622-3561.

Pownal

Bradbury Mountain State Park. Three miles of trails open to skiing and snowshoeing. ☎ 688-4712.

∎ Snowmobiling

 The area west of Bangor is alive with snowmobliers in winter. **Newport** is the hub. From Newport riders can head southwest toward Augusta, south down into Waldo County and Searsport or north to big snowmobiling country up around Dover-Foxcroft. While big, marked trails may be lacking in the **Augusta**, and **Lewiston-Auburn** area, there are plenty of club trails maintained by local volunteers. (See *Appendix* for a complete list of snowmobile clubs.)

Eco-Tours & Cultural Excursions

∎ Apple Picking

 Fall is the season for picking your own fresh apples. Here are the pick-your-own farms in the Mid-Maine area.

Pick-Your-Own Apples
Auburn
∎ **Apple Ridge Farm**, Perkins Ridge Road, ☎ 777-1696.
∎ **Wallingford's Orchard**, Perkins Ridge Road, ☎ 784-7958.

Brewer

- Harris Orchard, Wiswell Road, ☎ 989-3435.

Burnham

- Littlefield's Orchard, Troy Road, ☎ 948-3629.

Dresden

- Green Point Farms, Route 128, ☎ 737-2246.

East Winthrop

- Whit's Orchard, Case Road, ☎ 395-4436.

Fairfield

- North Star Orchards, Route 104, ☎ 696-5109.
- The Apple Farm, Back Road, ☎ 453-7656.

Kents Hill

- Kents Hill Orchard, Route 17, ☎ 685-3522.

Lewiston

- Bergeron's Orchards, Ferry Road, ☎ 783-0875.
- Stukas Farms, Ferry Road, ☎ 786-2639.

Livermore

- Clearview Orchard, Route 108, ☎ 897-6106.

Madison

- North Star Orchards, Route 43, ☎ 696-5109.

Manchester

- Lakeside Orchards, Readfield Road, ☎ 622-2479.

New Gloucester

- Thompson's Orchard, Gloucester Hill Road, ☎ 926-4738.

North Vassalboro

- Lemieux's Orchard, Priest Hill Road, ☎ 923-3518.
- Manter's Orchard, Oak Grove Road, ☎ 872-6078.

Skowhegan

- Snowbrook Orchard, Back Road, ☎ 474-6021.

Vassalboro

- **Brown's Orchard**, Taber Hill Road, ☎ 923-3113.

Whitefield

- **Bailey's Orchard**, Hunt's Meadow Road, ☎ 549-7282.

■ Blueberry Picking

 The blueberry harvest season in Maine is late July and early August. While pints and quarts of fresh-raked berries are available at most stores and farmstands, there is nothing like picking them yourself. Commercial picking fields charge a small fee, usually by the pint.

Pick-Your-Own Blueberries

Clinton

- **Beaudoin's Berry Farm**, Beaudoin Road. Call ahead for hours. ☎ 426-8131.

Mercer

- **Carol Zimmer Blueberries**, Route 137, Valley Road. Open Sunday-Friday. Call ahead to confirm. ☎ 634-2610.

Where to Stay & Eat

Rate Scale

All rates are for entrée or complete dinner, per person.

Inexpensive. . . . . under $10

Moderate . . . . $10-$20

Expensive . . . . More than $20

■ Favorite Restaurants

Augusta

 The majority of places in Augusta are fast-food joints, which you'll have no problem seeing as you drive through town. One establishment is worth a special mention:

The Senator, Inn and Spa, Western Avenue at I-95, Augusta 04330. This modern motel is often a hub of political intrigue in the state's capital. Politicians and those seeking to curry their favor frequently gather for lunch in the hotel restaurant or toss back a few brews in the lounge. Moderate to expensvie. ☎ 622-5804.

Bangor

Bangor's restaurant scene is being slowly overrun by chains such as Outback Steak House, Red Lobster, etc. Still, the number of independently-owned establishments remains high. There is something for every taste in this city from, Indian cooking to vegetarian.

Captain Nick's, 1165 Union Street (across from airport entrance), Bangor 04401. Family restaurant and lounge with one of the broadest menus in Eastern Maine. Seafood is a specialty, but steaks are great too. Daily lunch and dinner specials. Their triple lobster special is unique in Maine. Full cocktail service. Moderate. ☎ 942-6444.

Dysart's Truck Stop, Exit 44 off I-95, Bangor 04401. This sprawling truck stop's food is hot, a lot of it is brown, and there's plenty of it. It's delicious enough to make it a favorite spot for all who visit. Open 24 hours a day with traditional diner fare such as fried seafood and steaks. Breakfast available at any hour. Daily specials. Inexpensive. You can ask for gravy on your French fries (a favorite with Canadians) without anyone raising an eyebrow. ☎ 942-4878.

Lemon Tree, 167 Center Street, Bangor 04401. This funky establishment offers a unique menu featuring vegetarian and pasta entrées as well as fresh seafood. Full cocktail service. Live jazz and blues on Friday and Saturday nights. Open weekdays for lunch, Monday through Saturday for dinner. Moderate to expensive. ☎ 945-3666.

Miller's Restaurant, 427 Main Street, Bangor 04401. Home of one of the world's largest salad bar, featuring more than 200 items. Many folks make a meal from that alone! Full menu and cocktail service. The second dining room, The Lion, features fresh seafood, prime rib and the establishment's signature sirloin. Off-track betting parlor located in the back. Moderate to expensive. ☎ 942-6361.

Lewiston/Auburn

Luiggi's Restaurant, 63 Sabattus Street, Lewiston 04243. Italian fare with focus on pizza, lasagna, spaghetti and sandwiches. Eat in or take out. In business since 1953. Boasts "Your home is our only competition." Delivery available. Inexpensive. ☎ 782-0701.

Mac's Grill, 1052 Minot Avenue, Auburn 04210. Southwestern theme restaurant offers Black Angus steaks, beef and seafood. Homemade barbecue sauces and desserts. Cocktails. Weekly lunch and dinner specials. Closed Mondays. Moderate. ☎ 783-6885.

■ Brewpubs/Microbreweries

Auburn

 Great Falls Brewing Company, 36 Court Street. Beers include Auburn Amber, Bobcat Brown, Raspberry Wheat, and Bartlett's Pale Ale. Many seasonals. Tours on request. ☎ 784-3919.

Bangor

Sea Dog Brewing Company, 26 Front Street. Black Irish Winter Stout, Penobscot Maine Pilsener, Windjammer Blonde Ale, Owl's Head Light, Old East India Pale Ale, and nearly a dozen others. Lunch at the Sea Dog's dining room, located near the Penobscot River, is a favorite with the locals. At night, the place hops. The menu includes plenty of fresh Maine Seafood as well as traditional pub fare. Alcohol-free beverages are available. Call for tour times. ☎ 947-8720.

Orono

Bear Brewpub, 36 Main Street. Named for the Black Bear, official mascot of the University of Maine (the major industry in town). Beers include Crow Valley Blonde, Great Works Blonde, I'll Be Darned Amber, Honey Bear Brown and Midnight Stout. Small cozy bar room and beer garden. Standard college-town pub fare such as onion rings, gourmet pizza nachos and burgers. Tours available on request. No gift shop. ☎ 866-2739.

Whitefield

Sheepscot Valley Brewing Company, Townhouse Road. Beers include Madgoose Belgian Ale, White Rabbit, and Highlander Scottish Ale. Tours by appointment. ☎ 549-5530.

■ B&Bs, Hotels & Motels

Price Scale
All rates are based on double occupancy.
Inexpensive . . . . Under $65
Moderate . . . . $66-$100
Expensive. . . . . Above $100

Augusta

There are plenty of chain hotels in Augusta, which you'll easily see as you drive through.

The Senator, Inn and Spa, Western Avenue at I-95, Augusta 04330. This modern motel is often a hub of political intrigue in the state's capital. Several dozen regular rooms and suites available. Heated indoor and outdoor pools, health club, cable TV, phones. Moderate to expensvie. ☎ 622-5804.

Bangor

The Lucerne Inn, Route 1A, Dedham (15 minutes from Bangor). Sitting on the side of a hill overlooking an attractive lake and surrounding hills, the stately Lucerne Inn offers country inn accommodations and casual fine dining. Golf course across the road. Nearly all rooms have great views and fireplaces. Dinner served daily. Sunday brunch is especially popular from 9 am until 1 pm. Moderate to expensive. ☎ 843-5123.

The Ramada, 357 Odlin Road, Bangor 04401. Most of the motels in the Bangor area are the modern, concrete-box type. If you're going to stay at one of those, go for one that rocks. Just three minutes from the airport the Ramada sports an indoor, heated pool, fitness center, restaurant and busy bar. Popular with flight crews layover from international flights at Bangor International Airport, just three minutes away. Data/modem jacks in all rooms. Moderate. ☎ 947-6961.

Belgrade Lakes

Castle Island Camps, PO Box 251, Belgrade Lakes 04918. Located on Castle Island Road. Traditional sporting camps on small island (crossed by road) on Long Pond. Fully-equipped cabins on the water. Nice open fireplace in community building. Boat dock, rentals, and sun deck. Open seasonally. Daily and weekly rates include meals. Brochures advise "plan to diet some other time." Inexpensive to moderate. ☎ 495-3312.

Lewiston/Auburn

The Auburn Inn, 1777 Washington Street, Auburn 04210. 114 spacious guest rooms in conventional, two-story motel. Pool, cable TV, phones, non-smoking rooms, restaurant and lounge. Convenient to Exit 12 on Maine Pike. Moderate. ☎ 777-1777.

Poland

The Inns of Poland Spring, 47 Ricker Road, Poland Spring 04274. This company operates a cluster of inns that includes the stately Maine Inn, the gloriously Victorian Presidential Inn, a standard Motor Inn, housekeeping cottages and The Roosevelt House (built for Teddy in 1902). Underground flows the famous Poland Spring water, which is used to fill the pool! Weekend and golfing packages available. Outdoor pool, tennis court, game room, library, entertainment and band concerts. No phones. No children. Rates vary from inexpensive to expensive. ☎ 998-4351.

Wolf Cove Inn, 5 Jordan Shore Drive, Poland 04274. Located on the shore of Tripp Lake, this seven-room inn offers full B&B service. It is a quiet country location, but close to the coast. Only 10 minutes away from the Shaker Village at Sabbathday Lake. Porch overlooks lake and has good sunset views. No children, no pets, no smoking. Moderate. ☎ 998-4976.

■ Camping

 Facilities indicated as "nearby" are located within one mile of the campground.

Bangor

Paul Bunyan Campground, 1862 Union Street, Bangor 04401. A friendly family campground with many activities planned throughout the summer. RV's, pop-ups, tent trailers, and tents welcome. Hayrides Friday and Saturday nights. 52 sites, tenting area, 50 amp, sewer, dump station, store, rec hall, swimming, fishing, pool, group area, LP gas. Laundry nearby. Pets allowed. Open April 15-November15. ☎ 941-1177.

Pleasant Hill Campground, RR 3, Box 180, Bangor 04401. Quiet family campground with very clean restrooms. Spacious sites, big rigs welcome. Explore Bangor's lumber and seafaring history. Easy day trips to Central and Coastal Maine. 105 sites, tenting area, 50 amp, sewer, dump station, store, laundry, rec hall, fishing, pool, on-site rentals, group area, LP gas. Pets allowed. Open May 1-Columbus Day. ☎ 848-5127.

Wheeler Stream Camping Area, RR 2, Box 2800, Bangor 04401. Nothing fancy. Simply a quiet, family place to call home while you explore Maine. Shop Bangor's stores or take a day trip to Bar Harbor (50 miles). 24 sites, tenting area, 30 amp, dump station, laundry. Store nearby. Pets allowed. Open May 15-October 15. ☎ 848-3713.

Belgrade

Great Pond Campground, RFD #1, Box 913, Belgrade 04917. Located on Central Maine's largest lake with state record pike. Clean, friendly, easily accessible to Waterville and Augusta. 45 sites, tenting area, 30 amp, sewer, dump station, store, laundry, swimming, boating, fishing, pool. Pets allowed. Open May 1-October 15. ☎ 495-2116.

Canaan

Skowhegan/Canaan KOA, PO Box 87, Canaan 04924. Quiet and clean campground on Route 2. Amenities include heated pool, mini-golf, hiking and biking trails, softball field, volleyball, badminton, horseshoes, playground, game room, snacks, stove. Free hot showers. 100 sites, tenting area, 50 amp, sewer, dump station, store, laundry, rec hall, swimming, pool, on-site rentals, group area, LP gas. Pets allowed. Open May 10-October 20. ☎ 474-2858.

Carmel

Shady Acres RV Park, RR 2, Box 7890, Carmel 04419. Clean park only 10 miles to Bangor. Catering to large RVs, 5th wheels, motorhomes and group gatherings. Mostly adults here. Drop in or make reservations. 50 sites, 30 amp, sewer, dump station, rec hall, swimming, fishing, pool, on-site rentals. Store nearby. Pets allowed. Open May 15-October 15. ☎ 848-5515.

Clifton

Parks Pond Campground, 800 Airline Road, Clifton 04428. Small family area on spring-fed pond, 15 miles east of Bangor on Route 9, 80 miles to Canada. Rock climbing, swimming and canoeing. 70 sites, tenting area, 30 amp, dump station, laundry, rec hall, swimming, boating, fishing. Pets allowed. Open Memorial Day-Labor Day. ☎ 843-7360.

Eddington

Greenwood Acres Campground, RR 2, Box 2210, Eddington 04428. Large pool, large playground, horseshoes, games room, public phone, café on premises. Theme events: Pot luck suppers, Christmas in July, Halloween in August, and much more. 40 sites, tenting area, 30 amp, sewer, dump station, store, laundry, rec hall, pool, on-site rentals, swimming. Boating and fishing nearby. Pets allowed. Open year-round. ☎ 989-8898.

Farmingdale

Foggy-Bottom RV Campground, 195 Maine Avenue, Farmingdale 04344. Nine sites located on the beautiful Kennebec River. Swimming, 50 amp, dump station, boating, fishing. Pets allowed. Open May 1-November 1. ☎ 582-0075.

Hartland

Tall Pines Campground, RFD#1, Box 3162, Morrill Pond Road, Hartland 04943. The fun place to camp. Gather around the central fireplace with friendly people, or just enjoy the enchanting call of the loons on the lake. Located on 65 acres in Central Maine. 25 sites, tenting area, 30 amp, dump station, swimming, boating, fishing, on-site rentals, group area, LP gas. Pets allowed. Open Memorial Day-Labor Day. ☎ 938-4589.

Holden

Red Barn RV Park, 602 Main Road, Holden 04429. Nestled on Route 1A between Bangor and Ellsworth – The Gateway to Downeast Maine. Spacious and grassy sites with your choice of amenities, including cable TV on designated sites. 100 sites, tenting area, 30 amp, sewer, dump station, store, laundry, rec hall, swimming, pool, on-site rentals, group area, LP gas. Pets allowed. Open May 15-October 15. ☎ 843-6011.

Madison

Abnaki Camping Center, RR 2, Box 1500, Madison 04950. Offers a 1,000-foot-long sandy beach, two pontoon swim floats, dredge boat docking, volleyball, horseshoes, ping pong tournament, heated hall, game room, canoe, boat, and tandem bike rentals. 96 sites, tenting area, 30 amp, dump station, store, rec hall, swimming, boating, fishing, group area. Pets allowed. Open Memorial Day-Labor Day. ☎ 474-2070.

Sandy Beach Lakeside Campground, RR 1, Box 729, Madison 04950. Quiet family campground with planned activities on weekends. Wooded sites, canoe and paddleboat rentals. On Wesserunset Lake, Madison. 72 sites, tenting area, 30 amp, sewer, dump station, store, laundry, rec hall, swimming, boating, fishing, on-site rentals, group area, LP gas. Pets allowed. Open Memorial Day-October1. ☎ 474-5975.

Newport

Christies Campground, Route 2, Box 565, Newport 04953. Park-like setting on Lake Sebasticook, a great place for family fun. 49 sites, tenting area, 30 amp, sewer, dump station, store, laundry, rec hall, swimming, boating, fishing, group area, LP gas. Pets allowed. Open May15-November 30. ☎ 368-4645.

Tent Village Travel Trailer Park, RR 2, Box 580, Newport 04953. Beautiful lakeside camping with large open and wooded sites, Swimming pool, boat rentals, arcade and much more. Cottage rentals and pull-through sites available also. 48 sites, tenting area, 30 amp, sewer, dump station, store, rec hall, fishing, group area, LP gas. Pets allowed. Open May 15-October15. ☎ 368-5047.

Norridgewock

Maine Roads Camping, 722 Mercer Road, Norridgewock 04957. 44 sites, tenting area, 30 amp, sewer, store, laundry, rec hall, swimming, pool, group area. Pets allowed. Open Memorial Day-October15. ☎ 634-4952.

North Monmouth

Beaver Brook Campground, RD 1, Box 1835 N, North Monmouth 04265. Enjoy your camping experience in the midst of 150 acres of tall pines, with a serene brook, a half-mile of lake frontage and large private sites. 191 sites, tenting area, 30 amp, dump station, store, laundry, rec hall, swimming, boating, fishing, pool, group area, LP gas. Pets allowed. Open May 1-Columbus Day. ☎ 933-2108.

Oakland

Pleasant Point Park, RFD #3, Box 5000, Oakland 04963. 47 sites, tenting area, 15 amp, sewer, dump station, store, rec hall, swimming, boating, fishing, on-site rentals. Pets allowed. Open Memorial Day-Labor Day. ☎ 465-7265.

Orono

The Villa Vaughn, RR 5, Box 205, Orono 04473. Quiet, wooded, family-oriented option with 2,000 feet of lake frontage. Gorgeous sunsets, sandy beach, snack bar, children's play area, boat launch, rowboat/canoe rentals. Seasonal sites available. 75 sites, tenting area, 30 amp, sewer, dump station, laundry, rec hall, swimming, boating, fishing, LP gas. Store nearby. Pets allowed. Open May 15-October 15. ☎ 945-6796.

Palmyra

Palmyra Golf and RV Resort, 147 Lang Hill Road, Palmyra 04965. Campground sits on beautiful 18-hole golf course. Discounts on golf when you stay in campground. 42 sites, tenting area, 30 amp, dump station, rec hall, store, pool, group area. Pets allowed. Open April 15-October 15. ☎ 938-5677.

Pittsfield

Ringwood Campground, PO Box 192, Pittsfield 04967. A wilderness campground the way camping used to be. All sites on the lake and in the woods. 12 sites, tenting area, swimming, boating, fishing, on-site rentals, group area. Store and laundry nearby. Pets allowed. Open Memorial Day-Labor Day. ☎ 487-3406.

Richmond

Augusta-Gardiner KOA, US 1, Box 2410, Richmond 04357. Large shaded pull-throughs, slide-outs welcome. Pancake breakfast, extra-clean free showers. Great fishing. 80 sites, tenting area, 50 amp, sewer, dump station, store, laundry, rec hall, swimming, boating, fishing, pool, on-site rentals, group area, LP gas. Pets allowed. Open May 20-October 15. ☎ 582-5086.

Skowhegan

Eaton Mountain Ski Area and Campground, HCR 71, Box 128, Skowhegan 04976. Relax on a mountain with hiking and biking trails, game room, restaurant, lounge, large sites for RV and tent, full hook-ups with 15-30 amp, and showers. 60 sites, tenting area, 30 amp, dump station, store, rec hall, swimming, pool, on-site rentals, group area. Laundry, boating, fishing and LP gas nearby. Pets allowed. Open Memorial Day-Columbus Day. ☎ 474-2666.

Two Rivers Campground, HCR 71, Box 14, Skowhegan 04976. Located on the banks of the Kennebec River and Wesserunsett Stream with full hook-up sites, tenting, some along the river, cable available. 65 sites, tenting area, 30 amp, sewer, dump station, store, laundry, swimming, boating, fishing, LP gas. Pets allowed. Open May 1-October 31. ☎ 474-6482.

Yonder Hill Campground, 17 Parlin Street, Skowhegan 04976. Yonder Hill has grass sites and wooded sites. Large pool. They cater to family campers, offering wagon rides on weekends. 80 sites, tenting area, 30 amp, sewer, dump station, store, laundry, rec hall, swimming, pool, on-site rentals, group area. Boating, fishing, LP gas nearby. Pets allowed. Open May 15- September 15. ☎ 474-7353.

Solon

The Evergreens Campground, PO Box 114, Route 201A, Solon 04979. Restaurant and lounge with deck on the banks of the Kennebec River. Excellent fishing, swimming, snowmobiling. Rentals and cabin rentals available. 40 sites, tenting area, 30 amp, dump station, store, rec hall, boating, group area, LP gas. Pets allowed. Open year-round. ☎ 643-2324.

Stetson

Stetson Shores Campground, PO Box 86M, Stetson 04488. A nice, relaxing, quiet campground off Route 143. 43 sites, tenting area, 20 amp, dump station, store, laundry, rec hall, swimming, boating, fishing, on-site rentals, group area. Pets allowed. Open May 15-September 30. ☎ 296-2041.

Vassalboro

Green Valley Campground, RFD #1, Box 1850, Cross Hill Rd, Vassalboro 04989. A family campground located 10 miles from Waterville and Augusta, 35 miles from the coast, in a peaceful setting situated on a lake. 80 sites, tenting area, 50 amp, sewer, dump station, store, laundry, rec hall, swimming, boating, fishing, on-site rentals, LP gas. Pets allowed. Open May 15-October 15. ☎ 923-3000.

Waterville

Countryside Campground, PO Box 666, Waterville 04903. Nestled in the pines off Route 104. A quiet relaxing campground close to golf, stores, movies, bowling, and much more. Great place to relax. 25 sites, tenting area, 30 amp, sewer, dump station, group area, laundry. Store, rec hall, swimming, boating, fishing and pool nearby. Pets allowed. Open May 2-October 1. ☎ 873-4603.

Winslow

Giordanos Camping and Recreation, RR 2, Box 3580, Winslow 04901. Features a large dance hall, live bands and country dancing on weekends. Hall rental for reunions and wedding receptions. Located on Pattee Pond. 10 sites, tenting area, 15 amp, dump station, rec hall, swimming, boating, fishing, group area. Pets allowed. Open Memorial Day-Labor Day. ☎ 873-2408.

Winthrop

Augusta West Lakeside Resort, Box 232, Winthrop 04364. Located on Holmes Road. Closest campground to Augusta with easy access for larger

RVs. 81 sites, tenting area, 30 amp, sewer, dump station, store, laundry, rec hall, swimming, boating, fishing, pool, on-site rentals, group area, LP gas. Pets allowed. Open May 15-October 15. ☎ 377-9993.

The Great North Woods

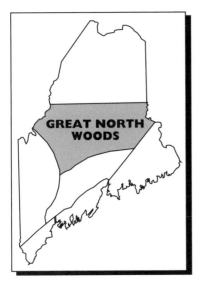

Maine's Great North Woods is a land where mighty rivers are born, the forest seems tractless, and where more deer and moose roam today than 100 years ago. It is a place the great nature writer Henry David Thoreau would still recognize today, although he would find it greatly changed.

Gone are the sprawling lumber camps peopled by hard-working loggers who spent months at a time felling and moving timber by river to the hungry mills to the South. In their place today heavy equipment allows just a handful of people to process as much wood in a day as a dozen men could do in a week a century ago. In their air-conditioned cabs these machine operators look out on a forest much different than that visited by Thoreau. Granted, the mix of species of trees remain the same – although mechanized harvesting and planned replanting have resulted in wide areas of a single species, most the same age. This groomed monoculture seems out of place in the lush, chaotic landscape that characterizes wilder areas.

Most of Maine's woods have been cut two or even three times now. In some areas, massive clear-cuts shock even those who understand the economic and silvacultural reasons behind the practice. Some argue clear-cutting amounts to land control by large, multi-national corporations concerned only with short-term profits. Others argue the cuts were needed to salvage trees ravaged by disease that would have only rotted anyway. The debate over the practice has been raging for years in Maine and will undoubtedly continue long into the future.

Still, it is the paper and lumber companies that drive the economic engines of the Great North Woods. They are the ones who put in the roads enjoyed by mountain bikers, campers, canoers, fishermen and hunters – most with little or no fees. And while no traditional working lumber camps remain (clusters of cabins and campers do, however), lakeside sporting camps continue the frontier traditions of catering to visitors. These camps, known as "sports," are serviced by Registered Maine Guides eager to show not only where the trophy trout or deer can be found, but also where less consumptive recreational pursuits such as mountain biking, canoeing, photography and hiking can best be enjoyed.

Nearly 30-feet tall, this statue of North Woods legend Paul Bunyan stands next to Bangor's visitor center on Main St.

In the west sits Jackman, home of the renowned wild and scenic Moose River. Sometimes referred to as the Switzerland of Maine, Jackman lies at the edge of a tranquil lake in sight of the Boundary Mountains with Quebec. While busy during fishing, hunting and canoeing season, Jackman really comes alive during the winter, when snowmobiles outnumber cars on the busy Main Street.

Farther south sits the village of The Forks, at the confluence of the Kennebec and Dead Rivers. It is Maine's whitewater rafting headquarters and has more rafting companies per capita than anyplace else.

Greenville is the centerpiece, the hub at the south end of massive Moosehead Lake, Maine's largest freshwater body. the town is home to Mount Kineo, a towering flint edifice that has attracted visitors since prehistoric times. Here the cove nearest town buzzes daily with the sound of seaplanes taking off and landing on trips to the more remote camps and ponds scattered across millions of acres of undeveloped land. Greenville too, like all communities in this part of Maine, sports unique seasonal personalities. Summer brings its own crop of visitors, as does winter, with snowmobilers and ice fishermen invading at the first sign of lasting snow.

North of Greenville, along the fabled Golden Road roads reach out in every direction. The Golden Road is actually a dirt highway through the wild where lumber rigs four trailers long have the right of way, even at speeds in excess of 60 miles per hour. Here, those in the know visit remote Telos Lake, a body of water that played a pivotal role in the state's lumbering history when it and surrounding waters were harnessed to make streams flow in reverse and send logs from the remote Allagash region to

Bangor instead of Canada. From this one lake a canoeist can, with no portage of more than two miles, traverse three of the state's mightiest river systems – the Allagash, Kennebec and Penobscot.

To the east lies Millinocket, a proud paper mill town that is gateway to Baxter State Park. The park's 205,000 acres of pristine wilderness incorporates Maine's highest peak, mile-high Katahdin, which looms over an ocean of greenery.

Maine's Great North Woods require more effort to reach and may not always offer as many creature comforts as other parts of the state. But that is usually just fine with those who seek to cast off the burdens of civilization and find escape in true wild lands.

- Note: Maine has one area code – 207.

Parks & Preserves

■ Private Lands

 The vast majority of land in the Great North Woods is private, owned by paper companies and land holding firms. As a matter of tradition it is open to the public for fishing, hunting, camping, hiking and canoeing. Some paper company roads are gated and modest fees are charged for day use and for use of campsites or cabins maintained by these companies. Occasionally, a small area may be closed for safety reasons during timber harvesting operations.

Travel Hazards on Private Lands

- Lumber and log trucks always have the right of way on paper company roads. They are not bound to the same weight or speed limits as on state roads and the trucks are large and fast. If you see one coming – get out of the way! Be especially wary on the one-lane bridges.
- Hazards on the dirt portions include dust clouds, unexpected ruts and potholes, and wandering animals.
- Dirt roads can be remarkably slippery after a rain so be careful.
- Make sure your vehicle is in good condition and gas up before heading into the outback.
- Most intersections and connecting roads are not signed; if you are lucky they may be numbered. Pick up a good map.

Great Northern Paper Company Lands

Great Northern, a division of Bowater Corp., controls nearly 2.1 million acres of wild lands mostly along the West Branch of the Penobscot River. The primary artery providing access is along the Golden Road, a privately owned byway that begins in Millinocket and heads west to the Canadian Border. From Millinocket to Chesuncook Lake the road is paved.

Access via the gate house just north and west of Millinocket.

The **Golden Road** is the main route to connect with the Telos Road (the main way into the Allagash Region) as well as access to Ripogenus Gorge, where whitewater rafting trips on the West Branch of the Penobscot begin.

The **Telos Bridge,** and **Cribwork** rapids just a short walk downstream, is a great place to stop and watch rafts come by each day. The rapid, a dangerous Class V, is among the toughest in Maine.

Because nearly every major lake and stream in the West Branch region is part of the hydropower system for the mills, stream levels may change at any moment without notice. Lake levels also fluctuate widely, but due to their size the water rises or falls more slowly.

 Be prepared at any time for water levels to change. Near dams alarm sirens or horns sound to warn people immediately downstream if additional flood gates are to be opened.

The last chance to fuel up north of Millinocket is Pray's Store, which is on the side road leading to Ripogenus or, as the locals call it, "Rip" dam.

Detailed maps of company lands and camping permits are available from the company (see address below) or at the Katahdin General Store in Millinocket and Wortman's Store in Greenville. Instead of gated checkpoints, which were used in the past, roving attendants check the company campsites to be sure visitors have paid the fee.

There is a daily charge of $4 for all vehicles. The camping fee is $5 per person, per night. Children under age nine camp free. Season passes are available.

For specific information on services in Great Northern Lands, contact the Public Relations Department at One Katahdin Avenue, Millinocket 04462. ☎ 723-2229.

Great Northern Paper is also part of the **North Maine Woods,** an umbrella organization that administers recreational use on diverse paper company lands in Northern Maine. It is based in Ashland and also offers helpful maps for $3 each. It can be reached by writing to North Maine Woods Inc., PO Box 421, Ashland 04732.

A more detailed description of North Maine Woods activities and responsibilities is included in the Far North section, pages 452-454. ☎ 435-6213.

■ Baxter State Park

Geographically and spiritually Baxter State Park is the center of the Maine outdoors, which is why we are covering it first, in a special section.

History

This 205,000-acre preserve is testament to the drive and vision of one man, Gov. Percival Baxter. After efforts to get the state to purchase land in the area failed, he came up with the money and over several decades purchased it privately. He then gave it to the people of the state to be kept forever wild.

> ### In Memory of Gov. Percival Baxter
>
> Gov. Baxter's words are immortalized on a bronze plaque affixed to a boulder near the base of Katahdin, the highest mountain in Maine and the northern terminus of the Appalachian Trail.
>
> *Man is born to Die,*
> *His Works are Short-lived*
> *Buildings Crumble, Monuments Decay, Wealth Vanishes*
> *But Katahdin, in All Its Glory, Forever Shall Remain the*
> *Mountain of the People of Maine.*

Gov. Baxter's first land purchase was in 1930, when he bought about 10 square miles, including barren and windswept Katahdin. His last purchase was made in 1962. The Baxter Park Commission, which oversees operation, has added several thousand acres since, most recently nearly 2,000 acres in the southern corner of the preserve along the West Branch of the Penobscot River.

> ### Baxter Not A True State Park
>
> While it is called a state park, Baxter is not controlled by political forces in Augusta. Feisty and controversial long-time superintendent Irvin "Buzz" Caverly, Jr. answers to a triad authority, which includes the state's attorney general, the director of the Forest Service and the commissioner of the Maine Department of Inland Fisheries and Wildlife. A volunteer commission advises the authority.

The park operates on fees and interest from a modest endowment. The only state funds used are for maintenance of the rough gravel perimeter road, which is one of the few places where cars and trucks are allowed.

Park Rules

- No pets.

- Camping is allowed in designated areas only.

- Vehicle size limited to 22 feet for a single vehicle, 44 feet for vehicle and trailer.

- Motorcycles and ATVs are banned. Bicycles permitted on roads only.

- Speed limit: 20 miles per hour.

- Vehicles parked outside designated areas are subject to towing at owner's expense.

- Group size limited to 12. Camping only in group areas.

- No children under age six allowed above timberline.

- Technical climbers must register with the park.

- Hunting allowed only in two small areas in the far north and south.

- Use of chainsaws, generators and other power equipment is prohibited.

- General Maine laws and regulations on drugs, alcohol, fishing are in effect.

- All trash and waste must be packed out.

The best place to get acquainted with the park is at the visitor center and reservation office in Millinocket. There is a short audio-visual orientation program about the park and books, maps and arm patches can be purchased.

Gov. Baxter saw his park as a place where people could go to escape the shackles of civilization and refresh themselves with nature. His gift and vision accomplished that and more.

Winter In Baxter

Winter use is strictly regulated, with a system of color-coded days indicating allowable activity according to weather conditions. Snow depths of five to seven feet are average. Windchill temperatures of 50° or even 60° below zero are not unusual.

Long backcountry Nordic ski excursions with stays in bunkhouses are possible. Often, parties will use snowmobile track shortcuts created by park staff who use the machines to bring summer supplies, fuel and equipment to remote campgrounds and ranger cabins. Snowmobiling is allowed only on the perimeter road, which is not groomed and is often impassable due to downed trees, etc.

All winter users must register with the park and will be quizzed on their experience level and physical condition. Equipment is also inspected to be sure users literally "have the right stuff."

Applications for winter use must be filed two weeks in advance.

Campsites & Cabins

Use of any campsite in Baxter is by reservation only. In peak summer, when the campgrounds are full and when trailhead parking lots are clogged with day hikers staying outside the park, the gates are, in effect, closed. Day hikers often arrive by 5:30 am to insure a spot when the gates open at 6 am.

Reservations at Baxter are not taken by phone. Callers can check on availability by phone, but must send a check and written request by mail or appear at park headquarters on Balsam Drive in Millinocket in person. Mail-in reservations from Maine residents are given priority over other mail-in reservation requests.

The park begins taking reservations each year on the first weekday after New Year's Day. In order to get favorite spots – particularly the rustic cabins at Daicey and Kidney Ponds offering glorious views on prime summer weekends – some people get in line days in advance. They camp out in sleeping bags and tents in the parking lot of a nearby hotel where opening day registrations are processed. It is not unusual for more than 150 people to be in line when the door opens. Some have endured nights with temperatures of 20-below zero!

In addition to the cabins, Baxter boasts 10 traditional campgrounds with tent and lean-to sites. Bunkhouses holding varying numbers of people are also available. Backcountry lean-tos and tent sites are also scattered throughout the park.

Great North Woods

One prime wilderness spot is **Russell Pond**, in the park's center. Reachable only by foot trail, it has lean-tos, a bunkhouse and canoes for rent. It is a great base camp for exploring the rusting remains of the lumbering era's heydays which lay in nearby woods and fields. It is also a good jumping-off point for the **Davis Pond** lean-to, a solitary shelter that is without a doubt the most remote camping location in Maine. Baxter rules require a night's stay at Chimney Pond or Russell Pond before heading to Davis.

South Branch Pond Campground (tent sites, lakeside lean-tos and bunkhouse) is also a favorite. Mountains rise steeply from the lakes here and moose and deer are frequent visitors to the shores.

There are no motels, stores or gas stations in the park. Cellular telephones are banned, as are noise-making electronic devices such as radios and tape players.

Hiking

In all, there are 180 miles of hiking trails in the park. Many lead into remote, foot-access-only campgrounds and lean-tos. There are 46 different mountain peaks, some with no paths to the top save the one you'll metaphorically blaze. Nearly 20 peaks exceed 3,000 feet in elevation. The highest are on Katahdin, where Baxter Peak tops out at just 13 feet shy of a mile at 5,267 feet. Here, in the treeless alpine zone, rare Arctic flowers bloom in spring, and snow can fall in any month of the year.

By far the busiest section of the park is the south end around Katahdin. Because of the big mountain hiking it is the most popular destination. Even people who have hiked in the Presidential Range in New Hampshire's White Mountains concede that a hike here is a major undertaking. Baxter's terrain is basically steep slopes of boulders and precipitous cliffs intertwined with almost impenetrable brush and stunted trees.

 Hikers above the treeline are urged to stay on the trail to avoid harming fragile alpine vegetation. Katahdin is a busy place in summer with as many as 300 people on the summit at one time on busy weekends. Without due care the terrain would be quickly trampled to dust.

WATCHABLE WILDLIFE: *Nearby* **Sandy Stream Pond**, *an easy half-hour walk, is a spectacular spot to moose watch. Moose frequently wade along the shore with the peaks of Katahdin and Hamlin Mountains in the background.*

Baxter State Park

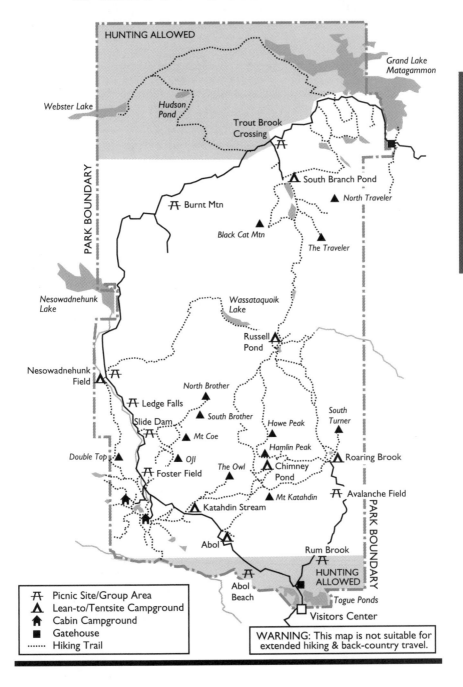

HUNTING ALLOWED

Grand Lake
Matagammon

Webster Lake

Hudson
Pond

Trout Brook
Crossing

🎋 South Branch Pond

▲ North Traveler

🎋 Burnt Mtn

▲ Black Cat Mtn

▲ The Traveler

Nesowadnehunk
Lake

Wassataquoik
Lake

Russell ▲
Pond

Nesowadnehunk
Field

North Brother

🎋 Ledge Falls

Slide Dam

▲ South Brother

South
Turner

▲ Howe Peak

▲ Mt Coe

Hamlin Peak

Double Top ▲

▲ OJI

The Owl ▲

▲ Chimney
Pond

🎋 Roaring Brook

🎋 Foster Field

▲ Mt Katahdin

🎋 Avalanche Field

▲ Katahdin Stream

Abol ▲

Rum Brook
🎋

HUNTING
ALLOWED

PARK BOUNDARY

PARK BOUNDARY

Abol
Beach

Togue Ponds

Visitors Center

Great North Woods

🎋	Picnic Site/Group Area
▲	Lean-to/Tentsite Campground
♠	Cabin Campground
■	Gatehouse
......	Hiking Trail

WARNING: This map is not suitable for
extended hiking & back-country travel.

Here are some recommended hikes in the park.

Freezeout Trail, Baxter State Park. Extended backpacking trips of up to 22 miles are possible on this seldom-used path in the park's northern reaches. The trail begins at Trout Brook Farm on the Perimeter Road and heads due north along an abandoned woods road that occasionally skirts Mattagamon Lake.

Unique slate ridges and a two-acre sawdust pile at the site of an old sawmill are passed. There is a good tenting area and lean-to at Little East where Webster Stream meets the East Branch of the Penobscot River. Other lean-tos are available by advanced reservation. From here the trail gets rougher as it passes spectacular Grand Falls and then parallels the Webster Stream, although most of the route is not near the water.

You'll see the rusting remains of several old logging camps. At about 13 miles the recently relocated trail cuts back south to a new lean-to on Hudson Pond (no views – the lean-to is stuck back in damp woods). It is another 9½ miles back to the Perimeter Road through very thick and tangled woods where the occasional moose may be spotted. For reservations for other multi-day trips contact park authorities (☎ 723-5140).

Katahdin, Abol, Baxter State Park: Although long, Abol Trail up the south side of Katahdin is perhaps the quickest way up Maine's highest mountain. The three-mile trip begins at the Abol Campground on the park's perimeter road and carves north and slightly east up the face, following for a time the path of an avalanche of rock. Most of the route is exposed and above treeline. Footing is often loose and slippery. The total elevation gain is just under 4,000 feet and there is no reliable water. Still, along with the 5.2-mile Hunt Trail, which is the route the Appalachian Trail takes to the top, Abol is often a preferred path, especially by day trippers. Views begin quickly and you can see for more than 100 miles on a clear day.

Katahdin, Chimney Pond, Baxter State Park: Chimney Pond is a favorite destination for hikers and backpackers who want to make an extended trip out of a climb of Katahdin. The four-mile Chimney Pond Trail from Roaring Brook Campground (where you park) to Chimney Pond has an impressive elevation gain of 1,500 feet. This well-worn and marked foot trail criss-crosses a tumbling stream and passes a good view spot at Basin Ponds.

Ice cold Chimney Pond, nestled at the foot of the 2,000-foot headwall in the Great South Basin, is perhaps the most spectacular scenic location in the state. A small reservation-only campground here has several lean-tos and a bunkhouse that sleeps 12. Four trails from the campground offer access to the summit of Baxter Peak and nearby ridges. It is the best place to begin and end a transit of the infamous Knife-Edge using the Cathedral and Dudley Trails (see below).

Katahdin, Knife Edge, Baxter State Park: Maine's most spectacular trail is also one of its most dangerous; not merely due to the precipitous drops of up to 1,500 feet from this narrow arête, but because of the exposure climbers face if the weather turns ugly – a frequent occurence in any month.

The Knife Edge, which must be accessed from any number of other trails in the area, runs from Pamola Peak to Baxter Peak over a series of sawtooth ridges. In some places it is only six feet wide with sheer drop-offs.

 In many places hikers must use their hands to ascend or descend near-vertical sections. Take care, as there are precious few places where a misstep would not end in calamity.

The actual Knife Edge is only about a mile long but can take two hours or longer to traverse depending on conditions and the number of users (hikers must frequently wait for others to safely pass in narrow sections). Most hikers prefer to ascend over the Knife Edge and return to their start by other trails, although travel in either direction is possible.

 There are no shortcuts. In the past, those who thought a slope looked like an easy alternate route soon discovered their folly. Many have died after falling off or becoming stranded near the Knife Edge.

Kayaking

South Branch Pond. Nestled between high mountains in the northern reaches of Baxter State Park, South Branch Pond is one of the most beautiful lakes in Maine. And, best of all, there are rentable lean-tos right on the water's edge. Access is from the campground at the north end of the lake reachable on a side road off the Baxter State Park Perimeter Road. You will share the shoreline with moose and deer as you paddle the 1½-mile length of this lake. Hiking trails at the south end lead to upper South Branch Pond and to a waterfall on Howe Brook.

You can bring you own boat or rent an aluminum canoe from the ranger.

Fees

Bunkhouse spots go for $7 per night, per person. In most cases three or four parties will be sharing. Lean-tos cost $6 per night, per person. Most lean-tos sleep four (but at less than 10-feet wide, things will be tight!)

Tent space is $6 per night, per person. Most sites have restrictions on the number of tents allowed (on backcountry sites it is two tents).

Cabins are $17 per night, per person, with a $30 per-night minimum. There is also a $8 fee per vehicle, per day, for non-Maine residents. A season pass is $25.

Contact Information

Baxter State Park, 64 Balsam Drive, Millinocket 04462. ☎ 723-5140.

■ State Parks

 Lily Bay State Park, Beaver Cove: Located on the eastern shore of Moosehead Lake not far from Greenville, this is one of the prettiest parks in Maine. Lakeside campsites, picnic ground, swimming beach, two boat ramps, dump station, great fishing, playground, toilets. On Lily Bay Road. ☎ 695-2700.

Moosehead Lake is big water and should not to be taken lightly. Still, the park makes the best jumping-off place for paddlers and boaters planning to visit remote campsites on Sugar Island, a very large undeveloped island in the middle of the lake. ☎ 695-2700.

Mattawamkeag Wilderness Park, Mattawamkeag: Run by the town, this 1,000-acre forested preserve along the Mattawamkeag River is a great place to hike, fish, swim or camp. Scenic falls. Campground with toilets, lean-tos, picnic grounds and showers. Located on the end of a long dirt road (The Park Road), off Route 2. ☎ 736-4881.

Peaks-Kenny State Park, Dover-Foxcroft: Situated on Sebec Lake, this modest-sized park is seldom visited by tourists. Good fishing, sand swimming beach with bath house and toilets, picnic grounds, camping with dump station, boating, and canoeing. Take Route 153 out of Dover-Foxcroft as far as you can, then follow the signs. ☎ 564-2003.

■ Wildlife Refuges

Owens Marsh Wildlife Area, Concord Township: One mile west of the Kennebec River just south of Bingham off Route 16, this 45-acre marshy area was set aside in 1998 as prime migratory waterfowl habitat. A trail leads to an old dam which was partially restored to restablish the marsh. Off Route 16.

Great North Woods

Major Parks & Preserves in the Great North Woods

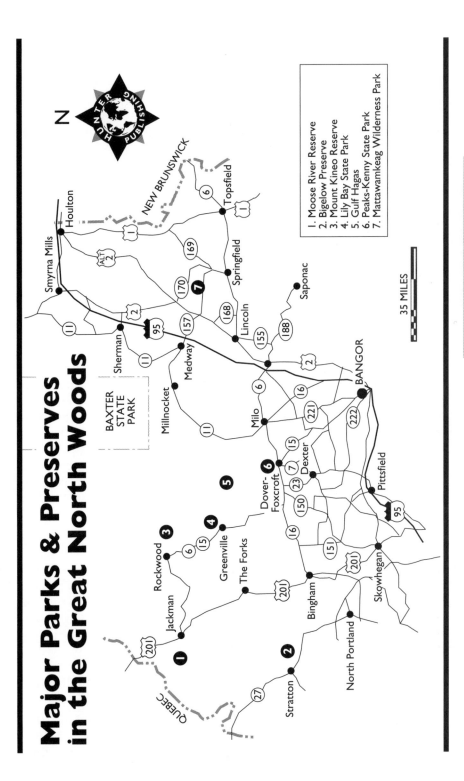

1. Moose River Reserve
2. Bigelow Preserve
3. Mount Kineo Reserve
4. Lily Bay State Park
5. Gulf Hagas
6. Peaks-Kenny State Park
7. Mattawamkeag Wilderness Park

35 MILES

■ Natural Areas/Preserves

 Mount Kineo: This unusual monadnock of volcanic flint-like rock, called rhyolite, towers 700 feet above Moosehead Lake. Native peoples traded pieces of this rock with tribes hundreds of miles away. The summit offers 360° views, taking in Katahdin to the east. The Nature Conservancy protects 800 acres or so here.

 DID YOU KNOW? *Henry David Thoreau is believed to have camped on the north end of the peninsula during one of his many canoe trips in Northern Maine.*

Peregrine falcons nest on the towering cliffs. Hiking trails range from moderate to strenuous. Access by boat in summer, snowmobile in winter. Faded resort at foot on south side. Golf course still active.

Nature Conservancy of Maine office is located at 14 Maine Street, Brunswick 04011. ☎ 729-5181.

See *Cruises* section, page 433, for information about the boat shuttle from Rockwood.

The Hermitage, Katahdin Iron Works: Accessible only on foot, the Nature Conservancy's Hermitage is a 36-acre grove of towering white pines that have not been touched in nearly 200 years. Located along the banks of the Pleasant River, it is reached by taking a section of the Appalachian Trail east from where it cross a dirt road just west of the river. Access can also be had by trails on the east side of the river. Pugwash Pond, a National Natural Landmark, and other kettle ponds are waterholes left by retreating glaciers. Nearby is Gulf Hagas, considered the Grand Canyon of the East. (See *Hiking* section, below.) Several attractive falls nearby including Screw Auger Falls and Hay Brook Falls.

Nature Conservancy of Maine office is located at 14 Maine Street, Brunswick 04011. ☎ 729-5181.

Katahdin Iron Works, Brownville Junction: In the 1800s a bustling industrial complex and village produced tons of pig iron each year. Only the stone remains of a crude blast furnace, and there are also the remains of one of the original 16 charcoal kilns, and some old foundations. A State Historic Site. At its high point the iron works employed more than 400 men and used 200 horse and oxen to haul an incredible 20,000 cords of wood a year to feed the kilns. No fee. Located at the site of the North Maine Woods KI Checkpoint. Access to camping and nearby Gulf Hagas. ☎ 435-6213.

Borestone Mountain Sanctuary, Elliotsville Township: More than 1,500 acres on a unique mountain with three high ponds (Sunset, Midday and Sunrise) and great views of Barren Mountain and other ridgelines.

The trail to twin peaks at the summit follows an old logging road for part of the way. Open daytime only from June through October. There is a nominal fee. Take Elliotsville Road from Route 15 in Monson. ☎ 631-4050.

Bowater River Pond Outdoor Classroom, Millinocket: Two self-guided trails – one six miles, the other 4½ miles – traverse 230 acres adjacent to the Golden Road. Nearly 50 acres are in tree plantation, 110 in harvest crops. Sixty acres were cut in the 1930s. Stops along the trail include a borrow pit (gravel pit), riparian zone, wildlife sites and exhibits on tree harvesting techniques. Brochures available by mail or at the Debsconeag checkpoint on the Golden Road. Adequate parking, no fee. Bowater Public Relations Department, 1 Katahdin Avenue, Millinocket 04462. ☎ 723-2229.

Sightseeing

■ Historic Sites/Museums

> ### NOTE
>
> *Many museums and historic sites in Maine are small, and operate for only part of the year, staffed by volunteers. The opening days and times of these institutions vary, depending upon weather, available staff and other factors; some are open by appointment only. We recommend that you call ahead to find out the latest opening times.*

Brownville

Katahdin Iron Works (1843). From Route 11, five miles north of Brownville Jct., take gravel road (left) six miles to Iron Works. Restored stone blast furnace and charcoal kiln on site of 19th-century iron works that produced some 18-20 tons of raw iron daily during its periods of peak operation in the 1880s. ☎ 941-4014.

Burlington

Stewart M. Lord Memorial Historical Society, Route 188. Displays depict life in Maine during the 1800s. ☎ 732-4121.

Dover-Foxcroft

Blacksmith Shop Museum (1863), 98 Dawes Road. Restored Civil War period shop retains much of the original equipment. ☎ 564-8618.

Sebec Historical Society/Harriman School Museum, North Road. ☎ 564-7259.

Greenville

Moosehead Historical Society, Pritham Avenue. ☎ 695-2909.

S/S *Katahdin* (1914) and **Moosehead Marine Museum**, N. Main Street, East Cove. Artifacts and photographs concerning the marine history of the region and Mount Kineo Peninsula. ☎ 695-2716.

Guilford

Guilford Historical Society, N. Main Street. One of the oldest buildings in Guilford, erected in 1825. ☎ 876-2787.

Lee

Lee Historical Society Museum, Main Street. Route 6. ☎ 738-3533.

Millinocket

Millinocket Town Museum, Municipal Building, Main Street. Collections relating to paper mill towns. ☎ 723-5766.

Northern Timber Cruisers Snowmobile Museum, Route 157, Lake Road. A history on snowmobiling and the part that Maine and Millinocket played in the development of the industry. ☎ 723-6344.

Monson

Monson Museum (1889), Main Street. Route 15. Local memorabilia and artifacts, some pertaining to the local narrow gauge railroad and the slate quarries. By appointment. ☎ 997-3792.

Patten

Lumberman's Museum, Route 159, Shin Pond Road. Spread over several old buildings housing historic equipment and displays of logging life. Many old photos. On way to Baxter State Park North entrance. ☎ 528-2650.

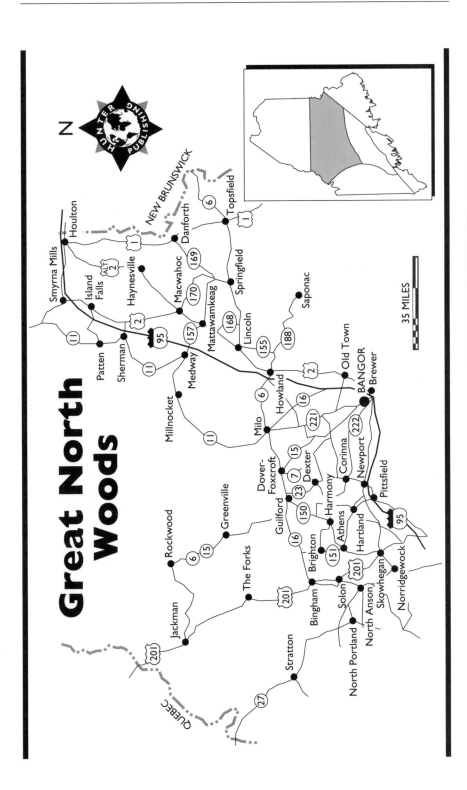

Great North Woods

Solon

South Solon Meeting House (1842), off Route 201. ☎ 474-8274.
List Source-Maine Department of Tourism.

■ Covered Bridge

In an era when stern chaperones kept a constant eye on courting couples, young lovers particularly liked the privacy afforded by these structures, many of which have succumbed to old age, fire, or flood. To romancers, a trip across a covered bridge was the perfect opportunity to steal a kiss.

Low's Bridge - 1857, Piscataquis River. This structure was originally built in 1857, carried away by flood in 1987, and then rebuilt in 1990. It is located off Routes 6 and 15, three-quarters of a mile east and one mile north of Sangerville, between the towns of Sangerville and Guilford.

Adventures On Foot

■ Hiking

For hikes in Baxter State Park, see that section at the beginning of this chapter.

Boarstone Mountain, Elliotsville Township. With a pair of open summits, attractive ponds and great views of the surrounding ranges, Boarstone is one of the finest day hikes in Maine. The elevation gain on the two-mile hike is just over 1,000 feet.

The trail begins off the Elliotsville Road a short distance after it crosses the Canadian Pacific Railroad tracks. Park across from the gate that blocks the private auto road that comprises the first mile of this trip. After a series of switchbacks on the road the route become a bona fide trail, skirting the south end of Sunrise Pond, part of a series of three small jewel-like lakes on the mountain. The last part of the trail to the top of West Peak is very steep and may require use of hands.

The best views are from the slightly higher East Peak, another quarter-mile further. Sights from here Lake Onawa below to the east and Barren Mountain beyond that. Moderate to strenuous. Owned by the Audubon Society and operated as a preserve for day use only with nature program and interpretive center part way up the trail. Small fee charged. Dogs not allowed.

Gulf Hagas, Bowdoin College Grant East: Dubbed the Grand Canyon of the East, Gulf Hagas sports some of the most spectacular scenery and most rugged terrain in the state. It is on the National Register of Natural Areas. The gulf is formed by the West Branch of the Pleasant River as it drops nearly 400 feet in four miles through a series of rapids and falls, all wedged between canyon walls that get narrower.

 INTERESTING FACT: *At The Jaws, the cliffs are so close that pulp sticks (less than four feet in length) would often get wedged during log drives, causing major backups. Loggers went to work with dynamite and made the gorge six feet wide.*

In places, cliffs tower 200 feet above the water. The trail and side routes traverse the cliffs and mossy woods and can be very slippery. Several people each summer are carried out after breaking an ankle. Most hikers follow a long loop that uses the trail along the river and an old woods road further back.

Depending on the route you choose distances can range from eight to 12 miles. You can access the site and get information on the latest road conditions, parking areas and campsite rental at the gate house at Katahdin Iron Works (see page 414). The Appalachian Trail, the Hermitage (a preserve saving old-growth white pine), and other waterfalls such as Screw Auger Falls, make this an extremely attractive area for adventure.

Mount Kineo, Kineo Township: Mount Kineo is one of the few mountains of inland Maine which must be accessed by ferry. Take the shuttle boat across Moosehead Lake from nearby Rockwood and follow the bridle trail along the Kineo Peninsula's west side. You can access either the steep Indian Trail or the more gradual bridle trail from this path.

There is a good 750-foot of elevation gain over the trail's 1½-mile length. The view from the top of this flint monadnock is spectacular and includes all of Moosehead, Squaw Mountain to the south, Katahdin to the northeast and Big Spencer to the north. Several side trails from the fire tower site at the summit lead to dizzying views off the sheer cliffs to the lake below. Strenuous.

Moxie Falls, Moxie Gore: Maine and New England's highest waterfall, Moxie Falls, requires some walking effort to see but is well worth the hike. From a parking area off the Moxie Pond Road, the trail heads roughly north through relatively flat terrain. About a half-mile from the start take a trail leading to the right. This will bring you to the top of the falls, which first fall 40 feet through a series of three cascades and then a little farther on plunge 90 feet. The trail continues downstream, providing excellent views looking back toward the falls. You can go back the way you came or continue on the loop trail that follows Moxie Stream to its confluence with the Kennebec River. At the Kennebec Gorge see if you can spot any whitewater rafters. The trail then cuts back through the woods to the parking area. Moderate.

Sally Mountain, Attean Township: In recent years, Jackman has increased its focus on hiking and on mountain biking. From the Attean Pond Road, which is used to access the popular Bow Trip on the Moose River, you can reach the Sally Mountain Trail by either paddling a short distance across to the trailhead on the north side of the lake or by parking near the end of Big Wood Pond and following the Canadian Pacific Railroad tracks (over the Moose River Bridge) for 1.7 miles. The trail starts out gradually enough but quickly becomes steep for the last 1½ miles to the fire tower at the top. Great views of the entire Moose River Basin and nearby ponds, hills all the way into Canada. Strenuous.

■ Golfing

Greens fees vary greatly according to the popularity of the course and the time of year.

Foxcroft Golf Club, Foxcroft Center Road, off Milo Road, Dover-Foxcroft. 2,922 yards, par 36. April-October. 9 holes. ☎ 564-8887.

Green Valley Golf Course, Route 2, West Enfield. 2,824 yards, par 35. April-October. 9 holes. ☎ 732-3006.

Piscataquis Country Club, Dover Road, Route 15, Guilford. Front 9, 2,656 yards, par 34; back 9, 2,639 yards, par 34. 18 holes. Late April until October. ☎ 876-3203.

Moose River Golf Course, Route 201, Jackman. 1,976 yards, par 31. 9 holes. Mid-May through mid-October. ☎ 668-4841.

Katahdin Country Club, 70 Park Street, Milo. 2,986 yards, par 36. 9 holes. April 15-November 5. ☎ 943-2686.

Mount Kineo Golf Course, on Moosehead Lake. 3,011 yards, par 36. 9 holes. May 25-September. ☎ 534-2221.

Adventures On Wheels

■ Mountain Biking

Jackman may have first found fame as a canoeing and snowmobiling paradise, but it is quickly becoming a popular destination for bikers. The same woods roads that open up the wilds for those other sports make for challenging riding (although single-track routes are in short supply). Many trips follow attractive streams and end at sandy beaches on the area's many ponds.

> Maps and information are available from the chamber of commerce. ☎ 668-4171.

South Lagrange to Medford Railbed. Like other rails-to-trails conversions in Maine the 12-mile route from South Lagrange to Medford offers easy grades and comparatively smooth riding. It is a multi-use trail open to ATVs in summer and snowmobiles in winter. There is a signed parking area where the old rail line once crossed Route 16. The trail heads pretty much north through wet woods and open fields. There are several major road crossings to watch for. When you get to the village of Medford, you'll find a nice picnic spot on the banks of the Piscataquis River.

Shirley Mills to Greenville Railbed. This route starts where the Upper Shirley Mills Corner Road passes close to the south end of a pond. The trailhead and a good place to park are on the east shore. The route follows an abandoned rail bed due north into Greenville on a gradual grade. It passes by several smaller ponds and through swampy areas. Keep an eye out for moose! Popular snowmobile route in winter. Another ride is possible to the south on the same abandoned railbed. It continues all the way south to Dover Foxcroft.

Arnold's Landing to Bingham Railbed, Solon. Hugging the banks of the Kennebec River, this path starts out at a dam and massive abandoned steel truss railroad bridge built on a large falls in river.

 DID YOU KNOW? *This place is called Arnold's Landing because it is a spot where Col. Benedict Arnold portaged his colonial fighting force in 1775 on an ill-fated mission to attack Quebec City.*

The trail is a seven-mile gradual grade with only a few wet spots. Used by snowmobiles in winter.

Mountain Bike Rentals

North Woods Outfitters
Main Street, Greenville 04441
Full-service bike shop with rentals for all ages and abilities. Bikes, accessories and clothing sold. Delivery of rental bikes. Free advice on where to ride. Also sells and rents canoes, kayaks and camping equipment. ☎ 695-3288.

The Birches
PO Box 41, Rockwood 04478
Rental mountain bikes, helmets, canoes, kayaks and sailboats.
50 miles of roads and trails right outside their front door. ☎ 534-2242.

■ Foliage/Motor Tours

 Here's a selction of driving routes that will show you woods, mountains, lakes and more.

Moosehead & the Maine Woods

210 miles, 5¼ hours, round trip

Highlights: *This getaway leads you to the southern reaches of the great North Maine Woods and to Moosehead Lake, the largest lake in the northeast. With its miles of majestic pines and hardwood forests, this unspoiled region serves up a virtual feast of glorious fall color.*

Route: From **Skowhegan**, take US 201 north to **Bingham**, site of **Wyman Dam** and whitewater rafting on the West Branch of the Kennebec River. Head to **Caratunk** along US 201, a road high above the river featuring stunning views of the Kennebec River and Wyman Lake. East of The Forks, **Moxie Falls** – a 90-foot cascade and gorge – is an easy and worthwhile half-mile hike. Continue north on US 201 to Route 15 just outside of **Jackman**. Take 15 southeast through **Rockwood**, watching for dramatic views of Mt. Kineo and Moosehead Lake. Continue on to **Greenville**, where you can hop on a bush plane and take leaf-peeping to new heights. Stay on 15 to **Dover-Foxcroft**, site of the rustic **Blacksmith Shop Museum**, then travel south on 7 to **Dexter** and the **Grist Mill Museum**.

Head for **Newport**, then west on 151 to **Corson Corner**. Continue west on 43 to **Athens**, then head south on 150 back to Skowhegan.

Aroostook & Katahdin/Moosehead

214 miles, 5 hours round trip

Highlights: *One of the most notable features of this region is the unpopulated territory between towns. This vast, sweeping and color-rich area of land is a sportsman's paradise, offering the perfect setting for canoeing, hiking, fishing and camping.*

Route: From **Howland**, go east on 6 through West Enfield and Lincoln to Lee; then north on 168 to **Winn**. Take US 2 northeast to **Macwahoc**, stopping en route in **Mattawamkeag,** home to a wilderness park (open until mid-September) that offers camping, hiking and canoeing facilities. From Macwahoc, take US 2A northeast through potato country to **Haynesville.** Go southeast on secondary road to **Danforth,** then north on US 1 to **Houlton,** home of the **Southern Aroostook History and Art Museum**

🌿 **Foliage Hotline:** The Maine foliage hotline, in service each fall, offers the latest color-peaking information for leaf-peepers. ☎ 800-932-3419.

(open through September). Drive west on US 2 to **Smyrna Mills,** then west on 212 to **Knowles Corner**; go south on 11 through Patten, which features the **Lumberman's Museum** (open weekends through Columbus Day), and an access route to **Baxter State Park.**

Continue on 11 south to **Sherman.** Take I-95 south to **Medway** (Exit 56), then west on 157 to 116. Go south on 116 through Chester back to Howland.

Routes courtesy Maine Department of Conservation

Route 15, Bangor to Greenville

71 miles, 1½ hours

Highlights: *Sitting at the south end of majestic Moosehead Lake, Greenville is often called the Gateway to the North Maine Woods. That's all fine, but first you have to get here. Route 15 from Bangor is the most direct and scenic route.*

Route: In the city of **Bangor** itself, Route 15 is actually called Broadway. It seems fitting that you start this trip surrounded by strip malls and fast food joints only to end in vast wilderness.

A short way north of Interstate 95 Broadway narrows and becomes two lane. It heads roughly north and crosses the Kenduskeag Stream at Six Mile Falls.

Canoe Race

Six Mile Falls is a popular place to watch thousands of canoeists test the fast-flowing water each spring in the **Kenduskeag Stream Race** (☎ 947-1018), one of the largest in New England.

Houses and businesses spread out as you pass through Glenburn and into the village of **Kenduskeag,** some 10 miles beyond the falls, where the race begins.

Route 15 then heads due north, favoring high ground through the farms and woods of Corinth and into **Charleston** with its intimidating **Bull**

Hill. Here, a former military radar installation has been converted into medium-security prison.

In downtown **Dover-Foxcroft** watch signs carefully. You need to take a relatively sharp left at the second traffic light. If you follows the signs at the second light and take Route 153, it leads straight to **Peaks-Kenny State Park**.

Next you will follow the Piscataquis River to **Guilford**. Keep an eye out for the **Low's Covered Bridge** (see page 418).

At the Guilford Industries Mill in Guilford take a left, cross the river and take the first hard right. No more tricky turns as you head through Abbott, Monson and Shirley on a straight north run to **Greenville**.

Greenville is a winter recreation Mecca as well as great place to catch a float plane to deep backcountry. There are miles of paper company dirt roads to explore on a mountain bike and the fishing in Moosehead Lake itself is steadily improving.

Route 201, Fairfield to Jackman

85 miles, 2¼ hours, one way

Highlights: *Often in Maine there is only one choice when it comes to deciding how to get somewhere and Route 201 is one of those roads. It's a pleasant route too.*

Route: From Interstate 95 in **Fairfield** (Exit 36) the road winds steadily north paralleling the Kennebec River. Open fields and hardwood forests characterize the 14 miles to **Skowhegan**.

Watch route signs carefully to keep from being diverted onto 201A. Cross the river and loop through town in a one-way traffic pattern. Go right after crossing the bridge, then get in the left lane for a left turn. As you come around 180 degrees, get into the right lane to make a right back onto 201 and to return heading north.

North of Skowhegan Route 201 traverses some pretty wild country. Here, Route 201 is called **The Arnold Trail**. It parallels the route taken by Col. Benedict Arnold during the revolution when, prior to his treason, he lead a force up the Kennebec and through the woods to attack Quebec. The trials and deprivations suffered as the men endured early snows, poor equipment and little food was profiled in Maine author Kenneth Roberts' novel Arundel. In the village of Solon, Col. Arnold was forced to portage around a tall falls with sharp rocks. A dam with abandoned railroad bridge atop now occupies the site.

The next village of any consequence is **Bingham**. Be sure to stop in at **Thompson's Restaurant** for some of their famous gingerbread, rumored to be the best in the world.

Just north of town a large earthen dam and power station holds back the river into Wyman Lake. Route 102 twists and turns as it climbs the hills on the eastern shore. Watch both the sharp, compound turns, and for moose, as well as for the seemingly endless parade of Canadian tractor trailers heading south.

About halfway up the lake a picnic area marks the spot where Benedict Arnold and his men left the river and attempted to haul their gear over a 1,000-foot-high mountain.

Up ahead is **Caratunk,** where the Appalachian Trail crosses the Kennebec. In peak through-hiker season, a ferryman with canoe is available to take walkers across, especially when water is being released upstream to facilitate whitewater rafting.

The tiny village of **The Forks**, where the Kennebec and Dead Rivers meet, is the whitewater rafting capital of Maine. There are more raft outfitters based here than anyplace else in the state. Most trips leave from base camps along Route 201. It is a quick bus trip to the nearby Harris Station Dam on Indian Pond where float trips begin.

A short side trip down Moxie Pond Road in The Forks brings you to the small pullout where the trail leads about a mile north to **Moxie Falls**, the tallest waterfall in Maine.

The next 30 miles or so of Route 201 to Jackman is a pretty lonely road. Watch out for moose!

Jackman, which bills itself as the Switzerland of Maine, is becoming a recreational destination of its own. In addition to its busy snowmobiling season, it is popular with hunters and fishermen as well as canoeists looking to take in the Moose River Bow Trip, one of the quintessential paddle journeys in the state (see page 429). It is just a short distance further on up Route 201 to the border checkpoint (staffed 24 hours a day).

Millinocket to Greenville via Golden Road

A long ways, half the day, one way

Highlights: *This trips is for the decidedly adventurous, since most of these roads are used for the timber industry or for backcountry recreation and not for sightseeing. There are few stops, and even fewer opportunities for food, fuel or mechanical assistance. See page 54-56 for advice on using remote dirt roads before heading out on this route. The Golden Road from Millinocket to Chesuncook is paved.*

Route: Begin on the **Golden Road** just north of **Millinocket**. There is an entrance station to the Golden Road about 10 miles north of town just off the paved road that heads toward Baxter State Park. Pay your day-use fee here. The store and seaplane base at Spencer Cove, just before the gate, is one of the last pit stops.

Great North Woods

For most of its length the Golden Road follows the fabled West Branch of the Penobscot River, once home to woodsmen and river drivers and immortalized in the writings of Henry David Thoreau. Slow up for the one-lane bridge at **Abol**. Remember that log trucks have the right of way. There is a small store and campground here and spectacular views of Katahdin to the north. Abol is also the name of a falls just downstream from the bridge. The next 10 miles follow the river.

 DID YOU KNOW? *At one point during the early 1980s plans called for a new dam here. It would have flooded the valley more than 100 feet deep. Luckily, it was never built.*

Ahead is **Pray's Campground**, rustic in a sort of benign road warrior sense, with tent sites, lots of seasonal trailers, and good fishing in the eddy.

A right just beyond the campground takes you toward Telos Lake. The bridge is a good place to watch whitewater rafters challenge the Class V Cribworks rapids.

The next major right dead-ends at a hydroelectric station where most raft trips begin. Just ahead, a right turn takes you to **Ripogenus Dam**, one of the largest in Maine. You'll pass Pray's Store which offers several rental cabins in the area.

You can drive across the dam or just get out and walk across. Marvel at the sound when the gates are open and water surges through the narrow gorge below.

Ahead, the Golden Road turns to well-groomed dirt as you pass the south tip of **Chesuncook Lake** and then the south end of **Caribou Lake** – which is really the western arm of Chesuncook. When you see this second lake, slow down and look to your left. There is an attractive waterfall.

The right turn to Greenville, via Kokadjo, is only a few hundred yards ahead on the left.

 WATCHABLE WILDLIFE: *Greenville Road, a stretch of paper company highway, is prime moose-watching territory. Often, you'll sense one is ahead before you see it as gawking traffic backs up in "moose jams."*

The exit fee station is just head at **Silas Hill**.

Take a break when you get to the tiny village of **Kokadjo**, which has bumper stickers for sale at the trading post noting its year-round population of three.

The **Roach River,** renowned for its prized salmon, begins at the dam here that holds back First Roach Pond.

Back on pavement now, the Lily Bay Road will take you south toward **Greenville**. From time to time Moosehead Lake is visible to the west. The road goes by **Lily Bay State Park**, which offers fine camping and canoeing opportunities.

■ Foliage Recommendations

Squaw Mountain ski area just outside of Greenville offers fall foliage rides on its chairlift. The views from the top of this 3,200-foot peak are grand and there is a short side trail – half a mile or so in length – to an abandoned forest fire warden's tower on a nearby peak. Especially on the ride down, when the endless forests surrounding the lake are ablaze in color, it will take your breath away. The lift is open 9 am until 4 pm weekends through October, weather and foliage permitting. The cost is just $6. Best to call ahead. ☎ 695-1000.

 You have the option of walking down, but the ski trails are steep, covered in slippery vegetation when damp, and not really good for hiking.

■ Riding the Rails

During the summer months the **Bangor and Aroostook Railroad** schedules a variety of passenger trips over rails that haven't seen regular passenger service for nearly 40 years. The equipment includes diesel locomotives, passenger coaches, sleepers, an observation car, baggage car and a first-class car. Double-decked observation cars are often used for fall foliage trips. Call to check the schedule as the trips are sandwiched between regular freight service and times vary.

Tours range from between two to six hours and provide a rare opportunity to see some of the most spectacular scenery in Northern Maine. The trains leave from Bangor, Brownville, Oakfield, Millinocket, Greenville and Jackman. Some include a picnic or a box lunch, but usually light refreshments such as chips and sodas are offered on the train. There are restrooms on board. Smoking is not allowed on board, although there are short breaks where passengers may disembark to stretch their legs and smoke, if they wish.

The Brownville trip, which stops to pick up passengers in Greenville, takes nearly all day. Part of its route parallels the hills where the Appalachian Trail runs. The tracks cross the spectacular 130-foot-tall Onawa trestle and for a time run along Moosehead Lake. The train eventually stops in Jackman and then turns around, allowing passengers good view of both sides of the tracks during the round trip.

Prices start at $12 for an adult and go as high as $28 for an all-day trip. First class is 15-20% higher. Prices for children start at $8.

In the past, folks were not allowed off the train at Jackman while the engines were running. Most likely this was so no one got left behind, but after four or five hours on a train small children not enamored with scenery and the occasional moose sighting may get fidgety. Bangor and Aroostook officials are looking into providing more breaks. The possibility of a shuttle bus to run people between the station in Greenville Junction and downtown Greenville is also under discussion.

Tickets may be purchased on the day of the trip for cash on a first-come, first-served basis. Most excursions sell out a week or two in advance. You can make reservations with a credit card by calling ☎ 800-847-1505 on weekdays between noon and 6 pm.

Adventures On Water

■ Places to Paddle

South Branch Pond in Baxter State Park offers some pleasant paddling. See the Baxter section at the beginning of this chapter.

East Branch Penobscot River. In its 27-mile run from Mattagamon Lake to Whetstone Falls the East Branch of the Penobscot is one tough, @ %&# river. The trip is a mix of flat water, Class I, Class II, Class III rapids and several brutal portages around unrunnable falls and drops that have struck fear into the hearts of river drivers since the earliest days of settlement. Portages run as long as half a mile, seem to be all uphill, and are very muddy. In some cases you'll need to do two in one day. But these portages allow you to avoid places like the Hulling Machine, a churning maelstrom of foam so named because every log driven through emerged at the other end without a shred of bark left on it.

The reward, however, is a trip through some of the most spectacular countryside in the state. The views of the back side of Traveller Mountain in Baxter State Park are particularly impressive. There are numerous fine campsites along the way.

Avoid this river in high water. Also, portages are discernable but not marked. If you miss them the next turn in the river could be a 20-foot drop. Proceed carefully.

Lobster Lake. With so many good canoeing rivers nearby many people forget to consider a paddle on Lobster Lake.

Lobster Legend

Legend has it that the lake was named for either some crayfish spotted on the bottom or because its shape is like that of a lobster claw. Either way don't expect to find any lobster there.

You will find quiet solitude, sandy beaches and campsites with great views. Access the lake by taking Lobster Stream from the boat launch ramp just off the Golden Road. Depending on lake and river levels the stream has been known to flow in both directions. The west shore is marshy and there is one sporting camp on the east shore. Most campsites are sprinkled along the southwest and southern shore along Ogden Point. The stream in is about 1½ miles long and it's another mile across the open lake to reach the campsites. The Big Island in the center of the lake is uninhabited by humans and perfect for exploring. Fee (payable at gate) and fire permit (available from Forest Warden) required for camping.

Canoes on the West Branch of the Penobscot River. Naturalist, writer Henry David Thoreau camped nearby.

Moose River Bow Trip, Jackman. The Moose River trip is special, not only for its pristine wilderness character, but also because it is one of the few excursions anywhere that can begin and end in the same spot. The trip starts at the landing on Attean Pond on the end of the Attean Road.

 The one major hazard along this route is Holeb Falls. A tricky set of turns on unmarked channels are necessary to avoid tumbling over a 20-foot drop.

Great North Woods

Paddling due west past islands studded with camps brings voyagers to a one-mile uphill portage to Holeb Pond. A stream leads from the pond to the Moose River, which may be followed for 25 miles back to the landing at Attean Pond. There are numerous fine campsites, and only minor rips and rapids. The trip is 34 miles and can be done in three to four days.

 WATCHABLE WILDLIFE: *Paddlers are almost sure to see at least one moose. While some paddlers may shun the slow flat water and the tight oxbow turns, it is exactly that terrain that gives paddlers a chance to get a chance to view these otherwise skittish critters.*

The **Maine Bureau of Parks and Lands** puts out an excellent map of the Bow Trip, including details on avoiding Holeb Falls. Contact them at ☎ 287-3821.

North Woods Ways, A Unique Outfitter

Canoe trips are offered with renowned authors and guides Garrett and Alexandra Conover. They focus on traditional methods and materials. These folks have written books on everything from winter travel to traditional canoe techniques. Trips: West Branch Penobscot, Allagash, and St. John. RR 2, Box 159A, Guilford 04443. ☎ 997-3723.

West Branch Penobscot River. The ghost of Henry David Thoreau, who first traveled these waters in the late 1800s, still hides in the mist that rises each dawn from the waters of the West Branch of the Penobscot. While the lower reaches, below Ripogenus Dam, are popular with whitewater rafters, the upper section from Seboomook Dam to Chesuncook Lake is home to canoeists and fly fishermen. Most trips begin at the campsite at Roll Dam, the name of a ledge running nearly across the river. There is also a put-in at Northeast Carry, the level route once used to ferry people and gear across the two miles of land between Moosehead Lake, which is part of the Kennebec River's watershed, and the Penobscot. The river turns north where it meets Lobster Stream. An alternate put-in is at the Lobster Landing with a short paddle to the West Branch.

Paddlers heading north now are in attractive, wild country with campsites located on both shores and on islands in mid-stream. Moose sightings are common. This is a broad, fast river with only a few rapids but good current. The river broadens out and the wind picks up where it enters the lake.

There is an especially nice campsite at the Boom House site at the tip of Chesuncook Peninsula. A once-thriving village here has quietly faded. Camps and cabins remain. The only access is by boat, float plane or a long walk on foot.

Paddling the length of Chesuncook, Maine's third largest water body, can be a challenge. Often southeast or northwest winds will whip up waves more than six feet tall. If you don't have time to work your way along the shore, inquire at the Chesuncook Lake House about a boat shuttle that can carry you, your boat and gear to the southern end of the lake.

Canoeing & Kayaking Outfitters

Overnight trips average $100-150 per person, per day. Half-day guided trips are $50. Basic rentals cost between $25 and $45 per day. Most rentals include life jackets, paddles & car-topping gear.

Upper Kennebec Valley Canoe Trips
HCR 64, Box 22, Bingham 04920
Canoe rentals, Chadbourne's Wyman Lake Cabins, Wyman Lake, Moscow. ☎ 672-3371.

Moosehead Adventures
178 East Main Street, Dover-Foxcroft 04426
Canoe, kayak trips in Northern Maine. ☎ 564-3452/695-4434

Allagash Canoe Trips
PO Box 713, Pleasant Street, Greenville 04441
Canoe trips on Allagash, St. John, Upper West/East Penobscot, and Moose River. May-September. ☎ 695-3668.

Beaver Cove Camps
PO Box 1233, Greenville 04441. Canoe rentals. ☎ 695-3717.

Beaver Creek Guide Service
PO Box 1347, Greenville 04441. Canoe trips. ☎ 695-2265/3091.

Chesuncook Lake House, Chesuncook Village (on lake)
Route 76, Box 656, Greenville 04441
Canoe rentals, canoe trips, lake shuttle. Trips: Upper West Branch Penobscot River. Radio phone, ☎ 745-5330.

Cry of the Loon Kayak Adventures
PO Box 238, Jackman 04945
Guided kayak trips of three days or more on Northwestern Lakes and flat water rivers. Specialty includes the Moose River Bow Trip. Size limited to eight people. May-October. Wildlife watching. Run by Maine Guides Andy and Leslie McKendry. ☎ 668-7808.

Sally Mountain Cabins
HCR 64, Box 50, Jackman 04945
Canoe rentals, canoe trips, year-round. ☎ 668-5621.

Penobscot River Outfitters
Route 157, PO Box 45, Medway 04460
Canoe rentals, canoe trips, kayak rentals, Katahdin Shadows Campground and Cabins. Trips: East/West Branch Penobscot, Allagash and St. John River. ☎ 746-9349.

Allagash Wilderness Outfitters
36-P Minuteman Drive, Millinocket 04462
Canoe rentals. May 15-September 30. Radio phone, ☎ 695-2821.

The Birches
PO Box 41, Rockwood 04478
Canoe & kayak rentals and trips on the Kennebec, Penobscot, Dead, Rapid, Allagash and St. John. ☎ 534-7305.

North Country Outfitters on Moosehead Lake
P.O. Box 41, Rockwood 04478
Canoe & kayak rentals and trips on the Allagash, St. John, Moose, West Branch of Penobscot. May-November. ☎ 534-2242/7305.

Moose Country Guiding Adventures
US 1, Box 524D, Sangerville 04479
Canoe trips. ☎ 876-4907.

Gil Gilpatrick, Maine Guide
PO Box 461, Skowhegan 04976
Custom canoe trips on Allagash and Northern Maine Rivers. Gil also written books on guided canoe trips. ☎ 453-6959.

Rivers and Trails Northeast
PO Box 90, Route 201, The Forks 04985
Canoe trips. Canoe ferry on Appalachian Trail across Kennebec. April-November. ☎ 663-4441.

Unicorn Rafting Expeditions
Route 201, Forks 04985
Canoe & kayak rentals and trips. Canoeing: Moose River. Kayaking: the Penobscot. ☎ 725-2255/1-800-UNICORN.

Northern Outdoors
Route 201, PO Box 100, The Forks 04985
Spend the day paddling and exploring the pristine waters of a wilderness lake rich in Maine's logging history. Moose, loons, osprey abound – bring your camera. ☎ 800-765-7238.

■ Houseboat Rentals

Aquaflo Houseboat Rentals, PO Box 117, Greenville 04441. Perhaps the best way to explore Moosehead Lake's hundreds of miles of shoreline is to rent your own floating base camp. You can wander around the lake for a week or return each night to your slip at the marina in town. This firm rents 30-foot houseboats, all of which are very stable due to their catamaran design. Each has a cabin and topside sundeck. Ideal for four to six people. Houseboats include 50 hp motor, marine radio, life jackets and safety gear as well as a depth sounder. Amenities include hot-air furnace, fresh water tank, shower and flush toilets. The galley has a two-burner stove, ice chest, dishes, utensils, pots and pans. Towels, blankets and pillows are provided. Prices are $165 per day or a maximum of $1,000 per week. No pets. There is plenty of parking, and instruction on operating a houseboat is free. Security deposit required. Renter is responsible for deductible on insurance ($800) in the event of an accident or damage. ☎ 695-3494.

■ Cruises, Boat Rides

Kineo Boat Shuttle. An open shuttle boat from Rockwood on the west shore of Moosehead Lake to Mount Kineo (see *Parks & Preserves*) runs every hour in season, and every two hours in June. Round-trip fare is around $5 per person. Boat operated by Registered Maine Guide. Next door is a comfortable, intimate and friendly full-service inn, the Kineo House. ☎ 534-8812.

Katahdin Cruises. PO Box 1151, Greenville 04441. Pleasure cruises on Moosehead Lake aboard the steamship *Katahdin*, affectionately referred to by the locals as "The Kate."

This steamship is the last representative of a fleet of vessels that worked rafts of logs around the lake and delivered passengers and freight. This is the best way to see the area, particularly in foliage season (late September). Operated by the non-profit Moosehead Marine Museum. Tours vary from three to six hours in length. Adult ticket prices range from $13 to $32, children pay less. ☎ 695-2716.

The Wilderness Boat, Box 41, Rockwood 04478. Guided moose safari boat trips as well as tours of the Mount Kineo peninsula. Foliage cruises and charters available. Reservations suggested. ☎ 534-2242.

Jolly Roger's Moosehead Cruises, Box 41, Rockwood 04478. The 48-foot, 45-passenger vessel the *Socatean* conducts regular guided tours of Moosehead Lake and Kineo. Sunset cruises and charters available. ☎ 534-8827.

Great North Woods

Katahdin View Pontoon Boat Rides, 210 Morgan Lane, Millinocket 04462. Regular 1½- or two-hour trips on Millinocket Lake offering wildlife and sunset watching. Good views of Katahdin. Adults $12, children less. ☎ 723-9712.

■ Fishing

Maine Guide Fly Shop, PO Box 1202, Greenville 04441. Those in the know always stop by this Route 15 mainstay to ask how the fishing's been. Canoe rentals, weekly fly fishing clinics and guided trips are available. Product line includes Orvis, Sage, and Cortland. ☎ 695-2266.

Adventures In the Air

■ Air Charter, Transport

Greenville

With three float plane services offering transport into the wilds of the northern part of the state, Greenville is the busiest water-air hub in the state. Each September there is a special float plane fly-in that attracts pilots from all over North America. There is a small airport and paved runway just outside town.

Currier's Flying Service, off Route 15, Greenville Junction 04442. Custom sightseeing flights as well as passenger and freight service to the far north. Trips can be tailored to include Moosehead Lake and Katahdin. Passengers can also come along on occassional forest fire patrol flights. Prices range from $15 to $80 per person, depending on time aloft. ☎ 695-2778.

Folsom's Flying Service, PO Box 507, Greenville 04441. Legends in the north, members of the Folsom family have been ferrying people and goods into remote lakes and ponds for three generations. In operation since 1948. Custom sightseeing trips and shuttles to remote cabin locations. Folsom's base is easy to spot. Just look on the east side of the cove for the massive DC-3 on floats, a WW II-vintage craft that the company dusts off for the annual seaplane fly-in. ☎ 695-2821.

Jack's Air Service, PO Box 338, Greenville 04441. Operates Cessna float planes with custom services for hunters, anglers and canoeists. Fly in to this company's remote housekeeping cabins. Their base in town also rents boats and canoes. Sightseeing tours available. ☎ 695-3020.

Jackman

Coleman's Flying and Guide Service, HCR 76, Box 102, Jackman 04945. Scenic float plane rides evenings, weekends and other times by appointment. Flights into remote lakes for backcountry fishing. Rates start at $20. ☎ 668-4436.

Millinocket

Katahdin Air Service, Box 171, Millinocket 04462. Full air/float plane service offering everything from scenic flights to Appalachian Trail shuttle service, canoe trip shuttles and day trips to remote ponds all over Northern Maine. Furnished remote camps accessible only by float plane for rent. Canoes and boats available for fishermen at some remote ponds. Cost is $15 and up. ☎ 723-8378.

Shin Pond

Scotty's Flying Service. Float plane service for fishermen, campers, canoeists throughout Northern Maine. Camp, cabins and boat rentals. Guides available. ☎ 528-2626.

Adventures On Snow

■ Downhill Skiing

Bingham

 Baker Mountain. 460 feet vertical, four trails, one lift, ski school, snack bar. Basically a side-hill, straight shot, local slope. ☎ 672-5580.

Greenville

Squaw Mountain Resort, PO Box D, Greenville 04441. 1,750-foot vertical drop, 18 trails, four lifts, 20% snowmaking, ski shop, rentals, lessons, on-mountain lodging, cafeteria, restaurant, lounge, Nordic skiing nearby. Squaw Mountain is perhaps Maine's "sleeper" ski area. The trendy crowds have yet to discover Squaw, much to its credit. The lift tickets are reasonable, and a cup of hot chocolate in the snack bar won't set you back too much. Squaw has everything the big mountains have except the crowds and the high prices (call to find out the latest fees). Views of frozen Moosehead Lake and Katahdin from the trails are spectacular. ☎ 695-2272.

Lee

Mount Jefferson, HCR 65, Box 671, Lincoln Ct. 04458. 432-foot vertical drop, 10 trails, three lifts, night skiing, rentals, lessons, cafeteria. Adult lift ticket $15. ☎ 738-2377.

■ Cross-Country Skiing

Caratunk

 Sterling Inn, Box 21, Caratunk 04925. Guided backcountry ski tours. ☎ 800-766-7238.

Greenville

Moosehead Nordic Ski Center, Scammon Road, PO Box 61, Greenville 04441. Sixteen miles of groomed trails for all experience levels. Equipment rentals, lessons. ☎ 695-2870.

Northwoods Outfitters Inc., PO Box 160 Greenville 04441. Rentals, sales, service of canoes, kayaks, bikes, skis, snowshoes, camping gear, guided and self-guided trips. ☎ 695-3288.

Rangeley

Rangeley Lake State Park. One mile of groomed ski trails plus other trails open to snowshoeing and snowmobiling. ☎ 624-6080.

Rockwood

The Birches Ski Touring Center, Rockwood 04478. Thirty miles of backcountry trails. Snowshoeing, remote skiing to backcountry yurts, lessons, rentals, snack bar, hot tub/sauna. ☎ 800-825-WILD.

Shin Pond, RR 1, Box 280, Patten 04765. Shin Pond Village is a family-operated recreational facility offering campsites, five guest rooms and cabins. Cross-country ski rentals and trails from the door. At junction of snowmobile trails, with fuel, oil and food available. ☎ 528-2900.

■ Snowmobiling

Maine's Great North Woods is prime snowmobiling country. The machines allow riders access to areas that may be too remote or gated off in better weather.

Jackman

Located on the shore of Big Wood Pond, Jackman puts out its welcome mat for snowmobilers. There is no place in town – shop, restaurant, lodging establishment – that can't be reached by sled. Most have their own exits clearly marked off the ITS.

There are big woods around Jackman and plenty of trails and tote roads to explore. Favorite rides include a cruise up to the **Canadian border** where you can clear Customs on the sled and head another 30 miles into Quebec to a clubhouse. As long as you go only there and back there is no need to register your sled in Canada.

Other popular rides include south toward **Eustis**, and north and east to **Pittston Farm**, a former logging supply outpost well north of Moosehead Lake that now sells food and fuel to as many as 1,000 snowmobilers a day.

Greenville

Snowmobile trails branch out in every direction from Greenville. Including ITS, club, and local trails, there's probably more than 300 miles of trails. In fact, the town is so snowmobile friendly that it holds a parade each year and a fireworks show out on frozen Moosehead Lake. There are several day trips possible, including circumnavigations of the lake. The longer trip takes riders through Rockwood, up to Northeast Carry, and back down the east shore.

A shorter route follows the well-marked trail across the narrow part of the lake at Rockwood to **Mount Kineo**. You can ride right to the base of the 1,000-foot cliffs.

INTERESTING FACT: *A warden counting sleds crossing the lake at Kineo once clicked off 3,000 sleds on a single Saturday when the weather was good.*

On the east side of the Moosehead circuit plan to stop at the **Kokadjo Trading Post** for a hearty lunch. This one tiny outpost will often have more than 200 sleds parked outside.

From Greenville riders can also head over to **Jackman** or south to the **Monson, Dover-Foxcroft** area.

Great North Woods

Millinocket

It may be a mill town, but Millinocket is also a prime snowmobiling hub. Like other Northern Maine towns you can get anywhere you want by sled. An adult entertainment club in a nearby unorganized township even has its own trail signs beckoning riders to stop in.

One of the nicest rides starts at the East Branch Sno Rovers Clubhouse in **Medway** and heads north along the East Branch of the Penobscot River. Clubs like the Rovers run the large grooming machines that keep the trails in such fine shape. There will be occasional glimpses of snow-covered Katahdin to the north and west. At Bowlin Falls, the trail crosses the river on a 100-foot suspension bridge built especially for snowmobiles. Have lunch at Bowlin Camps or continue on to Shin Pond.

Trails also lead west from Millinocket toward **Chesuncook** and into **Baxter State Park**. Only the Baxter perimeter road, which is open in season to cars, is available for use by snowmobiles. The way is not groomed and downed trees may be a problem.

Eco-Tours & Cultural Excursions

■ Moose Safari

 The Float Boat, Route 15, Rockwood. Pontoon boat offers wildlife and moose-watching tours on the Moose River where it empties into Moosehead Lake. Trips also run along the lake shore. Leaves from Moose River Store. ☎ 534-7352.

■ Apple Picking

 Fall is the season for picking your own fresh apples. Here's a pick-your-own farm in the Great North Woods.

Pick-Your-Own Apples

Charleston

■ **Olmstead's Orchard**, Route 15, ☎ 285-3426.

Where to Stay & Eat

Rate Scale
All rates are for entrée or complete dinner, per person.
Inexpensive. . . . . under $10
Moderate . . . . $10-$20
Expensive . . . . More than $20

■ Favorite Restaurants

 Pittston Farm, Pittston Academy Grant, PO Box 525, Rockwood 04478. Located north and somewhat west of Moosehead Lake about 25 miles above Rockwood. Its location means that few people arrive here for breakfast, lunch or dinner by accident. This outpost of civilization was a working farm supling food for the logging industry in the late 1800s. Today, from May 10 through April 10, the 65-seat restaurant is open to the public and is especially busy during snowmobile season when as many as 300 sleds can crowd the yard at one time. Their tasty, home-cooked smorgasbord offers a mountain of delicious food.

The inn at Pittston farm can accommodate as many as 60 people in cabins and a carriage house. There is no phone. You can ask the folks at Folsom's Flying Service in Greenville (☎ 695-2821) to contact the farm by radio. Folsom's also has a special flight from their base to the farm for diners. You can also write ahead for reservations, but mail is picked up only three days a week. Inexpensive.

Greenville

Frog Rock Café, Pritham Avenue, Greenville 04441. This restaurant was the founding branch of the wacko Road Kill Café chain, but the original owners fell out with the Wall Street types fueling the expansion and went back to just the one establishment. They changed the name but the quality of service and food remains good. Open year-round for lunch and dinner with full cocktail service. Handicapped accessible. Take out available. Moderate. ☎ 695-2230.

Kelly's Landing, PO Box 336, Greenville Junction 04442. Popular family-style restaurant located right on the lake offers a wide, varied menu including steaks, seafood, chops, pasta, salad bar. Cocktail lounge. Motel on second floor has air-conditioning, cable TV, phones. Private beach and free docking on property. Inexpensive to moderate. ☎ 695-4438.

Jackman

Moose Point Tavern, Route 201, Jackman 04945. Former sporting camp lodge on the shore of Big Wood Pond. Great food with imaginative specials and appetizers. The dining room has hardwood floors and a fireplace. Full dinners to burgers offered. Hunters' plates and prime rib specials on weekends. Inexpensive to moderate. ☎ 668-4012.

Hog's Breath, Route 201, Jackman 04945. Located just north of town, this combination restaurant, motel and lounge offers a wide variety of standard fare from steaks to seafood. Full bar; live band on weekends. Inexpensive to moderate. ☎ 668-2721.

Millinocket

Hotel Terrace, 52 Medway Road, Millinocket 04462. Famous for their Sunday brunch buffet which brings people in from miles away. Open seven days a week for breakfast, lunch and dinner. Breakfast buffet every day beginning at 5:30 am. The large open dining room can get a bit noisy – it's a popular place. Cocktails available. Inexpensive to moderate. ☎ 723-4525.

River Drivers' Restaurant, Medway Road, Millinocket 04462. Located at the New England Outdoor Center's Rice Farm, this restaurant with a view of the Penobscot is open year-round for dinner. Lunch is served seasonally. Menu includes BBQ, fresh seafood, steaks, chicken, pasta and vegetarian dishes. Desserts and bread are made on-premises. Lounge. Moderate. ☎ 723-5438.

■ B&Bs, Hotels & Motels

Cabins

 Great Northern Cabins. In 1998 Great Northern Paper Company authorized construction of four rustic log cabins on their lands adjacent to Baxter State Park and along the West Branch of the Penobscot River near Millinocket. These isolated, snug units include bunks for six (more can crash on the floor), gas lights, a gas furnace, a sink with wash water, log table and chairs, a porch and a heated, insulated privy. Users need to bring sleeping pads, cooking gear, drinking and cooking water pots, pans, coolers etc. All units can be accessed year-round by vehicle or by a short walk, ski, or snowmobile trip. Some are on lakes with views of Katahdin and nearby mountains.

Rates for 1999 are $72 per night for six, not including tax. For reservations and information, contact Great Northern Paper Company, 1024 Central Street, Millinocket 04462. ☎ 877-622-2467 (toll-free) or 723-2105.

Bowlin Camps, PO Box 251, Patten 04765. Established in 1895, this cluster of wood stove-heated log cabins and cottages and a main lodge is located on the East Branch of the Penobscot River at the end of a 14-mile private road. Full American Plan available. For cabins without private baths there is a heated common bath house with showers, sinks and toilets. Located on ITS. The camp owns a spectacular suspension bridge, which is used by snowmobilers and fishermen. Electricity from the camp generator is available for most of the day. Satellite TV in lodge. Inexpensive. ☎ 528-2022.

Price Scale
All rates are based on double occupancy.
Inexpensive . . . . Under $65
Moderate . . . . $66-$100
Expensive. . . . . Above $100

Bingham

Bingham Motor Inn, PO Box 683, Bingham 04920. Modern motel and housekeeping units located on Route 201. Full bath with showers, phones, cable TV, restaurants nearby. Located on ITS. ☎ 672-4135.

Chesuncook Village

Chesuncook Lake House, Route 76, Box 656, Greenville 04441. Located in a quiet, simple, historic village on the west shore of windswept Chesuncook Lake. Unreachable by car; boat, foot, or float plane access only. Great views of Katahdin and mountains of Baxter State Park to the east. Offers Full American Plan to all guests. A popular stop-over by canoeists doing the West Branch of the Penobscot River. Boat and canoe rentals. Canoe, people and gear shuttle down the lake can be arranged. Reservations required. Inexpensive. Write or call Folsom's Flying Service in Greenville, ☎ 695-2821; Radio phone direct, ☎ 745-5330.

Greenville

Indian Hill Motel, PO Box 327, Greenville Junction 04442. Older, clean motel located on a hilltop on Route 15, with good views of Moosehead Lake. Cable TV with HBO and ESPN, telephones, store across the street. Handicapped access. Inexpensive. ☎ 695-2623.

Kineo View Motel, PO Box 514, Greenville 04441. Located on a hill just south of town on Route 15. Every room has great views of the lake and of Mount Kineo to the north. This is the area's newest motel. Satellite TV, phones, free Green Mountain coffee, hot tub. Private snowmobile trail connects to ITS. Inexpensive to moderate. ☎ 695-4470.

The Lodge At Moosehead, Box 1167, Lily Bay Road, Greenville 04441. Five luxury rooms with fireplaces and jacuzzis. No smoking. Magnificent views out over Moosehead Lake. Cable TV. Moose safaris offered in spring, summer and fall. Dogsledding on grounds in winter. The only AAA Four-Diamond establishment in inland Maine. Expensive. ☎ 695-4400.

Wilson Pond Camps, PO Box 1354, Greenville 04441. Situated on crystal-clear Lower Wilson Pond just a few miles from Greenville. Five attractive cottages each with ample sleeping quarters, kitchens, modern baths, porches, blankets and pillows. Ask about their newest cottage, "Top Secret," on a remote point of land, accessible only by a 30-minute boat ride or by float plane. It sports gas lights and appliances and has one of the best sunset views in Maine. Open year-round. Daily and weekly rates offered. Inexpensive. Boat, canoe and motor rentals available. ☎ 695-2860.

Guilford

Packard's Camps, RFD #2, Box 176, Guilford 04443. This cluster of cozy lakeside cabins and main lodge is now being run by the fifth generation of the Packard family. All housekeeping cottages come with bedrooms, baths, kitchens and living rooms. Most have screened porches. There is a tackle shop, small store, boat ramp and dock and boat rentals on property as well as several lakeside campsites. Inexpensive. ☎ 997-3300.

Jackman

Bishop's Motel, PO Box 158, Jackman 04945. Located in the heart of the village on Route 201. This is the town's newest motel. Very modern with phones, cable TV, in-room refrigerators, free continental breakfast. Kids stay free. Inexpensive. ☎ 888-991-7669.

Cedar Ridge Outfitters, PO Box 744, Jackman 04945. Guides Hal and Debbie Blood have built up their business over the years, and it now has a variety of modern housekeeping cabins and larger duplexes that are open year-round. Guided hunting, fishing, snowmobiling and canoe trips available. Handicapped accessible. All rentals include modern bath with shower, kitchens and linens. Modified American Plan available. Inexpensive. Just minutes from town on Attean Road. Private snowmobile trail to lake, ITS. ☎ 668-4169.

Sky Lodge, Route 201, Moose River 04945. Main lodge and lounge is in massive log building that was once a private home. Separate motel units and restaurant at two sites and housekeeping log cabins. Moderate. ☎ 668-2171.

Kokadjo

Kokadjo Trading Post and Camps, HC 76, Box 590, Kokadjo 04441. Nine fully-equipped housekeeping camps with gas lights and wood stoves. The restaurant and lounge at the trading post near Roach River dam is a popular snowmobile lunch spot. Gasoline, LP gas, and snowmobile rentals. Inexpensive. ☎ 695-3993.

Northern Pride Lodge, HC 76, Box 588, Kokadjo 04441. Five handsomely appointed rooms in lodge on shores of First Roach Pond. Public invited to dining room in main lodge (built 1896) with large stone fireplace. Also operates a small campground with hot showers, electricity from the lodge's generator, fire rings and picnic tables. Boat, canoe and motor as well as mountain bike and helmet rentals. Rates, which include breakfast, are inexpensive. Full American Plan available. ☎ 695-2890.

Millinocket

The Atrium, 740 Central Street, Millinocket 04462. Features 72 rooms and 10 king suites, indoor lap pool, health club, complimentary breakfast, hot tub, jacuzzi rooms, lounge. Moderate to expensive. Honestly, this place looks like a prison from the outside, but it will grow on you once you see the decor. ☎ 723-4555.

Gateway Inn, PO Box 380, Medway 04460. The newest motel in Millinocket/Baxter State Park area, located on Route 11. It has 36 modern rooms. Guests have use of hot tub, indoor pool and exercise room. Cable TV, phones, handicapped accessible, air-conditioned. Pets welcome. Moderate. ☎ 746-3193.

Nahmakanta Lake Camps, PO Box 544, Millinocket 04462. Located in the heart of a vast wilderness on Nahmakanta Lake, these seven cabins accommodate from two to eight people. All have lake views, screened porches, wood stoves and gas lights. Some have housekeeping facilities. There is a common shower and toilet building with plenty of hot and cold running water. Each cabin has a fresh water spigot out front and private privy in back. Linens provided. There is no electricity. Housekeeping cabins $35 per person, per day. Modified and Full American Plan available. FAP is $75 per person, per day. Family rates available. Boat rental on Nahmakanta Lake. Boats and canoes at remote ponds in area may be used at no charge. Hiking trails. Good fishing. Road access is rough. Float plane access allowed. ☎ 746-7356.

Rockwood

The Birches, PO Box 41, Rockwood 04478. Located on a point about midway up the west side of Moosehead Lake on Route 15, the Birches offers 15 log cabins with running water and electricity, one or two baths, cooking facilities, roofed porch and wood stoves. Pets allowed. The lakeside dining room in the main lodge serves up prime rib, seafood, chicken and vegetarian dishes. The lodge has four B&B rooms. The same firm also operates a system of backcountry yurts and cabin tents. Open year-round. Moderate. ☎ 534-2242.

Kineo House, PO Box 397, Rockwood 04478. You have to take a shuttle boat from Rockwood to reach this attractive inn on a peninsula at the base of 800-foot Mount Kineo. Six rooms. Cable television. Lounge. Lunch and dinner offered to the public. Nine-hole golf course. Moderate. ☎ 534-8812.

The Forks

Northern Outdoors, PO Box 100, The Forks 04985. A total adventure trip company that runs a variety of lodgings, as well as a brew pub. Located on Route 201. Activities offered: a climbing wall, whitewater rafting, rock climbing, guided canoe, kayak and float trips, fishing and snowmobiling. Accommodations include log cabins with ¾ baths and mini-kitchenettes, a large condo off the main lodge that sleeps 10, four-bedroom cottage, "logdominum" units that sleep up to eight each and standard motel-like lodge rooms. Pool, tennis court, sauna and 16-person hot tub. Owned by raconteur Wayne Hockmeyer, inventor of the famous Banjo Minnow lure that supposedly drives fish crazy. Moderate to expensive. ☎ 663-4466.

■ Camping

 Facilities indicated as "nearby" are located within one mile of the campground.

Abbot Village

Balsam Woods Campground, 112 Pond Road, Abbot Village 04406. A quiet, exceptionally clean, modern campground. Centrally located. Facilities and recreation for the entire family. Explore the surrounding woods. 50 sites, tenting area, 30 amp, sewer, dump station, store, laundry, rec hall, pool, on-site rentals, group area, LP gas. Pets allowed. Open May 15-November 22. ☎ 876-2731.

Greenville

Allagash Gateway Campsite, Star Route 76, Box 675, Greenville 04441. Enjoy camping, fishing, hunting, hiking, rafting, canoeing, moose-watching or just relaxing while staying on beautiful Ripogenus Lake. Camp rentals available also. 30 sites, tenting area, swimming, boating, fishing, on-site rentals, group area. Dump station and store nearby. Open May 1-November 30. ☎ 723-9215.

Casey's Spencer Bay Camps, PO Box 1190, Greenville 04441. Quiet wilderness family camping off Lily Bay Road. Moose and loons are abundant. Spectacular sunrises and sunsets. Beach, showers, marina and store. 50 sites, tenting area, 20 amp, sewer, dump station, swimming, boating, fishing, on-site rentals, group area. Pets allowed. Open May 15-October 15. ☎ 695-2801.

Frost Pond Campground, HCR 76, Box 620, Greenville 04441. Ten wooded campsites on wilderness trout lake (Chesuncook Lake), off the Golden Road. Eight fully-equipped housekeeping cabins. Minutes to Moosehead Lake. One hour to Baxter State Park. Showers, canoes, boats, motors. Great family vacation spot. Tenting area, swimming, boating, fishing. Pets allowed. Open May 15-September 30. ☎ 695-2821.

Moosehead Family Campground, PO Box 307, Greenville 04441. Near Greenville and all area amenities. Centrally located near favorite fishing and hiking areas on Route 15. Electric service of 20, 30 and 50 amps; well water. Pull-throughs available, all sizes. 35 sites, tenting area, dump station, store, rec hall. Swimming, boating, fishing, and LP gas nearby. Pets allowed. Open May 1-November 30. ☎ 695-2210.

Jackman

Jackman Landing Campground, PO Box 567, Jackman 04945. Jackman Landing sits on the Moose River off Route 201. It has boat access into Big Wood Pond. Electric and cable hook-ups with dumping station and laundromat on-site. Float plane rides on-site. 25 sites, tenting area, 30 amp, swimming, boating, fishing, group area. Pets allowed. Open year-round. ☎ 668-3301.

John's Four Season Accommodations, SR 64, Box 132, John Street, Jackman 04945. All wooded sites. Restaurant with beer/wine, winter center snowmobile area, numerous groomed trails. Any size group accommodations. Barbecues every Saturday, outside eating under tents with music. Handicap accessible. 12 sites, tenting area, 30 amp, sewer, dump station, laundry, rec hall, on-site rentals. Store, swimming, boating, fishing and LP gas nearby. Pets allowed. Open year-round. Remote cabin at Holeb makes a good jumping-off place for the Moose River. ☎ 668-7683.

The Last Resort Campground and Cabins, PO Box 777, Jackman 04945. Located on Route 15. Four wilderness tent sites with outhouse, fire rings, picnic tables in fir grove on Long Lake. Canoe/boat rentals, showers available. Swimming, hiking, moose watching. Tenting area, four sites, swimming, boating, fishing. Pets allowed. Open Memorial Day-Columbus Day. ☎ 668-5091.

Loon Echo Family Campground, PO Box 711, Jackman 04945. Quiet, nature-oriented camping on 900 feet of unspoiled lakefront away from crowds on Route 201. Friendly atmosphere, cozy gardens on site, clean, free hot showers. 15 sites, tenting area, dump station, swimming, boating, fishing, on-site rentals, group area. Pets allowed. Open May 15-Labor Day. ☎ 668-4829.

Moose River Campground, Heald Stream Road, PO Box 98, Jackman 04045. 52 sites, tenting area, 50 amp, sewer, dump station, store, laundry, rec hall, fishing, pool, on-site rentals, group area. Pets allowed. Open May 15-November 1. ☎ 668-3341.

Lincoln

Lakeside Camping and Cabins, PO Box 38, Lincoln 04457. Open camping on Route 155 alongside a spring-fed, crystal-clear, sand-bottom lake. Beautiful beach, great swimming, plenty of loons. Boat docking available. Quiet, laid-back camping. 32 sites, tenting area, 15 amp, sewer, dump station, store, rec hall, swimming, boating, fishing. Pets allowed. Open Memorial Day-September 30. ☎ 732-4241.

Medway

Katahdin Shadows Campground, PO Box H, Medway 04460. The crown jewel of Northern Maine campgrounds. A modern, friendly, full-service facility at the gateway to Baxter State Park, Katahdin, and the North Maine Woods. 115 sites, tenting area, 50 amp, sewer, dump station, store, laundry, rec hall, swimming, pool, on-site rentals, group area, LP gas. Boating and fishing nearby. Pets allowed. Open May 1-March 31. ☎ 746-9349.

Pine Grove Campground and Cottages, HCR 86, Box 107, Medway 04460. Beautiful waterfront sites and full hook-ups, free use of canoes (to use on-site), also canoe rentals (for use off-site). Three cottages, showers, flushes, basketball, horseshoes, and playground. 43 sites, tenting area, 30 amp, sewer, dump station, store, laundry, rec hall, swimming, boating, fishing. Pets allowed. Open May 15-September 30. ☎ 746-5172.

Millinocket

Abol Bridge Campground, PO Box 536, Millinocket 04462. Located on the West Branch of the Penobscot River on Great Northern's Golden Road with a beautiful view of Mount Katahdin. 36 sites, tenting area, store, swimming, fishing, LP gas. Pets allowed. Open May 15-September 30. No phone.

Big Moose Inn Cabins and Campground, PO Box 98, Millinocket 04462. Located between two freshwater lakes, eight miles from Baxter State Park on Baxter Park Road. Swimming, boating, fishing, canoeing, whitewater raft trips, showers, flush toilets, well water and restaurant. 44 sites, tenting area, store, boating, fishing, group area. Pets allowed. Open May 15-Columbus Day. ☎ 723-8391.

Hidden Springs Campground, 224 Central Street, Millinocket 04462. This new campground is located just outside of Millinocket, 15 minutes from Baxter State Park entrance. Tent and RV sites, free hot showers, bike trails, swimming pool. 120 sites, tenting area, 50 amp, dump station, store, laundry, swimming, group area. Pets allowed. Open May 15-November 8. ☎ 723-6337.

Jo-Mary Lake Campground, PO Box 329, Millinocket 04462. Located on a lake off Jo-Mary Road with a quarter-mile-long sand beach in the campground. Bean hole bean suppers every Wednesday. 60 sites, tenting area, dump station, store, laundry, rec hall, swimming, boating, fishing, on-site rentals, group area, LP gas. Pets allowed. Open May 15-September 30. ☎ 723-8117.

Bean Hole Beans

Bean Hole Beans are cooked the way log drivers and lumber men did it. A hole is dug, sometimes lined with rocks, and a large fire is set and kept going for a day. When the wood burns down to coals a cast iron pot of beans with water and spices is lowered into the hole. The pot is then covered with canvas and the entire hole is covered with dirt and left to cook for a day. The result is a pot of delicious baked beans not made "in a brick oven," as is fancied today, but rather right in the ground.

Great North Woods

Rice Farm Campground at N.E.O.C., PO Box 669, Millinocket 04462. Located on Route 11. Whitewater rafting adventures on Maine's Kennebec, Dead, and Penobscot Rivers. Lakeside lodging in B&B and cabins or camping. 38 sites, tenting area, store, rec hall, swimming, boating, fishing, on-site rentals, group area. Dump station nearby. Open May 1-October 31. ☎ 723-5438.

Patten

Matagamon Wilderness Campground, PO Box 220, Patten 04765. Wilderness campground bordering Baxter State Park on Grand Lake Road, on the East Branch Penobscot River, near Matagamon Lake. Fish for salmon, brook trout, and togue. Hot showers and cabins. 36 sites, tenting area, dump station, store, swimming, boating, fishing, on-site rentals, group area, LP gas. Pets allowed. Open April 1-December 1. Cabins open year-round. ☎ 528-2448.

Shin Pond Village Campground, RR 1, Box 280, Patten 04765. Located 15 miles from the northern entrance to Baxter State Park. Great fishing, scenic views, uncrowded hiking adventures, wildlife and family fun in a natural, peaceful setting. 25 sites, tenting area, 30 amp, dump station, store, laundry, rec hall, swimming, fishing, on-site rentals, group area. Boating and LP gas nearby. Pets allowed. Open year-round. ☎ 528-2900.

Richmond

Nesowadnehunk Campground, RR 1, Box 330H, Marston Road, Richmond 04357. Fly fisherman's paradise on Maine's largest fly fishing lake. Located next to Baxter State Park, for hiking and backpacking. 41 sites, tenting area, 15 amp, sewer, dump station, store, rec hall, swimming, boating, fishing, on-site rentals, group area, LP gas, pets allowed. Open May 15-October 15. ☎ 737-4739.

Rockwood

Old Mill Campground and Cabins, PO Box 189, Rockwood 04478. Located on the west shore of Moosehead Lake, overlooking Mount Kineo, on Route 15. Boat launch and docking area. 50 sites, tenting area, 15 amp, sewer, dump station, store, laundry, swimming, boating, fishing, on-site rentals. LP gas nearby. Pets allowed. Open May 15-Columbus Day. ☎ 534-7333.

Seboomook Campground, HC 85, Box 560, Rockwood 04478. Located on the northwest shore of Moosehead Lake, midway on Moosehead snowmobile trail. Heated year-round cabins, RV sites, tent sites, heated bathhouse. 84 sites, tenting area, 15 amp, sewer, dump station, store, swimming, boating, fishing, group area, LP gas. Pets allowed. ☎ 534-8824.

The Forks

Indian Pond Campground, HCR 63, Box 52, The Forks 04985. Central Maine Power Company welcomes you to the spectacular wilderness of Western Maine. 27 wooded sites with fishing, hiking, biking, and whitewater rafting. 27 sites, tenting area, dump station, store, laundry, swimming, boating, fishing, group area. Pets allowed. Open April 15-October 15. ☎ 371-7774.

The Far North

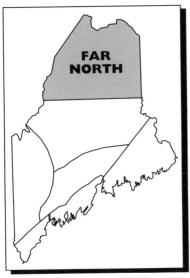

FAR NORTH

For years folks in the state have talked about there being two Maines. They refer to the economic disparity between the comparatively prosperous southern part of the state, with its more urban lifestyles and manufacturing and office jobs, and the distinctly rural parts of the state where folks still wrest a hard living from the land or the sea. In that respect, the two Maines are not so much actual locations, but rather distinct sets of circumstances.

When it comes to geography and culture, however, there are really *three* Maines. There is the coastal area, the central highlands (also referred to as the Great North Woods) and then there is the Far North, primarily Aroostook County.

Known as "The County," Aroostook opens up to visitors as they pass the towns of Medway and Patten on the way north on Interstate 95. A solid wall of trees gives way to rolling countryside planted with potatoes as far as the eye can see. More than 1½ million pounds of potatoes are produced annually in Aroostook County and there are plans to bring another 15,000 acres "on-line" at the turn of the century. In recent years, broccoli has become an important crop as well. Covering more than 4.2 million acres, Aroostook is the largest county in Maine and nearly double the size of the next two largest combined.

In this pastoral landscape, the culture and inhabitants feel strong ties to French-speaking Québec. In many cases, particularly at the tip of the state in places like Fort Kent, Madawaska and Van Buren, French is the primary language.

The area maintains a multi-cultural flair. Double Eagle Park on the Spragueville Road in Presque Isle marks the spot where the first ballonists to cross the Atlantic took off in 1978. The crew took less than a week to get to – you guessed it – France.

Even in the best of years you could not say times were good in Aroostook County. The closing of Loring Air Force Base in Limestone several years ago contributed to a population drop of more than 10,000. Still, despite economic disadvantage, the people of the country remain hard-working, generous and friendly. Most welcome the arrival of more than 70,000 young fans of the band Phish, who take over the former bomber base for several days of music and fun each summer.

Towns like Caribou and Houlton are strong commercial centers.

Sporting traditions such as hunting and fishing remain healthy in the Far North. The Allagash Wilderness Waterway continues to attract thousands of canoeists each year. Hidden to all but those with special knowledge, the hills here harbor caves where ice remains all year. It is a difficult journey by water and foot to find them, but they are unique places to visit.

An international extension of the famous Appalachian Trail – which will begin at the present terminus in Baxter State Park and end on the Gaspé Penninsula in Canada – is presently being constructed. Sections over Mars Hill near the New Brunswick border are already completed.

Aroostook holds the most remote and wild country in the Northeast United States. Evidence of the occasional visit by wolves has spurred hopes for their reintroduction. Small and pristine state parks seldom see the crowds endured by more popular areas to the south.

- ■ Note: Maine has one area code – 207.

Parks & Preserves

■ Private Lands

The vast majority of land in the Great North Woods is private, owned by paper companies and land holding firms. As a matter of tradition it is open to the public for fishing, hunting, camping, hiking and canoeing. Some paper company roads are gated and modest fees are charged for day use and for use of campsites or cabins maintained by these companies. Occasionally, a small area may be closed for safety reasons during timber harvesting operations. (See page 403 in the previous chapter for advice on traveling these lands.)

North Maine Woods, Ashland

North Maine Woods Inc. oversees more than three million acres of working forest for a consortium of more than 20 major landowners. There are more than 2,000 miles of gravel roads and most of the land is either being harvested for pulp and saw logs or has been in the past. Many areas are on their third cycle of cutting and regeneration.

While not billing itself as a wilderness, the North Maine Woods is home to two of the best scenic rivers in the Northeast – the Allagash and the St. John. It is also open to campers, hunters, fishermen and explorers who seek the rewards only found some distance from civilization. There are no tow trucks, gas stations, motels or restaurants out here. In all, the organization takes care of 280 remote campsites. Major areas of control include far Northern Maine, the Great Northern Paper-West Branch region and the KI, Jo-Mary Multiple Use Forest area near Brownville.

Write or call North Maine Woods for the latest information on checkpoint hours and hours the US and Canadian Customs officials work at border stations. (PO Box 421, Ashland 04732, ☎ 435-6213.)

North Maine Woods General Regulations

- Visitors must log in and log out at a checkpoint on each visit.
- Trucks have the right of way.
- Camp only where permitted by prior reservation.
- Do not block any road at any time.
- Carry out all trash.
- Obtain fire permits where required.
- Commercial users must obtain operator permits.
- Bicycles, motorcycles, ATVs, and horses are banned.
- All general Maine laws and hunting and fishing regulations apply.
- Cutting live trees for firewood or other uses is prohibited.

Far North

Campsites

There are two types of campsites in the North Maine Woods.

Authorized Campsites, which are marked on maps, have steel fire rings, picnic tables, and privies. Fire may be kindled in the rings without a permit.

Designated Fire Permit Campsites are generally more rustic and lack fire rings and privies. Fire permits must be obtained from the Maine Forest Service in advance. They can be reached in Ashland seven days a week at ☎ 435-7963. The fine for leaving a fire unattended is $50.

More than 40 businesses operate at various locations throughout the three million acres administered by North Maine Woods. A list can be obtained at the office.

For camping reservations, call ☎ 435-6213 weekdays. A maximum of two vehicles and six adults is permitted per site. The maximum length of stay is 14 days.

For those flying into remote campsites by float plane, proper permits must still be obtained in advance.

Large motor homes are banned from the North Maine Woods. Single vehicles longer than 28 feet or vehicles with trailers totalling more than 44 feet are prohibited. Large vehicles may be restricted to certain times of day depending on logging and hauling operations.

There is no charge for day use by anyone under age 15 or over age 70. Maine residents must pay a $4 per-day fee; non-residents pay $7. Commercial sporting camp visitors pay a one-time fee ($15 for Maine residents and $21 for non-residents). The additional fee for camping is $5 per per person, per night. Season passes are available at a substantial discount. There is a financial penalty for showing up at checkpoints after hours.

Mailing address: PO Box 421, Ashland 04732, ☎ 435-6213.

The Allagash Wilderness Waterway

With a length of nearly 100 miles and dozens of potential combinations of put-ins and take-outs, the Allagash Wilderness Waterway is considered the premier paddle trip on the East Coast. See *Adventures on Water*, pages 468-470, for in-depth descriptions of canoe/kayak routes.

From its southernmost point at a dam on Telos Lake in Township 6, Range 11, to its official terminus at Twin Brook in Allagash Village, near where the Allagash River melds with the St. John, this delightful waterway includes broad, windswept lakes, quiet backwaters, turbulent rapids and a spectacular falls. It is composed of a restricted zone, a strip 500 feet wide on both sides of the river, a new construction area roughly a quarter-mile from the edge of the inner zone, a one-mile area stretching back farther still, and areas simply visible from the river.

State officials call the north woods in this area "the heart of a working forest." The area holds unique opportunities to save not only the vestiges of wilderness but also historical artifacts and buildings from the bygone lumbering era as well as numerous prehistoric sites once used by indigenous people.

While tree-cutting is allowed throughout the area, the 500-foot "beauty" strip provides at least the illusion of untrammeled wilderness. Still, the calls of loons and coyotes will serenade you to sleep at night and moose, deer, and other wildlife abounds. Especially in spring, when black flies and mosquitos may be at their worst, the fishing can be very good. With detours of a day or less, Allagash travelers can visit several unique sites, including the **Ice Caves** on Allagash Lake, a series of natural openings on the slopes of a hill that fill with ice and snow in winter. Because summer is short here some ice remains year-round. The spot is a six-mile, upstream trip from Chamberlain to Allagash Lake and low water levels often make it more of a drag than a paddle. It is seldom visited.

The history and draw of Northern Maine has never been just about the land but rather a combination of the story of the land and the people who sought, often unsuccessfully, to tame it. Another popular spot at the north end of Chamberlain Lake is the site where to massive steam locomotives lay rusting (although in recent years an effort to cover them with sheds and set them back on short sections of rail have been underway). Before the railroad, logs were hauled overland by a massive tramway. Rusting remains of that machinery can also be seen as the forest reclaims the area.

Allagash Alliance Group

The not-for-profit organization Allagash Alliance Group welcomes any volunteer efforts to help preserve old buildings and trains. They can be reached at RR 1, 35 Tall Pines Road, West Buxton 04093. ☎ 929-8245.

There are fees for use of the Allagash and group size is limited to 10, although several larger groups such as scout troops, etc., who were frequent visitors before restrictions were imposed, are grandfathered.

Motor use is prohibited. But some lakes allow motors with a restriction on horsepower.

Use of this area has slowed somewhat in recent years. According to state officials, the Allagash had 27,008 visitor days (number of visitors multiplied by the number of days they stayed) during 1966. By 1981 that had soared to 51,194, but it has dropped to an average of 43,000 visitor days during the last few years. Because 75% or more of the visitors stay more than one day, that 43,000 amounts to about 12,000 visitors over 12 months spread among the waterway's 100 miles and 150 campsites. About 50% of that visitation comes in June and July. Still campsites, which are available on a first-come, first-served basis, are situated to provide as much privacy as possible to enhance the wilderness experience. Many parties plan to reach prime locations early in the day. The tradition is that people will remain at each site for only one night (weather delays excepted).

Far North

WISE WORDS: *Expect to have other wilderness-seekers nearby and be pleasantly surprised if you do not. The best time to go to avoid crowds is September, although the nights can be quite chilly.*

Allagash History

Logging and dams are the centerpoints of the Allagash's history. Originally most of the logs from the region flowed north into the St. John River and mills in Canada. One enterprising surveyor, however, realized that if dams were built on Chamberlain and Telos Lakes, and a shortcut made through the rock at the east end of Telos, logs could be sent into Webster Stream and into the Penobscot River watershed and processed in Bangor instead. A lock was also constructed between Chamberlain and Eagle Lakes to allow logs from that region to flow "backward." Eventually the trains and tramways mentioned above began hauling the lion's share of the wood.

Interestingly enough, Telos Lake is unique in the Northeast in that paddlers who start there can, with only a few portages of less than two miles each, enjoy trips on three of the region's largest rivers, including the Allagash, Penobscot and Kennebec.

Protection efforts for the Allagash begin in the early 1960s. The Allagash Wilderness Waterway was formally established in December of 1966 for the modest price of only $1.5 million.

Camping & Sports

Camping fees are $4 per night for Maine residents and $5 per night for non-residents. Fees can be paid at any of the several ranger stations located along the waterway. They include Headquarters at Umsaskis Lake, Michaud Farm, Churchill Dam, Lock Dam at Eagle Lake, and Chamberlain Bridge near Telos.

See *Adventures on Water*, pages 468-470, for in-depth descriptions of canoe/kayak routes.

There are several commercial sporting camps along the waterway, including **Willard Jalbert Camps** on Round Pond, and famed **Nugent's Camps** on Chamberlain Lake.

For a complete list of Allagash Rules and list of fees, contact the **Maine Bureau of Parks and Lands**, 106 Hogan Road, Bangor 04401. ☎ 941-4014.

⎕ Numerous maps and guidebooks are available at local stores.

■ State Parks

A casual reader may wonder why Northern Maine seems to have far fewer parks and preserves than the rest of the state. The answer is simple. With nearly all the privately-owned paper company land in Northern Maine open year-round to hunting, fishing, canoeing, camping and snowmobiling, the entire area is, in effect, one giant park. Still, its not unregulated or unsupervised. Check the sections on rules governing Great Northern Paper Company Lands (page 404) and on North Maine Woods Lands (page 452) for further details.

Aroostook State Park, Presque Isle. Good mountain views from this lakeside park with numerous trails including one to the top of 1,200-foot Quaggy Joe Mountain. The name is believed to be a corruption of the Indian name Quaquajo which, loosely translated, means "twin peaks." The north peak has views ranging from Canada to Katahdin. The south peak sports several radio and television antennas. Fish for trout and swim, canoe and boat in Echo Lake. Swimming beach, toilets, campground, bathhouse, picnic ground, boat launch ramp. Parking. Fee charged. ☎ 768-8341.

Arnold Brook Lake, Presque Isle. Located three miles from town on the Spragueville Road, this 400-acre lake and surrounding wooded park offers swimming, picnicing, nature trails and a boat launch ramp. Operated by the town of Presque Isle Recreation Department. Open daily May through September. Office at 270 Maine Street, Presque Isle 04769. ☎ 764-2914.

Riverside Park, Presque Isle. Just a few minutes walk from downtown, this small, pocket park features a picnic area, playground and boat ramp. Four-mile old railroad bed (paved) bicycle trail nearby. Office at 270 Maine Street, Presque Isle 04769. ☎ 764-2914.

■ Wildlife Refuges

A.E. Howell Wildlife Refuge, North Amity. A 64-acre tract along the Lycette Road devoted to wildlife management. Offers 5½ miles of hiking trails and an environmental group camping area. Stocked trout ponds and picnic areas available. Refuge also features a raptor and wildlife rehabilitation center. Open May through October, Tuesday through Saturday. ☎ 532-6880.

Aroostook National Wildlife Refuge, Limestone. This sprawling 4,800-acre refuge was recently carved from the territory formerly occupied by Loring Air Force Base. The built-up portions of the base are now used for non-heavy industrial and commercial purposes while the former runway and airfield are the frequent scene of Woodstock-like concerts by the group Phish. The refuge land was never developed by the military.

A former Alert Center for pilots of B-52 bombers has been renovated into a visitor's center. New trails have been created through the properties forests and marshy areas.

Major Parks & Preserves in the Far North

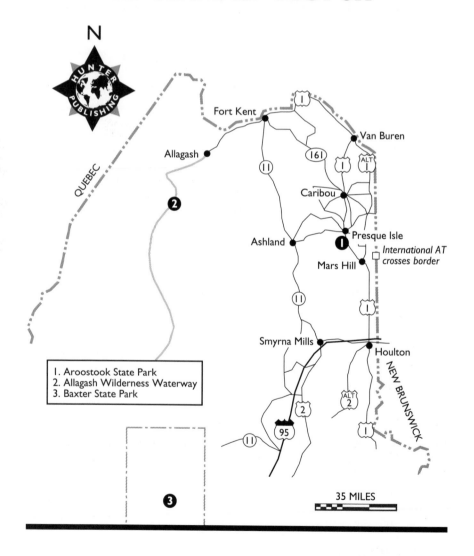

N

QUEBEC

Fort Kent

Van Buren

Allagash

161

ALT
1

2

Caribou

Ashland

Presque Isle
1

International AT
crosses border

Mars Hill

Smyrna Mills

Houlton

NEW BRUNSWICK

1. Aroostook State Park
2. Allagash Wilderness Waterway
3. Baxter State Park

3

35 MILES

Lt. Gordon Manuel Game Management Area, Hodgdon. A 500-acre area comprising woods and wetlands along the Meduxnekeag River. Prime waterfowl habitat. Hunting, canoeing and fishing allowed. Motors restricted. Picnic grounds and adequate parking.

■ Natural Areas/Preserves

Woodland Bog Preserve, Woodland. Located just west of Caribou, this 200-acre Nature Conservancy preserve protects several species of rare orchids and birds. Due to fragile nature of vegetation, casual visitation is discouraged. The Nature Conservancy of Maine office is located at 14 Maine Street, Brunswick 04011. ☎ 729-5181.

Sightseeing

■ Historic Sites/Museums

Allagash

Allagash Historical Society, Route 161. Log House containing local genealogical records, photos, history of area lumbering, artifacts, military section. ☎ 398-3335.

Ashland

Ashland Logging Museum, Garfield Road. Blacksmith shop and machine sheds housing artifacts and exhibits relating to the lumbering industry. ☎ 435-6039.

Far North

Caribou

Caribou Historical Society, Presque Isle Road. (A Whittier Memorial). Log T-shaped building. Artifacts, furniture, photographs, and documents from the community through the 1930s. ☎ 498-2556.

Lyndon School Museum, part of the Caribou Historical Society. ☎ 498-2556.

Nylander Natural History Museum, 393 Main Street. ☎ 493-4209.

Thomas Heritage House, 152 Main Street. ☎ 496-3011.

Fort Fairfield

Fort Fairfield Blockhouse, Main Street. Small settlement-era fort replica. Open in summer. ☎ 472-3802.

Fort Fairfield Railroad Museum, Main Street. ☎ 473-4045.

Frontier Heritage History, 3 Green Street. ☎ 768-4777.

Fort Kent

Fort Kent Blockhouse (1840), Block House Street. Erected to provide military protection from Canada resulting from the long-standing controversy about the location of Maine's northeastern boundary. ☎ 834-3155.

Fort Kent Historical Society Museum and Gardens, Market Street. Museum located in former Bangor and Aroostook Railroad station. ☎ 834-5248.

Houlton

Aroostook County Historical and Art Museum, 109 Main Street. Housed in a 1903 Colonial Revival building containing Aroostook County artifacts. On the National Register of Historic Places. ☎ 532-4216.

Island Falls

Island Falls Historical Society Museum. ☎ 463-2264.

Webb Museum of Vintage Fashion (1894), Sherman Street (Route 2). Family museum. All ages welcome. ☎ 862-3797.

Madawaska

Madawaska Historical Society, Madouesk Historic Center and Acadian Cross Historic Shrine, US 1. Features Acadian artifacts and those of local historical value. ☎ 728-4518.

Presque Isle

Aroostook County Historical Center, University of Presque Isle Library, 181 Main Street. Books about Aroostook history and culture, or by Aroostook authors. ☎ 764-0311.

Presque Isle Historical Society, 16 Third Street. ☎ 762-1151.

The Far North

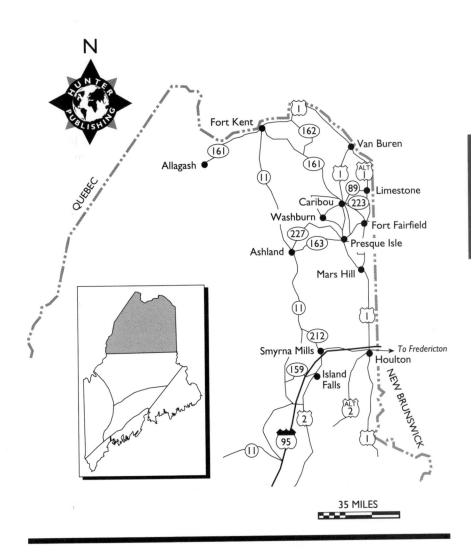

35 MILES

St. Agatha

St. Agatha Historical Society (1850s), Route 162, Main Street. Artifacts of everyday use by the people of the St. John Valley. ☎ 543-6364.

Van Buren

Acadian Village, US 1. ☎ 868-2691. Collection of 16 buildings with period furnishings designed to display and preserve Acadian culture.

Washburn

Salmon Brook Historical Society of Washburn Museum (1852), Main Street. ☎ 455-8110.

List Source-Maine Department of Tourism.

■ Covered Bridge

Covered bridges are a quintessential symbol of New England. Typical of Yankee frugality, the spans were covered over to afford the structure protection from wind and rain, make it easier to keep the decking free of snow and ice, and to help keep horses calm while crossing high over rushing streams. At their high point there were hundreds of covered bridges throughout the region. Most succumbed to old age, fire, or flood.

Watson Settlement Bridge - 1911, Meduxnekeag Stream. Located off US 1, on the road to Woodstock from Littleton, in the town of Littleton. This is the farthest north as well as the youngest covered bridge in the state.

Adventures On Foot

■ Hiking

Allagash Ice Caves: One of Maine's more unusual natural features is just a short walk from a campsite on Allagash Lake, which must be accessed by water. Canoeists often take two days to get into the lake by taking the difficult six-mile upstream passage from Chamberlain Lake, part of the official Allagash Wilderness Waterway. The ice caves, a boulder field with multiple underground entrances where winter's snow and ice lasts all year, can be found by following an unmarked but easy-to-follow trail from the Ice Caves campsite on the southwestern cove side of the lake. There is also a trail from the ranger cabin at the very southern end of the lake that leads up a steep and rock trail to the old fire tower on top of Allagash Mountain. The trail is strenuous with an elevation gain of more than 600 feet.

Deboullie Mountain, T-15, R-9 WELS: This hill gets its moniker from French and translates literally as "broken down mountain." That alone should be enough of a clue as to the nature of this rough and rocky trail that ascends to the old fire tower at the 1,981-foot peak. Begin on an old woods road at Red River Sporting Camps. Access the camps through the North Maine Woods road network approaching from St. Francis. The path descends gradually to the shores of Pushineer Pond and rises and falls along the edge of Deboullie Pond passing several potential lakeside overnight campsites. About 2½ miles from the start the trail turns northward and ascends 700 feet steeply up the east side of the hill to the top about three miles from the start. There are great views in all directions from the remote summit. Because of the wildness of the area this walk is moderate to strenuous.

Hedgehog Mountain T-15, R-6 WELS: Not to be confused with its much more diminutive cousin in Southern Maine, Hedgehog Mountain along Route 11 in the Far North is a much different climb. The trail begins near a ranger cabin at the official state picnic area on Route 11. There is a 600-foot elevation gain in the roughly half-mile walk to the summit through attractive hardwood forest. There are good views to the east and other views possible with a little exploring. The footings at the top belong to a fire watch tower that once occupied the site. Moderate.

Priestly Mountain, T-10, R-13 WELS: There are several paths to the top of 1,900-foot tall Priestly Mountain with its abandoned fire tower. One begins at Umsaskis Lake on the Allagash Wilderness Waterway. Another begins on the Churchill Dam Road, a dirt lumber road. The trailhead, marked by a small sign on the west side of the road, is about 7½ miles north of the Realty Road intersection.

The trail begins following an old tote road and rises and falls gently until it meets the trail from the lake near Drake Brook after 1½ miles. It then cuts southwest along Priestly Lake about a quarter-mile to an abandoned fire warden's camp with spring and outhouse. The real hiking begins right behind the camp as the trail rises steeply to the top, ascending nearly 800 feet in about half a mile. There are great views from the steel skeleton at the top including Katahdin some 58 miles to the south.

Quaggy Jo Mountain, Presque Isle: Hiking trails in Aroostook State Park climb to the top of this 1,200-foot, twin-peaked mountain. The 1¼-mile **North Peak Trail** begins in a well-marked day-use parking area and rises quickly through forests of hardwoods and conifers. Good views to the north from this unspoiled summit.

The .75-mile **South Peak Trail** begins in the campground and rises steeply through thick woods before emerging on open ledges near the top. There are several radio antennas at this summit. There is a one-mile trail connecting the two summits. You can make a loop by a walk of less than a mile on a park road between the two parking areas. Elevation gain, 600-700 feet.

■ Golfing

Greens fees vary greatly according to the popularity of the course and the time of year.

Caribou Country Club, Sweden Road, Caribou. 6,433 yards, par 72. 9/18 holes. May-October, or first snow. ☎ 493-3933.

Aroostook Valley Country Club, Russell Road, Fort Fairfield. 5,393/6,304 yards, par 72. 18 holes. ☎ 476-8083. May 15-October 1.

Fort Kent Golf Club, St. John Road, Fort Kent. 6,357 yards, par 71. 9/18 holes. May 1-November. ☎ 834-3149.

Houlton Community Golf Course, Nickerson Lake Road, Houlton. 2,979 yards, par 36. 9/18 holes. May 15-October 15. ☎ 532-2662.

Va-Jo-Wa Golf Club, Walker Settlement Road, Island Falls. 6,203 yards, par 72. 18 holes. May 1-October 31. ☎ 463-2128.

Vacationland Estates Resort, Golf Club Road, Island Falls. 18 holes, par 72. ☎ 463-2884.

Limestone Country Club, Sawyer Road, Limestone. 6,735 yards, par 72. 9/18 holes. May until first snow. ☎ 328-7277.

Birch Point Golf Club, Lakeshore Dr., Madawaska. 2,987 yards, par 35. 9 holes. May 1-October 31. ☎ 895-6957.

Mars Hill Country Club, York Road, Mars Hill. 3,143 yards, par 36. 9 holes. May 1-November. ☎ 425-4802.

Portage Hills Country Club, Route 11 North, Portage Lake. 3,268 yards, par 37. 9 holes. ☎ 435-8221.

Presque Isle Country Club, Parkhurst Siding Road, Presque Isle. 6,730 yards, par 72. 18 holes. May-October. ☎ 764-0430.

Adventures On Wheels

■ Mountain Biking

Houlton to Mars Hill Railbed. This 30-mile route is really the southern tip of a maze of old rail lines in Aroostook County that could take intrepid bikers weeks or even months to explore. You can start from the information center in Houlton. (The old rail line runs just a short ways away; staff can direct you down the local streets.) As it heads north, this trail passes through rolling potato farm country, lowland swamps, and attractive forests. Watch for road crossings and for logging vehicles that use the old roadbed from time to time. There is a unique trestle crossing over the Meduxnekeag River in Monticello and several picnic areas along the way. The trail crosses US 1 in Mars Hill. If you desire you can continue north.

Mars Hill is said to be one of the places where the rays of the rising sun hit the United States first each day. Ask at the ski area there for permission to take your bikes to the top. The new International Appalachian Trail also crosses Mars Hill just before plunging into Canada. ATVs are likely to be encountered in spring, summer and fall. All Aroostook County's railbeds are popular snowmobile routes in winter.

Stockholm to Van Buren Railbed. This 17-mile section of old railroad right-of-way passes through the woodlands and wetlands of the St. John Valley. From the parking area in Stockholm it heads due north and slightly east, avoiding major roads and crossing only small streams. In this remote land moose and coyote outnumber people. The trail ends in an old railroad yard at Van Buren at the information station there. A bike shop is located nearby. In all there are more than 70 miles of rail trails in Aroostook County.

■ Foliage/Motor Tours

Here are a few suggested driving routes in the Far North. The last one offers great views!

Aroostook County Circuit

200 miles, 5 hours, round trip

Highlights: *Aroostook County, known to Mainers as simply "The County" in recognition of its impressive size, is famed for its lumbering* *tradition, French-Acadian heritage and annual potato harvest. It is also where fall's bright foliage appears first.*

🌿Foliage Hotline: The Maine foliage hotline, in service each fall, offers the latest color-peaking information for leaf-peepers. ☎ 800-932-3419.

Route: Start in **Presque Isle**, watching for signs of the season's bountiful potato harvest. Travel west on 163 to **Ashland**, site of the **Ashland Logging Museum**, then head north on 11 through Eagle Lake to **Fort Kent**. Take US 1 east to **Frenchville**, named for its French-Acadian founders, then head south on 162 along **Long Lake**, stopping for a picnic or canoe trip. Continue on to **Guerette**, then southeast on 161 to **New Sweden**. Visit the **New Sweden Historical Museum** and take in the colorful panoramic vistas of Canada from the town's park benches. Take a secondary road to US 1 and go north to **Van Buren**, site of the **Village Acadien**, a detailed recreation of an early Acadian settlement. Go south on 1A to **Limestone**, then west on 89 to **Caribou**, stopping at the **Nylander Museum** to view geological and Native American artifacts. Drive south on 161 to US 1A at **Fort Fairfield**, on to **Mars Hill**, then northeast on US 1, returning to Presque Isle.

Route courtesy Maine Department of Conservation

US 1, Houlton to Fort Kent

100 miles, 2½ hours, one way

Highlights: *Houlton is literally the end of the road, at least as far as divided highway Interstate 95 goes. Even here, 300 miles from Kittery, there is still plenty of Maine to go. There are still 100 miles to Fort Kent and the way to go is US 1. Aroostook County is potato country, although in recent years the broad flat fields have been often planted in broccoli.*

Route: US 1 heads almost due north from **Houlton** passing through numerous neat villages including Littleton, Monticello, Bridgewater and **Mars Hill**. Many people believe Mars Hill is one of the first places in the United States to be touched by the rays of the rising sun on many days of the year. The new International Appalachian Trail, which runs from Baxter State Park to the Gaspé Peninsula, crosses the border here.

From Mars Hill US 1 leans toward the westard, passing through two good-sized towns – **Presque Isle** and **Caribou**. After a long run through very wild lands it passes through **Van Buren** on the Canadian border. For the remainder of its run US 1 hugs west side of the **St. John River**. The river forms the international border for much of its length. It was once the only highway for transporting pulp wood and saw logs from the vast woods to hungry mills.

Passing through the paper mill town of **Madawaska**, where for many people French is the first language, the road continues west until it ends in **Fort Kent**.

Allagash Village, the traditional terminus of voyagers enjoying the Allagash Wilderness Waterway, is another 25 miles or so down State Route 161.

Route 11, Fort Kent to Sherman Station

60 miles, 1½ hours, one way

Highlights: *Scenic drive through remote area with small villages but big views.*

Route: Instead of backtracking on US 1, head south on Route 11, also known as the **Aroostook Road**. It cuts due south from **Fort Kent**, passing through the attractive villages of **Soldier Pond** and **Eagle Lake**. The scenery, particularly along the lake, is spectacular.

Route 11 winds through hilly country roughly paralleling the south-flowing Fish River. There are several picnic areas and scenic turnouts along the way.

Drive carefully on the older sections, where unpaved shoulders wait to grab the steering wheel from unsuspecting drivers.

Further south, in **Portage**, the road passes the popular seaplane base on its way toward **Ashland**, headquarters for the Maine North Woods, an organization that oversees recreational use of the millions of acres of forest industry land to the west. Except for the occasional picnic area, the only landmark south of the tiny village of Masardis is the Oak Hill Fire Tower which is occasionally visible to the right. On this lonely road logging trucks frequently outnumber cars.

WISE WORDS: *If you haven't already, fill up the gas tank in Ashland and check your spare tire as the next 50 miles or so pass through some of the wildest and most undeveloped terrain in the state.*

Patten is a full-service town and is home to a logging museum. A right on Route 151 here takes you to Shin Pond and the north entrance of **Baxter State Park**. Interstate 95 is only another 10 miles or so straight ahead on Route 11.

Far North

■ Riding the Rails

During the summer months the **Bangor and Aroostook Railroad** schedules a variety of passenger trips over rails that have not seen regular passenger service for nearly 40 years. The equipment includes diesel locomotives, passengers coaches, sleepers, an observation car, baggage car and a first class car. Double-decker observation cars are used in the fall. Call to check the schedule, as the trips are sandwiched between regular freight service and times vary.

Trips range from from two to six hours and provide a rare opportunity to see some of the most spectacular scenery in Northern Maine. Trips leave from Fort Kent, Madawaska, Presque Isle, and Houlton. Some include a picnic or a box lunch. Only light refreshments such as chips and sodas is offered on the train. There are restrooms on board. Smoking is not allowed on the train, although it is allowed on short breaks where passengers are allowed off to stretch their legs.

Prices start at $12 for an adult and go as high as $28 for an all-day trip. First class is 15-20% higher. Prices for children start at $8. Tickets can be purchased on the day of the trip for cash on a first-come, first-served basis. Most trips sell out a week or two in advance. You can make reservations by calling ☎ 800-847-1505 weekdays between noon and 6 pm.

Adventures On Water

■ Places to Paddle

Allagash River

With its connecting system of lakes and miles of wild river frontage the Allagash Wilderness Waterway holds out the prospect of paddle trips ranging in length from a few days to nearly two weeks. The toughest part is on the lakes, where high winds can keep paddlers pinned down in campsites for days. The only real section of whitewater, Chases Rapids, just below Churchill Dam, is Class II and a ranger will truck your gear around for nominal fee. Most trips begin on Chamberlain Lake and end at the village of Allagash on the St. John, for a river distance of 100 miles. There are numerous campsites, logging-era relics and natural wonders to visit along the way. Because there are only unimproved paper company roads the vehicle shuttle alone can take a day or more. Many paddlers hire local folks to do the shuttle for them. A complete description of the waterway can be found on pages 454-456.

Paddlers along the Allagash Wilderness Waterway must portage the turbulent whitewater of Allagash Falls, where the ghost of an Indian maiden reportedly materializes from time to time in the mist.
Photo by Ted Koffman

The Allagash is not a grueling whitewater challenge, but rather a series of paddling challenges that test the skill and judgement of any paddler. With prime conditions, the entire trip can be done in a week. At the beginning there is a series of very large lakes where winds can keep parties pinned down for days at a time. Numerous shorter trips are possible. The large lakes can be avoided by putting in at Churchill Lake, although purists will insist that to do the river without the large lakes is to miss half the charm.

DID YOU KNOW? *Churchill Lake's Indian name was Allagas-kwigamook, which is translated to mean "bark cabin lake." From that Native American name the entire waterway gets its moniker.*

Float planes based out of Greenville, Millinocket or Shin Pond near Patten can be hired to drop you at almost any point along the way and pick you up at an appointed day and time.

Chase Rapids, which begin at the newly-rebuilt Churchill Dam, are a fun Class I and Class II romp. For those worried about getting gear wet, a ranger will shuttle the wannigan from the dam to the end of the fast water for a slight fee, allowing you to run light, empty, and just relax and have fun. Often the stronger portions of the rapids can be avoided by running river left or river right.

Below Chase Rapids the river becomes wide and comparatively shallow and is interspersed with several long, narrow lakes. Riffles and fast water are rare, with the exception of an old dam at Long Lake.

 *The only truly unrunnable section is **Allagash Falls**, a jagged 35-foot drop that should be approached with great caution. There is a well-defined portage trail and several attractive campsites at the base.*

Riffles and rips continue with only one other named "rapid," Twin Brook, which is rated Class II. Quick water continues to the traditional take out where the Allagash River joins the St. John at Allagash Village.

Aroostook River, Washburn

Flowing east from the remote lands north of Baxter State Park, the Aroostook River drains some of the wildest lands in the state. An easy 44-mile trip is possible from the Oxbow Landing and checkpoint on the Oxbow Road off Route 11. The entire trip is characterized by a mix of flat and quick water with only a handful of Class I rapids. One unique feature is the circular **Oxbow**, where the river has made an end run around itself. It is located just three miles downstream from the start.

There are several attractive campsites along the way, making trips of several days possible. The only major town encountered prior to the take-out (a the bridge off Route 164 in Washburn) is Ashland. This trip also passes through the tiny village of Masardis. Below Ashland the river winds among several small islands.

Deboullie Pond

Deboullie Pond is such a long way from anywhere that it is infrequently visited. Those searching for solitude will find Deboullie and associated nearby ponds a wonderful refuge. The best way in is to brave the rough dirt road into Pushineer Pond and put in there. Or, you can make arrangements to stay at Red River Sporting Camp (☎ 435-6000) and strike out from there. A small stream with moderate current connects the two. There are numerous campsites along the lakes and a hiking trail to the top of Deboullie Mountain. You can also portage from Deboullie Pond into nearby Gardner Pond.

Scraggly Lake, T-7, R-8 WELS

Located on public reserve land on a side road off the Huber Road north of Shin Pond, Scraggly Lake features pure water, remote lakeside camping and plenty of coves and islands to explore. There is even a stand of hemlock trees believed to be nearly 400 years old. These are located in a management area about a mile from the lake. In addition to the remote sites, which feature fire rings, picnic tables and pit toilets, there is a 10-site camping area at the boat launch ramp on the lake's southeastern shore. Owl's Head, a peninsula on the eastern shore, features a loop hiking trail to good views from the top.

Canoeing/Kayaking Outfitters

Overnight trips average $100-150 per person, per day. Half-day guided trips run in the vicinity of $50. Basic rentals cost between $25 and $45 per day. Most rentals include life jackets, paddles and car-topping gear.

Allagash Sporting Camps
Box 169A, Allagash 04774
Trips: Allagash, St. John, Big and Little Black Rivers. May-October. Canoe rentals, canoe trips. ☎ 398-3555.

Birch Point, Inc.
Box 120, Pleasant Lake, Island Falls 04747
Canoe rentals. May-October. ☎ 463-2515.

Maine Canoe Adventures
Box 105, Route 161, St. Francis 04774
Canoe rentals. Canoe trips, on the Allagash and St. John. May-October. ☎ 398-3191.

Pelletier's Campground
PO Box 67, Saint Francis 04774
Canoe rentals, canoe trips. May-October. ☎ 398-3187 days; 834-6118 evenings.

St. John River, T-9, R-17 WELS

Sister to the nearby Allagash, the St. John is a wild and remote river best run in the spring before low water takes too heavy a toll on fragile boats. It flows the sea in nearby New Brunswick and was named by French explorer Samuel de Champlain.

The 70-mile paddle from Moody Bridge (on the American Realty Road bridge in far northwestern Maine) to Allagash Village takes several days and features rapids up to Class III and some of the wildest most remote scenery in the East. There are numerous campsites and other points of

Far North

interest, including abandoned farms and logging camps. Only one other bridge and a single ranger station (Nine-Mile Bridge) is passed.

By early summer dropping water levels force canoes to be walked down several stretches. The rapids also become bony, causing rocks to rip at the bottoms of canoes and kayaks.

The North Maine Woods office receives daily readings on the water level in the St. John. Officials consider 3,000 CFS (cubic feet per second) the minimum for a good run. Call before leaving on a trip for the latest flow information. ☎ 435-6213.

Adventures In the Air

■ Air Charters

 Larson's Flying Service, Houlton. Scenic overflights offered by appointment as well as air taxi and flight school. Located at the Houlton International Airport. ☎ 532-9489.

North Star Wilderness Expeditions Inc., PO Box 276, Portage 04768. Fully licensed seaplane outfitter offering shuttle service, remote fly-in lake cabin rentals, canoe shuttles on the Allagash, hunting and fishing trips. ☎ 435-3002.

Adventures On Snow

■ Downhill Skiing

Fort Kent

 Lonesome Pines Ski Area, Fort Kent 04743. 500-foot vertical drop, 10 trails, one lift, night skiing, Nordic skiing available, snowboarding, lessons, rental, restaurant. ☎ 834-5202.

Mars Hill

Bigrock Ski Area, Mars Hill 04758. 1,000-foot vertical drop, 22 trails, two lifts, 40% snowmaking, night skiing, equipment rentals, lessons, restaurant. Trails for all abilities, including the challenging Ho Chi Min Trail. Adult lift ticket $22 weekend, $16 mid-week. ☎ 435-6711.

Presque Isle

Quoggy Jo Ski Club, PO Box, Presque Isle 04769. 175-foot vertical drop, eight trails, one lift, snowboarding, lessons, rentals, snack bar. ☎ 764-3248.

■ Cross-Country Skiing

Caribou

 Caribou Parks and Recreation Department, Caribou Country Club off Route 161. Offers 10 miles of groomed ski trails. Daily fees are $2 for adults and $1 for students. Children age nine and under ski free. Equipment rentals available. ☎ 493-4224.

Fort Kent

Lonesome Pines Ski Area. See info above.

Fort Kent Cross Country Ski Club. Three miles of trail near the Violet Settlement Road at intersection with Saint John Road. $2 per person, per day. Fees paid on honor system (box at trailhead).

Frenchville

Frenchville Trailmasters. Eight miles of trails on the Paradis Road, between Frenchville and Upper Frenchville. Non-member fee of $3 per day. Sign marks the beginning of the trail system. (No phone or other contact; this trail network is based on the honor system.)

Limestone

Trafton Lake Ski Trails. Seven miles of trails. No charge, but skiers can leave a donation in the box at the beginning of the trail off Ward Road.

Limestone Country Cub Ski Trails. Limestone Country Club has about seven miles of ski trails. Equipment rentals and small fee for trail use. ☎ 328-7277.

Littleton

Meduxnekeag Ramblers Ski Trails. This cross-country ski club grooms about 10 miles of trail that leads out from Littleton clubhouse. Trails to Houlton and nearby areas. (No phone.)

Far North

Presque Isle

Aroostook State Park offers 16 miles of groomed ski trails for all abilities. Snowshoeing and snowmobiling allowed. Warming lodge open on weekends. Maps available at park. ☎ 768-8341.

■ Snowmobiling

 This is premier snowmobile country. There are more than 1,600 miles of groomed and marked trails and many more local and club paths.

The folks in "The County" practically live on snow machines in winter, with many high school kids using them to commute to class. From Presque Isle and Caribou north trails fan out in every direction. One, ITS 81, roughly parallels the border with New Brunswick for more than 100 miles. The comparatively flat terrain is in marked contrast to the mountainous travel in other parts of the state.

Unlike trails to the south where riders heading in opposite directions share one groomed path, travel lanes are often separated in Aroostook County, allowing very fast riding. It is not unusual for riders to put 150 or even 200 miles a day on their machines with only a fraction of the fatigue endured by riders on bumpier, more serpentine trails.

Most businesses have special parking areas for snowmobiles. Riders often park at a clubhouse in Houlton and head north, spending the night at a camp or hotel in Fort Kent before returning by a different trail the next day. More than 100 motels, inns and sporting camps are accessible by snowmobile.

> Detailed trail maps, available from Aroostook Chamber of commerce and from snowmobile clubs, also note locations of warming huts, fuel stations and restaurants.

The clubs have earned a reputation as maintaining the best trail network in the Northeast. The work involves operating large grooming machines and pulling drags to smooth the snow behind snowmobiles. Most of the work is done at night to avoid traffic. Since groomers are able to do only a few miles per hour, sometimes the volunteers can begin at supper time and not return until breakfast!

Most clubs in Aroostook take care of more than 100 miles of trail each. In Presque Isle, the snowmobile club there boasts 400 members and has its own clubhouse on ITS 83.

Clubhouses, which usually feature warming rooms, snack bars, and restrooms, can be found at Castle Hill, Squa Pan Lake, Fort Fairfield, Limestone, Allagash, Frenchville, Fort Kent, and Black Lake. In St.

Francis, the Sno Angels have a warming shack on ITS 92 affectionately dubbed the "Love Shack."

Where to Stay & Eat

Rate Scale
All rates are for entrée or complete dinner, per person.
Inexpensive. . . . . under $10
Moderate . . . . $10-$20
Expensive . . . . More than $20

■ Favorite Restaurants

Caribou

Joe Hackett's Steaks and Seafood, Presque Isle Road, Caribou 04736. Another theme restaurant like the Road Kill, with menu items sporting weird names. But the food isn't half-bad and is very affordable. Open daily for dinner. Entrée selection has something for everyone, from tyrannosaurs to grazers. ☎ 469-2501.

Reno's Family Restaurant, 217 Sweden Street, Caribou 04736. A family restaurant that specializes in pizza, but also serves standard fare for breakfast, lunch and dinner. Inexpensive. ☎ 496-5331.

Fort Kent

Sirois' Restaurant, 84 West Main Street, Fort Kent 04743. Bills itself as having the best prime rib north of Bangor. Menu includes a wide range of entrées from steaks and seafood to salads and Italian dishes. Open daily year-round for breakfast, lunch and dinner. Sunday breakfast buffet until 12:30 pm. Inexpensive to moderate. ☎ 834-6548.

Houlton

Joe's Family Restaurant, 99½ Military Street, Houlton 04730. Serving breakfast, lunch and dinner seven days a week, year-round. Friday and Sunday buffet lunches and breakfast served all day. Open weekdays and Saturday at 5:30 am, Sunday at 6 am. Complete dinners, pizza and subs as well as homemade pies and pastries. Delivery service available. Inexpensive. ☎ 532-6394.

Elm Tree Diner, Bangor Road, Houlton 04730. You've got to love a place in business for 50 years that boasts about its homemade food and its large portions. Often there are as many as a dozen daily specials on the menu. Don't look for an old stainless-steel railroad car; this diner is in a wood-frame building (outside the big city, diners in Maine come in any shape or size). Take-out service available. Open most mornings at 5 am. Inexpensive. ☎ 532-3181.

Presque Isle

The Mai Tai, A Polynesian Chinese American Restaurant, 449 Main Street, Presque Isle 04769. You can tell by the name this place wants to be all things to all people and by most measures it succeeds. But hey, once you've come this far in Maine you're probably tired of lobster and baked beans. Daily buffet, take-out and delivery service. Open seven days a week. ☎ 764-4426.

Winnie's Restaurant and Dairy Bar, 79 Parson's Street, Presque Isle 04769. Home of the Winnie Burger and famous for their "LeBlanc's Gourmet lobster stew," this laid-back place offers good, wholesome, tasty food. Cheap. Busy in summer and again in winter when snowmobilers flock to its location at the end of ITS 88 extension. ☎ 769-4971.

St. Agatha

The Lakeview Restaurant, Lakeview Drive, St. Agatha 04772. Seating is available on the outdoor deck or indoors in booths and at tables. Nearly every seat has a view, making this a popular stop. Traditional steak and seafood restaurant with lounge. Inexpensive to moderate. Open daily, year-round. Snowmobile access. ☎ 543-6331.

■ B&Bs, Hotels & Motels

Price Scale
All rates are based on double occupancy.
Inexpensive . . . . Under $65
Moderate . . . . $66-$100
Expensive . . . . Above $100

Allagash Wilderness Waterway

 Nugent's Camps on Chamberlain Lake, HCR 76, Box 632, Greenville 04441. This rustic collection of private cabins and main lodge are accessible only by boat or float plane. Some cabins have gravity-feed showers, others are without running water. Common shower area in lodge. Private privies. One of the most remote and scenic locations in Maine with authentic sporting camp atmosphere. Guides available for hire. Rates are very reasonable: $25 per-person/day for housekeeping cabins, $60 per-person/day for Full American Plan (includes all meals). ☎ 944-5991.

Ashland

Four Seasons Inn, Presque Isle Road, Ashland 04732. 16-unit motel with restaurant is open year-round. Inexpensive prices. Phones and cable television. ☎ 435-8310.

Caribou

Crown Park Inn, Access Highway, Caribou 04736. A total of 60 rooms with phones and cable. Room rate includes gourmet continental breakfast. Exercise room and nightclub on premises. Moderate rates. Open year-round. ☎ 493-3311.

The Old Iron Inn B&B, 155 High Street, Caribou 04736. Down comforters, high-back oak beds and plush towels make a statement of the comfort offered by owners Kate and Kevin McCartney (no relation to Paul). Open year-round. Four rooms, one with private bath. The rooms have names including The Old Iron Room, The Lincoln Room, The Rose Room and the Amoeba Room. Inexpensive. ☎ 492-4766.

Eagle Lake

Overlook Motel, Route 11, Eagle Lake 04739. Good-sized lodging establishment offering all the trappings of civilization, including phones, air-conditioning, cable TV, microwaves, refridgerators, and continental breakfast. Good views from porches and popular with snowmobilers. Inexpensive. ☎ 444-4535.

Houlton

Ivy's Motor Lodge, North Road, Houlton 04730. AAA-approved 24-room motel with phones and cable. Open 24 hours, year-round. Inexpensive. ☎ 532-4206.

Far North

Shiretown Motor Inn, North Road, Houlton 04730. Modern 50-room motel with cable and phones. Health club, indoor pool, restaurant and lounge. Open 24 hours, year-round. Inexpensive. ☎ 532-9421.

Madawaska

River Watch B&B, 31 Riverview Street, Madawaska 04756. Watch the lights of Edmundston, a Canadian town directly across the St. John River from this establishment. All the stops are pulled out for breakfast, but you may be late for it if you can't drag yourself out from under the comfy homemade quilts. Moderately priced. ☎ 728-7109.

The Gateway Motel, US 1, Madawaska 04756. Older motel but the 34 rooms are clean and neat. Cable and phones in rooms. Dining room serves breakfast and dinner. Lounge on premises. Views of St. John River. Located on ITS. Inexpensive. ☎ 728-3318.

Presque Isle

The Northeastland Hotel, 436 Main Street, Presque Isle 04769. Downtown 50-room hotel is centrally located and has a coffee shop, restaurant and lounge. Cable and phones. In business since 1934, but decor is modern. Air-conditioned. Moderately priced. ☎ 768-5321.

Keddy's Motor Inn, PO Box 270, Presque Isle 04769. Located on Route 1. 150-room motel with indoor heated pool and individual saunas. Two lounges with dancing on weekends. Free HBO, coin-operated laundry. Air-conditioned. Moderately priced. On ITS. ☎ 764-3321.

Northern Lights Motel, 72 Houlton Road, Presque Isle 04769. One-story, 14-unit motel that is open year-round in a quiet location not far from downtown. Cable television, free coffee, phones, air-conditioning. Inexpensive rates. ☎ 764-4441.

St. Agatha

Cozy Log Cabin Rentals, 766 Main Street, St. Agatha 04772. With a name like this, what more do you need to know? Newly-built real log cabins offer amenities that include kitchens, oil heat and hot water. Cabins sleep six-eight persons, with one private bedroom and two lofts. Linens, towels and fixings for coffee included. Inexpensive to moderate. ☎ 543-6349.

Top O'Maine Cottage Rentals, RR 1, Box 2143A, St. David 04773. Cottages located on Cyr's Cove on Long Lake in St. Agatha. Private baths, running water, full kitchens, oil heat. All linens, towels, blankets, etc., provided. Cabins accomodate four to six people. Open year-round. Inexpensive to moderate. ☎ 728-4740.

Van Buren

The Farrell-Michaud House B&B, 231 Main Street, Van Buren 04785. A wrap-around porch encloses this blend of Victorian charm and period reproduction furniture that is on the National Registry of Historic Places. Rooms available with private or shared baths. Afternoon tea. Continental or full breakfast. Inexpensive. ☎ 868-7729.

■ Camping

 Facilities indicated as "nearby" are located within one mile of the campground.

Eagle Lake

Birch Haven Campground, Box 960, Sly Brook Road, Eagle Lake 04739. 80 sites, tenting area, 20 amp, sewer, dump station, store, laundry, swimming, boating, fishing. Pets allowed. Open Memorial Day-Columbus Day. ☎ 444-5102.

Winterville Lakeview Campground, PO Box 397, Eagle Lake 04739. A small campground with wooded sites. Very peaceful. Let the loons sing you to sleep. 16 sites, tenting area, 50 amp, dump station, swimming, boating, fishing, group area. Pets allowed. Open Memorial Day-Columbus Day. ☎ 444-4581.

Houlton

My Brother's Place, RR 3, Box 650, Houlton 04730. On the Canadian border with paved roads and grass sites, all pull-throughs. New bathrooms, showers and laundry. Meals available for groups – reservation suggested. 100 sites, tenting area, 50 amp, sewer, dump station, laundry, rec hall, swimming, boating, fishing, group area. Store and LP gas nearby. Pets allowed. Open May 1-October 31. ☎ 532-6739.

Island Falls

Birch Point, RR 1, Box 120 Pleasant Lake, Island Falls 04747. Nestled among the trees along the shoreline. Relax and refresh your spirit on a beautiful lake and enjoy the enchanting calls of loons. 65 sites, tenting area, 30 amp, sewer, dump station, store, laundry, rec hall, swimming, boating, fishing, group area. Pets allowed. Open May 1-October 31. ☎ 463-2515.

Far North

Monticello

Wilde Pines Campground, Box 1095, Monticello 04760. Plan to get a good night's sleep under the pines before entering Canada. Fifteen minutes from I-95, but very quiet. Campfires on-site. 88 sites, tenting area, 50 amp, sewer, dump station, store, swimming, pool, group area. Boating and fishing nearby. Pets allowed. Open Memorial Day-Columbus Day. ☎ 538-9004.

Presque Isle

Arndt's Aroostook River Campground, 95 Parkhurst Siding Road, Presque Isle 04769. Fragrant forests, bright blue skies, lush green fields, and crystal-clear waters. 75 sites, tenting area, 50 amp, sewer, dump station, store, laundry, rec hall, swimming, boating, fishing, pool, group area, LP gas. Pets allowed. Open May 15-October 15. ☎ 764-8677.

Neil E. Michaud Campground, 164 Houlton Road, Presque Isle 04769. Experience the stunning beauty in the heart of Maine's potato empire on grassy pull-through sites on US 1, 2½ miles south of Presque Isle. 45 sites, tenting area, 30 amp, sewer, dump station, store, laundry, rec hall, on-site rentals, group area. Swimming, boating, fishing, pool and LP gas nearby. Pets allowed. Open year-round. ☎ 769-1951.

St. Agatha

Lakeview Camping Resort, 9 Lakeview Drive, St. Agatha 04772. Walking distance to many activities throughout the summer. Canteen, restaurant, lounge, full-stock convenience store and shower house. 70 sites, tenting area, 50 amp, sewer, dump station, store, swimming, pool, on-site rentals, group area. Boating and fishing nearby. Pets allowed. Open Memorial Day-Columbus Day. ☎ 543-6331.

Appendix

Where Can I Learn More?

■ Books

📖 Abrell, Diana. *A Pocket Guide to the Carriage Roads of Acadia National Park* (with maps). Down East Books, 1996.

📖 *AMC Mountain Guide To Maine*. Appalachian Mountain Club Books, 1993.

📖 *AMC River Guide To Maine*. Appalachian Mountain Club Books, 1991.

📖 Brechlin, Earl. *A Pocket Guide to Hiking on Mount Desert Island* (with maps). Down East Books, 1996.

📖 Brechlin, Earl. *A Pocket Guide to Paddling the Waters of Mount Desert Island* (with maps). Down East Books, 1996.

📖 Clark, Stephen. *Katahdin, A Guide to Baxter State Park*. North Country Press, 1996.

📖 Collins, Jan and Joseph E. McCarthy. *Nature Walks in Southern Maine*. Appalachian Mountain Club Books, 1996.

📖 Gibson, John. *50 Hikes in Maine*. Backcountry Press, 1983.

📖 Gibson, John. *50 Hikes in Southern Maine*. Backcountry Press, 1989.

📖 Gilpatrick, Gil. *The Canoe Guide's Handbook*. DeLorme Publishing, 1987.

📖 Gorman, Stephen. *AMC Guide to Winter Camping*. Appalachian Mountain Club Books, 1991.

📖 Grierson, Ruth. *Acadia Wildlife Watcher's Guide*. NorthWord Press, 1995.

📖 Hale, Sarah and David Gibbs. *Maine, Mountain Bike!* Menasha Ridge Press, 1998.

📖 Katona, Steven et al. *Field Guide to Whales, Porpoises and Seals of the Gulf of Maine*. Scribners, 1983.

📖 Minutolo, Audrey. *A Pocket Guide to Biking on Mount Desert Island* (with maps). Down East Books, 1996.

📖 Morison, Samuel E. *The Story of Mount Desert Island*. Little, Brown, and Co, 1960.

📖 Newlin, William. *Lakes and Ponds of Mount Desert*. Down East Books, 1989.

📖 Paigen, Jennifer. *Sea Kayaker's Guide to Mount Desert Island*. Down East Books, 1998.

📖 Roberts, Ann Rockefeller. *Mr. Rockefeller's Roads: The Untold Story of Acadia's Carriage Roads and Their Creator*. Down East Books, 1990.

📖 Seymour, Tom. *Hiker's Guide to Maine*. Falcon Press, 1995.

📖 Slack, Nancy and Allison Bell. *A Field Guide to New England Alpine Summits*. Appalachian Mountain Club Books, 1995.

📖 Wilson, Alex and John Hayes. *AMC Quiet Water Canoe Guide To Maine*. Appalachian Mountain Club Books, 1995.

■ Magazine

Down East, the Magazine of Maine (monthly). PO Box 679, Camden 04843. ☎ 800-727-7422.

■ Map

Maine Atlas and Gazetteer. 78 pages of color maps. DeLorme, 1998.

■ On Video

Gift of Acadia, with Jack Perkins, Dobbs Productions.

Maine, America's Coast, with Jack Perkins, Dobbs Productions.

Light Spirits, Maine's lighthouses profiled, with Jack Perkins, Dobbs Productions.

Maine, An Ecotourism Guide, with Jennifer Skiff. Dobbs Productions.

Maine Coast Symphony, Acanthus Video.

The Four Seasons of Acadia, Acanthus Video.

■ Chambers of Commerce

For information on lodging, activities and restaurants contact the organizations below. A good, general-information Website is **www.visitmaine. com**. All area codes are 207.

■ ACADIA NATIONAL PARK
See Mount Desert Island, below.

■ ANDROSCOGGIN COUNTY
Androscoggin County, PO Box 59, 179 Lisbon Street, Lewiston 04243-0059; ☎ 783-2249; fax 783-4481. Areas covered: Auburn, Greene, Leeds, Lewiston, Lisbon, Lisbon Center, Livermore, Livermore Falls, Mechanic Falls, Minot, Poland, Sabattus, Turner, Wales.

■ BANGOR
Bangor Region Chamber of Commerce, 519 Main Street, Bangor 04402-1443; ☎ 947-0307, fax 990-1447; E-mail chamber@ bangorregion.com.

■ BAR HARBOR
Bar Harbor, PO Box 158, 93 Cottage Street, Bar Harbor 04609; ☎ 288-5103; fax 288-2565. Areas covered: Acadia National Park, Bar Harbor.

■ BATH-BRUNSWICK
Bath Business Association, Suite 215, 9 Coastal Plaza, Bath 04530. Area covered: Bath.

Bath-Brunswick Region, 59 Pleasant Street, Brunswick 04011; ☎ 725-8797 or 443-9751; fax 725-9787 or 442-0808; E-mail ccbbr@horton.col.k12.me.us. Areas covered: Arrowsic, Bath, Bowdoinham, Brunswick, Georgetown, Harpswell, Phippsburg, Topsham, West Bath, Wiscasset, Woolwich.

■ BELFAST

Belfast Area, PO Box 58, Belfast 04915; ☎ 338-5900. Areas covered: Belfast, Belmont, Brooks, Northport, Searsmont, Swanville.

■ BETHEL

Bethel Area, PO Box 439, Main Street, Bethel 04217-0439; ☎ 824-2282. Areas covered: Andover, Bethel, Bryant Pond (Woodstock), Gilead, Hanover, Locke Mills (Greenwood), Newry, Waterford and adjoining communities.

■ BIDDEFORD

Biddeford-Saco, 180 Main Street, Biddeford 04005; ☎ 282-1567; fax 282-3149. Areas covered: Biddeford, Saco.

■ BLUE HILL

Blue Hill, PO Box 533, Blue Hill 04614; ☎ E-mail woisard@ bluehillme.com.

■ BOOTHBAY

Boothbay, PO Box 187, Route 27, Boothbay 04537; ☎ 633-4743 (summer only). Area covered: Boothbay.

Boothbay Harbor Region, PO Box 356, Route 27, Boothbay Harbor 04538; ☎ 633-2353; fax 633-7448; E-mail seamaine@boothbayharbor.com. Areas covered: Boothbay, Boothbay Harbor, East Boothbay, Edgecomb, Newcastle, Southport.

■ BRIDGTON

Bridgton-Lakes Region Chamber of Commerce, PO Box 236 Bridgton 04009; ☎ 647-3472; E-mail director@mainelakes-chamber.com.

■ BRUNSWICK

See Bath-Brunswick, above.

■ BUCKSPORT

Bucksport Bay Area, PO Box 1880, Bucksport 04416-1880; ☎ 469-6818. Areas covered: Bucksport, Orland, Verona.

■ CALAIS

Calais Regional Chamber of Commerce, PO Box 368, 235 Main Street, Calais 04619; ☎ 454-2308. Areas covered: Alexander, Baring, Calais, Charlotte, Grand Lake Stream, Meddybemps, Pembroke, Perry, Princeton, Robinston, Woodland (Baileyville).

■ CAMDEN

Camden-Rockport-Lincolnville Chamber of Commerce, PO Box 919 Camden 04843; ☎ 236-4404; fax 236-4315; E-mail chamber@ camdenme.org. Areas covered: Camden, Hope, Islesboro, Lincolnville, Northport, Rockport, Union, Warren.

■ CARIBOU

Caribou, PO Box 357, 111 High Street, Caribou 04736; ☎ 498-6156. Area covered: Caribou.

■ CHINA

China Area Business Betterment Association, PO Box 189, South China 04358; ☎ 445-2890. Areas covered: Albion, China, Palermo, South China, Vassalboro, Windsor.

■ DAMARISCOTTA

Damariscotta Region, PO Box 13, Main Street, Damariscotta 04543; ☎ 563-2690. Areas covered: Alna, Breman, Bristol, Damariscotta, Edgecomb, Jefferson, Newcastle, Nobleboro, South Bristol.

Damariscotta Region Information Bureau, PO Box 217 address Bus. US 1, Damariscotta 04543; ☎ 563-3175 or 563-3176; fax563-2690; E-mail damainfo@lincoln.midcoast.com.

■ DEER ISLE-STONINGTON

Deer Isle-Stonington Chamber of Commerce, PO Box 459, Stonington 04681-0459; ☎ 348-6124; E-mail dkdphotography@acadia.net.

■ EAST PENOBSCOT BAY

East Penobscot Bay Association, East Penobscot, Maine; ☎ 359-8235; E-mail info@penobscotbay.com.

■ EASTPORT

Eastport Area, PO Box 254, Eastport 04631; ☎ 853-4644. Areas covered: Charlotte, Dennysville, Eastport, Pembroke, Perry, Robbinston.

■ ELLSWORTH

Ellsworth Area Chamber of Commerce, PO Box 267, 163 High Street, Ellsworth 04605; ☎ 667-5584; fax 667-2617; E-mail eacc@downeast.net. Areas covered: Blue Hill, Castine, Ellsworth, Franklin, Hancock, Lamoine, Orland, Sorrento, Sullivan, Surry, Trenton.

■ FARMINGTON

Greater Farmington, PO Box 108, 30 Main Street, Farmington 04938; ☎ 778-4215; fax 778-6237. Areas covered: East Wilton, Farmington, Farmington Falls, Industry, New Sharon, New Vineyard.

■ FORT FAIRFIELD

Fort Fairfield, PO Box 607, 121 Main Street, Fort Fairfield 04742; ☎ 472-3802. Area covered: Fort Fairfield.

■ FORT KENT

Greater Fort Kent Area, 54 West Main Street, Fort Kent 04743; ☎ 834-5354, 800-733-3563; fax 834-6868. Areas covered: Allagash Region, Eagle Lake, Fort Kent, New Canada, Soldier Pond, St. Francis, and St. John.

■ FREEPORT

Freeport Merchants Association, PO Box 452, 16 Mill Street, Freeport 04032; ☎ 865-1212, 800-865-1994 (answering machine); fax 865-0881. Area covered: Freeport.

■ GRAND LAKE STREAM

Grand Lake Stream Chamber of Commerce, PO Box 124, Grand Lake Stream, Maine 04637. Areas covered: Grand Lake Stream, Princeton and Woodland.

■ HOULTON

Greater Houlton, 109 Main Street, Houlton 04730; ☎ 532-4216 or 532-4217. Area covered: Southern Aroostook County.

■ JACKMAN

Jackman-Moose River, PO Box 368, Jackman 04945; ☎ 668-4171. Areas covered: Dennis Plantation, Jackman, Long Pond, Moose River, Parlin Pond.

■ JAY

Jay, Livermore, Livermore Falls, PO Box 150, Jay 04239; ☎ 897-6755. Areas covered: Jay, Livermore, Livermore Falls.

Katahdin Area, 1029 Central Street, Millinocket 04462; ☎ 723-4443. Areas covered: Millinocket, Baxter State Park.

■ KENNEBEC VALLEY

Kennebec Valley, PO Box E, 21 University Drive, Augusta 04332-0192; ☎ 623-4559; fax 626-9342. Areas covered: Augusta, Chelsea, Dresden, Farmingdale, Fayette, Gardiner, Hallowell, Jefferson, Litchfield, Manchester, Monmouth, Pittston, Randolph, Readfield, Somerville, Wayne, West Gardiner, Whitefield, Windsor, Winthrop.

Kennebec Valley Tourism Council, 179 Main Street, Waterville 04901; ☎ 800-393-8629. Areas covered: The Upper Kennebec Valley-Moose River Valley. Call for a free four-season guidebook, bicycle guide and snowmobile map.

■ KENNEBUNK/KENNEBUNKPORT

Kennebunk-Kennebunkport, PO Box 740, 173 Port Road, Kennebunk 04043; ☎ 967-0857; E-mail kkcc@maine.org. Areas covered: Arundel, Cape Porpoise, Goose Rocks Beach, Kennebunk, Kennebunkport, West Kennebunk.

■ KITTERY

Kittery Outlet Association, PO Box 357, Kittery, 03904; ☎ 748-0852; fax 748-1197; www.thekitteryoutlets.com.

Kittery/Eliot, PO Box 526, Kittery 03904; ☎ 439-7545 or 800-639-9645. Areas covered: Kittery, Eliot.

■ LIMESTONE

Limestone, PO Box 361, Limestone 04750; ☎ 325-4025. Areas covered: Caswell, Limestone.

■ LINCOLN

Greater Lincoln Area, PO Box 164, 75 Main Street, Lincoln 04457; ☎ 794-8065. Areas covered: Burlington, Carroll, Chester, Enfield, Howland, Lakeville, Lee, Lincoln, Mattamiscontis, Mattawamkeag, Passadumkeag, Prentiss, Seboeis, Springfield, Topsfield, West Enfield, Webster Plantation, Winn.

■ LIVERMORE, LIVERMORE FALLS

See Jay, above.

■ LUBEC

Lubec, PO Box 123, Lubec 04652-0123; ☎ 733-4522.

■ MACHIAS
Machias Bay Area, PO Box 606, 65-67 Main Street, Machias 04654; ☎ 255-4402. Areas covered: Cutler, East Machias, Jonesboro, Jonesport, Machias, Machiasport, Marshfield, Northfield, Roque Bluffs, Whiting, Whitneyville.

■ MADAWASKA
Great Madawaska, 378 Main Street, Madawaska 04756; ☎ 728-7000. Areas covered: Frenchville, Grand Isle, St. Agatha, Sinclair, Upper Frenchville.

■ LINCOLNVILLE
See Camden, above.

■ MADISON-ANSON
Madison-Anson, PO Box 91, Madison 04950. Areas covered: Anson, Madison.

■ MID-MAINE
Mid-Maine Chamber of Commerce, PO Box 142, One Post Office Square, Waterville 04903-0142; ☎ 873-3315, 873-3316. Areas covered: Albion, Belgrade, Benton, Burnham, Clinton, Fairfield, Hinckley, Oakland, Pittsfield, Rome, Sidney, Unity, Vassalboro, Waterville, Winslow.

■ MOOSEHEAD LAKE
Moosehead Lake Region, PO Box 581, Main Street, Greenville 04441; ☎ 695-2702. Areas covered: Beaver Cove, Greenville, Kokajo, Rockwood, Shirley, Moosehead Trail.

■ MOUNT DESERT ISLAND
Mount Desert, PO Box 675, Northeast Harbor 04662; ☎ 276-5040. Areas covered: Pretty Marsh, Northeast Harbor, Otter Creek, Seal Harbor, Somesville, Acadia National Park.

■ NORTHERN KATAHDIN VALLEY
Northern Katahdin Valley, PO Box 14, Patten 04765; ☎ 463-2077 or 463-2995. Areas covered: Benedicta, Chrystal/Golden Ridge, Dyer Brook, Hersey, Island Falls, Merrill, Monada/Silver Ridge, Moro Plantation, Mount Chase/Shin Pond, Oakfield, Oxbow, Patten, Sherman, Smyrna Mills, Stacyville, T5-R8/Bowlin Pond, T6-R8/Mattagamon, T7-R5.

■ OGUNQUIT
Ogunquit, PO Box 2289, US 1 South, Ogunquit 03907; ☎ 646-2939. Area covered: Ogunquit.

■ OLD ORCHARD BEACH
Old Orchard Beach, PO Box 600, First Street, Old Orchard Beach 04064; ☎ 934-2500; fax 934-4994. Area covered: Old Orchard Beach.

■ OXFORD HILLS
Oxford Hills, PO Box 167, South Paris 04281; ☎/fax 743-5917. Areas covered: Harrison, Hebron, Norway, Otisfield, Oxford, Paris, South Paris, Waterford, West Paris.

Appendix

■ PORTLAND

Convention and Visitors Bureau of Greater Portland, 305 Commercial Street, Portland 04101-4641; ☎ 772-5800; business office, ☎ 772-4994; fax 874-9043.

Greater Portland Region, 145 Middle Street, Portland 04101; ☎ 772-2811; fax 772-1179. Areas covered: Cape Elizabeth, Cumberland, Cumberland Center, Falmouth, Freeport, Gorham, Gray, North Yarmouth, Portland, Pownal, Scarborough, South Portland, Westbrook, Windham, Yarmouth.

Portland's Downtown District, 400 Congress Street, Portland 04101; ☎ 772-6828; fax 774-4640.

■ PRESQUE ISLE

Presque Isle Area, PO Box 672, Three Houlton Road, Presque Isle 04769; ☎ 764-6561; fax 764-6571. Areas covered: Ashland, Blaine, Castle Hill, Chapman, Easton, Mapleton, Mars Hill, Masardis, Oxbow, Portage, Presque Isle, Washburn, Westfield.

■ RANGELEY LAKES

Rangeley Lakes Region, PO Box 317, Rangeley 04970; ☎ 864-5571; fax 864-5366; E-mail mtlakes@rangeley.org. Areas covered: Dallas Plantation, Oquossoc, Rangeley Plantation, Sandy River Plantation.

■ RIVER VALLEY

River Valley Chamber of Commerce, P.O. Drawer 598 23 Hartford Street Rumford 04276; ☎ 364-3241, fax 364-3241; E-mail rvcc@agate.net. Areas covered: Andover, Byron, Canton, Dixfield, Hanover, Mexico, Peru, Roxbury, Rumford.

■ ROCKLAND

Rockland-Thomaston Area, PO Box 508, Harbor Park, Rockland 04841; ☎ 596-0376; fax 596-6549. Areas covered: Cushing, Friendship, Matinicus Island, Monhegan Island (Knox County Area), North Haven, Owls Head, Rockland, St. George, South Thomaston, Thomaston, Union, Vinalhaven, Warren, Washington.

■ ROCKPORT

See Camden, above.

■ SAINT FRANCIS

Saint Francis, PO Box 12, Saint Francis 04774; ☎ 398-3431. Areas covered: Saint Francis, St.John, Allagash.

■ SANFORD

Sanford/Springvale, 261 Main Street, Sanford 04073; ☎ 324-4280/4281; fax 324-8290. Areas covered: Acton, Alfred, Berwick, Lebanon, North Berwick, Sanford, Shapleigh, Springvale, South Berwick.

■ SCHOODIC PENINSULA

Schoodic Peninsula Area, PO Box 381, Winter Harbor 04693; ☎ 800-231-3008 or 963-7658; fax 963-7789. Areas covered: Winter Harbor, Gouldsboro.

■ SEBASTICOOK VALLEY

Sebasticook Valley Chamber of Commerce, PO Box 464, Newport 04953; ☎ 368-4698. Areas covered: Corinna, Detroit, Hartland, Newport, Palmyra, Pittsfield, Plymouth, St. Albans.

■ SKOWHEGAN

Skowhegan Area, PO Box 326, Skowhegan 04976; ☎ 474-3621. Areas covered: Canaan, Norridgewock, Skowhegan.

Skowhegan Chamber of Commerce, Town of Skowhegan, 90 Water Street, Skowhegan 04976.

■ SOUTHERN PISCATAQUIS COUNTY

Southern Piscataquis County, PO Box 376, Dover-Foxcroft 04426; ☎ 564-7533. Areas covered: Abbot, Atkinson, Bowerbank, Brownville, Brownville Jct., Dexter, Dover-Foxcroft, Guilford, Medford, Milo, Monson, Sangerville, Sebec.

■ SOUTHWEST HARBOR

Southwest Harbor/Tremont, PO Box 1143, Southwest Harbor 04679; ☎ 800-423-9264 or 244-9264; fax 244-4185. Areas covered: Acadia National Park, Southwest Harbor, Tremont.

■ STONINGTON

See Deer Isle, above.

■ SUGARLOAF

Sugarloaf Area, Box 2151, RR 1, Kingfield 04947; ☎ 235-2100. Areas covered: Carrabasset Valley, Coplin, Eustis, Farmington, Kingfield, New Vineyards, North Anson, North New Portland, Stratton.

■ TRENTON

Trenton, PO Box 8008, Trenton 04605; ☎ 288-2308. Area covered: Trenton.

■ UPPER KENNEBEC VALLEY

Upper Kennebec Valley, PO Box 491, Bingham 04920; ☎ 672-4100 (summer only). Areas covered: Bingham, Caratunk, Concord, Moscow, Pleasant Ridge, Salon, The Forks, West Forks.

■ VAN BUREN

Greater Van Buren, 65 Main Street, Van Buren 04785; ☎ 868-5059. Areas covered: Cyr Plantation, Grand Isle, Hamlin, Keegan, Lille, Van Buren.

■ WALDO COUNTY

Waldo County Regional Chamber of Commerce, PO Box 577, Unity 04974; ☎ 948-5050; fax 948-5104; E-mail thurston@acadia.net.

■ WALDOBORO

Waldoboro, PO Box 698, Waldoboro 04572; ☎ 832-4883. Areas covered: Friendship, (Knox County Area), Nobleboro, North Waldoboro, Waldoboro (Lincoln County Area).

Appendix

■ **WALDO COUNTY**
Waldo County Regional Chamber of Commerce, PO Box 577 Unity 04988; ☎ 945-5050. Area covered: Waldo County.

■ **WELLS**
Wells, PO Box 356, US 1, Wells 04090; ☎ 646-2451. Areas covered: Wells, Moody.

■ **WILTON**
Wilton, PO Box 501, Wilton 04294; ☎ 645-2214. Area covered: Wilton.

■ **WISCASSET**
Wiscasset Region, PO Box 150, Wiscasset 04578; ☎ 882-4600; E-mailwrba@gwi.net. Area covered: Wiscasset.

■ **WINDHAM**
Windham, PO Box 1015, Windham 04062; ☎ 892-8265. Areas covered: Casco, Gray, Raymond, Sebago Lake, Standish, Windham.

■ **YARMOUTH**
Yarmouth, 16 US Route One, Yarmouth 04096; ☎ 846-3984. Areas covered: North Yarmouth, Yarmouth.

■ **YORK**
York, PO Box 417, York 03909; ☎ 363-4422. Areas covered: Southern Maine and Southern New Hampshire.

■ Newspapers

There is no better way to learn more about a community than to read its newspaper. When pondering a visit to a specific area of Maine, consider getting a subscription to or several back issues of the nearest newspaper. Be sure to ask if they also produce and have available seasonal visitor information.

Maine has a long history of quality newspapers. Some have been in business more than 150 years. While there are seven daily newspapers serving various areas of Maine, most towns are served by weekly newspapers (the majority publishing on Thursdays). Some towns have papers that come out two or three times per week.

Don't let names such as "Republican" or "Democrat" fool you. They harken back to the days when journals were house organs for political parties. Fortunately, that practice ended long ago.

■ **AUGUSTA**
Capital Weekly, PO Box 2788, Augusta 04338. ☎ 621-6000; fax 621-6006; E-mail cwmail@courierpub.com.

Kennebec Journal, 274 Western Avenue, Augusta 04330. ☎ 623-3811; fax 621-5621; E-mail kjedit@biddeford.com.

■ BANGOR

Bangor Daily News/Maine Weekend, PO Box 1329, Bangor 04402. ☎ 990-8040; fax 941-9476; E-mail bdnmail@bangornews.infi.net.

The Weekly, PO Box 2237, Bangor 04402. ☎ 942-2913; fax 947-7508; E-mail thewkly@bangornews.infi.net

■ BAR HARBOR

Bar Harbor Times, PO Box 68, Bar Harbor 04609. ☎ 288-3311; fax 288-5813; E-mail bhtmail@downeast.net.

■ BATH

Coastal Journal, PO Box 705, Bath 04530. ☎ 443-6241; fax 443-5605; E-mail cjournal@gwi.net.

■ BELFAST

The Republican Journal, PO Box 327, Belfast 04915. ☎ 338-3333; fax 338-5498; E-mail trjmail@agate.net.

The Waldo Independent, PO Box 228, Belfast 04915. ☎ 338-5100; fax 338-1810.

■ BETHEL

The Bethel Citizen, PO Box 109, Bethel 04217. ☎ 824-2444; fax 824-2426.

■ BIDDEFORD

The Journal Tribune, PO Box 627, Biddeford 04005. ☎ 282-1535; fax 282-3138; E-mail jtribune@GWI.com.

Biddeford-Saco-OOB Courier, PO Box 1894, Biddeford 04005. ☎ 282-4337; fax 282-4339; E-mail courier@int-usa.net.

■ BLUE HILL

The Weekly Packet, Box 646, Blue Hill 04614. ☎ 374-2341; fax 374-2343.

■ BOOTHBAY HARBOR

Boothbay Register, PO Box 357, Boothbay Harbor 04538. ☎ 633-4620; fax 633-7123.

■ BRIDGTON

The Bridgton News, PO Box 244, Bridgton 04009. ☎ 647-2851; fax 647-5001.

■ BRUNSWICK

The Times Record, 6 Industry Road, Brunswick 04011. ☎ 729-3311; fax 729-5728; E-mail news@timesrecord.com.

■ BUCKSPORT

The Enterprise, PO Box 829, Bucksport 04416. ☎ 469-6722; fax 469-2114; E-mail theenterpr@aol.com.

■ CALAIS

The Calais Advertiser, 19 Church Street, Calais 04619. ☎ 454-3561; fax 454-3458.

Courier Weekend, PO Box 777, Calais 04619. ☎ 506-466-3220; E-mail courier@nbnet.nb.ca.

Saint Croix Courier, PO Box 777, Calais 04619. ☎ 506-466-3220; fax 506-466-9950; E-mail courier@nbnet.nb.ca.

■ **CAMDEN**

The Camden Herald, PO Box 248, Camden 04843. ☎ 236-8511; fax 236-2816; E-mail cherald@courierpub.com.

■ **CAPE ELIZABETH**

The Cape Courier, PO Box 6242, Cape Elizabeth 04107. ☎ 767-5023; E-mail courier@gwi.net; Website www.biddeford.com~courier.

■ **CARIBOU**

Aroostook Republican & News, PO Box 608, Caribou 04736. ☎ 496-3251; fax 492-4351; E-mail aroosrep@bangornews.infi.net.

■ **CASTINE**

Castine Patriot, PO Box 205, Castine 04421. ☎ 326-9300; fax 326-4383.

■ **CUTLER**

The Downeast Coastal Press, HCR 69 Box 287, Cutler 04626. ☎ 259-7751; E-mail downeast@nemaine.com.

■ **DAMARISCOTTA**

Lincoln County Weekly, PO Box 1287, Damariscotta 04543. ☎ 563-5006; fax 563-3615; E-mail lcwmail@courierpub.com.

Lincoln County News, PO Box 36, Damariscotta 04543. ☎ 563-3171; fax 563-3171; E-mail lcn@lincoln.midcoast.com.

■ **DEXTER**

The Eastern Gazette, PO Box 306, Dexter 04930-0306. ☎ 924-7402; fax 924-6215; E-mail gazette@kynd.net.

■ **DOVER-FOXCROFT**

The Piscataquis Observer, PO Box 30, Dover-Foxcroft 04426. ☎ 564-8355; fax 564-7056; E-mail observer@kynd.net.

■ **EASTPORT**

The Quoddy Tides, PO Box 213, Eastport 04631. ☎ 853-4806; fax 853-4095; E-mail qtides@nemaine.com.

■ **ELLSWORTH**

Ellsworth Weekly, PO Box 1122, Ellsworth 04605. ☎ 667-5514; fax 667-0693; E-mail ewmail@courierpub.com.

The Ellsworth American, PO Box 509, Ellsworth 04605-0509. ☎ 667-2576; fax 667-7656; E-mail info@ellsworthamerican.com.

■ **FALMOUTH**

The Forecaster, PO Box 66797, Falmouth 04105. ☎ 781-3661; fax 781-2060; E-mail forecaster@compuserve.com.

■ **FARMINGDALE**

Community Advertiser, 324 Maine Avenue, Farmingdale 04344. ☎ 582-8486; fax 582-4530; E-mail tiser@powerlink.net.

■ **FARMINGTON**

The Franklin Journal & Farmington Chronicle, PO Box 750, Farmington 04938. ☎ 778-2075; fax 778-6970; E-mail mail@mtbluenewspapers.com.

■ FORT FAIRFIELD
Fort Fairfield Review, PO Box 411, Fort Fairfield 04742-0411. ☎ 472-3111; fax 473-7977; E-mail ffreview@ainop.com.

■ GRAY
The Gray News, PO Box 433Gray 04039. ☎ 657-2200; fax 657-5831; E-mail editor@graynews.maine.com.

■ GREENVILLE
Moosehead Messenger, PO Box 400, Greenville 04441. ☎ 695-3077; fax 695-3780; E-mail messenger@gwi.net.

■ HALLOWELL
Maine Times, PO Box 350, Hallowell 04347. ☎ 623-8955; fax 623-8970; E-mail mainetimes@maine.com.

■ HOULTON
Houlton Pioneer Times, PO Box 456, Houlton 04730. ☎ 532-2281; fax 532-2403; E-mail pioneer.times@houlton.com.

■ KENNEBUNK
York County Coast Star, PO Box 979, Kennebunk 04043. ☎ 985-2961; fax 985-9050; E-mail yccs@coaststar.com.

■ LEWISTON/AUBURN
Sun-Journal, PO Box 4400, Lewiston 04243-4400. ☎ 784-5411Fax784-5955; E-mail costello@exploremaine.com.

■ LINCOLN
Lincoln News, PO Box 35, Lincoln 04457. ☎ 794-6532; fax 794-2004; E-mail lincnews@midmaine.com.

■ LIVERMORE FALLS
Livermore Falls Advertiser, PO Box B, Livermore Falls 04254. ☎ 897-4321; fax 897-4322; E-mail mail@mtbluenewspapers.com.

■ LUBEC
The Lubec Light, RR 2 Box 380, Lubec 04652. ☎ 733-2939; fax 733-2946; E-mail lubeclgt@nemaine.com.

■ MACHIAS
Machias Valley News Observer, PO Box 357, Machias 04654. ☎ 255-6561; fax 255-4058.

■ MADAWASKA
Saint John Valley Times, PO Box 419, Madawaska 04756. ☎ 728-3336; fax 728-3825; E-mail stvt@nci1.net.

■ MILLINOCKET
Katahdin Times, 202 Penobscot Avenue, Millinocket 04462. ☎ 723-8118; fax 723-4434; E-mail ktimes@agate.net.

■ MILO
The Town Crier, PO Box 158, Milo 04463. ☎ 943-7384; fax 943-8799.

■ NEW GLOUCESTER
New Gloucester News, PO Box 102, New Gloucester 04260. ☎ 926-4036; fax 926-4036; E-mail ngnews@cybertours.com.

Appendix

■ **NORWAY**
Advertiser-Democrat, PO Box 269, Norway 04268. ☎ 743-7011; fax 743-2256.

■ **OLD TOWN**
Penobscot Times, PO Box 568, Old Town 04468. ☎ 827-4451; fax 827-2280.

■ **PORTLAND**
Casco Bay Weekly, 561 Congress Street, Portland 04101. ☎ 775-6601; fax 775-1615; E-mail editor@cbw.maine.com.

Portland Press Herald/Maine Sunday Telegram, PO Box 1460, Portland 04104. ☎ 791-6650; fax 791-6911; E-mail portlandpaper@server.nlis.net.

■ **PRESQUE ISLE**
The Star-Herald, PO Box 510, Presque Isle 04769. ☎ 768-5431; fax 764-7585; E-mail starhrld@bangornews.infi.net.

■ **RANGELEY**
The Rangeley Highlander, PO Box 542, Rangeley 04970. ☎ 864-3756; fax 864-2447; E-mail highpub@rangeley.org.

■ **ROCKLAND**
The Courier-Gazette, PO Box 249, Rockland 04841. ☎ 594-4401; fax 596-6981; E-mail cgmail@courierpub.com.

The Free Press, 6 Leland Street, Rockland 04841. ☎ 596-0055; fax 596-6698; E-mail freepres@midcoast.com.

■ **RUMFORD**
Rumford Times, PO Box 490, Rumford 04276. ☎ 364-7893; fax 369-0170.

■ **SANFORD**
Sanford News, PO Box DSanford 04073. ☎ 324-5986; fax 490-1431.

■ **SCARBOROUGH**
Scarborough Leader, PO Box 907, Scarborough 04070. ☎ 883-5944; fax 282-4339; E-mail courier@int-usa.net.

■ **SKOWHEGAN**
Somerset Gazette, PO Box 887, Skowhegan 04976. ☎ 474-0606; E-mail gazette@tdstelme.net.

■ **SOUTH CHINA**
The Town Line, PO Box 89, South China 04358. ☎ 445-2234; fax 445-2265; E-mail Townline@pivot.net.

■ **STONINGTON**
Island Ad-Vantages, PO Box 36, Stonington 04681. ☎ 367-2200; fax 367-6397.

■ **WATERVILLE**
Central Maine Morning Sentinel, 31 Front Street, Waterville 04901. ☎ 873-3341; fax 861-9223; E-mail msedit@biddeford.com.

■ **WESTBROOK**
American Journal, 4 Dana St., Westbrook 04092. ☎ 854-2577; fax 854-0018.

■ **WINDHAM**
The Suburban News, 733 Roosevelt Trail, Windham 04062. ☎ 892-1166; fax 892-1171; E-mail subnews@aol.com.

■ **WISCASSET**
Wiscasset Newspaper, PO Box 429, Wiscasset 04578. ☎ 882-6355; fax 882-4280.

■ Maine Libraries

Mainers love their libraries. Perhaps it's the long winters. Or maybe it's the population's traditional love affair with reading. But whatever the reason, there is barely a town or village in the state that doesn't have a library. Even larger sporting camps and stately hotels reserve a room full of books for patrons and staff to enjoy.

Libraries in Maine range from stately, well-endowed brick or granite buildings established by wealthy summer folk more than a century ago to modest, one-room affairs where the door is seldom locked and the selection is mostly dog-eared paperbacks and mystery novels.

Now that the US Post Office is closing many of its smaller units, the library is often the last remaining symbol of community. Often, the library is home to the local historical society. Frequently it is where the town's oldest records are kept. Libraries are great places, not just for a good read, but also for people researching genealogy or those just wishing to develop a better sense of place about a given community. Note: All phone numbers are in 207 area code.

■ **ACTON**
Acton Public Library . . . . ☎ 636-2781

■ **ADDISON**
Mayhew Library Association . . . . ☎ 483-6090

■ **ALBION**
Albion Public Library. . . . . ☎ 437-2616

■ **ALFRED**
Parsons Memorial Library . . . . ☎ 324-2001

■ **ANDOVER**
Andover Public Library. . . . . ☎ 392-4841

■ **ANSON**
Stewart Public Library . . . . no phone

■ **APPLETON**
Williams Memorial Library . . . . no phone

■ **ASHLAND**
Ashland Community Library . . . . ☎ 435-6532

■ **AUBURN**
Auburn Public Library . . . . ☎ 782-3191

■ **AUGUSTA**
Lithgow Public Library . . . . ☎ 626-2415
Maine State Library . . . . ☎ 287-5600

■ **BALDWIN**
Brown Memorial Library. . . . . ☎ 787-3155

■ **BANGOR**
Bangor Public Library . . . . ☎ 947-8336

■ **BAR HARBOR**
Jesup Memorial Library . . . . ☎ 288-4245

■ **BATH**
Patten Free Library . . . . ☎ 443-5141

■ **BASS HARBOR**
Bass Harbor Memorial . . . . ☎ 244-3798

■ **BELFAST**
Belfast Free Library . . . . ☎ 338-3884

■ **BERWICK**
Berwick Public Library . . . . ☎ 698-5737

■ **BETHEL**
Bethel Library Association . . . . ☎ 824-2520

■ **BIDDEFORD**
McArthur Public Library . . . . ☎ 284-4181

■ **BINGHAM**
Bingham Union Library . . . . no phone

■ **BLUE HILL**
Blue Hill Public Library . . . . ☎ 374-5515
East Blue Hill Public Library. ☎ 374-5577

■ **BOOTHBAY HARBOR**
Boothbay Harbor Memorial . . . . ☎ 633-3112

■ **BOWDOINHAM**
Bowdoinham Public Library . . . . ☎ 666-8405

■ **BRADFORD**
Curtis Free Public Library . . . . ☎ 327-2923

■ **BREMEN**
Bremen Public Library . . . . ☎ 529-5572

■ BREWER
Brewer Public Library . . . . ☎ 989-7943

■ BRIDGTON
Bridgton Public Library . . . . ☎ 647-2472
North Bridgton Public Library . . . . ☎ 647-8563

■ BRISTOL
Bristol Area Library . . . . ☎ 677-2115

■ BROOKLIN
Friend Memorial Public Library . . . . ☎ 359-2276

■ BROOKSVILLE
Brooksville Free Public Library . . . . ☎ 326-4560

■ BROWNFIELD
Brownfield Public Library . . . . ☎ 935-3003

■ BROWNVILLE
Brownville Public Library . . . . no phone

■ BRUNSWICK
Curtis Memorial Library . . . . ☎ 725-5242

■ BUCKFIELD
Zadoc Long Free Library . . . . ☎ 336-2171

■ BUCKSPORT
Buck Memorial Library . . . . ☎ 469-2650

■ BUXTON
West Buxton Public Library . . . . ☎ 727-5898
Berry Memorial Library . . . . ☎ 929-5484

■ CALAIS
Calais Free Library . . . . ☎ 454-2758

■ CAMDEN
Camden Public Library . . . . ☎ 236-3440

■ CANAAN
Canaan Public Library . . . . ☎ 474-6397

■ CAPE ELIZABETH
Thomas Memorial Library . . . . ☎ 799-1720

■ CARRABASSETT VALLEY
Carrabassett Valley Library . . . . ☎ 235-2211

■ CARIBOU
Caribou Public Library . . . . ☎ 493-4214

■ CASCO
Simpson Memorial Library . . . . ☎ 848-7145
Casco Public Library . . . . ☎ 627-4541

■ CASTINE
Witherle Memorial Library . . . . ☎ 326-4375

■ **CHARLESTON**
Charleston Public Library . . . . ☎ 285-3637

■ **CUMBERLAND**
Chebeague Island Library. . . . . ☎ 846-4351

■ **CHERRYFIELD**
Cherryfield Public Library. . . . . no phone

■ **CHINA**
Brown Memorial Library. . . . . ☎ 968-2926
South China Library . . . . ☎ 445-3094

■ **CLINTON**
Brown Memorial Library. . . . . ☎ 426-8686

■ **COOPER**
Cooper Free Public Library . . . . no phone

■ **CORINNA**
Stewart Free Library . . . . ☎ 278-2454

■ **CORINTH**
Atkins Memorial Library. . . . . no phone

■ **CORNISH**
Bonney Memorial Library. . . . . ☎ 625-8083

■ **CRANBERRY ISLES**
Great Cranberry Library. . . . . ☎ 244-7358
Islesford Library . . . . ☎ 244-9565

■ **CUMBERLAND**
Prince Memorial Library. . . . . ☎ 829-2215

■ **CUSHING**
Cushing Public Library . . . . ☎ 354-8860

■ **DAMARISCOTTA**
Skidompha Library . . . . ☎ 563-5513

■ **DANFORTH**
Danforth Public Library . . . . ☎ 448-2055

■ **DEER ISLE**
Chase Emerson Memorial Library . . . . ☎ 348-2899

■ **DENMARK**
Denmark Public Library . . . . ☎ 452-2200

■ **DENNYSVILLE**
Lincoln Memorial Library . . . . no phone

■ **DETROIT**
Fernald Library. . . . . ☎ 257-4488

■ **DEXTER**
Abbott Memorial Library . . . . ☎ 924-7292

■ **DIXFIELD**
Ludden Memorial Library. . . . . ☎ 562-8838

■ **DOVER-FOXCROFT**
Thompson Free Library. . . . . ☎ 564-3350

■ **DRESDEN**
Bridge Academy Public Library . . . . ☎ 737-8810

■ **EAST MACHIAS**
Sturdivant Public Library . . . . ☎ 255-0070

■ **EAST MILLINOCKET**
East Millinocket Public Library . . . . ☎ 746-3554

■ **EASTPORT**
Peavey Memorial Library . . . . ☎ 853-4021

■ **ELIOT**
William Fogg Library . . . . ☎ 439-9437

■ **ELLSWORTH**
Ellsworth Public Library . . . . ☎ 667-6363

■ **ENFIELD**
Cole Memorial Library. . . . . ☎ 732-4270

■ **EUSTIS**
Stratton Public Library. . . . . ☎ 246-4401

■ **FAIRFIELD**
Lawrence Public Library . . . . ☎ 453-6867

■ **FALMOUTH**
Falmouth Memorial Library. . . . . ☎ 781-2351

■ **FARMINGTON**
Farmington Public Library . . . . ☎ 778-4312

■ **FAYETTE**
Underwood Memorial Library. . . . . no phone

■ **FORT FAIRFIELD**
Fort Fairfield Public Library . . . . ☎ 472-3880

■ **FORT KENT**
Fort Kent Public Library . . . . ☎834-3048

■ **FRANKFORT**
Pierce Reading Room. . . . . no phone

■ **FREEPORT**
Freeport Community Library . . . . ☎ 865-3307

■ **FRENCHBORO**
Frenchboro Public Library. ☎ 334-2944

■ **FRIENDSHIP**
Friendship Public Library . . . . ☎ 832-5332

■ **FRYEBURG**
Fryeburg Public Library . . . . ☎ 935-2731

■ **GARDINER**
Gardiner Public Library . . . . ☎ 582-3312

■ **GARLAND**
Lyndon Oak Memorial Library . . . . no phone

■ **GEORGETOWN**
Richards Library . . . . no phone

■ **GLENBURN**
Glenburn Library . . . . ☎ 942-9897

■ **GORHAM**
Baxter Memorial Library . . . . ☎ 839-5031
North Gorham Public Library . . . . ☎ 892-2575

■ **GOULDSBORO**
Dorcas Library . . . . ☎ 963-4027

■ **GRAY**
Gray Public Library . . . . ☎ 657-4110

■ **GREENE**
Morse Memorial Library . . . . ☎ 946-5544

■ **GREENVILLE**
Shaw Public Library . . . . ☎ 695-3579

■ **GUILFORD**
Guilford Memorial Library . . . . ☎ 876-4547

■ **HALLOWELL**
Hubbard Free Library . . . . ☎ 622-6582

■ **HAMPDEN**
Dyer Community Library . . . . ☎ 862-3550

■ **HARPSWELL**
Cundys Harbor Library . . . . ☎ 725-1461
Orrs Island Library . . . . no phone

■ **HARRINGTON**
Gallison Memorial Library . . . . ☎ 483-4547

■ **HARRISON**
Caswell Public Library . . . . ☎ 583-2970
Bolsters Mills Village Library . . . . ☎ 583-6421

■ **HARTLAND**
Hartland Public Library . . . . ☎ 938-4702

■ **HIRAM**
Soldiers Memorial Library . . . . ☎ 625-4650

■ **HOLLIS**
Hollis Center Public Library . . . . ☎ 929-3911

Salmon Falls Library . . . . ☎ 929-3990

■ HOPE
Hope Library . . . . ☎ 763-3548

■ HOULTON
Cary Library. . . . . ☎ 532-1302

■ HOWLAND
Thomas Free Library . . . . no phone

■ ISLAND FALLS
Katahdin Public Library. . . . . no phone

■ ISLE AU HAUT
Revere Memorial Library . . . . no phone

■ ISLEBORO
Pendleton Library. . . . . ☎ 734-2218

■ JACKMAN
Thomas Jackman Public Library . . . . ☎ 668-2110

■ JAY
Jay-Niles Memorial Library . . . . ☎ 645-4062

■ JEFFERSON
Jefferson Public Library. . . . . ☎ 549-7491

■ JONESPORT
Peabody Memorial Library. . . . . no phone

■ KENDUSKEAG
Case Memorial Library . . . . ☎ 884-8598

■ KENNEBUNK
Kennebunk Free Library. . . . . ☎ 985-2173

■ KENNEBUNKPORT
Graves Memorial Library . . . . ☎ 967-2778
Cape Porpoise Library. . . . . ☎ 967-5668

■ KINGFIELD
Webster Free Library. . . . . ☎ 265-2052

■ KITTERY
Rice Public Library. . . . . ☎ 439-1553

■ LEBANON
Lebanon Area Library . . . . no phone

■ LEWISTON
Lewiston Public Library . . . . ☎ 784-0135

■ LIBERTY
Davis-Liberty Library . . . . ☎ 589-3161

■ LIMERICK
Limerick Public Library . . . . ☎ 793-8975

■ **LIMESTONE**
Frost Memorial Library . . . . ☎ 325-4706

■ **LIMINGTON**
Davis Memorial Library . . . . ☎ 637-2422

■ **LINCOLN**
Lincoln Memorial Library. . . . . ☎ 794-2765

■ **LISBON**
Lisbon Village Branch Library . . . . ☎ 353-2262
Lisbon Library Department . . . . ☎ 353-6564

■ **LIVERMORE**
Livermore Public Library. . . . . ☎ 897-7173

■ **LIVERMORE FALLS**
Treat Memorial Library. . . . . ☎ 897-3631

■ **LONG ISLAND**
Long Island Community Library. . . . . ☎ 766-2530

■ **LOVELL**
Hobbs Memorial Library. . . . . ☎ 925-3177
Hill Memorial Library . . . . ☎ 928-2301

■ **LUBEC**
Lubec Memorial Library . . . . ☎ 733-2491

■ **LYMAN**
Lyman Community Library . . . . ☎ 499-7114

■ **MACHIAS**
Porter Memorial Library. . . . . ☎ 255-3933

■ **MADAWASKA**
Madawaska Public Library . . . . ☎ 728-3606

■ **MADISON**
Madison Public Library. . . . . ☎ 696-5626

■ **MARS HILL**
Hansen Memorial Library. . . . . ☎ 429-9625

■ **MATTAWAMKEAG**
Mattawamkeag Public Library . . . . ☎ 736-7013

■ **MECHANIC FALLS**
Mechanic Falls Public Library. . . . . ☎ 345-9450

■ **MEXICO**
Mexico Free Public Library . . . . ☎ 364-3281

■ **MILBRIDGE**
Milbridge Public Library. . . . . ☎ 546-3066

■ **MILLINOCKET**
Millinocket Memorial Library . . . . ☎ 723-7020

■ **MILO**
Milo Free Public Library . . . . ☎ 943-2612

■ **MONHEGAN**
Monhegan Memorial Library . . . . no phone

■ **MONMOUTH**
Cumston Public Library . . . . ☎ 933-4788
North Monmouth Public Library . . . . ☎ 933-3010

■ **MONROE**
Monroe Community Library . . . . ☎ 525-3515

■ **MONSON**
Monson Public Library . . . . no phone

■ **MOUNT DESERT**
Somesville Library . . . . ☎ 244-7404
Northeast Harbor Library . . . . ☎ 276-3333
Seal Harbor Library . . . . ☎ 276-5306

■ **MOUNT VERNON**
Shaw Memorial Library . . . . ☎ 293-2565

■ **NAPLES**
Naples Public Library . . . . ☎ 693-6841

■ **NEW GLOUCESTER**
New Gloucester Public Library . . . . no phone

■ **NEW PORTLAND**
New Portland Community Library . . . . ☎ 628-6561

■ **NEW SHARON**
New Sharon Town Library . . . . ☎ 779-1128

■ **NEW VINEYARD**
New Vineyard Public Library . . . . ☎ 652-2250

■ **NEWFIELD**
Newfield Village Library . . . . no phone

■ **NEWPORT**
Newport Public Library . . . . ☎ 368-5074

■ **MERCER**
Shaw Public Library . . . . ☎ 587-2911

■ **NORRIDGEWOCK**
Norridgewock Free Public Library . . . . ☎ 634-2828

■ **NORTH BERWICK**
Hurd Library . . . . ☎ 676-2215

■ **NORTH HAVEN**
North Haven Public Library . . . . ☎ 867-9797

■ **NORWAY**
Norway Memorial Library . . . . ☎ 743-5309

■ **OAKLAND**
Oakland Public Library . . . . ☎ 465-7533

■ **OLD ORCHARD BEACH**
Ocean Park Memorial Library . . . . ☎ 934-4351
Libby Memorial Library . . . . ☎ 934-4351

■ **OGUNQUIT**
Ogunquit Memorial Library . . . . ☎ 646-9024

■ **OLD TOWN**
Old Town Public Library . . . . ☎ 827-3972

■ **ORONO**
Orono Public Library . . . . ☎ 866-5060

■ **ORRINGTON**
Orrington Public Library . . . . ☎ 825-4938

■ **OTIS**
Otis Public Library . . . . ☎ 537-2211

■ **OWLS HEAD**
Owls Head Village Library . . . . no phone

■ **OXFORD**
Freeland Holmes Library . . . . no phone

■ **PARIS**
Hamlin Memorial Library . . . . ☎ 743-2980
Paris Public Library . . . . ☎ 743-6994

■ **PARKMAN**
Harvey Memorial Library . . . . ☎ 876-3730

■ **PARSONSFIELD**
Kezar Falls Circulating Library . . . . ☎ 625-2424
Parsonsfield Public Library . . . . ☎ 625-4689

■ **PATTEN**
Veterans Memorial Library . . . . ☎ 528-2164

■ **PORTLAND**
Portland Public Library . . . . ☎ 871-1700
Munjoy Branch Library . . . . ☎ 772-4581
Reiche Branch Library . . . . ☎ 774-6871
Riverton Branch Library . . . . ☎ 797-2915
Cliff Island Library . . . . no phone
Burbank Branch Library . . . . ☎ 774-4229
Peaks Island Branch . . . . ☎ 766-5540

■ **PHILLIPS**
Phillips Public Library . . . . ☎ 639-2665

■ **PHIPPSBURG**
Totman Library . . . . ☎ 389-2309

■ **PITTSFIELD**
Pittsfield Public Library . . . . ☎ 487-5880

■ **POLAND**
Ricker Memorial Library . . . . ☎ 998-4390

■ **PRESQUE ISLE**
Turner Memorial Library . . . . ☎ 764-2571

■ **PRINCETON**
Princeton Public Library . . . . ☎ 796-5333

■ **RANGELEY**
Rangeley Public Library . . . . ☎ 864-5529

■ **RAYMOND**
Raymond Village Library . . . . ☎ 655-4283

■ **READFIELD**
Readfield Community Library . . . . ☎ 685-4089

■ **RICHMOND**
Umberhine Public Library . . . . ☎ 737-2770

■ **ROCKLAND**
Rockland Public Library . . . . ☎ 594-0310

■ **ROCKPORT**
Rockport Public Library . . . . ☎ 236-3642

■ **RUMFORD**
Rumford Public Library . . . . ☎ 364-3661

■ **SACO**
Dyer Library . . . . ☎ 283-3861

■ **SANFORD**
Goodall Memorial Library . . . . ☎ 324-4714
Springvale Public Library . . . . ☎ 324-4624

■ **SANGERVILLE**
Sangerville Public Library . . . . ☎ 876-3491

■ **SEBAGO**
Spaulding Memorial Library . . . . ☎ 787-2321

■ **SEDGWICK**
Sargentville Library . . . . no phone

■ **SCARBOROUGH**
Scarborough Public Library . . . . ☎ 883-4723

■ **SEARSMONT**
Searsmont Town Library . . . . ☎ 342-5549

■ **SEARSPORT**
Carver Memorial Library . . . . ☎ 548-2303

■ **SHAPLEIGH**
Shapleigh Community Library . . . . ☎ 636-3630

■ **SHERMAN**
Sherman Public Library . . . . ☎ 365-4882

■ **SKOWHEGAN**
Skowhegan Public Library . . . . ☎ 474-9072

■ **SOLON**
Coolidge Library . . . . ☎ 643-2562

■ **SOMERVILLE**
Somerville Town Library . . . . no phone

■ **SOUTH BERWICK**
South Berwick Public Library . . . . ☎ 384-3308

■ **SOUTH BRISTOL**
Rutherford Library . . . . no phone

■ **SOUTHPORT**
Southport Memorial Library . . . . ☎ 633-2741

■ **SOUTH PORTLAND**
South Portland Public Library . . . . ☎ 767-7660
Memorial Branch Library . . . . ☎ 775-1835

■ **SOUTHWEST HARBOR**
Southwest Harbor Public Library . . . . ☎ 244-7065

■ **STANDISH**
Richville Library . . . . ☎ 642-4698
Steep Falls Library . . . . ☎ 675-3132

■ **STETSON**
Stetson Library . . . . ☎ 296-2020

■ **STEUBEN**
Moore Library . . . . ☎ 546-7301

■ **STONINGTON**
Stonington Public Library . . . . ☎ 367-5926

■ **STRONG**
Strong Public Library . . . . ☎ 684-4003

■ **SULLIVAN**
Frenchmans Bay Library . . . . ☎ 422-2307

■ **SWANS ISLAND**
Swans Island Public Library . . . . ☎ 526-4330

■ **ST. GEORGE**
Jackson Memorial Library . . . . ☎ 372-8961

■ **THOMASTON**
Thomaston Public Library . . . . ☎ 354-2453

■ **TOPSHAM**
Topsham Public Library . . . . ☎ 725-1727

■ **TURNER**
Turner Public Library . . . . ☎ 225-2030

■ **UNION**
Vose Library . . . . ☎ 785-4733

■ **UNITY**
Dorothy W. Quimby Library . . . . ☎ 948-3131

■ **VAN BUREN**
Morneault Memorial Library . . . . ☎ 868-5076

■ **VASSALBORO**
Vassalboro Public Library . . . . ☎ 923-3233

■ **VINALHAVEN**
Vinalhaven Public Library . . . . ☎ 863-4401

■ **WALDOBORO**
Waldoboro Public Library . . . . ☎ 832-4484

■ **WARREN**
Warren Free Public Library . . . . ☎ 273-2900

■ **WASHBURN**
Washburn Memorial Library . . . . ☎ 455-4814

■ **WASHINGTON**
Gibbs Library . . . . ☎ 845-2663

■ **WATERBORO**
Waterboro Public Library . . . . ☎ 247-3363

■ **WATERFORD**
Waterford Library Association . . . . ☎ 583-2546

■ **WATERVILLE**
Waterville Public Library . . . . ☎ 872-5433

■ **WAYNE**
Cary Memorial Library . . . . ☎ 685-3612
North Wayne Village Library . . . . ☎ 685-3689

■ **WELD**
Weld Public Library . . . . ☎ 585-2439

■ **WELLS**
Wells Public Library . . . . ☎ 646-8181

■ **WEST PARIS**
West Paris Public Library . . . . ☎ 674-2004

■ **WESTBROOK**
Walker Memorial Library . . . . ☎ 854-0630
Warren Memorial Library . . . . ☎ 854-5891

■ **WHITNEYVILLE**
Whitneyville Public Library . . . . ☎ 255-8077

Appendix

■ **WILTON**
Wilton Free Public Library . . . . ☎ 645-4831

■ **WINDHAM**
Windham Public Library . . . . ☎ 892-1908
South Windham Public Library . . . . ☎ 892-1908

■ **WINSLOW**
Winslow Public Library . . . . ☎ 872-1978

■ **WINTER HARBOR**
Winter Harbor Public Library . . . . ☎ 963-7556

■ **WINTERPORT**
Winterport Memorial Library . . . . ☎ 223-5540

■ **WINTHROP**
Bailey Public Library . . . . ☎ 377-8673

■ **WISCASSET**
Wiscasset Public Library . . . . ☎ 882-7161

■ **WOODLAND (Washington County)**
Woodland Public Library . . . . ☎ 427-6210

■ **WOODSTOCK**
Whitman Memorial Library . . . . ☎ 665-2505

■ **YARMOUTH**
Merrill Memorial Library . . . . ☎ 846-4763

■ **YORK**
York Public Library . . . . ☎ 363-2818

■ Snowmobile Clubs

Snowmobile clubs are primarily responsible for the maintenance and grooming of Maine's 12,000 mile of trails. Grooming funds pay for fuel and equipment. Most operators are unpaid volunteers. Clubs often provide warming huts and/or restrooms and parking for vehicles and trailers. They sometimes produce and publish detailed maps of local trails. None of the clubs have a phone contact.

When riding on any trail, or using club facilities, be sure to send along a donation to help defray costs.

■ **ABBOT**
Big Pine Riders, 109 Pond Road, Abbot 04406

■ **ALBION**
Night Roadrunners Snowmobile Club, RFD, Box 3510, Albion 04910

■ **ALFRED**
Shaker Valley Sno Traveler, RR 1, Box 258, Alfred 04002

■ **ALLAGASH**
Allagash Eagles Snowmobile Club, Box 232-A, Allagash 04774
Moose Town Riders, RR 1 Box 161, Allagash 04774

■ **ANDOVER**
Snow Valley Sno Goers, PO Box 159, Andover 04216
Anson-North Anson Snowmobile Club, PO Box 437, Anson 04911

■ **ASHLAND**
Ashland Snowmobile Club, PO Box 370, Ashland 04732

■ **ATHENS**
A C Lineriders Snow Club, 5088 Fox Hill Road, Athens 04912

■ **ATKINSON**
Cold Smoke Riders, 101 S. Stagecoach Road, Atkinson 04426

■ **AUBURN**
Auburn Sno Groomers, PO Box 3204, Auburn 04212
Andy Valley Sno Gypsies, 83 Boulder Drive, Auburn 04210
Perkins Ridge Sno Travelers, 147 Lake Street, Auburn 04210

■ **AUGUSTA**
Calumet Snowmobile Club, RR 3, Box 1242, Augusta 04330
Fox Glen Snowmobile Club, PO Box 4654, Augusta 04330
North Augusta Trailblazers, PO Box 213, Augusta 04330
State of Maine Snowmobile Club, RR 7, Box 1965, Augusta 04330

■ **BANGOR**
Maine Conn. Snowmobile Club, Apt. 4, 153 Husson Ave., Bangor 04401
Paul Bunyan Snowmobile Club, PO Box 2144, Bangor 04401
Penobscot Snowmobile Club, RR 2, Box 1680, Bangor 04401

■ **BAR MILLS**
Sokokis Riders Snowmobile Club, PO Box 422, Bar Mills 04004

■ **BATH**
Bath River Runners, PO Box 1114, Bath 04530

■ **BELFAST**
Belfast Area Snow Packers, RR 1, Box 5622, Belfast 04915

■ **BELGRADE**
Belgrade Draggin Masters, RFD 1 Box 200, Belgrade 04917
North Belgrade Trail Riders, Route 2, Box 4341, Belgrade 04746

■ **BENEDICTS**
Benedicta Sno-Gang, PO Box 39, Main Road, Benedicts 04733

■ **BENTON**
Country Cousins Snow Club, 201 Richards Road, Benton 04927

■ **BETHEL**
Bethel Snow Twisters, 815 Intervale Road, Bethel 04217

Appendix

■ BINGHAM
Lexington Highlanders Snowmobile Club, PO Box 410, Bingham 04920

Valley Riders, Box 12, Bingham 04920

■ BOWDOINHAM
Bowdoinham Snowbirds, 511 White Road, Bowdoinham 04008

Bowdoin Flurry Flyers , PO Box 27, Store West Road, Bowdoin 04287

■ BRADFORD
Bradford Snow Blazers, PO Box 66, Bradford 04410

■ BREWER
Eastern Maine Snowmobilers, PO Box 226, Brewer 04412

■ BRIDGTON
Bridgton Easy Riders, RR 3, Box 1031, Bridgton 04009

■ BRISTOL
Route 66 Snowmobile Club, PO Box 231, Bristol 04539

■ BROOKS
Harvest Valley Snowmobile Club, PO Box 187, Brooks 04921

■ BROWNFIELD
Burnt Meadow Snowmobile Club, PO Box 412, Brownfield 04010

■ BROWNVILLE
Brownville Snowmobile Club, PO Box 296, Brownville 04414

Ebeemee Snowmobile Club, RR 1, Box 2730, Brownville 04414

■ BRYANT POND
Milton Lucky Riders, RR 2, Box 3560, Bryant Pond 04219

■ BUCKFIELD
Streaked Mountaineers, PO Box 203, Buckfield 04220

■ BUCKSPORT
Family Snowmobile Club, HC 78, Box 124, Bucksport 04416

■ BURLINGTON
Back Country Snowmobilers, Box 14, Burlington 04417

Nicatous Lodge Snowmobile Club, Box 100, Burlington 04417

■ CALAIS
Sunrise Snowmobilers, US 1, Box 177, Calais 04619

■ CAMBRIDGE
Cambridge Supertrails, RR 1, Box 1855, Cambridge 04923

■ CANAAN
Canaan Bog Bouncers, PO Box 439, Canaan 04924

Smokey's Angels Snowmobile Club, RR 2, Box 8930, Canaan 04924

■ CANTON
Canton Hi-Riders, PO Box 614, Canton 04221

■ CAPE ELIZABETH
Cape Elizabeth Coastal Riders, PO Box 6206, Cape Elizabeth 04758

■ CARIBOU
Caribou Snowmobile Club, PO Box 143, Caribou 04736

■ CARMEL
Carmel Snowmobile Club, PO Box 141, Carmel 04419

■ CARRABASSETT VALLEY
JV Wing Snowmobile Club, RR 1, Box 2060, Carrabassett Valley 04947

■ CHARLESTON
Charleston Stump Jumpers, RFD #1, Box 3340, Charleston 04422

■ CHERRYFIELD
Narraguagus Snowmobile Club, PO Box 234, Cherryfield 04622

■ CLINTON
Town & Country Trail Riders, PO Box 23, Clinton 04927

■ CORINNA
Corundel Raiders Snowmobile Club, RR 1, Box 4875, Corinna 04928

■ CORNISH
Cornish Sno-Cruisers, PO Box 12, Cornish 04020

■ COSTIGAN
G & G Trailblazers, HC 63, Box 460, Costigan 04423

■ CUMBERLAND
Moonlite Sno Skimmers, 19 Crystal Lane, Cumberland 04021

■ DANFORTH
East Grand Snowmobile Club, PO Box 182, Danforth 04424

■ DEBLOIS
Airline Riders, HCR 72, Box 32D, Deblois 04622

■ DENMARK
Denmark Draggers, PO Box 103, Denmark 04022

■ DETROIT
Night Drifters, Box 98, Detroit 04929

■ DEXTER
Ripleys Trail Riders, RFD 3 Box 580, Dexter 04930
Wassookeag Snowmobile Club, PO Box 121, Dexter 04930

■ DIXFIELD
Webb River Valley Snowmobile Club, HCR 67 Box 850, Dixfield 04224
Poodunck Snowmobile Club, PO Box 276, Dixfield 04224

■ DIXMONT
Dixmont Goldcrest Riders, PO Box 13, Dixmont 04932

■ FOXCROFT
Piscataquis Valley Snowmobile Club, PO Box 52, Dover Foxcroft 04426

Appendix

■ **DRESDEN**
Sno Valley Riders, PO Box 175, Dresden 04342

■ **EAGLE LAKE**
Eagle Lake Winter Riders, PO Box 294, Eagle Lake 04739
Sno Hawgs, PO Box 276, Eagle Lake 04739

■ **EAST BALDWIN**
Baldwin Beltburners, PO Box 35, East Baldwin 04024

■ **EAST CORINTH**
Good Time Riders, RR 2, Box 2645, East Corinth 04427
Maine Snow Sports, Route 2, Box 1575, East Corinth 04427
Powerline Prowlers Snowmobile Club, PO Box 451, East Corinth 04427

■ **EAST LIVERMORE FALLS**
Jug Hill Riders, PO Box 126, East Livermore Falls 04228

■ **EASTON**
Easton Trail Breakers, PO Box 198, Easton 04740

■ **EAST SEBAGO**
Sebago Branch Duckers, HC 75 Box 270, E. Sebago 04029

■ **EAST STONEHAM**
Stoneham Knight Riders, PO Box 3, E. Stoneham 04231
Kezar Trailbreakers, PO Box 950, East Stoneham 04231

■ **EAST WATERBORO**
Ossipee Mountaineers, PO Box 273 East Waterboro 04030

■ **WINTHROP**
Seboomook Timber Cruisers, PO Box 62, East Winthrop 04343

■ **ELLSWORTH**
Ellsworth Snowmobile Club, RR 3, Box 200, Ellsworth 04605
Frenchmans Bay Riders, RFD 2, Box 61, Ellsworth 04605
Graham Lake Trail Riders, RFD 4, Box 181A, Ellsworth 04605
Waltham-Eastbrook Rough Riders Sno Club, HC 31, Box 2080, Ellsworth 04605

■ **ENFIELD**
Coldstream Sno Riders, HCR 67, Box 1184, Enfield 04433

■ **EXETER**
Cross Country Cruisers, PO Box 101, Exeter 04435

■ **FAIRFIELD**
Fairfield Country Riders, 24 Wood Street, Fairfield 04937

■ **FALMOUTH**
Falmouth Sno Voyagers, 199 Winn Road, Falmouth 04105

■ **FARMINGTON FALLS**
Chesterville Country Ramblers, PO Box 173, Farmington Falls 04940

Northern Lites Snow Club, RR 1, Box 1310-A, Farmington 04938

■ **FORT FAIRFIELD**
Fort Fairfield Snowmobile Club, PO Box 233, Fort Fairfield 04742

■ **FORT KENT**
Twin Lakes Sno Riders, RFD 2, Box 1145, Fort Kent 04743
Valley Sno Riders, PO Box 131, Fort Kent 04743
Black Lake Snowsledders, PO Box 101, Fort Kent 04743
Carter Brook Sno Birds, PO Box 211, Fort Kent 04743
Frontier Snowmobile Club, PO Box 179, Fort Kent 04746

■ **FREEDOM**
Frye Mountain Snow-Riders, PO Box 115, Freedom 04941
North Star Riders, P.O. 24, Freedom 04941

■ **FREEPORT**
Tri-Town Penguins Snowmobile Club, 5 Baker Road, Freeport 04032

■ **FRENCHVILLE**
Frenchville Snowmobile Club, PO Box 209, Frenchville 04745

■ **FRIENDSHIP**
Stormy Riders, PO Box 146, Friendship 04547

■ **FRYEBURG**
Interstate Sno Goers, PO Box 15, Fryeburg 04037

■ **GARDINER**
Cobbosseecontee Snowmobile Club, Box 1505, US 1, Gardiner 04354

■ **GARLAND**
Frosty Valley Snowsledders, PO Box 94, Garland 04939

■ **GILEAD**
Gilead Wildriver Snow Riders, RFD 2 Box 1350, Gilead 04217

■ **GORHAM**
Gorham Sno Goers, 315 Sebago Lake Road, Gorham 04038
Moonlighters Limited, RR 3, Box 112A, Gorham 04038

■ **GRAND ISLE**
Cold Mtn. Snowmobile Club, PO Box 172, Grand Isle 04746

■ **GRAND LAKE STREAM**
Grand Lake Snowmobile Club, PO Box 132, Grand Lake Stream 04637

■ **GRAY**
Crystal Lake Sno Cruisers, PO Box 293, Gray 04039
Gray Snowmobile Club, PO Box 164, Gray 04039

■ **GREENVILLE**
Kokadjo Roach Riders, HCR 76, Box 588, Greenville 04441
Moosehead Riders, PO Box 1145, Greenville 04441

■ **GREENE**
Greene Dragons Snowmobile Club, PO Box 147, Greene 04236

■ **GUILFORD**
Four Winds Snowmobile Club, PO Box 543, Guilford 04443
Parkman Trail Blazers, RFD 1, Box 208, Guilford 04443
West Road Riders, RFD 1, Box 264, Guilford 04443

■ **HALLOWELL**
Barnstormers Snowmobile Club, PO Box 161, Hallowell 04347

■ **HAMPDEN**
Goodwill Riders Inc., 844 Western Avenue, Hampden 04444

■ **HARMONY**
Heart of Gold Snow Club, PO Box 251, Harmony 04942

■ **HARRISON**
Harrison Friendly Riders, PO Box 817, Harrison 04040

■ **HEBRON**
Bouncing Bogies Snowmobile Club, PO Box 69, Hebron 04238

■ **HIRAM**
Hiram Hillclimbers, PO Box 275, Hiram 04041

■ **HOLDEN**
Bald Mountain Snowriders (Dedham), RR 2, Box 1188, Holden 04429

■ **HOLLIS CENTER**
Hollis Honkers Snowmobile Club, PO Box 48, Hollis Center 04042

■ **HOPE**
Hatchet Mountain Sno Riders, RR 3, Box 5665, Hope 04847

■ **HOULTON**
Linneus Sno Sports, PO Box 529, Houlton 04730
Meduxnekeag Ramblers, RFD 3, Box 2530, Houlton 04730
Sno Rovers (Hodgdon), RFD 4, Box 1880, Houlton 04730

■ **HOWLAND**
Twin Rivers Snowmobile Club, PO Box 275, Howland 04448

■ **HUDSON**
Pushaw Lake Snowmobile Club, PO Box 103, Hudson 04449

■ **ISLAND FALLS**
Big Valley Sno Club Inc., PO Box 86, Island Falls 04747

■ **JACKMAN**
Border Riders, PO Box 413, Jackman 04945
Parlin Pond Snowmobile Riders, HCR 64, Box 564, Jackman 04945

■ **JAY**
Andy Valley Riders, 20 Forest Circle, Jay 04239

■ **JEFFERSON**
Jefferson Sno Packers, PO Box 963, Jefferson 04348

■ **KENDUSKEAG**
Kenduskeag Stream Riders, RR 1, Box 6400, Kenduskeag 04450

■ KENTS HILL
Rainbow Riders, PO Box 282, Kents Hill 04349

■ KEZAR FALLS
Sacopee Valley Snowdrifters, RR 1, Box 37, Kezar Falls 04047

■ KINGFIELD
Salem Sno Drifters, PO Box 161, Kingfield 04947

Sno Wanderers Snowmobile Club, PO Box 12, Kingfield 04947

■ LEE
Dwinal Pond 4 Seasons Snow Hogs, RR 1, Box 1085, Lee 04455

Lee Mogul Pounders, RR 1, Box 4440, Lee 04455

■ LEEDS
Leeds Stumpthumpers, PO Box 93, Leeds 04263

■ LEVANT
Hungry Hollow 76'ers, RR 1, Box 3940, Levant 04456

■ LEWISTON
Hillside Family Riders Snowmobile Club, P.O Box 7044, Lewiston 04240

■ LIMESTONE
Limestone Snow Hawks, PO Box 48, Limestone 04750

■ LIMINGTON
Limington Crankers Snowmobile Club, PO Box 81, Limington 04049

■ LINCOLN
Snowhound Snowmobile Club, Town Farm Road, Lincoln 04457

■ LINCOLNVILLE
Lincolnville Mtn. Goats, PO Box 275, Lincolnville 04849

■ LISBON/LISBON FALLS
Riverside Snowmobile Club, PO Box 177, Lisbon 04250

Night Owls, RFD 1 Box 1760, Lisbon Falls 04252

Pejepscot Sno Chiefs, PO Box 1, Lisbon Falls 04252

■ LITCHFIELD
Litchfield Snowmobile Club, PO Box 218, Litchfield 04350

■ LIVERMORE FALLS
Bear Mountain Blazers, RFD 2, Box 2450, Livermore Falls 04254

■ LOCKE MILL
Greenstock Snowsports, PO Box 115, Locke Mill 04255

■ LUBEC
Quoddy Blazers Inc., RR 2 Box 4330, Lubec 04652

■ MADAWASKA
Madawaska Snowmobile Club, PO Box 755, Madawaska 04756

■ MANCHESTER
Manchester Country Riders, PO Box 405, Manchester 04351

Appendix

■ MAPLETON
Chapman Ridge Runners, PO Box 282, Mapleton 04757

Walker Siding Swampers, PO Box 60, Mapleton 04757

■ MARS HILL
Central Aroostook Snowmobile Club, PO Box 528, Mars Hill 04758

■ MATTAWAMKEAG
Mattawamkeag Roadrunners, RR 1, Box 249A, Mattawamkeag 04459

■ MECHANIC FALLS
Bog Hooters Snowmobile Club, P.O Box 351, Mechanic Falls 04256

■ MEXICO
Mexico Trailblazers, PO Box 160, Mexico 04257

■ MILFORD
Pine Tree Snowmobile Club, P.O Box 503, Outer Call Road, Milford 04461

■ MILLINOCKET/EAST MILLINOCKET
East Branch Sno Rovers, PO Box 397, East Millinocket 04430

Twin Pines Snowmobile Club, PO Box 152, Millinocket 04462

Northern Timber Cruisers, PO Box 269, Millinocket 04462

■ MILO
Devils Sledders, Route 2, Box 130C, Milo 04463

■ MINOT
Minot Moonshiners, PO Box 61, Minot 04268

■ MONMOUTH
Cochnewagan Trailblazers, PO Box 153, Monmouth 04259

■ MONSON
Narrow Gauge Riders, PO Box 296, Monson 04464

■ MORRILL
Tri-Town Sno-Riders, Brown Road, Morrill 04952

■ MOUNT VERNON
Minnehonk Ridge Riders, US 1, Box 3320, Mt. Vernon 04352

■ NAPLES
Muddy River Sno-Seekers, PO Box 794, Naples 04055

■ NEWBURGH
Newburgh Countryside Riders, 2926 Kennebec Road, Newburgh 04444

■ NEW GLOUCESTER
Royal River Riders, 97 Lewiston Road, New Glouceter 04260

■ NEWPORT
Sebasticook Valley Snowmobile Club, PO Box 61, Newport 04953

■ NEW SHARON
Missing Link Snowmobile Club, PO Box 142, New Sharon 04955

■ NEW VINEYARD
New Vineyard Trailmasters, PO Box 272, New Vineyard 04956

■ NEWRY
Windy Valley Snowmobile Club, General Delivery, Newry 04261

■ NORRIDGEWOCK
Mercer Bog Riders, Route 2, Box 1058, Norridgewock 04957

Norridgewock Sportsmens Association, PO Box 115, Norridgewock, 04857

■ NORTH ANSON
Embden Travelers Snowmobile Club, PO Box 82, North Anson 04958

■ NORTHEAST CARRY
Northeast Carry Sno Riders, Box 642, Northeast Carry 04478

■ NEW PORTLAND
Wire Bridge Sno Travelers, PO Box 139, N. New Portland 04961

■ NORTH WATERFORD
Waterford Snowpackers, Box 101, North Waterford 04267

■ NORTHPORT
Northport Ridge Riders, 257 Rocky Road, Northport 04849

■ NORWAY
Norway Trackers, PO Box 541, Norway 04268

■ OAKFIELD
Smoki Haulers Snowmobile Club, PO Box 331, Oakfield 04763

■ OAKLAND
Oakland Sno Goers, PO Box 566, Oakland 04963

Rome Ruff Riders, PO Box 261, Oakland 04963

■ OLD TOWN
L A Sledders Snow Club, RR 1 Box 382B, Old Town 04468

■ ORRINGTON
Orrington Trail Riders, PO Box 202, Orrington 04474

■ OTISFIELD
Otisfield Trail Blazers, 421 Scribner Hill Road, Otisfield 04270

■ OXBOW
Oxbow-Masardis Snowmobile Club, General Delivery, Oxbow 04764

■ OXFORD
Rock-O-Dunbee Riders, PO Box 6, Oxford 04270

■ PALERMO
Palermo Snowmobile Club, 280 North Palermo Road, Palermo 04354

■ PALMYRA
Palmyra Snowmobile Club, PO Box 57, Palmyra 04965

■ PATTEN
Bowlin-Matagamon Snowmobile Club, RR 1, Box 280, Patten 04765

Appendix

Rockabema Snow Rangers, PO Box 592, Patten 04765

■ **PERHAM**
Washburn Trail Runners, PO Box 5, Perham 04766

■ **PERRY**
Downeast Stump Jumpers, PO Box 271, Perry 04667

■ **PERU**
Peru Snowmobile Club, PO Box 252, Peru 04290

■ **PHILLIPS**
North Franklin Snowmobile Club, RR 2, Box 1285, Phillips 04966

■ **PITTSFIELD**
Pittsfield Driftbuilders, PO Box 491, Pittsfield 04967

■ **PITTSTON**
Pittston Prowlers Snowmobile Club, 33 Stage Road, Pittston 04345

■ **PLYMOUTH**
Plymouth Snowmobile Club, PO Box 56, Plymouth 04969

■ **POLAND**
Poland Sno Travelers Inc. , PO Box 442, Poland Spring 04274

■ **PORTAGE LAKE**
Portage Lakers Snowmobile Club, PO Box 149, Portage Lake 04768

■ **PORTLAND**
Ragged Riders, 201 Maine Avenue, Portland 04103

■ **PRESQUE ISLE**
Aroostook River Snowmobile Club, PO Box 108, Presque Isle 04769
Presque Isle Snowmobile Club, PO Box 1368, Presque Isle 04769

■ **PRINCETON**
Princeton Pathfinders, PO Box 774, Princeton 04668

■ **RANGELEY**
Rangeley Lakes Snowmobile Club, Box 950, Rangeley 04970

■ **RAYMOND**
Raymond Rattlers Snowmobile Club, PO Box 994, Raymond 04071

■ **READFIELD**
Readfield Blizzard Busters, PO Box 62, Readfield 04355

■ **RICHMOND**
Merrymeeting Sno Rovers, PO Box 6, Richmond 04357

■ **ROCKWOOD**
Blue Ridge Riders, PO Box 345, Rockwood 04478
Pittston Farm Snowmobile Club, Box 525, Rockwood 04478
Tauton-Raynham Boundary Riders, Route 15, PO Box 27, Rockwood 04478

■ **ROXBURY**
Slippery Sliders Snowmobile Club, HC 62, Box 62, Roxbury 04275

■ **RUMFORD**
Rumford Polar Bear Club, PO Box 634, Rumford 04276

■ **SABATTUS**
Sabattus Mountaineers, PO Box 696, Sabattus 04280

■ **SANFORD**
Southern Maine Sno-Goers, PO Box 1083, Sanford 04073

■ **SCARBOROUGH**
Saco Pathfinders Snowmobile Club, 228 Broadturn Road, Scarborough 04074

■ **SEARSMONT**
Appleton Trail Makers, C/O HC 81, Box 2235, Searsmont 04973

■ **SEARSPORT**
Seacoast Riders, PO Box 129, Searsport 04974

■ **SEBAGO LAKE**
Standish Sno Seekers, Box 9850, Route 114 , Sebago Lake 04075

■ **SEBEC VILLAGE**
Big Bear Snowmobile Club, PO Box 21, Sebec Village 04481

■ **SHAPLEIGH**
Mousam Valley Snowmobile Club, PO Box 109, Shapleigh 04076
Squash Hollow Sno Goers, PO Box 547, Shapleigh 04076

■ **SHERMAN MILLS**
Molunkus Valley Snodrifters, PO Box 323, Sherman Mills 04776

■ **SIDNEY**
Sidney Trail Riders, Goodhue Road, Sidney 04330

■ **SKOWHEGAN**
Abnaki Sno Riders, PO Box 114, Skowhegan 04976
Skowhegan Sno Hawks, PO Box 916, Skowhegan 04976

■ **SMITHFIELD**
Moonshiners Snowmobile Club, Box 134, Smithfield 04978

■ **SOLDIER POND**
Sly Brook Snow Riders, PO Box 76, Soldier Pond 04781

■ **SOLON**
Solon Snow Hawks, PO Box 251, Solon 04979

■ **SOMERVILLE**
Black Woods Bouncers, 84 Sand Hill Road, Somerville 04348

■ **SOUTH CASCO**
Crooked River Snow Club, PO Box 42, South Casco 04077

■ **SOUTH CHINA**
China Four Seasons, PO Box 474, South China 04358

■ **SOUTH GARDINER**
Gardiner Ridge Riders, General Delivery, South Gardiner 04359

Appendix

■ SOUTH PARIS
Hungry Hollow Hustlers, 430 Old Buckfield Road, South Paris 04746

Snow Hoppers (South Paris), 29 East Oxford Road, South Paris 04281

■ SPRUCE HEAD
Snow Owls, PO Box 127, Spruce Head 04859

■ ST. AGATHA
Red Arrow Snowmobile Club, PO Box 202, St. Agatha 04772

■ ST. ALBANS
Sno-Devils Snow Club, 689 Todds Corner Road, St. Albans 04971

■ ST. FRANCIS
Snow Angels Snowmobile Club, PO Box 42, St. Francis 04774

■ STANDISH
York County Snowmobile Club, PO Box 61, Standish 04084

■ STOCKHOLM
Nordic Lakers, RFD 1, Box 47A, Stockholm 04783

■ STRATTON
Arnold Trail Snowmobile Club, PO Box 573, Stratton 04982

■ STRONG
Narrow Gauge Snowmobile Club, PO Box 21, Strong 04983

Kennebec Scenic Sno Riders, Berry's General Store, Route 201, The Forks 04985

■ TOPSFIELD
Cross Roads Snowmobile Club, PO Box 5, Topsfield 04490

■ TROY
Troy Snow Beaters, RR 1- Box 2060, Troy 04987

■ TURNER
Turner Ridge Riders, RFD 2, Box 401A, Turner 04282

■ UNITY
Snow Dusters, PO Box 61, Unity 04988

■ VAN BUREN
Gateway Snowmobile Club, PO Box 407, Van Buren 04785

■ VANCEBORO
Vanceboro-Lambert Snowhounds, PO Box 131, Vanceboro 04491

■ VASSALBORO
Kennebec Valley Trail Riders, PO Box 13, Vassalboro 04989

■ WALDBORO
Rocky Ridge Riders, 615 North Nobleboro Road, Waldoboro 04572

Sno-Crawlers of Waldoboro, PO Box 156, Waldoboro 04572

■ WALES
Wales Ridge Runners, RR 1, Box 1765A, Wales 04280

■ WARREN
Bog Brigade Snowmobile Club, 2121 Atlantic Highway, Warren 04864

■ WASHINGTON
Hill & Gully Riders, PO Box 212, Washington 04574

■ WAYNE
Thirty Mile River Snowmobile Club, PO Box 238, Wayne 04284

■ WELD
Winter Wildcats, PO Box 74, Weld 04285

■ WEST NEWFIELD
Route 11 Streakers, PO Box 190, West Newfield 04746

■ WEST PARIS
Mollyockett Sportsman Club, PO Box 88, West Paris 04289

■ WEST ROCKPORT
Goose River Snowmobile Club, PO Box 252, West Rockport 04865

■ WEST SUMNER
Mt. Tom Snowmobile Club, HCR 64, Box 835, West Sumner 04292

■ WHITFIELD
King's Mills Eager Beavers, RR 1, Box 429, Whitefield 04353

■ WILTON
Woodland Wanderers Snowmobile Club, PO Box 638, Wilton 04294

■ WINDHAM
Windham Drifters, PO Box 869, Windham 04062

■ WINSLOW
Central Maine Snowmobile Club, RR 2, Box 3000, Winslow 04901
Fort Halifax Snowdrifters, PO Box 8175, Winslow 04901

■ WINSOR
WJW Snowmobile Club, RR 1, Box 5505, Winsor 04363

■ WINTERPORT
Winterport Riverside Riders, PO Box 544, Winterport 04496

■ WINTHROP
Hillandalers Snowmobile Club, PO Box 49, Winthrop 04364

■ WISCASSET
Wiscasset Sno Goers, RR 5, Box 910, Wiscasset 04578

■ WOODLAND
Breakneck Mtn. Sno Riders, RR 9, Box 480, Woodland 04694
St. Croix Trail Riders, PO Box 547, Woodland 04694

■ WOOLWICH
Nequasset Trailbreakers, PO Box 4, Woolwich 04579

■ YARMOUTH
Royal River Snowmobile Club, PO Box 1061, Yarmouth 04096

Appendix

Index

Index